25x3/11-3/11

D0601111

NP

BARRON'S

HOW TO PREPARE FOR THE

CSET

MULTIPLE SUBJECTS

CALIFORNIA SUBJECT MATTER EXAMINATIONS FOR TEACHERS: MULTIPLE SUBJECTS

Robert D. Postman, Ed.D.
Professor and Education Dean

SAN DIEGO PUBLIC LIBRARY
NORTH PARK BRANCH
FEB   2005

WITHDRAWN

3 1336 06750 3913

BARRON'S

To my wife
Liz
and my children
Chad, Blaire, and Ryan
This book is dedicated to you.

Copyright 2004, 1998 by Barron's Educational Series, Inc.
Some material in this book was adapted from the following Barron's books:
How to Prepare for the Praxis
How to Prepare for the PPST
How to Prepare for the CLAST

All rights reserved.
No part of this book may be reproduced in any form, by photostat, microfilm,
xerography, or any other means, or incorporated into any information retrieval
system, electronic or mechanical, without the written permission of the copyright
owner.

All inquiries should be addressed to:
Barron's Educational Series, Inc.
250 Wireless Boulevard
Hauppauge, New York 11788
http://www.barronseduc.com

Library of Congress Catalog Card No. 2004046137

International Standard Book No. 0-7641-2351-3

Library of Congress Cataloging-in-Publication Data

Postman, Robert D.
    How to prepare for the CSET Multiple Subjects : California Subject Matter
Examinations for Teachers, Multiple Subjects / by Robert D. Postman.
        p.   cm.
    Includes index.
    ISBN 0-7641-2351-3
    1. CSET: Multiple Subjects—Study guides. 2. Elementary school
teachers—Certification—California. 3. Teaching—California—Examinations—Study guides.
I. Title: How to prepare for the CSET Multiple Subjects. II. Title: CSET Multiple Subjects.
III. Title: California Subject Matter Examinations for Teachers, Multiple Subjects. IV. Barron's
Educational Series, Inc. V. Title.

LB1766.C74P67 2004
372.112'09794—dc22

                                                2004046137

PRINTED IN THE UNITED STATES OF AMERICA

9 8 7 6 5 4 3 2 1

CONTENTS

PART VII: BEGINNING A CAREER IN TEACHING   515

PREFACE

This book shows you how to get a passing score on the CSET: Multiple Subjects Examination and helps you get started in a teaching career. The book has been field-tested by college students and prospective teachers and reviewed by experienced teachers and subject matter specialists.

The practice tests in this book have the same question types and the same question-and-answer formats as the real tests. Review sections provide a clear overview of subject matter, strategies for passing the CSET, and extra CSET practice items.

My wife, Liz, a teacher, was a constant source of support, and she made significant contributions to this book. I hope she accepts my regrets for the lost months and believes my promises that it won't happen again. My children, Chad, Blaire, and Ryan have also been a source of support as I worked on this and other books over the years.

I can attest that Barron's is simply the best publisher of test preparation books. The editorial department, under the leadership of Mark Miele, spared no effort to assure that this book is most helpful to you, the test taker.

Anna Damaskos at Barron's, did a masterful job with this manuscript.

Particular thanks go to Mary Lou Pagno, a professor of reading, who reviewed the reading section and the reading items. I am very grateful to Martin Shields, a presidential-award–winning science teacher, for reviewing the science section and the science items. My gratitude goes also to Ryan Postman, who holds a master's degree in mathematics from Wake Forest University, for reviewing the mathematics section and the mathematics items. I am particularly indebted to Andy Schmidth, past president of the state AHPERD Chapter, for reviewing the physical education section and the physical education items.

Mark O'Shea, a professor at CSU Monterey Bay, was particularly helpful. He took the CSET: Multiple Subjects and shared his thoughts about the test during an interview found in this book.

I am also grateful to several colleagues. Dominic Angiello, professor of English and a published poet, reviewed the language and literature items. James Melville, professor of science and science department chair, reviewed the science items. Sean Dugan, professor of English and English department chair, reviewed the language and literature section.

Special thanks to the undergraduate and graduate students and those changing careers who field-tested sections of this book, and to those at the Metropolitan Museum of Art, the Crocker Museum of Art, the Duke University Music Library, and Texas Instruments for their assistance. I am also grateful to those at the California Education Department and to those at colleges and other organizations in California who talked to me about the CSET.

During the past three decades, teaching opportunities have shifted from promising to sparse to promising again. You are entering teaching during a time of tremendous opportunity, and I wish you well in your pursuit of a rewarding and fulfilling career. The next generation awaits. You will help them prepare for a vastly different, technological world.

Robert D. Postman

CSET TEST DATES
2004–2005

TEST DATE	Regular Internet *RECEIPT* *Mail POSTMARK*	Late* Internet *RECEIPT*	EMERGENCY* REGISTRATION *Online and Phone:*	SCORE MAILING DATE (Scores available online)
September 18, 2004	August 20, 2004	September 7, 2004	September 14, 2004	October 18, 2004
November 6, 2004	October 8, 2004	October 26, 2004	November 2, 2004	December 6, 2004
January 22, 2005	December 27, 2004	January 11, 2005	January 18, 2005	February 22, 2005
March 19, 2005	February 18, 2005	March 8, 2005	March 15, 2005	April 18, 2005
May 21, 2005	April 22, 2005	May 10, 2005	May 17, 2005	June 20, 2005
July 16, 2005	June 17, 2005	July 5, 2005	July 12, 2005	August 15, 2005

* Late and Emergency registration require an additional fee.

PART I

Your Review Plan

This section helps you set up a review plan for the CSET. We begin with a brief discussion of the test.

THE CSET

The CSET consists of three subtests. You may take one, two, or all three subtests during the five-hour administration period. Each subtest consists of multiple choice items and constructed response items that require a written answer. You must pass each subtest, but you do not have to pass them all during a single test administration. Here is the list.

SUBTEST I—52 Multiple Choice Items and 4 Constructed Response Items

Reading, Language, and Literature
   26 Multiple Choice Items
     2 Constructed Response Items
History and Social Science
   26 Multiple Choice Items
     2 Constructed Response Items

SUBTEST II—52 Multiple Choice Items and 4 Constructed Response Items

Science
   26 Multiple Choice Items
     2 Constructed Response Items
Mathematics
   26 Multiple Choice Items
     2 Constructed Response Items

SUBTEST III—39 Multiple Choice Items and 3 Constructed Response Items

Visual and Performing Arts
   13 Multiple Choice Items
     1 Constructed Response Item
Physical Education
   13 Multiple Choice Items
     1 Constructed Response Item
Human Development
   13 Multiple Choice Items
     1 Constructed Response Item

CALIFORNIA SUBJECT MATTER FRAMEWORKS

The CSET is based on the California academic content standards for all subjects. The link to these standards at press time is *www.cde.ca.gov/standards*. The California Subject Matter Frameworks, particularly Grade 4 through Grade 6, provide detailed information about these standards and are the best online source for detailed standards information. The link to the frameworks at press time is *www.cde.ca.gov/cdepress/downloads.html*.

PASSING THE CSET

Estimates are you need about 65 percent to 70 percent correct on the multiple choice items and an average of two points out of three points on the constructed response items to pass a subtest. Even the best students will encounter questions they cannot answer. One person who conducts CSET study groups likened the CSET to a game of Trivial Pursuit, where the goal is to know enough to pass, not to know everything. Passing the CSET is just that—passing the CSET. You do what is necessary.

As a college professor and dean, I recoil at my own thoughts, but it's true. The CSET is not like the SAT or the ACT. It does not matter how high your score is as long as the score is at or above the minimum passing score. You want to prepare effectively and efficiently. You certainly don't want too little, but you don't want to do too much.

HOW MUCH REVIEW IS ENOUGH?

That is the first question to ask for this test. A complete review is a stack of books many thousands of pages thick. That's too much. Just doing nothing, for most people that's too little. We need something that's just right—not too much, not too little.

Our analysis indicates that what is in this book meets that goal. It will be appropriate preparation for about 85 percent to 90 percent of the people who will take the CSET. The other 10 percent to 15 percent who have a very poor educational background or who are just very poor test takers will need more help, probably more than they will find in any book.

It's almost an urban legend in California to supplement your CSET preparation with a middle grade-level book from the series edited by E. D. Hirsch, such as *What Your Fifth Grader Needs to Know: Fundamentals of a Good Fifth-Grade Education*. It is not a bad idea to supplement your review in this way. However, our analysis and feedback from education advisors and professors has not confirmed the value of these books.

APPROACHES TO TAKING THE CSET

The CSET is given in a five-hour block of time, six hours with instructions. You may take one, two, or all three subtests during that time. The general consensus is your first test session should include the subtest you believe will be most difficult. You should take the online practice CSET, currently available at *http://www.cset.nesinc.com/* to diagnose your ability on the subtests.

You may take as many months, or years, as you want to pass all three subtests. You may retake the subtests as many times as you want. The CSET is fairly expensive; at press time it cost over $70 to register for each subtest. That fee can increase significantly if you have to pay late or emergency registration fees. Waivers may be available for late registration fees.

You have some strategic decision making to do about which subtests and how many subtests to take during any one five-hour test administration. Consider these factors: your knowledge of the subject matter, your ability as a test-taker, time span for completing the subtests, cost, and your emotional well-being. There are three fundamental approaches.

Careful Approach

Many education advisors and professors counsel a careful approach. They recommend taking just one subtest during a test administration. The CSET is given every two months, so you can take all three subtests during a five-month period. You may have to register for a test before you have the previous test results to avoid paying a late fee. This approach may be particularly appropriate if you are a poor test-taker or if your first language is not English. One advisor tells a student to use this approach if the student has a GPA below 3.0 in a liberal studies program.

Moderate Approach

Quite a few advisors and professors say you should take no more than two subtests at one administration. They advise taking first the single subtest test you believe will be most difficult. Then they say you should take the remaining two subtests during a single administration. Usually, these two subtests will include Subtest III and either Subtest I or Subtest II. Using this approach, you can take all the subtests during a three-month period.

Aggressive Approach

A significant but smaller number of advisors and professors say to take all three subtests at a single administration and then just retake the subtests you don't pass. They point out that there is no penalty for failing a subtest. You just have to pay the fee and take it over; although, retaking all three subtests can raise the total cost of the testing to over $400. They also acknowledge there can be an emotional downside to failing and that this approach is not for everyone.

Time Available to Answer Items

The following chart summarizes the time available to answer items if you take one, two, or all three subtests at a single administration. There are 300 minutes in each CSET administration.

SUBTESTS	MULTIPLE CHOICE ITEMS	TIME TO ANSWER EACH MULTIPLE CHOICE ITEM	CONSTRUCTED RESPONSE ITEMS	TIME TO ANSWER EACH CONSTRUCTED RESPONSE ITEM
JUST SUBTEST I or JUST SUBTEST II	52	4.2 minutes	4	20 minutes
JUST SUBTEST III	39	6.1 minutes	3	20 minutes
SUBTESTS I AND II	104	1.7 minutes	8	15 minutes
SUBTEST III WITH EITHER I OR II	91	2.1 minutes	7	15 minutes
ALL THREE SUBTESTS	143	0.9 minutes	11	15 minutes

You can see that taking all three subtests may create time pressure. There is not much time pressure if you take two subtests, and time pressure is not an issue at all if you take just one subtest. Now you have all the information; it's time to choose your review plan.

YOUR REVIEW PLAN

Weigh all the factors. Decide which subtest(s) to take at the next administration. Then choose one of these review plans.

CSET REVIEW PLANS

Choose your review plans for the next CSET test administration. Read the plans over, put a check next to your review plan, and let's get started. Check off each step as you go.

Quick Review

Use this plan if you are supremely confident, or if you'll be taking the CSET very soon.

- Review Chapter 1 for an overview of the test.   page 7
- Review Chapter 2 for test preparation and test-taking strategies.   page 13

Take the practice subtests you will take at the next administration. Then review the answers and explanations.

Core Reviews

Use one or more of these core reviews as a thorough preparation for the subtest or subtests you will take at the next test administration. All core reviews include Chapter 1 and Chapter 2.

- Review Chapter 1 for an overview of the test.   page 7
- Review Chapter 2 for test preparation and test-taking strategies.   page 13

Subtest I

Use this plan if you are taking Subtest I at the next test administration.

Subtest II

Use this plan if you are taking Subtest II at the next test administration.

Subtest III

Use this plan if you are taking Subtest III at the next test administration.

1 THE CSET: MULTIPLE SUBJECTS

CALIFORNIA SUBJECT EXAMINATIONS FOR TEACHERS

TEST INFO BOX

Most chapters begin with a Test Info Box. Read it for information about the CSET.

The CSET is offered by National Evaluation Systems (NES). Go to the Web site listed below for an online registration, a test booklet, test dates, score reports, and other information about the CSET.

www.cset.nesinc.com

National Evaluation Systems can also be contacted by mail or by phone.

National Evaluation Systems
P.O. Box 340813
Sacramento, CA
95834-0813
(916) 928-0244

THE TEST

The CSET: Multiple Subjects is usually required for a Multiple Subjects (elementary) teaching credential in California. The CSET: Multiple Subjects consists of three subtests that include both multiple choice and constructed response (essay) items. You may take one, two, or all three subtests during a five hour administration.

SUBTEST I (Language/Social Studies) 52 Multiple Choice and 4 Constructed Response
SUBTEST II (Science/Mathematics) 52 Multiple Choice and 4 Constructed Response
SUBTEST III (Arts/Phys. Ed/Human Development) 39 Multiple Choice and 3 Constructed Response

PASSING SCORES

An overall scale score of 220 is passing for each test. Estimates are that about 65 percent to 70 percent correct multiple choice answers and an average of two out of three on the constructed response items is passing for each subtest.

OTHER CALIFORNIA CSET TESTS

CSET: Single Subjects tests are required for most secondary school teaching certificates.

READ ME FIRST

This section describes the CSET, discusses scoring, and explains the steps you should take in the beginning of your preparation. Read it before going on.

WHAT'S GOING ON WITH THE CSET: MULTIPLE SUBJECTS?

The CSET Multiple Subjects is a test based on the California Curriculum Standards. The material is mainly at an introductory college level. Each CSET test administration takes five hours, so it lasts an entire day. You must get a passing score on each of the three subtests, which were described earlier.

THE GOOD NEWS

The good news is that the CSET focuses on a central core of information. The information covered by the test is at an introductory level. You can use a calculator for the mathematics section. This book will show you how to successfully prepare for this test.

There is more good news. You can take one, two, or three subtests during the five-hour period and this is a huge advantage over the MSAT, which used to be the required test. Students and advisors alike also agree that the CSET is a more reasonable test than the MSAT.

At the end of the book you will learn how to begin your career in teaching, how to get certified, how to write your first resume, and how to look for your first job.

GETTING A PASSING SCORE

Raw Scores and Scale Scores

Your raw score is the number of items you answer correctly, or the number of points you actually earn. Your scale score shows your raw score on a single scale compared to everyone else who has taken that CSET subtest.

It works this way. CSET test items and different forms of the test have different difficulty levels. For example, a mathematics item on one form of the CSET might be harder than a mathematics item on another form. To make up for this difference in difficulty, the harder mathematics item might earn 0.9 scale points, while the easier item might earn 0.8 scale points.

This is the fair way to do it. To maintain this fairness, CSET passing scores are given as scale scores. The scale scores range from 100 to 300.

Test Scoring

No one can be absolutely sure what raw scores will convert to what scale scores. However, we can make some reasonable estimates. These estimates are based on reports from those who have previously taken the test, and from those at NES who like to be helpful.

Passing Scores

Scale Scores and Raw Scores

You pass a subtest if your overall scale score is 220 or better. The table below shows the raw scores likely to earn passing scale scores.

PASSING SCALE SCORE AND ESTIMATED PASSING RAW SCORES

Subtest	Passing Scale Score	Estimated Minimum Passing Raw Scores
Subtest I	220	34–37 multiple choice correct out of 52 (65%–70%) 8–10 points on constructed response items (out of 12)
Subtest II	220	34–37 multiple choice correct out of 52 (65%–70%) 8–10 points on constructed response items (out of 12)
Subtest III	220	25–27 multiple choice correct out of 29 (65%–70%) 6–8 points on constructed response items (out of 9)

Finding Out If You Passed

You don't have to wait for the score report. Test scores are posted at *www.cset.nesinc.com* on the day the reports are mailed.

REGISTERING FOR THE CSET

Most people will register online through *www.cset.nesinc.com*. Click on Internet Registration. You can also register by phone or by mail. The CSET Registration booklet is also available at that site. You'll also find CSET registration materials at most California colleges. You will need the paper copy of the registration booklet to register by mail.

TEST LOCATION

Where you take the test is very important. Check for test locations near you and list as your first choice the location in which you feel most comfortable. Never list any locations you really don't want to go to. If you do, you can be sure that's where you'll end up.

Given below is a list of the California areas and the out of state areas in which the CSET was recently administered.

California Areas

Anaheim	Sacramento
Bakersfield	San Bernardino
Chico	San Diego
Costa Mesa	San Diego North Counties
Fresno	San Francisco
Humboldt County/Arcata	San Jose
Long Beach	San Luis Obispo
Los Angeles East	Santa Barbara
Los Angeles West	Santa Cruz
Oakland	Santa Rosa
Pasadena/San Gabriel	Stockton Modesto
Riverside/Moreno Valley	Woodland Hills

Out of State Areas

Atlanta, Georgia	New York, New York
Austin, Texas	Phoenix, Arizona
Boston, Massachusetts	Pittsburgh, Pennsylvania
Chicago, Illinois	Salt Lake City, Utah
Detroit, Michigan	Seattle, Washington

Register as soon as possible. Early registrants are more likely to get their first choice location.

TEST SCHEDULE

The CSET takes five hours. There is a morning and an afternoon session. The CSET Multiple Subjects is given in the morning session.

WHERE TO SEND YOUR SCORES

The CSET Bulletin lists a code for each organization that can receive scores. You should list the code for each certification agency or college you want to receive your scores. The scores must usually be sent directly to the agencies from NES.

You may feel that you should wait until you know you have gotten a passing score before sending it in, but that's not necessary. You will just slow down the process and incur extra expense. Certification agencies do not use these scores for evaluative purposes. They just need to see a passing score.

SPECIAL TEST ARRANGEMENTS

NES offers special arrangements or considerations for the following categories. If you qualify for special test arrangements, take advantage of the opportunity.

Remember that NES will likely conclude that the five-hour test administration offers a full opportunity for extra time to complete the test.

Do You Have a Disability, a Learning Disability or a Physical, Visual, or Hearing Handicap?

These accommodations are readily available to CSET test centers.

- frequent breaks
- wheelchair-accessibility
- magnifying glass, color overlays, ruler
- written copy of directions read by the test administrator

Submit the following to request one of these arrangements.

Submit the following to request alternative testing arrangements not listed above.

1. registration form with full payment
2. Alternative Testing Arrangements form
3. A statement on official letterhead from a medical professional or other professional qualified to assess the disability with specific information about the disability

As a practical matter, you should contact NES to discuss alternative testing arrangements well before the test date.

Do You Celebrate Your Sabbath on Saturday?

The alternative test date will be on the Sunday following the regular test date. You must submit the following by the regular registration deadline.

1. registration form with full payment
2. Alternative Testing Arrangements form
3. letter from a clergy member on official letterhead, stating that your religion prohibits Saturday testing

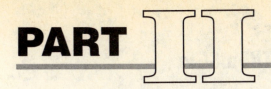

PART II

CSET Overview and Test Strategies

2 CSET PREPARATION AND TEST-TAKING STRATEGIES

TEST INFO BOX

The chapter shows you how to set up a test preparation schedule and shows you test-taking strategies that will help you improve your score.

The two most important test-taking strategies are discussed below.

Multiple Choice

- Eliminate and then guess.

- There is no penalty for wrong answers on the CSET. Never leave any answer blank.

On average, if you just guess the answer you have a 25 percent chance of being correct. Eliminate one answer and your chances of being correct increase to 33 percent. Eliminate two answers and you have a 50 percent chance of being correct. Of course, if you can definitely eliminate three answers, the remaining answer is always correct.

Say you know the answer to 26 of 52 items, that you eliminate two answers and guess on 10 items, eliminate one answer, then guess on 9 items, and just guess on the remaining 7 items. On average you will answer 36 items correctly. That's 69 percent correct and likely a "passing" score on the multiple choice items.

Say you know 31 answers and just guess on the remaining 21. On average that's also 36 correct and a likely "passing" score on the multiple choice items.

These are averages and things could turn out worse or better than the scenarios described above. But eliminate and guess is a powerful test-taking strategy and you should always use it when you don't know the answer.

Constructed Response

- Always write something. That is usually worth 1 point.

- Write for a 2, avoid a 0.

PREPARING FOR THE CSET

By now you've sent in the registration form and the test is at least four to nine weeks away. This section describes how to prepare for the CSET.

Wait! Why Test Me? I'm a Good Person!

Why indeed? Life would be so much easier without tests. If anyone tells you that they like to take tests, don't believe them. Nobody does. Tests are imperfect. Some people pass when they should have failed, while others fail when they should have passed. It may not be fair, but it is very real. So sit back and relax. You're just going to have to do it, and this book will show you how.

Who Makes Up These Tests and How Do They Get Written?

Consider the following scenario. It is late in the afternoon in Sacramento, California. Around a table sit teachers, deans of education, parents, and representatives of state education departments. In front of each person is a preliminary list of skills and knowledge that teachers should possess. The list comes from comments by an even larger group of teachers and other educational professionals.

Those around the table are regular people just like the ones you might run into in a store or on the street. They all care about education. They also bring to the table their own strengths and weaknesses—their own perspectives and biases. What's that? An argument just broke out. People are choosing up sides and, depending on the outcome, one item on the list will stay or go.

The final list goes to professional test writers to prepare test items. These items are tried out, refined, and put through a review process. Eventually the test question bank is established, and a test is born. These test writers are not geniuses. They just know how to write questions. You might get a better score on this test than some of them would.

The test writers want to write a test that measures important things. They try not to ask dumb or obscure questions that have strange answers. For the most part, they are successful. You can count on the test questions to ask about things you should know.

You can also be sure that the test writers will ask questions that will make you think. Their questions will ask you to use what you know. They will not ask for rote responses.

Keep those people around the table and the test writers in mind as you use this book. You are preparing for their test. Soon, you will be like one of those people around the table. You may even contribute to a test like this one.

Get Yourself Ready for the Test

Most people feel at least a little bit uncomfortable about tests. You are probably one of them. No book is going to make you feel comfortable. But here are some suggestions.

Most people are less tense when they exercise. Set up a reasonable exercise program for yourself. The program should involve exercising in a way that is appropriate for you 30 to 45 minutes each day. This exercise may be just as important as other preparation.

Prepare with another person. You will feel less isolated if you have a friend or colleague to study with.

Accept these important truths. You are not going to get all the answers correct. You don't have to. You can take this test over again if you have to. Remember the score you have to get. There is no penalty for taking the test again. This is not a do or die, life or death situation.

Follow This Study Plan

Begin working four to ten weeks before the test. Use the study schedule that follows.

Most review chapters start with a review quiz. Take each review quiz. Use the answer key to mark the review quiz. Each incorrect answer will point you to a specific portion of the review. Use the subject matter review indicated by the review quiz. Don't spend your time reviewing things you already know.

CSET STUDY SCHEDULE

This plan starts ten weeks before the test and it is designed for all three subtests. Adjust the time line if you have less time to study or if you are only taking one or two subtests. Write your target completion date for each step of the review in the space provided.

Ten weeks to go   **Target Completion Date**_____
Set up your study plan on pages 4–5.
Review Chapters 1 and 2.

Nine weeks to go   **Target Completion Date**_____
Review Chapter 3–Reading, Language and Literature

Eight weeks to go   **Target Completion Date**_____
Review Chapter 4–History and Social Studies

Seven weeks to go   **Target Completion Date**_____
Review Chapter 5–Science

Six weeks to go   **Target Completion Date**_____
Review Chapter 6–Mathematics

Five weeks to go   **Target Completion Date**_____
Review Chapter 7–Visual and Performing Arts
Chapter 8–Physical Education
Chapter 9–Human Development
Review the test-taking strategies on pages 20–43.

Four weeks before the actual test   **Target Completion Date**_____
Take Practice CSET (page 395)
Try to take the test on Saturday under exact test conditions.
Score the test and review the answer explanations.

**Four weeks to go and
Three weeks to go**   **Target Completion Date**_____
Review the errors you made on Practice CSET 1.
Review the test-taking strategies on pages 20–43.

Two weeks before the actual test   **Target Completion Date**_____
Take Practice CSET 2 (page 456)
Try to take the test on Saturday under exact test conditions.
Score the test and review the answer explanations.

Two weeks to go   *Target Completion Date*_____

During this week look over those areas you got wrong on the second Practice CSET. Go over the answer explanations and go back to the review sections. Read the newspaper every day until the day before the test.

One week to go   *Target Completion Date*_____

The hard work is over. You're coasting in for a landing. You know the material on the test. You don't even have to get an A. You just have to pass.

Get up each day at the time you will have to get up the following Saturday. Sit down at the time the test will start and spend about one hour answering questions on practice tests. It's okay that you have answered these questions before.

MONDAY

Make sure you have your admission ticket.
Make sure you know where the test is given.
Make sure you know how you're getting there.

TUESDAY

Visit the test site, if you haven't done it already. You don't want any surprises this Saturday.

WEDNESDAY

Get some sharpened No. 2 pencils, a digital watch or pocket clock, and a good big eraser and put them aside.

THURSDAY

Take a break from preparing for the test, and relax.

FRIDAY

Complete any forms you have to bring to the test.
Prepare any snacks or food you want to bring with you.
Talk to someone who makes you feel good or do something enjoyable and relaxing.
Have a good night's sleep.

SATURDAY—TEST DAY

Dress comfortably. There are no points for appearance.
Eat the same kind of breakfast you've been eating each morning.
Don't stuff yourself. You want your blood racing through your brain, not your stomach.
Get together things to bring to the test including: registration ticket, identification forms, pencils, calculator, eraser, and snacks or food.

Get to the test room, not the parking lot, about 10 to 15 minutes before the start time.
Remember to leave time for parking and walking to the test site.
Hand in your forms–you're in the door. You're ready. This is the easy part.
Follow the test-taking strategies in the next section.

Interview with a College Professor Who Took the CSET: Multiple Subjects

About a month before the final deadline for this book, this author had a conversation with Dr. Mark O'Shea, Professor of Education at the California State University—Monterey Bay. Dr. O'Shea and I each claim Columbia University as our graduate alma mater. He took quite a bit of time to share his reactions and his students' reactions to the CSET. You should consider these views as you prepare for the test.

Bob Postman:	Dr. O'Shea, it is nice to talk to you today.
Mark O'Shea:	Dr. Postman, I am glad we were able to find this time to get together.
Bob:	I understand that you have taken all three subtests of the CSET: Multiple Subjects.
Mark:	That's right.
Bob:	It is unusual for a college professor to take the CSET. How did you come to take the test?
Mark:	I wanted to be certified as an elementary school teacher in California. I took the CSET: Multiple Subjects to get my California teaching certificate in support of my role as a teacher educator.
Bob:	That puts you in a unique position to help the readers of this book as they prepare for the CSET: Multiple Subjects.
Mark:	Yes, and I will help, but I will not be able to talk specifically about any of the CSET test questions.
Bob:	Fair enough—where's a good place to start.
Mark:	Well, I passed all three subtests.
Bob:	That is important.
Mark:	I took all three subtests on the same day. It is true that I am not the standard test taker, and I was fortunate to have an excellent undergraduate education. However, there were over two hours left when I finished all three subtests.
	That makes me think that a good student, who usually does well on tests, could take all three parts and usually pass them all. It's up to the student and how many months they want to spend to pass all three subtests. I think it's good to get it over with as soon as possible so the student can concentrate on other things.
Bob:	What type of student should take fewer than three tests?
Mark:	There is a lot of reading on the CSET. Students whose first language is not English may have some trouble finishing all three subtests. I've also heard that from students here at the college.
	I would advise those students to take just one or two subtests during each testing period.
	You should also only take one or two subtests if you just do not do well on tests or if you usually take a long time to answer questions.

Bob:	There is a table on page 3 in this book that shows about how long a student has to answer a question if that student takes one, two, or three subtests.
Mark:	That should help, and you just have to use common sense. Failing a test may not be the best thing; however, if you don't pass you just take it over again. There is no other penalty. You have to pay again, of course. A student should not be concerned if they do not pass. That student should just keep going until he or she is successful.
Bob:	How about the test itself?
Mark:	I have very specific reactions to the test in five areas.
Bob:	What are they?
Mark:	First is the usefulness of the state standards.
	Second is the usefulness of the Hirsch books.
	Third is the usefulness of the online test posted by NES.
	Fourth is the overall content and difficulty of the test.
	Fifth is the reason that students usually give for not passing the CSET.
Bob:	That is an excellent list.
Mark:	Let me add that the things I am going to talk about here are generally validated by those students here at the college who have taken the CSET: Multiple Subjects.
Bob:	Okay—first the standards—the California standards give the subject matter that students are supposed to learn in schools.
Mark:	That's right. I reviewed the standards both before and after I took the test. The CSET I took did not test information in the detail and at the depth that you find in these standards. My advice to students, based on the test I took, is not to be intimidated by all the information in the standards. It will just cause you to be unnecessarily concerned. You should be familiar with these topics, but not in anywhere near that detail.
Bob:	Next, what about the E. D. Hirsch "What Every ___ Grader Needs to Know" books?
Mark:	I worked through the Fourth Grade book in that series. It is a good book, but it was really not that related to the test I took. The only place I found useful help was in a brief section about music. Your book gives a music review.
Bob:	Yes, this book has a music review section.
Mark:	I would say that the Hirsch books could be appropriate for someone who does not have a sound undergraduate education. My impression is that these books do not need to be a regular part of the review for most students.

Bob:	Third is the usefulness of the sample CSET posted online by National Evaluation Systems. This sample CSET is available at *http://www.cset.nesinc.com/*.
Mark:	This sample test was very useful. It gave a good indication of what the CSET was like, both in scope and in difficulty. Students need additional practice. Your book has two practice tests with explained answers.
Bob:	Fourth was the overall content and difficulty of the CSET.
Mark:	The CSET I took tested information at about the tenth or eleventh grade level. Most of the questions did not ask for detailed information. This makes the CSET: Multiple Subjects test different from the Multiple Subjects Assessment Test (MSAT) from ETS. The MSAT was previously required in California and it was more difficult. You do need a general knowledge of subject matter for the CSET, but there is a lot of common sense too.
	The Reading/Language test may have been the most difficult, and it included questions about teaching reading.
	The History/Social Studies test had more questions about California history than I was expecting, particularly compared with the relatively few world history questions I came across. My test did not include any items that asked for specific dates.
	California history is something worth brushing up on. Your book includes a review of California history.
Bob:	Yes, there is a California history review section.
Mark:	On the science part, the questions were pretty much evenly divided among the various science areas. The mathematics test had a different emphasis and different question types than the CBEST, but it seemed to me that the test was about at the same difficulty level. The mathematics test also included some questions about teaching mathematics. A student should brush up on mathematics skills and concepts and practice a little with a four-function calculator.
	Subtest III seemed fairly straightforward to me. There was some art to comment on but it did not require a sophisticated analysis. The music questions were very fundamental. I thought the questions on physical education and child development could be answered from experience. Much of this subtest was common sense.
	Overall I would say it is a reasonable test that you should prepare for, but don't over-prepare for it. I think it is actually easier for many students to over-prepare than under-prepare.
Bob:	What is your overall advice?
Mark:	Most successful students spend about 30 hours preparing for the CSET. That is about 15 hours for review and another 15 hours to take two practice tests and to review the answer explanations. That sounds about right to me for most students.

Bob: Some students are not successful the first time they take the test. You have feedback from some of these about why they did not pass.

Mark: I do. First, let me say that I have never had a student tell me they did not know enough to pass the test. Certainly, there are some students in that category, but I have not heard from any.

Many students point to the constructed response items as the source of their problem. There is a relatively small box to write the response for each item. Some students could not fit their answer in that area and wrote outside the box. It was clear that the person rating the answers did not look at what was written outside the response box.

Other students realized they had not responded to some of the points raised in the constructed response item. Just be sure to write in the space provided and be sure to respond to all the points raised in the item.

Others students with English as their second language who took two or three tests said they did not have enough time to respond appropriately to all of the items.

Other students who did not pass wished they had taken several practice tests and wished they had used some of the tips for answering multiple choice questions that I know are in your book.

Bob: Any last thoughts?

Mark: We talked about this informally before the interview began, and so I know we agree.

The CSET is a test to be passed. The test is not your life and it does not define you as a person. It does not predict how successful you will be as a teacher. Prepare for it, take it, pass it, and then move on with life and your teaching career.

Bob: Is there a way students can contact you?

Mark: They can email me at Mark_OShea@csumb.edu

Bob: Dr. O'Shea, thank you very much, and thanks also to your students at CSU—Monterey Bay.

Mark: Thank you Dr. Postman, and good luck on the CSET to all who read this book.

PROVEN TEST-TAKING STRATEGIES

Testing companies like to pretend that test-taking strategies don't help that much. They act like that because they want everyone to think that their tests only measure your knowledge of the subject. Of course, they are just pretending; test-taking strategies can make a big difference.

However, there is nothing better than being prepared for the subject matter on this test. These strategies will do you little good if you lack this fundamental knowledge. If you are prepared, then these strategies can make a difference. Use them. Other people will be. Not using them may very well lower your score.

Be Comfortable

Get a good seat. Don't sit near anyone or anything that will distract you. Stay away from your friends. If you don't like where you are sitting, move or ask for another seat. You paid money for this test, and you have a right to favorable test conditions.

You Will Make Mistakes

You are going to make mistakes on this test. The people who wrote the test expect you to make them.

You Are Not Competing with Anyone

Don't worry about how anyone else is doing. Your score does not depend on theirs. When the score report comes out it doesn't say, "Nancy got a 230, but Blaire got a 245." You just want to get the score required for your certificate. If you can do better, that's great. Stay focused. Remember your goal.

Taking More Than One Subtest

Most advisors recommend you register first for the subtest that will be most difficult for you. But once you've registered and it's test day, always complete first the subtest that is easiest for you. Take the time to do everything you can to pass that subtest. Only then move on to the other subtests. It's fine if you only have time to guess the multiple choice answers and sketch in constructed responses on the other subtests. It's also fine if you don't have enough time to complete the second or third subtest you signed up for. But you don't want to leave the test session without giving yourself the best chance to pass at least one subtest.

MULTIPLE CHOICE STRATEGIES

It's Not What You Know That Matters, It's Just Which Circle You Fill In

No one you know or care about will see your test. An impersonal machine scores all multiple choice questions. The machine just senses whether the correct circle on the answer sheet is filled in. That is the way the test makers want it. If that's good enough for them, it should be good enough for you. Concentrate on filling in the correct circle.

You Can Be Right but Be Marked Wrong

If you get the right answer but fill in the wrong circle, the machine will mark it wrong. We told you that filling in the right circle was what mattered. We strongly recommend that you follow this strategy.

Write the letter for your answer big in the test booklet next to the number for the problem. If you change your mind about an answer, cross off the "old" letter and write the "new" one. At the end of each section, transfer all the answers together from the test booklet to the answer sheet.

Do Your Work in the Test Booklet

You can write anything you want in your test booklet. The test booklet is not used for scoring and no one will look at it. You can't bring scratch paper to the test so use your booklet instead.

Some of the strategies we recommend involve writing in and marking up the booklet. These strategies work and we strongly recommend that you use them.

Do your work for a question near that question in the test booklet. You can also do work on the cover or wherever else suits you. You may want to do calculations, underline important words, mark up a picture, or draw a diagram.

Watch That Answer Sheet

Remember that a machine is doing the marking. Fill in the correct answer circle completely. Don't put extra pencil marks on the answer section of the answer sheet. Stray marks could be mistaken for answers.

Some Questions Are Traps

Some questions include the words *not*, *least*, or *except*. You are being asked for the answer that doesn't fit with the rest. Be alert for these types of questions.

Save the Hard Questions for Last

You're not supposed to get all the questions correct, and some of them will be too difficult for you. Work through the questions and answer the easy ones. Pass the other ones by. Do these more difficult questions the second time through. If a question seems really hard, draw a circle around the question number in the test booklet. Save these questions until the very end.

They Show You the Answer

Every multiple choice test shows you the correct answer for each question. The answer is staring right at you. You just have to figure out which one it is. There is a 20 or 25 percent chance you'll get it right by just closing your eyes and pointing.

Some Answers Are Traps

When someone writes a test question, they often include distracters. Distracters are traps— incorrect answers that look like correct answers. It might be an answer to an addition problem when you should be multiplying. It might be a correct answer to a different question. It might just be an answer that catches your eye. Watch out for this type of incorrect answer.

Eliminate the Incorrect Answers

If you can't figure out which answer is correct, then decide which answers can't be correct. Choose the answers you're sure are incorrect. Cross them off in the test booklet. Only one left? That's the correct answer.

Guess, Guess, Guess

If there are still two or more answers left, then guess. Guess the answer from those remaining. Never leave any item blank. There is no penalty for guessing.

CONSTRUCTED RESPONSE STRATEGIES

You should have about 15 minutes to write each constructed response. Look over the table on page 3 for estimates of the amount of time available to answer items for various combinations of subtests. The test company estimates that it will take about ten or fifteen minutes to write each response.

You will write each constructed response answer on a special single-page, lined sheet provided with the test. There is only room for 150 to 200 words and you may not use additional sheets. You should always print your answer. A useful part of your preparation is learning to fit your answer in the space provided.

Scoring Criteria

There are three scoring criteria.

> **Purpose:** How well does the response address the assignment based on CSET content.
> **Subject Matter Knowledge:** How well does the response demonstrate CSET subject knowledge.
> **Support:** How well does the response support the answer with CSET content.

You get the idea. Answer the question. Show that you know something. Provide as much support as you can. You don't have to support every single thing you write. Include everything that belongs in your response even if you can't provide support.

Here's How They Score You

Two California teachers or college professors, trained to evaluate answers using holistic scoring, will score your response. Holistic scoring means the scorer rates the response based on their informed impression, not a detailed analysis.

The highest possible total score from both raters for a response is 6. Scorers use this rating scale.

3 This rating indicates the response shows a mastery of the CSET knowledge and skills. That means the response directly addresses the assignment and includes accurate content and appropriate evidence.

2 This rating indicates the response shows a partial mastery of the CSET knowledge and skills. That means the response partially addresses the assignment and includes somewhat accurate content and incomplete evidence.

1 This rating indicates the response shows a limited mastery of the CSET knowledge and skills. That means the response may not directly address the assignment and may not include accurate content and appropriate evidence.

U This rating indicates the response is unscorable. That means the response is too short, unrelated to the assignment, illegible, or primarily written in a language other than English.

B This rating indicates the response is blank.

Set your goal at 3. Write for a minimum of 2. Avoid a U.

Most responses rated 3 by NES standards have about 120 to 150 words. That does not mean that a response this long will always receive a 3 or that some responses will not be longer. It does mean you will usually have to write that many words to qualify for a 3.

You can usually get a 2 with a solid paragraph or two with about 80 to 100 words. Always write enough to get a 1. You can usually think of something to write about the topic. Two sentences on the topic should be good enough for a 1.

You have to communicate clearly, but English grammar, itself, is not evaluated.

Use Your Time Wisely

Let's say you have 15 minutes to write your response. Here is a plan for using your time.

1. Read and Understand the Item (1 minute)

Read the item carefully to be sure you understand what it asks for. If you write a great answer that is not about the topic the rater will give you a "U." Do not waste your time supplying information not called for in the item. Extraneous information will just detract from your rating.

2. Jot Down a Brief Outline (3 minutes)

Jot down two topic sentences that convey the main points you want to include in your response. Write a supporting detail or two under each topic sentence. I say sentences, but these can just be phrases—ideas.

Do this directly in the text booklet below the item. Use these three minutes to think about your answer and chart your course. If you just start to write on the response sheet you might well write yourself into a corner. The limited space for the answer would require you to erase your work, and that's when real problems will begin.

3. Write Your Response (8 minutes)

Write directly and clearly. Print your answer on the response sheet. Plan to write about 100 to 150 words. We follow the guidelines from NES that show responses in paragraph form. However, it is also fine to outline your answers or number responses. Do not restate the item. The next section gives detailed steps for writing your response.

Use this approach when you write your response. Write your response on the sheet provided in the test materials. Responses written in the test booklet or outside the response sheet will not be scored.

Rewrite the first topic sentence from your outline. Write the topic sentence on the sheet provided in the test materials. Raters expect at least one clear statement about the topic. Write yours and stick to it. Make sure the topic sentence directly addresses the topic.

Write two or three more sentences with details to support the topic sentence. Details support the topic sentence. Details tell how, what, or why the topic sentence is true. Details can be explanations or examples.

Rewrite the second topic sentence from your outline to begin another paragraph. Then write at least one other sentence with details.

4. Review and Revise (3 minutes)

Compare your response to the item to be sure you have responded completely. Delete, add, or change words to clarify your response.

Leave time to read your response. Raters understand that your response is a first draft and they expect to see corrections. However, do not spend your time correcting minor grammatical or punctuation errors.

PRACTICE CONSTRUCTED RESPONSE ITEMS

Given below are seven constructed response items from each of the seven test areas. Write responses for the subtest or subtests you are preparing for. Use the space provided on the response sheet to write your response. Assignments are numbered sequentially 1 through 7.

Pages 33–43 provide a step-by-step explanation of the first item, and three rated examples for all seven items. You should show your responses to a qualified professor or teacher for an evaluation and for suggestions on how to improve your work.

Assignment 1 (Reading, Language, and Literature)
Subtest I

Read this passage from Act 2 Scene 2 of Shakespeare's *Romeo and Juliet* (circa 1595), then complete the exercise that follows.

JULIET

Well, do not swear. Although I joy in thee,
I have no joy of this contract to-night:
It is too rash, too unadvised, too sudden;
Too like the lightning, which doth cease to be
Ere one can say "It lightens." Sweet, good night!
This bud of love, by summer's ripening breath,
May prove a beauteous flower when next we meet.
Good night, good night! as sweet repose and rest
Come to thy heart as that within my breast!

Write a response in which you describe how Shakespeare uses simile and metaphor in this passage. You should cite specific examples from the passage.

_____

_____

_____

_____

_____

_____

_____

_____

_____

_____

End of Assignment 1

Assignment 2 (History and Social Science)
Subtest I

In the late 1800s, following decades of disagreements, Southern states announced their withdrawal from the United States and formed the Confederate States of America. The American Civil War followed.

Using what you know of United States History, write a response in which you

- identify three important causes of the Civil War

- provide an explanation of why one of these three causes led to the Civil War

_____

_____

_____

_____

_____

_____

_____

_____

_____

_____

_____

_____

_____

_____

End of Assignment 2

Assignment 3 (Science)
Subtest II

In a classroom experiment, students drop different objects from the same height to the ground below. They accurately measure how long it takes an object to reach the ground below. In particular, the students drop a bowling ball, a tennis ball, a large blanket, and a small marble. The students observe that all the objects take the same time to fall to the ground, except the blanket, which takes longer. From this experiment the students conclude that all objects do not fall at the same rate.

Use what you know of physics to write a response that

- discusses the validity of the conclusion that the students draw from this experiment.

- provides an explanation of why the blanket took longer to fall than the other objects.

End of Assignment 3

Assignment 4 (Mathematics)
Subtest II

 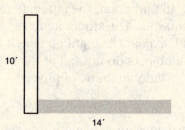

The picture above accurately represents the height of a stick on the length of its shadow and the length of a tree's shadow at exactly the same time. The stick and the tree are both perpendicular to the ground.

Use what you know of algebra and geometry to

• write a proportion that represents the relationship between the heights of objects and the length of shadows shown in the diagram.

• show how to use the proportion to find the height of the tree.

_____

_____

_____

_____

_____

_____

_____

_____

_____

_____

End of Assignment 4

Assignment 5 (Physical Education)
Subtest III

Locomotor skills and learning activities are an important part of any elementary school physical education program. Locomotor skills and learning activities are different from nonlocomotor activities.

Using your knowledge of physical education activities, write a response that

- identifies three locomotor activities and explains why these are locomotor and not non-locomotor activities.

- Then choose one of these locomotor activities and describe two appropriate learning activities for the skill you have chosen.

_____

_____

_____

_____

_____

_____

_____

_____

_____

_____

_____

_____

_____

End of Assignment 5

Assignment 6 (Human Development)
Subtest III

Child abuse is one of the most pervasive problems in society today.
Use what you know of human development to write a response that

- describes the impact of child abuse on that child's performance in school and actions in life.

- identifies who is most likely to be the person who abused a child.

_____

_____

_____

_____

_____

_____

_____

_____

_____

_____

_____

_____

_____

End of Assignment 6

Assignment 7 (Visual and Performing Arts)
Subtest III

Base your response on this photograph by Arnold Genther, which shows a scene on Sacramento Street looking toward the bay in San Francisco after the San Francisco Earthquake.

["Photograph: After the San Francisco Earthquake" by Arnold Genther. The Metropolitan Museum of Art, The Alfred Stieglitz Collection, 1933. (33.43.223)]

Using your knowledge of visual and performing arts, write a response that

• describes the most striking elements of form and composition in the picture.

• discusses why this picture would be an appropriate one for elementary school students to analyze and discuss.

End of Assignment 7

APPLYING THE STEPS

This section shows you how to apply these steps and gives examples of rated responses for a practice Assignment 1 from Subtest I. No book can evaluate the quality of your response. You must ask an experienced professor or teacher to review the practice responses you write and ask them to suggest improvements. Two raters score your response 1–3, and the highest total score is 6.

Assignment 1—Subtest I.

Read this passage from Act 2 Scene 2 of Shakespeare's *Romeo and Juliet* (circa 1595), then complete the exercise that follows.

JULIET

Well, do not swear. Although I joy in thee,
I have no joy of this contract to-night:
It is too rash, too unadvised, too sudden;
Too like the lightning, which doth cease to be
Ere one can say "It lightens." Sweet, good night!
This bud of love, by summer's ripening breath,
May prove a beauteous flower when next we meet.
Good night, good night! as sweet repose and rest
Come to thy heart as that within my breast!

Write a response in which you describe how Shakespeare uses simile and metaphor in this passage. You should cite specific examples from the passage.

1. Read and Understand the Item (1 minute)

This item asks me to explain how this passage uses metaphor. A metaphor is a figure of speech that makes a comparison of two unlike things without using the words like or as. A simile uses the words like or as.

2. Jot Down a Brief Topic Sentence Outline (3 minutes)

Simile—Compares contract with lightning
  Contract to-night
  Doth cease to be
Metaphor—Compares love to a flower
  Bud of love
  Beauteous flower

Juliet is saying don't rush.

This response would likely receive a total score of 5 or 6 out of 6.
There are 142 words in this response.

Shakespeare uses simile when in the second and fourth line Juliet says the "contract tonight" is "too like the lightning, which doth cease to be." The word like in the passage identifies this as a simile. Shakespeare uses metaphor in this passage when he compares love to a flower. You see the comparison in lines five and seven when Juliet says that the "bud of love" she feels now may grow into a "beauteous flower" by the next time they meet.

We know from the play's title that Juliet is speaking to Romeo. Through simile and metaphor, she is saying that things are moving too quickly. Time spent together tonight could be too temporary. While she likes Romeo, Juliet feels the beginning of love she has for Romeo now, "by summer's ripening breath," may blossom fully by the next time they meet.

This response would likely receive a total score of 3 or 4 out of 6.
There are 81 words in this response.

Shakespeare is using the comparison of being together with someone tonight with lightning because it does not last and uses comparison of what she calls a bud of love she says she feels now with a full flower of love she says she may feel some time in the future. Juliet is telling Romeo to stop being so aggressive and to stop pushing her for a date. It is as though she's telling him "I'll call you — don't you call me."

This response would likely receive a total score of 2 out of 6.
There are 108 words in this response.

This passage is from Romeo and Juliet about two sweethearts, and it was written by William Shakespeare about 550 years ago. But some people think Shakespeare may not really have written all the things they say he has written. They wrote differently back then and the words he uses do not have their literal meanings. So it can be hard to follow but it seems that Juliet has some sort of bud of a feeling for Romeo that she wants the summer to ripen into a full-blossomed rose. That is a very nice thought and Shakespeare is known for writing those sort of nice thoughts in his works.

RATED EXAMPLES

Given below are rated examples for practice Assignments 2, 3, 4, 5, 6, and 7.

Assignment 2 (History and Social Studies)
Subtest I

Likely score of 5 or 6 out of 6.

> There were many causes of the Civil War.
> 1- Slavery.
> 2- State's rights.
> 3- The shift of population from southern states to northern states.
> Slavery - most significant cause
>
> Leading up to the Civil War there were tremendous disagreements over whether a state would be admitted as a free state or a slave state. Slavery was legal in all states but slavery was required to support the economy of southern states. Slavery was not required to support the economy of the more populous northern states. After Lincoln was elected president southern states were not able to get assurances that slavery would continue to be legal. This concern that slavery would eventually be ruled illegal, among other factors, led to secession and the Civil War.

Likely score of 3 or 4 out of 6

> The Civil War was caused by slavery, concern over states' rights, and arguments over which states would be free and which states would be slave states.
>
> Slavery was the main cause of the Civil War. Southern states needed slave labor to harvest the crops and southerners were just used to having people waiting on them. Southerners would not accept the fact that northerners wanted to do away with slavery, even though a lot of Southerners did not think slavery was right. The Underground Railway helped slaves escape to the north as another indication of the problems with southern slavery.

Likely score of 2 out of 6

> The Civil War was caused by slavery the battles in Kansas and by the attack on Fort Sumter in South Carolina. Without that attack on the fort the Civil War would not have started and that would have given the politicians more time to try to straighten things out. That is why I think the attack on the fort is the most important cause of the Civil War.

Assignment 3 (Science)
Subtest II

Likely score of 5 or 6 out of 6.

> The student's conclusion about falling objects is not valid because they did not take all factors into account. Effective controls are one of the most important aspects of designing an experiment. The falling bowling ball, tennis ball and marble fall in reaction to gravity. We know that the force of gravity causes all objects to fall at the same rate. That means all these objects will reach the ground at the same time, as the experiment for just these objects shows.
>
> The blanket takes longer to reach the ground because it is slowed as it encounters air and wind. The blanket really falls at the same rate as the other objects but the experiment does not measure what it was designed to measure because of these other forces. It is almost impossible to take these factors into account during the experiment. The students did not control for that variable and so they ended up with an invalid conclusion.

Likely score of 3 or 4 out of 6.

> The student's conclusion is not valid because they did not take all the factors into account. The blanket is very different from the other objects and it falls in a different way. That is what makes the conclusion invalid.
>
> The blanket falls at a different rate because it spreads out and floats down on the air currents. It is these air currents that lead the students to their incorrect conclusion.

Likely score of 2 out of 6

Every experiment just has the results that can be observed. For that very reason it is not correct to say that this experiment is invalid. It is true that the results do not agree with the results of other experiments, which means that these students should go back and to view their experiment to see if they can find a more appropriate approach.

Assignment 4 (Mathematics)
Subtest II

Likely score of 5 or 6 out of 6.

The proportion is the height of the tree/tree's shadow equals that height of the stick divided by the length of the stick's shadow. You show the proportion this way.

The T is the tree's height

$$\frac{T}{21} = \frac{10}{14}$$

Cross multiply to find T

$$14T = 21 \times 10$$
$$14T = 210$$
$$T = \frac{210}{14} = 15$$

The tree height is 15 feet.

Likely score of 3 or 4 out of 6

The T is the tree's height

$$\frac{T}{21} = \frac{10}{14}$$

Then you cross multiply to find T

Write this proportion.

$$\frac{T}{10} \quad X \quad \frac{21}{14}$$

Then Multiply.

$$\frac{21T}{140} = \frac{T}{15}$$

That means the tree is about 15 feet tall.

Likely score of 2 out of 6

The height of the tree is going to be less than the length of its shadow. So as I measure the drawing and I use 75% that seems to be the percent I get.

$$0.75 \times 21 = 15.75 \text{ or about 16 feet}$$

Assignment 5 (Physical Education)
Subtest III

Likely score of 5 or 6 out of 6.

Crawl, jump, and run are all examples of locomotor activities. These locomotor activities "move" the body from one place to another. These activities are very different from nonlocomotor activities, which do not move the body from one place to another. Examples of nonlocomotor activities include stretching and bending.

Running means transferring the weight from the ball of one foot to the ball of the other foot. Both feet are frequently off the ground and the arms swing in the opposite direction from leg movement.

Initially, a teacher can actually help a student understand how they run by asking the child to run at a different pace. Ask the student to run as slowly as they can over a 50 yard distance. The teacher should point out that both feet are off the ground as the child runs. Students can eventually be taught to run for fitness. They should be helped to maintain an appropriate pace and to monitor their heart rate as they run.

Likely score of 3 or 4 out of 6

Running, jumping and crawling are all examples of locomotor activities. These are locomotor and not nonlocomotor activities because they move the body from one place to the other.

Running is almost a natural activity and most students learn to run well before they come to school. So there is not much left for the teacher to do when it comes to teaching about running. What a teacher can do is to be sure that children actually do run, whether that running comes as a part of regular play or in races or in games such as soccer and tennis that include running at different rates.

Likely score of 2 out of 6

Locomotor activities move the body from one place to the other and there are more than just three locomotor activities. But any activity that moves the body around is a locomotor activity.

One of the most common locomotor activities is running. A teacher can show students how to run as a part of many field games such as soccer and softball. In soccer you run most of the time but in softball you are sitting most of the time or standing in the field.

Assignment 6 (Human Development)
Subtest III

Likely score of 5 or 6 out of 6

Child abuse has a devastating impact on a child's school learning. Abused children often have such a disruptive home environment that they cannot work there and cannot receive help from parents. Child abuse frequently leads to learning disabilities or other problems that interfere with a child's learning. Abused students are often absent from school and can't keep up with work. Abused students are often killed I remember reading that about 2000 children die from child abuse each year and that number is probably underreported. Abused children go on to be abusers themselves and are more likely to become criminals and to have other serious problems in life than those who were not abused.

The child abuser is almost always well know to the child and is most likely a family member. So with all the concern there is about abuse by others who care for children, the most likely abuser is the person most responsible for the child's care.

Likely score of 3 or 4 out of 6

Abused children perform more poorly in school than children who are not abused. These abused children cannot concentrate on school work and may think only of the fate waiting for them out of school. These children are often embarrassed or intimidated and will not tell anyone about what is happening to them. But it is the responsibility of a teacher to contact the appropriate authority if the teacher thinks that a child my be abused. But their problems also cause disruptions in the classroom for other students. Even then the person they contact may not do anything to help that child. Abused children do not enjoy a very good life. All of the problems they had in school just continue to show up in life.

Someone living with the abused child is the person most likely to be the abuser. It is not usually a priest or a teacher even though we hear a lot about those cases.

Likely score of 2 out of 6

A lot of children who have been abused turn out to have problems in school. They may have trouble with reading or writing or mathematics. You really never know where the problem will pop up. There are many abused children who do fine in school but they are having so many problems that you know they could do better.

Lots of times the abuser is someone like a clergyman or a baby sitter. The abuser could also be someone like the child's stepfather or uncle.

Assignment 7 (Visual and Performing Arts)
Subtest III

Likely score of 5 or 6 out of 6

This photograph captures so much about what happened after the San Francisco earthquake. You can see the damage done to the buildings right near where the photographer was standing. The rubble is still on the street. You see people standing in groups and talking or sitting. Everyone is looking down the hill on Sacramento Street. I first thought the people were looking down toward the bottom of the hill. And then I thought they were looking at a dust cloud. Then I realized the smoke in the photograph was from the fire that started after the earthquake and that the people were looking in the direction of that fire.

This photograph is very appropriate for elementary school students. It shows them the kind of photographs that were taken about 100 years ago. It also shows how the photographer captured so much of what was going on in one single still photo. Perhaps most importantly the photograph shows a link to the past that helps integrate the teaching of art and the teaching of California history.

Likely score of 3 or 4 out of 6

The San Francisco earthquake is one of the most important events in California history and this photograph gives just a little insight at that event. It shows the natural tendency of people to gather together in groups after a catastrophe like this and to talk. The whole street is filled with people and some of them seem very well dressed. You can also see lots damaged buildings.

This photograph would be wonderful to use in an elementary school class. Students could use the photo as a starting point to discuss the San Francisco earthquake. They could also wonder aloud about human nature and what brings people out to the street after a disaster and what individual people in the street are looking at or thinking about.

Likely score of 2 out of 6

This photograph shows Sacramento Street about 100 years ago after the San Francisco earthquake. You can see that the photographer stood in the middle of the street to frame this picture to get a balance on the left and right with buildings and people. The dust cloud must be from the collapsed buildings.

The picture shows a lot of interesting information and it helps students understand that the streets of San Francisco were as hill a hundred years as as they are today.

USING THE CALCULATOR

Reproduced with permission
Copyright (c) Texas Instruments Incorporated

At the test site, you will be given a TI-108 calculator to use just during Subtest II – Mathematics and Science. You can't bring your own calculator and you can't use the calculator on any other subtests.

The TI-108 is a basic four-function calculator with a square root key, memory keys, and a percent key. It's probably the calculator used most often in elementary schools. This section explains how to use the calculator on the CSET.

It is a good idea to get an inexpensive calculator that works exactly like the TI-108 to prepare for the CSET.

Key Entry Errors

Many calculator mistakes come from key entry errors. I would want to avoid that at all costs. Let me explain.

When you work with paper and pencil, you see all your work. On this calculator, you see only the last entry or the last answer. So it is possible to make a key entry error and, in a flurry of entries, never catch your mistake. We all put an enormous amount of trust in the calculator answer, and we don't usually question the answer it produces. This makes us particularly vulnerable to the results of these key entry errors.

How Should I Use a Calculator?

Use your calculator to calculate. Remember that the calculator is best at helping you find answers quickly. Use it to calculate the answers to numerical problems. Use it to try out answers quickly to find which is correct. Whenever you come across a problem involving calculation, you can use the calculator to do or check your work.

Estimate before you calculate. Earlier we mentioned that many calculator errors are caused by key entry mistakes. You think you put in one number, but you really put in another. One way to avoid this type of error is to estimate before you calculate. Then compare the estimate to your answer. If they aren't close, then either your estimate or your calculation is off.

Recognize when your calculator will be helpful. Let's think of problems in three categories. The calculator can be a big help, some help, or no help. The idea is to use your calculator on the first two types of problems and not to use it when it won't help.

Big Help

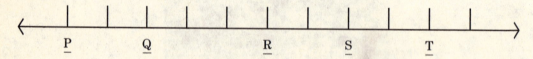

The segment $\overline{PT}$ has a length of 31.5. What is the length of segment $\overline{QS}$?

A calculator is a big help here. There are 9 units from P to T. So divide 31.5 by 9 = 3.5 to find the length of each unit. Multiply 3.5 by 5 = 17.5 to find the length of QS.

Some Help

A rectangle has a length 3 and width 5. What is the area?

You can do this computation in your head. A calculator could help you check the answer, but you don't absolutely need it.

No Help

Calculators are no help with problems involving equations or nonnumerical solutions. Using a calculator when it won't help will cause trouble and waste time.

ORDER OF OPERATIONS

There is a difficulty with the TI-108 that you'll have to work around during the test. The TI-108 does not use order of operations and it does not include keys with parentheses. The TI-108 just does the calculations in the order you press the keys

When there is more than one operation, calculations are done according to a particular order of operations.

1. Parentheses (Operations in parentheses are done first.)
2. Exponents
3. Multiplication
4. Division
5. Addition
6. Subtraction

Find the answer: $4 + 6 \times 5$

Using order of operation: $4 + 6 \times 5 = 4 + 30 = 34$
That's because you multiply first and then add.

But press $4 + 6 \times 5$ on a TI-108 and the answer is 50.
That's because the TI-108 just completes the calculation in the order you press the keys.

You have to press the TI-108 calculator keys as shown below to find the correct answer.
$6 \times 5 + 4 =$

How Are Calculator Keys Used?

Press the numeral keys and the decimal point to represent numbers.
Press the $\boxed{+}$, $\boxed{-}$, $\boxed{\times}$, and $\boxed{\div}$ keys to add, subtract, multiply, and divide.
Press the equal $\boxed{=}$ key when you are through to get the final answer.

4 $\boxed{\times}$ 7 $\boxed{+}$ 9 $\boxed{=}$ *37*   12 $\boxed{-}$ 18 $\boxed{=}$ *-6*

6 $\boxed{\times}$ 4 $\boxed{\times}$ 3 $\boxed{=}$ *72*   10 $\boxed{\div}$ 3 $\boxed{=}$ *3.3333333*

Square Root Key. $\boxed{\sqrt{}}$ To find the square root of 38.44 enter 38.44 $\boxed{\sqrt{}}$ =. Note also that the square root key will not simplify a square root. So the square root shows up as 2.8284, not $2\sqrt{2}$.

Integer Key. $\boxed{+/-}$ The subtraction key on the calculator cannot be used to represent negative integers. Use the $\boxed{+/-}$ key on the calculator after a number to change the sign. For example, to subtract $^-62 - {^+25}$, enter 62 $\boxed{+/-}$ $\boxed{-}$ 25 $\boxed{=}$. To multiply $^-8 \times {^-6}$, enter 8 $\boxed{+/-}$ $\boxed{\times}$ 6 $\boxed{+/-}$ $\boxed{=}$.

Percent Key $\boxed{\%}$

Use the percent key to find percent of increase or percent of decrease, such as the price after a sales tax is added or the price after a percent discount.

Find the cost of an item sold for $16 after a 7% sales tax.

Use these key strokes.

16 $\boxed{+}$ 7 $\boxed{\%}$ 17.12 [Do not press the equal sign.]

The cost with sales tax is $17.12.

Find the price of a $15.50 item sold at a 20% discount.

Use these key strokes.

1 5 . 5 0 $\boxed{-}$ 2 0 $\boxed{\%}$ 12.40   [Do not press the equal sign.]

The cost after the discount is $12.40.

Memory Keys $\boxed{M+}$ $\boxed{M-}$ $\boxed{MRC}$

The memory can be a handy place to store a number. The keys let you add and subtract values in memory, recall the value from memory and erase that number.

13 $\boxed{M+}$ places the 13 in memory.

5 $\boxed{M-}$ subtracts 5 from memory.

32.5 $\boxed{M+}$ adds 32 to the memory

Press $\boxed{MRC}$ after this series of key strokes and the display shows 40.5, the value stored in memory.

Press the $\boxed{MRC}$ a second time and the value in memory is erased.

$\boxed{ON/C}$

This key turns the calculator on. Press the key once after the calculator is on to erase the display. Press the key a second time to erase all the work you have done. Pressing this key does not erase the memory.

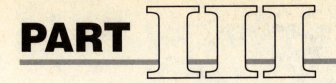

PART III

Subtest I Review

③ READING, LANGUAGE, AND LITERATURE

TEST INFO BOX

26 Multiple Choice items   Half of Subtest I items
2 Constructed Response items   Half of Subtest I items

READING, LANGUAGE, AND LITERATURE ITEMS

Multiple choice items look like this.

In which sentence is the underlined word used correctly?

(A) The rider grabbed the horse's <u>reign</u>.
(B) The teacher had just begun her <u>lessen</u>.
(C) The dog's collar showed its <u>address</u>.
(D) The road offered a steep <u>assent</u> to the plateau.

Constructed Response items look like this.

Write two brief paragraphs, one using argumentation and one using narration, to support Pacific Coast ecological movements.

USING THIS CHAPTER

This chapter prepares you to take the Reading, Language, and Literature subtest of the CSET.

❏ Read the Language and Linguistics Review on page 48.
❏ Read the Non-Written and Written Communication Review on page 62.
❏ Read the Texts Review on page 87.
❏ Complete the Targeted Test on page 98.

Reading, Language, and Literature topics on the CSET are partitioned into three domains, and this chapter is partitioned in the same way. However, these topics overlap and are related to one another. You will find that a review for one domain will help with the review in the other domains.

Chapter 2, CSET Preparation and Test-Taking Strategies includes annotated steps for writing essays and constructed response answers, which are related to the review in this chapter.

LANGUAGE AND LINGUISTICS

LEARNING TO READ

Reading is the most important subject addressed in school. Students who cannot read effectively are denied access to most other learning. There are dire practical consequences for those who cannot read. Teaching reading is a sophisticated, technical process that requires careful study.

This section reviews five areas of reading instruction: phonemic awareness, phonics, fluency, vocabulary, and text comprehension. You'll find a description of each topic, some specific examples and a summary of the most current research about reading instruction.

Phonemic Awareness

Here are some essential definitions related to phonemic awareness.

Phoneme

A phoneme is the smallest part of *spoken* language that makes a difference in the meaning of words. Phonemes are represented by letters between slash marks. English has about 41 phonemes. A few words have one phoneme, but most words have more than one phoneme: The word "at" has two phonemes, one for each letter; "check" has three phonemes (/ch/ /e/ /k/).

Grapheme

A grapheme is the smallest part of *written* language that represents a phoneme in the spelling of a word. A grapheme may be just one letter, such as "b" or "s" or several letters, such as "sh" or "ea."

Phonics

Phonics is the fairly predictable relationship between phonemes and graphemes.

Phonemic Awareness

Phonemic awareness is the ability to hear, identify, and manipulate the individual sounds—phonemes—in spoken words.

Phonological Awareness

Phonological awareness is a broad term that includes phonemic awareness. In addition to phonemes, phonological awareness activities can involve work with rhymes, words, syllables, and onsets and rimes.

Onset and rime

Onsets and rimes are parts of spoken language that are smaller than syllables but larger than phonemes. An onset is the initial consonant(s) sound of a syllable (the onset of bag is b-; of swim, sw-). A rime is the part of a syllable that contains the vowel and all that follows it (the rime of bag is -ag; of swim, -im).

Children learn phonemes—the sounds of a language—before they learn to read. Phonemic awareness is the ability to notice, think about, and work with those individual sounds in spoken words. Children who have well-established phonemic awareness skills generally find it easier to read and spell than children who do not.

Phonemic awareness is not phonics, as we can see from the definitions above. Phonemic awareness is not the same as phonological awareness, although phonemic awareness is a subcategory of phonological awareness. The focus of phonemic awareness is narrow—identifying and manipulating the individual sounds in words. The focus of phonological awareness is much broader. It includes identifying and manipulating larger parts of spoken language, such as words, syllables, and onsets and rimes—as well as phonemes. It also encompasses awareness of other aspects of sound, such as rhyming, alliteration, and intonation.

Here are some activities to build phonemic awareness.

Phoneme isolation - recognize individual sounds in a word.
Phoneme identity - recognize the same sounds in different words.
Phoneme categorization - recognize a word with a sound that does not match the sounds in other words.
Phoneme blending - combine the phonemes to form a word. Then they write and read the word.
Phoneme segmentation - break a word into its separate sounds, saying each sound.
Phoneme deletion - recognize the word that remains when a phoneme is removed from another word.
Phoneme addition - make a new word by adding a phoneme to an existing word.
Phoneme substitution - substitute one phoneme for another to make a new word.

Phonemic awareness instruction helps children learn to read.

Phonemic awareness instruction aids reading comprehension primarily through its influence on word reading. For children to understand what they read, they must be able to read words rapidly and accurately. Rapid and accurate word reading frees children to focus their attention on the meaning of what they read. Of course, many other things, including the size of children's vocabulary and their world experiences, contribute to reading comprehension.

Phonemic awareness instruction helps children learn to spell.

Teaching phonemic awareness, particularly how to segment words into phonemes, helps children learn to spell. The explanation for this may be that children who have phonemic awareness understand that sounds and letters are related in a predictable way. Thus, they are able to relate the sounds to letters as they spell words.

Phonemic awareness instruction is most effective when children are taught to manipulate phonemes by using the letters of the alphabet.

Phonemic awareness instruction makes a stronger contribution to the improvement of reading and spelling when children are taught to use letters as they manipulate phonemes than when instruction is limited to phonemes alone. Teaching sounds along with the letters of the alphabet is important because it helps children to see how phonemic awareness relates to their reading and writing.

If children do not know letter names and shapes, they need to be taught them along with phonemic awareness. Relating sounds to letters is, of course, the heart of phonics instruction, which is discussed later in this section.

Phonemic awareness instruction is most effective when it focuses on only one or two types of phoneme manipulation.

Children who receive instruction that focuses on one or two types of phoneme manipulation make greater gains in reading and spelling than do children who are taught three or more types of manipulation.

Phonics

Phonics is the relationships between the letters (graphemes) of written language and the individual sounds (phonemes) of spoken language. It teaches children to use these relationships to read and write words. Phonics instruction teaches children a system for remembering how to read words. The alphabetic system is a mnemonic device that supports our memory for specific words.

Systematic phonics instruction is more effective than non-systematic or no phonics instruction.

Systematic phonics instruction is the direct teaching of a set of letter–sound relationships in a clearly defined sequence. The set includes the major sound/spelling relationships of both consonants and vowels.

Systematic and explicit phonics instruction significantly improves kindergarten and first-grade children's word recognition and spelling.

Systematic phonics instruction produces the greatest impact on children's reading achievement when it begins in kindergarten or first grade.

Both kindergarten and first-grade children who receive systematic phonics instruction are better at reading and spelling words than kindergarten and first-grade children who do not receive systematic instruction.

Systematic and explicit phonics instruction significantly improves children's reading comprehension.

Systematic phonics instruction results in better growth in children's ability to comprehend what they read than non-systematic or no phonics instruction. This is not surprising because the ability to read the words in a text accurately and quickly is highly related to successful reading comprehension.

Systematic and explicit phonics instruction is effective for children from various social and economic levels.

Systematic phonics instruction is beneficial to children regardless of their socioeconomic status. It helps children from various backgrounds make greater gains in reading than non-systematic instruction or no phonics instruction.

Systematic and explicit phonics instruction is particularly beneficial for children who are having difficulty learning to read and who are at risk for developing future reading problems.

Systematic phonics instruction is significantly more effective than non-systematic or no phonics instruction in helping to prevent reading difficulties among at risk students and in helping children overcome reading difficulties.

Systematic and explicit phonics instruction is most effective when introduced early.

Phonics instruction is most effective when it begins in kindergarten or first grade. To be effective with young learners, systematic instruction must be designed appropriately and taught carefully. It should include teaching letter shapes and names, phonemic awareness, and all major letter–sound relationships. It should ensure that all children learn these skills. As instruction proceeds, children should be taught to use this knowledge to read and write words.

Phonics instruction is not an entire reading program for beginning readers.

Along with phonics instruction, young children should be solidifying their knowledge of the alphabet, engaging in phonemic awareness activities, and listening to stories and informational texts read aloud to them. They also should be reading texts (both out loud and silently) and writing letters, words, messages, and stories.

Examples of Non-Systematic Programs

Here are examples of non-systematic programs that may be important in other ways but that do not achieve the essential outcomes of systematic phonics instruction.

Literature-based programs that emphasize reading and writing activities.

Phonics instruction is embedded in these activities, but letter–sound relationships are taught incidentally, usually based on key letters that appear in student reading materials.

Basal reading programs that focus on whole-word or meaning-based activities. These programs pay only limited attention to letter–sound relationships and provide little or no instruction in how to blend letters to pronounce words.

Sight-word programs that begin by teaching a sight-word reading vocabulary of from 50 to 100 words. Only after they learn to read these words do children receive instruction in the alphabetic principle.

Adding phonics workbooks or phonics activities. Just adding phonics workbooks or phonics activities to these programs has not been effective. Such "add-ons" tend to confuse rather than help children to read.

Fluency

Fluency means to read a text accurately and quickly. Fluent readers recognize words automatically and they group words quickly to help them gain meaning. Fluent readers read aloud effortlessly and with expression. Readers who have not yet developed fluency read slowly, word by word. Their oral reading is choppy and plodding.

Fluency is the bridge between word recognition and comprehension. Fluent readers can concentrate on meaning because they do not have to concentrate on decoding words. Less fluent readers, however, must focus their attention on the words and not on meaning.

Fluency develops gradually through substantial practice. At the earliest stage of reading development, students' oral reading is slow and labored and even when students recognize many words automatically, their oral reading may still not be fluent. To read with expression, readers must be able to divide the text into meaningful chunks and know when to pause appropriately.

Fluency varies, depending on what readers are reading. Even very skilled readers may read in a slow, labored manner when reading texts with many unfamiliar words or topics. For example, readers who are usually fluent may not be able to fluently read unfamiliar technical material.

Repeated and monitored oral reading improves reading fluency and overall reading achievement.

Students who read and reread passages orally as they receive guidance and/or feedback become better readers. Repeated oral reading substantially improves word recognition, speed, and accuracy as well as fluency. To a lesser but still considerable extent, repeated oral reading also improves reading comprehension. Repeated oral reading improves the reading ability of all students throughout the elementary school years. It also helps struggling readers at higher grade levels.

Round-robin reading means students take turns reading parts of a text aloud (though usually not repeatedly). But round-robin reading in itself does not increase fluency. This may be because students only read small amounts of text, and they usually read this small portion only once.

Students should read and reread a text a certain number of times or until a certain level of fluency is reached. Four rereadings are sufficient for most students. Oral reading practice is increased through the use of audiotapes, tutors, and peer guidance.

No research evidence currently confirms that silent, independent reading with minimal guidance improves reading fluency and overall reading achievement.

One of the major differences between good and poor readers is the amount of time they spend reading. But research has not yet confirmed whether independent silent reading with minimal guidance or feedback improves reading achievement and fluency. Neither has it proven that more silent reading in the classroom cannot work. But the research does suggest that there are more beneficial ways to spend reading instructional time than to have students read independently in the classroom without reading instruction.

Students should hear models of fluent reading.

Primary teachers should read aloud daily to their students. By reading effortlessly and with expression, the teacher is modeling how a fluent reader sounds during reading. After a teacher models how to read students should reread the selection.

A teacher should encourage parents or other family members to read aloud to their children at home. The more models of fluent reading the children hear, the better. Of course, hearing a model of fluent reading is not the only benefit of reading aloud to children. Reading to children also increases their knowledge of the world, their vocabulary, their familiarity with written language, and their interest in reading.

Students should read orally from text they can easily master.

Fluency develops as a result of many opportunities to practice reading with a high degree of success. Therefore, students should practice orally rereading text that contains mostly words that they know or can decode easily. In other words, the texts should be at the students' independent reading level, which means the student can read it with about 95% accuracy. If the text is more difficult, students will focus so much on word recognition that they will not have an opportunity to develop fluency.

The text your students practice rereading orally should also be relatively short—probably 50–200 words, depending on the age of the students. You should also use a variety of reading materials, including stories, nonfiction, and poetry. Poetry is especially well suited to fluency practice because poems for children are often short and they contain rhythm, rhyme, and meaning, making practice easy, fun, and rewarding.

Vocabulary

Vocabulary refers to the words we must know to communicate effectively. In general, vocabulary can be described as oral vocabulary or reading vocabulary. Oral vocabulary refers to words that we use in speaking or recognize in listening. Reading vocabulary refers to words we recognize or use in print.

Vocabulary plays an important part in learning to read. As beginning readers, children use the words they have heard to make sense of the words they see in print. Beginning readers have a much more difficult time reading words that are not already part of their oral vocabulary.

Vocabulary also is very important to reading comprehension. Readers cannot understand what they are reading without knowing what most of the words mean. As children learn to read more advanced texts, they must learn the meaning of new words that are not part of their oral vocabulary.

Children learn the meanings of most words indirectly, through everyday experiences with oral and written language.

Children learn word meanings indirectly in three ways:

Children engage in oral language daily.

Young children learn word meanings through conversations with other people, especially adults. As they engage in these conversations, children often hear adults repeat words several times. They also may hear adults use new and interesting words. The more oral language experiences children have, the more word meanings they learn.

Children listen to adults read to them.

Children learn word meanings from listening to adults read to them. Reading aloud is particularly helpful when the reader pauses during reading to define an unfamiliar word and, after reading, engages the child in a conversation about the book. Conversations about books help children to learn new words and concepts and to relate them to their prior knowledge and experience.

Children read extensively on their own.

Children learn many new words by reading extensively on their own. The more children read on their own, the more words they encounter and the more word meanings they learn.

Teaching specific words before reading helps both vocabulary and reading comprehension.

Before students read a text, it is helpful to teach them specific words they will see in the text. Teaching important vocabulary before reading can help students both learn new words and comprehend the text.

Extended instruction that promotes active engagement with vocabulary improves word learning.

Children learn words best when they work actively with the words over an extended period of time. The more students use new words and the more they use them in different contexts, the more likely they are to learn the words.

Repeated exposure to vocabulary in many contexts aids word learning.

Students learn new words better when they encounter them often and in various contexts. When the students read those same words in their texts, they increase their exposure to the new words.

Word-Learning Strategies

Of course, it is not possible for teachers to provide specific instruction for all the words their students do not know. Therefore, students also need to be able to determine the meaning of words that are new to them but not taught directly to them. They need to develop effective word-learning strategies. Word-learning strategies include:

(1) how to use dictionaries and other reference aids to learn word meanings and to deepen knowledge of word meanings;

(2) how to use information about word parts to figure out the meanings of words in text; and

(3) how to use context clues to determine word meanings.

Using dictionaries and other reference aids. Students must learn how to use dictionaries, glossaries, and thesauruses to help broaden and deepen their knowledge of words, even though these resources can be difficult to use. The most helpful dictionaries include sentences providing clear examples of word meanings in context.

Parts of Words

Word parts include *affixes* (prefixes and suffixes), *base words*, and *word roots*.

> **Affixes** are word parts that are "fixed to" either the beginnings of words (prefixes) or the ending of words (suffixes). The word "unremarkable" has two affixes, a prefix "un" and a suffix "able."
>
> **Base words** are words from which many other words are formed. For example, many words can be formed from the base word migrate: migration, migrant, immigration, immigrant, migrating, migratory.
>
> **Word roots** are the words from other languages that are the origin of many English words. About 60% of all English words have Latin or Greek origins.

Using Context Clues

Context clues are hints about the meaning of an unknown word that are provided in the words, phrases, and sentences that surround the word. Context clues include definitions, restatements, examples, or descriptions. Because students learn most word meanings indirectly, or from context, it is important that they learn to use context clues effectively.

Text Comprehension

Comprehension is the reason for reading. Without comprehension, reading is a largely meaningless activity. Good readers are both purposeful and active as they read.

Good readers are purposeful.
Good readers have a purpose for reading. They may read to find out how to use a food processor, read a guidebook to gather information about national parks, read a textbook to satisfy the requirements of a course, read a magazine for entertainment, or read a classic novel to experience the pleasures of great literature.

Good readers are active.
Good readers think actively as they read. To make sense of what they read, good readers engage in a complicated process. Using their experiences and knowledge of the world, their knowledge of vocabulary and language structure, and their knowledge of reading strategies (or plans), good readers make sense of the text and know how to get the most out of it. They know when they have problems with understanding and how to resolve these problems as they occur.

Research over 30 years has shown that instruction in comprehension can help students understand what they read, remember what they read, and communicate with others about what they read.

Specific comprehension strategies help improve text comprehension.
Comprehension strategies are conscious sets of steps that good readers use to make sense of text. Comprehension strategy instruction helps students become purposeful, active readers who are in control of their own reading comprehension.

The following six strategies appear to have a firm scientific basis for improving text comprehension.

Metacognition. Metacognition can be defined as "thinking about thinking." Good readers use metacognitive strategies to think about and have control over their reading. Before reading, they might clarify their purpose for reading and preview the text. During reading, they might monitor their understanding, adjusting their reading speed to fit the difficulty of the text and "fixing up" any comprehension problems they have. After reading, they check their understanding of what they read.

Comprehension monitoring. Comprehension monitoring is a critical part of metacognition. Students who are good at monitoring their comprehension know when they understand what they read and when they do not. They have strategies to "fix up" problems in their understanding as the problems arise. Research shows that instruction, even in the early grades, can help students become better at monitoring their comprehension.

Using graphic and semantic organizers. Graphic organizers illustrate concepts and interrelationships among concepts in a text, using diagrams or other pictorial devices. Graphic organizers may be maps, webs, graphs, charts, frames, or clusters. Semantic organizers (also called semantic maps or semantic webs) are graphic organizers that look somewhat like a spider web. In a semantic organizer, lines connect a central concept to a variety of related ideas and events.

Regardless of the label, graphic organizers can help readers focus on concepts and how they are related to other concepts. Graphic organizers help students read to learn from informational text in the content areas, such as science and social studies textbooks and trade books. Used with informational text, graphic organizers can help students see how concepts fit common text structures. Graphic organizers are also used with narrative text, or stories, as story maps.

Recognizing story structure. Story structure refers to the way the content and events of a story are organized into a plot. Students who can recognize story structure have greater appreciation, understanding, and memory for stories. In story structure instruction, students learn to identify the categories of content (setting, initiating events, internal reactions, goals, attempts, and outcomes) and how this content is organized into a plot. Often, students learn to recognize story structure through the use of story maps. Story maps, a type of graphic organizer, show the sequence of events in simple stories. Instruction in the content and organization of stories improves students' comprehension and memory of stories.

Summarizing. A summary is a synthesis of the important ideas in a text. Summarizing requires students to determine what is important in what they are reading, to condense this information, and to put it into their own words. Instruction in summarizing helps students identify or generate main ideas; connect the main or central ideas; eliminate redundant and unnecessary information; and remember what they read.

Students can be taught to use comprehension strategies.

In addition to identifying which comprehension strategies are effective, scientific research provides guidelines for how to teach comprehension strategies.

Effective comprehension strategy instruction is explicit, or direct.

Research shows that explicit teaching techniques are particularly effective for comprehension strategy instruction. In explicit instruction, teachers tell readers why and when they should use strategies, what strategies to use, and how to apply them. The steps of explicit instruction typically include direct explanation, teacher modeling ("thinking aloud"), guided practice, and application.

Direct explanation. The teacher explains to students why the strategy helps comprehension and when to apply the strategy.

Modeling. The teacher models, or demonstrates, how to apply the strategy, usually by "thinking aloud" while reading the text that the students are using.

Guided practice. The teacher guides and assists students as they learn how and when to apply the strategy.

Application. The teacher helps students practice the strategy until they can apply it independently.

Effective comprehension strategy instruction can be accomplished through cooperative learning.

Cooperative learning (and the closely related concept, collaborative learning) involves students working together as partners or in small groups on clearly defined tasks. Cooperative learning instruction has been used successfully to teach comprehension strategies in content-area subjects. Students work together to understand content-area texts, helping each other learn and apply comprehension strategies. Teachers help students learn to work in groups, demonstrate comprehension strategies, and monitor student progress.

Effective instruction helps readers use comprehension strategies flexibly and in combination.

Good readers must be able to coordinate and adjust several strategies to assist comprehension. Multiple-strategy instruction teaches students how to use strategies flexibly as they are needed to assist their comprehension. In a well-known example of multiple-strategy instruction called "reciprocal teaching," the teacher and students work together so that the students learn these four comprehension strategies.

1. Ask questions about the text they are reading;
2. Summarize parts of the text;
3. Clarify words and sentences students don't understand;
4. Predict what might occur next in the text.

Teachers and students use these four strategies flexibly as they are needed in reading literature and informational texts.

Language

We use language, including gestures and sounds, to communicate. Humans first used gestures, but it was spoken language that opened the vistas for human communication. Language consists of two things: the thoughts that language conveys and the physical sounds, writing, and structure of the language itself.

Human speech organs (mouth, tongue, lips, etc.) were not developed to make sounds but they uniquely determined the sounds and words humans could produce. Human speech gradually came to be loosely bound together by unique rules of grammar.

Many believe that humans developed their unique ability to speak with the development of a specialized area of the brain called Broca's area. If this is so, human speech and language probably developed in the past 100,000 years.

The appearance of written language about 3500 B.C. separates prehistoric from historic times. Written language often does not adequately represent the spoken language. For example, English uses the 26-letter Latin alphabet, which does not represent all the English sounds.

The English Language

The English language emerged 1500 years ago from Germanic languages on the European continent and developed primarily in England. American English is based on the English language and includes words from every major language including Latin, Greek, and French.

English is spoken throughout Australia, Canada, the United Kingdom, and the United States. It is the most universally accepted language in the world, and only Chinese is spoken by more people. In all likelihood, English will become even more prominent as the world's primary language.

Some experts estimate that there are over 1,000,000 English words, more than any other language in the world. Sounds and letters do not match in the English language. For example the word spelled t-o-u-g-h is pronounced *tuf*. The rock group Phish also reminds us of this variation, which often makes English words difficult to pronounce and spell.

Language has a structure and a function. The structure of a language refers to the way words and sentences are combined to create effective communication. The function of a language is the ability to use language to think and communicate. Understanding language development means understanding how each of these aspects develops.

Much of the recent work on structural language development is related to Chomsky's work. Chomsky says that the "old" explanations of language development, modeling and reinforcement, were incorrect. This is not to say that language cannot be learned through these methods because this task is accomplished every day as people learn a foreign language. Rather, Chomsky says that this model-repeat-reinforce approach is not the way that children actually learn language.

Chomsky holds that children possess an innate ability to learn language, both words and structure, merely through exposure. To bolster his argument, Chomsky points out that most grammatical mistakes made by children actually follow the general grammatical rules of the language and that the children's errors represent exceptions to these rules.

For example, a child may say "Lisa goed to the store" instead of "Lisa went to the store." Chomsky would say, *goed* is structurally sound and represents a good grasp of the English language. The child would certainly say *hopped* if Lisa had gotten to the store that way. The problem is created because the past tense for *go* is an exception to the past tense formation rule.

Vygotsky is a prominent psychologist who studied the relationship between thought and language. A contemporary of Piaget, he pointed out that thought and language are not coordinated during the sensorimotor and most of the preoperational stages. That is, from birth through about age 6 or 7, thought and language develop independently, with language being primarily functional.

As students move toward the concrete operational stage, their language also becomes operational. That is, thought and the structural and functional aspects of language become integrated, and students can use language to think and solve problems.

Teachers can foster language development most effectively by constantly encouraging and enabling students to express themselves by speaking and writing. Students should be encouraged to integrate writing and speaking with all subject matter, and writing and speaking should be the overarching classroom objectives to be developed in every lesson. In all cases, teachers should help children communicate in standard English while in school.

Linguistics

Linguistics is the scientific study of language. Linguistics studies the development of languages and language groups, vocabulary and meaning, the structure of contemporary languages, and how speech and language is learned and taught. A list of some areas of language studied by linguistics follows.

Morphology studies morphemes, the building blocks of language.

Phonetics studies all speech sounds in a language and the way speech sounds are produced. Phonetics is reflected in many school curricula.

Phonology studies the important sounds in a language.

Syntax studies the logical or grammatical structure of sentences.

Semantics studies meaning in language.

Discourse analysis studies longer spoken and written discourses such as verbal exchanges or written texts.

Pragmatics studies how different contexts and social settings impact the way language is used.

Transformational grammar is an approach to understanding language developed by Noam Chomsky, an American linguist. He said sentences had a "deep structure" (what the writer or speaker is thinking) and the sentences "surface structure" (what is actually written or spoken). He posited that a universal linguistic structure was present in all humans. He further said that this structure naturally leads people to "transform" their thoughts into sentences that follow natural grammatical rules. There are also grammatical rules for individual languages. Chomsky pointed out that many errors found in children's grammar follow these natural grammatical rules.

Assessment Program

Every teacher evaluates instruction. The assessment program and the assessment instruments should measure mastery and understanding of important topics. The assessment program should also be used as a teaching tool. That is, the program should be used to help students learn and to improve instruction. The program should include authentic assessment of students' work as well as teacher-made and standardized tests.

Formative assessment information is usually gathered before or during teaching. Formative information is used to help you prepare appropriate lessons and assist students. Formative evaluations help teachers decide which objectives to teach, which instructional techniques to use, and which special help or service to provide to individual students.

Summative assessment information is usually gathered once instruction is complete. Summative evaluation is used to make judgments about student achievement and the effectiveness of the instructional programs. Summative evaluations lead to grades, to reports about a student's relative level of accomplishment, and to alterations of instructional programs.

Assessment information may be used for both purposes. For example, you may give a test to determine grades for a marking period or unit. You may then use the information from this test to plan further instruction and arrange individual help for students.

You may informally gather formative and summative information. Just walking around the room observing students' work can yield a lot of useful information. You can frequently discern the additional work that students need and identify different levels of student achievement.

Assessment

Tests have long been used to determine what students have learned and to compare students. Every test is imperfect. Many tests are so imperfect that they are useless. It is important to realize how this imperfection affects test results.

Some students are poor test takers. Every test assumes that the test taker has the opportunity to demonstrate what he or she knows. A student may know something but be unable to demonstrate it on a particular test. We must also consider alternative assessment strategies for these students.

Familiarize yourself with these basic assessment concepts.

- Errors of Measurement—Every test contains errors of measurement. In other words, no one test accurately measures a student's achievement or ability. Carefully designed standardized tests may have measurement errors of 5 percent or 10 percent. Teacher-designed tests typically have large errors of measurement.

  A test result shows that a student falls into a range of scores and not just the single reported score. Focusing on a single score and ignoring the score range is among the most serious of score-reporting errors.

- Reliability—A reliable test is consistent. That is, a reliable test will give similar results when given to the same person in a short time span. You can't count on unreliable tests to give you useful scores. Use only very reliable standardized tests and be very aware of how important reliability is when you make up your own tests.

- Validity—Valid tests measure what they are supposed to measure. There are two important types of validity: content validity and criterion validity.

  A test with high content validity measures the material covered in the curriculum or unit being tested. Tests that lack high content validity are unfair. When you make up a test it should have complete content validity. This does not mean that the test has to be unchallenging. It does mean that the questions should refer to the subject matter covered.

A test with high criterion validity successfully predicts the ability to do other work. For example, a test to be an automobile mechanic with high criterion validity will successfully predict who will be a good mechanic.

Norm-Referenced and Criterion-Referenced Tests

Norm-referenced tests are designed to compare students. Intelligence tests are probably the best-known norm-referenced tests. These tests yield a number that purports to show how one person's intelligence compares to everyone else's. The average IQ score is 100.

Standardized achievement tests yield grade-level equivalent scores. These tests purport to show how student achievement compares to the achievement of all other students of the same grade level.

A fifth grader who earns a grade level equivalent of 5.5 might be thought of as average. A second-grade student with the same grade equivalent score would be thought of as above average. About half of all the students taking these tests will be below average.

Standardized tests also yield percentile scores. Percentile scores are reported as a number from 0 through 100. A percentile of 50 indicates that the student did as well as or better than 50 percent of the students at that grade level who took the test. The higher the percentile, the better the relative performance.

Criterion-referenced tests are designed to determine the degree to which an objective has been reached. Teacher made tests and tests found in teachers' editions of texts are usually criterion referenced tests. Criterion referenced tests have very high content validity.

Authentic Assessment

Standardized and teacher-made tests have significant drawbacks. These types of tests do not evaluate a student's ability to perform a task or demonstrate a skill in a real-life situation. These tests do not evaluate a student's ability to work cooperatively or consistently.

In authentic assessment, students are asked to demonstrate the skill or knowledge in a real-life setting. The teacher and students collaborate in the learning assessment process and discuss how learning is progressing and how to facilitate that learning. The idea is to get an authentic picture of the student's work and progress.

The student has an opportunity to demonstrate what he or she knows or can do in a variety of settings. Students can also demonstrate their ability to work independently or as part of a group.

Portfolio assessment is another name for authentic assessment. Students evaluated through a system of authentic assessment frequently keep a portfolio of their work. Authentic assessment might include the following approaches.

- The student might be observed by the teacher, or occasionally by other students. The observer takes notes and discusses the observation later with the students.

- Students establish portfolios that contain samples of their work. Students are told which work samples they must include in their portfolios. The students place their best work for each requirement in the portfolio. Portfolios are evaluated periodically during a conference between the teacher and the student.

- Students maintain journals and logs containing written descriptions, sketches, and other notes that chronicle their work and the process they went through while learning. The journals and logs are reviewed periodically during a conference between the teacher and the student.

Interpreting Test Scores

The grade level at which you are teaching determines the approach you will take to grading. In the primary grades, you are often asked to check off a list of criteria to show how a student is progressing. Starting in intermediate grades, you will usually issue letter grades.

You should develop a consistent, fair, and varied approach to grading. Students should understand the basis for their grades. You should give students an opportunity to demonstrate what they have learned in a variety of ways.

It is not necessary to adopt a rigid grading system in the elementary grades. Remember, the purpose of a grading system should be to help students learn better, not just to compare them to other students.

Beginning about sixth or seventh grade, the grade should reflect how students are doing relative to other students in the class. By this age, students need to be exposed to the grading system they will experience through high school and college. The grading system should always be fair, consistent, and offer students a variety of ways to demonstrate their mastery.

You will need to interpret normed scores. These scores may be reported as grade equivalents or as percentiles. You may receive these results normed for different groups. For example, one normed score may show performance relative to all students who took the test. Another normed score may show performance relative to students from school districts that have the same Socioeconomic Status (SES) as your school district.

When interpreting normed scores for parents, point out that the student's performance falls into a range of scores. A student's score that varies significantly from the average score from schools with a similar SES requires attention followed by remediation or enriched instruction.

When interpreting district-wide normed scores, remember that these scores correlate highly with SES.

WRITTEN AND NON-WRITTEN COMMUNICATION

VOCABULARY

This vocabulary review will help you prepare for the Reading, Language, and Literature items. It will also help you prepare to read all the other CSET items. This section begins with roots and prefixes followed by a vocabulary list. It shows you how to find the meaning of a word from context clues, roots, and prefixes.

CONTEXT CLUES

Many times you can figure out a word from its context. Look at these examples. Synonyms, antonyms, examples, or descriptions may help you figure out the word.

1. The woman's mind wandered as her two friends *prated* on. It really did not bother her though. In all the years she had known them, they had always *babbled* about their lives. It was almost comforting.
2. The wind *abated* in the late afternoon. Things were different yesterday when the wind had *picked up* toward the end of the day.
3. The argument with her boss had been her *Waterloo*. She wondered if the *defeat* suffered by Napoleon *at this famous place* had felt the same.
4. The events swept the politician into a *vortex* of controversy. The politician knew what it meant to be spun around like a toy boat in the *swirl of water* that swept down the bathtub drain.

    Passage 1 gives a synonym for the unknown word. We can tell that *prated* means babbled. *Babbled* is used as a synonym of *prated* in the passage.

    Passage 2 gives an antonym for the unknown word. We can tell that *abated* means slowed down or diminished because *picked up* is used as an antonym of *abated*.

    Passage 3 gives a description of the unknown word. The description of *Waterloo* tells us that the word means *defeat*.

    Passage 4 gives an example of the unknown word. This example of a *swirl of water* going down the bathtub drain gives us a good idea of what a *vortex* is.

ROOTS

A root is the basic element of a word. The root is usually related to the word's origin. Roots can often help you figure out the word's meaning. Here are some roots that may help you.

Root	Meaning	Examples
bio	life	biography, biology
circu	around	circumference, circulate
frac	break	fraction, refract
geo	earth	geology, geography
mal	bad	malicious, malcontent
matr, mater	mother	maternal, matron
neo	new	neonate, neoclassic
patr, pater	father	paternal, patron
spec	look	spectacles, specimen
tele	distant	telephone, television

PREFIXES

Prefixes are syllables that come at the beginning of a word. Prefixes usually have a standard meaning. They can often help you figure out the word's meaning. Here is a list of prefixes that may help you figure out a word.

Prefix	Meaning	Examples
a-	not	amoral, apolitical
il-, im-, ir-	not	illegitimate, immoral, incorrect
un-	not	unbearable, unknown
non-	not	nonbeliever, nonsense
ant-, anti-	against	antiwar, antidote
de-	opposite	defoliate, declaw
mis-	wrong	misstep, misdeed
ante-	before	antedate, antecedent
fore-	before	foretell, forecast
post-	after	postfight, postoperative
re-	again	refurbish, redo
super-	above	superior, superstar
sub-	below	subsonic, subpar

THE VOCABULARY LIST

Here is a list of a few hundred vocabulary words. This list includes everyday words and a few specialized education terms. Read through the list and visualize the words and their definitions. After a while you will become very familiar with them.

Of course, this is not anywhere near all the words you need to know for the CSET. But they will give you a start. These words also will give you some idea of the kinds of nonspecialized words you may encounter on the CSET.

Another great way to develop a vocabulary is to read a paper every day and a news magazine every week, in addition to the other reading you are doing. There are also several inexpensive books, including *1100 Words You Need to Know, Pocket Guide to Vocabulary*, and *Vocabulary Success* from Barron's, which may help you develop your vocabulary further.

abhor To regard with horror
I abhor violence.

abstain To refrain by choice
Ray decided to abstain from fattening foods.

abstract Not related to any object, theoretical
Mathematics can be very abstract.

acquisition An addition to an established group or collection
The museum's most recent acquisition was an early Roman vase.

admonish To correct firmly but kindly
The teacher admonished the student not to chew gum in class.

adroit Skillful or nimble in difficult circumstances
The nine year old was already an adroit gymnast.

adversary A foe or enemy
The wildebeast was ever-alert for its ancient adversary, the lion.

advocate To speak for an idea; a person who speaks for an idea
Lou was an advocate of gun control.

aesthetic Pertaining to beauty
Ron found the painting a moving aesthetic experience.

affective To do with the emotional or feeling aspect of learning
Len read the Taxonomy of Educational Objectives: Affective Domain.

alias An assumed name
The check forger had used an alias.

alleviate To reduce or make more bearable
The hot shower helped alleviate the pain in her back.

allude To make an indirect reference to, hint at
Elaine only alluded to her previous trips through the state.

ambiguous Open to many interpretations
That is an ambiguous statement.

apathy Absence of passion or emotion
The teacher tried to overcome their apathy toward the subject.

apprehensive Fear or unease about possible outcomes
Bob was apprehensive about visiting the dentist.

aptitude The ability to gain from a particular type of instruction
The professor pointed out that aptitude alone was not enough for success in school.

articulate To speak clearly and distinctly, present a point of view
Chris was chosen to articulate the group's point of view.

assess To measure or determine an outcome or value
There are many informal ways to assess learning.

attest To affirm or certify
I can attest to Cathy's ability as a softball pitcher.

augment To increase or add to
The new coins augmented the already large collection.

belated Past time or tardy
George sent a belated birthday card.

benevolent Expresses good will or kindly feelings
The club was devoted to performing benevolent acts.

biased A prejudiced view or action
The judge ruled that the decision was biased.

bolster To shore up, support
The explorer sang to bolster her courage.

candid Direct and outspoken
Lee was well known for her candid comments.

caricature Exaggerated, ludicrous picture, in words or a cartoon
The satirist presented world leaders as caricatures.

carnivorous Flesh eating or predatory
The lion is a carnivorous animal.

censor A person who judges the morality of others; act on that judgment
Please don't censor my views!

censure Expression of disapproval, reprimand
The senate acted to censure the congressman.

cessation The act of ceasing or halting
The eleventh hour marked the cessation of hostilities.

chronic Continuing and constant
Asthma can be a chronic condition.

clandestine Concealed or secret
The spy engaged in clandestine activities.

cogent Intellectually convincing
He presented a cogent argument.

cognitive Relates to the intellectual area of learning
Lou read the Taxonomy of Educational Objectives: Cognitive Domain.

competency Demonstrated ability
Bert demonstrated the specified mathematics competency.

complacent Unaware self-satisfaction
The tennis player realized she had become complacent.

concept A generalization
The professor lectured on concept development.

congenital Existing at birth but nonhereditary
The baby had a small congenital defect.

contemporaries Belonging in the same time period, about the same age
Piaget and Bruner were contemporaries.

contempt Feeling or showing disdain or scorn
She felt nothing but contempt for their actions.

contentious Argumentative
Tim was in a contentious mood.

corroborate To make certain with other information, to confirm
The reporter would always corroborate a story before publication.

credence Claim to acceptance or trustworthiness
They did not want to lend credence to his views.

cursory Surface, not in depth
Ron gave his car a cursory inspection.

daunt To intimidate with fear
Harry did not let the difficulty of the task daunt him.

debacle Disastrous collapse or rout
The whole trip had been a debacle.

debilitate To make feeble
He was concerned that the flu would debilitate him.

decadent Condition of decline/decay
Joan said in frustration, "We live in a decadent society."

deductive Learning that proceeds from general to specific
He proved his premise using deductive logic.

demographic Population data
The census gathers demographic information.

denounce To condemn a person or idea
The diplomat rose in the United Nations to denounce the plan.

deter To prevent or stop an action, usually by some threat
The president felt that the peace conference would help deter aggression.

diligent A persistent effort; a person who makes such an effort
The investigator was diligent in her pursuit of the truth.

discern To perceive or recognize, often by insight
The principal attempted to discern which student was telling the truth.

discord Disagreement or disharmony
Gail's early promotion led to discord in the office.

discriminate To distinguish among people or groups based on their characteristics
It is not appropriate to discriminate based on race or ethnicity.

disdain To show or act with contempt
The professional showed disdain for her amateurish efforts.

disseminate To send around, scatter
The health organization will disseminate any new information on the flu.

divergent Thinking that extends in many directions, is not focused
Les was an intelligent but divergent thinker.

diverse Not uniform, varied
Alan came from a diverse neighborhood.

duress coercion
He claimed that he confessed under duress.

eccentric Behaves unusually, different from the norm
His long hair and midnight walks made Albert appear eccentric.

eclectic Drawing from several ideas or practices
Joe preferred an eclectic approach to the practice of psychology.

eloquent Vivid, articulate expression
The congregation was spellbound by the eloquent sermon.

emanate To flow out, come forth
How could such wisdom emanate from one so young?

embellish To make things seem more than they are
Art loved to embellish the truth.

empirical From observation or experiment
The scientist's conclusions were based on empirical evidence.

employment A job or professional position (paid)
You seek employment so you can make the big bucks.

enduring Lasting over the long term
Their friendship grew into an enduring relationship.

enhance To improve or build up
The mechanic used a fuel additive to enhance the car's performance.

enigma A mystery or puzzle
The communist bloc is an "enigma wrapped inside a mystery." (Churchill)

equity Equal attention or treatment
The workers were seeking pay equity with others in their industry.

equivocal Uncertain, capable of multiple interpretations
In an attempt to avoid conflict, the negotiator took an equivocal stand.

expedite To speed up, facilitate
Hal's job at the shipping company was to expedite deliveries.

exploit Take maximum advantage of, perhaps unethically
Her adversary tried to exploit her grief to gain an advantage.

extrinsic Coming from outside
The teacher turned to extrinsic motivation.

farce A mockery
The attorney objected, saying that the testimony made the trial a farce.

feign To pretend, make a false appearance of
Some people feign illness to get out of work.

fervent Marked by intense feeling
The spokesman presented a fervent defense of the company's actions.

fiasco Total failure
They had not prepared for the presentation, and it turned into a fiasco.

formidable Difficult to surmount
State certification requirements can present a formidable obstacle.

fracas A noisy quarrel or a scrap
The debate turned into a full-fledged fracas.

gamut Complete range or extent
Waiting to take the test, her mind ran the gamut of emotions.

glib Quickness suggesting insincerity
The glib response made Rita wonder about the speaker's sincerity.

grave Very serious or weighty
The supervisor had grave concerns about the worker's ability.

guile Cunning, crafty, duplicitous
When the truth failed, he tried to win his point with guile.

handicapped Having one or more disabilities
The child study team classified Loren as handicapped.

harass Bother persistently
Some fans came to harass the players on the opposing team.

heterogeneous A group with normal variation in ability or performance
Students from many backgrounds formed a heterogeneous population.

homogeneous A group with little variation in ability or performance
The school used test scores to place students in homogeneous groups.

hypocrite One who feigns a virtuous character or belief
Speaking against drinking and then driving drunk make him a hypocrite!

immune Protected or exempt from disease or harm
The vaccination made Ray immune to measles.

impartial Fair and objective
The contestants agreed on an objective, impartial referee.

impasse Situation with no workable solution
The talks had not stopped, but they had reached an impasse.

impede To retard or obstruct
Mason did not let adversity impede his progress.

implicit Understood but not directly stated
They never spoke about the matter, but they had an implicit understanding.

indifferent Uncaring or apathetic
The teacher was indifferent to the student's pleas for an extension.

indigenous Native to an area
The botanist recognized it as an indigenous plant.

inductive Learning that proceeds from specific to general
Science uses an inductive process, from examples to a generalization.

inevitable Certain and unavoidable
After the rains, the collapse of the dam was inevitable.

infer To reach a conclusion not explicitly stated
The viewer could infer that this product is superior to all others.

inhibit To hold back or restrain
The hormone was used to inhibit growth.

innovate To introduce something new or change established procedure
Mere change was not enough, they had to innovate the procedure.

inquiry Question-based Socratic learning
Much of science teaching uses inquiry-based learning.

intrinsic inherent, the essential nature
The teacher drew on the meaning of the topic for an intrinsic motivation.

inundate To overwhelm, flood
It was December, and mail began to inundate the post office.

jocular Characterized by joking or good nature
The smiling man seemed to be a jocular fellow.

judicial Relating to the administration of justice
His goal was to have no dealings with the judicial system.

knack A talent for doing something
Ron had a real knack for mechanical work.

languid Weak, lacking energy
The sunbather enjoyed a languid afternoon at the shore.

liaison An illicit relationship or a means of communication
The governor appointed his chief aid liaison to the senate.

lucid Clear and easily understood
The teacher answered the question in a direct and lucid way.

magnanimous Generous in forgiving
Loretta is a magnanimous to a fault.

malignant Very injurious, evil
Crime is a malignant sore on our society.

malleable Open to being shaped or influenced
He had a malleable position on gun control.

meticulous Very careful and precise
Gina took meticulous care of the fine china.

miser A money hoarder
The old miser had more money than he could ever use.

monotonous Repetitive and boring
Circling the airport, waiting to land, became monotonous.

mores Understood rules of society
Linda made following social mores her goal in life.

motivation Something that creates interest or action
Most good lessons begin with good motivation.

myriad Large indefinite number
Look skyward and be amazed by the myriad of stars.

naive Lacking sophistication
Laura is unaware, and a little naive, about the impact she has on others.

nemesis A formidable rival
Lex Luthor is Superman's nemesis.

novice A beginner
Her unsteady legs revealed that Sue was a novice skater.

nullified Removed the importance of
The penalty nullified the 20-yard gain made by the running back.

objective A goal
The teacher wrote an objective for each lesson.

oblivious Unaware and unmindful
Les was half asleep and oblivious to the racket around him.

obscure Vague, unclear, uncertain
The lawyer quoted an obscure reference.

ominous Threatening or menacing
There were ominous black storm clouds on the horizon.

palatable Agreeable, acceptable
Sandy's friends tried to make her punishment more palatable.

panorama A comprehensive view or picture
The visitors' center offered a panorama of the canyon below.

pedagogy The science of teaching
Part of certification tests focus on pedagogy.

perpetuate To continue or cause to be remembered
A plaque was put up to perpetuate the memory of the retiring teacher.

pompous Exaggerated self-importance
Rona acted pompous, but Lynne suspected she was very empty inside.

precarious Uncertain, beyond one's control
A diver sat on a precarious perch on a cliff above the water.

precedent An act or instance that sets the standard
The judge's ruling set a precedent for later cases.

preclude To act to make impossible or impracticable
Beau did not want to preclude any options.

precocious Very early development
Chad was very precocious and ran at six months.

prolific Abundant producer
Isaac Asimov was a prolific science fiction writer.

prognosis A forecast or prediction
The stock broker gave a guarded prognosis for continued growth.

provoke To stir up or anger
Children banging on the cage would provoke the circus lion to growl.

psychomotor Relates to the motor skill area of learning
I read the Taxonomy of Behavioral Objectives: Psychomotor Domain.

quagmire Predicament or difficult situation
The regulations were a quagmire of conflicting rules and vague terms.

qualm Feeling of doubt or misgiving
The teacher had not a single qualm about giving the student a low grade.

quandary A dilemma
The absence of the teacher aide left the teacher in a quandary.

quench To put out, satisfy
The glass of water was not enough to quench his thirst.

rancor Bitter continuing resentment
A deep rancor had existed between the two friends since the accident.

rationale The basis or reason for something
The speeder tried to present a rationale to the officer who stopped her.

reciprocal Mutual interchange
Each person got something out of their reciprocal arrangement.

refute To prove false
The lawyer used new evidence to refute claims made by the prosecution.

remedial Designed to compensate for learning deficits
Jim spent one period a day in remedial instruction.

reprove Criticize gently
The teacher would reprove students for chewing gum in class.

repudiate To reject or disown
The senator repudiated membership in an all male club.

resolve To reach a definite conclusion
A mediator was called in to resolve the situation.

retrospect Contemplation of the past
Ryan noted, in retrospect, that leaving home was his best decision.

revere To hold in the highest regard
Citizens of the town revere their long time mayor.

sanction To issue authoritative approval or a penalty
The boxing commissioner had to sanction the match.

scrutinize To inspect with great care
You should scrutinize any document before signing it.

siblings Brothers or sisters
The holidays give me the chance to spend time with my siblings.

skeptical Doubting, questioning the validity
The principal was skeptical about the students' reason for being late.

solace Comfort in misfortune
Her friends provided solace in her time of grief.

solitude Being alone
Pat enjoyed her Sunday afternoon moments of solitude.

stagnant Inert, contaminated
In dry weather the lake shrank to a stagnant pool.

stereotype An oversimplified generalized view or belief
We are all guilty of fitting people into a stereotype.

subsidy Financial assistance
Chris received a subsidy from her company so she could attend school.

subtle Faint, not easy to find or understand
Subtle changes in the teller's actions alerted the police to the robbery.

subterfuge A deceptive strategy
The spy used subterfuge to gain access to the secret materials.

superficial Surface, not profound
The inspector gave the car a superficial inspection.

tacit Not spoken, inferred
They had a tacit agreement.

taxonomy Classification of levels of thinking or organisms
I read each Taxonomy of Educational Objectives.

tenacious Persistent and determined
The police officer was tenacious in pursuit of a criminal.

tentative Unsure, uncertain
The athletic director set up a tentative basketball schedule.

terminate To end, conclude
He wanted to terminate the relationship.

transition Passage from one activity to another
The transition from college student to teacher was not easy.

trepidation Apprehension, state of dread
Erin felt some trepidation about beginning her new job

trivial Unimportant, ordinary
The seemingly trivial occurrence had taken on added importance.

ubiquitous Everywhere, omnipresent
A walk through the forest invited attacks from the ubiquitous mosquitoes.

ultimatum A final demand
After a trying day, the teacher issued an ultimatum to the class.

usurp To wrongfully and forcefully seize and hold, particularly power
The association vice president tried to usurp the president's power.

vacillate To swing indecisively
He had a tendency to vacillate in his stance on discipline.

valid Logically correct
The math teacher was explaining a valid mathematical proof.

vehement Forceful, passionate
The child had a vehement reaction to the teacher's criticism.

vestige A sign of something no longer there or existing
Old John was the last vestige of the first teachers to work at the school.

vicarious Experience through the activities or feelings of others
He had to experience sports in a vicarious way through his students.

virulent Very poisonous or noxious
The coral snake has a particularly virulent venom.

vital Important and essential
The school secretary was a vital part of the school.

waffle To write or speak in a misleading way
The spokesperson waffled as she tried to explain away the mistake.

wary Watchful, on guard
The soldiers were very wary of any movements in the field.

Xanadu An idyllic, perfect place
All wished for some time in Xanadu.

yearned Longed or hoped for
Liz yearned for a small class.

zeal Diligent devotion to a cause
Ron approached his job with considerable zeal.

CONVENTIONS OF ENGLISH

This review section begins with a review of English conventions that may be tested on the CSET.

SENTENCE

A sentence conveys a complete thought or idea. Every sentence has a subject and a predicate. Most sentences are statements. The sentence usually names something (subject). Then the sentence describes the subject or tells what that subject is doing (predicate). Sentences that ask questions also have a subject and a predicate. Here are some examples.

Subject	Predicate
The car	moved.
The tree	grew.
The street	was dark.
The forest	teemed with plants of every type and size.

Many subjects are nouns. Every predicate has a verb. A list of the nouns and verbs from the preceding sentences follows.

Noun	Verb
car	moved
tree	grew
street	was
forest, plants	teemed

CLAUSE

A clause is part of a sentence that contains a subject and a verb.

Independent Clauses

Independent clauses can stand alone as a sentence. The underlined words below form an independent clause.

"Ron has been going to the gym, and he feels much better."

Dependent Clauses

Dependent clauses can not stand alone as a sentence. The underlined section below is a dependent clause. It has a subject and a predicate, but it could not stand alone as a sentence.

"Since Ron has been going to the gym, he feels much better."

Subordinate Clauses

Subordinate clause is another name for a dependent clause because it is subordinate to, or depends on, the independent clause for its meaning.

Relative Clauses

Relative clauses are dependent clauses that begin with a relative pronoun (*of which, that, which, whichever, who, whoever, whom, whomever, whose*). The relative pronoun is the subject and refers to something that came before the clause.

The relative clause is underlined in the sentence below. The relative clause refers to the "gym."

"Ron has been going to the gym, which is just five minutes away."

The relative clause underlined below refers to the entire clause about Ron's exercise.

"Ron exercised for 15 minutes, which made him a little tired."

Nouns

Nouns name a person, place, thing, characteristic, or concept. Nouns give a name to everything that is, has been, or will be. Here are some simple examples.

Person	Place	Thing	Characteristic	Concept (Idea)
Abe Lincoln	Lincoln Memorial	beard	mystery	freedom
judge	courthouse	gavel	fairness	justice
professor	college	chalkboard	intelligence	number

Singular and Plural Nouns

Singular nouns refer to only one thing. Plural forms refer to more than one thing. Plurals are usually formed by adding an *s* or dropping a *y* and adding *ies*. Here are some examples.

Singular	Plural
college	colleges
professor	professors
Lincoln Memorial	Lincoln Memorials
mystery	mysteries

Possessive Nouns

Possessive nouns show that the noun possesses a thing or a characteristic. Make a singular noun possessive by adding *'s*. Here are some examples.

The *child's* sled was in the garage ready for use.
The *school's* mascot was loose again.
The rain interfered with *Jane's* vacation.
Ron's and *Doug's* fathers were born in the same year.
Ron and *Doug's* teacher kept them after school.

Make a singular noun ending in *s* possessive by adding *'s* unless the pronunciation is too difficult.

The teacher read *James's* paper several times.
The angler grabbed the *bass'* fin.

Make a plural noun possessive by adding an apostrophe (') only.

The *principals'* meeting was delayed.
The report indicated that *students'* scores had declined.

Verbs

Some verbs are action verbs. Other verbs are linking verbs that link the subject to words that describe it. Here are some examples.

Action Verbs	Linking Verbs
Blaire *runs* down the street.	Blaire *is* tired.
Blaire *told* her story.	The class *was* bored.
The crowd *roared*.	The players *were* inspired.
The old ship *rusted*.	It *had been* a proud ship.

Tense

A verb has three principal tenses: present tense, past tense, and future tense. The present tense shows that the action is happening now. The past tense shows that the action happened in the past. The future tense shows that something will happen. Here are some examples.

Present:	I *enjoy* my time off.
Past:	I *enjoyed* my time off.
Future:	I *will enjoy* my time off.

Present:	I *hate* working late.
Past:	I *hated* working late.
Future:	I *will hate* working late.

Regular and Irregular Verbs

Regular verbs follow the consistent pattern noted previously. However, a number of verbs are irregular. Irregular verbs have their own unique forms for each tense. A partial list of irregular verbs follows. The past participle is usually preceded by *had, has* or *have*.

SOME IRREGULAR VERBS

Present Tense	Past Tense	Past Participle
am, is, are	was, were	been
begin	began	begun
break	broke	broken
bring	brought	brought
catch	caught	caught
choose	chose	chosen
come	came	come
do	did	done
eat	ate	eaten
give	gave	given
go	went	gone
grow	grew	grown
know	knew	known
lie	lay	lain
lay	laid	laid
raise	raised	raised
ride	rode	ridden
see	saw	seen
set	set	set
sit	sat	sat
speak	spoke	spoken
take	took	taken
tear	tore	torn
throw	threw	thrown
write	wrote	written

PRONOUNS

Pronouns take the place of nouns or noun phrases and help avoid constant repetition of the noun or phrase. Here is an example.

> *Blaire* is in law school. *She* studies in *her* room every day.
> [The pronouns *she* and *her* refer to the noun *Blaire*.]

Pronoun Cases

Pronouns take three case forms: subjective, objective, and possessive. The personal pronouns *I, he, she, it, we, they, you* refer to an individual or individuals. The relative pronoun *who* refers to these personal pronouns as well as to an individual or individuals. These pronouns change their case form depending on their use in the sentence.

Subjective Pronouns: I, we, he, it, she, they, who, you
Use the subjective form if the pronoun is, or refers to, the subject of a clause or sentence.

> *He* and *I* studied for the CSET.

> The proctors for the test were *she* and *I*.
> [*She* and *I* refer to the subject *proctors*.]

> She is the woman *who* answered every question correctly.

> I don't expect to do as well as *she*.
> [*She* is the subject for the understood verb *does*.]

Objective Pronouns: me, us, him, it, her, them, whom, you
Use the objective form if the pronoun is the object of a verb or preposition.

> Cathy helps both *him* and *me*.

> She wanted *them* to pass.

> I don't know *whom* she helped most.

Possessive Pronouns: my, our, his, its, her, their, whose, your
Use the objective form if the pronoun shows possession.

> I recommended they reduce the time they study with *their* friends.

> He was the person *whose* help they relied on.

Clear Reference

The pronoun must clearly refer to a particular noun or noun phrase. Here are some examples.

> *Unclear*

> Gary and Blaire took turns feeding *her* cat.
> [We can't tell which person *her* refers to.]

> Gary gave *it* to Blaire.
> [The pronoun *it* refers to a noun that is not stated.]

Clear

> Gary and Blaire took turns feeding Blaire's cat.
> [A pronoun doesn't work here.]

> Gary got the book and gave it to Blaire.
> [The pronoun works once the noun is stated.]

Agreement

Each pronoun must agree in number (singular or plural) and gender (male or female) with the noun it refers to. Here are some examples.

Nonagreement in Number

> The children played all day, and *she* came in exhausted.
> [*Children* is plural, but *she* is singular.]

> The child picked up the hat and brought *them* into the house.
> [*Hat* is singular, but *them* is plural.]

Agreement

> The children played all day, and *they* came in exhausted.

> The child picked up the hat and brought *it* into the house.

Nonagreement in Gender

> The lioness picked up *his* cub.
> [*Lioness* is female, and *his* is male.]

> A child must bring in a doctor's note before *she* comes to school.
> [The child may be a male or female but *she* is female.]

Agreement

> The lioness picked up *her* cub.

> A child must bring in a doctor's note before *he* or *she* comes to school.

SUBJECT-VERB AGREEMENT

Singular and Plural

Singular nouns take singular verbs. Plural nouns take plural verbs. Singular verbs usually end in *s*, and plural verbs usually do not. Here are some examples.

Singular:	My father want*s* me home early.
Plural:	My parents want me home early.
Singular:	Ryan run*s* a mile each day.
Plural:	Ryan and Chad run a mile each day.
Singular:	She trie*s* her best to do a good job.
Plural:	Liz and Ann try their best to do a good job.

Correctly Identify Subject and Verb

The subject may not be in front of the verb. In fact, the subject may not be anywhere near the verb. Say the subject and the verb to yourself. If it makes sense, you probably have it right.

- Words may come between the subject and the verb.

    Chad's final exam score, which he showed to his mother, improved his final grade.

The verb is *improved*. The word *mother* appears just before improved.

Is this the subject? Say it to yourself. [Mother improved the grade.]

That can't be right. Score must be the subject. Say it to yourself. [Score improved the grade.] That's right. *Score* is the subject, and *improved* is the verb.

    The racer running with a sore arm finished first.

Say it to yourself. [Racer finished first.] *Racer* is the noun, and *finished* is the verb.

It wouldn't make any sense to say the arm finished first.

- The verb may come before the subject.

    Over the river and through the woods romps the merry leprechaun.

Leprechaun is the subject, and *romps* is the verb. [Think: Leprechaun romps.]

    Where are the car keys?

Keys is the subject, and *are* is the verb. [Think: The car keys are where?]

Examples of Subject-Verb Agreement

Words such as *each, neither, everyone, nobody, someone,* and *anyone* are singular pronouns. They always take a singular verb.

    Everyone *needs* a good laugh now and then.
    Nobody *knows* more about computers than Bob.

Words that refer to number such as *one-half, any, most,* and *some* can be singular or plural.

    One-fifth of the students *were* absent. [*Students* is plural.]
    One-fifth of the cake *was* eaten. [There is only one cake.]

Tense Shift

Verbs in a sentence should reflect time sequence. If the actions represented by the verbs happened at the same time, the verbs should have the same tense.

Incorrect:	Beth sits in the boat while she wore a life jacket.
Correct:	Beth sits in the boat while she wears a life jacket. [Both verbs are present tense.]
Correct:	Beth sat in the boat while she wore a life jacket. [Both verbs are past tense.]
Correct:	Beth wears the life jacket she wore last week. [The verbs show time order.]

ADJECTIVES AND ADVERBS

Adjectives

Adjectives modify nouns and pronouns. Adjectives add detail and clarify nouns and pronouns. Frequently, adjectives come immediately before the nouns or pronouns they are modifying. At other times, the nouns or pronouns come first and are connected directly to the adjectives by linking verbs. Here are some examples.

Direct	With a Linking Verb
That is a *large* dog.	That dog is *large*.
He's an *angry* man.	The man seems *angry*.

Adverbs

Adverbs are often formed by adding *ly* to an adjective. However, many adverbs don't end in *ly* (for example, *always*). Adverbs modify verbs, adjectives, and adverbs. Adverbs can also modify phrases, clauses, and sentences. Here are some examples.

Modify verb:	Ryan *quickly* sought a solution.
Modify adjective:	That is an *exceedingly* large dog.
Modify adverb:	Lisa told her story *quite* truthfully.
Modify sentence:	*Unfortunately*, all good things must end.
Modify phrase:	The instructor arrived *just* in time to start the class.

Avoiding Adjective and Adverb Errors

• Don't use adjectives in place of adverbs.

Correct	Incorrect
Lynne read the book quickly.	Lynne read the book quick.
Stan finished his work easily.	Stan finished his work easy.

• Don't confuse the adjectives *good* and *bad* with the adverbs *well* and *badly*.

Correct	Incorrect
Adverbs	
She wanted to play the piano well.	She wanted to play the piano good.
Bob sang badly.	Bob sang bad.
Adjectives	
The food tastes good.	The food tastes well.
The food tastes bad.	The food tastes badly.

• Don't confuse the adjectives *real* and *sure* with the adverbs *really* and *surely*.

Correct	Incorrect
Chuck played really well.	Chuck played real well.
He was surely correct.	He was sure correct.

Comparison

Adjectives and adverbs can show comparisons. Avoid clumsy modifiers.

Correct	Incorrect
Jim is more clingy than Ray.	Jim is clingier than Ray.
Ray is much taller than Jim.	Ray is more taller than Jim.
Jim is more interesting than Ray.	Jim is interesting than Ray.
Ray is happier than Jim.	Ray is more happy than Jim.

Word comparisons carefully to be sure that the comparison is clear.

Unclear:	Chad lives closer to Ryan than Blaire.
Clear:	Chad lives closer to Ryan than Blaire does.
Clear:	Chad lives closer to Ryan than he does to Blaire.

Unclear:	The bus engines are bigger than cars.
Clear:	The bus engines are bigger than cars' engines.

CONJUNCTIONS

Conjunctions are words that connect and logically relate parts of a sentence.

• These conjunctions connect words: *and, but, for, or, nor.*

Dan *and* Dorie live in Pittsburgh.
Tim *or* Sarah will get up to feed the baby.

• These conjunctive pairs establish a relationship among words: *either-or, neither-nor, not only-but also.* Words in these pairs should not be mixed.

Neither David *nor* Noel wants to get up to feed the baby.

The baby cries *not only* when she is hungry, *but also* when she is thirsty.

• These conjunctions connect and modify clauses in a sentence: nevertheless, however, because, furthermore.

Matt's mother was coming to visit; *however,* a snowstorm prevented the trip.
Because the baby was sleeping, Julie and Bill decided to get some sleep too.

PREPOSITIONS

Prepositions connect a word to a pronoun, noun, or noun phrase called the object of the preposition. A partial list of prepositions follows.

PREPOSITIONS

above	across	after	among
as	at	before	below
beside	by	except	for
from	in	into	near
of	on	over	to
toward	up	upon	without

A prepositional phrase consists of a preposition, its object and any modifiers. Here are some examples.

Preposition	Object
in	the book
with	apparent glee
without	a care

Some sentences with prepositional phrases follow.

> Chad found his book *in the room.*
> Liz rode *on her horse.*
> Trix is the dog *with the brown paws.*
> *Over the river* and *through the woods to grandmother's house* we go.

Negation

Words such as *no, never, nobody, nothing,* and *not* (with contractions such as *would not—wouldn't*) are used to express a negative. However, only one of these words is needed to express a negative thought. Two negative words create a double negative, which is not standard English.

Incorrect:	The politician *didn't say nothing* that made sense.
Revised:	The politician *didn't say anything* that made sense.
Revised:	The politician *said nothing* that made any sense.

Incorrect:	The politician *wouldn't do nothing* that did no good. [A triple negative.]
Revised:	The politician *would do nothing* good.
Revised:	The politician *wouldn't do* good things.

Misplaced and Dangling Modifiers

Modifiers may be words or groups of words. Modifiers change or qualify the meaning of another word or group of words. Modifiers belong near the words they modify.

Misplaced modifiers appear to modify words in a way that doesn't make sense.

The modifier in the following sentence is *in a large box.* It doesn't make sense for *in a large box* to modify *house.* Move the modifier near *pizza* where it belongs.

Misplaced:	Les delivered pizza to the house in a large box.
Revised:	Les delivered pizza in a large box to the house.

The modifier in the next sentence is *paid well. Paid well* can't modify *city.* Move it next to *the job* where it belongs.

Misplaced:	Gail wanted the job in the city that paid well.
Revised:	Gail wanted the well-paying job in the city.

Dangling modifiers modify words not present in the sentence. The modifier in the following sentence is *waiting for the concert to begin.*

This modifier describes the audience, but audience is not mentioned in the sentence. The modifier is left dangling with nothing to attach itself to.

Dangling:	Waiting for the concert to begin, the chanting started.
Revised:	Waiting for the concert to begin, the audience began chanting.
Revised:	The audience began chanting while waiting for the concert to begin.

The modifier in the next sentence is *after three weeks in the country*. The modifier describes the person, not the license. But the person is not mentioned in the sentence. The modifier is dangling.

Dangling:	After three weeks in the country, the license was revoked.
Revised:	After he was in the country for three weeks, his license was revoked.
Revised:	His license was revoked after he was in the country three weeks.

COMMA SPLICES AND RUN-ON SENTENCES

An *independent clause* is a clause that could be a sentence.

Independent clauses should be joined by a semicolon, or by a comma and a conjunction.

A *comma splice* consists of two independent clauses joined by just a comma.

A *run-on* sentence consists of two independent clauses incorrectly joined.

Correct:	The whole family went on vacation; the parents took turns driving. [Two independent clauses are joined by a semicolon.]
	The whole family went on vacation, and the parents took turns driving. [Two independent clauses are joined by a comma and a conjunction.]
Incorrect:	The whole family went on vacation, the parents took turns driving. [Comma splice. Two independent clauses are joined by just a comma.]
	The whole family went on vacation the parents took turns driving. [Run-on sentence. Two independent clauses are incorrectly joined.]

SENTENCE FRAGMENTS

English sentences require a subject and a verb. Fragments are parts of sentences written as though they were sentences. Fragments are writing mistakes that lack a subject, a predicate, or both subject and predicate. Here are some examples.

Since when.

To enjoy the summer months.

Because he isn't working hard.

If you can fix old cars.

What the principal wanted to hear.

Include a subject and/or a verb to rewrite a fragment as a sentence.

Fragment	Sentence
Should be coming up the driveway now.	The *car* should be coming up the driveway now.
Both the lawyer and her client.	Both the lawyer and her client *waited* in court.
Which is my favorite subject.	*I took math*, which is my favorite subject.
If you can play.	If you can play, *you'll improve with practice.*

Verbs such as *to be, to go, winning, starring*, etc., need a main verb.

Fragment	Sentence
The new rules to go into effect in April.	The new rules *will* go into effect in April.
The team winning every game.	The team *was* winning every game.

Often, a fragment is related to a complete sentence. Combine the two to make a single sentence.

Fragment:	Reni loved vegetables. *Particularly corn, celery, lettuce, squash, and eggplant.*
Revised:	Reni loved vegetables, particularly corn, celery, lettuce, squash, and eggplant.
Fragment:	*To see people standing on Mars.* This could happen in the 21st century.
Revised:	To see people standing on Mars is one of the things that could happen in the 21st century.

Sometimes short fragments can be used for emphasis. However, you should not use fragments in your essay. Here are some examples.

Stop! Don't take one more step toward that apple pie.

I need some time to myself. *That's why.*

PARALLELISM

When two or more ideas are connected, use a parallel structure. Parallelism helps the reader follow the passage more clearly. Here are some examples.

Not Parallel:	Toni stayed in shape by eating right and exercising daily.
Parallel:	Toni stayed in shape by eating right and *by* exercising daily.
Not Parallel:	Lisa is a student who works hard and has genuine insight.
Parallel:	Lisa is a student who works hard and *who* has genuine insight.
Not Parallel:	Art had a choice either to clean his room or take out the garbage.
Parallel:	Art had a choice either to clean his room or *to* take out the garbage.
Not Parallel:	Derek wanted a success rather than failing.
Parallel:	Derek wanted a success rather than a failure.
Parallel:	Derek wanted success rather than failure.

DICTION

Diction is choosing and using appropriate words. Good diction conveys a thought clearly without unnecessary words. Good diction develops fully over a number of years; however, there are some rules and tips you can follow.

- Do not use slang, colloquialisms, or other non-standard English. One person's slang is another person's confusion. Slang is often regional, and slang meanings change rapidly. We do not give examples of slang here for that very reason. Do not use slang words in your formal writing.

  Colloquialisms are words used frequently in spoken language. This informal use of terms such as *dog tired*, *kids*, and *hanging around* is not generally accepted in formal writing. Save these informal terms for daily speech and omit or remove them from your writing except as quotations.

  Omit any other non-standard English. Always choose standard English terms that accurately reflect the thought to be conveyed.

- Avoid wordy, redundant, or pretentious writing. Good writing is clear and economical.

  Wordy: I chose my career as a teacher because of its high ideals, the truly self-sacrificing idealism of a career in teaching, and for the purpose of receiving the myriad and cascading recognition that one can receive from the community as a whole and from its constituents.

  Revised: I chose a career in teaching for its high ideals and for community recognition.

Given below is a partial list of wordy phrases and the replacement word.

Wordy Phrases and Replacements

at the present time	now	because of the fact that	because
for the purpose of	for	in the final analysis	finally
in the event that	if	until such time as	until

HOMONYMS

Homonyms are words that sound alike but do not have the same meaning. These words can be confusing and you may use the incorrect spelling of a word. If words are homonyms, be sure you choose the correct spelling for the meaning you intend.

HOMONYMS

accept (receive)	ascent (rise)
except (other than)	assent (agreement)
board (wood)	fair (average)
bored (uninterested)	fare (a charge)
led (guided)	lessen (make less)
lead (metal)	lesson (learning experience)
past (gone before)	peace (no war)
passed (moved by)	piece (portion)

rain (precipitation)	to (toward)
reign (rule)	too (also)
rein (animal strap)	two (a number)
their (possessive pronoun)	its (shows possession)
there (location)	it's (it is)
they're (they are)	

Spelling Rules

There are a great many rules for spelling English words. Here are some of the rules used in schools today along with examples of words that follow the rules. There are many exceptions to most spelling rules.

Put *i* before *e*, except after *c* or when sounded as *a* as in "neighbor" and "weigh."
> sieve
> receive
> freight
> deceive

Leave the word when a prefix is added.
> submarine
> remove
> disallow

Drop the final *e* from a word when a suffix with a vowel is added.
> Sensible not senseible
> desirable not desireable
> admiring not admireing

Leave the word when adding a suffix to a word that ends in a vowel followed by a y.
> played
> paying
> laying

Change y to i when adding a suffix to a word that ends in a consonant followed by a y.
> happiness not happyness
> married not marryed
> happiest not happyest

Double the final consonant in one syllable words when adding ing, ed, or er to words that end in a single vowel followed by a consonant.
> tapped not taped
> trapper not traper
> hottest not hotest

Double the final consonant in words of more than one syllable when the final consonant is stressed.
> beginning not begining
> exiting not exitting

Add es to form the plural of a noun that ends in *s, x, z, ch*, or *sh*
> bunches
> wishes
> foxes

Spelling Lists

This list shows some of the most frequently misspelled words along with the corrected spelling.

Words Frequently Spelled Incorrectly with the Corrected Spelling

Incorrect Spelling	Corrected Spelling
accidently	accidentally
accomodate	accommodate
allot	a lot
annoint	anoint
batallion	battalion
broccli	broccoli
cematery	cemetery
concensus	consensus
coolley	coolly
definately	definitely
desparate	desperate
developement	development
disippate	dissipate
dispair	despair
drunkeness	drunkenness
ecstacy	ecstasy
embarassment	embarrassment
excede	exceed
existance	existence
harrass	harass
inadvertant	inadvertent

Incorrect Spelling	Corrected Spelling
independant	independent
indispensible	indispensable
innoculate	inoculate
insistant	insistent
irresistable	irresistible
irritible	irritable
judgement	judgment
liason	liaison
liquify	liquefy
momento	memento
occassion	occasion
occurence	occurrence
persue	pursue
priviledge	privilege
reccomend	recommend
recieve	receive
repitition	repetition
sacreligious	sacrilegious
seperate	separate
sieze	seize
subpena	subpoena
tyrrany	tyranny
wierd	weird
yeild	yield

IDIOMS

Idioms are expressions with special meanings and often break the rules of grammar. Idioms are acceptable in formal writing, but they must be used carefully. Here are some examples.

IDIOMS

in accordance with	inferior to
angry with	occupied by (someone)
differ from (someone)	occupied with (something)
differ about (an issue)	prior to
independent of	rewarded with (something)

PUNCTUATION

The Comma (,)

The comma may be the most used punctuation mark. This section details a few of these uses.

A clause is part of a sentence that could be a sentence itself. If a clause begins with a conjunction, use a comma before the conjunction.

| Incorrect: | I was satisfied with the food but John was grumbling. |
| Correct: | I was satisfied with the food, but John was grumbling. |

| Incorrect: | Larry was going fishing or he was going to paint his house. |
| Correct: | Larry was going fishing, or he was going to paint his house. |

A clause or a phrase often introduces a sentence. Introductory phrases or clauses should be set off by a comma. If the introductory element is very short, the comma is optional. Here are some examples.

However, there are other options you may want to consider.

When the de-icer hit the plane's wing, the ice began to melt.

To get a driver's license, go to the motor vehicle bureau.

It doesn't matter what you want, you have to take what you get.

Parenthetical expressions interrupt the flow of a sentence. Set off the parenthetical expression with commas. Do not set off expressions that are essential to understanding the sentence. Here are some examples.

Tom, an old friend, showed up at my house the other day.

I was traveling on a train, in car 8200, on my way to Florida.

John and Ron, who are seniors, went on break to Florida.
[Use a comma. The phrase "who are seniors" is extra information.]

All the students who are seniors take an additional course.
[Don't use a comma. The phrase "who are seniors" is essential information.]

Commas are used to set off items in a list or series. Here are some examples.

Jed is interested in computers, surfing, and fishing.
[Notice the comma before the conjunction *and*.]

Mario drives a fast, red car.
[The sentence would make sense with *and* in place of the commas.]

Andy hoped for a bright, sunny, balmy day.
[The sentence would make sense with *and* in place of the commas.]

Lucy had a pale green dress.
[The sentence would not make sense with *and*. The word *pale* modifies *green*. Don't use a comma.]

Randy will go to the movies, pick up some groceries, and then go home.

Semicolon and Colon

The Semicolon (;)

Use the semicolon to connect main clauses not connected by a conjunction. Include a semicolon with very long clauses connected by a conjunction. Here are some examples.

The puck was dropped; the hockey game began.

The puck was dropped, and the hockey game began.

The general manager of the hockey team was not sure what should be done about the player who was injured during the game; but he did know that the player's contract stipulated that his pay would continue whether he was able to play or not.

The Colon (:)

Use the colon after a main clause to introduce a list. Here are some examples.

Liz kept these items in her car: spare tire, jack, flares, and a blanket.

Liz kept a spare tire, jack, flares, and a blanket in her car.

Period, Question Mark, Exclamation Point

The Period (.)

Use a period to end every sentence, unless the sentence is a direct question, a strong command, or an interjection.

You will do well on the CSET test.

The Question Mark (?)

Use a question mark to end every sentence that is a direct question.

What is the passing score for the CSET test?

The Exclamation Point (!)

Use an exclamation point to end every sentence that is a strong command or interjection. Do not overuse exclamation points.

Interjection: Pass that test!

Command: Avalanche, head for cover!

TEXTS

LITERARY FORMS

Children's Literature

Children's literature, as we know it, did not exist until the late 1700s. Jean Rousseau, in his influential *Emile*, was among the first writers to popularize the view that children were not just small adults. A collection of age-old fairy tales, *The Tales of Mother Goose*, was published in France about 1700. The first illustrated book was probably *The Visible World in Pictures*, which was written in Latin about 1760 by John Comenius.

Before this time, most children's literature conveyed a religious or moral message or was designed for instruction. A few adult books appealed to children including *Robinson Crusoe* and the satirical *Gulliver's Travels*.

In the United States during the 1800s, James Fenimore Cooper wrote *The Last of the Mohicans*, Washington Irving wrote *The Legend of Sleepy Hollow*, and Nathaniel Hawthorne wrote *A Wonder Book for Boys and Girls*. Louisa May Alcott wrote *Little Women* and Samuel Clemens, writing as Mark Twain, wrote *The Adventures of Huckleberry Finn*. Horatio Alger wrote a series of "rags to riches" books at the end of the century.

On the European continent, the Brothers Grimm published *Grimm's Fairy Tales*, which included "Snow White and the Seven Dwarfs." Hans Christian Anderson published a number of stories including "The Ugly Duckling." *Heidi* and the *Adventures of Pinocchio* were also published about this time.

In England, Charles Dodgson, writing as Lewis Carroll, penned *Alice's Adventures in Wonderland*. John Tenniel provided the illustrations for this famous work. Robert Louis Stevenson wrote *Treasure Island*, Rudyard Kipling wrote *The Jungle Book*, and Edward Lear wrote the *Nonsense Book*.

At the beginning of this century, Frank Baum wrote the first *Wizard of Oz* book and Lucy Maud Montgomery wrote *Anne of Green Gables*. Also in this century, Hugh Loftig penned the famous Dr. Doolittle books, A. A. Milne published a series of Winnie-the-Pooh books and P. L. Travers wrote the Mary Poppins books. Albert Payson Terhune wrote a series of dog stories, most notably *Lad a Dog*.

The Little Prince and *Charlotte's Web* were published in the mid 1900s. About this time, Theodore Geisel, writing as Dr. Seuss, began to write a popular series of books, including *Green Eggs and Ham*. Notable books of the past twenty years include *The Snowy Day*, and *Where the Wild Things Are*.

The Newbery Award and Caldecott Medal are given annually to the most notable American children's books. The Newbery Award is named after publisher John Newbery and is awarded to the best American children's book. The Caldecott Medal is named after illustrator Randolph Caldecott and is given to the best picture book.

Poetry

Poetry usually communicates through linguistic imagery, sounds of words, and a rhythmic quality. Poetry and poems are among the oldest forms of literature and date to ancient Greece. Ancient poems were originally sung, and poetry has been slowly emancipated from this reliance on music, replacing it with a linguistic cadence.

Poetry is often associated with rhyming. However, many poems do not rhyme. Some poems rely on their rhythmic patterns alone, others are composed of open verses, while still others, such as Japanese haiku, rely on special features such as the number of syllables in a line.

The epic, the lyric, and some romances are examples of early poetry.

Epic

The epic is a very long narrative poem, usually about a single heroic person. Epics have a monumental sweep, embrace the essence of an entire nation, and frequently include mythical forces that influence the inevitable battles and conflicts. Epics include the *Odyssey* and the *Illiad*, which were written by Homer and embrace Greek national themes, as well as the Scandinavian *Beowulf*.

Lyric

The lyric is related to the epic, but it is shorter and presents profound feelings or ideas. The terms elegy and ode both refer to lyric poems. Lyric poems were called rondeaus when sung by French troubadours and madrigals when sung by English balladeers. During the 1800s both Robert Browning and Tennyson wrote lyrics. Modern lyrics are still written but no longer occupy a central place in culture.

> **fable** A short literary piece designed to present a moral or truth. Fables frequently involve animals. The most famous fables are attributed to a reputed Greek slave, Aesop, who lived in the sixth century.

Romance

The romance and the epic are similar. However, the romance is concerned with love and chivalry and, originally, was written in one of the romance languages. This genre of literature dates from the 1100s and was most popular during the 1200s. Stories of *King Arthur and the Knights of the Round Table* are romances.

> **legend** A heroic story or collection of stories about a specific person or persons. Legends are presented as fact but are actually a combination of fact and fiction. Legends with differing degrees of factual content have been built around Davy Crockett, who "kilt him a bar when he was only three," and the gigantic logger Paul Bunyan and his blue ox Babe. Paul Bunyan reputedly cleared out entire Maine forests with one swing of the ax.

Satire

Satire exposes the frailty of the human condition through wit, irony, mockery, sarcasm, or ridicule. For example, the sentence, "The doctor looked down at the man sneaking away from the impending flu shot and said, 'At least he knows to avoid sharp objects,'" is an example of satire. Occasionally, entire works such as Jonathan Swift's *Gulliver's Travels* are satirical.

> **doggerel** A work that features awkward or rough verbiage. Most often, this clumsy verse is the result of an inept writer, although it may occasionally be intended as humor.

Short Story

The short story is a short fictional piece, usually with a single theme. The first short stories date from ancient Egypt. O. Henry and Mark Twain were famous writers who penned short stories in the early 1900s. Hemingway and Faulkner wrote short stories before mid-century with John Cheever and Eudora Welty noted as prominent short story writers in the latter half of the century.

Novel

The novel is a fictional story that depicts characters in a plot. The novel builds on the epic and the romance. The first novels were written during the Renaissance (1300–1600) and were developed more fully during the 1700s and 1800s in England.

The modern novel developed in the 1800s. Novels with strong historical and social themes, including dialogue, were written by the English authors Dickens, Thackeray, and Eliot. American novels written during this time tended to be allegorical.

American novels in the early 1900s focused on social ills. These novels include *The Jungle* by Sinclair Lewis, *Studs Lonigan* by James Farrell, and *The Grapes of Wrath* by John Steinbeck. In the late 1900s American novels of great strength appeared including *The Naked and the Dead* by Norman Mailer and *Catch-22* by Joseph Heller.

> **biography** A full account of a person's life. An autobiography is a biography written by the person.

APPROACHES TO READING AND INTERPRETING LITERATURE

This section shows how to interpret passages on the Literature and Language Studies sections of the CSET.

Recognize the Author's Purpose

The author's primary purpose explains why the author wrote the passage. The purpose is closely related to the main idea. You might think. "Fine, I know the main idea. But why did the author take the time to write about that main idea?" "What is the author trying to make me know or feel?"

The author's purpose will be in one of the following five categories.

Describe	Present an image of physical reality or a mental image.
Entertain	Amuse, Perform
Inform	Clarify, Explain, State
Narrate	Relate, Tell a story
Persuade	Argue, Convince, Prove

There is no hard and fast rule for identifying the author's purpose. Rely on your informed impression of the passage. Once in a while a passage may overtly state the author's purpose. But you must usually figure it out on your own. Remember, one of the answer choices will be correct. Your job is to decide which one it is.

Distinguish Between Fact and Opinion

Facts can be proven true *or* false by some objective means or method. *A fact refers to persons, things, or events that exist now or existed at some time in the past.* Note that a fact does not have to be true. For example, the statement "The tallest human being alive today is 86 inches tall" is false. This statement is a fact because it can be proven false.

Opinions, however, cannot be proved or disproved by some objective means or method. Opinions are subjective and include attitudes and probabilities. Some statements, which seem true, may still be opinions. For example, the statement "A car is easier to park than a bus" seems true. However, this statement is an opinion. There is no way to objectively prove this statement true or false.

Examples:

Fact: Abraham Lincoln was President of the United States during the Civil War. We can check historical records and find out if the statement is true. This statement of fact is true.

Fact: Robert E. Lee went into exile in Canada after the Civil War. We can check historical records. This factual statement is true. Lee later became president of Washington College, now called Washington and Lee University.

Fact: It is more than 90°F. outside. We can use a thermometer to prove or disprove this statement.

Fact: More people were born in November than in any other month. We can check statistical records to prove or disprove this statement.

Opinion: If Lincoln had lived, Reconstruction would have been better. This sounds true, but there is no way to prove or disprove this statement.

Opinion: Lee was the Civil War's most brilliant general. Sounds true, but there is no way to prove it.

Opinion: It will always be colder in November than in July. Sounds true! But we can't prove or disprove future events.

Detect Bias

Bias
A statement or passage reveals bias if the author has prejudged or has a predisposition to a doctrine, idea, or practice. Bias means the author is trying to convince or influence the reader through some emotional appeal or slanted writing.

Bias can be positive or negative.

Positive Bias: She is so lovely, she deserves the very best.
Negative Bias: She is so horrible, I hope she gets what's coming to her.

Forms of Bias
Biased writing can often be identified by the presence of one or more of the following forms of bias.

Emotional Language Language that appeals to the reader's emotions, and not to common sense or logic.

Positive: If I am elected, I will help your family get jobs.
Negative: If my opponent is elected, your family will lose their jobs.

Inaccurate Information	Language that presents false, inaccurate, or unproved information as though it were factual.
	Positive: My polls indicate that I am very popular. Negative: My polls indicate that a lot of people disagree with my opponent.
Name Calling	Language that uses negative, disapproving terms without any factual basis.
	Negative: I'll tell you, my opponent is a real jerk.
Slanted Language	Language that slants the facts or evidence toward the writer's point of view.
	Positive: I am a positive person, looking for the good side of people. Negative: My opponent finds fault with everyone and everything.
Stereotyping	Language that indicates that a person is like all the members of a particular group.
	Positive: I belong to the Krepenkle party, the party known for its honesty. Negative: My opponent belongs to the Perplenkle party, the party of increased taxes.

Recognize the Author's Tone

Tone

The author's tone is the author's attitude as reflected in the passage. Answering this question means choosing the correct tone word. How do you think the author would sound while speaking? What impression would you form about the speaker's attitude or feeling? The answer to the latter question will usually lead you to the author's tone. A partial list of tone words is given below.

absurd	excited	outraged
amused	formal	outspoken
angry	gentle	pathetic
apathetic	hard	pessimistic
arrogant	impassioned	playful
bitter	indignant	prayerful
cheerful	intense	reverent
comic	intimate	righteous
compassionate	joyous	satirical
complex	loving	sentimental
concerned	malicious	serious
cruel	mocking	solemn
depressed	nostalgic	tragic
distressed	objective	uneasy
evasive	optimistic	vindictive

Recognize Invalid Arguments

Valid arguments are reasonable. Valid arguments are objective and supported by evidence. Invalid arguments are *not* reasonable. They are not objective. Invalid arguments usually reflect one of the following fallacies.

Ad hominem	Arguing against a person to discredit their position, rather than an argument against the position itself
Ad populum	An argument that appeals to the emotions of the person
Bandwagon	Arguing for position because of its popularity
Begging the question	Assuming that an argument, or part of an argument, is true without providing proof
Circular logic	Using a statement of a position to argue in favor of that position
Either/or	Stating that the conclusion falls into one of two extremes, when there are more intermediate choices
Faulty analogy	Using an analogy as an argument when the analogy does not match the situation under discussion
Hasty generalization	Reaching a conclusion too quickly, before all the information is known
Non sequitur	A conclusion that does not logically follow from the facts
Post hoc, ergo propter hoc	Falsely stating that one event following another is caused by the first event (faulty cause and effect)
Red herring	An irrelevant point, diverting attention from the position under discussion

LITERARY TERMS

allegory Expression in which the characters, story, and setting actually represent other people, settings, or abstract ideas. This symbolic meaning is more important than the literal meaning. For example, Jonathan Swift's *Gulliver's Travels* is allegorical when it uses horses and other creatures to represent people. *Aesop's Fables* use allegory to represent moral or ethical ideas. Parables such as the Prodigal Son use allegory to teach a lesson.

alliteration The repetition of an initial consonant in nearby words. For example, the selections "Neither rain, nor sleet nor dark of night," and "Peas?—Please. Peanuts?—Possibly. Potatoes?— Potentially. Pigs knuckles?—Please!" use alliteration.

anthropomorphism Attributing the human body or human qualities to nonhuman things or entities. Initially, anthropomorphism meant depicting a god or gods as humans with human qualities.

connotation The secondary meanings that the word represents.

couplet Two successive poetic lines that form a single unit because they rhyme.

denotation Actual meaning of the word.

essay A fairly brief work that tries to get across a particular point of view or to persuade the reader about the correctness of that point of view.

Figures of Speech Figurative language that is not meant to be taken literally. Figures of speech are used to create some special meaning or imagery.

euphemism Figure of speech in which an inoffensive term is substituted for one that may be offensive or cause distress. For example, *pass away* may be substituted for *die*, and *indisposed* may be substituted for *ill*.

hyperbole Figure of speech in which a drastic overstatement or understatement is used. Hyperbole may be used to emphasize a point or for comic effect. For example, after an argument between friends one might exclaim, "You are the worst person who has ever lived." In another example, the winner of the Olympic decathlon may be referred to as "Not that bad an athlete."

metaphor Figure of speech in which one thing is discussed as though it were something else. The words *like* or *as* are not used. For example, "My life's a tennis match, but I never get to serve" and "The night crept through til dawn" are metaphors.

mixed metaphor Figure of speech in which two or more unrelated metaphors are combined. For example, "Running on empty, the soccer player plowed through the rest of the match" is a mixed metaphor.

onomatopoeia Figure of speech that refers to words that imitate natural sounds. Onomatopoeia appears in the words of a once popular song, "*Buzz, buzz, buzz* goes the bumble bee, *twiddely, diddely, dee* goes the bird."

simile Figure of speech that compares two different things, usually using the words *like* or *as*. For example, "Her eyes are like deep, quiet pools" or "Her nails are like tiger claws" are similes.

haiku Poetry of Japanese origin with three nonrhyming lines with a pattern of five-seven-five syllables.

HOW TO ANALYZE POETRY AND PROSE FICTION

This is a brief overview of some steps to analyze poetry and prose. Analyzing these written forms can be thought of as answering a series of questions. The answers to the short list of questions below are your analysis.

Poetry

1. What is the poem's genre?
Draw from the discussion on page 88 to identify the genre of a poem. Each genre has a purpose as described on that page.

2. Who is the speaker?
The "speaker" may not be identified, or it may be the authors of the poem, or it may be some other person. What is the speaker's perspective—It may be political, social or some other. Does the speaker have a point of view, an opinion? What is the speaker trying to accomplish—Is there a specific goal.

3. What is the setting?

Where in time is the poem set? Is it in recent years, the past, the future—is there a specific time or date? Does the date have significance? Can you tell if the poem is set in the day or at night?

Where in physical space is the poem set? Is it in a particular country, in a field, in the city, by the roadside?

Does the poem have a symbolic setting? The Literary Terms on page 92 lists some of the literary devices you may encounter in a poem with a symbolic setting.

4. What is the main purpose or subject?

Why did the poet create this work? Was it to convey an emotional tone, a visual image or was it to communicate an idea or make a poem. The Author's Purpose section on page 89 offers some suggestions.

5. What is the structure?

Is it a rhyming poem; does it have a formal structure; is a free form verse; is it haiku? Is it a sonnet, or an epic or a lyric poem? The partial list of poetic forms on page 87 suggests some possibilities.

6. What is the tone?

What is the author's tone? A list of tone words on page 91 will help you identify and describe the author's tone.

7. What is the imagery?

What imagery does the author employ? Are there emotional images, or physical images, or symbolic images? What are they?

8. Does the poem rely primarily on connotation or denotation?

Does the poem rely primarily on the figurative meaning of words or does it rely primarily on the literal meaning?

9. How does the sound of the poem contribute to its meaning?

Does the sound or tempo of the poem contribute to its meaning or message? Does the poem use alliteration?

10. What else do you notice?

There are literally hundreds of features that one might find in a poem. What else did you notice that should be mentioned in an analysis?

11. What is your reaction to the poem?

The same poem often draws different reactions from different people. What is your reaction to the poem? What did you take from it?

Gather together your brief answers to these 11 questions and form them into two paragraphs to summarize your analysis of the poem.

Prose Fiction

Prose fiction typically has plot, a setting or settings, and characters along with a narrator to tell the story, which often tries to make some point that goes beyond the story itself.

As with poetry analysis, your prose fiction analysis will consist of answers to a series of questions.

1. What is the plot?

A fictional story uses a series of "scenes" which may or may not occur in time order. These scenes are related to one another in a way that tells the story. Each scene usually has a specific purpose to further the story and may, among other things, clarify or obscure, simplify or complicate, set a scene and develop characters.

2. What is the setting?

These questions are very similar to poetry. Where in time is the story set? Is it in recent years, the past, the future—is there a specific time or date? Does the date have significance? What time span does it cover?

Where in physical space is the story set? Is it in a particular country, in a field, in the city, by the roadside? Are there many different settings?

Does the story have a symbolic setting? Literary Terms on page 92 lists some of the literary devices you may encounter in a story with a symbolic setting.

3. Who are the characters, what do they represent, and what are the conflicts?

A work of fiction generally has a relatively small central cast of characters. These characters usually represent something. The characters may represent other people, or they may represent particular human traits or they may represent ideas or basic principles, or may have strictly symbolic meaning. Some conflict or tension between and among the characters is usually at the center of the story.

4. Who is narrating and what is his or her perspective?

The narrator is the person or persons who tell the story. The narration may come from a character in the story or from outside the story. Typically, an external narrator is presumed to be objective while a narrator from within the story may or may not have this trait. A narrator will always have a unique perspective from which they tell the story.

5. How does the story use language?

Does the story rely primarily on the figurative meaning of words or does it rely primarily on the literal meaning?

6. What is the tone?

What is the author's tone? A list of tone words on page 91 will help you identify and describe the author's tone.

7. What is the imagery?

What imagery does the author employ? Are there emotional images, physical images, or symbolic images? What are they?

8. What is the point?

Almost every fictional story has a larger point the author wants to make. What is the larger point that the story attempts to make.

9. What is the poem's genre?

Draw from the discussion on page 88 to identify the genre of a story. Each genre has a purpose as described on that page.

10. What else do you notice?

There are literally hundreds of features that one might find in a fictional story. What else did you notice that should be mentioned in an analysis?

11. What is your reaction to the story?

The same story often draws different reactions from different people. What is your reaction to the story? What did you take from it?

Gather together your brief answers to these 11 questions and form them into two paragraphs to summarize your analysis of the prose fiction.

Retrieval of Information from Print and Nonprint Sources

Information can be retrieved from books, magazines, and other print sources by simply picking up the reading materials and turning and flipping through the pages. The book, newspaper, or periodical remains one of the most efficient ways to access print information.

Libraries

Print materials are also found in libraries or other repositories on microfilm and microfiche. Microfilms are 35mm films of books, while microfiche are flat and can contain hundreds of pages of text material. Microfilm and microfiche are read with specialized readers.

Computers

Other information can be retrieved on or through the computer. Written materials can be entered on a computer, usually with a word processor. This information can be accessed directly through the computer's hard disk. Special features of most word processors and other utilities permit the user to search electronically for words and phrases. Sound, graphics, and animation may also be stored on a computer's hard disk. These sounds and images may be accessed using specialized computer programs.

Print materials, images, sounds and animation may also be stored on CD-ROMs designed for computer use. Information on these CD-ROMs may be accessed through a CD-ROM player that is connected to the computer. Images and sounds on videotapes, audiotapes, music CD-ROMs, and videodisk may also be accessed through the computer.

Computers can be connected to telephone lines and television cables using a modem. Modems allow computers to upload and download data from other computers, usually via the Internet. "Going on line" has become a popular way to gather information.

Internet

The Internet is a vast collection of computers around the world. These computers are connected by cables and phone lines, forming a huge net. Once on the Internet, a person can have access to enormous amounts of information.

Browsers

Browsers such as Microsoft Explorer and Netscape Navigator turn the Internet's electronic signals into viewable text and images. You can retrieve text, pictures, video, and sound with these browsers. Almost all periodical and newspaper information is available online, and you can hold Internet conversations and Internet videoconferences.

World Wide Web

The World Wide Web is the collection of sites on the Internet. Web addresses identify the different sites and the information contained at these sites. For example the Web address *http://www.barronseduc.com* connects you directly to the Barron's Web site.

Search engines such as Google and Yahoo help you to find sites containing the information you want. If you entered "teacher testing," these search engines would return a list of WWW sites in their catalog containing these key words.

Rhetorical Conventions of Argumentation, Persuasion, Exposition, Narration, and Reflection

In **argumentation** the writer or speaker tries to convince the readers or listeners to accept a particular view or idea. There are several rules to follow to construct a well-ordered argument. Your presentation should appear moderate and reasoned, and you should acknowledge the reasonableness of those who differ with you.

The statements must be believable in form and in fact. That is, the statements must distinguish among fact, opinion, and the conclusions you have drawn. The presentation should clarify the meanings of key ideas and words. The presentation must also squarely address the question and not beg the question as described in the preceding example.

The presentation must support any views or conclusions with solid evidence and arguments. The arguments can be inductive or deductive. However, these arguments must avoid the invalid and fallacious arguments noted previously.

> **Expository** presentations simply explain. This book is essentially expository presentation. It explains about the CSET and how to pass it.

> **Narration** presents a factual or fictional story. A written fictional account or a spoken presentation about your life as a child is a narration.

> **Reflection** describes a scene, person, or emotion. A spoken description of your neighborhood or a written note describing how you felt when you graduated from high school are reflections.

READING, LANGUAGE, AND LITERATURE TARGETED TEST

Use these test items to strengthen and extend your review.

Instructions

Mark your answers on the sheet provided below. Correct your answer sheet using the answers on page 102.

1 Ⓐ Ⓑ Ⓒ Ⓓ		9 Ⓐ Ⓑ Ⓒ Ⓓ		17 Ⓐ Ⓑ Ⓒ Ⓓ		25 Ⓐ Ⓑ Ⓒ Ⓓ		33 Ⓐ Ⓑ Ⓒ Ⓓ
2 Ⓐ Ⓑ Ⓒ Ⓓ		10 Ⓐ Ⓑ Ⓒ Ⓓ		18 Ⓐ Ⓑ Ⓒ Ⓓ		26 Ⓐ Ⓑ Ⓒ Ⓓ		34 Ⓐ Ⓑ Ⓒ Ⓓ
3 Ⓐ Ⓑ Ⓒ Ⓓ		11 Ⓐ Ⓑ Ⓒ Ⓓ		19 Ⓐ Ⓑ Ⓒ Ⓓ		27 Ⓐ Ⓑ Ⓒ Ⓓ		35 Ⓐ Ⓑ Ⓒ Ⓓ
4 Ⓐ Ⓑ Ⓒ Ⓓ		12 Ⓐ Ⓑ Ⓒ Ⓓ		20 Ⓐ Ⓑ Ⓒ Ⓓ		28 Ⓐ Ⓑ Ⓒ Ⓓ		36 Ⓐ Ⓑ Ⓒ Ⓓ
5 Ⓐ Ⓑ Ⓒ Ⓓ		13 Ⓐ Ⓑ Ⓒ Ⓓ		21 Ⓐ Ⓑ Ⓒ Ⓓ		29 Ⓐ Ⓑ Ⓒ Ⓓ		37 Ⓐ Ⓑ Ⓒ Ⓓ
6 Ⓐ Ⓑ Ⓒ Ⓓ		14 Ⓐ Ⓑ Ⓒ Ⓓ		22 Ⓐ Ⓑ Ⓒ Ⓓ		30 Ⓐ Ⓑ Ⓒ Ⓓ		38 Ⓐ Ⓑ Ⓒ Ⓓ
7 Ⓐ Ⓑ Ⓒ Ⓓ		15 Ⓐ Ⓑ Ⓒ Ⓓ		23 Ⓐ Ⓑ Ⓒ Ⓓ		31 Ⓐ Ⓑ Ⓒ Ⓓ		39 Ⓐ Ⓑ Ⓒ Ⓓ
8 Ⓐ Ⓑ Ⓒ Ⓓ		16 Ⓐ Ⓑ Ⓒ Ⓓ		24 Ⓐ Ⓑ Ⓒ Ⓓ		32 Ⓐ Ⓑ Ⓒ Ⓓ		40 Ⓐ Ⓑ Ⓒ Ⓓ

1. Which of the following would NOT be supported by a basal reading approach?
   (A) Skills are taught and developed in a systematic sequential manner.
   (B) Meeting individual differences and needs of the child.
   (C) A basic vocabulary is established and reinforced.
   (D) Manuals provide a detailed outline for teaching.

2. A child has difficulty pronouncing a printed word. The problem may reflect all of the following EXCEPT
   (A) phonetic analysis.
   (B) sight vocabulary.
   (C) language comprehension.
   (D) context analysis.

3. Personal journals should NOT be used as a
   (A) record of feelings.
   (B) way to share thoughts with others.
   (C) means of expressing thought.
   (D) means for writing ideas.

4. Reading books for different grades first appeared in the 1800s as
   (A) *McGuffey's Readers*
   (B) *The Horn Book*
   (C) *The New England Primer*
   (D) *The American Readers*

5. Which of the following is NOT furthered by a phonics approach?
   (A) associating sounds with printed letters
   (B) reading comprehension
   (C) attacking new works independently
   (D) developing a sight vocabulary

6. The second-grade teacher is considering a whole language approach. Which of the following is the best reason to institute the program?
   (A) Whole language instruction is widely accepted.
   (B) It is not necessary to teach word recognition.
   (C) Children comprehend more after using a whole language approach.
   (D) Children have a better attitude toward reading.

7. During a unit on animal stories, sixth-grade students read *Lad a Dog,* by Albert Payson Terhune. The teacher wants to use transactional strategy instruction to help students develop a deeper understanding of the cognitive process involved in understanding Lad's "motivations" as described in the book. Which of the following indicates the teacher is using this approach?
   (A) The teacher explicitly explains the processes involved in successful reading comprehension.
   (B) The teacher encourages students to explore the processes involved in successful reading comprehension.
   (C) The teacher and students cooperate to jointly explore the processes involved in successful reading instruction.
   (D) The teacher asks students to explore the processes involved in successful reading comprehension.

8. A fourth-grade student hands in a writing assignment containing this sentence.

   I are going swimming.

   This assignment indicates that the student needs more help with which of the following?
   (A) subject-verb agreement
   (B) pronouns
   (C) sentence fragments
   (D) adjectives and adverbs

9. Your class reads a science fiction story about space travel. Which of the following actions on your part is most likely to help students differentiate between science fact and science fiction?
   (A) Guide students to understand that science fiction stories are creative writing and not based on science fact.
   (B) Guide students as they identify examples of science fact and science fiction based on the story they just completed.
   (C) Ask students to work independently to make their own list of science fact and science fiction.
   (D) Ask students to work independently as they identify examples of science fact and science fiction in the story they just completed.

10. You have a number of long newspaper articles about whales. Which of the following approaches on your part is most likely to best inform students about the main idea(s) of each article.
    (A) Students work independently and summarize for themselves the main point(s) of each article.
    (B) Students work in cooperative learning groups to summarize and present the main point(s) of each article.
    (C) You present a brief summary of the main point(s) of each article.
    (D) You prepare a brief summary of the main point(s) of each article and distribute them to your students.

11. A young student writes about a sailor on a four-masted schooner. The student's writing contains this sentence.

    He had enuf rope to tie up the boat.

    Which of the actions on the part of the teacher listed below addresses the errors in the sentence?

(A) instruction on phonics-based word attack skills.
(B) instruction on context-based word attack skills
(C) instruction on the use of homonyms
(D) instruction on variable spelling phonemes

12. Which of the following would be the best opportunity for a formative evaluation of student's writing?
    (A) a discussion with the student
    (B) a portfolio of student's writing samples
    (C) Iowa Test of Basic Skills
    (D) end of unit test

13. A teacher is using an ESL approach to teach reading to a group of LEP students. Which of the following actions on the part of the teacher is most consistent with that approach?
    (A) Use context clues to help students identify English words.
    (B) Help students learn to read in the student's native language.
    (C) Translate English reading passages into the student's native language.
    (D) Ask students to bring in original literature in the student's native language.

14. A fifth-grade student hands in this writing sample.

    I sat in the audience while my sister play the clarinet. I saw her play while sit there. I guess I will never be a profesional musician.

    The teacher is most likely to help improve this student's writing by providing instruction in which of the following areas?
    (A) nouns
    (B) pronouns
    (C) spelling
    (D) verbs

15. A primary teacher wants to produce the most significant reading benefits for his students. Which of the following actions on the part of the teacher is most likely to create that benefit?
    (A) providing a literature-rich environment
    (B) providing effective phonics instruction
    (C) providing opportunities for oral expression and listening
    (D) using real literature sources instead of basal texts

16. The speaker described her teen years and spoke about the arguments she had with her brothers and sisters. Then the speaker told the audience that she and her siblings were now the best of friends.

    This account of the speaker's presentation best characterizes
    (A) argumentation.
    (B) exposition.
    (C) narration.
    (D) propaganda.

17. The stories of *King Arthur and the Knights of the Round Table* originated between about 1000 A.D. and 1200 A.D. To which genre of literature do these stories belong?
    (A) poetry
    (B) epic
    (C) lyric
    (D) romance

18. You ain't going to no party.

    Which of the following statements most accurately describes this quote?
    (A) The quote effectively communicates in function and structure.
    (B) The quote effectively communicates in function but not structure.
    (C) The quote effectively communicates in structure but not function.
    (D) The quote effectively communicates in neither function nor structure.

19. The novels *The Jungle* by Sinclair Lewis and the *Grapes of Wrath* by John Steinbeck share what main common theme?
    (A) They exposed American social problems.
    (B) They focused on overpricing in the food industry.
    (C) They exposed the plight of California migrant workers.
    (D) They exposed the dangers of imported meat and produce.

20. Which of the following examples does NOT point out the difficulty of using the 26-letter alphabet to represent spoken English?
    (A) "Live and on stage, the rock group Phish"
    (B) "The new tuf truck line from Tough Trucks"
    (C) "'I' before 'e' except after 'c' and when sounded as 'a' in neighbor and weigh."
    (D) "It's a terrrr-iffic day here at the car wash."

21. The Newbery Award and Caldecott Medal are given annually to the best American books for young people. Which type of book receives which recognition?
    (A) Newbery, elementary grade book; Caldecott, young adult book
    (B) Newbery, young adult book; Caldecott, elementary grade book
    (C) Newbery, children's book; Caldecott, picture book
    (D) Newbery, picture book; Caldecott, children's book

22. Which sentence below is *incorrect*?
    (A) The dinner tastes good.
    (B) The dinner tastes badly.
    (C) The chef cooked badly.
    (D) The chef cooked well.

23. Which sentence below is correct?
    (A) The cowboy reigned in his horse to accept a cup of water.
    (B) The cowboy led his horse and spoke of times passed.
    (C) The cowboy gave his assent to their request for a ride.
    (D) The cowboy only wanted peace on they're section of the plains.

24. What does *ante* in the word *antebellum* mean?
    (A) Before
    (B) Against
    (C) After
    (D) During

Questions 25–27 refer to the following poem.

My love falls on silence nigh
I am alone in knowing the good-bye
For while a lost love has its day
A love unknown is a sadder way

25. The word *nigh* in line 1 means
    (A) clear.
    (B) complete.
    (C) near.
    (D) not.

26. This passage describes
    (A) loving someone and being rebuffed.
    (B) being loved by someone you do not love.
    (C) loving someone who loves another person.
    (D) loving someone without acknowledgment.

27. The subject and the verb in line 2 are
(A) I . . . am.
(B) I . . . alone.
(C) I . . . knowing.
(D) alone . . . knowing.

_____

28. *Peter Piper picked a peck of pickled peppers.*

The sentence above is an example of
(A) alliteration.
(B) euphemism.
(C) hyperbole.
(D) metaphor.

29. *The Odyssey* is best categorized as
(A) an epic.
(B) a lyric.
(C) a novel.
(D) a romance.

30. I grew up in Kearny, New Jersey, now known as Soccer Town, USA. I played football in high school and barely knew that the soccer team existed. However, a look back at my high school yearbook revealed that the soccer team won the state championship. We had a 0.500 season.

Which of these techniques is used by the author of this passage?
(A) exposition
(B) reflection
(C) argumentation
(D) narration

31. [1] Their heads were filled with thoughts of laughing children and whirling rides. [2] Finally they were on their way. [3] Now every school day seemed like a month. [4] The children had been waiting for months to visit their favorite amusement park.

Which of the following choices represents the most logical way to order the sentences from the paragraph above?
(A) 3, 1, 4, 2
(B) 3, 4, 1, 2
(C) 4, 3, 1, 2
(D) 4, 2, 3, 1

32. Which of the following words or word pairs would NOT be used to coordinate sentence elements?
(A) and
(B) either or
(C) but
(D) when

33.   ah autumn coolness
          hand in hand paring away

Which of the following could be the third line in the haiku poem above?
(A) in the wetness
(B) branches and leaves
(C) eggplants cucumbers
(D) til the end of day

34. The word *paring* in the poem above means
(A) putting together.
(B) doubling up.
(C) cutting off.
(D) planting fruit.

35. How is haiku different from a cinquain?
(A) The cinquain has a 5-5-5 scheme instead of 5-7-5.
(B) Lines can rhyme in haiku but not in a cinquain.
(C) A cinquain has five lines instead of three.
(D) A cinquain is of Spanish origin, and haiku originated in Japan.

36. The root *frac* in the word *fraction* means
(A) break.
(B) eighths.
(C) part.
(D) piece.

37. [1] All of my visits came before the series of fires that burned the park. [2] I have some very happy memories about Yellowstone National Park. [3] The United States National Park system is extensive. [4] Although most land dedicated to the park system is in western states.

Which of the following choices represents the most logical way to order the sentences from the paragraph above?
(A) 4, 3, 2, 1
(B) 4, 3, 1, 2
(C) 3, 4, 1, 2
(D) 3, 4, 2, 1

38. In which sentence is the underlined word used correctly?
    (A) The rider grabbed the horse's <u>reign</u>.
    (B) The teacher had just begun her <u>lessen</u>.
    (C) The dog's collar showed <u>its</u> address.
    (D) The road offered a steep <u>assent</u> to the plateau.

39. Which of the following shows the correct syllables for *simultaneous*?
    (A) simul ta neous
    (B) sim ul ta neous
    (C) si mul ta ne ous
    (D) sim ul ta ne ous

40. Japanese students have always been considered to be well prepared for life in the world's business and engineering communities. The mathematics and science curricula of Japanese schools are considered to be superior to those in American schools. With the daily advancement of Japanese technological prowess, how can American children ever hope to compete with their Japanese counterparts?

Which of the following is the best descriptor of the author's tone in this passage?
    (A) disbelief
    (B) anger
    (C) pride
    (D) concern

TARGETED TEST ANSWERS EXPLAINED

1. **B** Note the word NOT in the item. A basal reading program is not designed to meet the individual needs of students. A basal program is designed for all students, typically with all students in the United States. A basal program must be supplemented to meet the individual needs of students.

2. **C** Choice C is correct. Note the word EXCEPT in the item. You don't have to understand the meaning of a word to pronounce it. This item points out the important distinction between recognizing a word and knowing what the word means. Word recognition and comprehension are both important parts of reading instruction.

3. **B** Note the word NOT in the item. Personal journals are just that—personal. These journals are not a way to share thoughts with others. Students should use a different format, such as a response journal, to share their thoughts.

4. **A** *McGuffey's Readers* were the first schoolbooks written for different grade levels.

5. **B** Note the word NOT in the item. A phonics approach does not address word meaning or reading comprehension. Phonics addresses word recognition and word pronunciation. Educators frequently criticize overreliance on phonics for just this reason.

6. **D** Students develop a better attitude toward reading when they use the real literature found in a whole language approach.

7. **C** The word "transactional" in the term "transactional strategy instruction" means a give-and-take between students and teachers as they explore the processes involved in successful reading comprehension.

8. **A** The singular subject "I" does not agree with the plural verb "are." Nonagreement of subject and verb should be addressed in the early grades.

9. **B** Guiding students as they work is a very effective strategy for teaching reading. Picking out science fact and science fiction in a space exploration science fiction story is certainly the best kind of guidance among the choices given.

10. **B** This is exactly the situation in which cooperative learning groups excel. Students learn from interaction in the group, from the presentation made by other groups, and from your reaction and others' reaction to the presentations.

11. **D** This student is a phonetic speller. "Enuf" is misspelled, but the student correctly followed phonics rules. This student

needs instruction in the alternative spelling used for phonemes (sounds associated with letters and groups of letters). For example, English spelling uses the letters "gh" to represent the "f" sound in "enough." Using many spellings for the same sound can make English a difficult language to learn.

12. **B** A formative evaluation helps a teacher plan lessons. Samples of a student's writing best furthers that goal.

13. **A** ESL means English as a Second Language. This approach encourages the teaching and use of English.

14. **D** Choice D is correct. The student's writing contains several verb tense shifts. In the first sentence, "sat" is past tense, while "play" is present tense. In the second sentence, "saw" is past tense, while "sit" is present tense.

15. **B** Reading is a unique skill, and different from language. Studies show that students benefit most from early, effective phonics instruction. This should not be taken to mean that every phonics program is effective.

16. **C** The speaker is telling a story about her life.

17. **D** The King Arthur legends showing brave men, defenseless women, and stories of love are the classic romance. The epic and the lyric appeared much earlier.

18. **B** Language has two main aspects—function and structure. Language function refers to the ability to communicate. Language structure refers to the way words are used in a language. The structure of the quote is inappropriate; however, we know what it means.

19. **A** Both of these novels exposed American social ills. *The Jungle* described the problems with the meat and meat-packing industry, while *Grapes of Wrath* described the plight of migrant workers in the Depression.

20. **D** Choices A, B, and C point out the kind of spelling difficulties regularly encountered in the English language. Choice D does not have such a problem but emphasizes the *r* sound by repeating the letters a number of times.

21. **C** The Newbery Award was first given in 1922, while the Caldecott Award dates to 1938.

22. **B** This sentence uses the adverb *badly* to modify the noun *dinner*. Choice A cor-

rectly uses the adjective *good*. Choices C and D correctly use the adverbs *badly* and *well*.

23. **C** Other choices contain "classic" word usage errors. These errors: (A) *reigned* instead of *reined* (B) *passed* instead of *past*, and (D) *they're* instead of *their*.

24. **A** *Ante* means before. *Anti* means against, and *post* means after.

25. **C** The word *nigh* means near in space or time.

26. **D** The passage tells us that love falls on silence and that love unknown is sad, leading to the conclusion that the passage is about loving without acknowledgment.

27. **A** I is the subject; am is the verb. Alone is not a verb, and knowing is a part of the prepositional phrase.

28. **A** Alliteration refers to the repetition of an initial consonant in nearby words.

29. **A** *The Odyssey* is an epic, a very long narrative with great scope.

30. **D** The author is narrating, or telling a story, about a part of his life.

31. **C** Sentence 4 is the opening sentence followed in order by sentences, 3, 1, and 2. Some other arrangements not listed could also be logical.

32. **D** The word *when* is used to subordinate sentence elements. All of the other choices are used to coordinate sentence elements.

33. **C** Haiku follows a 5-7-5 syllabic scheme with no rhyming. Choice C alone meets these criteria.

34. **C** The word *paring* means to cut off. Do not confuse this word with its homonym *pairing*.

35. **C** A cinquain is a five-line poem with no particular rhyming scheme. The cinquain originated in France.

36. **A** The word *fraction* developed from the root *frac*, which means breaking something into pieces.

37. **D** Sentence 4 only makes sense after reading sentence 3. Sentence 1 only makes sense after reading sentence 2. Choice D, alone, shows this arrangement.

38. **C** This sentence correctly uses the possessive form of *its*. The other underlined words are homonyms (words that sound the same but are spelled differently) of the correct word.

39. **C** This is the correct syllabication for *simultaneous*.

40. **D** The author is concerned that American children will have limited opportunities.

4 HISTORY AND SOCIAL STUDIES

TEST INFO BOX

26 Multiple Choice items   Half of Subtest I items
2 Constructed Response items   Half of Subtest I items

HISTORY AND SOCIAL STUDIES ITEMS

History and Social Studies multiple choice items look like this.

The main effect of the Treaty of Utrecht in 1742 was that

(A) France lost North American possessions to England.
(B) the Spanish Empire was partitioned.
(C) Britain recognized the United States after the Revolutionary War.
(D) Holland and Switzerland were officially formed.

Social Studies constructed response items look like this.

Describe the view supported by the *Federalist Papers* and the impact of the debate between the Jeffersonians and the Federalists on the American political system.

USING THIS CHAPTER

This chapter prepares you to take the History and Social Studies part of the CSET. Choose one of these approaches.

There are four History and Social Studies sections

Apply the steps given below to each section.

I want all the review I can get.

❏ Skip the Review Quiz and read the entire review section.
❏ Take the Review Quiz.
❏ Correct the Review Quiz and reread the indicated parts of the review.
❏ Complete the Practice Questions.

I want a thorough review.

❏ Take the Review Quiz.
❏ Correct the Review Quiz and reread the indicated parts of the review.
❏ Complete the Practice Questions.

I want a quick review.

❏ Take and correct the Review Quiz.
❏ Complete the Practice Questions.

I want to practice History and Social Studies questions.

❏ Complete the Practice Questions.

CALIFORNIA HISTORY

CALIFORNIA HISTORY REVIEW QUIZ

This quiz uses a short answer format to help you find out what you know. The quiz results direct you to the portions of the chapter you should read.

This quiz will also help focus your thinking, and these questions and answers are a good review in themselves. It's not important to answer all these questions correctly, and don't be concerned if you miss many of them.

The answers are found immediately after the quiz. It's to your advantage not to look at them until you have completed the quiz. Once you have completed and corrected the review quiz, use the answer checklist to decide which sections of the review to study.

Write the answers in the space provided or on a separate sheet of paper.

1. What are the four main regions in California?

2. About how far each year does the Pacific plate move along the San Andreas Fault?

3. The northern border of California is closest to which degree of latitude?

4. California been inhabited for about how many years?

5. Which Spanish explorer is credited as the first European to land in California?

6. Which port did Spanish galleons sail from as they traveled down the California coast on their way to Acapulco?

7. Who is credited with establishing the first Christian mission in California?

8. Overall, what was the main impact of the mission system on Native Americans?

9. California came under the control of which country after Mexico gained its independence from Spain?

10. What was the status of American Indians during the rancho period?

11. What is the most notable cause of the survival of half the members of the Donner party?

12. About how long did the Bear Flag Republic exist in California?

13. Who were the Californios?

_____

_____

14. What was the outcome of the Capitulation of Cahuenga?

_____

_____

15. What was the fastest way from the eastern part of the United States to California during the gold rush?

_____

_____

16. What was the California government's official position toward Native Americans during the gold rush?

_____

_____

17. What was the original California Constitution's position on women?

_____

_____

18. What event of 1861 speeded communication between California and the rest of the United States?

_____

_____

19. What was the main responsibility of federal troops from California during the Civil War?

_____

_____

20. Who is credited with planning the transcontinental railroad?

_____

_____

21. What was the main reason the railroad could continue after the death of its founder?

_____

_____

22. What were the relations between business and California government like at the turn of the twentieth century?

_____

_____

23. How does the 1906 San Francisco earthquake compare with the 1989 Loma Prieta earthquake?

_____

24. Which book chronicles the lives of dust bowl immigrants to California?

_____

_____

25. Which group of Japanese Americans did the United States government consider a particular threat?

_____

_____

26. Approximately what percent of the Californian population is Caucasian?

_____

_____

ANSWER CHECKLIST

The answers are organized by review sections. Check your answers. If you miss an answer in a section, check the box and review that section.

California History

❑ *An Overview, page 110.*
1. Coast, Central Valley, Desert, Mountains

❑ *Beginnings, page 112.*
2. 1 inch

❑ *Latitude and Longitude, page 113.*
3. 42 degrees

❑ *Earliest Inhabitants, page 115.*
4. About 13,000 to 15,000 years

❑ *Spanish Exploration, page 116.*
5. Juan Cabrillo
6. Manila

❑ *The Mission Period, page 117.*
7. Father Sierra

❑ *The Mission System, page 118.*
8. The Native Americans became dependent; the Native American population was reduced by 75%.

❑ *Mexican Independence from Spain, page 118.*
9. Mexico
10. The Native Americans were essentially indentured servants.

❑ *Wagon Trains, page 119.*
11. Members of the Donner party resorted to cannibalism.

❑ *Bear Flag Revolt, page 119.*
12. less than a month

❑ *Mexican American War, page 119.*
13. Californios were Spanish-speaking people who came from Spain or Mexico to settle in California before the Mexican American War.
14. It effectively made California a part of the United States.

❑ *Gold Rush, page 120.*
15. by boat, with overland transfer through the Isthmus of Panama
16. Extermination

❑ *Statehood, page 120.*
17. Women could own land but could not vote.

❑ *Early Transportation and Communication, page 121.*
18. The telegraph began operation on October 21, 1961.

❑ *The Civil War and Aftermath, page 121.*
19. Control Native Americans

❑ *The Railroads, page 122.*
20 Theodore Judah
21. Inflated mileage payments from the government

❑ *Into the Twentieth Century, page 123.*
22. Business controlled government; bribes and favoritism were common

❑ *The San Francisco Earthquake and Fires, page 123.*
23. The San Francisco quake was about 15 to 20 times stronger.

❑ *The Great Depression, page 123.*
24. *The Grapes of Wrath,* by John Steinbeck

❑ *World War II, page 124.*
25. Nisei—those Japanese Americans born in the United States who had returned to Japan for their education

❑ *Predictable Diversity, page 124.*
26. Less than 50 percent (about 47%)

CALIFORNIA HISTORY REVIEW

An Overview

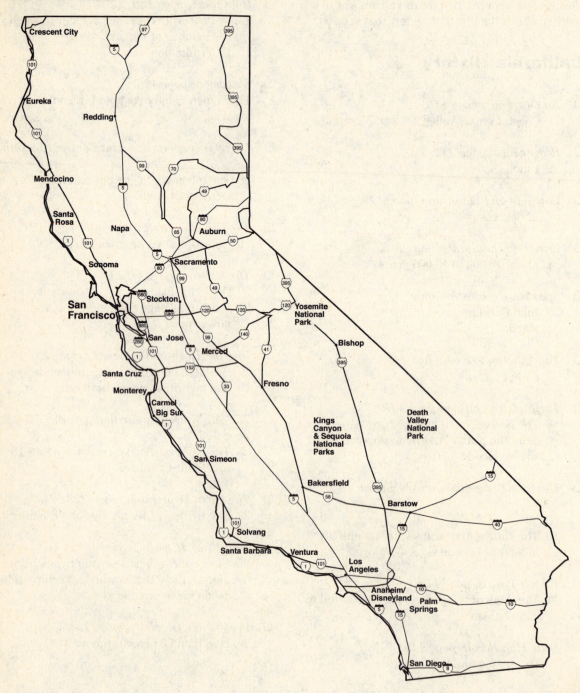

About 35,000,000 people live in California, making it the most populous state in the United States. About 13 percent of United States residents live in California. California was admitted as the 31st state on September 9, 1850. The state capital is in Sacramento. The state governor and 40 state senators are elected for four-year terms, while 80 members of the Assembly are elected for two-year terms.

The entire 840 miles of the western border consists of coastline. The highest point in the 48 Contiguous United States at the peak of Mount Whitney (14,495 feet above sea level and the state's lowest point in the United States at Death Valley (282 feet below sea level) are just about 100 miles apart in the southeast part of the state.

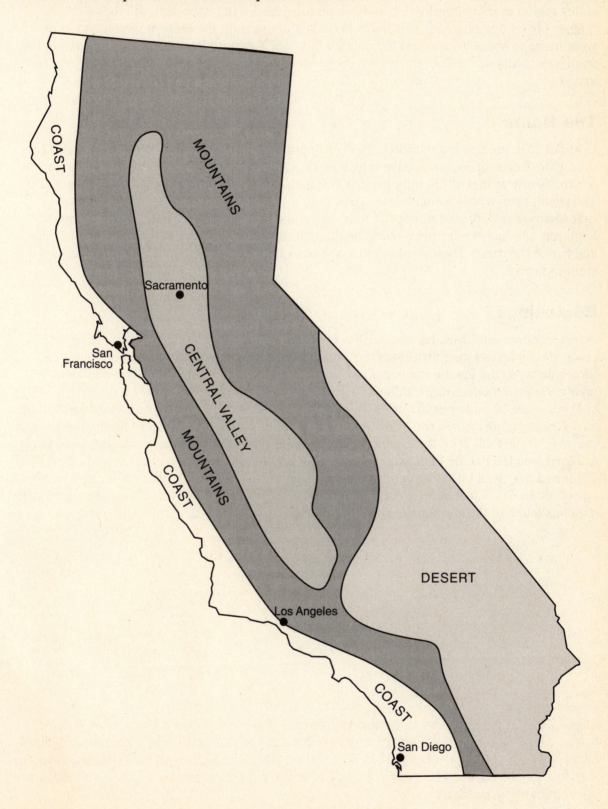

California has four main regions. These regions are the Coast, the Central Valley, the Desert in the southeast, and the Mountains that surround central valley. Much of the coastal region includes the San Andreas Fault, a center of earthquake activity. Statistics indicate that almost 6 percent of the population of the United States is in the southern coastal region. The central valley region is agriculturally rich and is a national leader in production of crops such as grapes, olives, and peaches. The Sierra Nevada Mountains in the eastern mountain region were home to the gold rush and the current home of Yosemite Park. The desert region in the southeast is among the hottest regions on Earth and parts of this region may receive no rain in a year.

The Name

In about 1510 the Spanish explorer Garci Ordonez de Montalvo wrote *Las Sergas de Esplandian* (The Deeds of Esplandian) in which he describes a fictional place called California. He wrote, "Know ye that at the right hand of the Indies there is an island named California . . . The island everywhere abounds with gold."

It seems that Cortes or someone in his entourage was familiar with this story. When the explorer marched north from Mexico he thought they were approaching this fabled island, and hence the name. These explorers expected to find gold as abundant in California as the story indicates.

Beginnings

Fossil evidence confirms that the earth is covered with geologic "plates," land masses that creep slowly across the Earth's surface. Most of California was underwater until geologic forces between the Pacific Plate and the North American Plate pushed up mountains to create much of modern-day California.

For the last 30 million years or so, the Pacific Plate has been moving northwest an inch or so a year scraping against the North American plate along the San Andreas Fault. The land to the west of the fault is on the Pacific Plate. Tens of millions of years ago that part of coastal California on the Pacific Plate was in Mexico. In another 30 million years that part of coastal California may well be in current-day Alaska. That means the Pacific Plate will move an average of about 6 or 7 feet in an average lifetime. The movement tends to occur suddenly, which explains much of the earthquake risk in California.

Latitude and Longitude

Latitude and longitude lines form a grid on the Earth's surface. Latitude lines run east to west, longitude lines run north to south.

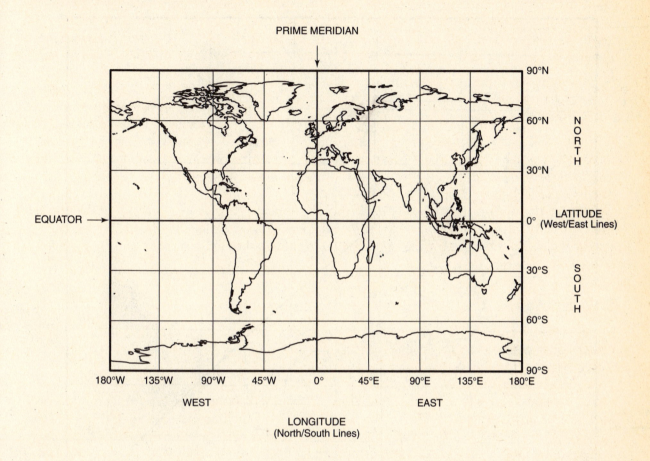

PRIME MERIDIAN

EQUATOR →

90°N
60°N
30°N
0° LATITUDE (West/East Lines)
30°S
60°S
90°S

N O R T H

S O U T H

180°W   135°W   90°W   45°W   0°   45°E   90°E   135°E   180°E

WEST   EAST

LONGITUDE
(North/South Lines)

Latitude lines run parallel to the equator and measure the distance north or south of the equator.

Latitude ranges from 0 degrees at the equator to 90 degrees North or 90 degrees South at the poles. Longitude lines run parallel to the Prime Meridian, which runs through Greenwich, England. Longitude measures the distance east and west of this line. Longitude ranges from zero degrees at the Prime Meridian to 180 degrees East or 180 degrees West.

We express latitude and longitude in degrees, minutes, and sometimes seconds. Each degree is subdivided into 60 minutes ('). The easternmost part of the state along the Colorado River is about 115 degrees West Longitude. The westernmost part of the coast is between 123 degrees and 124 degrees West Longitude. The southernmost part of the state at the Mexican border is between 32 degrees and 33 degrees North Latitude. The northernmost part of the state at the Oregon border is at 42 degrees North Latitude.

The map below shows latitude and longitude in California. The map faces North, and on this map you can see that the longitude lines become closer together as they converge on the North Pole.

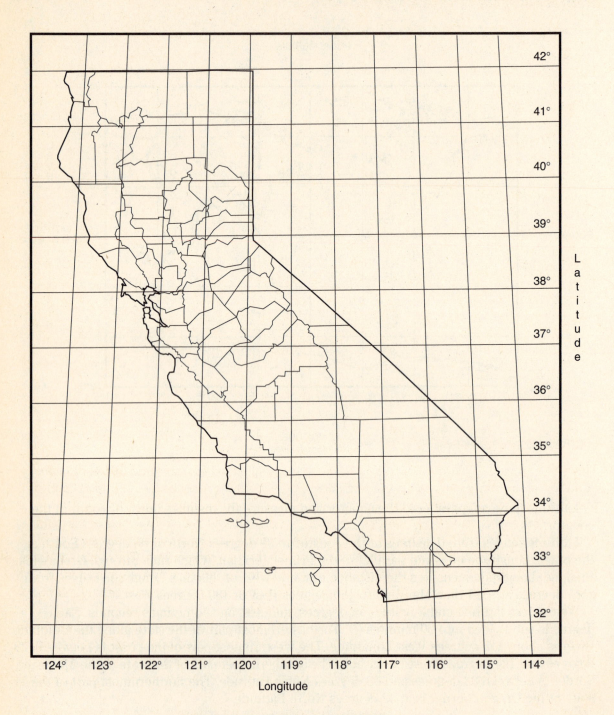

CAIFORNIA LATITUDE and LONGITUDE

Here are some representative latitudes and longitudes for California.

California
Representative Latitude and Longitude

Blythe	33° 37' N 114° 43' W
Crescent City	41° 46' N 124° 12' W
Eureka/Arcata	40° 59' N 124° 6' W
Lompoc	34° 43' N 120° 34' W
Long Beach	33° 49' N 118° 9' W
Los Angeles	34° 3' N 118° 14' W
Merced-Castle AFB	37° 23' N 120° 34' W
Napa	38° 13' N 122° 17' W
Needles AP	34° 36' N 114° 37' W
Oakland AP	37° 49' N 122° 19' W
Palm Springs	33° 49' N 16° 32' W
Redlands	34° 3' N 117° 11' W
Sacramento	38° 31' N 121° 30' W
Salinas	36° 40' N 121° 36' W
San Diego	32° 44' N 117° 10' W
San Francisco	37° 37' N 122° 23' W
San Luis Obispo	35° 20' N 120° 43' W
Santa Ana	33° 45' N 117° 52' W
Santa Barbara	34° 26' N 119° 50' W
Santa Cruz	36° 59' N 122° 1' W
Ukiah	39° 9' N 123° 12' W
Yreka	41° 43' N 122° 38' W

Earliest Inhabitants

There is a story that about 400 C.E. (A.D.) a Chinese ship sailed east, instead of west because of a malfunctioning compass. In the story, the ship eventually reaches the shores of California. When the sailors realize their error, they turn around and sail back to China.

If the story were true, these sailors would have encountered Native Americans who had been living in California for about 12,000 years. Nomadic hunters most likely crossed the Bering Strait between Asia and North America when it was a grassy area. These Native Americans were the first people to inhabit what is now California, and the first people to inhabit what is now the United States. The immigration continued and these groups slowly migrated throughout California and east throughout the Unites States.

About 5500 B.C.E. (B.C.) these nomadic people started to settle and established villages near the coast. It was about this time that the first native settlers arrived in the San Francisco area. The Native American tribes grew to over 100 with many different language groups. This marked linguistic diversity meant that people from different tribal groups could not communicate effectively.

Even though there were many different languages, these California Native Americans were truly prehistoric. That means they did not use a written language. Contrast these with the African continent where writing was introduced about 3000 B.C.E. (B.C.). This absence of writing means that scholars have to rely on archaeological evidence to find out about these early people.

The Native American population of California was over 250,000 by 1500 C.E. (A.D.). Even by that date, most Native American tribes in California were not well organized. The lack of distant communication, the absence of organization and the relative isolation spelled trouble for these Native Americans with the start of European exploration and settlement. The native population was ill prepared to resist these new settlers. In the centuries that followed a striking percent of these Native Americans were killed by disease, slaughtered by modern weapons, separated from their families, and enslaved in the name of religion.

Spanish Exploration

Christopher Columbus made four voyages under Spanish patronage to the Caribbean in the 1490s and early 1500s. His voyages sparked interest in further European exploration. The Spanish monarchy was particularly interested in spreading Christianity. It was in this climate that Hernando Cortes sailed from Spain to Cuba and then in 1519 he commanded eleven ships and sailed west to Mexico. Spain established a colony there called New Spain. Indigenous people in the colony were enslaved and mistreated, setting the trend for future encounters between settlers and the original inhabitants.

As Spanish explorers moved west in Mexico, they heard of a body of water that connected the Atlantic Ocean and the Pacific Ocean. This passage did not exist until construction of the Panama Canal in 1912. In an attempt to find this passage, Juan Rodriguez Cabrillo sailed from the west coast of Mexico (New Spain) in 1542. Cabrillo with two ships sailed north along the Pacific Coast. His party eventually reached current-day San Diego and went as far north as current-day San Francisco.

During the voyage, Cabrillo died of injuries suffered following a battle with Native Americans on what historians now believe was Santa Rosa Island. Historians say that Cabrillo and his party were the first Europeans to set foot on what they called California, leaving open the possibility that Asian explorers may have previously visited the area. Spanish explorers came to use the name Alta (upper) California to distinguish it from Baja (lower) California.

Cabrillo's expedition was unable to find the passage between the oceans and unable to find gold. Interest in Alta California waned. However, the search for the Atlantic–Pacific passage was still underway. In 1579, Sir Frances Drake reached California after successful raids on Spanish ships. He crossed the Pacific Ocean to complete his voyage around the world. However, his landing in California was of little significance to settlements there.

A galleon was a large ship with three or more masts and square sails used by Spain from the 1400s to the 1700s. Spanish galleons made the six-month trip each year from Manila to Acapulco to transport goods to Mexico. The Spanish government sought a port along the northern California coast for the galleons to stop during their journey. Even though the death rates during a galleon's voyage could reach 50 percent, command of these sailing ships was much sought after. In 1602, Viceroy Monterey of New Spain (Mexico) entrusted Sebastian Vizciano with the task of finding a suitable port. Vizciano sailed the California coast and assigned many of the place names we are familiar with today. On his return he reported that a bay he named Monterey was a suitable port.

Vizciano was awarded his galleon, but Viceroy Monterey was transferred to Peru. The next viceroy did not believe Vizciano's reports and correctly disputed the importance of a California port. He pointed out that when galleons were just a few days' sail from Mexico they sighted California. California had not yielded the expected gold or the passage between the oceans. These factors coupled with California's isolation by sea, mountains, and desert meant that little attention was paid to this area for over 150 years.

The Mission Period

It was not until 10 years before the American Revolutionary War that Spain took a new and different interest in Alta California. The king of Spain directed the military to take control of Alta California and convert the Indians to Catholicism. A primary reason for this was that Spain could not convince settlers to travel to the region and they planned to substitute the Native Americans for these absent colonists. As in past Spanish conquests, the plan was to combine the power of the military and the power of the church (sword and cross).

In 1769, the governor of New Spain sent three expeditions to San Diego and Monterey, one by sea and two by land. The expeditions were under the command of Gaspar de Portolá. Father Serna, a Catholic priest, led one of the expeditions. In 1769, he established the first mission when he erected a wooden cross in San Diego. Other missions were established in relatively short order at Monterey and San Francisco. The Spanish also built pueblos (towns) and presidios (forts) to accompany the missions.

Early missions were constructed of wood, but later these missions were constructed of adobe with tiles for roofs. Eventually the missions, pueblos, and presidios formed a chain near the coast of California along El Camino Real. Serna headed the missions until his death in 1784. Given below is a map of El Camino Real showing the 21 missions, 2 pueblos, and 4 presidios including the date they were established.

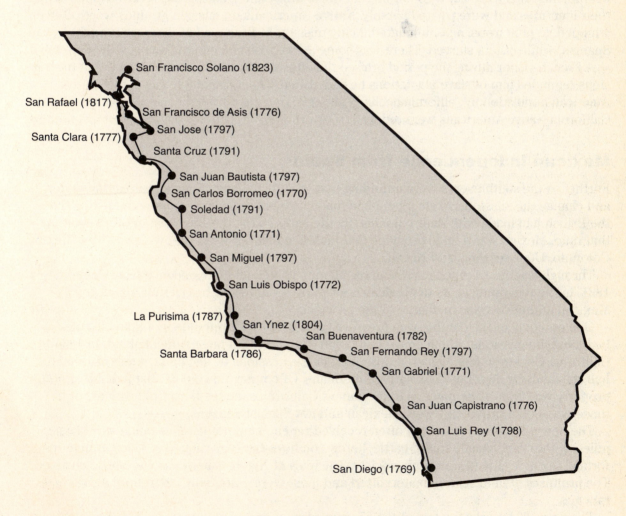

Spanish Missions on the Camino Real

By 1832, all the missions had been established. The American Revolutionary War was long over and the Civil War was a scant 30 years away. California was still a somewhat primitive Spanish colonial province.

The Mission System

It is important to note in all of this that we are talking about relatively few people. At the beginning of the mission period, the entire Native American population of California from San Francisco south was less than 75,000. On the missions themselves, at that time there were fewer than 1,500 Native Americans and fewer than 200 Spanish.

The mission system was based on the presumption that Native Americans needed help to become Roman Catholics. Some Native Americans came to the missions voluntarily, while others were offered trinkets or other rewards. Native Americans on the mission grounds were given food, shelter, and work along with religious and cultural "training." However, it was not the food or the culture to which they were accustomed. They were not allowed to leave the mission and those who did leave were often forcibly returned and punished.

There is no doubt that some Native Americans benefited from mission life. Historians point out that the mission system set the stage for much of what was to become California. But overall, missions were not a good thing for these first Californians. They were stripped of their identities and were treated harshly. Native Americans on mission grounds were often whipped, kept in irons, and humiliated. Many mission Indians died of diseases brought by the Spanish, while others starved. There was some active resistance but it was largely ineffective.

A French visitor during the period praised the efforts of Spanish priests but said that the missions reminded him of slave plantations he had visited. The indisputable fact is that Native American population in California declined about 75 percent during the mission period. The California Native Americans were reduced from a thriving if primitive culture to almost nothing.

Mexican Independence from Spain

Further to the south events were unfolding that would challenge Spanish rule in the region and change the mission system. Spain had made some of the same errors with Mexico that the British had made with their colonies. By the early 1800s, the stage was set for revolt. At that time, Mexico was a huge province that included most of what is now Texas, New Mexico, Colorado, Utah, Arizona, and Nevada.

Through a series of revolts and actions, Mexico gained its independence from Spain in 1821. In the remaining years of Mexican control over California, a governor appointed by Mexican authorities was in charge of the province.

One outcome of the conflict was pressure to do away with reminders of Spanish rule, including the missions, which controlled much of California's most valuable land. In 1834, California Governor José Figueroa ordered that the missions be secularized and ordered that half the lands be distributed to Native Americans. Of course, this did not happen. Most of the property was granted as ranchos to prominent Californios, native-born Californians, or to those who could prove they were Mexican and not Spanish citizens.

The new rancheros (ranchers) often received rancho land grants of as much as 75 square miles, where they usually raised cattle, herded on horseback by vaqueros. These rancheros formed the new elite of California society. The lives of Native Americans were little changed. The promises of land seldom materialized and most were essentially indentured servants on ranchos.

The date 1834 marks the end of the 65-year mission period, although in 1845 the remaining mission properties were sold to help close a budget deficit. Spain had ceased to be a colonial power in North America.

Wagon Trains

Shortly after Mexican independence, wagon trains set out from states such as Missouri for California. Most of these wagon trains had to cross the Sierra Nevada Mountains and the trip could take six months or more.

One of the most harrowing trips involved the Donner party, which left Independence, Missouri, in May 1886. The party was delayed en route and stranded by a terrible snowstorm near the summit of the mountains. The party was trapped for months, and despite escape attempts and rescue efforts, only about half of the party survived. The story of survival against terrible odds is punctuated by the survivors' cannibalism.

Bear Flag Revolt

Almost immediately after Mexican Independence, Texas declared its own independence from Mexico in 1836. Texas became a separate nation after a series of battles that included Goliad and the Alamo. Texas became a state in 1845. Texas independence, westward migration, and the sense of Manifest Destiny (a country bounded by both oceans) led the United States government to consider annexing California. In California, an edict was issued preventing non-Mexicans from owning land in California and threatening their expulsion.

In the midst of this was Captain John Fremont of the United States Army. Fremont was a surveyor and mapmaker who entered California late in 1845 with about 60 men. He was supposed to be there to map the California coast, but he traveled through California and created problems for the California government. When Fremont heard of the edict preventing settlers from owning land he decided to stay and "advise" the settlers.

Fremont's advice appears at least partially responsible for the Bear Flag Revolt on June 14, 1846. A small group of American settlers took control of a fort in Sonoma, California. They had a rather civil interchange with General Vallejo, the fort commander, before he surrendered. It seems he understood that Mexico did not have the resources to resist and wanted the United States to annex California. After his surrender, a crude flag was raised showing a poorly drawn bear and a star with the words "CALIFORNIA REPUBLIC."

The California government and the American settlers each sought to strengthen their forces in and around Sonoma. Fremont merged his forces with the American settlers. There was a brief conflict and approximately ten combatants were killed.

Mexican-American War

At this time, Commodore Stout, United States Navy commander in the Pacific, acting on orders, which likely came before the Bear Flag Revolt, sailed into Monterey Bay. Shortly after his arrival, he proclaimed California to be a possession of the United States. Within several days, the United States flag was flying over Monterey Bay and a few days later the United States flag replaced the Bear Flag in Sonoma. The Bear Flag Republic had lasted less than a month, but the symbolism of this time remains today in the California state flag.

Most of the Mexican-American War was fought outside of California. General Stephen Kearney and 300 troops marched from Fort Leavenworth, Kansas, to Santa Fe, New Mexico. Then with about 100 troops and the famous scout Kit Carson, Kearney moved on California. The Californios prevailed in a number of skirmishes, particularly at San Pasqual Valley, but the Californios were not strong enough to counter the United States. Mexico itself was battling the United States Army and could not come to the Californios' aid.

Eventually Andres Pico, the brother of the Mexican governor of California, surrendered the Californio forces to American forces at Cahuenga and signed the Capitulation of Cahuenga. The Capitulation effectively ended the Mexican-American War in California and made California part of the United States. Even though he had done none of the fighting, John Fremont signed the Capitulation for the United States.

The Mexican-American War continued, and on September 14, 1847, United States forces occupied Mexico City. Soon after, in 1848, the Treaty of Guadalupe Hidalgo ended the war. Mexico gave the United States all the lands Mexico claimed north of the current border and paid the United States $15,000,000. California was officially a part of the United States and the Manifest Destiny of the country had been fulfilled.

Gold Rush

As though the past 15 years had not presented much change, an event was about to occur that would forever transform California. It was mid-January in 1848, shortly after the decisive battle in the Mexican-American War. James Marshall reported it, but he may not have found it. He showed it to John Sutter who recognized it as high-quality gold. Gold was discovered on John Augustus Sutter's Mill, a fifty-thousand-acre compound Sutter had received as a land grant.

Word spread fast. In a short time everyone in the area from the coast of California to Mexico was searching for gold. Word spread across the United States and throughout the world by 1849, and the Gold Rush began. Of course, the vast majority who traveled to California in search of gold were worse off when they left than when they arrived.

Forty-niners, who journeyed to California in 1849, started a wave of immigration. Eventually all gold seekers during the Gold Rush were called forty-niners. Mining techniques changed quickly from panning and picks to hydraulic jets of water. Eventually, large companies conducted much of the gold mining in California.

The fastest way to California from the east was by boat and transfer by land over the Isthmus of Panama. Some immigrants traveled by boat around the tip of South America. Most easterners reached California by overland trail. By 1856, the California population, excluding Native Americans, increased from about 15,000 to about 300,000.

Before the Gold Rush, a small village called Yerba Buena stood on a hill where San Francisco is today. By 1856, San Francisco's population had increased almost 100 fold. Much of this immigration was to the eastern mountain area. Few miners found riches, became rich, and by 1856 or so many had left the state or blended in with the population. In fact, the merchants of the time usually fared better than the miners. It was during this period that Levi Strauss began his career selling "levis" to miners.

It seems that most groups were discriminated against during the Gold Rush era. The Californios lost their ranchos. Latinos, French, Asian, and Chinese miners were discriminated against. Laws, eventually declared unconstitutional, levied special taxes on these foreign miners.

The hardest hit minority group was the Native Americans. Many of the gold mines were in Native hunting lands and the stage was set for inevitable conflict. Historians agree that the Native American population was reduced by about 80 percent during this time, a staggering number. Many died from disease. However, the extermination of Native Americans was openly supported and it was funded with state and federal revenues. Some experts have put the Native American death toll from non-disease causes as high as 100,000. Native Americans were effectively eliminated as a meaningful presence in California.

Statehood

It was an unusual sight on September 3, 1849, when the 48 delegates met in Monterey to draw up California's first constitution. The delegates were primarily in their thirties. Eight delegates were original Californios, including Mariano Vallejo who had surrendered Sonoma at the beginning of the Bear Flag Revolt. Most of the Californios did not speak English.

Cooperation abounded and the delegates drew up a constitution that established one California with the state's current borders. The delegates deliberately chose to exclude the adjacent territory that Mexico had given to the United States at the end of the Mexican-American War.

The California Constitution also specifically permitted a woman to own property independent from their husband. This was the custom in Spanish-controlled California and California became the first state to give women land ownership rights. Voting rights were another matter. Women, Native Americans, Blacks, and Chinese were not granted the right to vote.

The delegates unanimously agreed that California should be a free state and not allow slaves. This created a problem when Congress was asked to approve statehood. The number of free states and slave states had been kept the same. It was only after an agreement to enact a tough fugitive slave law that California was admitted as a state when President Millard Fillmore signed the statehood resolution on September 9, 1850.

Early Transportation and Communication

California was a state, but it was isolated from the rest of the country. Travel was by wagon train or ship and it took over six months to send messages or ship goods from the east to California. In 1858, non-stop stagecoach service began between St. Louis and Los Angeles by a southern route. The 2,600-mile journey took about three weeks. In 1860, the Pony Express began carrying mail between Missouri and California. The 2,000-mile trip took about two weeks. The Pony Express ceased operation on October 21, 1861 when telegraph lines first carried messages across the nation by the dots and dashes of Morse code.

The Pony Express and the telegraph did not solve the problem of travel and the shipment of merchandise. The Civil War started just a few months before the telegraph began operations, making travel and commerce even more difficult. The solution for that time was the transcontinental railroad.

The Civil War and Aftermath

California was a Union state during the Civil War and the state, and about 17,000 California volunteers fought for the Union cause. This number included a Californio cavalry. The main duty of California troops was to control Native Americans. These troops also guarded overland mail and protected the west coast.

Immigration to California increased again after the Civil War. Again, there was conflict between the new immigrants and the Native Americans. Again, many Native Americans were killed or died from disease.

Historians often point to the Modoc War, the only Indian War in California, as an example of conflict between Native Americans and the government. The Modocs were placed on a reservation with their sworn enemies the Kalmath Indians. The Modocs left the reservation several times and went to their ancestral lands. By 1872, pressure was mounting to return them to the Kalmath reservation. On November 28, 1872 the Modoc War began when a group of Modoc resisted an action by government troops. A group of Modocs that escaped from the encounter killed 14 settlers near Tule Lake. A group of about 50 Modoc decisively won a subsequent engagement with a superior force of United States troops on the lava beds near Tule Lake. Forty soldiers were killed.

President Grant arranged for a peace committee, which met near the Modocs preferred reservation on the Lost River. Several government representatives including a general were killed at the peace meeting. Troops tracked down one group and members of that group helped the troops find those responsible for the peace meeting killings.

Some Modocs were hanged, while others were sent to Alcatraz after being pardoned by President Grant. The remaining Modocs were moved to a reservation in Oklahoma. In 1909, Modocs were allowed to return to the Kalmath Reservation. Some did, while others remained in Oklahoma. There are about 1,000 Modoc today, most on the Kalmath reservation with a few hundred in Oklahoma.

The Railroads

Theodore Judah developed the idea and the plan for the transcontinental railroad. Judah came to California to work on a single railroad only to develop an image of a rail line that stretched all across the country. Judah knew that the most difficult part of any transcontinental railroad would be crossing the Sierras. One of his first steps was to explore the mountains and find and map a suitable route.

Route and plan in hand, Judah set out to found a transcontinental railroad. However, he and his friends from Dutch Flat did not have enough money to form a corporation. His original appeals to bankers were rejected. Eventually he met with the four men who would finance his dream. Collis Huntington and Mark Hopkins owned the hardware store in Sacramento where the meeting took place. Leland Stanford was a merchant and unsuccessful California gubernatorial candidate. Charles Crocker was also a merchant.

All these men were well enough off, but they were not wealthy. All that would change in the years ahead as they emerged as the Big Four—the wealthiest men in California. Eventually they did provide modest additional investment to form the company that would earn $50 million for each of them. These profits made them the most powerful and perhaps the most hated men in California. As frequently happens in these situations, the investors were in charge, not the founder. Leland Stanford was chosen as the president.

Judah became a part of the committee structure in the United States Congress. From this position he helped draw up legislation that was favorable to the private company he partially owned. His efforts were primarily responsible for the Pacific Railroad Act of 1862/1864. The act essentially gave the Central Pacific the right to build the railroad from Sacramento, California, to Omaha, Nebraska. The Union Pacific would build the railroad from the east to Omaha. Both railway companies received huge land grants along the right of way and a payment for each mile of track that was laid.

Work began and there were immediate conflicts between the Big Four and Judah. They wanted to build the railroad to make money. Judah was more interested in quality than they were. However, in 1863 Judah had an agreement from the Big Four to buy their shares and he traveled east via the Isthmus of Panama to find backers. He contracted yellow fever and died at age 37.

There were problems after Judah's death and without some inflated mileage payments from the federal government the whole railroad project might have been abandoned. In the first two years, less than a half mile of track was laid each week.

Some of the most difficult construction was in the Sierra Nevada Mountains, where it might take a month to tunnel thirty feet. From 1863 until the railroad's completion in 1869, Chinese workers provided most of the labor. These workers were poorly paid, segregated, and discriminated against. But finally, California was connected to the rest of the country. Other rail lines were built to southern California by 1880. By 1890, trains were traveling from Omaha to San Francisco in just three days.

The immediate impact on California was not good. Completion of railroad work returned more workers to the California work force. Goods from the east competed with California goods. California entered a brief recession. However, the railroads provided a way to transport agricultural goods including wheat and oranges from California to the east. Migrant labor harvested the crops now as then. The railroads owned about 10 percent of the land in California and there were battles over land.

Into the Twentieth Century

Agriculture, oil, citrus, and the movie industry led California into the 1900s. The motion picture began around 1908 and grew into one of California's largest industries. In the 1920s, huge oil deposits were discovered in southern California that dwarfed the discoveries of the late 1800s. The growth in the number of automobiles was more than twice the population growth. The Panama Canal opened in 1914, making it much easier to ship goods to southern California.

Against the wishes of farmers and conservationists, dams and aqueducts were built to provide water for San Francisco and Los Angeles. Battles over water, including sabotage of the aqueduct system, continued through the first third of the century. A series of dams and canals were eventually built in the central valley that helped family farmers get water to irrigate their lands.

Railroads and other large companies had a stranglehold on California government. Graft, favoritism, and kickbacks were the rule rather than the exception. A progressive political movement emerged to counter these forces. By the early 1900s, railroads and business had been brought under reasonable control.

The San Francisco Earthquake and Fires

The date and time are precisely known. The first foreshock came on April 18, 1906 at 5:12 AM. The more powerful earthquake came less than a minute later. By 5:14 AM it was all over. One of the strongest earthquakes in the history of the world had shaken San Francisco and the surrounding region.

The land along the San Andreas fault had cracked for a distance of about 290 miles and had slipped up to 20 feet, an enormous distance. The magnitude was about 7.9 or 8.0 on the Richter scale. That would make the San Francisco earthquake about 15 to 20 times more powerful than the shorter, magnitude 7.0 Loma Prieta earthquake of 1989. Some seismologists think the next significant earthquake will be about as strong as the Loma Prieta quake but last about as long as the San Francisco earthquake.

San Francisco residents stood by helplessly as a fire started immediately after the earthquake and burned for four days. Troops used dynamite in unsuccessful attempts to stop the fire, officers and crew of the USS Chicago evacuated 20,000 inhabitants by sea. Some historians say this was among the largest seaborne evacuations in world history. About 30,000 buildings in four square miles were destroyed. Recent estimates indicate that 3,000 died because of the earthquake and fire. The successful rebuilding of San Francisco was marked by graft and bribes that led to many legal actions.

The Great Depression

The Great Depression of the 1930s hit California as hard as any part of the country. However, things were made worse by the huge immigration from the Dust Bowl, a huge area that had become impossible to farm in eastern Colorado, western Kansas, northern Texas, and smaller parts of New Mexico and Oklahoma. John Steinbeck's *The Grapes of Wrath* chronicles the lives of these migrants.

Many others came to California in search of work, only to find there was very little or none. Many worked in the fields or entered city ghettos. Many cite the 1932 Los Angeles

Olympics, construction of the Hoover Dam in nearby Nevada from 1932 to 1935, and the building of the Golden Gate Bridge from 1933 to 1937 as when California emerged from the Depression.

World War II

The Japanese attack on Pearl Harbor on December 7, 1941, led to a stark contrast in California. The war that followed created many defense-related jobs in California, as many as 700,000. There were jobs for Blacks, those of Mexican descent, and women. Things were different for those of Japanese descent.

The Issei were Japanese Americans born in Japan. The Nisei were the second generation of Japanese Americans and were born in the United States. The Kibei were Nisei who went to Japan for their education and returned to the United States. The Sansei were fourth-generation Japanese Americans who were very young at the start of the war. United States officials were concerned about the security risk posed by the Kibei.

However, all 120,000 Japanese in the military zones along the west coast of the United States were moved to ten internment camps. By August 1942, the move was complete and the internees were kept there until 1946. The internment was authorized by Executive Order 9066 signed by President Franklin Roosevelt on February 19, 1942. The camps were located in eastern California and in other states west of the Mississippi River. Camp Manzanar in Owens Valley is often discussed. A portion of this internment camp is preserved today as a National Park Service historic site.

Not a single Japanese American was convicted of espionage against the United States. Historians indicate that Japanese American soldiers, particularly the 442nd Regimental Combat Team, were among the most decorated units during World War II.

After the war, California entered an age of flight, space, and technology. Silicon Valley became a synonym for technological advancement. Agriculture and tourism flourished and the freeway mileage increased more than a thousand fold. New waves of immigrants crossed the Pacific from Asia and crossed the Mexico–United States border from the south.

Predictable Diversity

It was predictable. California has a striking and singular ethnic diversity unlike any other state. The successive waves of Asian and Latino immigration and the systematic eradication of the Native American population has produced the culture we find in California today. The recent census and other population studies indicate that the current ethnic makeup of California's population is approximately as shown below.

Asian	11%
Black (African)	7%
Caucasian	47%
Hispanic or Latino	33.5%
Native American	1%
Pacific Islander	0.5%

The percent of Asians and Hispanics is strikingly higher than in the rest of the United States, while the percent of Caucasians is strikingly lower. In a recent year, California's population increased about 50 percent faster than the population of the other states, and the growth rate will likely remain higher through the middle of this century.

The predictable diversity with its accompanying strengths and problems will only increase. Dealing with that diversity may be California's most significant challenge.

UNITED STATES HISTORY

UNITED STATES HISTORY REVIEW QUIZ

This quiz uses a short answer format to help you find out what you know. The quiz results direct you to the portions of the chapter you should read.

This quiz will also help focus your thinking, and these questions and answers are a good review in themselves. It's not important to answer all these questions correctly, and don't be concerned if you miss many of them.

The answers are found immediately after the quiz. It's to your advantage not to look at them until you have completed the quiz. Once you have completed and corrected the review quiz, use the answer checklist to decide which sections of the review to study.

Write the answers in the space provided or on a separate sheet of paper.

---

1. Which Indian group established a culture off southern Alaska about 7,000 years ago?

2. In what structure did plains Indians live?

3. Name a nonindigenous group that established North American settlements before Columbus.

4. In what year did Columbus reach the mainland of North America?

5. Where were African slaves first brought to America?

6. What did Spanish explorers bring that caused great devastation to Native Americans?

7. Which nation established the first settlement in Manhattan?

8. How many English colonies were there in the 1740s?

9. Which things frequently used by colonists were taxed by the original Townsend Acts?

10. What was the Boston Tea Party and why was it held?

11. Which riders spread the word about the English march on Concord?

12. Name two of the self-evident truths found in the Declaration of Independence.

    _____
    _____
    _____

13. Where did the Colonial army winter in 1777?

    _____
    _____

14. Which two main forces trapped Cornwallis at Yorktown, Virginia?

    _____
    _____

15. What was the first governing document for the United States?

    _____
    _____

16. Describe the effect of three of the first ten amendments to the Constitution.

    _____
    _____
    _____
    _____
    _____

17. Briefly describe the theory of nullification.

    _____
    _____
    _____
    _____

18. What tract of land did Jefferson purchase from France?

    _____
    _____

19. What action started the War of 1812?

    _____
    _____

20. What famous national song was written during the War of 1812?

    _____
    _____

21. What impact did the Missouri Compromise have on the state of Missouri?

    _____
    _____
    _____

22. What governmental group did Jackson ignore when he moved Native Americans onto reservations?

    _____
    _____

23. What was the status of Texas after it gained independence from Mexico?

    _____
    _____

24. What did the Underground Railroad transport?

    _____
    _____

25. What states seceded from the Union before hostilities began?

    _____
    _____
    _____

26. What action began the Civil War?

    _____
    _____

27. What was the effect of the Emancipation Proclamation?

    _____
    _____
    _____

28. What type of government did Lincoln call for in his Gettysburg Address?

    _____
    _____

29. Describe one of the three civil rights amendments adopted from 1865 and 1870.

    _____
    _____
    _____

30. Until what year were Northern troops in the South following the Civil War?

    _____
    _____

31. Who was the only president to be elected and re-elected during this period?

    _____
    _____

32. What was the goal of the Dawes Severalty Act?

_____

_____

33. What inventions drew women to the workplace?

_____

_____

34. Name a territory the United States gained in the treaty ending the Spanish American War.

_____

_____

35. Teddy Roosevelt was awarded the Nobel Prize for helping to end what war?

_____

_____

ANSWER CHECKLIST

The answers are organized by review sections. Check your answers. If you miss any question in a section, check the box and review that section.

United States History

Native American Civilizations
❑ *Primitive Cultures, page 129*
  1. Aleuts

❑ *Recent Cultures, page 129*
  2. tepees

European Exploration and Colonization
❑ *Visitors Before Columbus, page 130*
  3. Celtic/Norse (Vikings)

❑ *Columbus, page 130*
  4. never

❑ *English Colonization, page 130*
  5. Jamestown in 1619

❑ *Spanish Exploration, page 130*
  6. disease

❑ *Other Explorers, page 131*
  7. Holland (Dutch)

❑ *Colonies in the 1700s, page 131*
  8. thirteen

The American Revolution and the Founding of America
❑ *Road to the Revolutionary War, page 131*
  9. just about everything
  10. Tea was dumped in Boston harbor to protest the British tax on tea.

❑ *War's Beginnings, page 132*
  11. Revere and Dawes
  12. (1) equality of all persons; (2) inalienable rights of life, liberty, and the pursuit of happiness; (3) rights of government come from the governed; (4) the right of the people to alter or abolish a destructive government
❑ *Revolutionary War, page 133*
  13. Morristown, N.J.
  14. American army and the French fleet

Growth of the New Republic
❑ *The New Nation, page 134*
  15. Articles of Confederation

❑ *First Constitutional Government, page 134*
  16. I. Freedom of religion, speech, press, assembly, and petition
  II. Right to bear arms
  III No troops can be quartered in homes without permission
  IV. Warrants and probable cause needed for search and seizure
  V. Rights of the accused are assured
  VI. Right to a speedy public trial and the right to a lawyer
  VII. Right to a jury trial
  VIII. Excessive bail, excessive fines, and cruel and unusual punishment are forbidden
  IX. Rights not spelled out are retained by the people
  X. Powers not specifically federal are retained by the states.

❑ *Adams to Madison, page 135*
  17. States can nullify federal laws in that state.
  18. Louisiana Purchase

❑ *War of 1812, page 135*
  19. American invasion of Canada
  20. "The Star Spangled Banner"

❑ *Movements and Accomplishments 1800–1850, page 137*
  24. It moved slaves from the South to the North.

Civil War and Reconstruction: Causes and Consequences

❑ *Road to Civil War, page 137*
  25. South Carolina, Alabama, Georgia, Florida, Louisiana, Mississippi, and Texas seceded before hostilities began. Other states seceded once hostilities had begun.

❑ *Civil War, page 138*
  26. Confederate attack on Fort Sumter, S.C.
  27. It freed slaves in Confederate states.
  28. "A government of the people, by the people, for the people"

❑ *Reconstruction, page 139*
  29. XIII. Prohibits slavery
     XIV. Former slaves given citizenship
     XV. Voting rights for former slaves
  30. 1877

Industrialization of America

❑ *1877–1897, page 139*
  31. McKinley
  32. to move Indians from reservations into society
  33. sewing machine, typewriter

❑ *Spanish-American War, page 141*
  34. Puerto Rico, Guam, and the Philippines

❑ *1900–1916, page 141*
  35. Russo-Japanese War

UNITED STATES HISTORY REVIEW

NATIVE AMERICAN CIVILIZATIONS

Immigration

Current scholarship indicates that Native Americans, "Indians," came to this continent about 30,000 years ago. They passed over a land bridge near what is now the Bering Strait between Siberia and Alaska. These Native Americans eventually spread throughout all of North, Central, and South America. Christopher Columbus was likely the person who first used the name Indian because he believed he had arrived at the Indies in Asia.

Scholars estimate that when Europeans arrived there were between 70 million to 90 million Native Americans throughout North and South America. About 40 percent of this number lived in South America, most in the Andes. About 30 percent lived in Mexico, with another 10 percent in Central America and less than a million on the Caribbean Islands. That means that less than 10 percent of Native Americans lived in what is now the United States and Canada.

Primitive Cultures

Some of the earliest civilizations developed in and around California about 10,000 years ago and lasted largely unchanged until hundreds of years after European immigration. These Native Americans lived in thatched huts or wooden houses and used boats to fish. They had a sophisticated culture and a monetary system based on shell money. Tribes in and near California included the Paiute, Pomo, Shoshone, Ute, and Yurok.

Even with a glacier covering Alaska, the Aleuts had established a culture on the Aleutian islands off southern Alaska by 5000 B.C.E. (B.C.) This hunting/fishing society has retained much of its ancient character.

Primitive northern woodland cultures developed in the northeastern United States about 3000 B.C.E. (B.C.) These cultures included the Algonquin-speaking tribes, such as the Shawnee, and the Iroquois Federation. There is evidence that Native Americans in the northern woodlands may have been exposed to outside contact five hundred years before the arrival of Europeans after Columbus.

Also at about 3000 B.C.E. (B.C.), civilizations developed in southeast North America, in and around what is now Florida and Georgia. These sophisticated cultures built cities with central plazas. The tribes of this area included the Cherokee, Choctaw, and Seminole. These tribes had highly organized governments and economic systems.

Once glaciers melted in the area, the Eskimo and Inuit Indians established a culture in northern Alaska about 1800 B.C.E. (B.C.) Their use of igloos, kayaks, and dogsleds in harsh conditions was a remarkable adaptation to their environment.

Recent Cultures

In the Southwest United States the Anasazi (Pueblo) culture developed by about 500 C.E. (A.D.) Pueblo and Hopi Indians built walled towns, some on the sides of inaccessible mountains or on mesas.

Around 600 C.E. (A.D.) a mound-building culture developed from the Mississippi River into Ohio. This culture probably built a town called Cahokia with a population of over 30,000 on the east side of the Mississippi River near St. Louis. Cahokia had hundreds of mounds.

Starting about 750 C.E. (A.D.), a nomadic culture was established on the great plains of the United States. These Native American nomads lived in tepees as they followed and hunted herds of bison. These are probably the most popularized of Native Americans. Original tribes of this area include the Blackfoot.

Around 1400 C.E. (A.D.), Native Americans who became the Navajos and the Apaches migrated from Canada to the southwestern United States.

The Nez Pierce Spokane, Okanagon, and Walla Walla tribes inhabited the northwestern United States. Each had advanced agricultural and cultural traditions.

By 1500 C.E. (A.D.), advanced Native American cultures existed across North America. However, these cultures did not rival the Aztec, Inca, and Mayan cultures of Central and South America, which are discussed on pages 156–157. They were nonetheless sophisticated, organized cultures that lacked only the technological developments of Europe and Asia.

EUROPEAN EXPLORATION AND COLONIZATION

Visitors Before Columbus

A number of groups visited what is now the United States before Columbus sailed. Whether by accident or design, sailors from Iceland, Europe, and Africa came to this continent before 1000 C.E. (A.D.) It appears that Celtic and Norse settlements were established in North America between 1000 and 1300 C.E. (A.D.) These settlements were not maintained.

Columbus

Notoriety greeted Columbus as he returned to Spain from the first of his four voyages. Columbus never reached the mainland of North America, but he landed throughout the Caribbean and established a settlement in what is now the Dominican Republic.

English Colonization

John Cabot reached the North American mainland in 1497 and claimed the land for England. In 1584 Sir Walter Raleigh established the "lost colony" on Roanoke Island just off the North Carolina coast. The settlement failed when all the settlers disappeared, leaving the word CROATOAN carved in a tree.

In 1607 the English established Jamestown, Virginia, under John Smith. Tobacco exports sustained the colony, and slaves from Africa were brought to Jamestown in 1619. One third of African slaves died on ships during their journey. In that same year, the House of Burgesses was formed in Virginia as the first elected governing body in America.

In 1620 Pilgrims left England on the Mayflower to escape religious persecution. The Pilgrims established a colony at Provincetown and then a second colony at Plymouth in December 1620. The Pilgrims drafted and received popular approval for the Mayflower Compact as a way of governing their colony.

Spanish Exploration

Cortez conquered Mexico about 1520, and Pizarro conquered Peru about 1530. The Spaniards imported slaves from Africa at this time. Records of the native civilizations were destroyed, and natives were forced to convert to Catholicism. The Spanish also imported diseases, which effectively wiped out whole populations of natives. In North America the Spanish established a fort in St. Augustine, Florida, about 1565 and in Santa Fe, New Mexico, about 1610.

Other Explorers

In the 1500s the French through Jacques Cartier explored the Great Lakes. The French city of Quebec was founded about 1609.

Henry Hudson, under Dutch contract, explored the East Coast and the Hudson River in the 1600s. The Dutch established settlements under Peter Minuit in Manhattan about 1624. The Dutch built the first road for wheeled vehicles in America about 1650.

Disease was the most devastating impact of European colonization. Native Americans did not have a natural immunity to measles, smallpox, typhoid, and influenza. These diseases decimated the Native American population. By the early 1700s, there were more Europeans than Native Americans living in the Americas.

Colonies in the 1700s

By 1740 there were 13 English colonies, all located along the eastern seaboard. These colonies grew in size and prosperity and developed diversified populations by the time of the Revolutionary War. The colonists were in an almost constant state of conflict with Native Americans, with Spanish colonists, and with the French in the French and Indian wars. In 1739 an early slave revolt took place in Stono, South Carolina.

THE AMERICAN REVOLUTION AND THE FOUNDING OF AMERICA

ROAD TO THE REVOLUTIONARY WAR

This chronology details the causes up to the Revolutionary War. Note how cumulative the causes are and how a change in English policy might have averted the conflict.

Proclamation of 1763

After the British won the French and Indian War they signed the Proclamation of 1763, which forbade English colonial expansion west of the Appalachian Mountains. The proclamation was designed to avoid conflicts with Indians and to make it easier to tax the colonists. It angered many colonists.

1764 Sugar Act

The English government was in serious financial debt after the French and Indian War. The English government levied a sugar tax on the colonies to help pay for the war. Colonists protested this tax saying it was "taxation without representation."

1765

In 1765 Britain passed a law called the Quartering Act. The act required colonial governments to pay for supplies for British troops and to quarter these troops in barracks and inns and taverns.

The Stamp Act required legal papers, college degrees, policies, newspapers, and playing cards to carry a tax stamp. The act was protested vehemently and eventually repealed by Britain.

These acts led to many colonial reactions. Patrick Henry spoke against the acts in the Virginia House of Burgesses. Revolutionary groups called Sons of Liberty were formed.

1767 Townshend Acts

The Townshend Acts were named for Charles Townshend, British Chancellor of the Exchequer. Import duties (taxes) were on most things used by colonists. Colonists objected, and some tax officials in Boston were attacked. British troops were sent to Boston. Three years later, the British repealed all the Townshend duties except for the duties on tea!

1770 Boston Massacre

British troops fired on colonial protesters, killing five including Crispus Attucks, an escaped slave, in the Boston Massacre. The British soldiers were defended in court by patriots including John Adams, leading to the acquittal of most of the soldiers by a Boston jury. Other tensions continued for the next three years.

1773 Boston Tea Party

To protest the remaining import tax on tea, men dressed as Indians boarded English ships in Boston Harbor. They dumped hundreds of chests of tea into Boston Harbor in what has come to be known as the Boston Tea Party. In retaliation Britain closed Boston Harbor and took more direct control of the colony.

1774 First Continental Congress

In September, representatives from each colony except Georgia met at the First Continental Congress in Philadelphia. The congress called on the colonies to boycott goods from England until the English repealed the tax on tea and opened Boston Harbor. Massachusetts minutemen armed themselves and were declared in rebellion by Parliament.

WAR'S BEGINNINGS
1775

On April 18, 1775, British General Gage left Boston to commandeer arms at Concord. Paul Revere and William Dawes rode out to alert the minutemen. The British troops first encountered minutemen in Lexington. The first shot was fired, but no one knows by whom. There were American and English dead. British troops destroyed supplies at Concord but were decimated by minuteman attacks on the march back to Boston. Hostilities had begun.

The Second Continental Congress named George Washington commander-in-chief. The Congress asked Britain for discussions about American independence, but was rebuked. George Washington, a slave owner, encouraged blacks who were not slaves to join the Continental Army. The British promised freedom to slaves who joined the British Army.

Gage attacked colonists on the top of Breeds Hill (the colonists went to occupy Bunker Hill, but they occupied nearby Breeds Hill instead). The British won the battle but at a tremendous cost, establishing the fighting ability of colonial forces.

1776

In this year Thomas Paine wrote his pamphlet *Common Sense*, which favored American independence. On July 4, 1776, the Continental Congress approved the Declaration of Independence authored by Thomas Jefferson.

The Declaration included four self-evident truths:

1. Equality of all persons.
2. Inalienable rights of life, liberty, and the pursuit of happiness.
3. Rights of the government come from the governed.
4. The right of the people to alter or abolish a destructive government.

REVOLUTIONARY WAR

1775

The battles of "Bunker Hill" and Concord and Lexington took place in 1775. Fighting also broke out in Virginia.

1776

In March, Washington laid siege to Boston. The British sent forces to New York. Washington failed in his attempt to drive the British out of New York and withdrew across New Jersey to Pennsylvania. Washington led a successful surprise attack against Hessian mercenaries fighting for the British in Trenton, New Jersey, in December 1776.

1777

In January 1777, Washington followed up his Trenton victory with a successful attack at Princeton, New Jersey. Washington spent the remainder of the winter in camp at Morristown, New Jersey. The British, under Howe, attacked and occupied the American capital at Philadelphia. The fighting delayed Howe's planned move to Saratoga, New York. This action enabled American militia under Horatio Gates to defeat British troops invading from Canada at Saratoga.

The American victory at Saratoga moved the French to openly recognize America. The French joined the war as allies in 1778. This action by France was the decisive moment in the Revolutionary War. Washington's forces spent the winter in Valley Forge, Pennsylvania.

1778

American forces suffered through a harsh winter in Valley Forge, while British forces were much better accommodated in New York and Philadelphia. The forces from Philadelphia marched to New York under the new British general, Clinton. The British forces narrowly avoided defeat at the Battle of Monmouth in June. Late that year, British forces conquered Georgia.

1779

Fighting took place primarily around the British main headquarters in New York. Late in the year Clinton took the British army south.

1780

When Clinton captured Charleston, South Carolina, Cornwallis took over the southern army, while Clinton returned to New York. Cornwallis defeated American forces under Gates. Things were looking bleak for American forces, and American General Benedict Arnold became a traitor.

Then American forces under George Rogers Clark won a battle in the northwest while frontiersmen defeated Cornwallis in North Carolina.

1781

Cornwallis was beset by American guerrillas including Francis Marion, the Swamp Fox. Cornwallis moved into Virginia and maneuvered himself into a trap at Yorktown. Surrounded by American forces on the land and the French fleet in Chesapeake Bay, Cornwallis surrendered on October 17, 1781.

1782–1783

Great Britain decided to withdraw from the colonies. In 1783 Britain and the United States signed the Treaty of Paris, which gave the United States lands east of the Mississippi.

GROWTH OF THE NEW REPUBLIC

The New Nation

In 1781 the Articles of Confederation, drawn up in 1777, were approved by Congress as the "first constitution" of the United States. The Land Ordinance of 1785 established surveys of the Northwest Territories. (These territories became states such as Ohio and Illinois.) The Northwest Ordinance detailed the way in which states would be carved out of these territories.

The Articles of Confederation proved too weak and a Constitutional Convention convened during 1787 in Philadelphia. A compromise Constitution was written with special efforts by James Madison. The Constitution was sent to Congress, which approved it and in turn submitted it to the states for ratification. The Constitution supported slaveholders.

The state ratification process fostered a brisk debate. Alexander Hamilton, John Jay, and James Madison authored *The Federalist Papers* to support ratification. Anti-Federalists were concerned that the Constitution did not sufficiently protect individual rights.

Delaware was the first state to ratify the Constitution in 1787 and Rhode Island was the last to ratify in 1790. Many of the ratification votes were very close. Strict versus loose construction of the Constitution has been a contentious issue since its ratification.

First Constitutional Government

New York City was chosen as the temporary capital. Once the required nine states had ratified the Constitution, George Washington was sworn in as the first president on April 30, 1789. John Adams was sworn in as vice president.

The concern of the Anti-Federalists was partially answered in 1791 when the first ten amendments to the Constitution were ratified. A summary of the Bill of Rights follows.

I. Freedom of religion, speech, press, assembly, and petition
II. Right to bear arms
III. No troops can be quartered in homes without permission
IV. Warrants and probable cause needed for search and seizure
V. Rights of the accused are assured
VI. Right to a speedy public trial and the right to a lawyer
VII. Right to a jury trial
VIII. Excessive bail, excessive fines, and cruel and unusual punishment are forbidden
IX. Rights not spelled out are retained by the people
X. Powers not specifically federal are retained by the states.

In 1793, Congress passed a weak fugitive slave act, which made it illegal to hide "escaped slaves." In the same year, Eli Whitney invented the cotton gin, which led to a dramatic increase in the need for slaves.

The issue of a stronger versus a weaker central government was an active debate then as it is now. Washington was elected without opposition for his second term. The differences between Jeffersonians (less government, Democrat-Republicans) and Hamiltonians (more government, Federalists) led to a two party system.

In 1796 Washington bade farewell as president with three gems of advice for the country:

1. Avoid political parties based on geographic boundaries.
2. Avoid permanent alliances with foreign powers.
3. Safeguard the ability of America to pay its national debts.

Adams to Madison

In the 1796 presidential election, John Adams eked out a victory over Thomas Jefferson. In the controversial XYZ affair, France sought bribes from America. Concern about France led to the Alien and Sedition Acts. These acts put pressure on noncitizens and forbade writing that criticized the government.

Some western states opposed these acts and wanted to nullify the Federal Acts in their state. This Theory of Nullification, and the states' rights mentioned in the tenth amendment to the Constitution, raised issues still important today.

In 1800 Aaron Burr and Jefferson were tied for the presidency in the Electoral College. Alexander Hamilton supported Jefferson. Jefferson won the vote in the House of Representatives and went on to serve a second term. Four years later, Burr killed Hamilton in a duel. Also in 1800 over 1,000 armed slaves revolted in Virginia leading to the execution of their leader Gabriel Prosser along with a number of his followers. Some twenty years later, a planned rebellion of many thousands of slaves in South Carolina was thwarted leading to the execution of the leader Denmark Vesey and many of his followers.

Jefferson resisted the demands of Barbary pirates for tribute. The four North African Barbary States of Algiers, Morocco, Tripoli, and Tunis had raided shipping for hundreds of years. In 1801 Tripoli declared war on the United States, and Jefferson successfully blockaded the coast of Tripoli. Tribute continued to be paid to other Barbary states.

Jefferson also arranged the purchase of the Louisiana Territory from France, doubling the size of the country. In 1804 Jefferson sent Lewis and Clark to explore the territory and open it for settlement.

Madison was elected president in 1808 and again in 1812. For a number of years, British ships had been impressing American sailors at sea, forcing them to serve on British ships. In response to this practice, the war hawks pressed for war with Britain in 1811.

War of 1812

The War of 1812 began with a failed American invasion of Canada. The U.S.S. *Constitution* (Old Ironsides) and "We have met the enemy and they are ours." Admiral Perry were active in this conflict. The British sacked and burned Washington and unsuccessfully attacked Fort McHenry in Baltimore, Maryland. Francis Scott Key wrote "The Star Spangled Banner" while a prisoner on a British ship off Fort McHenry. After the war had been declared officially over, communication was so slow that Andrew Jackson fought and defeated the British at the Battle of New Orleans.

Federalists had opposed the war and ceased to exist as a viable political party. In the wake of the Federalist collapse, Monroe was elected president in 1816 and again in 1820. In treaties with Spain and England, under the leadership of John Quincy Adams, the United States established borders with Canada, acquired Florida from Spain, and gave up any claims to Texas.

Missouri Compromise

The Missouri Compromise of 1820 was a response to rapid westward expansion and the slavery issue. It admitted Maine as a free state and Missouri as a slave state and excluded slavery in the northern part of the Louisiana Purchase. The compromise maintained the balance of free and slave states.

Monroe

James Monroe and John Quincy Adams established the Monroe Doctrine in 1823. The doctrine said: (1) the Americas were off limits for further, colonization, (2) the political system in the United States was different from Europe, (3) the United States would see danger if European states meddled in the Western Hemisphere, and (4) the United States would not interfere in the internal affairs of other states or their established colonies.

Jackson

In 1824 Andrew Jackson entered the electoral college with more electoral votes than any other candidate, but not a majority. He still lost in the House of Representatives to J.Q. Adams.

In 1828 Jackson was elected president. In this year, people voted directly for electors in all but 2 of 24 states. Jackson used a "kitchen cabinet" of friends to advise him on important issues. Jackson favored the removal of Native Americans to reservations and ignored Supreme Court decisions in favor of the Native Americans. This "trail of tears" is an uncomfortable American story. The age of Jackson marks a time of increased democracy in the United States.

Van Buren

Martin Van Buren was elected president in 1836. On the heels of the financial panic of 1837, Van Buren lost the presidency to William Henry Harrison in 1840. Harrison died less than a month after his inauguration. John Tyler, the vice president, succeeded to the presidency.

Manifest Destiny

The Manifest Destiny of the United States as a country that stretched from the Atlantic Ocean to the Pacific Ocean explained the expansion of the United States into Texas, Oregon, and California. Manifest Destiny was a prominent focus of American political thought during this period.

Primarily during the 1840s, settlers traveled six months and 2,000 miles along the Oregon Trail to reach Oregon. The phrase "54°40' or Fight!" described the latitude of the northern Oregon boundary preferred by many Americans. This saying served as Polk's campaign slogan in his successful campaign to become president in 1844. The actual border was established further south at 49 degrees.

Texan independence from Mexico occurred in a single year. The battle for Texan independence began in March 1836 with a loss at the Alamo that included the death of defenders James Bowie, David Crockett, and William Travis. At almost the same time, 350 Texan prisoners were executed at Goliad under orders from Mexican President Antonio López de Santa Ana. A little over a month later, Texan forces won a decisive battle at the battle of San Jacinto and Santa Ana was captured. About six months later, Samuel Houston became president of the Republic of Texas, a sovereign country. After years of debate and infighting, Polk was able to obtain congressional approval and Texas was admitted as a slave state in 1844.

Mexico objected to Texas statehood, and the Mexican-American War started in 1846. U.S. generals, including Robert E. Lee, led troops into Mexico and captured Mexico City. The Treaty of Guadeloupe Hidalgo ended the war, and the United States acquired Texas north of the Rio Grande as well as the California and New Mexico Territories. Much of the Manifest Destiny of the United States to stretch from sea to sea had been achieved under Polk.

Taylor

Zachary Taylor, a general in the Mexican-American War, was elected president in 1848. Slavery remained a significant and contentious issue. In 1849 gold was discovered near Sutters Mill in California. The gold rush brought thousands of prospectors and settlers to California.

The Compromise of 1850 specified whether territories would be granted statehood as a free or slave state and contained a strict fugitive slave law. *Uncle Tom's Cabin* by Harriet Beecher Stowe was published in 1852.

Movements and Accomplishments 1800–1850

In 1839, African slaves aboard the ship *Amistad* revolted, killing several members of the crew. The ship was intercepted off Long Island and the Africans were charged with murder. The Africans were acquitted but remained confined, only to be freed after a Supreme Court decision two years later. The current president Martin Van Buren favored deporting the Africans, while past president John Quincy Adams represented the Africans before the Supreme Court.

Estimates are that over 75,000 slaves escaped from southern states to northern states on the Underground Railroad. The Underground Railroad was a series of paths with stops and way stations by land and sea that led north, aided by "conductors" along the way. These paths led slaves to a sort of semi-freedom in the North.

Many in the South reacted against the success of these escape routes. In 1842, the United States Supreme Court ruled that states were not required to help capture escaped slaves. In 1850, Congress changed the Fugitive Slave Bill to give slave owners the right to forcibly pursue and capture slaves throughout the country and requiring state and local officials and citizens to assist them under threat of fines or imprisonment.

Horace Mann and others established public schools and training schools for teachers. The women's movement, featuring an 1848 meeting in Seneca Falls, New York, did not achieve much success. The temperance movement reduced the consumption of alcohol. Transcendentalist writers, who believed in the sanctity and importance of individual experience, were active during this period. These writers included James Fenimore Cooper, Ralph Waldo Emerson, Henry David Thoreau, and Herman Melville.

Large groups of non-English, Catholic immigrants arrived in New York. In the 1840s there was regular steamship travel between Liverpool, England, and New York City.

THE CIVIL WAR AND RECONSTRUCTION: CAUSES AND CONSEQUENCES

The Road to Civil War

Pierce

Franklin Pierce was elected president in 1852. There was bloody warfare in Kansas over whether Kansas should enter the union as a free or slave state. Kansas gained its statehood in 1861 as a free state. Another significant event was Commodore Perry's visit to Japan, opening Japan to the West.

Buchanan

James Buchanan was elected president in 1856. In 1857 the Supreme Court decided the *Dred Scott* case. They found that Dred Scott, a slave, was property, not a citizen, and had no standing in the court.

John Brown

In 1859 an erratic John Brown launched an ill-prepared raid on the arsenal in Harpers Ferry, Virginia. Brown was tried, executed, and became a martyr in the abolitionist movement.

Lincoln

In 1860, and again in 1864, Abraham Lincoln was elected president. Southern states sought assurances about their right to hold slaves. Slaves were too important to the southern economy, and attempts at compromise failed. South Carolina seceded in December 1860. Alabama, Georgia, Florida, Louisiana, Mississippi, and Texas soon followed. In February 1861 the Confederate States of America (CSA) was formed with Jefferson Davis as its president.

The Civil War

On April 12, 1861, Confederate forces attacked Fort Sumter in South Carolina. Arkansas, North Carolina, Tennessee, and Virginia seceded once hostilities began.

The war pitted brother against brother, and one in every 30 Americans was killed or wounded. The North had a larger population and an industrialized economy. The South had an agrarian economy.

While Northern troops performed poorly in initial battles, the North was too strong and too populous for the South. Lee's generalship during the early war years sustained the South.

Monitor *and* Merrimac

Northern ships blockaded Southern ports. This blockade effectively denied foreign goods to the South. The Confederate ironclad *Merrimac*, renamed the *Virginia*, sailed out to challenge blockading ships in 1862, sinking several Union ships. The *Merrimac* was challenged and repulsed by the Union ironclad *Monitor* in March 1862.

Emancipation Proclamation

In 1862 Lincoln issued the Emancipation Proclamation. The proclamation freed all the slaves in Confederate states. The Proclamation prevented Great Britain and France from recognizing the slaveholding Confederate States of America.

Sherman's March

The Union launched a successful attack on the South through Tennessee. New Orleans was captured in 1862. A final wedge was driven through the South with the capture of Vicksburg, Mississippi, in 1863. Atlanta fell in 1864. Sherman then launched his infamous march to the sea, which cut a 20-mile wide swath of destruction through the South. Sherman reached Charleston, South Carolina in December 1864.

Gettysburg

Confederate forces did much better in and around Virginia, and there were draft riots in New York City during 1863. Lee brilliantly led his army and invaded Pennsylvania in 1863. The advance ended with Lee's questionable decision to launch Pickett's charge against the massed Union forces at Gettysburg.

Four months after the battle, Lincoln delivered the Gettysburg Address at the dedication of the Union Cemetery near Gettysburg. The brief transcendent address ends "...government of the people, by the people, for the people shall not perish from the earth."

War's End

In 1864 Grant took command of the Union Army of the Potomac. He waged a war of attrition against Lee. Richmond fell on April 2, 1865. On April 9, 1865, Lee surrendered at Appomattox Court House, Virginia.

Lincoln was assassinated five days later on April 15, 1865.

Homestead Act

In 1862 the Homestead Act made public lands available to Western settlers. Public lands were granted to the Union Pacific and Central Pacific companies to build rail lines from Omaha to California. After the war, farmers and settlers moved west.

Reconstruction

Three civil rights amendments were adopted between 1865 and 1870.

XIII. Prohibited slavery (1865)
XIV. Slaves given citizenship and rights (1868)
XV. Voting rights for former slaves (1870)

Johnson

Andrew Johnson became president after Lincoln was assassinated. During his administration, William Seward arranged to acquire Alaska (Seward's Folly) and occupied Midway Island. Johnson's dismissal of Secretary of War Stanton led to Johnson's impeachment (legislative indictment). Johnson survived the impeachment ballot by one vote.

Southern states slowly returned to the Union, but troops stayed in the South until 1877. During Reconstruction, former slaves gained some power in the South. This power did not last beyond 1877. Carpetbaggers from the North collaborated with white scalawags from the South and former slaves to keep Confederates out of power. In turn, the Black Codes and the KKK emerged as ways to subjugate and terrorize former slaves. Grandfather clauses, which stated that you couldn't vote if your grandfather didn't, were used to deny former slaves the vote.

Grant

In 1868 and again in 1872, Ulysses S. Grant was elected president. Corruption was widespread in Grant's government. The "Whiskey Ring" involved members of Grant's administration in fraud. Boss Tweed and the Tweed Ring were looting the New York City treasury.

The Indian Wars continued. In 1876 Sioux chiefs Sitting Bull and Crazy Horse defeated Custer and his cavalry at the Little Big Horn River in Montana.

INDUSTRIALIZATION OF AMERICA

1877–1899

Individual presidents in the late 1800s were not notable, and this was the era of caretaker presidents. The highlights of this era were the growth of business, economic conditions, and other national events and issues. The presidents in this period were:

Rutherford B. Hayes	1876	Wins a close disputed election, similar to the election of 2000
James A. Garfield	1880	Shot and killed in 1881
Chester Arthur	1881	Succeeds Garfield

Grover Cleveland   1884, 1892

William Henry Harrison   1888

William McKinley   1896, 1900   Shot and killed in 1901

In 1877 Hayes directed the removal of troops from the South and southern whites reestablished their control over the South. Reconstruction was over.

The Jim Crow South

In 1896 the United States Supreme Court in *Plessy v. Ferguson* ruled that it was legal to provide separate but equal accommodations for black Americans. In 1899, that court ruled in *Cumming v. County Board of Education* that separate schools for blacks were acceptable.

These decisions set a climate in which former Confederate states and some other states instituted Jim Crow laws that re-imposed racial segregation. These laws evolved from the Black Codes from 30 years earlier and from a national practice of segregation in rail travel. While there were some changes in these laws in the early 1900s, it was not until the United States Supreme Court ruling in *Brown v. Board of Education* that the ruling in *Plessy v. Ferguson* was reversed and not until the 1960s that most Jim Crow laws were changed.

Indian Wars

During this period most of the Indian Wars were concluded. Until then the government moved Native Americans onto reserved areas (reservations). But in 1887, under the Dawes Severalty Act, the federal government tried to move Native Americans from reservations into society. The effort failed, and Native Americans continued to be treated poorly.

Railroads

The unfenced frontier, which had produced most of American western folklore, was shrinking. By 1890 railroads, settlers, and farmers had brought it to a final end.

The railroads brought other changes to American life. Chinese immigrants who came to work on the railroads were banned from immigration by 1890. Huge herds of buffalo were killed so that they could not interfere with train travel. Railroads stimulated the economy and created a unified United States.

Business and Commerce

Inventions during this period included the telephone (Alexander Graham Bell) and the light bulb (Thomas Alva Edison).

But it was business and profits that ruled the time. John D. Rockefeller formed the Standard Oil Trust. A trust could control many companies and monopolize business. Business owners cut wages and hired new workers if there was a strike. Social Darwinism, popular during this time, stressed the survival of the fittest. Trusts grew so rapidly that the Sherman Anti-Trust Act was passed in 1890. Any trust "in restraint of trade" was illegal.

Sewing machines and typewriters drew many women to the workforce. Clara Barton founded the Red Cross in 1881.

Unions

Unions tried to respond. In 1878 the Knights of Labor started to organize workers successfully. The union collapsed after the Chicago Haymarket Riot in 1888 when eight police officers died. The American Federation of Labor, under Samuel Gompers, successfully organized workers in 1886.

The government intervened in several strike situations. In 1894 Grover Cleveland used troops to break the Pullman Strike. In 1902 Teddy Roosevelt sided with coal miners in the Anthracite Coal Strike.

Another issue was hard versus cheap money. Hard money meant that currency was linked to something valuable (gold), limiting inflation. Cheap money removes the linkage, hastening inflation.

Immigration

Immigration increased dramatically after 1880. The new immigrants to the United States now came from eastern and southern Europe. Many immigrants settled in urban areas in the eastern United States. Living conditions were difficult in tenements. Urban gangs and crime were common during this period.

Literature

Horatio Alger's rags to riches stories were very popular. Mark Twain (Samuel Clemens) wrote *The Adventures of Tom Sawyer* (1876) and *The Adventures of Huckleberry Finn* (1884). Joseph Pulitzer (Pulitzer Prize) introduced a yellow comic page in his newspaper. "Yellow journalism" came to mean sensationalized journalism.

Temperance and Suffrage

The temperance movement was making steady progress to prohibition (enacted in 1919). Carrie Nation was famous for smashing liquor bottles with a hatchet. Elizabeth Cady Stanton and Susan B. Anthony led the women's suffrage movement. Women's suffrage is a woman's right to vote. (Suffrage for women came with the Nineteenth Amendment in 1920, nearly 125 years after the U.S. Constitution was adopted.)

Spanish-American War

During Spanish suppression of a Cuban revolt in 1898, the battleship *Maine* was sunk in Havana Harbor. Popular reaction led to the Spanish-American War in Cuba and the Philippines. The war lasted eight months with most casualties coming from disease. The Battle of San Juan Hill that involved Teddy Roosevelt and his Rough Riders occurred during this conflict. The treaty ending the war gave the United States Puerto Rico, Guam, and the Philippines. In unrelated actions, the United States also annexed Wake Island and Hawaii.

1900–1916

Teddy Roosevelt

In 1901 Teddy Roosevelt, credited with leading the charge up San Juan Hill, succeeded McKinley. Roosevelt was reelected in 1904. Roosevelt was a progressive opposed to monopolies. Roosevelt was particularly moved by the novel *The Jungle* (Upton Sinclair), which exposed abuses in the meat-packing industry and championed conservation. Roosevelt used "big stick diplomacy," and the United States started to become policeman of the world. Roosevelt earned the Nobel Peace Prize for arranging a cessation to the Russo-Japanese War.

Taft

William Howard Taft was elected president in 1908. Taft continued Roosevelt's campaign against monopolies and established the Bureau of Mines. Some of Taft's policies on conservation offended Teddy Roosevelt. Roosevelt established the Bull Moose Party for the 1912 election.

WORLD HISTORY

WORLD HISTORY REVIEW QUIZ

This quiz uses a short answer format to help you find out what you know. The quiz results direct you to the portions of the chapter you should read.

This quiz will also help focus your thinking, and these questions and answers are a good review in themselves. It's not important to answer all these questions correctly, and don't be concerned if you miss many of them.

The answers are found immediately after the quiz. It's to your advantage not to look at them until you have completed the quiz. Once you have completed and corrected the review quiz, use the answer checklist to decide which sections of the review to study.

Write the answers in the space provided or on a separate sheet of paper.

---

1. Give the approximate population of the world in 1 C.E. (A.D.)_____ 1992 C.E. (A.D.)_____

2. Approximately when was writing invented?
_____
_____

3. What is the name of the justice codes formulated in ancient Mesopotamia?
_____
_____

4. Approximately when were most Egyptian pyramids built?
_____
_____

5. Who fought in the Peloponesian Wars?
_____
_____

6. Name two of the three greatest thinkers of the Greek Classic age.
_____
_____

7. What event marked the beginning of the Greek Hellenistic age?
_____
_____

8. What was the outcome of the Punic wars?
_____
_____

9. Which leaders were defeated at the Battle of Acton?
_____
_____

10. Approximately when was Christianity declared the national religion of Rome?
_____
_____

11. Who was the original founder of Islam and approximately when was he born?
_____
_____

12. What was the original Japanese religion?
_____
_____

13. Why did the Samurai revolt in 1876?
_____
_____

14. Who was named emperor of the Holy Roman Empire in the late 700s C.E. (A.D.)?
_____
_____

15. What were the stated reasons for the Crusades?

16. Joan of Arc fought for which country in what war?

17. About what percent of the European population was killed by the bubonic plague?

18. Approximately when was Confucius born?

19. During what centuries did the Mongol Kahns rule China?

20. What was the cause of the Chinese-British Opium War?

21. What name was given to the earliest inhabitants of the Indus Valley in India?

22. What ideal did Buddha preach?

23. What was the beginning of Muslim and Hindu strife in India?

24. Where did the first towns in Africa appear?

25. During what century did Northern Africa become predominately Islamic?

26. What role did African kingdoms play in the slave trade?

27. What was the dominant civilization of the Yucatan peninsula until about 900 C.E. (A.D.)?

28. What was the dominant civilization in South America in 1500 C.E. (A.D.)?

29. The ideas of which ancient civilization were dominant during the Renaissance?

30. Which practice of the Catholic church was particularly repugnant to Protestants?

31. What was the significant difference between the English queens Mary I and her successor Elizabeth I?

32. What was the main effect of European exploration on American Indians?

33. What major trade was begun during the Age of Exploration?

34. What major discovery did Copernicus make?

35. What was the average life expectancy in the early 1700s?

36. Who was the most famous Baroque painter?

37. Which Romanov leader began the modernization of Russia?

_____

_____

38. Which action began the French Revolution?

_____

_____

39. Which leader oversaw the reign of terror following the French Revolution?

_____

_____

40. Where was Napoleon exiled?

_____

_____

41. Which industries were the first to develop after the Industrial Revolution?

_____

_____

42. Which ideals were stressed by the Romantic Movement?

_____

_____

43. With which country were Great Britain and France allied during the Crimean War?

_____

_____

44. What do anarchists believe?

_____

_____

45. What continent drew the most attention from European countries during the period of New Imperialism?

_____

_____

ANSWER CHECKLIST

World History

The answers are organized by review sections. Check your answers. If you miss any question in a section, check the box and review that section.

Prehistory and Early Civilizations
❑ *World Population, page 146*
   1. 1 C.E. (A.D.), 200 million; 1992 C.E. (A.D.), 5.7 billion

❑ *Early Civilizations, page 147*
   2. 3500 B.C.E. (B.C.)

❑ *Mesopotamia (4000–500 B.C.E. [B.C.]), page 146*
   3. Codes of Hammurabi

Classical Civilizations
❑ *Egypt (5000–30 B.C.E. [B.C.]), page 149*
   4. 2600–2100 B.C.E. (B.C.)

❑ *Greece, page 149*
   5. Athens and Sparta
   6. There were three: Plato, Aristotle, and Socrates.
   7. the death of Alexander the Great

❑ *Rome, page 149*
   8. Rome gained control of both sides of the Mediterranean.
   9. Antony and Cleopatra

Development of World Religions
❑ *Judaism and Christianity, pages 150, 151*
   10. 300s C.E. (A.D.)

❑ *Islam, Buddhism, Hinduism, pages 150, 151*
   11. Mohammed, 570 C.E. (A.D.)

Feudalism in Japan and Europe
❑ *Japan, page 151*
   12. Shinto
   13. They had lost power and were forbidden to wear their swords.

❑ *Europe, page 152*
   14. Charlemagne
   15. to force Muslims from the Holy Land

The Middle and Late Ages
❑ *The Middle and Late Ages (1300–1500), page 152*
  16. She fought for France in the Hundred Years War.
  17. About 50 percent.

Chinese and Indian Empires
❑ *China to 1900, page 153*
  18. 550 B.C.E. (B.C.)
  19. 1200–1400 C.E. (A.D.)
  20. The Chinese resisted importation of opium.
❑ *India to 1900, page 154*
  21. Dravidians
  22. Nirvana
  23. the invasion of India about 1200 C.E. (A.D.) by Turk and Afghan Muslims

Sub-Saharan Kingdoms and Cultures
❑ *Early Africa, page 155*
  24. around the Nile River

❑ *Sub-Saharan Africa, pages 155–156*
  25. 1000–1100 A.D.
  26. They captured and sold African slaves.

Civilizations of the Americas
❑ *Mayan Culture, page 156*
  27. Mayans

❑ *Aztec, Incan Culture, pages 156, 157*
  28. Incas

Rise and Expansion of Europe
❑ *Renaissance (1300–1600), page 157*
  29. Greece

❑ *Reformation (1500–1600), page 157*
  30. selling indulgences
  31. Mary killed Protestants; Elizabeth was a Protestant.

❑ *Age of Exploration (1500–1650), page 158*
  32. death from disease
  33. slaves

❑ *Scientific Revolution (1550–1650), page 158*
  34. The sun is at the center of the solar system.

❑ *Enlightenment (c. 1650–1790), page 158*
  35. about 30
  36. Michelangelo

❑ *Romanov Russia, page 159*
  37. Peter the Great

❑ *French Revolution, page 159*
  38. storming of the Bastille
  39. Robespierre

❑ *Napoleon, page 160*
  40. to Elba and then to St. Helena

❑ *Industrial Revolution (1750–1850), page 160*
  41. textiles and metal

❑ *Romanticism (1790–1850), page 160*
  42. nature, feelings, personal freedom, and humanitarianism

European Developments
❑ *Crimean War, page 161*
  43. Turkey

❑ *Capitalism, Marxism, and Anarchism, page 161*
  44. There should be no authority.

❑ *New Imperialism, page 161*
  45. Africa

WORLD HISTORY REVIEW

PREHISTORY AND THE DEVELOPMENT OF EARLY CIVILIZATIONS

WORLD POPULATION

World population grew steadily from 1 C.E. (A.D.) through 1650 C.E. (A.D.) After 1650 C.E. (A.D.), world population exploded. Rapid population growth has made it more difficult to provide for everyone. A table showing population growth follows.

1 C.E. (A.D.)	500	1000	1650	1850	1930	1975	2000
200 million	220 million	300 million	500 million	1 billion	2 billion	4 billion	6.1 billion

EARLY CIVILIZATIONS

Current knowledge of human history stretches back about 8,000 years to 6000 B.C.E. (B.C.). The earliest established date is around 4500 B.C.E. (B.C.). Most historians agree that civilization began when writing was invented about 3500 B.C.E. (B.C.). This date separates prehistoric from historic times.

In prehistoric time, humans used calendars, invented and used the wheel, played flutes and harps, and alloyed copper. These humans also created pottery and colored ceramics. There was an active trade in the Mediterranean Sea with Cretan shipping most prominent. What follows is a brief summary of historic times.

MESOPOTAMIA

The earliest recorded civilizations were in Mesopotamia and probably developed in the lined area on the map below. This region was centered near the Tigris and Euphrates Rivers in what is now Iraq and extended from the western Mediterranean to Palestine to the Persian Gulf. The Sumerians inhabited Mesopotamia from 4000 B.C.E. (B.C.) to 2000 B.C.E. (B.C.) and probably invented the first writing—wedge-shaped symbols called cuneiform.

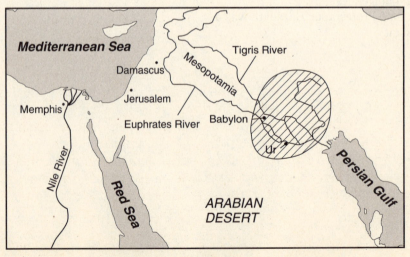

MESOPOTAMIA

The Old Babylonians (2000–1550 B.C.E. [B.C.]) inhabited this area and established a capital at Babylonia (hanging gardens). King Hammurabi, known for the justice code named after him, ruled during the middle of this period. The militaristic Assyrians ruled from 1000 to about 600 B.C.E. (B.C.) The Assyrians were followed by the New Babylonians under King Nebuchadnezzar from about 600 to 500 B.C.E. (B.C.). A defeat by the Persians in the fifth century B.C.E. (B.C.) led to a dissolution of Mesopotamia.

EARLY AFRICA

Humans (*Homo sapiens*) are believed to have developed in Africa about 250,000 years ago. Humans formed nomadic bands that spread throughout Africa about 30,000 years ago. The first "towns" were founded in the Nile River Valley about 4500 B.C.E. (B.C.).

By about 3000 B.C.E. (B.C.) sophisticated civilizations developed throughout Egypt, which occupied a swath of land along the Nile River and extending to the Mediterranean. The Egyptians had writing (hieroglyphics) and invented a calendar still in use today.

EARLY CIVILIZATIONS

EGYPT

Egyptian history is usually divided into seven periods. Pharaohs became deities during the Old Kingdom (2685–2180 B.C.E. [B.C.]). Most pyramids were built during the Fourth Dynasty of the Old Kingdom (about 2600–2500 B.C.E. [B.C.]). Our vision of Egyptians in horse-drawn chariots marked the Second Intermediate Period (1785–1560 B.C.E. [B.C.]). The Egyptians invaded Palestine and enslaved the Jews during the New Kingdom (1560–1085 B.C.E. [B.C.]). King Tutankhamen reigned during this period. In the first millennium B.C.E. (B.C.) Egypt was controlled by many groups and leaders, including Alexander the Great.

Beginning around 2150 B.C.E. (B.C.), a century of weak pharaohs, civil wars, and famines weakened and fragmented Egypt. From about 2050 to 1650 B.C.E. (B.C.), Egypt came together in the Middle Kingdom. In 1650 B.C.E. (B.C.), foreign armies invaded and conquered Egypt. In about 1550 B.C.E. (B.C.) the Egyptians overthrew the foreign leaders and the New Kingdom began (1550–1100 B.C.E. [B.C.]).

In the beginning of the New Kingdom, Egypt stretched along the Nile and occupied the coast of the Mediterranean out of Africa and in Palestine and Syria. By 1250 B.C.E. (B.C.), the Egyptian Empire was in decline. Egypt ceased to be the dominant force in the area about 750 B.C.E. (B.C.). In about 30 B.C.E. (B.C.). Egypt came under the control of the Roman Empire.

Kush Kingdom

The Nile River flows north some 3,500 miles from Lake Victoria into Egypt and the Mediterranean Sea. There are six cataracts, waterfalls, south of Egypt numbered north to south along the Nile.

The region south of the first cataract was called the Kingdom of Kush by the ancient Egyptians. That area has been called Nubia for the last 1,500 years. This area roughly corresponds to the modern country of Sudan. Much is unknown about the Kush civilization, which may have stretched over 5,000 years and many scholars do not use the term Kush for that entire period. This section summarizes generally agreed on information.

Kush was the first African Kingdom. It originated around the capital called Kerma near the Nile's third cataract and named after the current Sudanese town on the plain there. Studies indicate the area around Kerma may be the oldest settlement in Africa, dating from about 4800 B.C.E. (B.C.).

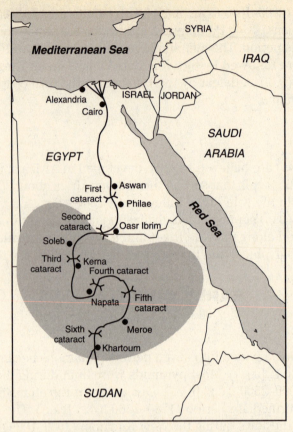

NILE RIVER REGION DURING THE KUSH KINGDOM
AND SHOWING MODERN COUNTRIES

There was constant strife between Egypt and the Kingdom of Kush, which was frequently dominated by Egypt. Some scholars speculate about a very early relationship between the Kush Kingdom and Egypt. Between 1700 B.C.E. (B.C.) and 1500 B.C.E. (B.C.) Egypt's domination of the Kush Empire diminished, leading to a growth of Kush culture. But the new dynasty kings reasserted their dominance over the Kush Empire at the end of this time. By about 1000 B.C.E. (B.C.) the capital of the Kush Kingdom was moved south to Napata near the fourth cataract.

The Kush Kingdom started to reassert itself and in 730 B.C.E. (B.C.), the Kush Kingdom defeated Egypt and established a Kush (XXV) dynasty. This dynasty united Egypt and the Kush Empire. Black Kush pharaohs ruled Egypt until the Assyrians forced a withdrawal in 661 B.C.E. (B.C.).

Until about 300 B.C.E. (B.C.) the Kush retained their Egyptian identity and the Egyptian language as though they were still the rulers of Egypt. Assyrian and Persian attacks forced the Kush Kingdom further south to Meroe between the fifth and sixth cataract. This moved the Kush civilization away from Egyptian influence and closer to the kingdom's sub-Saharan African roots.

In 30 B.C.E. (B.C.), Rome conquered Egypt and about five years later the Kushites attacked the now Roman-controlled territories around Aswan near the first cataract. A Roman army drove back the Kush forces apparently under the command of a queen. The Kush counterattacked the Romans at Oasr Ibrim but were repulsed. Eventually the Kush and Roman Empires signed a truce that held until near the end of the Kush Empire. By about 350 C.E. (A.D.) the third Meroite phase of the Kush Empire had disintegrated.

More pyramids were built in the Kush Kingdom than in Egypt, although Egyptian pyramids were larger. The Kush Meroites developed their own form of script writing, which is not able to be translated. The Kush Meroites' king was elected from among royal family members. Women enjoyed relative equality in the Kush culture and a number of women served as monarchs. This was a striking and singular breakthrough for the time. In the Kush religion,

Amon was the most significant god, but the Kush Meroites worshipped many gods, including the Egyptian gods.

CLASSICAL CIVILIZATIONS

GREECE

Greece has always been linked to its nearby islands. One of these islands, Crete, was inhabited by the Minoans (about 2600–1250 B.C.E. [B.C.]). During this time the ancient city of Troy was built. The mainland, inhabited by the Myceneans since about 2000 B.C.E. (B.C.), eventually incorporated Crete and the Minoan Civilization about 1200 B.C.E. (B.C.).

Dorian invasions from the north around 1200 B.C.E. (B.C.) led to the defeat of the Myceneans and to the Greek Dark Ages from 1200 to 750 B.C.E. (B.C.). The Trojan War, which occurred during this period, was described by Homer in the *Iliad*.

Athens (founded 1000 B.C.E. [B.C.]) and Sparta (founded 750 B.C.E. [B.C.]) were famous Greek city-states. Draco was a harsh Athenian leader and democracy was established only in 527 B.C.E. (B.C.). During this period, the Parthenon was built in Athens. In Sparta, each male citizen became a lifetime soldier at the age of 7.

Classic Age

The Classic Age of Greece began about 500 B.C.E. (B.C.) when Athens defeated Persia at Marathon and declined with the Peloponnesian War (430–404 B.C.E. [B.C.]) between Athens and Sparta.

The Classic Age was a time for the development of great literature and great thought. During this period, Socrates, Plato, and Aristotle taught and wrote in Greece. Aristotle tutored Alexander the Great after Alexander conquered Greece. In this relatively brief period, Aeschylus wrote his *Orestia Tiology* and Sophocles wrote *Oedipus Rex*. Also writing during this period were Aristophanes, Euripides, Herodotus, and Thucydides.

Hellenistic Age

This age begins with the death of Alexander the Great. Alexander lived for only 33 years (356–323 B.C.E. [B.C.]) but during his brief life he carved out a huge empire. His conquests led to the spread of Greek culture and thought to most of that region of the world. This age ended about 30 B.C.E. (B.C.) when Greece, like Egypt, was incorporated in the Roman Empire.

Epicurus and Zeno wrote during this time. The Hellenistic Age was a time of great scientific and mathematical development. Euclid wrote his *Elements* in the third century B.C.E. (B.C.) while Archimedes, and Erasthotenes made important discoveries later in the period.

ROME

Some say that Rome was founded between 700 and 800 B.C.E. (B.C.). The real founding of Rome may be closer to 500 B.C.E. (B.C.). The Roman Senate consisting of landowners was eventually replaced by the plebeian Assembly about 300 B.C.E. (B.C.) as the governing body of Rome.

Rome acquired all of Italy by about 300 B.C.E. (B.C.), defeated Carthage (in North Africa) during a series of Punic Wars, and controlled both sides of the Mediterranean by about 150 B.C.E. (B.C.). The Roman victories were marked by one defeat at the hands of the Carthaginian general Hannibal. Julius Caesar and Pompeii were leaders in the first century B.C.E. (B.C.) and Spartacus led a rebellion by slaves. Caesar was assassinated on the Ides of March, 44 B.C.E. (B.C.) in a conspiracy led by Brutus ("et tu Brute") and Cassius.

Roman Empire

Octavius defeated Antony and Cleopatra at the Battle of Acton around 38 B.C.E. (B.C.). Following this, Octavius was crowned the first "God-Emperor." The 200 years of peace that followed, called the Pax Romana, is the longest period of peace in the Western World.

The birth of the Roman Empire coincided roughly with the beginning of the C.E. (A.D.) era. During the first century C.E. (A.D.), the Emperor Nero committed suicide. Jewish zealots also committed suicide at Masada following the destruction of their temple by the Romans. The empire reached its greatest size during this century. A code of law was established. Scientists Ptomely and Pliny the Elder were active, and the Colosseum was constructed.

Following the death of Emperor Marcus Aurelius, the Roman Empire began its decline. Civil war raged in the 200s C.E. (A.D.) and there were defeats of provinces by the Persians and the Goths. Constantine's attempts to stop the empire's decline were ultimately fruitless, and the Visigoths looted Rome in about 400 C.E. (A.D.).

DEVELOPMENT OF WORLD RELIGIONS

Most of the world's religions emerged in Africa and Asia. About two billion people follow some Christian religion, and one billion Christians are Roman Catholics. There are about one billion Muslims, 800 million Hindus and 350 million Buddhists. There are fewer who follow tribal religions or who are Sikhs, Jews, Shamanists, Confucians, and followers of other religions. About one billion people are nonreligious and about 250 million people are atheists.

Hinduism

Hinduism emerged in India about 2500 B.C.E. (B.C.). Hindu beliefs are a mixture of the religious beliefs of invaders of India and the religious beliefs of native Indians. Hinduism embraces a caste system with religious services conducted by members of the priestly caste. Most Hindus worship one of the gods Vishnu and Shiva, and the goddess Shakti.

Hindus believe that a person's *karma*, the purity or impurity of past deeds, determines a person's ultimate fate. A karma can be improved through pure acts, deeds, and devotion.

Judaism

Judaism developed from the beliefs of the Hebrew tribes located in and around Israel before 1300 B.C.E. (B.C.). From about 1000 B.C.E. (B.C.) to 150 B.C.E. (B.C.) a number of different authors wrote a series of books describing the religion, laws, and customs which are now known as the Old Testament of the Bible. The Old Testament describes a single just God. Judaism is an important world religion because elements of Judaism can be found in both Islam and Christianity.

Hebrews trace their ancestry to Abraham and his grandson Jacob, whose 12 sons are said to have founded the 12 tribes of Israel. About 1000 B.C.E. (B.C.) David is believed to have united these 12 tribes into a single religious state. Modern Jews refer to the Talmud, a book of Jewish law and tradition written around 400 C.E. (A.D.).

Buddhism

Buddhism was founded around 525 B.C.E. (B.C.) in India. The religion was founded by the Buddha, Siddhartho Gautama, who lived from about 560 B.C.E. (B.C.) to about 480 B.C.E. (B.C.). The Triptika contains Buddha's teachings. A large number of *Sutras* contains a great body of Buddhiso beliefs and teachings. Monastic life provides the main organizational and administrative structure for modern-day Buddhism.

It is said that Buddha achieved his enlightenment through meditation, and meditation is an important Buddhist practice. Buddhism holds that life is essentially meaningless and without reality. Buddhists seek to achieve Nirvana, a great void of perfection, through meditation and just acts.

Christianity

Jesus was probably born about 5 B.C.E. (B.C.). He acquired a small following of Jews who believed he was the Messiah. Later this belief was developed into a worldwide religion known as Christianity. Christianity was generally tolerated in Rome, although there were periods of persecution. The Emperor Constantine converted to Christianity about 300 C.E. (A.D.). In the mid 300s Christianity was decreed the state religion of Rome. Augustine (St. Augustine) converted to Christianity in the late 300s.

In the Byzantine Era, starting after the Visigoths looted Rome, there was an Eastern and Western emperor. Constantinople was the capital in the East. This division led in 1054 to the great schism of the Catholic church, which survives to this day. The Crusaders captured Constantinople and defeated the Eastern Byzantines in 1204. In 1453 Constantinople was captured by the Turks and renamed Istanbul.

Islam

Mohammad was born in 570 C.E. (A.D.) and went into Mecca in 630 and founded Islam. Muslims believe Mohammad is the greatest prophet of God. The Quran contains the 114 chapters (suras) of Islamic religion and law. The Quran is the holiest book of Islam and Muslims believe it contains God's final revelation to man. Around 640 C.E. (A.D.) the Omar, religious leader, established an Islamic empire with Damascus as the capital. The capital was eventually moved to Baghdad. The Muslims enjoyed a prosperous economy, and in the late days of the empire Omar Khayyam wrote the *Rubaiyat*.

Muslim armies conquered Spain and much of France by about 730. A series of Caliphs ruled from 750 until 1250 when an army originally led by Genghis Khan sacked Baghdad and killed the last caliph.

FEUDALISM IN JAPAN AND EUROPE

Japan

The Japanese Islands had an early civilization by 3000 B.C.E. (B.C.). Throughout the whole B.C.E. (B.C.) period Japan remained a primitive society overrun by successive invasions of Mongols and Malays. Around the beginning of the C.E. (A.D.) period, Chinese writers referred to Japan as a backward nation.

The first religion in Japan was Shinto, a cult of nature and ancestor worship. Around 550 C.E. (A.D.), Buddhism was introduced in Japan and quickly spread throughout the country. Throughout this period Japan existed in the shadow of China. Chinese words are still found today in the Japanese language.

Shoguns

Japanese emperors had always been powerful, godlike figures. But around 1150 C.E. (A.D.), Shoguns were installed as the permanent leaders of Japan, leaving the emperor with only ceremonial duties. Until that time Shoguns had been only military leaders. In the following years a succession of Shoguns were ultimately unsuccessful in unifying Japan. Japan was reduced to a group of warring states.

Around 1600 the strong Tokugawa Shogunate was formed. This Shogunate ruled Japan until 1868. Japan was at peace for most of this period. Under this Shogunate, Christians were persecuted, and in 1639 foreign ships were forbidden in Japanese waters. This period of isolation lasted until American Commodore Perry forced Japan to sign a treaty in 1853, opening limited trade with the West.

Meiji Period

The Meiji period of Japan lasted from 1868 until 1912. Feudalism established under the Shogunates was outlawed, and Japan started to develop an industrial economy. As lords lost their feudal manors, the importance of the samurai (a lord's private soldiers) declined. In 1876 samurai were forbidden to wear their swords. Some 250,000 samurai rebelled in 1876 but were easily defeated by soldiers bearing modern weapons.

Buddhism declined, and Shintoism enjoyed a rebirth during this period. Japan actively sought contact with Western nations and adopted a number of Western customs and institutions. In 1889 the first Diet or parliament was established.

Wars

In 1894 Japan entered into war with China (Sino-Japanese War) over a dispute about Korea. Japan defeated China, establishing Japan as a military power. In 1904 Japan entered into war with Russia (The Russo-Japanese War). Japan also emerged victorious in this war and established a new balance of power between East and West. This new balance of power set the stage for conflicts yet to come.

Europe

Charlemagne

Charles the Great, Charlemagne, halted a Muslim advance in what is now France. Later he ruled the Frankish kingdom from about 770–815 C.E. (A.D.). He was named emperor of the Holy Roman Empire in 800 C.E. (A.D.) by Pope Leo III. Charlemagne's authority was also accepted in the East. After much fighting in Europe, the Normans, under William the Conqueror, defeated the Saxons in England at the Battle of Hastings in 1066.

The High Middle Ages lasted from the Battle of Hastings until about 1300. During this time the Roman road system was rebuilt, and Europe grew larger than the Muslim and Byzantine Empires.

In England a long series of battles with the Danes and Danish occupation preceded the Battle of Hastings. Henry II arranged for Archbishop Thomas Becket's murder in the late 1100s followed by the reign of Richard the Lionhearted and the signing of the Magna Carta in 1215.

Crusades

There were at least seven crusades from 1100 and 1300 to dislodge Muslim "infidels" from Jerusalem and the Holy Land. The third crusade was led by Richard the Lionhearted. Ultimately, these crusades were unsuccessful, and many Muslims and Jews were massacred. Jews were persecuted throughout Europe beginning with the first crusade. Hundreds of Jewish communities were destroyed in the area of present-day Germany alone.

Scholasticism, an attempt to bring together the Christian faith and logic, was active during this period with leaders such as St. Anselm, Thomas Aquinas, Albertus Magnus, and Peter Abelard.

THE MIDDLE AND LATE AGES (1300–1500)

Hundred Years War

For much of this period, England and France were engaged in the Hundred Years War (actually about 120 years long). Most of the war was fought in France. Joan of Arc led the French army to a great victory. She was burned at the stake at age 19. England was ultimately defeated. During this time, Chaucer wrote the *Canterbury Tales*.

Black Death

The bubonic plague, carried by rats' fleas, was epidemic in Europe by 1350. According to some estimates, almost half of the European population was killed by the plague.

CHINESE AND INDIAN EMPIRES

CHINA TO 1900

Early civilization developed near the Yellow River in ancient times. It appears that cities developed in China after they appeared in Egypt. The Shang Dynasty emerged in China about 1500 B.C.E. (B.C.) and lasted until about 1100 B.C.E. (B.C.). This dynasty is known for its works of art, particularly its fine bronze castings and walled cities. Life in this dynasty did not emphasize religion, a trait noted also in modern China.

The Chou Dynasty ruled from about 1100 to 250 B.C.E. (B.C.) Jade carvings and Chinese calligraphy were developed during this time.

Confucius

Confucius was born near the end of the Chou Dynasty around 550 B.C.E. (B.C.). He was a philosopher who was concerned with the way people acted. He emphasized regard for authority, self-control, conformity, and respectful behavior. Confucius had little impact during his lifetime. His disciples carried his thoughts and ideas throughout China. Eventually he came to be revered, and his ideas and sayings give a distinct shape and form to Chinese thought.

250 B.C.E. (B.C.)–220 C.E. (A.D.)

Following the Chou Dynasty were the Ch'in rulers, including the first emperor of China. During this time the Great Wall of China was expanded and built along the northern Chinese border. Confucian writings were destroyed by these leaders.

A successor in this period founded the Han Dynasty, which ruled China from about 200 B.C.E. (B.C.) to 220 C.E. (A.D.). During this period Confucius became a revered figure, and his writings were the objects of careful study.

Invaders

Invaders from the north attacked China around 315 C.E. (A.D.) and controlled north China until about 560 C.E. (A.D.). The Chinese maintained their independence in the south, but China was divided into a number of states. Influence from India established Buddhism in China during this time.

580 C.E. (A.D.)–1279 C.E. (A.D.)

China was reunited under the Sui Dynasty about 580 C.E. (A.D.). In 618 the Sui Dynasty was overthrown. The T'ang Dynasty that followed lasted until about 906 C.E. (A.D.). During this time Turkish incursions were halted, and Chinese influence grew to include Korea and northern Indochina. The T'angs developed a civil service testing apparatus, and the Chinese economy improved during this time.

During the Sung Dynasty (960–1279 C.E. [A.D.]) gunpowder was used for weapons. The nation prospered during this time, and the standard of living rose to new heights.

Mongols

The Mongols, under Genghis Khan, invaded and controlled much of northern China by 1215. Kublai Khan followed, and his successors ruled China until 1368. During this time the Chinese launched a fleet to attack Japan. The fleet was destroyed in a typhoon. The Japanese refer to this typhoon as the divine wind—*kamikaze.*

Ming Dynasty

In 1368 the Khan Dynasty was overthrown, and the Ming Dynasty was born. Rulers of the Ming Dynasty launched a campaign to stamp out any remnants of the Mongol occupation. Even though there were some contacts with the West, the rulers of this dynasty forbade sea travel to foreign lands. Beginning in 1433 Chinese isolation and suspicion of foreigners grew. The Ming Dynasty reigned until 1644 when it was overthrown by the Manchu Dynasty.

Western Contacts

Contacts with the West increased under the Manchu Dynasty. However, in 1757 the Chinese government became offended by some Western traders. They allowed trade only through the port of Canton and under very strict regulations. At that time, opium was one of the few Chinese imports. The Chinese government objected to these imports, and this led to the Opium War of 1839, won by the British. Western intervention in China continued through 1900.

India to 1900

Early, advanced civilizations developed in the Indus Valley. The inhabitants were called Dravidians. Around 2500 B.C.E. (B.C.), a series of floods and foreign invasions appears to have all but destroyed these civilizations. Between 2500 and 1500 B.C.E. (B.C.) the Dravidians were forced into southern India by a nomadic band with Greek and Persian roots.

The conquerors brought a less sophisticated civilization and it was this latter group that formed the Indian civilization. An early caste system was established with the Dravidians serving as slaves.

After a time the society developed around religious, nonsecular concerns. The Mahabarata became a verbal tradition around 1000 B.C.E. (B.C.) It describes a war hero Krishna. The Mahabarata's most significant impact was the frequent descriptions of correct conduct and belief. The Mahabarata also describes how the soul remains immortal through transmigration— the successive occupation of many bodies.

Castes

From about 1000 to 500 B.C.E. (B.C.) the caste system became fixed and it was almost impossible for people to move out of their caste. The priests, or Brahmans, were at the top of the caste system. Next were rulers and warriors and then farmers and tradesmen. Near the bottom were workers. Finally, there were those who had no caste at all—outcastes—who could not participate in society.

Buddha

Buddha was born in India about 580 B.C.E. (B.C.). His teachings developed the Buddhist religion. Buddha preached nirvana—a rejection of worldly and material concerns and a surrender of individual consciousness. During his lifetime his ideas spread throughout India.

Maurya Empire

The Maurya Empire ruled India from about 320 to 185 B.C.E. (B.C.). During this time Buddhism was spread throughout Asia, China, and Southeast Asia. The Andrhan Dynasty ruled India proper to 220 C.E. (A.D.). Buddhism became less popular in India during this period while Brahmans gained more prominence.

Gupta Dynasty

After disorder following the collapse of the Andhran Dynasty, the Gupta Dynasty ruled from about 320 to 500 C.E. (A.D.). Arts, literature, and mathematics flourished during this period.

Indian mathematicians used the decimal system and probably introduced the concept of zero. Hinduism developed from earlier religions and became the dominant religion in India. Most people in India worshipped many gods including Brahma (creator), Vishnu (preserver), and Shiva (destroyer).

The Gupta Dynasty declined with the invasion of the Huns in the fifth century C.E. (A.D.). Successors of these invaders, called Rajputs, intermarried, joined Hindu society, and dominated northern India until 1200 C.E. (A.D.). Other kingdoms were established in central and southern India.

By this time the caste system and the power of Brahman priests were dominant throughout India.

Muslims

Around 1200 C.E. (A.D.) Muslims (Turks and Afghans) invaded India from the north. The invaders controlled all but the southern part of India by about 1320. The Delhi Sultanate lasted in a state of intrigue until about 1530. Muslim sultans oppressed Hindus while their supporters killed or converted many Hindus. Remnants of this strife between Muslims and Hindus can be seen to this day.

In 1530 the Mongols, also Muslims, invaded India and by 1600 controlled most of India. The Mongol leader Akbar assumed the throne about 1560. His reign featured religious tolerance, the development of arts and literature, and a massive building campaign. In 1756 the Mongol Dynasty was overthrown by internal strife and Hindu resistance. India became a divided state.

Britain

Into this void stepped the European powers, particularly England. The East India Company of England virtually ruled India through 1857. In 1857, sepoys, Indian soldiers in the British army, mutinied. The revolt was eventually put down after two years of savage fighting. The British government began to rule India directly. This form of British rule was superior to that provided by the East India Company. Indian troops fought with Britain in World War I and World War II.

SUB-SAHARAN KINGDOMS AND CULTURES

The Sudan, south of Egypt, developed a culture mentioned earlier. The Kush civilization of Sudan flourished in middle Africa and was dominant until about 250 C.E. (A.D.). The C.E. (A.D.) period marks the conquest of North Africa by the Roman Empire. Christian European influence was dominant until about 640 C.E. (A.D.).

ISLAM

Islam spread throughout Africa in the seventh century C.E. (A.D.). During this time Muslims conquered the area occupied by Egypt and the rest of North Africa, including Morocco and Libya. By about 1050 C.E. (A.D.) most of northern Africa was an Islamic land.

WEST AFRICA

The earliest state in West Africa was probably Ghana [established about 700 C.E. (A.D.)]. By 1050 Ghana was also a Muslim state. In about 1100 C.E. (A.D.), the Mali evolved from tribes near the headwaters of the Senegal and Niger Rivers. Around 1300 Mali became a Muslim state. Songhai emerged as the dominant state in West Africa about 1400 C.E. (A.D.). Islam became the dominant faith in Songhai around 1500 and the capital, Timbuktu, became a major center for trade and learning. Songhai was overrun by Morocco in 1591.

EAST AFRICA

East African civilizations had an early exposure to Asian peoples. Most towns were established by Arab and Indonesian settlers. There was a great deal of intermarriage among natives and settlers. Mogadishu and Mombassa were among a number of smaller states, which emerged around 1250 C.E. (A.D.).

CENTRAL AFRICA

Civilizations in central Africa are shrouded in mystery. Bantu-speaking people apparently settled there around 700 C.E. (A.D.). In the fourteenth century the Kongo Kingdom was formed. The area around Lake Tanganyika was formed in the Luba Empire about the time Columbus made his first voyage. South Africa is best known for the Zulu people. They conquered most of South Africa between 1816 and 1850.

Slaves

European conquest and domination of Africa began in the late fifteenth century. Slave trade by Europeans began at this time. Many slaves were supplied by African kingdoms, which grew rich on the slave trade.

CIVILIZATIONS OF THE AMERICAS

EARLY CULTURES

Before 1500 the inhabitants of the Americas were related to the Native Americans. This group had migrated over the land bridge from Siberia about 30,000 years before. About 90 percent of the tens of millions of ancestors of this migratory tribe were found in Latin America in 1500.

By 7000 B.C.E. (B.C.), primitive cultures existed throughout the Americas. Cultures developed more slowly in the jungle areas of South America. Primitive cultures still exist there today. Agriculture seems to have been widespread by about 2500 B.C.E. (B.C.).

MAYAN CULTURE

The dominant civilization in Mexico until about 900 C.E. (A.D.) were the Mayans. They began to occupy the Yucatan peninsula of Mexico and surrounding areas about 1700 B.C.E. (B.C.). The Mayans probably developed the most sophisticated indigenous American culture. The Mayan civilization ended suddenly with the mysterious desertion of Mayan cities and migration of the Mayan population.

Striking Mayan cities, plazas, and pyramids survive to this day. Mayans had a written language and wrote books about astronomy. Their calendar was the most accurate in the world at that time. Many Mayan descendants live as peasants in Mexico and speak dialects of their ancient language.

From about 1500 to 600 C.E. (A.D.), the Olmec civilization was a sophisticated culture in eastern Mexico. About this time a culture centered in Teotihuacan, near Mexico City, also grew in prominence. This culture was to dominate central Mexico until about 900 C.E. (A.D.).

AZTEC CULTURE

In about 900 C.E. (A.D.) the Aztecs began their rise to power in northern Mexico. Aztecs referred to themselves as Mexica. Aztecs were warlike and sacrificed humans. By about 1300 C.E. (A.D.) they established a capital city in a marsh, which is now the site of Mexico City.

The Spaniards, under Cortez, entered Mexico in 1519, and duped the Aztec Emperor Montezuma II and easily defeated the Aztec confederation in 1521. Over a million descendants of the Aztecs still live in Mexico, mainly living a subsistence existence and speaking their ancient language.

INCAN CULTURE

The Incas were the dominant pre-Columbian civilization in South America. This culture existed in Peru by about 500 C.E. (A.D.). From about 1100 to about 1500 C.E. (A.D.) the Incas expanded their empire to most of the western coast of South America and included parts of Argentina.

The Incas had the best developed system of government in the Americas. They built extensive systems of stone roads and huge stone structures such as the Temple of the Sun. The Incas also built the fortress Machu Picchu high in the Andes. Machu Picchu may have been the last stronghold of the Incas after the Spaniard Pizzaro overcame the Incan empire in 1532 with about 200 troops and palace intrigue.

RISE AND EXPANSION OF EUROPE

RENAISSANCE (1300–1600)

The Renaissance, which means the rebirth, arose in Italy and particularly in Florence. It was a time for the discovery and rediscovery of literature and art. Humanism, reading, and the ideas of Classical Greece were dominant during this period. Dante wrote the *Inferno* and the *Divine Comedy* early in the Renaissance and Machiavelli wrote *The Prince* near the end of the period. Leonardo da Vinci painted the Mona Lisa and designed many workable mechanical devices. Michelangelo painted the ceiling of the Sistine Chapel, among other accomplishments.

LUTHER AND THE REFORMATION (1500–1600)

The abuses of the Catholic church, then monolithic in Europe, drew much criticism. The practice of selling indulgences (relief from punishment in purgatory) was considered particularly repugnant. Martin Luther drew particular attention these abuses when, on October 31, 1517, he nailed his *95 Theses* to the Wittenberg Church door. Luther authored many books and wrote the most popular hymn of the time, *A Mighty Fortress Is Our God*. Since Luther's teachings *protested* church practice, his followers were called Protestants.

The reform movement spread beyond Luther in Germany to England and other parts of Europe. Henry VIII in England broke with the pope and formed the Church of England. Protestantism was effectively blocked in Spain and Italy and was the subject of warfare in France.

RELIGIOUS WARFARE

The 90 years that followed were marked by religious strife. Gunpowder, available since the 1300s, was now used in cannons. Warfare became more regimented and more deadly. There were no fewer than seven civil wars in France. The St. Bartholomew's Day Massacre occurred in 1572, when Catherine de' Medici arranged the death of about 20,000 French Huguenots (Calvinist Protestants).

Mary I (Bloody Mary) of England killed many Protestants in her brief five-year reign (1553–1558). Her successor, Elizabeth I, was a Protestant and achieved some degree of religious peace in England. Later attempts were made to force England back to Catholicism.

By 1575 governments were in shambles, and many religious groups were discriminated against. In England the Puritans objected to what they saw as a pro-Catholic shift in the Church of England. Many Puritans escaped to the New World.

AGE OF EXPLORATION (1500–1650)

Countries sponsored exploration throughout the world toward the end of the Renaissance. These countries were seeking new trade and easily accessible trade routes.

The New World had already been visited when Columbus sailed from Spain in 1492. His voyage followed on other explorations by Prince Henry the Navigator and Vasco da Gama, although these explorers never reached the New World. Many other explorers traveled to the New World and circumnavigated the world during this period. Cortes conquered the Aztecs, in Mexico, and Pizarro, in Peru, conquered the Incas.

The effect of exploration on the Native Indian population of the Americas was disastrous. Some estimates indicate that 80 percent of the native population was wiped out by disease in one of the greatest epidemics on earth. Gold and food were shipped back to Europe. A large number of English settled in North America. Small numbers of Spanish settlers went to South and Central America. Still smaller numbers of French settled in Canada following the explorations of Champlain.

Europeans, with the complicity of some African kingdoms, began transporting slaves from Africa to the Americas. About 5 percent of the slaves from Africa reached the English colonies and the United States. Over 50 percent of the African slaves went to the Caribbean, with over 30 percent to Brazil and about 10 percent to other Spanish colonies. The first African slaves arrived in Jamestown, Virginia, about 1620. By the early 1800s there were about one million slaves in the United States. By 1860 there were more than four million slaves in the United States.

We will return later to the development of the New World following this period of exploration.

SCIENTIFIC REVOLUTION (1550–1650)

The scientific revolution took place toward the end of the Renaissance and spilled over into the age of exploration. Copernicus showed that the sun was at the center of the solar system. Kepler discovered the orbits of the planets. Galileo made significant discoveries in astronomy, mechanics, and surveying. He proved that all falling bodies fall at the same rate.

Francis Bacon championed inductive investigations in which data are gathered and used to form hypotheses. Rene Decartes (Cartesian coordinates) provided leadership in mathematics and championed the deductive, step-by-step method of proof.

ENLIGHTENMENT (C. 1650–1790)

In 1650 Europe consisted of 300–500 smaller states and a Germany devastated by the Thirty Years War. A series of treaties and wars brought a kind of order out of this chaos.

Peace of Westphalia (1648)—Holland and Switzerland officially formed.

First Dutch War (1667–1668)—Warfare between France and Spain led to the Triple Alliance (England, Holland, and Sweden).

War of the League of Augsburg (1688–1697)—France fought England and Holland. The conflict between England and France continued on and off for about 125 years.

The Grand Alliance (1701)—A coalition of Spain and France against England led to the formation of the Grand Coalition (Holy Roman Empire, England, Holland, and Prussia).

Treaty of Utrecht (1742)—The Spanish Empire was partitioned. England received Gibraltar, Newfoundland, Hudson Bay, and Nova Scotia.

King William's War (1744–1748)—Prussia emerged as a world power.

Seven Years War (1756–1763)—Prussia fought Austria, France, and Russia. With help from England and the withdrawal of Russia from the conflict, Prussia held onto its lands.

Treaty of Paris (1763)—France, which had already given Spain all its western American lands, lost the rest of its North American possessions to England. England traded Cuba to Spain for the Floridas.

Treaty of Paris (1783)—Britain recognized the United States following the Revolutionary War, but no lands were given to France, even though France (Lafayette, Rochambeau) had aided the United States in the Revolutionary War.

Life was still difficult in the 1700s. In the early 1700s the average life expectancy was 30, and almost no one lived to see their grandchildren. Famine and disease (including smallpox, bubonic plague, and typhus) were rampant. But, slowly, the economies and social institutions of Europe began to change for the better.

Mercantilism, an emphasis on material wealth, became a leading force in Europe. In Holland and England productivity became important. As a result, these countries became leading economic powers.

TECHNOLOGY, ART, AND LITERATURE

In the early 18th century, technology provided a means for further economic development. Watt refined and developed the steam engine, while other inventors devised power-driven textile equipment.

The Enlightenment established intellect as distinct from God and sought to establish a rational basis for life. Descartes paused in his scientific work to proclaim, "I think; therefore, I am."

This period included the Baroque art movement. Baroque art featured grandeur and included the works of Rembrandt. Rubens, Bach, and Handel were great Baroque artists and composers.

The impact of the Enlightenment can be seen in the theories of Jean Jacques Rousseau who believed that common people should have a wider role in their own government. The centralized mercantilist theory was attacked by economist Adam Smith and others, who believed in free trade and the law of supply and demand.

ROMANOV RUSSIA

The Romanovs ruled Russia from about 1613 until 1917. From 1682 until 1725 the giant (7 feet tall), driven, and cruel Peter the Great ruled Russia. He used secret police to identify and punish those who opposed him. Despite his bizarre behavior, he spent time among the common people. He modernized and westernized Russia. He built St. Petersburg as a modern western city with slave labor. Many of the companies begun during his reign were controlled by the state. After six short-lived emperors, Catherine the Great (1762–1796) continued the modernization of Russia.

THE FRENCH REVOLUTION

King Louis XVI was on the throne as France became bankrupt in the late 1780s. Food was in short supply and food prices were inflated as the Third Estate (commoners) asserted themselves and took over the national assembly. They forced recognition by the king.

Galvanized by food shortages, repression, and unemployment, Parisian workers armed themselves and stormed the fortress Bastille on July 14, 1789. The French Revolution was born. After two years of fighting and intrigue, the newly formed national assembly condemned and executed Louis XVI and Marie "let them eat cake" Antoinette in 1793.

Robespierre emerged to direct a Committee of Public Safety, which conducted the Reign of Terror from 1793–1794. During the Reign thousands were summarily found guilty of real or imagined wrongs and guillotined. Robespierre was executed under orders from the National Convention on July 28, 1794.

NAPOLEON

Napoleon was born in 1769, and while in Paris in 1795, he helped put down a royalist uprising. He was also there to lead the overthrow of the government in 1799 and soon become the dictator (Consul for Life in 1801) of France. Napoleon was a brilliant, charismatic man and a true military genius. He led France on an unsuccessful quest for an expanded empire from 1799 to 1815.

However, he was unable to complete his militaristic expansion successfully. He was deposed and exiled to Elba only to return to "meet his Waterloo" at the battle of that name. He was exiled again and died on the island of St. Helena in 1821.

The Quadruple Alliance (Austria, England, Prussia, and Russia), who had defeated Napoleon, reached a settlement that encircled France. This settlement maintained a balance of power in Europe until Germany was unified 60 years later.

THE INDUSTRIAL REVOLUTION (1750–1850)

Increased population, cheap labor, available capital, raw materials, and industrial skill led to the beginning of the Industrial Revolution in England about 1750. Textiles and metal industries were the first to develop. These industries were helped along by the steamboat and the locomotive. During the early 1800s this industrialism moved to the continent.

The Industrial Revolution produced a new class of factory workers. These workers did not benefit from the Industrial Revolution until late in the 1800s. Until then, work had centered around the family, but all that changed. Generally speaking, men worked outside the home, and women worked in the home.

ROMANTICISM (1790–1850)

Romanticism had its biggest impact from the late 1700s through 1850. This movement stressed nature, feelings, personal freedom and humanitarianism. The names of many Romantic writers, painters, and composers are familiar to us. Some writers were Balzac, Burns, Browning, Byron, Coleridge, Cooper, Dostoyevsky, Dumas, Emerson, Longfellow, Poe, and Thoreau. Painters included Goya and Delacorte. Composers of the era were Brahms, Chopin, and Schubert.

Romanticism broadened thought and led to a number of different philosophies and approaches to living. Liberalism celebrated the individual and proclaimed that individuals have certain natural rights. Conservatism proposed that some people were better prepared to rule and lead than others. Nationalism stressed loyalty to a group or country rather than the individual. Socialism expressed the view that all should receive their share of a nation's wealth. Marxism developed by Marx and Engels was a popular form of socialism. Marxism is described in *Das Kapital* and *Communist Manifesto*.

A series of revolutions swept Europe in 1820, 1825, and 1830, culminating in 1848. Italy and Germany were unified as an aftermath of these revolutions.

EUROPEAN DEVELOPMENTS

CRIMEAN WAR

The year 1854 found Great Britain and France allied with the Turks against Russia in the Crimean War. It was this war that sparked the writing of "The Charge of the Light Brigade" and featured the nursing work of Florence Nightingale and her disciples. The war ended in 1856 with the Peace of Paris.

CAPITALISM, MARXISM, AND ANARCHISM

Following the revolutions of 1848, capitalism and communism competed for economic supremacy in Europe. Anarchists believed that there should be no authority. They used violent means to further their ends.

NEW IMPERIALISM

Beginning about 1870, Europe was producing more goods than it could consume. So European powers began to vie for colonies. Much of the early activity focused on Africa. By 1914 Belgium, Britain, France, Germany, Italy, Portugal, and Spain controlled about 90 percent of Africa, with Britain and then France controlling the most territory.

During this time the German Empire developed under Bismarck. In Great Britain the House of Commons reduced the power of the House of Lords. The Third French Republic survived infighting and socialist challenges and solidified support of the majority of the French populace.

This period also saw the emergence of new and revolutionary ideas. Freud established psychoanalytic psychology, Einstein presented his theory of relativity, and Darwin wrote the *Origin of the Species*.

OTHER SOCIAL STUDIES TOPICS

Other social studies topics may also be the subject of test questions. These topics, which include anthropology, government/politics, geography, and graph interpretation, are discussed next.

OTHER SOCIAL STUDIES TOPICS REVIEW QUIZ

This quiz uses a short answer format to help you find out what you know. The quiz results direct you to the portions of the chapter you should read.

This quiz will also help focus your thinking, and these questions and answers are a good review in themselves. It's not important to answer all these questions correctly, and don't be concerned if you miss many of them.

The answers are found immediately after the quiz. It's to your advantage not to look at them until you have completed the quiz. Once you have completed and corrected the review quiz, use the answer checklist to decide which sections of the review to study.

Write the answers in the space provided or on a separate sheet of paper.

1. What do physical anthropologists study?

2. What are the three primary determinants of culture?

3. What is the relationship of the legislative and executive branches in a parliamentary government?

4. What percentage of United States Representatives are elected every two years?

5. What percent of the popular vote is required to elect the president of the United States?

ANSWER CHECKLIST

Other Social Studies Review

The answers are organized by review sections. Check your answers. If you miss any question in a section, check the box and review that section.

❑ *Anthropology, page 163*
1. the evolution of primates including humans
2. material aspects of life—food, energy, and technology

❑ *Government and Political Science, page 164*
3. The executive branch is subordinate to the legislative branch

❑ *United States Government, page 164*
4. 100 percent
5. There is no set percent. Presidents are not elected by popular vote.

❑ *Interpreting Maps, page 166*

ANTHROPOLOGY

Anthropology is a holistic study of humans. Anthropologists study the biology, culture, and development of human species and communities. Anthropologists rely on field work, fossils, and observation in their work.

Physical Anthropology

Physical anthropology is concerned with the evolution of primates and humans. Physical anthropologists are seeking to trace the evolution of humans through human fossils. Louis Leakey is probably the most famous physical anthropologist. He discovered the three-million-year-old remains of "Lucy" at the Olduvai gorge in Africa.

Biological Anthropologists

Human biology is another focus of anthropologists. Biological anthropologists study the genetic development of primates and humans. They seek to identify the cause of human diseases such as high blood pressure. Other biological anthropologists such as Jane Goodall study the behavior of apes and other primates. These anthropologists have found that primates can use tools and communicate.

Cultural Anthropologists

Cultural anthropology is concerned with the social systems, customs, languages, and religion of existing cultures. Cultural anthropologists classify cultures as patrilineal, matrilineal, or bilateral depending on whether the family roots are traced through the father, mother, or both father and mother.

Anthropological Development

The simplest cultures are associated with nomadic hunter-gatherers. About 13,000 years ago, humans began domesticating livestock and raising crops. More stable communities developed as cultures became more stationary. Then these communities became linked together to form tribes with a shared tradition (religion). Political systems developed, and leaders or chiefs of these tribes appeared. Some of these tribes developed unevenly into kingdoms with a shared language. Occasionally a kingdom would develop into a civilization with different hierarchies of individuals.

More advanced cultures featured complex religious systems, important priests, and codified religious rules. Early cultures typically had a single religious system. Until recently there was a close relationship between religion and government.

Most cultural anthropologists agree that the primary determinants of culture are the material conditions of life—food, energy sources, and technology. Geography and climate have a tremendous influence on these factors. Ideas, movements, and personalities also have a significant impact on a culture.

GOVERNMENT AND POLITICAL SCIENCE

Government and political science are studies of the ways governments are organized and how governments function.

There are a number of ways to classify governments. Aristotle placed governments in one of three categories:

Democracy—government by the populace

Aristocracy—government by a few

Monarchy—government by one

Current classifications of government include the following.

Parliamentary, or Cabinet (England)—The executive branch is subordinate to the legislative branch.

Presidential (United States)—The executive branch is independent of the legislative branch, although some executive actions require legislative action.

Federal States (United States)—The power of the central government is limited by rights of the states.

Unitary (England)—The states are subordinate to the central government.

Dictatorship (Nazi Germany)—Rule by a single individual or a small group in which the needs of the state are generally more important than the needs of the people.

Republic (United States)—Rule through the will of the people within which the needs of the people are generally more important than the needs of the state.

UNITED STATES GOVERNMENT

The United States government is based on the Constitution of the United States. The Constitution can be amended by a two-thirds vote of both houses of Congress with concurrence of three-fourths of the state legislatures. The first ten amendments to the Constitution are called the Bill of Rights. Other important amendments provided protection by due process of law, abolished slavery, and gave women the right to vote.

The Constitution established a federal form of government. States have rights and hold all power not expressly granted to the federal government.

The federal government of the United States has three branches: legislative, executive, and judicial. The framers of the Constitution established these as three complementary, overlapping branches to provide checks and balances in the governmental process.

Legislative

The Congress of the United States consists of the Senate and the House of Representatives. The 100 senators, two from each state, serve for six years with one-third standing for election every two years. The 435 representatives in the House are partitioned among the states according to population. Every state must have at least one representative. All representatives stand for election every two years.

Measures passed by a majority of Congress present and voting are sent to the president as a bill. The president may sign the bill into law or veto it. If the bill is vetoed, the Congress may still make the bill law by a two-thirds vote of each body.

Executive

The president and the vice president are the elected heads of the federal government. Their election takes place through a cumbersome process in which electors are chosen from each state by popular vote. These electors then gather in an Electoral College to cast votes for the president and vice president.

The president is Commander-in-Chief of the Armed Forces, but only Congress has the power to declare war. The president also has the right to negotiate treaties. Two-thirds of the Senate must vote to ratify any treaties. Treaties are null and void without this ratification.

Judicial

The Constitution established the Supreme Court as the final arbiter of whether a law adhered to the Constitution. Other federal courts established by Congress can also rule on a law's constitutionality.

Supreme Court justices are nominated by the president. A majority of the Senate must consent to any Supreme Court nomination.

Checks and Balances

The three branches of government provide adequate checks and balances. There are ways to remove presidents, legislators, and judges from office.

READING AND INTERPRETING MAPS

The items below are the sorts of map questions you might find on the CSET.

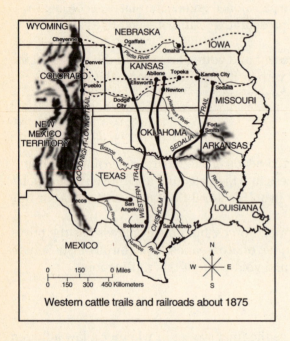

Western cattle trails and railroads about 1875

1. Which cattle trail goes from San Antonio to Abilene?
   (A) Chisholm
   (B) Sedalia
   (C) Goodnight-Loving
   (D) Western Trail

2. Which cattle trail crosses the Pecos River?
   (A) Chisholm
   (B) Sedalia
   (C) Goodnight-Loving
   (D) Western Trail

3. Which cattle trail passes through the fewest states?
   (A) Chisholm
   (B) Sedalia
   (C) Goodnight-Loving
   (D) Western Trail

4. About how far is it by train from Sedalia to Abilene?
   (A) 150 miles
   (B) 300 miles
   (C) 450 miles
   (D) 600 miles

5. The Goodnight-Loving Trail turns north after Pecos because
   (A) that's the way to Denver
   (B) cattle drovers did not want to go into Mexico
   (C) of the mountains
   (D) of the Rio Grande River

6. Which state contains the final railhead for the largest number of cattle trails?
   (A) Texas
   (B) Kansas
   (C) Oklahoma
   (D) Nebraska

7. If drovers move a herd of cattle about 25 kilometers per day, about how many days would it take to move a herd from Fort Smith to Sedalia on the Sedalia Trail?
   (A) 8
   (B) 16
   (C) 24
   (D) 32

READING AND INTERPRETING MAPS

ANSWERS EXPLAINED

1. **A** Find San Antonio in southern Texas and trace the Chisholm Trail to Abilene, Kansas. Notice that the trail splits as it gets into Kansas.

2. **C** The Pecos River flows through Pecos in southwest Texas. You can trace the Goodnight-Loving Trail across the river.

3. **A** The Chisholm Trail passes through just three states, while the other four trails pass through at least four states. Notice that the trails go generally south to north while the railroads go generally east to west.

4. **B** Use the scale at the bottom of the page to see that the distance is about 300 miles. The scale shows miles on the top and kilometers on the bottom.

5. **C** The map shows that the Goodnight-Loving Trail turns north because of the mountains.

6. **B** Two trails have railheads in Kansas, at Dodge City, and at Abilene.

7. **B** Use the kilometer scale to find that it is about 400 kilometers from Fort Smith to Sedalia. Divide 400 by 25 to find that it would take about 16 days to make the trip.

HISTORY AND SOCIAL STUDIES TARGETED PRACTICE ITEMS

These items will help you practice for the real CSET. These items have the same form and test the same material as the CSET items and test material. The items you encounter on the CSET may have a different emphasis and may be more complete.

Instructions

Mark your answers on the sheet provided below. Complete the items in 20 minutes or less. Correct your answer sheet using the answers on page 173.

1 Ⓐ Ⓑ Ⓒ Ⓓ	9 Ⓐ Ⓑ Ⓒ Ⓓ	17 Ⓐ Ⓑ Ⓒ Ⓓ	25 Ⓐ Ⓑ Ⓒ Ⓓ	33 Ⓐ Ⓑ Ⓒ Ⓓ
2 Ⓐ Ⓑ Ⓒ Ⓓ	10 Ⓐ Ⓑ Ⓒ Ⓓ	18 Ⓐ Ⓑ Ⓒ Ⓓ	26 Ⓐ Ⓑ Ⓒ Ⓓ	34 Ⓐ Ⓑ Ⓒ Ⓓ
3 Ⓐ Ⓑ Ⓒ Ⓓ	11 Ⓐ Ⓑ Ⓒ Ⓓ	19 Ⓐ Ⓑ Ⓒ Ⓓ	27 Ⓐ Ⓑ Ⓒ Ⓓ	35 Ⓐ Ⓑ Ⓒ Ⓓ
4 Ⓐ Ⓑ Ⓒ Ⓓ	12 Ⓐ Ⓑ Ⓒ Ⓓ	20 Ⓐ Ⓑ Ⓒ Ⓓ	28 Ⓐ Ⓑ Ⓒ Ⓓ	36 Ⓐ Ⓑ Ⓒ Ⓓ
5 Ⓐ Ⓑ Ⓒ Ⓓ	13 Ⓐ Ⓑ Ⓒ Ⓓ	21 Ⓐ Ⓑ Ⓒ Ⓓ	29 Ⓐ Ⓑ Ⓒ Ⓓ	37 Ⓐ Ⓑ Ⓒ Ⓓ
6 Ⓐ Ⓑ Ⓒ Ⓓ	14 Ⓐ Ⓑ Ⓒ Ⓓ	22 Ⓐ Ⓑ Ⓒ Ⓓ	30 Ⓐ Ⓑ Ⓒ Ⓓ	38 Ⓐ Ⓑ Ⓒ Ⓓ
7 Ⓐ Ⓑ Ⓒ Ⓓ	15 Ⓐ Ⓑ Ⓒ Ⓓ	23 Ⓐ Ⓑ Ⓒ Ⓓ	31 Ⓐ Ⓑ Ⓒ Ⓓ	39 Ⓐ Ⓑ Ⓒ Ⓓ
8 Ⓐ Ⓑ Ⓒ Ⓓ	16 Ⓐ Ⓑ Ⓒ Ⓓ	24 Ⓐ Ⓑ Ⓒ Ⓓ	32 Ⓐ Ⓑ Ⓒ Ⓓ	40 Ⓐ Ⓑ Ⓒ Ⓓ

1. In California, the Mexican era ended about what date?
   (A) The battle of the Alamo
   (B) The signing of the Declaration of Independence
   (C) 1877
   (D) 1846

2. The primary impact of early colonization on the North American continent was that
   (A) more than half of the indigenous population died from disease.
   (B) trade goods were available for shipment back to Europe.
   (C) religiously oppressed minorities came in large numbers to North America.
   (D) England expanded the British Empire to include North America.

3. In which region of the United States did Algonquin-speaking people live?

4. Which quotation is attributed to the Nez Percé Indian Chief Joseph?
   (A) "The white man covers the land like the buffalo."
   (B) "We wanted only food—not war."
   (C) "I will fight no more—forever."
   (D) "Your prison can hold my body but not my spirit."

5. Who was the first European to explore what is now California?
   (A) Juan Rodriguez Cabillero
   (B) Sir Francis Drake
   (C) Antonio de Mendoza
   (D) Herman Cortes

6. What impact did the Russian Revolution have on World War I?
   (A) The Russian Revolution had no impact because it occurred much earlier than World War I.
   (B) The Russian Revolution had no impact because the fighting was in Europe.
   (C) The Russian Revolution had an impact because Russia left the war.
   (D) The Russian Revolution had an impact because it was a cause of World War I.

7. President Hoover's approach to the Depression can best be characterized in the following way.
   (A) He acted immediately to establish work and relief programs.
   (B) He acted immediately by making loan programs available to the unemployed.
   (C) He acted slowly but imposed strict rules that stabilized the stock market.
   (D) He acted slowly but established a program that loaned money to employers.

8. What was the intent of Lincoln's Emancipation Proclamation?
   (A) To free all slaves
   (B) To free slaves, but not in Washington D.C.
   (C) To free slaves in the confederate states
   (D) To free immediately all slaves who fought for the North and all other slaves at war's end.

9. What was the federal government's reaction to management and unions during the Pullman and Anthracite strikes in the late 1800s and early 1900s?
   (A) The government was even handed in the Pullman and Anthracite strikes.
   (B) The government favored management in both the Pullman strike and the Anthracite strike.
   (C) The government favored the unions in the Pullman strike and management in the Anthracite strike.
   (D) The government favored management in the Pullman strike and unions in the Anthracite strike.

10. What happened to the English soldiers who fired on colonial protesters, killing five including Crispus Attucks, during the Boston Massacre?
    (A) They returned to England before they could be tried for the crime.
    (B) They were defended by colonial patriots including John Adams.
    (C) They were found guilty but were freed by English soldiers dressed as colonials.
    (D) They were acquitted primarily because Crispus Attucks was African American.

11. In the debate during the late 1700s over a stronger versus a weaker federal government, which group took the position for a weaker federal government?

(A) The Federalists
(B) The Jeffersonians
(C) The Whigs
(D) The Hamiltonians

12. Which of the following denotes the activity that separates prehistoric from historic times?
    (A) Use of tools
    (B) Use of fire
    (C) Writing on clay tablets
    (D) Use of the wheel

13. Which South American civilization featured human sacrifice?
    (A) Aztec
    (B) Incan
    (C) Manchu
    (D) Mayan

14. What was Robespierre's role during the French Revolution?
    (A) He was an advisor to Marie Antoinette and a defender of the throne who opposed the Reign of Terror.
    (B) He headed the Committee of Public Safety which conducted the Reign of Terror.
    (C) He was an advisor to Napoleon and in this role reported to Napoleon about the Reign of Terror.
    (D) He headed the storming of the Bastille but later opposed the excesses of the Reign of Terror.

15. How were the negotiations about the Common Market concluded?
    (A) The United States was accepted as a provisional member of the Common Market.
    (B) Britain and Western Europe agreed to form a Common Market.
    (C) A Common Market including England, Western Europe, China and Russia was established.
    (D) The Common Market was denied most favored nation status by the United States.

16. What people conquered most of South Africa between 1816 and 1850?
    (A) The British
    (B) The Dutch
    (C) The Bantu
    (D) The Zulu

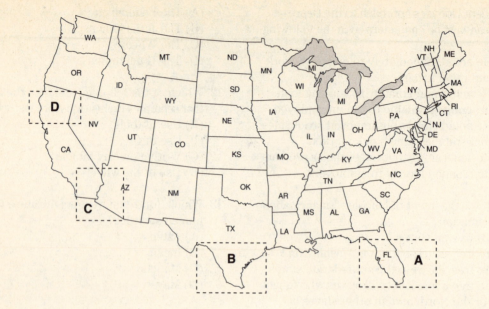

17. Which Allied leaders met at Potsdam in 1945?
    (A) Churchill, de Gaulle, Roosevelt, Stalin
    (B) Churchill, de Gaulle, Truman, Stalin
    (C) Churchill, Truman, Stalin
    (D) Churchill, Roosevelt, Stalin

18. For religious guidance a person of Islamic faith is most likely to turn to
    (A) the Bible.
    (B) the Koran.
    (C) the Rubaiyat.
    (D) the Mahabarata.

19. Which of the following led to the great schism of the Catholic church?
    (A) establishment of Constantinople as the Eastern capital of the Roman Empire
    (B) establishment by Queen Elizabeth I of the Protestant Church of England
    (C) conversion of the Emperor Constantine and (St.) Augustine to Catholicism
    (D) nailing by Martin Luther of his *95 Theses* to the Wittenberg Church door

20. During which of the following conflicts involving England did the nursing efforts of Florence Nightingale become famous?
    (A) American Revolutionary War
    (B) Crimean War
    (C) World War I
    (D) World War II

21. The Manifest Destiny of the United States refers primarily to acquiring lands
    (A) north of the Mason-Dixon line.
    (B) south of the Mason-Dixon line.
    (C) east of the Mississippi.
    (D) west of the Mississippi.

22. The main effect of the Treaty of Utrecht in 1742 was that
    (A) France lost North American possessions to England.
    (B) Spanish Empire was partitioned.
    (C) Britain recognized the United States after the Revolutionary War.
    (D) Holland and Switzerland were officially formed.

23. In an election of the president of the United States, a candidate who receives the most popular votes for the entire country
    (A) wins the election because he or she receives the most electoral votes.
    (B) wins the election even if he or she does not receive the most electoral votes.
    (C) wins the election because he or she receives the most popular votes.
    (D) wins the election only if he or she receives the most electoral votes.

24. Which of the four lettered areas on the map above of the United States has the highest daily temperatures?
    (A) A
    (B) B
    (C) C
    (D) D

25. Which of the following shows the correct order of the listed events in United States history?

    I. Reconstruction
    II. Sherman's March to the Sea
    III. the Gettysburg Address
    IV. approval of the XIII Amendment

    (A) I, II, III, IV
    (B) II, III, I, IV
    (C) II, I, III, IV
    (D) IV, II, III, I

26. Say that Company A and Company B try to raise money by selling bonds to the public. Which of the following could cause the interest rate for Company A's bonds to be much higher than the rates for Company B's bonds?
    (A) The bonds for Company A have a higher risk.
    (B) The bonds for Company B have a higher risk.
    (C) The management of Company A wants to reward its investors.
    (D) The management of company B wants to reward its investors.

27. When Julius Caesar uttered the words "et tu Brute,"
    (A) he was talking to his collaborator, Brutus.
    (B) he was talking to his assassin, Brutus.
    (C) he was preparing Brutus to become his second in command.
    (D) he was preparing Brutus for fateful days to come in the Ides of May.

28. "The cause of liberty becomes a mockery if the price to be paid is the wholesale destruction of those who are to enjoy it."

    The quote above from Mohandas Gandhi is best reflected in which of the following statements about the American civil rights movement?
    (A) Bus boycotts are not effective because boycotters are punished.
    (B) Nonviolence and civil disobedience are the best approach to protest.
    (C) Desegregation laws were a direct result of freedom marches.
    (D) America will never be free as long as minorities are oppressed.

29. Anthropology is a holistic study of human beings. Which of the following types of anthropology is concerned with tracing the evolution of primates?
    (A) Biological Anthropology
    (B) Cultural Anthropology
    (C) Physical Anthropology
    (D) Political Anthropology

30. During the Spanish-American War in the late 1890s, the battleship *Maine* was sunk in the harbor at
    (A) Boston.
    (B) Havana.
    (C) New York.
    (D) Madrid.

31. In the United States, the Senate and the House of Representatives combine to form
    (A) the Legislature.
    (B) the Parliament.
    (C) the Congress.
    (D) the judiciary.

32. The way in which humans learn to live in different habitats is called
    (A) acculturation.
    (B) adaptation.
    (C) climatization.
    (D) imprinting.

33. Which of the following would you turn to for a primary source of information about World War II?
    (A) The film *The Longest Day*
    (B) A handwritten log by the Captain of the *Lusitania*
    (C) An essay on war by George Sherman
    (D) Letters written by an Italian soldier fighting in North Africa to his sister in Sicily

34. Which of the following is the best definition of representative democracy?
    (A) Political and social equality exist in spirit and in practice.
    (B) The various states have rights and power not expressly assigned to the national government.
    (C) The populace of individual regions elect those who will represent them.
    (D) A set of checks and balances exists among the legislative, judicial, and executive branches of government.

35. What is the connection among the following items?

    • FDIC
    • Tennessee Valley Authority
    • Civilian Conservation Corps
    • Agricultural Adjustment Act

    (A) They are all programs enacted by President Herbert Hoover.
    (B) They are all federal works programs.
    (C) They all resulted from World War II.
    (D) They are all programs enacted by President Franklin Roosevelt.

36. What event is often identified as the cause of the American Revolution?
    (A) The death of Catherine the Great
    (B) The defeat of Napoleon at Waterloo
    (C) The French Revolution
    (D) The Townshend Acts

37. All the following happened in full or part as a result of World War I EXCEPT
    (A) World War II.
    (B) the Depression.
    (C) the growth of the Nazi Party.
    (D) the Yalta Agreement.

38. Go west young man.

    Which of the following items is best characterized by this statement?
    (A) The age of exploration
    (B) Manifest destiny
    (C) Zionism
    (D) The Peace Corps

39. The cause of liberty becomes a mockery if the price to be paid is the wholesale destruction of those who are to enjoy liberty.

    The quote from Mohandas Gandhi is best reflected in which of the following statements about the American civil rights movement?
    (A) Bus boycotts are not effective because innocent boycotters are punishes.
    (B) Nonviolence and civil disobedience are the best approaches to protest.
    (C) Desegregation laws were a direct result of freedom marches.
    (D) America will never be free as long as minorities are oppressed.

Question 40 is based on this map.

40. You can deduce from the map that teachers' salaries are probably lowest in
    (A) Georgia, Alabama, and Idaho.
    (B) South Dakota, Tennessee, and Oklahoma.
    (C) Kentucky, Louisiana, and New Mexico.
    (D) Florida, Hawaii, and Iowa.

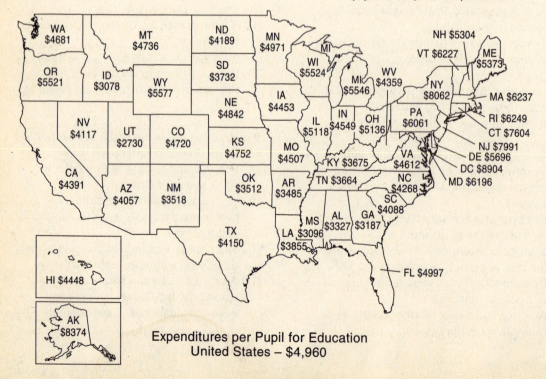

Expenditures per Pupil for Education
United States – $4,960

TARGETED TEST ANSWERS EXPLAINED

1. **D** American settlement in California preceded the Civil War. This settlement brought an end to the Mexican era.

2. **A** The mass death of indigenous Americans began as soon as the first colonists arrived.

3. **A** The Algonquin-speaking tribes included the Iroquois Federation and other Northeast Indians.

4. **C** Choice C is correct.

5. **A** Cabillero explored southern California. Sir Frances Drake came later. Mendoza and Cortes never explored California.

6. **C** Withdrawal from the war had been a revolutionary promise. Russia left the war and gave up vast expanses of land and resources.

7. **D** Hoover adopted a hands off policy and only attempted a "trickle down" approach by making money available to employers.

8. **C** The Emancipation Proclamation applied only to slaves in confederate states.

9. **D** The United States government had been pro business until Roosevelt came into office and sided with the strikers in the Anthracite strike.

10. **B** They were successfully defended by patriots, including John Adams, on the grounds that they acted in self defense.

11. **B** The Jeffersonians favored a weaker federal government, and they were opposed by the Federalists (Hamiltonians) who favored a stronger federal government.

12. **C** Introduction of writing separates prehistoric from historic times, and the first symbols were cuneiform symbols.

13. **A** The Aztecs who inhabited the area around Mexico City featured human sacrifice.

14. **B** Robespierre was executed for his role as head of the Committee on Public Safety, which arranged the deaths of over 20,000 people.

15. **B** The Common Market includes only England and European countries.

16. **D** The Zulu were dominant in South Africa in the early 1800s.

17. **C** Roosevelt died just months before. De Gaulle never participated in this conference.

18. **B** Those of the Islamic faith consider the Koran to be the direct word of God.

19. **A** The great schism of the Catholic church refers to the division of the church into eastern and western churches. This schism was the direct result of the establishment of an eastern capital of the Roman Empire.

20. **B** It was during the Crimean War, which pitted Great Britain, France, and Turkey as allies against Russia, that Florence Nightingale became famous.

21. **D** The Manifest Destiny of the United States referred to a country that spread from the Atlantic Ocean to Pacific Ocean. Most eastern lands were under American control, so lands west of the Mississippi had to be acquired for this country to realize its manifest destiny.

22. **B** As a result of the Treaty of Utrecht the Spanish Empire was partitioned.

23. **D** In presidential elections, each state has a certain number of electoral votes based on that state's population. The candidate who wins the popular vote for each state gets those electors. So it is possible for a candidate to win the national popular vote and not win the election.

24. **C** This section of the Southwest, which includes Death Valley, is a desert region. The highest temperatures are recorded here.

25. **B** Sherman's March to the Sea occurred during the Civil War followed by the Gettysburg Address. Reconstruction and then the XIII Amendment followed the war.

26. **A** Companies only pay higher rates to attract investors. The main reason one company pays a higher rate than another company is that their bonds are riskier.

27. **B** Julius Caesar supposedly spoke the words "and you, Brutus" to his "friend" Brutus who had joined others in assassinating Julius Caesar during the Ides (middle days) of March.

28. **B** The quote supports the nonviolent, nondestructive approach to protest supported by Gandhi.

29. **C** Physical anthropologists study the evolution of human beings. Louis and Mary Leakey are probably the most famous physical anthropologists.

30. **B** The Spanish American War was fought in Cuba and the Philippines.

31. **C** These two legislative bodies combine to form the Congress

32. **B** Adaptation is correct. Acculturation refers to adopting a culture, and climatization refers to adapting to a particular climate.

33. **D** Choices B, C, and D are all primary sources. Only D refers to World War II.

34. **C** Representative democracy means that people elect others to represent them.

35. **D** These are just a few of the measures FDR implemented during the Depression.

36. **D** These taxation acts moved many colonists to revolution.

37. **B** The Depression occurred some 15 to 20 years after World War I.

38. **B** The Manifest Destiny of the United States was to stretch from ocean to ocean.

39. **B** Gandhi believed in and "popularized" non-violence.

40. **A** These states have the lowest per pupil expenditures.

PART 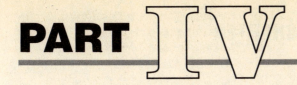IV

Subtest II Review

5 SCIENCE

TEST INFO BOX

26 Multiple Choice items   Half of Subtest II items
2 Constructed Response items   Half of Subtest II items

SCIENCE ITEMS

Science multiple choice items look like this.

During which period did the dinosaurs appear on earth?

(A) Cambrian
(B) Carboniferous
(C) Triassic
(D) Tertiary

Science short answer items look like this.

USING THIS CHAPTER

This chapter prepares you to take the Science part of the CSET. Choose one of these approaches.

I want all the Science review I can get.

❑ Skip the Science Review Quiz and read the entire review section.
❑ Take the Science Review Quiz on page 177.
❑ Correct the Review Quiz and reread the indicated parts of the review.
❑ Go over the Interpreting Graphs items and the Science Terms glossary on pages 212–216.
❑ Complete the Science Multiple Choice Practice Questions on page 217.

I want a thorough Science review.

❑ Take the Science Review Quiz on page 177.
❑ Correct the Review Quiz and reread the indicated parts of the review.
❑ Go over the Interpreting Graphs items and the Science Terms glossary on pages 212–216.
❑ Complete the Science Multiple Choice Practice Questions on page 217.

I want a quick Science review.

❑ Take and correct the Science Review Quiz on page 177.
❑ Go over the Interpreting Graphs items and the Science Terms glossary on pages 212–216.
❑ Complete the Science Multiple Choice Practice Questions on page 217.

I want to practice Science questions.

❑ Go over the Interpreting Graphs items and the Science Terms glossary on pages 212–216.
❑ Complete the Science Multiple Choice Practice Questions on page 217.

SCIENCE REVIEW QUIZ

This quiz uses a short answer format to help you find out what you know about the Science topics reviewed in this chapter. The quiz results direct you to the portions of the chapter you should read.

This quiz will also help focus your thinking about Science, and these questions and answers are a good review in themselves. It's not important to answer all these questions correctly, and don't be concerned if you miss many of them.

The answers are found immediately after the quiz. It's to your advantage not to look at them until you have completed the quiz. Once you have completed and corrected this review quiz, use the answer checklist to decide which sections of the review to study.

Write the answers in the space provided or on a separate sheet of paper.

1. What name is given to the cells that make up most living things?

2. Name the two methods of cell reproduction.

3. What does photosynthesis create?

4. What do cells create when they respire?

5. Where are genes located?

6. What type of life could have developed spontaneously in earth's early atmosphere?

7. What is the name of the very first cells to develop?

8. What is the dominant invertebrate animal species?

9. Which animal has the most striking genetic similarity to humans?

10. What types of organisms make up the Protistae kingdom?

11. What three main functions do bacteria perform?

12. What plant group includes the most deciduous trees?

13. What are the four stages of complete metamorphosis?

14. What part of the circulatory system carries blood back to the heart?

15. What part of a cell transmits signals?

16. What does the endocrine system consist of?

17. What function do granulocytes perform in the immune system?

18. What do ecologists study?

19. What survival options do subdominant individuals have?

20. How do plants and animals balance the carbon cycle?

21. What do cosmologists study?

22. About how long does it take for light to travel from the North Star to the earth?

23. What causes seasons on earth?

     _____

     _____

24. What percent of earth's atmosphere is nitrogen? _____ oxygen? _____

25. About what percent of the earth's surface is covered by water?

     _____

     _____

26. What is the temperature in the earth's inner core?

     _____

     _____

27. In which direction does Coriolis force pull air in the Southern Hemisphere?

     _____

     _____

28. About what percent of sea water is salt?

     _____

     _____

29. How were the earth's continents arranged during the Permian period about 280,000,000 years ago?

     _____

     _____

30. How are metamorphic rocks formed?

     _____

     _____

31. What subatomic particles do atoms consist of?

     _____

     _____

32. How can matter be destroyed?

     _____

     _____

33. When do chemical reactions occur?

     _____

     _____

34. Does a body's mass vary?

     _____

     _____

35. What two factors determine a body's velocity?

     _____

     _____

36. How does Newton's Second Law describe the relationship between mass and acceleration?

     _____

     _____

37. What type of energy does fuel in a car's gas tank represent?

     _____

     _____

38. What must happen for work to occur?

     _____

     _____

39. What method of transfer moves heat from a heating pad to a person's back?

     _____

     _____

40. What determines a wave's frequency?

     _____

     _____

41. What three things may happen when light strikes a surface?

     _____

     _____

42. Through which medium does sound travel most quickly?

     _____

     _____

43. What charges may an object possess?

     _____

     _____

44. What does an ampere measure?

     _____

     _____

45. Where is the magnetic North Pole?

     _____

     _____

46. Name the three types of energy radioactive material can release.

     _____

     _____

47. What is the advantage of nuclear fusion over nuclear fission?

     _____

     _____

ANSWER CHECKLIST

The answers are organized by review sections. Check your answers. If you miss any question in a section, check the box and review that section.

Life Science

Cellular Biology

❑ *Cells, page 181*
 1. eukaryotes

❑ *Reproduction, page 181*
 2. mitosis and meiosis

❑ *Photosynthesis, page 182*
 3. carbohydrates, water, and oxygen

❑ *Cell Activities, page 182*
 4. energy

❑ *Genes, page 182*
 5. Genes are located on chromosomes.

Biology of Organisms and Evolution

❑ *Evolution, page 183*
 6. early life
 7. first cells
 8. plants
 9. animals & humans

❑ *Cell Classification, page 184*
 10. single-celled eukaryotes including algae and protozoa
 11. Bacteria live on dead material, are helpful in human bodies, and function as parasites.

❑ *Plants, page 185*
 12. Anglosperms

❑ *Arthropods, page 186*
 13. egg, larva, pupa, adult

❑ *Human Biology, page 188*
 14. veins
 15. dendrites
 16. glands that secrete hormones
 17. They ingest antigens already killed by cell enzymes.

❑ *Ecology, page 193*
 18. the relationship between organisms and their ecosystems
 19. They accept a poorer habitat, give up resources, immigrate, or perish.

❑ *Life Cycles, page 194*
 20. Plants use carbon dioxide and give off oxygen. Animals use oxygen and give off carbon dioxide.

Earth and Space Science

❑ *Astronomy, page 195*
 21. the universe
 22. 300 years
 23. the tilt of the Earth's axis

❑ *Meteorology, page 199*
 27. Southeast

❑ *Oceanography, page 200*
 28. 3.5 percent (0.035)

❑ *Geology, page 201*
 29. Earth's land mass consisted of a single continent.
 30. Existing rocks are subjected to enormous pressure.

❑ *The Earth's Parts, page 201*
 24. 78 percent nitrogen, 21 percent oxygen
 25. about 75 percent
 26. 10,000° F

Physical Science

Chemistry

❑ *Atoms, page 203*
 31. protons, neutrons, and electrons

❑ *Matter, page 205*
 32. Matter cannot be destroyed; it can only be converted.

❑ *Chemical Reactions, page 206*
 33. when bonds between atoms form or break

Physics

❏ *Matter and Mass, page 206*
   34. A body's mass is constant although it varies near the speed of light.

❏ *Motion, page 206*
   35. magnitude and direction
   36. The more the mass, the less the acceleration.

❏ *Energy, page 207*
   37. potential

❏ *Work, page 208*
   38. There must be some movement.

❏ *Heat, page 208*
   39. conduction

❏ *Wave Phenomena, page 208*
   40. vibrations per second

❏ *Light, page 209*
   41. Light can be reflected, absorbed, or scattered.

❏ *Sound, page 209*
   42. solid

❏ *Electricity, page 209*
   43. positive, negative, neutral
   44. rate of current flow

❏ *Magnetism, page 210*
   45. northeastern Canada

❏ *Modern Physics and Radioactivity, page 211*
   46. alpha, beta, and gamma
   47. Fusion is much safer because it releases less radioactivity.

LIFE SCIENCE

Cells

The cell is the smallest unit of life that is capable of reproduction. There are two types of cells, prokaryotes and eukaryotes. Prokaryotes are bacteria, including cyanobacteria (previously called blue-green algae). Plant cells and animal cells are eukaryotes. In this overview we focus primarily on plant cells and animal cells.

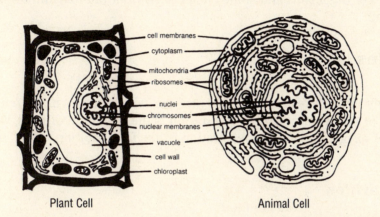

Plant Cell   Animal Cell

Plant cells and animal cells have many common components. Both types of cells have a membrane at the outer edge of the cell. The gel-like cytoplasm in the interior of the cell contains organelles (cell organs). A nucleus, the cell's "brain," is surrounded by a nuclear membrane. The nucleus contains genetic material. The Golgi apparatus packages hormone and enzyme material for plant cells. They differ from animal cells in two primary ways: plant cells have a thick cell wall outside the membrane; plant cells contain plastids, which may include chloroplasts, where photosynthesis takes place.

Reproduction

Cells reproduce in five stages. Four of these stages are called mitosis. In mitosis, a cell duplicates its own set of chromosomes. The chromosomes migrate to opposite ends of the cell. Then the cell splits, making an exact copy of itself in cytokenesis.

Prophase   MITOSIS BEGINS as the cell begins to divide.
Metaphase   Chromosomes align around the equator of the cell.
Anaphase   Sister chromosomes are formed and move toward opposite ends of the cell.
Telophase   MITOSIS ENDS as two new nuclei are formed.
Cytokinesis The cell splits into two daughter cells in the final stage of reproduction.

Prophase   Metaphase   Anaphase   Telophase   Cytokinesis

Humans reproduce sexually following the combination of sperm cells and egg cells. Meiosis creates sperm cells and egg cells, each with half the number of chromosomes (haploid) found in a human cell. When a sperm cell and egg cell combine, a single cell, zygote, is created with a complete (diploid) set of chromosomes. The zygote develops into a human.

Photosynthesis

Photosynthesis occurs primarily in green plants and uses light energy to create organic compounds. Chlorophyll in a plant's chloroplasts captures solar energy. The solar energy combines with carbon dioxide (CO_2) from the atmosphere and water (H_2O) to produce glucose (sugar). Plant photosynthesis releases oxygen (O_2) into the atmosphere. Photosynthesis also occurs in some other organisms and some bacteria. Without photosynthesis we would not have breathable air.

Cell Activities

Respiration

Cells create energy through respiration. This process, which occurs in the mitochondria, can be either aerobic or anaerobic. Aerobic respiration is the oxidation of food, which takes place in the presence of oxygen. Anaerobic respiration is like fermentation, which takes place without oxygen.

Other Cell Activities

Ingestion	Take in food
Digestion	Break down food to usable forms
Secretion	Create and release useful substances
Excretion	Eliminate waste material
Homeostasis	Maintain the cell's equilibrium

Genes

A chromosome is a rodlike structure located in the cell nucleus. Each gene occupies a specific location on one of the chromosomes. Genes carry specific bits of genetic information.

Deoxyribonucleic acid (DNA) is the genetic material tightly coiled as a chromosome. DNA provides the genetic codes that determine many traits of an organism. There are very large quantities of noncoding DNA, which does not affect the makeup of an organism.

The DNA creates ribonucleic acid (RNA). The DNA cannot leave the nucleus; RNA serves as the messenger that carries the genetic code throughout the cell.

BIOLOGY OF ORGANISMS AND EVOLUTION

Early Life

There was very little oxygen in the earth's atmosphere about 3.5 billion years ago. Research has shown that atoms can combine spontaneously in this type of environment to form molecules. This is how life may have begun on earth about 3.4 billion years ago.

Eventually these molecules linked together in complex groupings to form organisms. These earliest organisms must have been able to ingest and live on nonorganic material. Over a period of time, these organisms adapted and began using the sun's energy. When photosynthesis released oxygen into the oceans and the atmosphere, the stage was set for more advanced life forms.

First Cells

The first cells were prokaryotes (bacteria), which converted energy (respired) without oxygen (anaerobic). The next cells to develop were cyanobacterium (blue-green algae) prokaryotes, which were aerobic (created energy with oxygen) and used photosynthesis. Advanced eukaryotes developed from these primitive cells.

It took about 2.7 billion years for algae to develop. When this simple cell appeared 950 million years ago, it contained an enormous amount of DNA. This very slow process moved somewhat faster in the millennia that followed as animal and plant forms slowly emerged.

Plants

Scientists believe plants developed from algae. Algae are often found as green plankton in the ocean or living together with a fungus to form lichen. Algae reproduce by cell division and use photosynthesis to make food. Scientists also believe that mosses and ferns developed next and that many of today's plants developed from ferns. Mosses and ferns use spores to reproduce, but they still use photosynthesis to make food.

Animals

Animals developed into vertebrate (backbone) and invertebrate (no backbone) species. Mammals became the dominant vertebrate class, and insects became the dominant invertebrate class. As animals developed, they adapted to their environment. Those species that adapted best survived. This process is called natural selection. Entire species have vanished from the earth.

Mammals and dinosaurs coexisted for over 100 million years. During that time, dinosaurs were the dominant class. When dinosaurs became extinct 65 million years ago, mammals survived. Freed of dinosaurian dominance, mammals evolved into the dominant creatures they are today. Despite many years of study, it is not known what caused the dinosaurs to become extinct or why mammals survived.

Humans

Humans are in the primate (upright) family of mammals. Very primitive primates, along with other mammals, were found on earth before the dinosaurs became extinct. Modern humans demonstrate striking genetic similarities to other members of the primate group, particularly to African apes.

Scientists believe that early sapiens developed about 250,000 years ago and that modern Homo sapiens developed about 75,000 years ago.

The History of Life

Era	Period	Epoch	Approximate Beginning Date	Life Forms Originating
Cenozoic	Quaternary	Recent	10,000	Humans
		Pleistocene	2,500,000	
	Tertiary	Pilocene	12,000,000	Grazing and Meat-eating Mammals
		Miocene	26,000,000	
		Oligocene	38,000,000	
		Eocene	54,000,000	
		Paleocene	65,000,000	
Mesozoic	Cretaceous		136,000,000	Primates-Flowering Plants
	Jurassic		195,000,000	Birds
	Triassic		225,000,000	Dinosaurs-Mammals
Paleozoic	Permian		280,000,000	
	Carbonifurous — Pennsylvanian		320,000,000	Reptiles
	Mississippian		345,000,000	Ferns
	Devonian		395,000,000	Amphibians-insects
	Silurian		430,000,000	Vascular Land Plants
	Ordovician		500,000,000	Fish-Chordates
	Cambrian		570,000,000	Shellfish-Trilobites
Precambrian			(700,000,000)	Algae
			(1,500,000,000)	Eukaryotic Cells
			(3,500,000,000)	Prokaryotic Cells

CELL CLASSIFICATION

Living things are generally classified into six kingdoms. Three kingdoms are dedicated to one-celled living things (prokaryote or eukaryote). There are three kingdoms of multicelled eukaryotes based on whether nutrition is obtained through absorption, photosynthesis, or ingestion.

Single Cells

The former Moneran Kingdom is now two kingdoms—Kingdom Archaea and Kingdom Eubacteria. These two kingdoms include all prokaryotes. The organisms include bacteria and blue-green algae. These microscopic organisms are limited to respiration and reproduction.

The Protista kingdom includes all single-celled eukaryotes. These organisms include algae and protozoa. These cells have a fully functional organ system and some get their energy through photosynthesis.

Multi Cells

The Fungi kingdom includes multicelled eukaryotes that gain their nutrition through absorption. These organisms include mushrooms and are rootlike with caps and filaments.

The Plantae kingdom includes multicelled eukaryotes that gain their energy through photosynthesis. These organisms have thicker cellulose cell walls.

The Animalae kingdom includes multicelled eukaryotes that gain their nutrition through ingestion. Most of these organisms are mobile at some time in their existence.

Bacteria

Bacteria are small, single-celled organisms (prokaryotes) found everywhere in the environment. As noted already, bacteria were the earliest organisms to develop. Bacteria are classified as bacilli (rod-shaped), cocci (circular or spherical), and spirilla (coiled). Bacteria that can move "swim" with flagella.

One type of bacteria live on dead animal and vegetable material. Without the decomposition these bacteria bring, the earth would quickly be covered with dead organic material. A second type of bacteria helps humans and is often needed for regular physiological processes. The third type, parasites, harm the organisms in which they live. About 200 types of bacteria cause diseases in humans.

Viruses

A virus is a bit of genetic material surrounded by a protective coat of protein. The virus itself is lifeless, lacks the ability to reproduce by itself, and is not classified in one of the six kingdoms. Viruses cannot be seen in even the most powerful regular microscope. The smallest virus is about one millionth of a centimeter long.

Viruses are parasitic and remain a major challenge in battling infectious diseases. Once in a living cell, a virus can send its own genetic material into the cell, reproduce, and do significant damage to the host cell and the host organism.

Plants

Plants are living things that belong to the kingdom Plantae. Plants are different from animals in that plants have cells with rigid walls and chlorophyll. Plants usually do not move because they have no nervous system. There are two dominant plant groups. Angiosperms are the largest group of plants. Angiosperms have flowers and true leaves. This plant group includes trees such as oak, cherry, beech, and most other deciduous trees (shed leaves). Gymnosperms are the other type of common plant. Gymnosperms have no flowers and have needles for leaves. This plant group includes trees such as pines, spruces, firs, and most other evergreens.

Stems and stalks support the plant structure. Roots are the underground portion of a plant that gets nutrients and water from the soil. Photosynthesis takes place in a leaf, which is usually green, flat, and attached to a stem. Fruit is the mature ovary of a flower, which contains the seed. A seed may be a fertilized ovule, or less frequently a bulb or a tuber. Tubers and bulbs grow underground. A potato is a tuber; an onion is a bulb. A plant's phloem tissue brings food produced in the leaves to the rest of the plant. A plant's xylem tissue brings water and nutrients from the roots.

Flower
The flower is the reproductive unit of most plants.

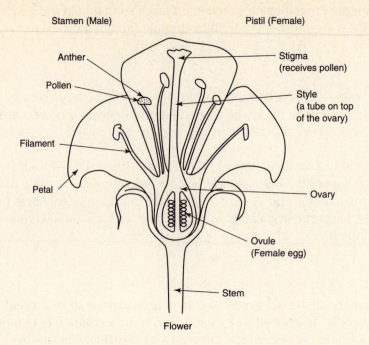

The pistil contains the female reproductive organs. The ovules (eggs) are produced in the ovary. The stamen contains male reproductive flower parts. A stamen includes the anther, which produces pollen.

Pollination

Pollen fertilizes an ovule to produce a seed. Bees, wind, and other animals usually carry the pollen. The process begins when pollen is deposited on the stigma. Pollen tubes bend down and the pollen fertilizes the ovule and the ovule becomes a seed.

Fungus

Mushrooms and other funguses belong to the Fungi Kingdom. A fungus is not a plant, and fungi do not have flowers. A fungus may live in a symbiotic relationship with a plant. Fungi use spores to reproduce, but a fungus has no chlorophyll and so it does not use photosynthesis.

ARTHROPODS

Arthropods include insects (ants, beetles, butterflies, etc.), arachnids (spiders, scorpions, etc.), and crustaceans (crabs, lobsters, etc.), among others. Insects are the dominant arthropod and a dominant animal species. However, spiders, centipedes, and millipedes, are arthropods, not insects.

Insects

Insects are cold-blooded animals. A mature insect must have three body parts (head, thorax, abdomen), six-jointed legs, two antennae, and an exoskeleton. Most insects fly, but an insect need not have wings. The diagram below shows the body parts of a winged insect.

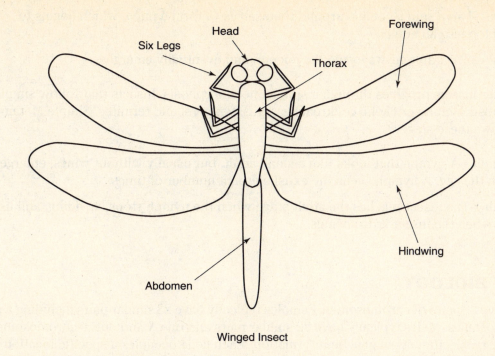

Winged Insect

Insects comprise about 25 percent of all the animals on earth. There are more different kinds of insects than there are different kinds of any other animal. Only about 5 percent of animal species are not species of insects. There are about a half-million species of beetles. About 20 percent of the total amount of animals in the world consists of ants and termites.

Metamorphosis Most insects progress through distinct changes of individual development from an egg to an adult. Over 85 percent of insects go through a complete metamorphosis, as shown in the diagram below.

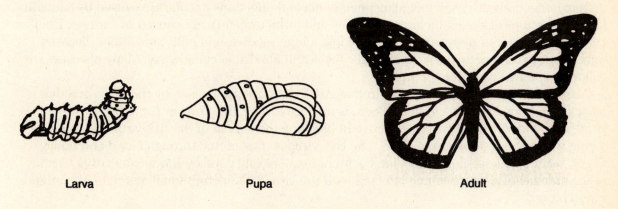

Larva   Pupa   Adult

Complete Metamorphosis

Insects that follow complete metamorphosis include ants, beetles, bees, butterflies, flies, and wasps. Complete Metamorphosis follows these stages.

Egg—The female lays an egg.

Larva—The larva that emerge from the egg do not look like the adult insect. Caterpillars and grubs are examples of larva. Larva usually shed their skin as they grow.

Pupa—Larva spin a cocoon around themselves to form a pupa, which begins to develop into an adult.

Adult—The adult grows inside the cocoon and eventually emerges.

Most other insects progress through a simple metamorphosis. Insects that follow simple metamorphosis include crickets, cockroaches, grasshoppers, and termites. Simple Metamorphosis follows these stages.

Nymph—A nymph that looks like a small adult, but usually without wings, emerges from the egg. A nymph sheds the exoskeleton a number of times.

Adult—The insect reaches the adult stage when the nymph stops shedding, and usually when the insect grows wings.

HUMAN BIOLOGY

Humans have 23 pairs of chromosomes. Females typically have 23 similar pairs including a pair of X chromosomes. Males typically have 22 similar pairs and one X and one Y chromosome.

Genes carry specific bits of genetic information. Each gene occupies a specific location on one of the chromosomes. Researchers today have identified and mapped the exact location of each gene. Scientists can even identify whether or not a person has certain hereditary traits. For example, scientists have identified a gene linked to hereditary breast cancer.

Disease

Diseases compromise the body's defense system. Most diseases can be recognized by symptoms that may include fever, aches and pains, fatigue, growths, changes in blood cell composition, and high blood pressure.

Many infectious diseases, including pneumonia and infections in cuts, are caused by bacteria. Other infectious diseases, including measles and influenza (flu), are caused by viruses. Environmental causes of disease include smoking, a high-fat diet, and pollution. Other diseases may result from genetic or occupational causes and abnormal cell growth. Many diseases are related to mental disorders or stress.

Acquired Immune Deficiency Syndrome (AIDS) is a disease caused by the HIV virus that attacks the body's immune system. There is no cure for the HIV virus or for AIDS. However, protease inhibitors have proven effective in blocking the spread of the HIV virus and interfering with the development of AIDS. The HIV virus is transmitted through blood and bodily fluids, including those fluids associated with intimate sexual contact. Intravenous drug users who share needles may become infected with the virus by injecting small amounts of contaminated blood.

Human Body Systems

Parts of the human body are made up of highly specialized cells. These cells combine to make tissue. Some tissues combine to form organs. Various organs combine in systems that enable the body to function.

Cells → Tissue → Organ → Organ System → Body

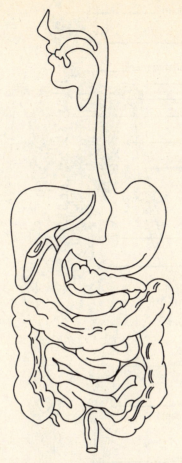

The Human Digestive System

Digestive System

Food is usually taken in through the mouth. The teeth and tongue break the food down mechanically, and the saliva begins the digestive process. When food reaches the stomach, the stomach churns to mix the food while digestive enzymes break down the proteins. The semiliquid, digested food moves into the small intestine.

Nutrients are absorbed through the small intestine into the bloodstream. Waste and undigested food move into the large intestine. The large intestine carries the waste and undigested food to the rectum.

Skeletal System

The body gets its shape from a system of bones as shown in the accompanying illustration. The bones consist of a living marrow, blood vessels, and nerves surrounded by a hard calcium exterior.

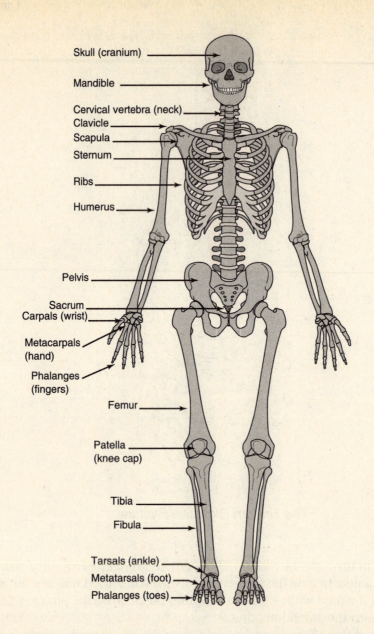

Skull (cranium)

Mandible

Cervical vertebra (neck)
Clavicle
Scapula
Sternum

Ribs

Humerus

Pelvis

Sacrum
Carpals (wrist)

Metacarpals
(hand)

Phalanges
(fingers)

Femur

Patella
(knee cap)

Tibia

Fibula

Tarsals (ankle)
Metatarsals (foot)
Phalanges (toes)

The *thorax* consists of the ribs and the sternum. The *pelvis* consists of the hip bones and the sacrum. The *femur* refers to the thighbone, the *patella* refers to the kneecap, and the *tibia* refers to the shinbone. *Tarsal* refers to the seven anklebones. Five *metatarsals* form the sole and instep of the foot.

The *clavicle* is the shoulder bone and the *scapula* is the shoulder blade. The *humerus* refers to the upper arm bone. The *radius* and *ulna* refer to the two bones that form the forearm. *Carpal* refers to the eight wrist bones and *metacarpal* refers to the five bones that form the palm.

A *joint* is where two or more bones meet. Joints are typically held together by ligaments. In most joints, cartilage between the bones absorbs the shock of the bones moving against one another.

The *cranium* refers to the skull atop the body that contains the brain. Nerves extend from within the skull, through the spinal column to the rest of the body. The *spinal column* consists of vertebra and is partitioned into cervical, thoracic, lumbar, sacrum, and coccyx sections as shown below.

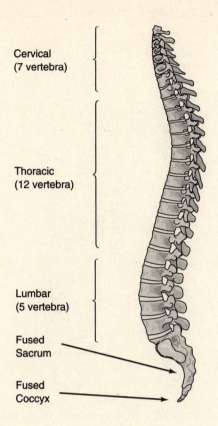

Cervical
(7 vertebra)

Thoracic
(12 vertebra)

Lumbar
(5 vertebra)

Fused
Sacrum

Fused
Coccyx

Nervous System

The nervous system consists of an incredibly complex set of nerve cells (*neurons*). Neurons receive stimuli and transmit information to and from the brain and the spinal cord. The nervous system can be partitioned into the central nervous system and the peripheral nervous system.

Central nervous system—The central nervous system consists of the *brain* and the *spinal cord.* The brain permits humans to reason and enables the human body to perform its functions. The brain's *cerebrum* takes up about three quarters of the brain's mass and is partitioned into left and right hemispheres. The temporal lobe of the cerebrum controls hearing and smell; the occipital lobe controls sight. Each side of the brain controls sensations and reactions on the other side of the body.

The *cerebral cortex* surrounds the cerebrum. The *cerebellum* controls muscle activity and is located below the cerebrum. The brain stem extends from the base of the brain to the spinal cord. The spinal cord carries impulses to and from the brain and nerves along the cord to control functions in various parts of the body.

Peripheral nervous system—The peripheral nervous system consists of *nerve cells* that exit the spinal cord and extend to all parts of the body. This system is partitioned into voluntary and involuntary (autonomic) systems. The voluntary system controls the senses and motor activity. The autonomic system controls activities not consciously controlled such as heartbeat and digestion.

Respiratory System

The respiratory system introduces oxygen into the body from the air. Air moves in the nose, down the throat (*pharynx*), down the windpipe (*trachea*), through one of two bronchial tubes and into the *lungs*. The lungs filter out oxygen and transfer oxygen to the bloodstream. Carbon dioxide is removed from the blood and is exhaled along with other gases.

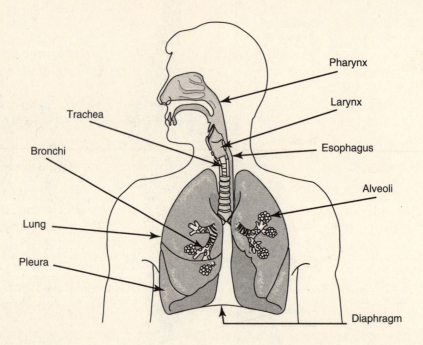

Circulatory System

The circulatory system is a vast array of blood vessels that deliver oxygen-rich blood to the body's cells and carry waste-filled blood away from these cells. A powerful heart drives this system.

The heart—The heart has a left and right side. Each side has an upper portion (atrium) and lower portion (ventricle). The heart contracts and relaxes.

> **Heart contracts.**
> Oxygen-poor blood goes from the right ventricle, through the lungs to the left atrium. Oxygen-rich blood goes from the left ventricle, through the body and back to the right atrium.

> **Heart relaxes.**
> Oxygen-rich blood enters the left atrium from the lungs.
> Oxygen-poor blood enters the right atrium from the body.

Blood vessels—*Arteries* are strong tubes that carry blood away from the heart. Arteries branch into increasingly smaller and smaller vessels and finally into very tiny *capillaries* that deliver oxygen to individual cells. At the cell level, the other capillaries start to carry oxygen-poor carbon dioxide rich blood away from the cells. These capillaries join into larger and larger *veins* and finally back to the heart.

Blood—The plasma in blood transports the red blood cells, white blood cells, and platelets throughout the body. Red blood cells carry oxygen. White blood cells are a part of the immune system. Platelets aid clotting.

Muscular System

The muscular system consists of dense fibers. There are three types of muscles: skeletal muscles, smooth muscles, and cardiac muscles. Skeletal muscles control voluntary acts such as chewing, jumping, and turning the head. Smooth muscles control involuntary activities and are found in blood vessels and the urinary tract. Cardiac muscles are highly specialized and are found only in the heart.

Endocrine System

The endocrine system is a complex system that produces and distributes hormones through the bloodstream. The system consists of glands that secrete hormones and other substances.

The **pituitary gland** is located near the brain and is the primary gland in the body. Hormones from this gland control the operation of other endocrine glands, sex glands, milk production, and pigmentation.

The **adrenal glands** are found near the kidney. Hormones from these glands affect heart rate, blood pressure, blood vessels, and blood sugar.

The **thyroid** is found in the neck. It regulates mental and physical alertness. The parathyroid glands are found near or inside the thyroid and regulate calcium in the blood.

Immune System

The immune system resists the spread of disease by destroying disease-causing agents (antigens). This system is exceptionally complex and not fully understood. Normally, a combination of the following immune responses is needed to defeat an antigen.

The lymphatic system produces lymphocytes in bean-sized lymph glands located throughout the body. The lymphocytes are transported throughout bodily tissue by lymphatic capillaries. Lymphocytes control the immune system and kill antigens directly.

Granulocytes are very numerous. They ingest antigens already killed by cell enzymes. Monocytes exist in small numbers. They ingest and kill antigens and more importantly alter antigens in a way that makes it easier for lymphocytes to destroy them.

Immunoglobins (antibodies) combine with antigens to disable them. There are thousands of antibodies, each targeted for a specific antigen. Other proteins called cytokines complement proteins and aid the immune response.

ECOLOGY

Ecology refers to the relationship between organisms and their ecosystem (habitat). An ecosystem includes interdependent life forms and supports life through food, atmosphere, energy, and water. Organisms, including plants and animals, interact with and adapt to their ecosystem.

Earth is surrounded by a thin layer of atmosphere. Within that atmosphere lies earth's biosphere where life exists. The biosphere contains a number of biomes or living areas. Aquatic biomes include ocean, shallow water, and tidal marshes. Land biomes are classified by the predominant form of plant life and include forest, grassland, and desert.

Each organism in a biome occupies a place in the food web. Each organism, at some point in its life or death, is food for some other organism. In this way, energy is transferred among organisms in the biome.

A community refers to the interdependent populations of plants and animals. The dominance of one species in a community can affect the diversity (number of species and specie members). The community includes the habitat where a particular plant or animal lives and its niche (role).

Within a community, the primary interactions are predation, parasitism, commensalism, competition, and cooperation. Predators and prey adapt and develop more effective ways of hunting or defense. Cooperation may develop due to the dependence of one organism on another.

Organisms may compete within their species or with other species for resources. Successful competitors survive and become dominant. Subdominant individuals either accept poorer habitats, give up the resources, migrate, or perish.

LIFE CYCLES

A number of essential life cycles take place on earth.

Water Cycle

Most of the earth's water is salty, but humans need fresh water to survive. Fresh water is renewed through the water cycle. The cycle consists of three phases: evaporation, condensation, and precipitation.

Evaporation occurs when heat from the sun changes ocean water, and some water from other sources, into water vapor. Condensation follows when water vapor turns into water droplets, which form clouds. Precipitation occurs when the droplets become too heavy and water falls as rain, snow, sleet, or hail.

Oxygen Cycle

Humans and other animal organisms need oxygen to survive. Plants give off oxygen. An appropriate balance between plant photosynthesis and animal respiration ensures that enough oxygen is available.

Carbon Cycle

Carbon is used by all living things. Plants need carbon dioxide for photosynthesis. Animals get the carbon from the plant and animal tissues they eat and exhale carbon dioxide as a by-product of respiration. Here again, the balance between animal respiration and plant photosynthesis ensures that enough carbon will be available. In recent times, however, industrialization has added extra carbon to the atmosphere, jeopardizing the balance of this cycle.

Pollution

Air, water, and soil pollution are serious environmental problems. Some lakes, rivers, and streams are so polluted they can not be used by humans. Fish from many of these waters cannot be eaten. Air in some areas has been very polluted by factories and power plants, which use sulfur based fuels such as oil and coal. Land has been polluted by dumping hazardous wastes, including radioactive wastes. Pollution may lead to disease and premature death.

EARTH AND SPACE SCIENCE

ASTRONOMY

Astronomy is the study of space and the relationship of objects in space. Astronomers use optical telescopes and radio telescopes, including the orbiting Hubble Telescope, to study space and objects in space.

Solar System

Our solar system has one star (the sun), nine planets, some comets, and lots of satellites (moons), asteroids, and meteors. A diagram of the solar system is shown below. Only the planets are shown to rough scale in this diagram.

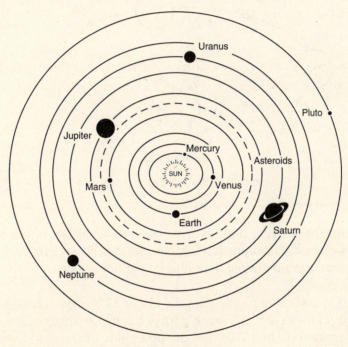

Our Solar System

The Sun

Our sun is a star, a turbulent mass of incredibly hot gases exploding with repeated nuclear fusion reactions. Without the heat and light from the sun, our universe would not exist as we know it. About 1,000,000 earths could fit inside the sun. The sun's diameter is about 864,000 miles, and the surface temperature is over 10,000° Fahrenheit. Still, the sun is just average size by galactic standards.

The sun is at the center of our solar system, although this was not realized until the time of Copernicus in the 1500s. The most noticeable features of the sun's surface are the sunspots, cooler areas that move across the sun's surface. Sunspots appear in somewhat predictable cycles and are associated with interruptions in radio and television transmissions.

The Earth and the Moon

Earth is the name of our planet. The earth is the third plant from the sun. The earth's distance from the sun ranges from about 91,000,000 to 95,000,000 miles. It takes light about eight minutes to travel from the sun to earth. The earth's diameter is about 7,900 miles. The earth's rotation and revolution have a tremendous impact on life here.

Rotation. The earth *rotates* around its axis, which roughly runs through the geographic north and south poles. This rotation creates day and night as parts of the earth are turned toward and then away from the sun.

Revolution. The earth *revolves* in an orbit (path) around the sun. The earth's axis is tilted about 23° from perpendicular with the orbit around the sun. The tilting and revolving creates seasons as regions of the earth are tilted toward the sun and away from the sun.

The diagram here shows the earth's tilt and earth's relation to the sun at the beginning of each season in the Northern Hemisphere. Seasons are opposite in the Southern Hemisphere.

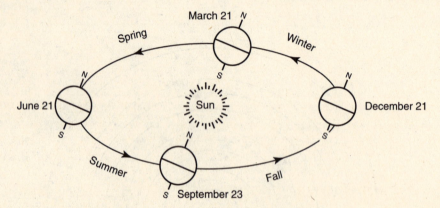

Seasons in the Northern Hemisphere

Moon is the name for the satellite that revolves around earth. The moon also rotates around its axis. The moon's diameter is about 2,100 miles and it is about 240,000 miles from the earth to the moon. The moon has no atmosphere and its surface is covered with craters from meteorites and from volcanoes.

The moon's rotation and revolution each take about 27 ½ days. These equal periods of rotation and revolution mean that the same part of the moon always faces the earth. It was not until lunar exploration in the 1970s that the other side of the moon was viewed and photographed.

The Moon's Phases

Different parts of the moon's surface reflect light to the earth, creating the different phases of the moons as shown on the next page.

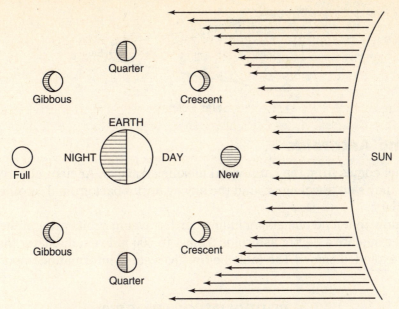

Appearance of the Moon During Different Phases

Tides

The phases of the moon are also integrally related to tides on earth. High tides occur on the parts of earth directly under the moon and on the other side of earth directly opposite this point. Low tides occur halfway between the two high tides. The tides move around the earth as the moon revolves around the earth, creating two high and two low tides each day at each place on earth.

The lowest and highest tides occur when the sun and the moon are in a straight line. These tides are called spring tides. The moon is either new or full during this direct alignment.

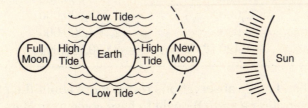

Alignment During Spring Tides

Eclipses

The position of the sun, earth, and moon can create eclipses. A lunar eclipse occurs when the moon is in the earth's shadow. A solar eclipse occurs when the sun is "hidden" behind the moon. Look at the diagrams below.

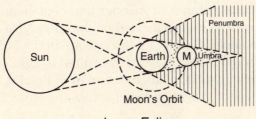

Lunar Eclipse

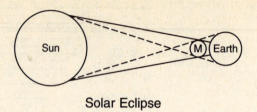

Solar Eclipse

Planets and Asteroids

The word planet comes from the Latin word meaning traveler. Ancient observers were taken by the "lights" they saw traveling around the sky against a background of other "lights" that seemed stationary.

Today we know that nine planets including earth travel in orbits around the sun. Also in orbit around the sun are a belt of asteroids from 1 to 500 miles in diameter that may be the remains of an exploded planet. The table below gives some information about the planets and asteroids.

BODIES IN SOLAR ORBIT

Name	Approximate diameter in miles	Approximate distance from sun in miles	Revolution Period
Mercury	3,100	36,000,000	88 days
Venus	7,700	67,000,000	225 days
Earth	7,900	93,000,000	365¼ days
Mars	4,200	142,000,000	687 days
Asteroids		161,000,000	
Jupiter	88,700	483,000,000	12 years
Saturn	75,000	886,000,000	29½ years
Uranus	32,000	1,783,000,000	84 years
Neptune	28,000	2,794,000,000	165 years
Pluto	1,420 (?)	3,670,000,000	248 years

Unmanned spacecraft and other observations reveal more about the planets each year. Recent discoveries of meteorites on earth thought to have come from Mars and evidence of ice and a former ocean bed on Mars have fueled speculation that some life forms might exist, or might have existed, on Mars.

COSMOLOGY

Cosmology is the study of the universe. Cosmological theories are about the origin, development, and ultimate fate of the universe.

The universe consists of a large number of galaxies that contain an enormous number of stars and other material. Our solar system is located on the outer edge of the Milky Way galaxy. All the stars you can see from earth without a telescope are in the Milky Way galaxy.

Intergalactic distances are so huge that they are measured in light years. Light travels about 6 trillion miles in a year. It takes light 300 years to travel from Polaris, the North Star, to earth. It would take about 100,000 years for light to travel across the Milky Way galaxy.

Scientists have discovered a great many other galaxies. The Andromeda galaxy is over 2 million light years away from earth. The most distant detectable galaxies are about 10 to 15 billion light years from earth.

Scientists have discovered that galaxies are moving away from each other. This, among other factors, has led most scientists to embrace the Big Bang theory. This theory proposes that helium and hydrogen combined to create a gigantic explosion 15 billion to 20 billion years ago. This explosion led to the development of the stars, galaxies, and eventually planets.

METEOROLOGY

Meteorology is the study of the earth's atmosphere. We are most attentive to meteorologist's predictions about weather.

Weather observations are taken on the ground, in the upper atmosphere, and from satellites in space. All these observations inform us about likely weather events and add to our knowledge about the atmosphere.

The complex movement of air masses creates our weather. This movement begins because air around the equator is heated, causing it to rise and air at the poles is cool. Air in the lower atmosphere moves toward the equator to replace the rising heated air, while upper air moves toward the poles. Added to this is the effect of Coriolis force, caused by the rotation of the planet. Coriolis force pulls air to the right in the Northern Hemisphere and to the left in the Southern Hemisphere.

Weather fronts move from west to east in the United States. High pressure systems are usually associated with good weather. Wind circulates to the right (left in the Southern Hemisphere) around a high pressure system. Low pressure systems are usually associated with bad weather. Wind circulates to the left (right in the Southern Hemisphere) around a low pressure system.

Humidity

Humidity refers to the percent of water vapor in the air. Dew point is the temperature below which the air will become so humid that it is saturated with water. Humidity above 60 or 65 percent makes us more uncomfortable because perspiration evaporates slowly.

Fog and Clouds

When the temperature is below the dew point, the air is saturated with water droplets or ice crystals, and fog or clouds are formed. Fog is a cloud that touches the ground. Clouds are formed well above the ground.

Stratus clouds refer to low-hanging clouds. Rain or snow may fall from nimbostratus clouds. Other stratus clouds can appear after rain has fallen. Stratus clouds may be just a few thousand feet above the ground.

Cumulus can be puffy cotton-like clouds that appear in the afternoon. The base of these clouds is about a mile above the ground. Cumulonimbus clouds are huge dark cumulus clouds that produce thunderstorms and hail. All cumulus clouds have strong convective, upward wind currents.

Cirrus clouds are high wispy clouds made up of ice crystals. Cirrus clouds are frequently three to five miles above the ground.

Precipitation

When condensed water or ice crystals become too dense for the air to support the precipitate, they fall toward the ground. *Rain* is water droplets that fall to the ground. *Snow* crystallizes from water droplets in clouds and falls to the earth. *Sleet* begins as rain and freezes or partially freezes as it falls to the earth. *Freezing rain* is rain that freezes when it strikes the surface. *Hail* is rain that freezes in cumulonimbus clouds and is blown up and falls only to be blown up again. This cycle is repeated many times, forming noticeable layers of ice in a hailstone.

Lightning

Lightning is an instantaneous, high energy electrical discharge in the atmosphere. Lightning occurs when positive and negative charges are separated in the atmosphere. While this occurs most often in violent thunderstorms it can occur also in sandstorms or in clouds above volcanoes. Lightning can be from cloud to cloud, or from cloud to ground.

Weather Maps

Weather maps show the position of pressure systems and fronts. A *warm front* signals that the air behind the front is warmer than the air in front. A *cold front* signals that the air behind the front is colder. The map below shows the symbols for fronts and pressure systems.

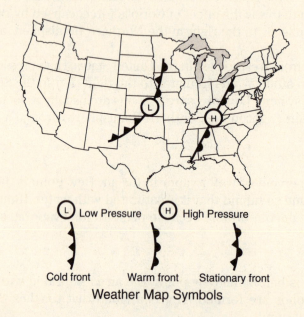

Weather Map Symbols

OCEANOGRAPHY

Oceanography is the study of the world's oceans and ocean beds. Oceanographers are concerned with 71 percent of the earth's surface. The ocean floor is covered by sediment, which reveals information about life on earth. Midocean ridges are the source of many volcanic eruptions.

Seawater itself is about 3.5 percent salt. Ocean currents, such as the Gulf Stream, are like rivers of water within the ocean. The sea provides over one-quarter of the protein needed in the world. Off-shore wells provide about 15 percent of the world's petroleum. Pollution by petroleum spills and other factors has had a noticeable impact on the oceans and on marine life.

GEOLOGY

Geology is the study of the earth, its development and origin. The History of Life table on page 184 shows the different periods in earth's development and when living organisms appeared on earth.

Using this time scale, geologists are fairly certain that, during the Permian period, earth's land mass consisted of a single continent called Pangea. During the Triassic period, Pangea split into two continents. During the Jurassic period, the Atlantic Ocean was formed. During the Cretaceous period, the Rocky Mountains rose. During the Tertiary period, the land bridge between North America and Europe disappeared. During the Quaternary period, glaciers covered most of North America.

THE EARTH'S PARTS

The earth has five parts—atmosphere, crust, mantle, outer core, and inner core.

The atmosphere is the gaseous region that surrounds the earth; it consists of 78 percent nitrogen and 21 percent oxygen. The remaining 1 percent consists of carbon dioxide, argon, water vapor, and other gases. The atmosphere extends out about 650 miles. But air becomes thinner as you travel away from earth and only the bottom 3 ½ miles or so of the atmosphere is habitable by humans without special equipment. The ozone layer, which protects earth from ultraviolet rays, is about 20 miles up.

The hydrosphere is the layer of water that covers about three-quarters of earth's surface. Ocean water, salt water, makes up about 95 percent of all earth's water. Oceans average about 12,400 feet deep. Below 100 feet, water temperature decreases rapidly. At 5,000 feet, the ocean temperature is near freezing.

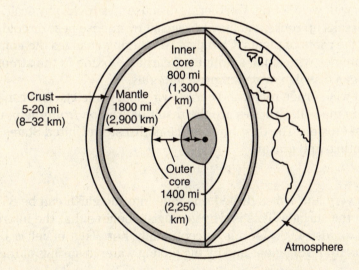

It is about 4,000 miles from the surface to the center of earth. Pressure and density increase with depth.

The lithosphere includes the rigid crust (20 miles thick) and upper mantle (40 miles thick) of the earth. The lithosphere is divided into a number of tectonic plates, which drift across earth's surface on the partially molten asthenosphere. The asthenosphere separates the lithosphere from the mantle.

The rigid mantle reaches to a depth of about 1,800 miles. The outer core is about 1,400 miles thick and consists of dense rigid materials. The inner core has a radius of about 800 miles and is very dense and hot with temperatures over 10,000° F. The heat generated in the inner core is transferred to the surface and provides the energy for continental drift and for molten rock, which erupts on land and in the ocean.

Rocks

Geologists study rocks. Three types of rocks are found in the earth's crust—sedimentary, igneous, and metamorphic. Sedimentary rocks form in water when sediments and remains of dead organisms harden. Igneous rocks form when molten rock, magma, crystallizes. Metamorphic rocks form when other rocks are subjected to extreme pressure. Sedimentary rocks are found near the surface of the earth while igneous and metamorphic rocks are usually found beneath the surface.

Fossils

Fossils are evidence of living organisms. Geologists and other scientists use fossils to learn about earth's history. Fossils usually form when organisms die and are buried in the sediment that forms sedimentary rocks. Other fossils include footprints or tracks of animals. Fossils of animals help us date rocks and other layers of the earth. Rocks are dated through radioactive isotope dating, which helps date the fossils found in the rock layers.

Geologic Processes

External Processes

As new rocks are being created, old ones are being destroyed, and earth's surface is being worn away. This process is called erosion.

Most erosion begins with weathering. Weathering disintegrates rocks physically and chemically. Physical weathering breaks up rocks and may be caused by intense heat or cold, by frost, or by the action of vines or the roots of plants. Chemical weathering changes the composition of the rocks. Rain water combines with small amounts of carbon dioxide in the atmosphere to form carbonic acid, which can dissolve or decompose minerals.

Streams, rivers, and wind erode rocks and carry away soil, while glaciers can gouge out huge grooves in rocks and in the soil. Beaches are the result of erosion from the pounding surf or oceans. Humans cause erosion. The dust bowl in the midwestern United States was caused by careless plowing, planting, and grazing.

Internal Processes

The earth's interior is very hot. Holes drilled one mile into the earth can be 85° to 90° warmer at the bottom than on the surface. This is why geologists believe that the interior of the earth, which extends down almost 4,000 feet, is exceptionally hot. This belief is bolstered by the molten rock that erupts from volcanoes and by the boiling water in springs at the earth's surface.

New Land Masses

New mountains and land are constantly being created. Hot magma comes to the surface, seeps out, and is cooled. Land masses also rise as the land is eroded and pushed up from below.

PHYSICAL SCIENCE

CHEMISTRY

Chemistry refers to the composition, properties, and interactions of matter. Organic chemistry is about living things. Inorganic chemistry deals with all other substances.

Atoms

Matter consists of atoms, which are so small they have never been seen—not even with the most powerful microscope. Atoms contain three subatomic particles—protons, neutrons, and electrons. The nucleus contains positively charged protons and neutrons with a neutral charge. Negatively charged electrons revolve around the nucleus.

Elements

Elements are the building blocks of chemistry. They cannot be broken by chemical means into other elements. Some elements have been produced artificially and have not been found in nature. Atoms are the smallest piece of an element. Elements can be represented in a periodic table. The following table shows all the known elements and some elements that are under investigation. Patterns in the table allow scientists to predict where new elements will appear.

Each cell in this periodic table shows the atomic symbol and the atomic number of an element. The atomic number shows how many protons are in the nucleus of the element. In general, an element has the same number of electrons as protons. For the element hydrogen (H) the atomic number is 1. That means there is 1 proton and so there is 1 electron.

The electrons orbit around the nucleus in different layers (shells). The closest layer to the nucleus has room for 2 electrons; the second layer has room for 8 electrons; the third layer has room for 18 and so on. There may be fewer electrons than there is room for. The rule for the number of electrons that can occupy a particular layer is two times the square of the layer number $(2n^2)$.

Adding or taking away protons from an atom creates a different element. However, in general, electrons can be added or taken away and only the charge of the element is changed. Some periodic tables show the atomic weight of an element. Here is the entry for carbon (C).

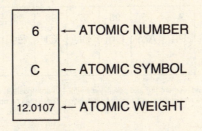

Round the atomic weight to the nearest whole number to find the atomic mass. The atomic mass shows the total number of protons and neutrons. Use this information to find the number of protons, electrons, and neutrons in hydrogen.

PERIODIC TABLE OF THE ELEMENTS

1 H																	2 He
3 Li	4 Be											5 B	6 C	7 N	8 O	9 F	10 Ne
11 Na	12 Mg											13 Al	14 Si	15 P	16 S	17 Cl	18 Ar
19 K	20 Ca	21 Sc	22 Ti	23 V	24 Cr	25 Mn	26 Fe	27 Co	28 Ni	29 Cu	30 Zn	31 Ga	32 Ge	33 As	34 Se	35 Br	36 Kr
37 Rb	38 Sr	39 Y	40 Zr	41 Nb	42 Mo	43 Tc	44 Ru	45 Rh	46 Pd	47 Ag	48 Cd	49	50 Sn	51 Sb	52 Te	53 I	54 Xe
55 CS	56 Ba	57-71 BELOW	72 Hf	73 Ta	74 W	75 Re	76 Os	77 Ir	78 Pt	79 Au	80 Hg	81 Tl	82 Pb	83 Bi	84 Po	85 At	86 Rn
87 Fr	88 Ra	89-103 BELOW	104 Rf	105 Db	106 Sg	107 Bh	108 Hs	109 Mt	110 Rf	111 Uuu	112 Uub	113 Uut	114 Uuq	115 Uup	116 Uuh	117 Uus	118 Uuo

57 La	58 Ce	59 Pr	60 Nd	61 Pm	62 Sm	63 Eu	64 Gd	65 Tb	66 Dy	67 Ho	68 Er	69 Tm	70 Yb	71 Lu
89 Ac	90 Th	91 Pa	92 U	93 Np	94 Pu	95 Am	96 Cm	97 Bk	98 Cf	99 Es	100 Fm	101 Md	102 No	103 Lr

Elements 113, 115, and 117 are unknown and element 118 and possibly element 116 are uncertain a press time. Elements 114 and 116 are very recent additions to the periodic table and may require further investigation. There may be additional changes.

1

← ATOMIC NUMBER

H ← ATOMIC SYMBOL

Carbon (C)
Atomic number = 6   Atomic mass = 12 (12.0107 rounded to the nearest whole number)

Number of protons = the atomic number.   There are 6 protons.
Number of electrons = number of protons.   There are 6 electrons.
Number of neutrons = mass – protons.   There are 12 – 6 = 6 neutrons.

Isotopes
Atoms of the same element can have different numbers of neutrons. The different versions of each element are called isotopes. The atomic number is the same for each isotope, but the atomic mass varies. The symbol for an isotope is written as the element symbol and the number of neutrons.

The isotope of hydrogen with 2 neutrons is written ^{2}H. The isotope of carbon with 12 neutrons is written ^{12}C.

Mass of Protons, Neutrons, and Electrons
The atomic mass of the nucleus of a carbon-12 isotope (^{12}C) is 12. Scientists use one-twelfth of this mass as the atomic mass unit (amu) for measuring atomic particles. While not precisely correct, the mass of a proton and a neutron are said to be 1 amu. The mass of an electron is said to be 1/1836 amu.

This table summarizes the mass and charge of protons, neutrons, and electrons.

Particle	mass in au	charge
Proton	1	+1
Neutron	10	neutral
Electron	1/1836	–1

This table gives information about carbon isotopes.

Isotope	Protons	Neutrons	Mass in amu
carbon-12	6	6	12
carbon-13	6	7	13
carbon-14	6	8	14

Matter

Matter is anything that has mass and takes up space. Matter can exist as a solid, liquid, or gas. The form of matter may change. For example, water becomes solid below freezing, and lead can be heated to a liquid.

All matter is made up of atoms. The weight of matter is a measure of the force that gravity places on its mass. Matter is conserved. That is, it cannot be created or destroyed, but it can be converted into energy.

Compound

A compound is formed when two or more elements unite chemically. A molecule is the smallest part of a compound with the properties of that compound.

There are three important types of chemical compounds—acids, bases, and salt. Acids dissolved in water produce hydrogen. Bases dissolved in water produce hydroxide. When acids and bases are combined chemically, they form salt.

Solution

A solution is formed when element(s) or compound(s) are dissolved in another substance. Club soda is a solution with carbon dioxide dissolved in water. Lemonade is a solution of lemon juice and sugar dissolved in water.

Chemical Reaction

A chemical reaction is when one or more new substances are formed. A chemical reaction involves the rearrangement of electrons. One example of a chemical reaction is when concrete is created from mixing water and cement. Chemical reactions also occur when elements are heated, cooled, and burned.

PHYSICS

Physics began at the earliest time with an attempt to understand matter and forces. This study has progressed through relativity and atomic physics to today when physicists are concerned with elementary particles. Physics seeks to describe nature through a number of general statements or laws. These laws are often stated in mathematical form.

Matter and Mass

Mass is the amount of matter in a body and is a measure of the body's inertia (resistance to change of motion). Weight is a measure of the force of gravity on a body. Weight and mass are different. Mass at rest is the same everywhere, but mass increases as it approaches the speed of light. Weight varies depending on its location in a gravitational field.

The density (specific gravity) of matter describes how compact the matter is. Archimedes discovered density and is reputed to have shouted "Eureka" in the process. He found that, in similar weights of lead and gold, the gold displaced less water, showing that it was more dense.

Motion

Physics is concerned with an object's response to force and the resulting movement. Force is energy that causes a change in an object's motion or shape. To explain force completely, you must describe both the magnitude and the direction. For example, two forces of the same magnitude pushing in the same direction are different from these same forces pushing at one another.

Velocity is described as magnitude (e.g., miles per hour) and direction (e.g., from 220 degrees). The magnitude portion of velocity is speed. The following formula describes the distance traveled for a constant velocity and a known time. For a time t and a constant velocity v the distance traveled d is:

$$d = vt$$

Newton's three laws of motion are still most important in everyday life. We must remember, though, that recent theories have shown that these laws do not apply to objects traveling near the speed of light or for very small subatomic particles.

Newton's First Law (Inertia). A body maintains its state of rest or uniform motion unless acted upon by an outside force.

Newton's Second Law (Constant Acceleration). As force is applied to an object, the object accelerates in the direction of the force. Both the mass and the force affect how the object accelerates. The more the mass the less the acceleration. The formula for this law follows:

$$F(\text{orce}) = M(\text{ass}) \times A(\text{cceleration}) \text{ or } A(\text{cceleration}) = \frac{F(\text{orce})}{M(\text{ass})}$$

Newton's Third Law (Conservation of Momentum). This law states that for every action there is an equal and opposite reaction. If two objects bump into each other, they are pushed away from each other with an equal force. The net effect of this event is 0, and the momentum is conserved.

Energy

Energy is the ability to do work. Energy can be mechanical, solar, thermal, chemical, electrical, or nuclear. Potential energy is stored energy or energy ready to be released. Kinetic energy is energy resulting from motion. Activation energy converts potential energy into kinetic energy.

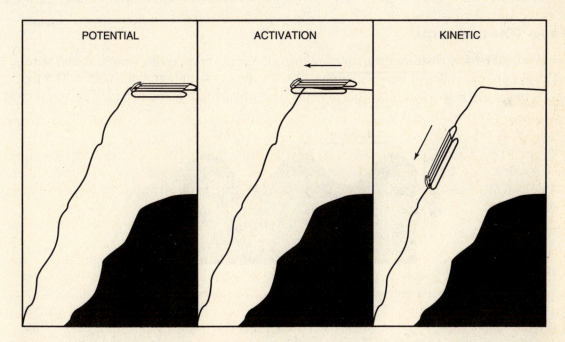

In one simple example, a sled at the top of a hill possesses potential energy. The push of the sledder is the activation energy needed to set the sled in motion. While in motion, the sled possesses kinetic energy.

In another example, the fuel in a rocket car has potential energy. This potential energy is activated by energy from a flame and transformed into the kinetic energy of the moving car.

Work

Work is the movement of a body by a force. If there is no movement, there is no work. Work occurs when you pick up an object. Trying without success to move a heavy object or holding an object steady involves no work. It does not matter that a lot of effort was involved. The rate of work is power. Power is measured in foot-pounds. A foot-pound is the amount of work it takes to raise one pound, one foot at sea level.

Heat

In physics, heat is energy in motion. Heat transfers energy within a body or from one body to the other when there is a temperature difference. Heat moves from higher temperature to lower temperature, lowering the former and raising the latter. Heat is measured in calories.

Temperature measures how fast the molecules in a substance are moving. The faster the molecules move, the hotter the substance. Temperature is commonly measured on two scales, Fahrenheit (freezing 32 degrees, boiling [water] 212 degrees) and Celsius (freezing 0 degrees and boiling [water] 100 degrees). The Kelvin scale is used in science. Zero on the Kelvin scale is absolute zero—molecules are not moving at all—and is equal to −273°C or −460°F.

Heat is transferred by conduction (physical contact), convection (from moving liquid or gas), and radiation (no physical contact). A heating pad *conducts* heat to your back. Moving hot water transfers heat to the radiator by *convection*. The sun *radiates* heat to the earth.

Wave Phenomena

Waves transfer energy without transferring matter. Microwaves, radio waves, sound waves, and x-rays are examples of waves in action. Most waves resemble the one below. The frequency of a wave is the vibrations per second. The wavelength is the distance between crests.

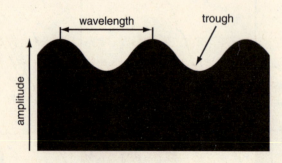

Light

Most light is produced by heated electrons vibrating at high frequencies. Light makes it possible for us to see things and to observe colors. Plants need light to carry out photosynthesis.

Light travels in straight lines and spreads out as it travels. When light strikes a rough surface it may be absorbed or scattered. When light strikes a highly polished surface it is reflected away at the angle of the original ray (angle of incidence equals the angle of reflection). Black surfaces absorb all light, while white surfaces scatter all light. This is why white clothes are recommended for sunny, warm days.

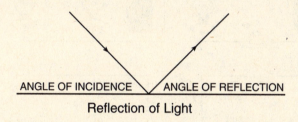

ANGLE OF INCIDENCE   ANGLE OF REFLECTION

Reflection of Light

Sound

Sounds are waves. For the human ear to hear a sound it must travel through a medium—a gas, a solid, or a liquid. As the sound waves travel through the medium, molecules in the medium vibrate.

Sound travels more quickly through solid media because the molecules are more closely packed together. Sound travels through air at about 1,100 feet per second, through water at about 5,000 feet per second, and through stone at about 20,000 feet per second.

ELECTRICITY AND MAGNETISM

Atoms are composed of protons (positive charge), electrons (negative charge), and neutrons (neutral charge). All things have either a positive (more protons), negative (more electrons), or neutral (balance of protons and electrons) charge.

Electricity

Electricity is based on these charges and follows these rules. Like charges repel, unlike charges attract. Neutral charges are attracted by both positive and negative charges, but not as strongly as opposite charges.

In a static electricity experiment, the experimenter shows that the glass rod does not attract bits of paper. Then the glass rod is rubbed with a piece of silk. This process removes electrons from the rod, creating a negative charge. Then the rod attracts the neutral bits of paper.

Electricity speeds through conductors such as copper. Electricity moves slower through semiconductors such as ceramics. Electricity does not move through nonconductors or insulators such as rubber and glass.

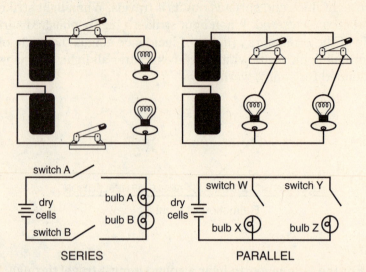

Electricity moves through wires to form circuits. Most circuits in this country use alternating current (AC). Circuits in other countries may use direct current (DC). Most circuits are wired parallel—if a light burns out, or a switch is off, all other switches or lights work. Some circuits are wired in series—if a switch is off or a light is missing or burned out, all lights go out.

Three units are used to measure electricity as it flows through wires. The volt measures the force of the current. The ampere (amp) measures the rate of current flow. The ohm tells the resistance in the wire to the flow of electricity.

Batteries are used to produce, store, and release electricity. Batteries used in a toy or flashlight are dry cell batteries. Car batteries are wet cell batteries.

Magnetism

Magnets occur naturally in magnetite, although most magnets are manufactured from iron. Magnetism is very similar to electricity, and electromagnets can be made from coils of wire. Magnets have a north and south pole—like poles repel, while opposite poles attract. The magnetic field is strongest around the poles.

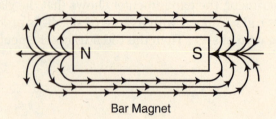

Bar Magnet

Earth has a magnetic field that aids navigation. Magnetic north is located in northeastern Canada. It is not located at the North Pole. Compass needles point to magnetic north, not to the geographic North Pole.

MODERN PHYSICS

Modern physics studies very small particles of energy. Energy as very small discrete quantities gives scientists a different view than energy as a continuous flow. Particle physics is particularly useful as scientists study atomic energy. For example, scientists study light as the transmission of tiny particles called photons. In fact, it is believed that energy is transmitted as both particles and waves.

Modern physics also studies the conversion of matter into energy and energy into matter. Einstein's famous equation quantifies the conversion between mass to energy.

$$E = mc^2$$

(E is energy, m is mass, and c is the speed of light, 186,000 miles per second.)

Calculations with this equation reveal that very small amounts of mass can create huge amounts of energy. Similarly, calculations reveal it would take huge amounts of energy to create a very small amount of mass.

RADIOACTIVITY

Materials are radioactive when they have unstable nuclei. Uranium is an example of a naturally occurring radioactive substance. Radioactive materials decay, losing their radioactivity at a certain rate. The decay of radioactive materials is very useful for dating rocks and other materials.

Other radioactive material is created through nuclear fission in nuclear power plants. The energy from the reaction can be used as a power source.

Radioactive materials release energy including alpha, beta, and usually gamma radiation. Gamma rays penetrate living organisms very deeply and can destroy living cells and lead to the death of humans.

Fusion

The sun creates energy through fusion. Attempts are underway to create energy through nuclear fusion. Fusion creates much less radioactivity and could be fueled by deuterium, which is found in limitless quantities throughout the ocean.

INTERPRETING GRAPHS

You will encounter four main types of graphs on the test.

The Pictograph

The pictograph uses symbols to stand for numbers. In the following graph, each picture represents 1,000 phones.

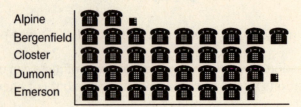

Number of Phones in Five Towns
(in thousands)

Try these questions:

1. According to this graph, about how many more phones are there in Bergenfield than in Emerson?
   (A) 10,000
   (B) 15,000
   (C) 1,000
   (D) 1.5 thousand

2. This graph *best* demonstrates which of the following?
   (A) More people live in Bergenfield.
   (B) People in Alpine make the fewest calls.
   (C) There are about twice as many phones in Emerson as in Alpine.
   (D) There are about four times as many phones in Bergenfield as in Alpine.

Answers are on page 214.

The Bar Graph

The bar graph represents information by the length of a bar. The graph below shows the rainfall during two months in each of five towns.

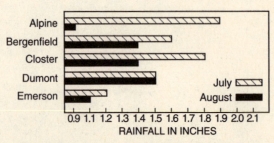

RAINFALL IN INCHES
Rainfall in July and August for Five Towns

Try these questions:

3. You wanted to get the least rainfall. Based on this graph, which town would you go to in July and which town would you go to in August?
   (A) Closter, Bergenfield
   (B) Alpine, Dumont
   (C) Closter, Alpine
   (D) None of the above

4. This graph *best* demonstrates which of the following?
   (A) The rainiest town yearly is Closter.
   (B) Alpine has the largest rainfall difference between July and August.
   (C) The driest town yearly is Emerson.
   (D) In August, Alpine has more rain than Emerson.

The Line Graph

The line graph plots information against two axes. The graph below shows monthly sales for two corporations.

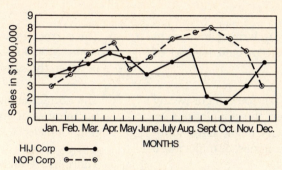

Sales for Two Companies During the Year

You might be asked two types of questions.

5. What was the approximate difference in sales between the HIJ and the NOP Corporations in June?
   (A) $15,000
   (B) $150,000
   (C) $400,000
   (D) $4.5 million

6. This graph *best* demonstrates which of the following?
   (A) NOP has more employees.
   (B) From August to September, the differences in sales grew by 400%.
   (C) In October, NOP had over $600,000 more in sales than HIJ.
   (D) In total, HIJ had more sales this year than NOP.

The Circle Graph

The circle represents an entire amount. In the graph below, each wedge-shaped piece of the graph represents the percent of tax money spent on different town services.

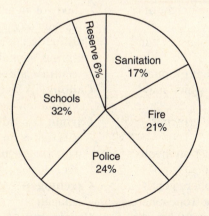

Percent of Tax Money Spent for Town Services

Use the circle graph to answer these questions.

7. The town collects $1,400,000 in taxes. How much will the town spend on schools?
   (A) $320,000
   (B) $60,000
   (C) $600,000
   (D) $448,000

8. The town collects $1,400,000 in taxes. The town needs to spend $392,000 for police. Any needed money will come from sanitation. The percents in the pie chart are recalculated. What percent is left for sanitation?
   (A) 21%
   (B) 17%
   (C) 13%
   (D) 10%

EXPLAINED ANSWERS

1. The correct answer is (D). Writing answers in a different format (1.5 thousand instead of 1,500) is common.

2. The correct answer is (D). You can't draw any valid conclusions about the populations or calls made. Some towns might have more businesses, own fewer phones, or make more calls per household.

3. The correct answer is (D). Emerson, Alpine are the towns you would choose. No need to compute. Find the smallest bar for each month.

4. The correct answer is (B). That fact is clear. We only have information about July and August, so we can't be sure about (A) or (C). Choice (D) is not true.

5. The correct answer is (B). Each space represents $100,000 and there are 1.5 spaces between the sales figures in June.

6. The correct answer is (B). You can't predict the number of employees from this information. Choices (C) and (D) are false.

7. The correct answer is (D). Multiply 0.32 × $1,400,000.

8. The correct answer is (C). It takes 28 percent of the taxes to get $392,000. That's 4 percent more than the police get now. Sanitation loses 4 percent, leaving 13 percent.

Science Terms

Use this glossary of a little over one hundred science terms to support and augment your science review.

Altimeter   An instrument that uses air pressure to record height, such as the height of a plane.

Anemometer   An instrument to measure wind speed.

Angiosperm   A group of plants that produce seeds enclosed within an ovary, which may mature into a fruit.

Annuals   Plants that die after one growing season.

Asexual reproduction   Reproduction involving only one parent.

Atmosphere   The Earth's atmosphere is primarily nitrogen and oxygen. The troposphere extends from the surface to about 10 km; the stratosphere from 10 km to 50 km; the mesosphere from 50 km to 80 km; and the thermosphere is the atmosphere beyond 80 km.

Aurora Borealis (Northern Lights)   Light emission from the upper atmosphere that appear in many shapes and colors.

Bacillus   A rod-shaped bacteria.

Blood   Fluid that circulates throughout the body of an animal, distributing nutrients, and usually oxygen.

California current   A dry, north wind in late spring, summer, and early fall in north and central California.

Canopy   A layer of tree branches and other vegetation elevated above the ground.

Carbon Dioxide (CO_2)   A colorless, odorless gas that is important in the Earth's atmospheric greenhouse effect. Frozen CO_2 is dry ice.

Carcinogen   A substance that can lead to cancer.

Carcinoma   A malignant tumor, which forms in the skin and outside of internal organs.

Carnivore   An organism that eats meat, which includes animals, fungi, and plants.

Ceilometer   An instrument that measures cloud height.

Cell   The fundamental unit of all life. The cell consists of an outer plasma membrane, the cytoplasm, and genetic material (DNA).

Celsius   A temperature scale in which water freezes at 0 degrees and boils at 100 degrees.

Chemotherapy   A cancer treatment that includes chemicals toxic to malignant cells.

Chinook wind   A warm, dry wind on the eastern side of the Rocky Mountains.

Chlorophyll   The green substance that absorbs light during photosynthesis.

Chromosome   A single DNA molecule, a tightly coiled strand of DNA, condensed into a compact structure.

Clone   An identical copy of an organism.

Cloud   A visible group of water or ice particles in the atmosphere.

Commensalism   A relationship between dissimilar organisms that is advantageous to one and doesn't affect the other.

Continental divide   In the United States, the part of the western mountains that separates water flowing toward opposite sides of the country.

Convection   The movement up in the atmosphere of heated moisture. Thunderstorms are often caused by convection.

Core   The portion of Earth from beneath the mantle to the Earth's center.

Cross-pollination   Fertilization of one plant by pollen from a different plant species.

Diabetes   A disease related to lowered levels of insulin.

Diploid Cell   A cell with two copies of each chromosome.

DNA (Deoxyribonucleic acid)   This primary component of chromosomes carries an organism's genetic code.

Double helix   A term used to describe the coiling strands of DNA molecule that resembles a spiral staircase.

Ecology   The study of the interactions of organisms with their environment and with each other.

Ecosystem   All the organisms in an area and the environment in which they live.

El Nino   Warming of Pacific Ocean seawater along the coast of South America that leads to significant weather changes in the United States.

Embryo   The stage of cellular divisions that develops from a zygote.

Enzyme   A protein that aids biochemical reactions.

Epicenter   The place on the surface of the Earth immediately above the *focus* of an earthquake.

Esophagus   The part of the gut that connects the pharynx and stomach.

Estuary   A place where fresh water and seawater mix.

Flower   The reproductive parts of flowering plants.

Fossil   Evidence of past life.

Fruit   The part of flowering plants that contains seeds.

Gamete   Reproductive haploid cells that combine to create a zygote.

Genus   The level of plant and animal between the species and the family.

Germination   The process by which seeds develop into seedlings.

Gill   The tissues aquatic animals use to breath in water.

Glucose   A simple sugar and a product of photosynthesis.

Gut   That part of the body cavity between the mouth and anus including in most animals the mouth, pharynx, esophagus, stomach, intestine, and the anus.

Haploid Cell   A cell with one set of chromosomes, which is half the regular (diploid) number.

Heart   A muscle that pumps to circulate the blood.

Herbivore   An organism that relies primarily on plants for food.

Hypothesis   A preliminary proposition that can be tested through scientific study.

Insulin   A hormone needed to transport glucose to cells.

Interferon   Small proteins that stimulate viral resistance in cells.

Intestine   The digestive tract between the stomach and anus where most nutrients are absorbed.

Isotope   Atoms of the same chemical element with a different number of neutrons but the same number of protons. Isotopes of an element have the same atomic number but may not have the same mass.

Jet stream   Strong upper wind currents in a narrow stream that flow west to east in the United States. Weather patterns are related to the position of the jet stream, which changes often.

Kelvin   A temperature scale in which 1° Kelvin equals 1° C. 0° Kelvin is about –273° C. 0° Kelvin is called absolute zero because there is no movement of molecules.

Knot   One nautical mile per hour or about 1.15 miles per hour.

Larva   In the metamorphosis of insects, the larva becomes a pupa before it becomes an adult.

Lenticular Cloud   An almond-shaped cloud usually seen on windy days.

Lipids   Compounds that are fats and oils.

Magma   Molten rock formed in the Earth that may appear on the surface.

Mantle   The part of Earth located between the crust and the core.

Marsupial   A mammal whose young crawl into its mother's pouch to complete development.

Meiosis   The process in which a diploid cell divides to form haploid cells.

Metamorphosis   In most amphibians, a process in which larva goes through significant changes, perhaps including a pupa stage, before becoming an adult.

Mirage   The phenomenon when refraction of light makes objects appear where they are not.

Mitosis   Cell division consisting of prophase, metaphase, anaphase, and telophase, that usually creates in two new nuclei, each with a full set of chromosomes.

Moraine   Material deposited by a glacier and often marking a glacier's furthest advance.

Nebula   An interstellar cloud of dust and gas.

Nerve   A bundle of neurons, or nerve cells.

Neuron   A cell that reacts to stimuli and transmits impulses consisting of a body with a nucleus and dendrites to receive and axons to transmit impulses.

Niche   An organism's unique place in the environment.

Nimbostratus   A dark cloud, but not a thundercloud, that frequently produces rain.

Nucleus   An organelle in a cell that contains chromosomes.

Nymph   The larval stage of an aquatic insect.

Paleontology   Study and interpretation of fossils.

Parasitism   A relationship between organisms in which one organism benefits and the other does not die, even though the second organism may be harmed.

Perennials   Plants that live through more than one growing season.

Permafrost   Soil beneath the earth's surface that stays frozen throughout the year.

Phloem   The tissue in plants that conducts nutrients.

Phylum   A level of plant and animal classification between class and kingdom.

Placenta   A tissue in the uterus through which nutrients pass from the mother to the fetus.

Plankton   Floating aquatic plants (phytoplankton) and animals (zooplankton).

Plate Tectonics   The movement of plates and the interaction across the Earth's surface to form land masses.

Pollination   Movement of pollen to a plant egg cell, often by wind, bees, or other animals.

Pupa   In metamorphosis, the stage between the larva and adult.

Radiocarbon dating   A way to date organic substances based on the carbon-14 remaining.

Rainbow   Light refracted through raindrops to form colors of a spectrum from red to blue.

Reef   A ridge built in water by organisms such as coral.

Seed   In plants, a seed includes the embryo.

Sonic Boom   A loud noise caused by a shock wave when an object exceeds the speed of sound.

Summer Solstice   When the sun is highest in the sky and directly above the Tropic of Cancer 23½° North Latitude. This date usually falls on June 22.

Tree rings   Rings that show how many years a tree has been growing. The thickness of the rings may reveal other information about climatic conditions.

Vernal Equinox   When the sun is directly over the equator. This date usually occurs on March 20.

Virga   Precipitation that evaporates before it reaches the Earth's surface.

Weathering   The physical, chemical, and biological processes by which rock is broken down into smaller pieces.

Wind chill   The combined cooling effect of wind and temperature. Higher wind chills indicate that a body will cool more quickly to the air temperature.

SCIENCE TARGETED TEST

These items will help you practice for the real CSET. These items have the same form and test the same material as CSET items and test material. The items you encounter on the real CSET may have a different emphasis and may be more complete.

Instructions

Mark your answers on the sheet provided below. Complete the items in 40 minutes or less. Correct your answer sheet using the answers on page 221.

1 Ⓐ Ⓑ Ⓒ Ⓓ	9 Ⓐ Ⓑ Ⓒ Ⓓ	17 Ⓐ Ⓑ Ⓒ Ⓓ	25 Ⓐ Ⓑ Ⓒ Ⓓ	33 Ⓐ Ⓑ Ⓒ Ⓓ
2 Ⓐ Ⓑ Ⓒ Ⓓ	10 Ⓐ Ⓑ Ⓒ Ⓓ	18 Ⓐ Ⓑ Ⓒ Ⓓ	26 Ⓐ Ⓑ Ⓒ Ⓓ	34 Ⓐ Ⓑ Ⓒ Ⓓ
3 Ⓐ Ⓑ Ⓒ Ⓓ	11 Ⓐ Ⓑ Ⓒ Ⓓ	19 Ⓐ Ⓑ Ⓒ Ⓓ	27 Ⓐ Ⓑ Ⓒ Ⓓ	35 Ⓐ Ⓑ Ⓒ Ⓓ
4 Ⓐ Ⓑ Ⓒ Ⓓ	12 Ⓐ Ⓑ Ⓒ Ⓓ	20 Ⓐ Ⓑ Ⓒ Ⓓ	28 Ⓐ Ⓑ Ⓒ Ⓓ	36 Ⓐ Ⓑ Ⓒ Ⓓ
5 Ⓐ Ⓑ Ⓒ Ⓓ	13 Ⓐ Ⓑ Ⓒ Ⓓ	21 Ⓐ Ⓑ Ⓒ Ⓓ	29 Ⓐ Ⓑ Ⓒ Ⓓ	37 Ⓐ Ⓑ Ⓒ Ⓓ
6 Ⓐ Ⓑ Ⓒ Ⓓ	14 Ⓐ Ⓑ Ⓒ Ⓓ	22 Ⓐ Ⓑ Ⓒ Ⓓ	30 Ⓐ Ⓑ Ⓒ Ⓓ	38 Ⓐ Ⓑ Ⓒ Ⓓ
7 Ⓐ Ⓑ Ⓒ Ⓓ	15 Ⓐ Ⓑ Ⓒ Ⓓ	23 Ⓐ Ⓑ Ⓒ Ⓓ	31 Ⓐ Ⓑ Ⓒ Ⓓ	39 Ⓐ Ⓑ Ⓒ Ⓓ
8 Ⓐ Ⓑ Ⓒ Ⓓ	16 Ⓐ Ⓑ Ⓒ Ⓓ	24 Ⓐ Ⓑ Ⓒ Ⓓ	32 Ⓐ Ⓑ Ⓒ Ⓓ	40 Ⓐ Ⓑ Ⓒ Ⓓ

1. The word *ecology* refers to what area of scientific endeavor?
   (A) The methods for keeping the environment clean
   (B) The relationship between organisms and their habitat
   (C) The effect of industrial and residential pollution on water resources
   (D) The methods for determining the quality of water and the atmosphere

2. During which period did dinosaurs appear on earth?
   (A) Cambrian
   (B) Carboniferous
   (C) Triassic
   (D) Tertiary

3. How are galaxies moving?
   (A) They are moving in a circular pattern.
   (B) They are moving away from the earth.
   (C) They are moving away from one another.
   (D) They are moving to a common point in the universe.

4. Which of the following most correctly shows the make-up of earth's atmosphere?
   (A) Oxygen 78 percent, nitrogen 21 percent
   (B) Oxygen 58 percent, nitrogen 41 percent
   (C) Oxygen 41 percent, nitrogen 58 percent
   (D) Oxygen 21 percent, nitrogen 78 percent

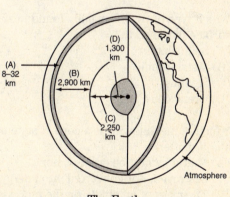

The Earth

5. In the diagram, what letter labels the mantle?

6. In electricity, what does the ohm measure?
   (A) Resistance
   (B) Current flow
   (C) Current force
   (D) Heat

7. Which of the following choices is a part of the carbon cycle?
   (A) Respiration
   (B) Evaporation
   (C) Condensation
   (D) Excretion

8. Which of the following is not a subatomic particle?
   (A) Neutron
   (B) Electron
   (C) Proton
   (D) Nucleus

9. What is the pattern of air circulation in the pressure system on this weather map?
   (A) Around it to the right
   (B) Around it to the left
   (C) Through it to the north
   (D) Through it to the east

10. Which type of rock is usually found near the surface of the earth?
    (A) Sedimentary
    (B) Metamorphic
    (C) Igneous
    (D) Cretaceous

11. Which of the following is a correct statement about matter?
    (A) Matter cannot be created, nor destroyed, nor converted into energy.
    (B) The mass of an object on the moon is the same as the mass on earth.
    (C) The weight of matter is the sum of its atomic numbers.
    (D) Once established, the form of matter cannot change.

12. What is produced when a base is dissolved in water?
    (A) Oxygen
    (B) Hydrogen
    (C) Hydroxide
    (D) Salt

13. What does heat measure?
    (A) The amount of reflection of energy off a surface
    (B) The ratio of friction to air temperature
    (C) The speed of moving molecules
    (D) The rate of connective activity

14. Through which of the media listed below will sound travel the fastest?
    (A) air
    (B) stone
    (C) water
    (D) vacuum

15. Which of the following represents the correct sequence of events that occurs during photosynthesis?

    I. CO_2 and water are broken down
    II. Carbohydrates are formed
    III. Sunlight is absorbed by chlorophyll
    IV. The plant emits O_2

    (A) I, III, II, IV
    (B) I, II, III, IV
    (C) III, I, II, IV
    (D) II, IV, I, III

16. A person puts a black cloth over a pile of snow to make the snow melt faster. Why is that?
    (A) The black material absorbs more sunlight and more heat.
    (B) The black material holds the heat in close to the snow.
    (C) The black material reflects more light and so it gets hotter.
    (D) The black cloth is the opposite color of the white snow.

17. When ironing clothes, heat is transferred from the iron to the clothes by
    (A) convection.
    (B) radiation.
    (C) conduction.
    (D) attraction.

18. Radioactive materials release particles because of
    (A) their environment.
    (B) their place in the periodic table.
    (C) their nuclear make-up.
    (D) the instability of the outer shell electrons.

19. All of the following examples represent potential energy EXCEPT
    (A) gasoline in a car's motor.
    (B) a sled at the top of a hill.
    (C) carbonated water in a sealed bottle.
    (D) a moving pendulum.

20. There are 12 electrons in an element with a neutral charge. How many protons does it have?
    (A) 3
    (B) 4
    (C) 6
    (D) 12

21. Which would not be found in our solar system?
    (A) asteroid
    (B) star
    (C) galaxy
    (D) moon

22. Which diagram could result in a solar eclipse?

A.
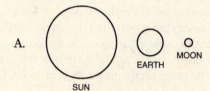

B.
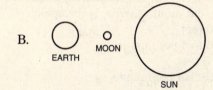

C.
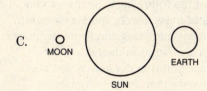

D.
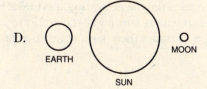

23. Which of the following paths best describes how blood circulates in the human body?
    (A) Out from the heart along veins and arteries and back to the heart through the same veins and arteries
    (B) Out from the heart through arteries and back to the heart through veins
    (C) Out from the heart along veins and back to the heart through ducts
    (D) Out from the heart through capillaries and back to the heart through arteries

24. Which of the following best describes plate tectonic theory?
    (A) Molten material from within the earth pushes up on portions of the earth called plates causing volcanoes and earthquakes.
    (B) Certain roughly circular portions of the earth's surface called plates are subjected to pressure causing them to turn left or right causing earthquakes.
    (C) The earth's surface consists of a series of plates that float slowly on the material beneath the surface.
    (D) Over time, portions of the earth's surface crack or break in a fashion similar to the way plates break when dropped.

25. According to the chapter, the cell wall
    (A) is narrower on animal cells than it is on plant cells.
    (B) occurs only on plant cells.
    (C) is not found on the cells of living things.
    (D) is thinner on plant cells than the cell wall on animal cells.

26. The word "diploid" most nearly means
    (A) double the
    (B) depleted by the
    (C) half the
    (D) part of the

27. Which of the following is NOT required for the process of photosynthesis?
    (A) Water
    (B) Sunlight
    (C) Glucose
    (D) Carbon dioxide

28. Which of the following is a true statement about DNA?
    (A) All DNA determines human traits.
    (B) Genes occupy specific locations on RNA.
    (C) DNA carries genetic code throughout the cell.
    (D) A chromosome is made up of DNA.

29. Where did the Earth's early oxygen supply come from?
    (A) It came from anaerobic cells.
    (B) Early molecules gave off oxygen.
    (C) It came from photosynthesis.
    (D) It came from aerobic cells.

30. Compared to cells, a virus is best characterized as
    (A) advanced.
    (B) parasitic.
    (C) primitive.
    (D) spirilla.

31. Intravenous (IV) drug users are at particular risk for acquiring the HIV virus because
    (A) the virus is transmitted through the injected drugs.
    (B) the virus is transmitted through blood.
    (C) the virus is transmitted through germs on the needle.
    (D) the virus is transmitted through intimate sexual contact.

32. Which of the following determines seasons on Earth?
    (A) the Earth's tilt
    (B) the Earth's revolution
    (C) the Earth's rotation
    (D) the Earth's distance from the sun

33. A solar eclipse occurs when
    (A) the moon hides the sun from some of the Earth.
    (B) the moon hides some of the sun from the Earth.
    (C) the moon covers the Earth with a shadow.
    (D) the Earth casts a shadow on the moon.

34. You're standing at the ocean's edge facing west in Northern California. A high pressure system is directly opposite you some miles off shore to the west. Where you are standing, the wind is most likely coming from which direction?
    (A) northwest
    (B) northeast
    (C) southwest
    (D) southeast

35. You weigh a lump of clay on Earth, and then weigh the same lump of clay on the moon. Which of the following accurately summarizes the result?
    (A) The weight and the mass both remain the same on the moon as on Earth.
    (B) The mass is altered by its presence on the moon, and so the clay will have a different weight on the moon than on Earth.
    (C) The mass of the object remains the same on the moon as on Earth, but the weight will be different on the moon than it is on Earth.
    (D) The clay weight is different on a scale while on the moon than it was on Earth, but the mass is the same on the moon as on Earth, so the actual weight of the clay is the same on the moon as it is on Earth.

36. An object travels at a constant speed over 90 feet in four minutes. What is the velocity?
    (A) 360 feet
    (B) 360 feet per minute
    (C) 22.5 feet
    (D) 22.5 feet per minute

37. Which of the following is a correct conclusion about mass, force, and acceleration?
    (A) As mass increases and force decreases then acceleration decreases.
    (B) As acceleration decreases and mass increases then force increases.
    (C) As mass stays constant and force increases then acceleration increases.
    (D) As force increases and acceleration stays constant then mass stays constant.

38. Which of the following statements is correct?
    (A) Where there's energy, there's work.
    (B) Where there's work, there's energy.
    (C) Where there's heat convection, there's heat conduction.
    (D) Where there's heat conduction, there's heat convection.

39. You are looking out the window and you see a single lightning flash. About 25 seconds later you hear the thunder clap. About how far away was the lightening bolt?

    (A) 1 mile
    (B) 3 miles
    (C) 5 miles
    (D) 7 miles

40. Which of the following is most likely when you remove one light from a string of lights and all the lights go out.
    (A) A circuit breaker burned out.
    (B) All the other lights burned out when you removed the light.
    (C) The lights are wired in parallel.
    (D) The lights are wired in series.

TARGETED TEST ANSWERS EXPLAINED

1. **B** Choice B is the definition of ecology.
2. **C** The Triassic period about 225,000,000 years ago saw the appearance of dinosaurs on earth.
3. **C** Computations that show all galaxies are moving away from each other are used as a basis for the big bang theory.
4. **D** Most of the earth's atmosphere is nitrogen. Oxygen makes up about 21 percent of the atmosphere. The remaining 1 percent of earth's atmosphere is partitioned among trace elements and gases.
5. **B** The earth's mantle is the first part of the earth beneath the surface.
6. **A** The amp measures the current flow, and the volt measures the current force.
7. **A** Choices B and C are part of the water cycle.
8. **D** The nucleus is the central part of the atom. The subatomic particles revolve around the nucleus.
9. **B** Air circulates counterclockwise around a low and clockwise around a high in the Northern Hemisphere. This pattern is reversed in the Southern Hemisphere.
10. **A** Sedimentary rocks are found near the surface. Igneous and metamorphic rocks are found beneath the surface. The term Cretaceous refers to a time period, not a rock type.
11. **B** Mass is the amount of an object and it does not vary. Weight is the force of gravity on mass, and weight does vary with gravity.
12. **C** Acids dissolved in water produce hydrogen. Acids and bases combined chemically form salt.

13. **C** Answers A and D might play a role in the speed of molecules. However, heat measures the speed of moving molecules.
14. **B** Sound travels through stone a little less than 20 times faster than it travels through air and about 4 times faster than it travels through water. Sound does not travel through a vacuum.
15. **A** This is the correct sequence of events.
16. **A** Dark colored material absorbs more sunlight and more heat than lighter colored material. Lighter colored material reflects more sunlight than darker colored material.
17. **C** Conduction means heat transfer by physical contact.
18. **D** The instability of this outer shell permits radioactive particles to be released.
19. **D** The pendulum represents kinetic energy—energy in use.
20. **D** Elements with neutral charges have a balance of electrons (negative charge) and protons (positive charge).
21. **C** Our solar system is part of a galaxy. The sun in a star.
22. **B** In a solar eclipse, the moon blocks the sun's light from reaching earth.
23. **B** Arteries carry blood away from the heart, and veins bring the blood back to the heart.
24. **C** Plate tectonic theory shows that all parts of the earth's surface are slowly moving.
25. **B** The cell wall is one of the features found only on plant cells. Choice D is incorrect because there is no cell wall on animal cells.

26. **A** Diploid refers to double the haploid number, a single set of chromosomes (half the full set) present in egg and sperm cells.

27. **C** Glucose is produced by photosynthesis, but it is not needed for photosynthesis to take place.

28. **D** The chapter explains that DNA is genetic material tightly coiled as a chromosome.

29. **C** The Earth's early supply of oxygen came from photosynthesis.

30. **C** A virus is primitive in that it is simpler and less developed than a cell. Answer B is incorrect because cells can also be parasitic.

31. **B** Intravenous (IV) drug users are at particular risk because sharing needles may transmit small quantities of infected blood.

32. **A** The Earth's tilt is the primary reason for seasons, and more important than the Earth's distance from the sun.

33. **A** A solar eclipse occurs when the moon hides some of the sun from the Earth. The moon casts a shadow on the Earth, but the shadow does not cover the Earth.

34. **D** Northwest, because the wind travels clockwise around a high-pressure system in the northern hemisphere. If a person is facing west, the wind will come from the front-right part of the body.

35. **C** Weight measures the force of gravity on an object. Since gravity is lower on the moon, the clay will weigh less on the moon.

36. **D** The formula is $d = vt$.
    Divide both sides by t to get $v = d/t$.
    Then substitute 90 feet for d and 4 minutes for t.
    $v = 90 \text{ feet}/4 \text{ minutes}$
    $v = 22.5$ feet per minute

37. **C** $\text{Acceleration} = \dfrac{\text{Force}}{\text{Mass}}$

    If the mass part of the fraction stays the same, and the force part increases, the value of the fraction increases. That means the acceleration increases.

38. **B** Work always involves energy; energy does not necessarily create work.

39. **C** In 25 seconds sound travels about 25×1100 feet = 27,500 feet. Divide by the number of feet in a mile $27,500 \div 5,280$ feet is about 5.2 miles. That's close to 5 miles. You can estimate this answer.

40. **D** The result described in this item is what happens when you remove a bulb from a string of lights wired in *series*.

6 MATHEMATICS

TEST INFO BOX

26 Multiple Choice items   Half of Subtest II items
2 Constructed Response items   Half of Subtest II items

MATHEMATICS ITEMS

Mathematics multiple choice items look like this.

If $x = 5/6$, which of the following inequalities is correct?

(A) $5/9 < x < 7/9$
(B) $5/8 < x < 3/4$
(C) $3/4 < x < 7/8$
(D) $7/8 < x < 15/16$

Mathematics constructed response items look like this.

You have a one-inch hollow paper cube and a pair of scissors. Display the different flat designs you can make by cutting the cube along the edges of the cube.

USING THIS CHAPTER

This chapter prepares you to take the Mathematics part of the CSET. Choose one of the approaches.

I want all the Mathematics review I can get.

❑ Skip the Review Quiz and read the entire review section.
❑ Take the Mathematics Review Quiz on page 225.
❑ Correct the Review Quiz and reread the indicated parts of the review.
❑ Go over the Special Strategies for Answering the Mathematics items on pages 306–307.
❑ Complete the Mathematics CSET Practice items on page 309.

I want a thorough Mathematics review.

❑ Take the Mathematics Review Quiz on page 225.
❑ Correct the Review Quiz and reread the indicated parts of the review.
❑ Go over the Special Strategies for Answering the Mathematics items on pages 306–307.
❑ Complete the Mathematics CSET Practice items on page 309.

I want a quick Mathematics review.

❑ Take and correct the Mathematics Review Quiz on page 225.
❑ Go over the Special Strategies for Answering the Mathematics items on pages 306–307.
❑ Complete the Mathematics CSET Practice items on page 309.

MATHEMATICS REVIEW QUIZ

This quiz uses a short answer format to help you find out what you know about the Mathematics topics reviewed in this chapter. The quiz results direct you to the portions of the chapter you should reread. You don't have to take the quiz in one sitting.

This quiz will also help focus your thinking about Mathematics, and these questions and answers are a good review in themselves. It's not important to answer all these questions correctly, and don't be concerned if you miss many of them. Just taking the quiz is a review in itself.

The answers are found immediately after the quiz. It's to your advantage not to look at them until you have completed the quiz. Once you have completed and corrected this review quiz, use the answer checklist to decide which sections of the review to study.

Write the answers in the space provided or on a separate sheet of paper.

---

1. Which number is missing from this sequence?

   3 6 _____ 12

Questions 2–4: *Use symbols for less than, greater than, and equal to, and compare these numbers:*

2. 23 _____ 32

3. 18 _____ 4 + 14

4. 9 _____ 10 _____ 11

5. Write the place value of the digit 7 in the numeral 476,891,202,593.

   _____

6. Write this number in words: 6,000,000,000,000.

   _____

7. $2^2 \times 2^3 =$ _____

8. $6^9 \div 6^7 =$ _____

9. $3^2 \times 2^3 =$ _____

10. Write 8342 in scientific notation.

    _____

11. Write the place value of the digit 4 in the numeral 529.354.

    _____

Questions 12–13: *Use symbols for less than, greater than, and equal to, and compare these numbers:*

12. 9,879 _____ 12,021

13. 98.1589 _____ 98.162

Questions 14–17:

   Round 234,489.0754 to the:

14. thousands place _____

15. hundredths place _____

16. tenths place _____

17. Write these fractions from least to greatest.

    $7/_8, \; 11/_{12}, \; 17/_{20}$

    _____, _____, _____

18. Which integer is one smaller than –6? _____

19. $5 + 7 \times 3^2$ _____

20. $5 \times 8 - (15 - 7 \times 2)$ _____

21. Write a seven-digit number divisible by 4.

    _____

22. Write the GCF and LCM of 6 and 14.

    _____

23. $426 \div 16 =$ _____

24. Write the property illustrated by:

_____

$$x(x+2) = x^2 + 2x$$

25. $30.916 - 8.72$ _____

26. 3.4×0.0021 _____

27. $0.576 \div 0.32$ _____

28. $1^2/_3 \times 3^3/_4$ _____

29. $1^2/_3 \div \, ^3/_8$ _____

30. $1^4/_9 + \, ^5/_6$ _____

31. $4^5/_6 - 2^3/_5$ _____

32. Simplify this square root $\sqrt{98} =$ _____

33. Complete the following ratio so that it is equivalent to $4:5$

   $28 :$ _____

34. Use a proportion and solve this problem. Bob uses jelly and peanut butter in a ratio of $5:2$. He uses 10 teaspoons of jelly. How much peanut butter will he use?

_____

Questions 35–40: *Change among decimals, percents, and fractions to complete the table.*

Decimal	Percent	Fraction
0.56	35. _____	36. _____
37. _____	15.2%	38. _____
39. _____	40. _____	$^3/_8$

41. What is 35 percent of 50? _____

42. What percent of 120 is 40? _____

43. A $25 item is on sale for $23.50. What percent of decrease is that? _____

44. What is the probability of rolling one die and getting a 7? _____

45. You flip a fair coin five times in a row and it comes up heads each time. What is the probability that it will come up tails on the next flip?

_____

46. You pick one card from a deck. Then you pick another one without replacing the first. Are these dependent or independent events? Explain.

_____

47. Anna has four pictures. How many different pairs can she make? _____

Questions 48–49: *Find the median and mode of this set of data*

   10, 5, 2, 1, 8, 5, 3, 0

48. Median _____

49. Mode _____

50. Draw a stem and leaf plot that shows this data: 12, 12, 23, 25, 36, 38.

51. A recreation center is going to be built. The builders randomly poll people in town of various ages, male and female, to find out what is wanted in the recreation center. Is this an appropriate or inappropriate form of sampling? _____

52. The graph below represents the percentage of money that is given to each department at Ryan's college. If there is $3,000,000 in available funds, how much does the mathematics department get. _____

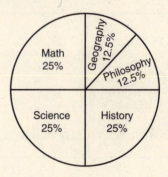

53. $^+85 + \, ^-103 =$ _____

54. $^-12 - \, ^+7 =$ _____

55. $^-72 - ^-28 =$ _____

56. $^-12 \times ^-6 =$ _____

57. $^-28 \div ^+7 =$ _____

58. $^-72 \div ^-9 =$ _____

59. Find the area of a triangle with a base of 3 and a height of 2.

_____

60. Find the area of a square with a side of 5.

_____

61. Find the area of a circle with a radius of 6.

_____

62. Add $(3x^2 + 4xy^2 - 2xy - 3) + (4\,x^2y - 2y)$

_____

Write the value of the variable.

63. $x - 35 = 26$ _____

64. $x + 81 = 7$ _____

65. $y \div 8 < 3$ _____

66. $3z \geq 54$ _____

67. $4y - 9 = 19$ _____

68. Write a linear factor of $6x^2 - 8x + 2$

_____

69. Find the solution to $x^2 - 6x + 4$

_____

70. Find the solution to the following system of equations _____

$$4x - 3y = 6$$
$$x\ - 2y = 4$$

71. Which letters below have rotational symmetry? _____

A   E   I   O   U

Questions 72–75: *Draw a model of:*

72. an acute angle

73. complementary angles

74. an isosceles triangle

75. a rectangle

76. Triangle *PQR* and triangle *LMN* are similar. What is the length of side *LN*? _____

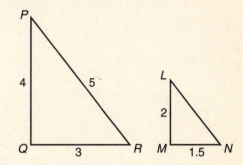

77. Use this coordinate grid and plot these points: $A\ (3,2)\ B\ (-4, -2)$.

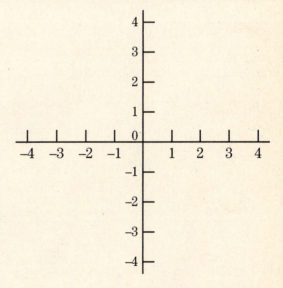

78. Graph the inequality $y \leq 2x - 4$.

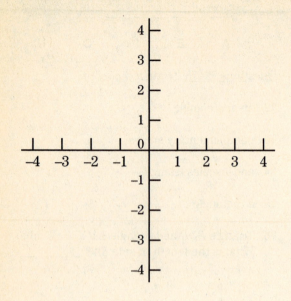

79. Draw a diagram to show that all vowels (a, e, i, o, u) are letters and that all consonants are letters, but that no vowels are consonants.

80. What is the difference between the mass of an object on earth and the mass of the same object on the moon?

_____

81. How many inches would it take to make 5 yards?_____

82. How many cups would it take to make 3 quarts? _____

83. A kilogram is how many grams? _____

84. A centimeter is how many meters? _____

85. It's 1:00 P.M. in Los Angeles. What time is it in New York? _____

86. It's 32° Celsius. How would you describe a day with that temperature?

_____

ANSWER CHECKLIST

The answers are organized by review sections. Check your answers. If you miss any questions in a section, check the box and review that section.

Number Sense

❑ *Understanding and Ordering Whole Numbers, page 232*
    1. 9
    2. <
    3. =
    4. <, <

❑ *Place Value, page 232*
    5. 10 billion
    6. six trillion

❑ *Positive Exponents, page 233*
    7. 32
    8. 36
    9. 72

❑ *Scientific Notation, page 234*
    10. 8.342×10^3

❑ *Understanding and Ordering Decimals, page 235*
    11. thousandths

❑ *Comparing Whole Numbers and Decimals, page 235*
    12. <
    13. <

❑ *Rounding Whole Numbers and Decimals, page 236*
    14. 234,000
    15. 234,489.08
    16. 234,489.1

❑ *Understanding and Ordering Fractions, page 237*
    17. $^{17}/_{20}$, $^{7}/_{8}$, $^{11}/_{12}$

❑ *Integers, page 240*
    18. −7

❑ *How and When to Add, Subtract, Multiply, and Divide, page 240*
    19. 00
    20. 39

❑ *Number Theory, page 242*
    21. The last 2 digits have to be divisible by 4.
    22. GCF is 2. LCM is 42.

❑ *Whole Number Computation, page 244*
    23. 26 R 11

❑ *Properties of Operations, page 246*
    24. Distributive

❑ *Add, Subtract, Multiply, and Divide Decimals, page 247*
    25. 22.196
    26. 0.00714
    27. 1.8

❑ *Multiplying, Dividing, Adding, and Subtracting Fractions and Mixed Numbers, page 248*
    28. $6 \frac{1}{4}$
    29. $4 \frac{4}{9}$
    30. $2 \frac{5}{18}$
    31. $2 \frac{7}{30}$

❑ *Square Roots, page 250*
    32. $7\sqrt{2}$

❑ *Ratio and Proportion, page 251*
    33. 35
    34. 4

❑ *Percent, page 252*

Decimal	Percent	Fraction
0.56	**35.** 56%	**36.** 14/25
37. 0.152	15.2%	**38.** 19/125
39. 0.375	**40.** 37.5%	3/8

❏ *Three Types of Percent Problems, page 254*
  41. 17.5
  42. 33 $\frac{1}{3}$%

❏ *Percent of Increase and Decrease, page 256*
  43. 6%

Probability, Statistics, and Data Analysis

❏ *Probability, page 257*
  44. Zero
  45. $\frac{1}{2}$

❏ *Dependent and Independent Events, page 258*
  46. Dependent. The outcome of one event affects the probability of the other event.

❏ *Permutations, Combinations, Counting Principle, page 259*
  47. 6

❏ *Statistics, page 260*
  48. 4
  49. 5

❏ *Stem-and-Leaf and Box-and-Whisker Plots, page 261*
  50.

1	2,2
2	3,5
3	6,8

Algebra

❏ *Adding and Subtracting Integers, page 264*
  51. −18
  52. −19
  53. −44

❏ *Multiplying and Dividing Integers, page 264*
  54. +72
  55. −4
  56. +8

❏ *Polynomials, page 265*
  57. $3x^2 + 4xy^2 - 4x^2y - 2xy - (-2y - 3)$

❏ *Formulas, page 268*
  58. 3
  59. 25
  60. about 113 (113.097...)

❏ *Equations and Inequalities, page 271*
  61. 61
  62. −74
  63. $y < 24$
  64. $z \geq 18$
  65. 7

❏ *Factor a Quadratic Expression, page 273*
  66. Either $(3x - 1)$ or $(2x - 2)$

Geometry and Measurement

❏ *Find the Root(s) of a Quadratic Expression, page 274*
  67. $x = 2$

❏ *Solve a System of Linear Equations, page 275*
  68. $x = 0, y = -2$ $(0, -2)$

❏ *Symmetry, page 278*
  69. I O

70. Acute angle   **71.** Complementary angles

 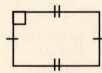

72. Isosceles triangle   **73.** Rectangle

❏ *Similar Triangles, page 284*
  74. 2.5

❑ *Coordinate Grid, page 286*
75.

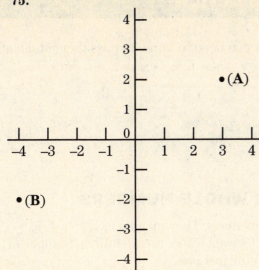

❑ *Graphing Equations on the Coordinate Grid, page 286*
76.

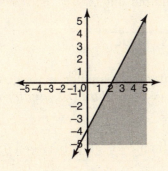

❑ *Using Diagrams, page 289*
77.

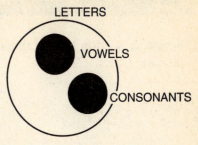

❑ *Measuring with a Ruler and a Protractor, page 290*

❑ *Weight and Mass, page 291*
78. None. Mass remains constant.

❑ *Customary (English) Units, page 291*
79. 180 inches
80. 12

❑ *Metric System, page 291*
81. 1,000
82. 0.01

❑ *Time and Temperature, page 293*
83. 4:00 P.M.
84. Hot — about 90°F.

☑ *Problem Solving, page 293*
Everyone should review this section.

MATHEMATICS REVIEW

This review section targets the skills and concepts you need to know to pass the mathematics part of the CSET.

NUMBER SENSE

UNDERSTANDING AND ORDERING WHOLE NUMBERS

Whole numbers are the numbers you use to tell how many. They include 0, 1, 2, 3, 4, 5, 6 . . . . The dots tell us that these numbers keep going on forever. There are an infinite number of whole numbers, which means you will never reach the last one.

Cardinal numbers such as 1, 9, and 18 tell how many. There are 9 players on the field in a baseball game. Ordinal numbers such as 1st, 2nd, 9th, and 18th tell about order. For example, Lynne batted 1st this inning.

You can visualize whole numbers evenly spaced on a number line.

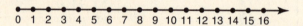

You can use the number line to compare numbers. Numbers get smaller as we go to the left and larger as we go to the right. We use the terms *equal to* (=), *less than* (<), *greater than* (>), and between to compare numbers.

12 equals 10 +2	2 is less than 5	9 is greater than 4	6 is between 5 and 7
12 = 10 + 2	2 < 5	9 > 4	5 < 6 < 7

PLACE VALUE

We use ten digits, 0–9 to write out numerals. We also use a place value system of numeration. The value of a digit depends on the place it occupies. Look at the following place value chart.

millions	hundred thousands	ten thousands	thousands	hundreds	tens	ones
3	5	7	9	4	1	0

The value of the 9 is 9,000. The 9 is in the thousands place. The value of the 5 is 500,000. The 5 is in the hundred thousands place. Read the number three million, five hundred seventy-nine thousand, four hundred ten.

Some whole numbers are very large. The distance from earth to the planet Pluto is about six trillion (6,000,000,000,000) yards. The distance from earth to the nearest star is about 40 quadrillion (40,000,000,000,000,000) yards.

Completed Examples

A. What is the value of 8 in the numeral 47,829?

The value of the 8 is 800; this is because the 8 is in the hundreds place.

B. Use <, >, or = to compare 2 and 7.

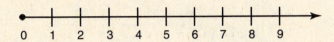

Use the number line to see that 2 < 7 (2 is less than 7).

Practice

Fill in the space with = , <, or > to make each statement true.

1. 2 ____ 3

2. 4 ____ 1

3. 8 ____ 9

4. 1 ____ 1

5. 7 ____ 6

6. Write a numeral in which the value of 7 is seven, the value of 9 is nine thousand, the value of 3 is thirty, and the 0 is in the hundreds place.

7. Write a numeral in which the value of 5 is fifty, the value of 2 is two thousand, the value of 1 is one, and the value of 8 is eight hundred.

8. What place values in the numeral 65,747 contain the same digit?

9. Write the whole numbers between 0 and 15.

10. How many whole numbers are there between 0 and 50?

Answers on page 316

POSITIVE EXPONENTS

You can show repeated multiplication as an exponent. The exponent shows how many times the factor appears.

$$\text{Base}—3^5 = 3 \times 3 \times 3 \times 3 \times 3 = 243$$

[Exponent]

[Factors]

Rules for Exponents

Use these rules to multiply and divide exponents with the *same base*.

$$7^8 \times 7^5 = 7^{13} \qquad a^n \times a^m = a^{m+n}$$
$$7^8 \div 7^5 = 7^3 \qquad a^n \div a^m = a^{n-m}$$

Completed Examples

    A. $4^3 + 6^2$ $= 4 \times 4 \times 4 + 6 \times 6$ $= 64 + 36 = 100$
    B. $(2^3)\,(4^2)$ $= (2 \times 2 \times 2) \times (4 \times 4) = 8 \times 16$ $= 128$
    C. $(3^2)^2$ $= 3^4$ $= 3 \times 3 \times 3 \times 3 = 81$
    D. $(10 - 9)^2 = 1^2$ $= 1$

Practice

1. $5^2 + 6^3 =$

2. $(3^2)^2 =$

3. $(8 - 6)^3 =$

4. $(5^2)\,(6^2) =$

5. $3^3 + 2^3 =$

6. $10^2 - 7^2 =$

7. $(4^3)^2 =$

8. $(2^4)^5 =$

9. $6^2 + 2^3 =$

10. $(25 - 15)^3 =$

11. $(4^2)^2 =$

12. $(2^3)\,(3^2) =$

Answers on page 316

SCIENTIFIC NOTATION

Scientific notation uses powers of 10. The power shows how many zeros to use.

$10^0 = 1$ $10^1 = 10$ $10^2 = 100$ $10^3 = 1,000$ $10^4 = 10,000$ $10^5 = 100,000$
               $10^{-1} = 0.1$ $10^{-2} = 0.01$ $10^{-3} = 0.001$ $10^{-4} = 0.0001$ $10^{-5} = 0.00001$

Write whole numbers and decimals in scientific notation. Use a decimal with one numeral to the left of the decimal point.

2,345	$=$	2.345×10^3	The decimal point moved three places to the left. Use 10^3.
176.8	$=$	1.768×10^2	The decimal point moved two places to the left. Use 10^2.
0.0034	$=$	3.4×10^{-3}	The decimal point moved three places to the right. Use 10^{-3}.
2.0735	$=$	2.0735×10^0	The decimal is in the correct form. Use 10^0 to stand for 1.

Completed Examples

    A. Write 7,952 in scientific notation.

    Move the decimal point three places to the left and write $7,952 = 7.952 \times 10^3$.

    B. Write 0.03254 in scientific notation.

    Move the decimal point two places to the right and write 3.254×10^{-2}.

Practice

Rewrite using scientific notation.

1. 0.0564

2. 0.00897

3. 0.06501

4. 0.000354

5. 545

6. 7,790

7. 289,705

8. 1,801,319

Answers on page 316

UNDERSTANDING AND ORDERING DECIMALS

Decimals are used to represent numbers between 0 and 1. Decimals can also be written on a number line.

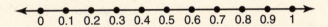

We also use ten digits 0–9 and a place value system of numeration to write decimals. The value of a digit depends on the place it occupies. Look at the following place value chart.

ones	tenths	hundredths	thousandths	ten thousandths	hundred thousandths	millionths	ten millionths	hundred millionths	billionths
0 .	3	6	8	7					

The value of 3 is three tenths. The 3 is in the tenths place. The value of 8 is eight thousandths. The 8 is in the thousandths place.

COMPARING WHOLE NUMBERS AND DECIMALS

To compare two numbers line up the place values. Start at the left and keep going until the digits in the same place are different.

Compare	9,879 and 16,459	23,801 and 23,798	58.1289 and 58.132
Line up the place values	9,879 16,459 9,879 < 16,459 Less than	23,**8**01 23,798 23,801 > 23,798 Greater than	58.1**2**89 58.1**3**2 58.1289 < 58.132 Less than

Completed Examples

A. What is the value of the digit 2 in the decimal 35.6829?

The 2 is in the thousandths place. $2 \times 0.001 = 0.002$.
The value of the 2 is 0.002 or 2 thousandths.

B. Use <, >, or = to compare 1248.9234 and 1248.9229

1248.9234 ◯ 1248.9229 The digits in the numerals are the same until you reach the thousandths place where 3 > 2. Since 3 > 2, then 1248.9234 > 1248.9229.

Practice

Use <, >, or = to compare.

---

1. 0.02 ____ 0.003

2. 4.6 ____ 1.98

3. 0.0008 ____ 0.00009

4. 1.0 ____ 1

5. 7.6274 ____ 7.6269

Write the answer.

---

6. Write a numeral in which the value of 5 is five tenths, the value of 2 is two, the value of 6 is six thousandths, and the value of 8 is eight hundredths.

7. Write a numeral in which the value of 4 is in the ten thousandths place, the value of 3 is three hundred, the 7 is in the hundredths place, the 1 is in the tens place, the 9 is in the ten thousands place, and the rest of the digits are zeros.

8. In the numeral 6.238935, which place values contain the same digit?

9. Using only the tenths place, write all the decimals from 0 to 1.

10. If you used only the tenths and hundredths places, how many decimals are between 0 and 1?

Answers on page 316

ROUNDING WHOLE NUMBERS AND DECIMALS

Follow these steps to round a number to a place.

- Look at the digit to the right of that place.

- If the digit to the right is 5 or more, round up. If the digit is less than 5, leave the numeral to be rounded as written.

Completed Examples

A. *Round 859,465 to the thousands place.*

Underline the thousands place.

Look to the right. The digit 4 is less than 5 so leave as written.

859,465 rounded to the thousands place is 859,000.

859,465 rounded to the ten-thousands place 860,000.

B. *Round 8.647 to the hundredths place.*

Underline the hundredths place.

Look to the right. The digit 7 is 5 or more so you round up.

8.647 rounded to the *hundredths* place is 8.65.

8.647 rounded to the *tenths* place is 8.6.

Practice

1. Round 23,465 to the hundreds place.

2. Round 74.1508 to the thousandths place.

3. Round 975,540 to the ten thousands place.

4. Round 302.787 to the tenths place.

5. Round 495,244 to the tens place.

6. Round 1508.75 to the hundreds place.

7. Round 13.097 to the hundredths place.

8. Round 198,704 to the hundred thousands place.

9. Round 51.8985 to the ones place.

10. Round 23,457 to the hundreds place.

Answers on page 316

UNDERSTANDING AND ORDERING FRACTIONS

A fractions names a part of a whole or of a group. A fraction has two parts, a numerator and a denominator. The denominator tells how many parts in all. The numerator tell how many parts you identified.

$\dfrac{3}{4}$ Numerator
     Denominator

Equivalent Fractions

Two fractions that stand for the same number are called equivalent fractions. Multiply or divide the numerator and denominator by the same number to find an equivalent fraction.

$$\frac{2\times 3}{5\times 3}=\frac{6}{15} \qquad \frac{6\div 3}{9\div 3}=\frac{2}{3} \qquad \frac{6\times 4}{8\times 4}=\frac{24}{32} \qquad \frac{8\div 2}{10\div 2}=\frac{4}{5}$$

Fractions can also be written and ordered on a number line. You can use the number line to compare fractions. Fractions get smaller as we go to the left and larger as we go to the right. We use the terms equivalent to (=), less than (<), greater than (>), and between to compare fractions.

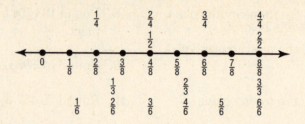

$\frac{1}{2}$ is equivalent to $\frac{2}{4}$ $\frac{2}{3}$ is less than $\frac{3}{4}$ $\frac{5}{8}$ is greater than $\frac{1}{2}$ $\frac{1}{3}$ is between $\frac{1}{4}$ and $\frac{3}{8}$

$$\frac{1}{2} = \frac{2}{4}$$ $$\frac{2}{3} < \frac{3}{4}$$ $$\frac{5}{8} > \frac{1}{2}$$ $$\frac{1}{4} < \frac{1}{3} < \frac{3}{8}$$

Compare Two Fractions

Use this method to compare two fractions. For example, compare $\frac{13}{18}$ and $\frac{5}{7}$. First write the two fractions and cross multiply as shown. The larger cross product appears next to the larger fraction. If cross products are equal then the fractions are equivalent.

$$91 = \qquad\qquad = 90$$

$$\frac{13 \quad \times \quad 5}{18 \qquad\qquad 7}$$

$$91 > 90 \text{ so } \frac{13}{18} > \frac{5}{7}$$

Mixed Numbers and Improper Fractions

Change an improper fraction to a mixed number:

$$\frac{23}{8} = 8\overline{)23}\,^{2\frac{7}{8}}$$

Change a mixed number to an improper fraction:

$$3\frac{2}{5} = \frac{17}{5}$$

Multiply denominator and whole number. Then add the numerator.

$$\frac{(3 \times 5) + 2}{5} = \frac{15 + 2}{5} = \frac{17}{5}$$

Completed Examples

A. Compare $\frac{5}{7}$ and $\frac{18}{19}$,

Use cross multiplication.

$5 \times 19 = 95$ and $7 \times 18 = 126$, therefore $\frac{5}{7} < \frac{18}{19}$.

B. Write $\frac{27}{7}$ as a mixed number.

$$\begin{array}{r} 3 \text{ R6} \\ 7\overline{)27} \\ \underline{21} \\ 6 \end{array}$$

$$\frac{27}{7} = 3\frac{6}{7}$$

C. Write $6\frac{5}{8}$ as a fraction.

$6 \times 8 = 48$. Multiply the denominator and the whole number.

$48 + 5 = 53$. Add the numerator to the product.

$$6\frac{5}{8} = \frac{53}{8}$$

Practice

Write the improper fraction as a mixed number.

1. $\frac{5}{3}$

2. $\frac{15}{7}$

3. $\frac{24}{9}$

Write the mixed number as an improper fraction.

4. $8\frac{1}{5}$

5. $6\frac{7}{8}$

6. $9\frac{5}{7}$

Use $>$, $<$, $=$ to compare the fractions.

7. $\frac{3}{7}, \frac{4}{9}$

8. $\frac{5}{6}, \frac{25}{30}$

9. $\frac{4}{5}, \frac{7}{8}$

Answers on page 316

INTEGERS

The number line can also show negative numbers. There is a negative whole number for every positive whole number. Zero is neither positive nor negative. The negative whole numbers, the positive whole numbers, and zero, together, are called integers. Integers are smaller as you go left on the number line and larger as you go to the right.

```
◄———•——•——•——•——•——•——•——•——•——•——•——•——•——•——•——•——•——•——•——•——•———►
  ⁻10 ⁻9 ⁻8  ⁻7 ⁻6 ⁻5  ⁻4 ⁻3 ⁻2 ⁻1  0  ⁺1 ⁺2 ⁺3 ⁺4 ⁺5 ⁺6 ⁺7 ⁺8 ⁺9 ⁺10
```

$$^-10 < {^-1} \qquad\qquad ^-8 < {^-3} \qquad\qquad ^+1 > {^-9} \qquad\qquad ^+6 > {^+4}$$

HOW AND WHEN TO ADD, SUBTRACT, MULTIPLY, AND DIVIDE

Order of Operations

Use this phrase to remember the order in which we do operations:

Please Excuse My Dear Aunt Sally

(1) **P**arentheses (2) **E**xponents (3) **M**ultiplication or **D**ivision (4) **A**ddition or **S**ubtraction

For example,

$$4 + 3 \times 7^2 = 4 + 3 \times 49 = 4 + 147 = 151$$
$$(4 + 3) \times 7^2 = 7 \times 7^2 = 7 \times 49 = 343$$
$$(6 - 10 \div 5) + 6 \times 3 = (6 - 2) + 6 \times 3 = 4 + 6 \times 3 = 4 + 18 = 22$$

Decide Whether to Add, Subtract, Multiply, or Divide

Before you can solve a problem, you should know which operation to use. You can use key words to decide which operation to use, or you can use a problem-solving strategy called choosing the operation. We'll discuss both of them here.

Key Words

Addition	sum, and, more, increased by
Subtraction	less, difference, decreased by
Multiplication	of, product, times
Division	per, quotient, shared, ratio
Equals	is, equals

You can't just use these key words without thinking. You must check to be sure that the operation makes sense when it replaces the key word. For example,

19 and 23 is 42	16 is 4 more than 12	What percent of 19 is 5.7
$19 + 23 = 42$	$16 = 4 + 12$	_____% $\times 19 = 5.7$

Completed Example

$7 + 3 \times 6 + 4^2 - (8 + 4) = 7 + 3 \times 6 + 4^2 - \underline{12} =$

$7 + 3 \times 6 + \underline{16} - 12 \quad = 7 + \underline{18} + 16 - 12 \quad = 29$

Practice

Find the answer.

1. $4 \times 5 + 4 \div 2 =$

2. $(5 + 7 - 9) \times 8^2 + 2 =$

3. $((7 + 4) - (1 + 4)) \times 6 =$

4. $6^2 + 3(9 - 5 + 7)^2 =$

5. $(12 + 5) \times 3 - 6^2 =$

6. $8 \times 5 + 4 - 8 \div 2 =$

7. $100 - 30 \times 5 + 7 =$

8. $((5 + 2)^2 + 16) \times 8 =$

Answers on page 317

Choosing the Operation

To use the choosing-the-operation strategy, you think of each situation in this way. What do I know? What am I trying to find? The answers to these questions lead you directly to the correct operation.

You Know	You Want to Find
Add	
1. How many in two or more groups	How many in all
2. How many in one group How many join it	The total amount
3. How many in one group How many more in the second group	How many in the second group
Subtract	
4. How many in one group Number taken away	How many are left
5. How many in each of two groups	How much larger one group is than the other
6. How many in one group How many in part of that group	How many in the rest of the group
Multiply	
7. How many in each group There is the same number in each group How many groups	How many in all
Divide	
8. Same number in each group How many in all How many in each group	How many groups
9. Same number in each group How many in all How many groups	How many in each group

NUMBER THEORY

Number theory explores the natural numbers {1, 2, 3, 4, . . .}. We'll review just a few important number theory concepts.

Factors

The factors of a number evenly divide the number with no remainder. For example, 2 is a factor of 6, but 2 is not a factor of 5.

The number 1 is a factor of every number. Each number is a factor of itself.

1	The only factor is 1
2	Factors 1, 2
3	1, 3
4	1, 2, 4
5	1, 5
6	1, 2, 3, 6
7	1, 7
8	1, 2, 4, 8
9	1, 3, 9
10	1, 2, 5, 10

Prime Numbers and Composite Numbers

A prime number has exactly two factors, itself and 1.
2 is prime. The only factors are 1 and 2.
3 Prime. Factors 1, 3.
5 Prime. Factors 1, 5.
7 Prime. Factors 1, 7.

A composite number has more than two factors.
4 is composite. The factors are 1, 2, 4.
6 is composite. Factors: 1, 2, 3, 6.
8 is composite. Factors: 1, 2, 4, 8.
9 is composite. Factors: 1, 3, 9.
10 is composite. Factors: 1, 2, 5, 10.

The number 1 has only one factor, itself. The number 1 is neither prime nor composite.

Least Common Multiple (LCM), Greatest Common Factor (GCF)

Multiples. The multiples of a number are all the numbers you get when you count by that number. Here are some examples.

Multiples of 1: 1, 2, 3, 4, 5, . . .
Multiples of 2: 2, 4, 6, 8, 10, . . .
Multiples of 3: 3, 6, 9, 12, 15, . . .
Multiples of 4: 4, 8, 12, 16, 20, . . .
Multiples of 5: 5, 10, 15, 20, 25, . . .

Least Common Multiple is the smallest multiple shared by two numbers.

The least common multiple of 6 and 8 is 24.

List the multiples of 6 and 8. Notice that 24 is the smallest multiple common to both numbers.

Multiples of 6: 6, 12, 18, **24**, 30, 36
Multiples of 8: 8, 16, **24**, 32, 40

Greatest Common Factor is the largest factor shared by two numbers.

The greatest common factor of 28 and 36 is 4.
List the factors of 28 and 36.

Factors of 28: 1, 2, **4**, 7, 28
Factors of 36: 1, 2, 3, **4**, 9, 12, 18, 36

Divisibility Rules

Use these rules to find out if a number is divisible by the given number. *Divisible* means the given number divides evenly with no remainder.

2 Every even number is divisible by 2.

3 If the sum of the digits is divisible by 3, the number is divisible by 3.

347   3 + 4 + 7 = 14   14 is not divisible by 3 so 347 is not divisible by 3

738   7 + 3 + 8 = 18   18 is divisible by 3 so 738 is divisible by 3

4 If the last two digits are divisible by 4, the number is divisible by 4.

484,8<u>42</u>   42 is not divisible by 4 so 484,842 is not divisible by 4.

371,9<u>56</u>   56 is divisible by 4 so 372,956 is divisible by 4.

5 If the last digit is 0 or 5, then the number is divisible by 5.

6 If the number meets the divisibility rules for both 2 *and* 3 then it is divisible by 6.

8 If the last three digits are divisible by 8, then the number is divisible by 8.

208,513,<u>114</u>   114 is not divisible by 8 so 208,513,114 is not divisible by 8.

703,628,<u>920</u>   920 is divisible by 8 so 703,628,920 is divisible by 8.

9 If the sum of the digits is divisible by 9 then the number is divisible by 9.

93,163   9 + 3 + 1 + 6 + 3 = 22   22 is not divisible by 9 so 93,163
                                        is not divisible by 9.

86,715   8 + 6 + 7 + 1 + 5 = 27   27 is divisible by 9 so 86,715 is
                                        divisible by 9.

10 If a number ends in 0, the number is divisible by 10.

Completed Examples

A. Find the factors of 24.

The factors are 1, 2, 3, 4, 6, 8, 12, and 24.
These are the only numbers that divide 24 with no remainder.

B. Find the GCF of 14 and 22.

Write out the factors of each number.
14: 1, 2, 7, 14
22: 1, 2, 11, 22

The greatest common factor is 2.

C. Find the LCM of 6 and 9.

List some of the multiples of each number.
6: 6, 12, 18, 24, ...
9: 9, 18, 27, ...

The least common multiple is 18.

Practice

Write the factors of each number.

1. 13	**2.** 26
3. 40	**4.** 23

Find the LCM of the two numbers.

5. 6 and 8	**6.** 5 and 12
7. 7 and 35	**8.** 4 and 14

Find the GCF of the two numbers.

9. 24 and 30	**10.** 15 and 40
11. 32 and 64	**12.** 56 and 84

Answers on page 317

WHOLE NUMBER COMPUTATION

Follow these steps to add, subtract, multiply, and divide whole numbers.
Estimate first and then check to be sure your answer is reasonable.

Add: 24,262 + 8,921.

Estimate first.

24,262 rounded to the nearest ten thousand is 24,000.
8,921 rounded to the nearest thousand is 9,000.
24,000 + 9,000 = 33,000. The answer should be close to 33,000.

Add.

```
                          1 1
    2 4 2 6 2          2 4 2 6 2
  +   8 9 2 1        +   8 9 2 1
                      3 3 1 8 3
```

Align digits.   Add.

33,183 is close to 33,000, so the answer is reasonable.

Subtract: 20,274 – 17,235.

Estimate first.

20,274 rounded to the nearest thousand is 20,000.
17,235 rounded to the nearest thousand is 17,000.
20,000 – 17,000 = 3,000.
The answer should be close to 3,000.

Subtract.

```
                      1 10  6 14
    2 0 2 7 4         2 0 2 7 4
  – 1 7 2 3 5       – 1 7 2 3 5
                       3 0 3 9
```

Align digits.   Subtract.

3,039 is close to 3000, so the answer seems reasonable.

Multiply: 32 × 181.

Estimate first.

Multiplication answers may look correct but may be wrong by a multiple of 10.

32 rounded to the nearest ten is 30.
181 rounded to the nearest hundred is 200.

$30 \times 200 = 6,000$

The answer should be near 6,000.

Multiply.

```
      181              181
    × 32             × 32
      362              362
      543              543
                       5792
```

Find the partial products.   Add the partial products.

The answer is close to 6,000.
The answer seems reasonable.

Divide: $927 \div 43$.

Estimate first.

You may make a division error if you misalign digits.

927 rounded to the nearest hundred is 900.
43 is close to 45.
$900 \div 45 = 20$

The answer should be somewhere near 20.

Divide.

$$43 \overline{)927}$$

$$\begin{array}{r} 21 \text{ R}24 \\ 43 \overline{)927} \\ \underline{86} \\ 67 \\ \underline{43} \\ 24 \end{array}$$

Divide.   Find the quotient and the remainder.

The answer is close to 20.
The answer seems reasonable.

Practice

Find the answer.

1.	97,218 + 1,187	2.	23,045 + 4,034	3.	67,914 +27,895	4.	48,549 +17,635
5.	20,591 − 4,578	6.	34,504 − 405	7.	57,895 − 23,207	8.	84,403 − 42,194
9.	240 × 57	10.	302 × 91	11.	725 × 41	12.	146 × 36

13. $328 \div 41 =$ 14. $240 \div 59 =$ 15. $754 \div 26 =$ 16. $2{,}370 \div 74 =$

Answers on page 317

Properties of Operations

Subtraction and division are not commutative or associative.

Commutative $a + b = b + a$ $a \times b = b \times a$

          $3 + 5 = 5 + 3$ $3 \times 5 = 5 \times 3$

Associative $(a + b) + c = a + (b + c)$ $(a \times b) \times c = a \times (b \times c)$

          $(3 + 4) + 5 = 3 + (4 + 5)$ $(3 \times 4) \times 5 = 3 \times (4 \times 5)$

Identity	$a + 0 = a$	$a \times 1 = a$
	$5 + 0 = 5$	$5 \times 1 = 5$

Inverse	$a + (-a) = 0$	$a \times \dfrac{1}{a} = 1$
	$5 + (-5) = 0$	$5 \times \dfrac{1}{5} = 1 \ (a \neq 0)$

Distributive property of $a\,(b + c) = (a \times b) + (a \times c)$
multiplication over addition $3\,(4 + 5) = (3 \times 4) + (3 \times 5)$

Completed Examples

A. Use a property of arithmetic to write an expression equivalent to $8y - 4x$.
These items ask you to identify equivalent statements produced by the properties.
The distributive property creates the equivalent expressions $4(2y - x)$ or $2(4y - 2x)$.

B. What property is illustrated by $7^2 + 8^3 = 8^3 + 7^2$?
This statement demonstrates the commutative property.

Practice Questions

1. Use a property to write an expression equivalent to $\% \times \%$.

2. What property is illustrated by $(2 + 3) + 4 = 2 + (3 + 4)$?

3. What property is illustrated by $3x(x + 2y) = 3x^2 + 6xy$?

4. Write an expression equivalent to $a(6) + a(3)$.

5. What property is illustrated by $3a + 3b = 3b + 3a$?

6. Choose a statement that is *not* true for all real numbers.
   (A) $A\,(1/A) = 0$ for $A \neq 0$.
   (B) $x^2\,(y^2) = (xy)^2$
   (C) $(3x + y)\,(x - y) = (x - y)\,(3x + y)$
   (D) $10^2 + 12 = 12 + 10^2$

Answers on page 317

ADD, SUBTRACT, MULTIPLY, AND DIVIDE DECIMALS

Add and Subtract Decimals

Line up the decimal points and add or subtract.

Add: $14.9 + 3.108 + 0.16$ Subtract $14.234 - 7.14$

$$
\begin{array}{r}
14.9 \\
3.108 \\
+\ 0.16 \\
\hline
18.168
\end{array}
\qquad
\begin{array}{r}
14.234 \\
-7.14 \\
\hline
7.094
\end{array}
$$

Multiply Decimals

Multiply as with whole numbers. Count the total number of decimal places in the factors. Put that many decimal places in the product. You may have to write leading zeros.

Multiply: 17.4×1.3

$$
\begin{array}{r}
17.4 \\
\times\ 1.3 \\
\hline
522 \\
174 \\
\hline
22\,6\,2
\end{array}
$$

Multiply: 0.016×1.7

$$
\begin{array}{r}
0.016 \\
\times\ 1.7 \\
\hline
112 \\
16 \\
\hline
.02\,7\,2
\end{array}
$$

Divide Decimals

Make the divisor a whole number. Match the movement in the dividend and then divide.

$0.16\overline{)1.328}$

$0.16.\overline{)1.32.8}$

$$
\begin{array}{r}
8.3 \\
16\overline{)132.8} \\
128 \\
\hline
48 \\
48 \\
\hline
0
\end{array}
$$

Practice

1. 12.79 8.1 + 5.2	**2.** 40.267 23.2 + 9.15	**3.** 940.17 36.15 + 12.07	**4.** 5290.3 167.81 + 15.09
5. 37.9 − 29.7	**6.** 136.804 − 65.7944	**7.** 513.72 − 59.75	**8.** 2451.06 − 683.19
9. 0.249 × 2.5	**10.** 46.7 × 3.5	**11.** 56.2 × 65.49	**12.** 93.57 × 40.2

13. $10.08 \div 2.1\,5$ **14.** $16.32 \div 1.7\,5$ **15.** $248.64 \div 7.4\,5$ **16.** $653.276 \div 5.2\,5$

Answers on page 000

MULTIPLYING, DIVIDING, ADDING, AND SUBTRACTING FRACTIONS AND MIXED NUMBERS

Multiplying Fractions and Mixed Numbers

Write any mixed number as an improper fraction. Multiply numerator and denominator. Write the product in simplest form. For example, Multiply $^3/_4$ and $^1/_6$.

$$
\frac{3}{4} \times \frac{1}{6} = \frac{3}{24} = \frac{1}{8}
$$

Now, multiply $3^1/_3$ times $^3/_5$.

$$
3\frac{1}{3} \times \frac{3}{5} = \frac{10}{3} \times \frac{3}{5} = \frac{30}{15} = 2
$$

Dividing Fractions and Mixed Numbers

To divide $1\frac{4}{5}$ by $\frac{3}{8}$:

$$1\frac{4}{5} \div \frac{3}{8} = \frac{9}{5} \div \frac{3}{8} = \frac{9}{5} \times \frac{8}{3} = \frac{72}{15} = 4\frac{12}{15} = 4\frac{4}{5}$$

Write any mixed numbers as improper fractions   Invert the divisor and multiply   Write the product   Write in simplest form

Adding Fractions and Mixed Numbers

Write fractions with common denominators. Add and then write in simplest form.

Add: $\frac{3}{8}+\frac{1}{4}$

$$\frac{3}{8}=\frac{3}{8}$$
$$+\frac{1}{4}=\frac{2}{8}$$
$$\frac{5}{8}$$

Add: $\frac{7}{8}+\frac{5}{12}$

$$\frac{7}{8}=\frac{21}{24}$$
$$+\frac{5}{12}=\frac{10}{24}$$
$$\frac{31}{24}=1\frac{7}{24}$$

Add: $2\frac{1}{3}+\frac{5}{7}$

$$2\frac{1}{3}=2\frac{7}{21}$$
$$+\frac{5}{7}=\frac{15}{21}$$
$$2\frac{22}{21}=3\frac{1}{21}$$

Subtracting Fractions and Mixed Numbers

Write fractions with common denominators. Subtract and then write in simplest form.

Subtract: $\frac{5}{16}-\frac{1}{3}$

$$\frac{5}{6}=\frac{5}{6}$$
$$-\frac{1}{3}=\frac{2}{6}$$
$$\frac{3}{6}=\frac{1}{2}$$

Subtract: $\frac{3}{8}-\frac{1}{5}$

$$\frac{3}{8}=\frac{15}{40}$$
$$-\frac{1}{5}=\frac{8}{40}$$
$$\frac{7}{40}$$

Subtract: $3\frac{1}{6}-1\frac{1}{3}$

$$3\frac{1}{6}=3\frac{1}{6}=2\frac{7}{6}$$
$$-1\frac{1}{3}=1\frac{2}{6}=1\frac{2}{6}$$
$$1\frac{5}{6}$$

Practice

1. $\frac{1}{3}\times\frac{5}{9}=$

2. $\frac{2}{3}\times\frac{1}{4}=$

3. $3\frac{3}{8}\times4\frac{1}{8}=$

4. $3\frac{1}{5}\times2\frac{4}{7}=$

5. $\frac{3}{4}\div\frac{7}{8}=$

6. $\frac{2}{5}\div\frac{7}{9}=$

7. $9\frac{5}{7} \div 4\frac{1}{3} =$

8. $2\frac{4}{5} \div 7\frac{3}{5} =$

9. $\frac{5}{9} + \frac{2}{3} =$

10. $\frac{7}{10} + \frac{2}{4} =$

11. $1\frac{6}{7} + 2\frac{3}{14} =$

12. $5\frac{2}{3} + 6\frac{5}{6} =$

13. $\frac{2}{7} - \frac{5}{21} =$

14. $\frac{2}{5} - \frac{3}{8} =$

15. $3\frac{4}{5} - 3\frac{2}{15} =$

16. $8\frac{1}{7} - 4\frac{2}{9} =$

Answers on page 317

SQUARE ROOTS

The square root of a given number, when multiplied by itself, equals the given number. This symbol means the square root of 25 $\sqrt{25}$. The square root of 25 is 5. $5 \times 5 = 25$.

Some Square Roots Are Whole Numbers

The numbers with whole-number square roots are called perfect squares.

$$\sqrt{1} = 1 \quad \sqrt{4} = 2 \quad \sqrt{9} = 3 \quad \sqrt{16} = 4 \quad \sqrt{25} = 5 \quad \sqrt{36} = 6$$

$$\sqrt{49} = 7 \quad \sqrt{64} = 8 \quad \sqrt{81} = 9 \quad \sqrt{100} = 10 \quad \sqrt{121} = 11 \quad \sqrt{144} = 12$$

The fractional exponent $a^{\frac{1}{2}}$ is another way to write square root.

$$16^{\frac{1}{2}} = \sqrt{16} = 4 \qquad\qquad 324^{\frac{1}{2}} = \sqrt{324} = 18$$

Use This Rule to Write a Square Root in Its Simplest Form

$$\sqrt{a \times b} = \sqrt{a} \times \sqrt{b} \qquad\qquad \sqrt{5 \times 3} = \sqrt{5} \times \sqrt{3}$$

$$\sqrt{72} = \sqrt{36 \times 2} = \sqrt{36} \times \sqrt{2} = 6 \times \sqrt{2}$$

Completed Examples

A. Write the square root of 162 in simplest form.

$$\sqrt{162} = \sqrt{81 \times 2} = \sqrt{81} \times \sqrt{2} = 9\sqrt{2}$$

B. Write the square root of 112 in simplest form.

$$\sqrt{112} = \sqrt{16 \times 7} = \sqrt{16} \times \sqrt{7} = 4\sqrt{7}$$

Practice

Simplify.

1. $\sqrt{256}$

2. $\sqrt{400}$

3. $\sqrt{576}$

4. $\sqrt{900}$

5. $\sqrt{1225}$

6. $\sqrt{48}$

7. $\sqrt{245}$

8. $\sqrt{396}$

9. $\sqrt{567}$

10. $\sqrt{832}$

Answers on page 318

RATIO, PROPORTION, AND PERCENT

Ratio

A ratio is a way of comparing two numbers with division. It conveys the same meaning as a fraction. There are three ways to write a ratio.

Using words   3 to 4   As a fraction   3/4   Using a colon   3 : 4

Proportion

A proportion shows two ratios that have the same value; that is, the fractions representing the ratios are equivalent. Use cross multiplication. If the cross products are equal, then the two ratios form a proportion.

$^3/_8$ and $^{27}/_{72}$ form a proportion. The cross products are equal. ($3 \times 72 = 8 \times 27$)

$^3/_8$ and $^{24}/_{56}$ do not form a proportion. The cross products are not equal.

Solving a Proportion

You may have to write a proportion to solve a problem. For example, the mason mixes cement and sand using a ratio of 2 : 5. Twelve bags of cement will be used. How much sand is needed?

To solve, use the numerator to stand for cement. The denominator will stand for sand.

$$\frac{2}{5} = \frac{12}{S} \qquad\qquad \frac{2}{5} = \frac{12}{S}$$

$$2 \times S = 5 \times 12$$
$$2S = 60$$
$$S = 30$$

Write the proportion   Cross multiply to solve

Thirty bags of sand are needed.

Completed Example

The problem compares loaves of whole wheat bread with loaves of rye bread. Let the numerators stand for loaves of whole wheat bread. The denominators stand for loaves of rye bread.

Ratio of whole wheat to rye. $\dfrac{3}{7}$ Ratio of whole wheat to rye for 51 loaves of whole wheat. $\dfrac{51}{R}$

Write a proportion. $\dfrac{3}{7} = \dfrac{51}{R}$

Solution: $3R = 357$ $R = 119$

There are 119 loaves of bread.

Practice

1. A salesperson sells 7 vacuum cleaners for every 140 potential buyers. If there are 280 potential buyers, how many vacuums are sold?

2. There is one teacher for every 8 preschool students. How many teachers are needed if there are 32 preschool students?

3. There are 3 rest stops for every 20 miles of highway. How many rest stops would there be on 140 miles of highway?

4. Does $\dfrac{7}{9}$ and $\dfrac{28}{36}$ form a proportion? Explain.

Answers on page 318

PERCENT

Percent comes from per centum, which means per hundred. Whenever you see a number followed by a percent sign it means that number out of 100.

Decimals and Percents

To write a decimal as a percent, move the decimal point two places to the right and write the percent sign.

$$0.34 = 34\% \qquad 0.297 = 29.7\% \qquad 0.6 = 60\% \qquad 0.001 = 0.1\%$$

To write a percent as a decimal, move the decimal point two places to the left and delete the percent sign.

$$51\% = 0.51 \qquad 34.18\% = 0.3418 \qquad 0.9\% = 0.009$$

Fractions and Percents

Writing Fractions as Percents

• Divide the numerator by the denominator. Write the answer as a percent.

Write $^3/_5$ as a percent.

$$5\overline{)3.0} = 0.6 \qquad 0.6 = 60\%$$

Write $^5/_8$ as a percent.

$$8\overline{)5.000} = 0.625 \qquad 0.625 = 62.5\%$$

• Write an equivalent fraction with 100 in the denominator. Write the numerator followed by a percent sign.

Write $^{13}/_{25}$ as a percent.

$$\frac{13}{25} = \frac{52}{100} = 52\%$$

• Use these equivalencies.

$\frac{1}{4} = 25\%$	$\frac{1}{2} = 50\%$	$\frac{3}{4} = 75\%$	$\frac{4}{4} = 100\%$
$\frac{1}{5} = 20\%$	$\frac{2}{5} = 40\%$	$\frac{3}{5} = 60\%$	$\frac{4}{5} = 80\%$
$\frac{1}{6} = 16\frac{2}{3}\%$	$\frac{1}{3} = 33\frac{1}{3}\%$	$\frac{2}{3} = 66\frac{2}{3}\%$	$\frac{5}{6} = 83\frac{1}{3}\%$
$\frac{1}{8} = 12\frac{1}{2}\%$	$\frac{3}{8} = 37\frac{1}{2}\%$	$\frac{5}{8} = 62\frac{1}{2}\%$	$\frac{7}{8} = 87\frac{1}{2}\%$

Writing Percents as Fractions

Write a fraction with 100 in the denominator and the percent in the numerator. Simplify.

$$18\% = \frac{18}{100} = \frac{9}{50} \qquad 7.5\% = \frac{7.5}{100} = \frac{75}{1000} = \frac{3}{40}$$

Completed Examples

A. Write 0.567 as a percent.

Move the decimal two places to the right and write a percent sign, therefore, 0.567 = 56.7%.

B. Write $\frac{1}{4}$ as a percent.

Write $\frac{1}{4}$ as a decimal $(1 \div 4) = 0.25$

Write 0.25 as a decimal 0.25 = 25%

    C. Write 26% as a fraction.

    Place the percent number in the numerator and 100 in the denominator.

$$26\% = \frac{26}{100} = \frac{13}{50}.$$

Simplify: $\frac{26}{100} = \frac{13}{50}$

Practice

Write the decimal as a percent.

1. 0.359   **2.** 0.78

3. 0.215   **4.** 0.041

Write the fraction as a percent.

5. $\frac{1}{9}$ **6.** $\frac{5}{8}$

7. $\frac{3}{10}$ **8.** $\frac{4}{9}$

Write the percents as fractions in simplest form.

9. 58%   **10.** 79%

11. 85.2%   **12.** 97.4%

Answers on page 318

THREE TYPES OF PERCENT PROBLEMS

Finding a Percent of a Number

To find a percent of a number, write a number sentence with a decimal for the percent and solve.

Find 40% of 90.

$0.4 \times 90 = 36$

It may be easier to write a fraction for the percent.

Find $62\frac{1}{2}$% of 64.

$\frac{5}{8} \times 64 = 5 \times 8 = 40$

Finding What Percent One Number Is of Another

To find what percent one number is of another, write a number sentence and solve to find the percent.

What percent of 5 is 3?

$n \times 5 = 3$

$n = {}^3/_5 = 0.6 = 60\%$

Finding a Number When a Percent of It Is Known

To find a number when a percent of it is known, write a number sentence with a decimal or a fraction for the percent and solve to find the number.

5% of what number is 2?

$0.05 \times n = 2$

$n = 2 \div 0.05$

$n = 40$

Completed Examples

A. What percent of 70 is 28?

$\square \times 70 = 28$

$\square = \dfrac{28}{70} = \dfrac{4}{10}$

$\square = 40\%$

B. 30% of 60 is what number?

$30\% \times 60 = \square$

$0.3 \times 60 = \square$

$\square = 18$

C. 40% of what number is 16?

$0.40 \times \square = 16$

$\square = \dfrac{16}{0.4}$

$\square = 40$

Practice

1. 120 is what percent of 240?

2. 15% of 70 is what number?

3. 60% of 300 is what number?

4. What percent of 60 is 42?

5. What percent of 25 is 2.5?

6. 40% of what number is 22?

7. 70% of what number is 85?

8. 25% of 38 is what number?

9. 35% of what number is 24?

10. 24 is what percent of 80?

Answers on page 318

PERCENT OF INCREASE AND DECREASE

Percent of Increase

A price increases from $50 to $65. What is the percent of increase?

Subtract to find the amount of increase.	$65 − $50 = $15 $15 is the amount of increase
Write a fraction. The amount of increase is the numerator. The original amount is the denominator.	$\dfrac{\$15}{\$50}$ Amount of increase Original amount
Write the fraction as a percent. The percent of increase is 30%.	$\begin{array}{r} 0.3 \\ 50\overline{)15.00} \end{array}$ $0.3 = 30\%$

Percent of Decrease

A price decreases from $35 to $28. What is the percent of decrease?

Subtract to find the amount of decrease.	$35 − $28 = $7 $7 is the amount of decrease
Write a fraction. The amount of decrease is the numerator. The original amount is the denominator.	$\dfrac{\$7}{\$35}$ Amount of decrease Original amount
Write the fraction as a percent. The percent of decrease is 20%.	$\dfrac{7}{35} = \dfrac{1}{5} = 20\%$

Completed Examples

A. The price increased from $30 to $36. What is the percent of increase?
$36 − $30 = $6
$$\frac{6}{30} = \frac{1}{5} = 20\%$$

B. An $80 item goes on sale for 25% off. What is the sale price?
$80 × 25% = $80 × 0.25 = $20
$80 − $20 = $60. $60 is the sale price.

Practice

1. The price increased from $25 to $35. What is the percent of increase?

2. A sale marks down a $100 item 25%. What is the sale price?

3. The price decreases from $80 by 15%. What is the new price?

4. The price increased from $120 to $150. What is the percent of increase?

5. A sale marks down a $75 item 10%. What is the sale price?

6. The price decreases from $18 to $6. What is the percent of decrease?

7. A sale marks down a $225 item to $180. What is the percent of decrease?

8. A sale price of $150 was 25% off the original price. What was the original price?

Answers on page 318

PROBABILITY, STATISTICS, AND DATA ANALYSIS

PROBABILITY

The probability of an occurrence is the likelihood that it will happen. Most often, we write probability as a fraction.

Flip a fair coin and the probability that it will come up heads is 1/2. The same is true for tails. Write the probability this way.

$$P(\text{H}) = 1/2 \qquad P(\text{T}) = 1/2$$

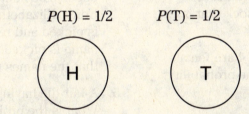

If something will never occur the probability is 0. If something will always occur, the probability is 1. Therefore, if you flip a fair coin,

$$P(7) = 0 \qquad P(\text{H or T}) = 1$$

Write the letters A, B, C, D, and E on pieces of paper. Pick them randomly without looking. The probability of picking any letter is $\frac{1}{5}$.

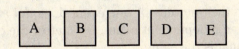

$$P(\text{vowel}) = \frac{2}{5} \qquad P(\text{consonant}) = \frac{3}{5}$$

Rules for Computing Probability

$$P(A \text{ or } B) = P(A) + P(B) = \frac{1}{5} + \frac{1}{5} = \frac{2}{5}$$

when A and B have no common elements

$$P(A \text{ and } B) = P(A) \times P(B) = \frac{1}{5} \times \frac{1}{5} = \frac{1}{25}$$

$$P(\text{not } C) = 1 - P(C) = 1 - \frac{1}{5} = \frac{4}{5}$$

Completed Example

In one high school, 40% of the students go on to college. Two graduates of the high school are chosen at random. What is the probability that they both went to college?

Write the probabilities you know.
$$P(\text{college}) = \frac{40}{100} = \frac{2}{5}$$

Solve the problem.
$P(A \text{ and } B)$ probability the two students went to college.

$$P(A \text{ and } B) = P(A) \times P(B) = \frac{2}{5} \times \frac{2}{5} = \frac{4}{25}$$

The probability that they both went to college is $\frac{4}{25}$.

Practice

1. There are 3 black, 2 white, 2 gray, and 3 blue socks in a drawer. What is the probability of drawing a sock that is not black?

2. Six goldfish are in a tank; 4 are female and 2 are male. What is the probability of scooping out a male?

3. A standard deck of 52 playing cards is spread facedown on a table. What is the probability of choosing a card that is a king or a queen?

4. Six names are written on pieces of paper. The names are Aaron, Ben, Carl, Edith, Elizabeth, and Phyllis. One name is picked and replaced. Then another name is picked. What is the probability that the names were Carl and Phyllis?

5. A fair die having six sides is rolled. What is the probability that the side facing up is a prime number?

6. A fair coin is tossed in the air 5 times. What is the probability of getting five tails?

Answers on page 319

DEPENDENT AND INDEPENDENT EVENTS

Events are *independent* when the outcome of one event does not affect the probability of the other event. Each coin flip is an independent event. No matter the outcome of one flip, the probability of the next flip remains the same.

Flip heads 10 times in a row with a fair coin. On the next flip, the $P(\text{H})$ is still 1/2. Coin flips are independent events.

Events are *dependent* where the outcome of one event does affect the probability of the other event. For example, you have a full deck of cards. The probability of picking the Queen of Hearts is 1/52.

You pick one card and it's not the Queen of Hearts. You don't put the card back. The probability of picking the Queen of Hearts is now 1/51. Cards picked without replacement are dependent events.

PERMUTATIONS, COMBINATIONS, AND THE FUNDAMENTAL COUNTING PRINCIPLE

Permutations

A permutation is the way a set of things can be arranged in order. There are 6 permutations of the letters A, B, and C.

ABC   ACB   BAC   BCA   CAB   CBA

Permutation Formula
The formula for the number of permutations of n things is **n! (n factorial)**.

$$6! = 6 \times 5 \times 4 \times 3 \times 2 \times 1 \qquad 4! = 4 \times 3 \times 2 \times 1 \qquad 2! = 2 \times 1$$

There are 120 permutations of 5 things.

$$n! = 5! = 5 \times 4 \times 3 \times 2 \times 1 = 120$$

Combinations

A combination is the number of ways of choosing a given number of elements from a set. The order of the elements does not matter. There are 3 ways of choosing 2 letters from the letters A, B, and C.

AB   AC   BC

Fundamental Counting Principle

The fundamental counting principle is used to find the total number of possibilities. Multiply the number of possibilities from each category.

Completed Example
An ice cream stand has a sundae with choices of 28 flavors of ice cream, 8 types of syrups, and 5 types of toppings. How many different sundae combinations are available?

28	$\times$	8	$\times$	5	=	1,120
flavors		syrups		toppings		sundaes

There are 1,120 possible sundaes.

Practice

1. There are 2 chairs left in the auditorium, but 4 people are without seats. In how many ways could 2 people be chosen to sit in the chairs?

2. The books *Little Women, Crime & Punishment, Trinity, The Great Santini, Pygmalion, The Scarlet Letter,* and *War and Peace* are on a shelf. In how many different ways can they be arranged?

3. A license plate consists of 2 letters and 2 digits. How many different license plates can be formed?

4. There are four students on line for the bus, but there is only room for three students on this bus. How many different ways can 3 of the 4 students get on the bus?

Answers on page 319

STATISTICS

Descriptive statistics are used to explain or describe a set of numbers. Most often we use the mean, median, or mode to describe these numbers.

Mean (Average)

The mean is a position midway between two extremes. To find the mean:

1. Add the items or scores.

2. Divide by the number of items.

For example, find the mean of 24, 17, 42, 51, 36.

$$24 + 17 + 42 + 51 + 36 = 170 \qquad 170 \div 5 = 34$$

The mean or average is 34.

Median

The median is the middle number. To find the median:

1. Arrange the numbers from least to greatest.

2. If there are an odd number of scores, then find the middle score.

3. If there is an even number of scores, average the two middle scores.

For example, find the median of these numbers.

6, 9, 11, <u>17</u>, <u>21</u>, 33, 45, 71

There are an even number of scores.

$$17 + 21 = 38 \qquad 38 \div 2 = 19$$

The median is 19.

Don't forget to arrange the scores in order before finding the middle score!

Mode

The mode is the number that occurs most often.
For example, find the mode of these numbers.

$$6, 3, 7, 6, 9, 3, 6, 1, 2, 6, 7, 3$$

The number 6 occurs most often so 6 is the mode.

Not all sets of numbers have a mode. Some sets of numbers may have more than one mode.

Completed Example

What is the mean, median, and mode of 7, 13, 18, 4, 14, 22?

Mean   Add the scores and divide by the number of scores.
$7 + 13 + 18 + 4 + 14 + 22 = 78 \div 6 = 13$ The mean is 13.

Median   Arrange the scores in order. Find the middle score.
$4, 7, 13, 14, 18, 22 \quad 13 + 14 = 27 \div 2 = 13.5$ The median is 13.5.

Mode   Find the score that occurs most often.
Each score occurs only once.   There is no mode.

Practice

1. A group of fourth graders received the following scores on a science test.

   80, 87, 94, 100, 75, 80, 98, 85, 80, 95, 92

   Which score represents the mode?

2. What is the mean of the following set of data?

   44, 13, 84, 42, 12, 18

3. What is the median of the following set of data?

   8, 9, 10, 10, 8, 10, 7, 6, 9

4. What measure of central tendency does the number 16 represent in the following data?

   14, 15, 17, 16, 19, 20, 16, 14, 16

5. What is the mean of the following set of scores?

   100, 98, 95, 70, 85, 90, 94, 78, 80, 100

6. What is the mode of the following data?

   25, 30, 25, 15, 40, 45, 30, 20, 30

Answers on page 319

STEM-AND-LEAF AND BOX-AND-WHISKER PLOTS

Stem-and-Leaf Plots

Stem-and-leaf plots represent data in place value-oriented plots. Each piece of data is shown in the plot. The following stem-and-leaf plot shows test scores. The stem represents 10, and the leaves represent 1. You can read each score. In the 50s the scores are 55, 55, and 58. There are no scores in the 60s. You can find the lowest score, 40, and highest score, 128.

```
Stem    Leaves

  4 | 0 7
  5 | 5 5 8
  6 |
  7 | 1 4 4 6
  8 | 2 3 4 5
  9 | 9 9
 10 |
 11 |
 12 | 3 4 8
```

Example: 7 | 4   means 74 people

Box-and-Whisker Plots

Box-and-whisker plots show the range and quartiles of scores. The plot is a box divided into two parts with a whisker at each end. The ends of the left and right whiskers show the lowest and highest scores. Quartiles partition scores into quarters. The left and right parts of the box show the upper and lower quartiles; the dividing line shows the median.

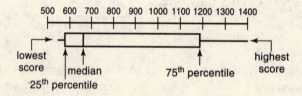

Completed Example

Use the stem-and-leaf plot above. How many people scored 100 on the test?

No one scored 100 on the test. Look at the stem and find 10, and see that there are no leaves attached to that stem.

Practice

1. Create a stem-and-leaf plot using the following test scores.

   15, 19, 94, 10, 56, 23, 106, 28, 36, 38, 42, 48, 45, 26, 42, 105, 55, 53, 76, 47, 77, 29, 79, 49, 92, 96, 17, 13, 101, 75, 33

   Check the answer before continuing.

Use the stem-and-leaf graph from exercise 1.

2. Which score is between 56 and 75?

3. What is the median of these test scores?

4. What is the mode of these test scores?

Answers on page 319

Choose a Process That Involves Random Selection

Random selection means that the sample is picked by chance. Every person in the larger population has an equal chance of being picked.

Examples of random sampling:

Pick a sample of names by chance out of a container with all the names.

Have a computer use a random selection program to choose the sample.

Partition a group into a male group and a female group, and then choose names at random from each group.

Examples of nonrandom sampling:

Sample the first 100 people you meet.

Choose every sixth person from a list of names.

Rely on voluntary responses.

Choose Your Sample from the Correct Population

The random selection must be from the group you want to study.

Examples of sampling from the wrong population:

Sample college alumni to determine current reactions to the cafeteria.

Sample from one town to determine statewide views.

Sample from 18–22-year-old military recruits to determine the views of college students.

Completed Example

The college cafeteria manager wants to find out which new selections students want added to the menu. What procedure would be appropriate for selecting an unbiased sample?

The manager could gather the names of all the students who ate in the cafeteria during the week and then draw a random sample from those names. The manager should not draw a sample from all the students in the school. You should not interview every fifth student entering the cafeteria during the week.

Practice Questions

1. A group is taking a poll to determine working parents' day-care needs. They interview parents at work. Give examples of good and poor sampling techniques.

2. The town architect wants to find out about senior community members' ideas for the new senior center. Give examples of good and poor sampling techniques.

Answers on page 320

ALGEBRA

ADD, SUBTRACT, MULTIPLY, AND DIVIDE INTEGERS

Addition

When the signs are the same, keep the sign and add.

$$\begin{array}{r} {}^+7 \\ +\ {}^+8 \\ \hline {}^+15 \end{array} \qquad \begin{array}{r} {}^-3 \\ +\ {}^-11 \\ \hline {}^-14 \end{array}$$

When the signs are different, disregard the signs, subtract the numbers, and keep the sign of the larger number.

$$\begin{array}{r} {}^+28 \\ +\ {}^-49 \\ \hline {}^-21 \end{array} \qquad \begin{array}{r} {}^-86 \\ +\ {}^+135 \\ \hline {}^+49 \end{array}$$

Subtraction

Change the sign of the number being subtracted. Then add using the preceding rules.

$$\begin{array}{r} {}^+13 \\ -\ {}^-18 \\ \hline \downarrow \end{array} \qquad \begin{array}{r} {}^-43 \\ -\ {}^-17 \\ \hline \downarrow \end{array} \qquad \begin{array}{r} {}^+29 \\ -\ {}^-49 \\ \hline \downarrow \end{array} \qquad \begin{array}{r} {}^-92 \\ -\ {}^+135 \\ \hline \downarrow \end{array}$$

$$\begin{array}{r} {}^+13 \\ +\ {}^+18 \\ \hline {}^+31 \end{array} \qquad \begin{array}{r} {}^-43 \\ +\ {}^+17 \\ \hline {}^-26 \end{array} \qquad \begin{array}{r} {}^+29 \\ +\ {}^+49 \\ \hline {}^+78 \end{array} \qquad \begin{array}{r} {}^-92 \\ +\ {}^-135 \\ \hline {}^-227 \end{array}$$

Multiply

Multiply as you would whole numbers. The product is *positive* if there are an even number of negative factors. The product is *negative* if there are an odd number of negative factors.

$$^-2 \times {}^+4 \times {}^-6 \times {}^+3 = {}^+144 \qquad ^-2 \times {}^-4 \times {}^+6 \times {}^-3 = {}^-144$$

Divide

Forget the signs and divide. The quotient is *positive* if both integers have the same sign. The quotient is *negative* if the integers have different signs.

$$^+24 \div {}^+4 = {}^+6 \qquad {}^-24 \div {}^-4 = {}^+6 \qquad {}^+24 \div {}^-4 = {}^-6 \qquad {}^-24 \div {}^+4 = {}^-6$$

Practice

1. $6 + 9 =$

2. $18 + {}^-17 =$

3. ${}^-24 + {}^-45 =$

4. ${}^-38 + 29 =$

5. $7 - 6 =$

6. $15 - {}^-39 =$

7. ${}^-36 - {}^-58 =$

8. ${}^-27 - 53 =$

9. $9 \times 11 =$

10. $26 \times {}^-25 =$

11. ${}^-31 \times {}^-59 =$

12. ${}^-42 \times 35 =$

13. $120 \div 8 =$

14. $68 \div {}^-4 =$

15. ${}^-352 \div {}^-8 =$

16. ${}^-66 \div 3 =$

Answers on page 320

Polynomials

Polynomials are made up of constants and variables.

> Constant—A constant is a number such as 9, ½, 0.56.

> Variable—A variable is represented by a letter (such as x, a, c) to show that we don't know the value.

Polynomials don't have equal signs.

We describe polynomials by the number of terms. Terms are separated by addition or subtraction.

A term can be a constant, a variable, or the product of constants and variables.

In a term with a constant and a variable or variables, the constant is called the coefficient.

In the term $9x$, the coefficient is 9 and the variable is x.

Monomials

A monomial has one term.

But there are no addition or subtraction signs in a monomial.

Here are some monomials.

$$7, x, 3x, 6/27, y^2, -16,$$

Binomials

A binomial has two terms.

Here are some binomials.

$$5x - 6, \quad 3y^2 + 7, \quad 13x^2 + 0.5y^2$$

Trinomials

A trinomial has three terms.
Here are some trinomials.

$$6x^2 + 12y^2 + 12y, \quad 13x^6z^5 + 12y^2 + 12y,$$

Simplify Polynomials

Combine similar terms to simplify a polynomial.
Similar terms have the same variable part. The order of the variables is not important.
$3x$ is similar to $5x$ and $0.9x$. The variable in each term is x.

$2\,x^3y$ is similar to $12\,yx^3$.
$3\,x^3y$ is not similar.$3\,y^3x$.

Combine Similar Terms

Add or subtract the coefficient and keep the variable part.

Combine the terms in $\qquad 5x + 9xy + 2y^3 - 8x + 2x^2 - 8\,y^3$

Rearrange the terms so that similar terms are next to one another.

The similar terms are $2y^3$ and $8y^3$.

$$5x + 9xy \underline{+ 2y^3 - 8\,y^3} - 8x + 2x^2$$
$$5x + 9xy \underline{-6y^3} - 8x + 2x^2$$

Operations on Polynomials

Add Polynomials

Combine similar terms.

Add: $\qquad\qquad\qquad (5x^6 + 7x^3y - y^2 + 9) + (7x^5 - 3x^3y + y^2z)$

Write as a polynomial: $\qquad 5x^6 + 7x^3y - y^2 + 9 + 7x^5 - 3x^3y + y^2z$

The common terms are $7x^3y$ and $3x^3y$.

Rearrange terms: $\qquad 5x^6 + \underline{7x^3y - 3x^3y} - y^2 + 9 + 7x^5 + y^2z$

Combine: $\qquad\qquad 5x^6 + 4x^3y - y^2 + 9 + 7x^5 + y^2z$

Subtract Polynomials

Change the signs in the polynomial being subtracted.
Then combine similar terms.

Subtract: $\qquad\qquad (2x^4 + 15x^2 - y^2 + x) - (x^4 - 8x^3y + y^2z - 3x + 4)$

Change the signs in the polynomial
being subtracted and add: $\qquad (2x^4 + 15x^2 - y^2 + x) + (-x^4 + 8x^3y - y^2z + 3x + 4)$

The common terms are $2x^4$ and $-x^4$, x and $3x$.

Rearrange terms: $\qquad \underline{2x^4 - x^4} + 15x^2 - y^2 + \underline{x + 3x} + 8x^3y - y^2z + 4$

Combine: $\qquad\qquad x^4 + 15x^2 - y^2 + 4\underline{x} + 8x^3y - y^2z + 4$

Multiply Polynomials
Multiply a binomial by a monomial.
Multiply each term of the polynomial by the monomial.

Multiply:

$$4x\,(12x^2 - 6x)$$
$$4x\,(12x^2) - (4x)\,(6x) =$$
$$48x^3 - 24x^2$$

Multiply a binomial by a binomial.

Multiply: $(2x + 3)\,(-4x - 5)$

Multiply the first terms: $(2x)\,(-4x) = \quad -8x^2$

Multiply the outer terms: $(2x)\,(-5) = \quad -10x$

Multiply the inner terms: $(3)\,(-4x) = \quad -12x$

Multiply the last terms: $(3)\,(-5) = \quad -15$

Add: $-8x^2 - 10x - 12x - 15$

Combine like terms: $-8x^2 - 22x - 15$

Practice
Combine terms.

1. $3x^2 + 4y + 3x^2y + 6y$

2. $7x + 3x^2y + 17x + 3yx^2 + 7x^2y^2$

Add.

3. $(3x^5 + 3x^2 - 5x^2y + 6xy^2) + (3x^5 - 2x^2 + 4x^3y - x^2y + 3xy^3 - y^2)$

4. $(x^4 - 4x^3 + 2x^2y^2 - 4xy^2) + (3x^5 - 7x^4 + 3x^3 - 2x^2y^3 + 7xy^2)$

Subtract.

5. $(6x^7 + 9x^4 - 3x^2y + 5xy^3) - (6x^8 - 15x^4 - 3x^3y + x^2y)$

6. $(7x^2 - 9x + 3xy^2 + 3y^3 - 12) - (x^3 - 9x^2 + 2xy^2 - 3y^5 - 18)$

Multiply.

7. $(5x + 6)\,(x + 2)$

8. $(6x + 4)\,(3x - 8)$

Answers on page 320

FORMULAS

Evaluating an Expression

Evaluate an expression by replacing the variables with values. Remember to use the correct order of operations. For example, evaluate

$$3x - \frac{y}{z} \text{ for } x = 3, y = 8, \text{ and } z = 4$$

$$3\left(3\right) - \frac{8}{4} = 9 - 2 = 7$$

Using Formulas

Using a formula is like evaluating an expression. Just replace the variables with values. Here are some important formulas to know. The area of a figure is the amount of space it occupies in two dimensions. The perimeter of a figure is the distance around the figure. Use 3.14 for π.

Figure	Formula	Description
Triangle	Area = $\frac{1}{2} bh$ Perimeter = $s_1 + s_2 + s_3$	
Square	Area = s^2 Perimeter = $4s$	
Rectangle	Area = lw Perimeter = $2l + 2w$	
Parallelogram	Area = bh Perimeter = $2s + 2h$	
Trapezoid	Area = $\frac{1}{2} h(b_1 + b_2)$ Perimeter = $b_1 + b_2 + s_1 + s_2$	
Circle	Area = πr^2 Circumference = $2\pi r$ or $= \pi d$	

Pythagorean Formula

The Pythagorean formula for right triangles states that the sum of the square of the legs equals the square of the hypotenuse:

$$a^2 + b^2 = c^2$$

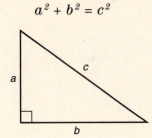

Other Polygons

Pentagon	5 sides		Octagon	8 sides
Hexagon	6 sides		Nonagon	9 sides
Heptagon	7 sides		Decagon	10 sides

Regular Polygon—All sides are the same length.

Completed Examples—Distance and Area

Let's solve the distance and area problems.

A. How many meters is it around a regular hexagon with a side of 87 centimeters?
A hexagon has 6 sides. It's a regular hexagon, so all the sides are the same length.
$6 \times 87 = 522$. The perimeter is 522 centimeters, which equals 5.22 meters.

B. What is the area of this figure?

The formula for the area of a circle is πr^2.
The diameter is 18, so the radius is 9. Use 3.14 for π.
$A = 3.14 \times (9)^2 = 3.14 \times 81 = 254.34$ or about 254.

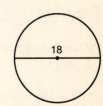

VOLUME

Volume—The amount of space occupied by a three-dimensional figure.

Formulas for Volume

Figure	Formula	Description
Cube	Volume $= s^3$	
Rectangular Prism	Volume $= lwh$	

Figure	Formula	Description
Sphere	Volume $= \dfrac{4}{3}\pi r^3$	
Cone	Volume $= \dfrac{1}{3}\pi r^2 h$	
Cylinder	Volume $= \pi r^2 h$ Surface Area $= 2\pi r(h+r)$	

Completed Example—Volume

A circular cone has a radius of 8 cm and a height of 10 cm. What is the volume?

Formula for the volume of a cone $= \dfrac{1}{3}\pi r^2 h$.

$$V = \left(\frac{1}{3}\right)(3.14)(8^2)(10) = \left(\frac{1}{3}\right)(3.14)(64)(10) = \left(\frac{1}{3}\right)(3.14)(640) = 669.87$$

The volume of the cone is 669.87 cubic centimeters or about 670 cubic centimeters.

Practice

1. A circle has a radius of 9 meters. What is the area?

2. The faces of a pyramid are equilateral triangles. What is the surface area of the pyramid if the sides of the triangles equal 3 inches and the height is 2.6 inches?

3. A regular hexagon has one side 5 feet long. What is the distance around its edge?

4. What is the surface area of the side of a cylinder (not top and bottom) with a height of 10 cm and a diameter of 2.5 cm?

5. A rectangle has a width x and a length $(x + 5)$. If the perimeter is 90 feet, what is the length?

6. The perimeter of one face of a cube is 20 cm. What is the surface area?

7. What is the length of the third side in the right triangle below?

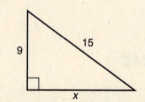

8. What is the area of a trapezoid whose height is 5 inches, the length of one base is 5 inches, and the length of the other base is 8 inches?

9. What is the volume of a sphere that has a diameter of length 20 cm?

10. What is the volume of a cube having a side length of 15 inches.

Answers on page 320

SOLVE LINEAR EQUATIONS AND INEQUALITIES

Equations and Inequalities

The whole idea of solving equations and inequalities is to isolate the variable on one side. The value of the variable is what's on the other side. Substitute your answer in the original equation or inequality to check your solution.

Solving Equations and Inequalities by Adding or Subtracting

$$\text{Solve: } y + 19 = 23$$

Subtract 19 $\quad y + 19 - 19 = 23 - 19$

$$y = 4$$

Check: Does **4** + 19 = 23? Yes. It checks.

$$\text{Solve: } x = 23 < 51$$

Add 23 $\quad x - 23 + 23 < 51 + 23$

$$x < 74$$

Check: Is **74** − 23 < 51. Yes. It checks.

Solving Equations and Inequalities by Multiplying or Dividing

$$\text{Solve: } \frac{z}{7} \geq 6$$

Multiply by 7 $\quad \frac{x}{7} \times 7 \geq 6 \times 7$

$$z \geq 42$$

Check: Is $\frac{\mathbf{42}}{7} \geq 6$? Yes. It checks.

$$\text{Solve: } 21 = -3x$$

Divide by −3 $\quad \frac{21}{-3} = \frac{-3x}{-3}$

$$-7 = x$$

Check: Does 21 = (−3) (−7)?
Yes. It checks.

Solving Two-Step Equations and Inequalities

Add or subtract before you multiply or divide.

$$\text{Solve: } 3x - 6 = 24$$

Add 6 $\quad 3x - 6 + 6 = 24 + 6$

$$3x = 30$$

Divide by 3 $\quad \frac{3x}{3} = \frac{30}{3}$

$$3x = 10$$

Check: Does 3 × **10** − 6 = 24? Yes. It checks.

Solve: $\frac{y}{7} + 4 > 32$

Subtract 4 $\frac{y}{7} + 4 - 4 > 32 - 4$

$$\frac{y}{7} > 28$$

Multiply by 7 $\frac{y}{7} \times 7 > (28)\,(7)$

$$y > 196$$

Check: Is $\dfrac{\mathbf{196}}{7} + 4 > 32?$

$28 + 4 = 32$. Yes. It checks.

Special Reminder About Inequalities

Multiplying or dividing by a *negative number* reverses the inequality sign.

$x < -7 \Rightarrow -x > 7$

Multiply both sides by (-1).

$5x - 4 \geq 9 \Rightarrow -10x + 8 \leq -18$

Multiply both sides by (-2).

$-3x - 12 \leq y \Rightarrow x + 4 \geq \dfrac{-y}{3}$

Divide both sides by (-3).

$\dfrac{2}{3}y - 4 > -x + 3 \Rightarrow -y + 6 < \dfrac{3}{2}x + 4\dfrac{1}{2}$

Multiply both sides by $\dfrac{(-3)}{(2)}$.

$-9 > -3x - 18 \Rightarrow 3 < x + 6$

Divide by (-3).

Completed Examples

A. Solve $6x - 7 = 4(-x + 3)$

Expand $4(-x + 3) = -4x + 12$

Solve for x: $6x - 7 \quad = -4x + 12$

Add 7 $\underline{ + 7 \qquad\quad + 7}$

                     $6x \quad\quad = -4x + 19$

Add $4x$ $\underline{+ 4x \qquad\quad +4x}$

Divide by 10 $\dfrac{10x}{10} \quad = \dfrac{19}{10}$

                     $x \qquad\; = 1.9$

B. Solve $7n - 11 > 17$

Solve for n: $7n - 11 \;\; > \; 17$

Add 11 $\underline{\quad +11 \quad\;\; +11}$

Divide by 7 $\dfrac{7n}{7} \;\; > \dfrac{28}{7}$

                  $n \quad\; > \; 4$

Practice Questions

1. Solve for y: $10y + 5 = 15 + 20y$

2. Solve for x: $10x + 3 = -5x + 33$

3. Solve for y: $-6y - 4 = y + 10$

4. Solve for x: $5 + 12x = -4x - 27$

5. Solve for n: $15 - 4n > -21$

6. Solve for k: $7k + 7 < -14$

7. Solve for x: $20 > 2x - 4$

8. Solve for y: $2 > 10 - 14y$

Answers on page 321.

FACTOR A QUADRATIC EXPRESSION

Quadratic Expression

An expression that can be written in the form $ax^2 + bx + c = 0$
(a, b, and c are real numbers, and $a \neq 0$.)

$$12x^2 + 2x - 2 \text{ is a quadratic expression.}$$

Linear Factors

Two expressions whose product is the quadratic equation.

$$(4x + 2) \text{ and } (3x - 1) \text{ are linear factors of } 12x^2 + 2x - 2$$

$$(4x + 2) \times (3x - 1) = 12x^2 - 4x + 6x - 2 = 12x^2 + 2x - 2$$

Use These Steps

ALWAYS work back from the answer choices. Try out each linear factor until you find the correct choice.

Completed Example

Which is the linear factor of $9x^2 - 6x - 8$?

(A) $(9x - 8)$
(B) $(3x + 4)$
(C) $(-3x + 4)$
(D) $(-9x + 8)$

Use a trial and error process.

Try choice (A) (9x–8)

Think: What would the other linear factor look like?
The second term would have to be -1. ($\_x - 1$).
There is no first term that will give $9x^2 - 6x$ for the rest of the quadratic.
Choice (A) is not correct.

Try choice (B) ($3x + 4$)

Think: What would the other linear factor look like?

The second term would have to be 2. (__x + 2).

There is no first term that will give $9x^2 - 6x$ for the rest of the quadratic.

Choice (B) is not correct.

Try choice (C) ($-3x + 4$)

Think: What would the other linear factor look like?

The second term would have to be –2. (__x – 2).

The first term $-3x$ will give $9x^2 - 6x$ for the rest of the quadratic.

$(-3x + 4)(-3x - 2) = 9x^2 + 6x - 12x - 4 = 9x^2 - 6x - 4$

Choice (C) is correct.

We don't have to try choice (D).

Practice Questions

1. Which is a linear factor of $6x^2 - x - 2$?

   (A) ($2x - 3$)

   (B) ($3x - 2$)

   (C) ($-2x + 3$)

   (D) ($-3x - 2$)

2. Which is a linear factor of $12x^2 - 14x - 6$?

   (A) ($6x - 2$)

   (B) ($6x + 2$)

   (C) ($2x + 1$)

   (D) ($-2x - 1$)

Answers on page 321.

Find the Roots of a Quadratic Equation

Quadratic Formula

The quadratic formula is used to solve a quadratic equation. The solutions, or roots, are values of the variable x: Every quadratic equation has two roots.

$$x = \frac{-b \pm \sqrt{b^2 - 4ac}}{2a}$$ (a, b, and c are the values in the quadratic equation)

Completed Example

Find the solutions to $x^2 - 2x = 1$.

Write the quadratic equation in standard form. ($ax^2 + bx + c = 0$)

$$\begin{array}{rcr} x^2 - 2x & = & 1 \\ -1 & & -1 \\ \hline x^2 - 2x - 1 = & & 0 \end{array}$$

Write the values for a, b, and c.

$a = 1, b = -2, c = -1$

Substitute the values of a, b, and c into the quadratic formula.

$$\frac{-b \pm \sqrt{b^2 - 4ac}}{2a}$$

$$\frac{-(-2) \pm \sqrt{(-2)^2 - 4(1)(-1)}}{(2)(1)}$$

$$\frac{2 \pm \sqrt{4+4}}{2}$$

$$\frac{2}{2} \pm \frac{\sqrt{8}}{2}$$

$$\frac{2}{2} \pm \frac{2\sqrt{2}}{2}$$

$$1 \pm \sqrt{2}$$

The roots (solutions) of the quadratic equation are $1 + \sqrt{2}$ and $1 - \sqrt{2}$.

Practice Questions

1. Find the roots of $2x^2 - 3x = 2$.   **2.** Find the solutions to $4x^2 = 2x + 5$.

Answers on page 321.

SOLVE A SYSTEM OF LINEAR EQUATIONS

Linear Equation

Any equation in the form $ax + by = c$ $(a \neq 0, b \neq 0)$
A linear equation produces a line.

Solving Two Linear Equations

The solution to a linear equation is an ordered pair (x, y).
The solution for two linear equations is a solution for each of the equations.

ALWAYS work back from the answer choices.
Try out each solution until you find the correct choice.

There are three possible answer types.
This section shows how to consider each answer type. CSET linear equations questions may not look like this.

  1. *The answer is a single ordered pair* [such as (2,3) or a statement such as $x = 2, y = 3$].
     (The lines meet at one point.)
     Substitute the ordered pair in each equation.
     If the ordered pair works for both equations, that is the correct answer.

  2. *The answer looks like $y = \frac{5}{6} x$.* The solution for both equations is $y = \frac{5}{6} x$. (The lines are the same.)
     Solve each equation for y.
     If both solutions match the answer choice, that answer is correct.

  3. *The answer states that there is no solution.* The solution is the empty set or null set.
     (The lines are parallel.)
     If the other choices don't work, this is the correct answer.

Completed Examples

A. $3x - 4y - 7 = 0$
$2x + 8y = -6$

    (A) $(1, -1)$
    (B) $x = 5, y = 12$
    (C) $y = 8x$
    (D)   the empty set

Try answer choice (A)
Substitute the ordered pair $(1, -1)$ in the
first equation. $(1, -1)$ means $x = 1, y = -1$. $3(1) - 4(-1) - 7 \stackrel{?}{=} 0$ $3 + 4 - 7 = 0$
The expression is correct. $(1, -1)$ is a
possible solution.

Try out $(1, -1)$ in the second equation. $2(1) + 8(-1) \stackrel{?}{=} -6$ $2 + -8 = -6$
This expression is correct also.

The ordered pair $(1, -1)$ worked for both equations.
This is the solution for these equations. Choose answer (A).

B. $8x - 2y = 4$
$-12x + 3y - 6 = 0$

    (A) $x = 2, y = 4$
    (B) $x = 3, y = 6$
    (C) $y = 4x - 2$
    (D)   the empty set

Try answer choice (A)
Substitute $x = 2, y = 4$ in the first equation. $8(2) - 2(4) \stackrel{?}{=} 4$ $16 - 8 \neq 4$
The expression is incorrect.
Choice (A) is not correct.

Try answer choice (B)
Substitute $x = 3, y = 6$ $8(3) - 2(6) \stackrel{?}{=} 4$ $24 - 12 \neq 4$
in the first equation.
Choice (B) is not correct.

Try answer choice (C)
Choice (C) means that the solution
is every pair of numbers for
which $y = 4x - 2$.

Solve the first equation for y. $8x - 2y = 4$ $8x - 4 = 2y$ $4x - 2 = y$
The solution matches the
equation in choice (C).

Try it for the second equation. $-12x + 3y + 6 = 0$ $-4x + y + 2 = 0$ $y = 4x - 2$
The solutions for both equations
match the answer choice.

Choice (C) is the correct answer.

C. $3x - y = 5$
    $-12x + 4y = 7$

    (A) $x = 2, y = 1$
    (B) $(3, 5)$
    (C) $y = \frac{3}{5}x$
    (D) the empty set

Try answer choice (A)
Substitute $x = 2, y = 1$
in the first equation. $3(2) - (1) \overset{?}{=} 5$ $6 - 1 = 5$
The expression is correct.
$x = 2, y = 1$ is a possible solution.

Try out $x = 2, y = 1$ in the second equation. $-12(2) + 4(1) \overset{?}{=} 5$ $-24 + 4 \neq 5$
$x = 2, y = 1$ does not work. Answer choice
(A) is not correct.

Try answer choice (B)
Try the ordered pair $(3, 5)$ $3(5) - (5) = 5$? $15 - 5 \neq 5$
in the first equation.
Answer choice (B) is not correct.

Try answer choice (C)
Solve the first equation for y. $3x - y = 5$ $3x - 5 = y$
Choice (C) is not correct. $3x - 5 = y$ does not match $y = \frac{3}{4}x$

Choice (D) must be correct.
If one of the choices is the empty set,
save that choice for last.

Practice Questions

1. Choose the correct solution for the
    system of equations.
    $-6y + 2x + 12 = 2$
    $4x + 7y = -1$
    (A) $x = -2, y = 1$
    (B) $x = 4, y = 2$
    (C) $y = 2x$
    (D) the empty set

2. Choose the correct solution for the
    system of equations.
    $3y - \frac{1}{2}x = 14$
    $3x + 2y + 5 = 1$
    (A) $x = -4, y = 4$
    (B) $x = -2, y = 3$
    (C) $y = x + 1$
    (D) the null set

3. Choose the correct solution for the sys-
    tem of equations.
    $4x + 2y - 3 = -7$
    $5y - 6x = 6$
    (A) $(0, 2)$
    (B) $(-1, 0)$
    (C) $y = 2x$
    (D) the empty set

Answers on page 321.

GEOMETRY AND MEASUREMENT

SYMMETRY

Symmetric objects, figures, and designs have a pleasing, balanced appearance.
There are three primary types of symmetry—line (reflection), rotational, and translational.

Line or Reflective Symmetry

A figure with line symmetry can be folded in half so that one half exactly matches the other half.

This letter M has line symmetry.

Fold the M in half at the line and one half exactly matches the other half.
Flip the M over the line and it looks the same.
Place a mirror on that line and half the M and the reflection will form the entire M.
The line is called the line of symmetry.

Rotational Symmetry

A figure has rotational symmetry if it can be turned less than a full turn and look exactly as it did before it was turned.

This letter N has rotational symmetry.

N ↧ Z ↧ N

Turn the Z half a turn and it looks exactly as it did before the turn.

Translational Symmetry

A design has translational symmetry if it repeats a pattern.
Many wallpaper patterns have translational symmetry.

This simple pattern has translational symmetry because it shows a repeating pattern.

A B C A B C

Completed Examples

A. Which of these letters has line symmetry?

B. Which of these letters has rotational symmetry?

    A   B   C   D   E   F   G   H   I

These letters have both line and rotational symmetry: H, I

These letters have only line symmetry: A, B, C, D, E

None of the letters has only rotational symmetry.

These letters have neither type of symmetry: F, G

Practice

1. Which of these numerals has rotational or line symmetry?

   1   **2**   **3**   **4**   **5**   **6**   **7**   **8**   **9**   **0**

2. Complete this pattern so that the final pattern has translational symmetry.

   2   **3**   **4**

Answers on page 321.

TWO-DIMENSIONAL GEOMETRY

We can think of geometry in two or three dimensions. A two-dimensional model is this page. A three-dimensional model is the room you'll take the test in.

Definition	Model	Symbol
Point—a location	. A	A
Plane—a flat surface that extends infinitely in all directions	A• .B .C	plane ABC
Line—a set of points in a straight path that extends infinitely in two directions	A B	$\overleftrightarrow{AB}$
Line segment—part of a line with two endpoints	B A	$\overline{AB}$
Ray—part of a line with one endpoint	A B	$\overrightarrow{AB}$
Parallel lines—lines that stay the same distance apart and never touch	A B / D F	

Definition	**Model**	**Symbol**

Perpendicular lines—lines that meet at right angles

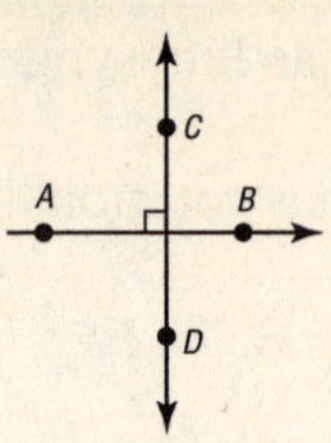

$AB \perp CD$

Angle—two rays with a common endpoint, which is called the vertex

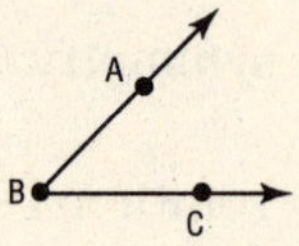

$\angle ABC$

Acute angle—angle that measures between 0° and 90°

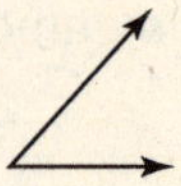

Right angle—angle that measures 90°

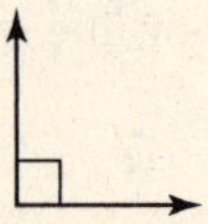

Obtuse angle—angle that measures between 90° and 180°

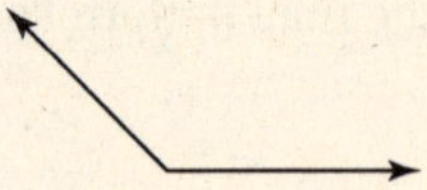

Complementary angles—angles that have a total measure of 90°

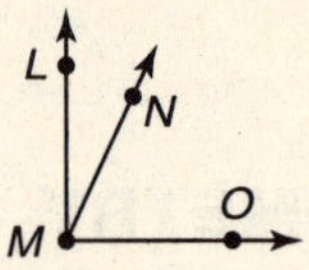

Supplementary angles—angles that have a total measure of 180°

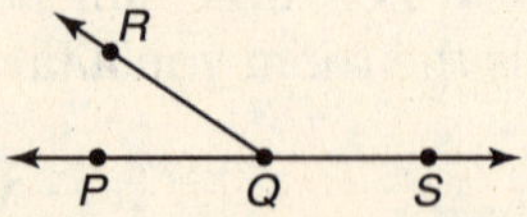

Congruent angles have the same angle measure.
$\angle p$ and $\angle q$ measure 90°.
$\angle p$ and $\angle q$ are congruent.
$m\angle p = m\angle q$

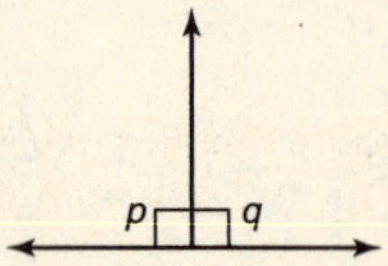

Vertical angles are formed when two lines intersect. Angles opposite each other are vertical angles. Vertical angles are congruent.

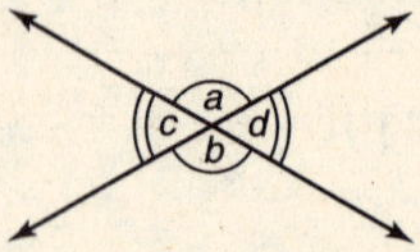

$\angle a$ and $\angle b$ are vertical angles.　　　$\angle c$ and $\angle d$ are vertical angles.

The measures of vertical angles are equal.　　$m\angle a = m\angle b$　　$m\angle c = m\angle d$

Definition	Model	Symbol

Parallel lines cut by a transversal form congruent angles.
Line *A* and line *B* are parallel.
Line *C* is the transversal.

Corresponding angles are congruent. The corresponding angles in this figure are
∠1 and ∠5   ∠2 and ∠6
∠3 and ∠7   ∠4 and ∠8

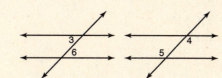

Alternate interior angles are congruent. The pairs of alternate interior angles in this figure are
∠3 and ∠6   m∠3 = m∠6
∠4 and ∠5   m∠4 = m∠5

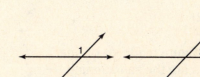

Alternate exterior angles are congruent. The pairs of alternate interior angles in this figure are
∠1 and ∠8   m∠1 = m∠8
∠2 and ∠7   m∠2 = m∠7

Completed Example

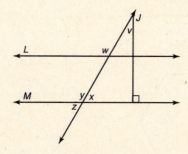

Lines *L* and *M* are parallel. Line *J* is perpendicular to line *M*.
What statements can we make about ∠v, ∠w, ∠x, ∠ y, and ∠z?

Statement	Reason
∠x and ∠z are congruent.	Vertical angles are congruent.
∠w and ∠y are congruent.	Corresponding angles are congruent.
∠y and ∠x are supplementary.	The sum of angles is 180°.
∠v and ∠x are complementary.	The large triangle contains a right angle *and* the sum of the other angle is 90°.

Practice Questions

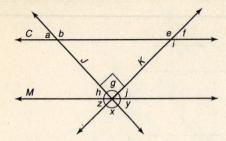

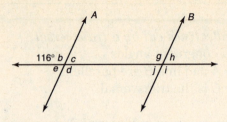

1. If $\overleftrightarrow{C} \parallel \overleftrightarrow{M}$, then which of the following is true?

    (A) $m\angle b = m\angle a$

    (B) $m\angle j = m\angle h$

    (C) $m\angle e + \angle f = 90$

    (D) $m\angle e = m\angle i$

2. If $\overleftrightarrow{A} \parallel \overleftrightarrow{B}$, what is the measure of $\angle j$?

    (A) 116°

    (B) 64°

    (C) 26°

    (D) 154°

Answers on page 321

Polygon—a closed figure made up of line segments; if all sides are the same length, the figure is a regular polygon

Pentagon

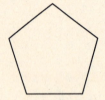

Five Sides

Hexagon

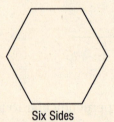

Six Sides

Octagon

Eight Sides

Triangle—polygon with three sides and three angles; the sum of the angles is always 180°.

Equilateral triangle—all the sides are the same length; all the angles are the same size, 60°.

Isosceles triangle—two sides the same length; two angles the same size.

Scalene triangle—all sides different lengths; all angles different sizes.

Congruent triangle—Two triangles are congruent if the lengths of each corresponding pair of sides are equal and the measures of each corresponding pair of angles are equal. That means one triangle fits exactly on top of the other triangle.

Quadrilateral—polygon with four sides

Square

Parallelogram

Rhombus

Trapezoid

Rectangle

Completed Example

Which types of quadrilaterals can be constructed using four congruent line segments *AB*, *BC*, *CD*, and *DA*?

You can create a square and a rhombus.

Practice Questions

Be certain to use proper markings to indicate congruent segments and congruent angles.

1. What is the name of a quadrilateral that has exactly one pair of parallel sides?

2. Use the figure below. The m∠1 = 45°. What is m∠2?

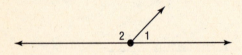

3. In the triangle below, *AB* = *AC* and m∠*BAC* = 80°.

   What are the measures of ∠*ABC* and ∠*ACB*?

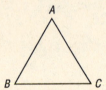

4. Draw a diagram of an equilateral triangle.

5. Which has more sides, an octagon or a hexagon?

   What is the difference in the number of sides for these figures?

6. What type of angle with a measure less than 180° is neither obtuse nor acute?

7. Draw a diagram in which ray (*AB*) intersects ray (*AC*) at point *A*, and name the new figure that is formed.

8. Draw a diagram of line *AB* intersecting line segment *CD* at point *E*.

9. Draw a diagram of two parallel lines perpendicular to a third line.

10. Given a triangle *ABC*, describe the relationship among the measures of the three angles.

Answers on page 321

Similar Triangles

In similar triangles, corresponding angles are congruent. The ratio of the lengths of corresponding sides are equal.
   These triangles are similar.

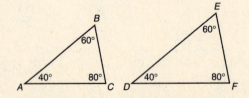

Corresponding angles of the two triangles are congruent.

$\angle A$ and $\angle D$
$\angle B$ and $\angle E$
$\angle C$ and $\angle F$

That means the measures of congruent angles are equal.

measure of $\angle A$ = measure of $\angle D = 40°$
measure of $\angle B$ = measure of $\angle E = 60°$
measure of $\angle C$ = measure of $\angle F = 80°$

Corresponding sides (Corresponding sides are opposite corresponding angles)

$\overline{BC}$ and $\overline{EF}$
$\overline{AC}$ and $\overline{DF}$
$\overline{AB}$ and $\overline{DE}$

The ratios of the lengths of corresponding sides are equal.

$$\frac{BC}{EF} = \frac{AC}{DF} = \frac{AB}{DE}$$

Are these triangles similar?

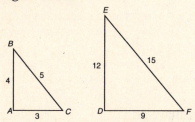

Corresponding sides: $\overline{AB}$ and $\overline{DF}$, $\overline{BC}$ and $\overline{EF}$, $\overline{AC}$ and $\overline{DF}$

Does $\dfrac{AB}{DE} = \dfrac{BC}{EF}$? $\quad \dfrac{AB}{DE} = \dfrac{4}{12}$; $\quad \dfrac{BC}{EF} = \dfrac{5}{15}$; $\quad \dfrac{4}{12} = \dfrac{1}{3}$; $\quad \dfrac{5}{15} = \dfrac{1}{3}$

These triangles are similar. Ratios of corresponding sides of the two triangles are equal.

Completed Example

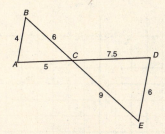

Are triangle ABC and triangle CDE similar triangles?

The ratios of the lengths of corresponding sides are equal.

$\overline{AB}$ and $\overline{DE}$ are corresponding sides.

Does $\dfrac{AC}{CD} = \dfrac{AB}{DE}$? $\quad$ Yes. $\dfrac{5}{7.5} = \dfrac{4}{6} \left(\dfrac{20}{30} = \dfrac{20}{30} \right)$

Practice Questions

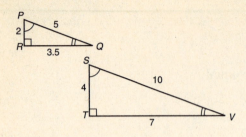

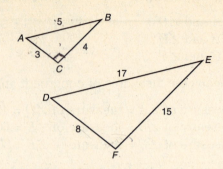

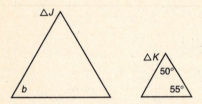

1. Are △*PQR* and △*SVT* similar?

2. The triangles above are similar. What is the measure of ∠*b*?

3. Which of these statements is true for the triangles above?
   (A) ∠*C* is congruent to ∠*F*
   (B) ∠*B* is congruent to ∠*E*

   (C) $\dfrac{AB}{DE} = \dfrac{CB}{FE}$

   (D) △*ABC* and △*DEF* are congruent

Answers on page 322

COORDINATE GRID

You can plot ordered pairs of numbers on a coordinate grid.

The *x* axis goes horizontally from left to right. The first number in the pair tells how far to move left or right from the origin. A minus sign means move left. A plus sign means move right.

The *y* axis goes vertically up and down. The second number in the pair tells how far to move up or down from the origin. A minus sign means move down. A plus sign means move up.

Pairs of numbers show the *x* coordinate first and the *y* coordinate second (*x*, *y*). The origin is point (0, 0) where the *x* axis and the *y* axis meet.

Plot these pairs of numbers on the grid.

A (⁺3, ⁻7)   **B** (⁺5, ⁺3)   **C** (⁻6, ⁺2)   **D** (⁻3, ⁻6)

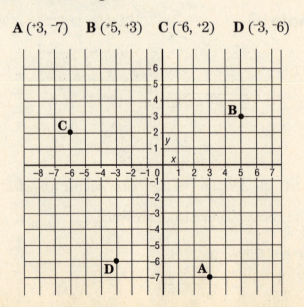

Practice Questions

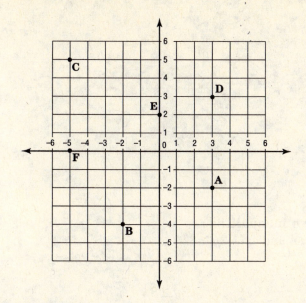

2. Plot these points on the grid below.

$G\,(3, -1)$	$H\,(2, -3)$	$I\,(5, 6)$
$J\,(-4, 0)$	$K\,(-5, -2)$	$L\,(-1, 6)$
$M\,(0, 3)$	$N\,(-5, 2)$	

3. Plot these points on the grid below and connect them in the order shown.

$Z\,(-5, 5)$	$Y\,(-2, 0)$	$X\,(2, -6)$
$W\,(3, 5)$	$V\,(-6, -2)$	$U\,(2, 0)$
$T\,(6, 1)$	$S\,(-5, 5)$	

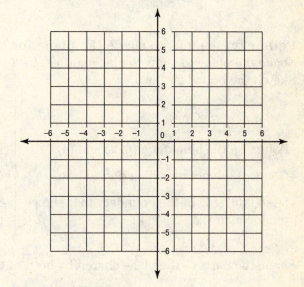

1. Write the coordinates of the points on the grid.

A _____
B _____
C _____
D _____
E _____
F _____

Answers on page 322

Graphing Inequalities on a Coordinate Grid

An inequality with two variables produces a region on the grid. The region is bounded by a line.

A solid line means the inequality is ≤ or ≥. A dotted line means the inequality is < or >.

Follow these steps to shade the plane for one inequality:

Shade the plane to show the inequality $x + 2y < 6$.

1. Sketch the boundary line. (Think: $x + 2y = 6$)

    Substitute 0 for x and solve.
    $0 + 2y = 6; y = 3$.
    One point on the boundary line is (0, 3).

    Substitute 0 for y and solve.
    $x + 0 = 6; x = 6$.
    One point on the boundary line is (6, 0).

    Plot the points. Connect them with a line.
    Draw a dotted line to show that the inequality is <.

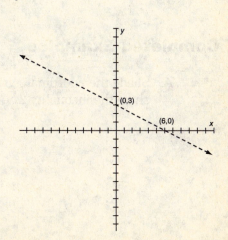

2. Shade the side of the boundary that satisfies the inequality $x + 2y < 6$.

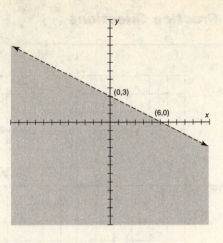

Follow these steps to shade the plane for two inequalities:
Shade the plane to show the inequalities $x + 2y < 4$ and $4x + 2y \geq 8$.
Sketch the boundary lines.

$x + 2y < 4$	$4x + 2y \geq 8$
–Points on the boundary: $(0, 2)$ and $(4, 0)$	–Points on the boundary: $(0, 4)$ and $(2, 0)$
–Connect the points with a dotted line.	–Connect the points with a solid line.
–Shade the side of the boundary that shows the inequality $x + 2y < 4$	–Shade the side of the boundary that shows the inequality $4x + 2y > 8$.

Shade the parts of the plane shared by both of the regions above.

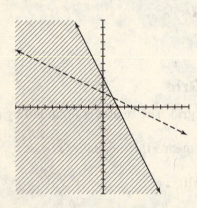   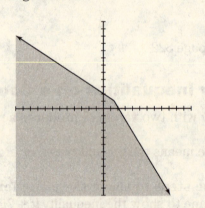

Completed Examples

A. Shade the coordinate grid to show the inequality $2x + y \leq 8$.

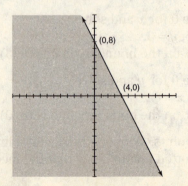

Practice Questions

Shade the plane on one of the graphs on pages 286–287 to show these inequalities.

1. $3x + 6y < 12$

3. $2x + 3y \geq 6$ and $4x + y < 12$.

2. $x + 4y \geq 8$

Answers on page 322

All, Some, and None

Diagrams can show the logical connectives all, some, and none. View the following diagrams for an explanation.

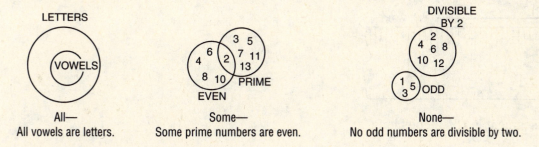

All—
All vowels are letters.

Some—
Some prime numbers are even.

None—
No odd numbers are divisible by two.

Deductive Reasoning

Deductive reasoning draws conclusions from statements or assumptions. Diagrams may help you draw a conclusion. Consider this simple example.

Assume that all even numbers are divisible by two and that all multiples of ten are even. Draw a diagram:

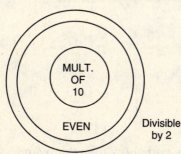

The multiple of ten circle is entirely within the divisible by two circle. Conclusion: All multiples of ten are divisible by two.

Practice Questions

Write whether the statement is true or false. Explain your answer.

1. A ball is used in all sports.

3. There are no even numbers divisible by 3.

2. Some numbers divisible by 5 are also divisible by 7.

4. Some prime numbers are divisible by 2.

Answers on page 322

MEASUREMENT

MEASURING WITH A RULER AND A PROTRACTOR

You may use a ruler that shows inches, halves, quarters, and sixteenths, or you may use a ruler that shows centimeters and millimeters.

Customary Rulers

Measure the length of a line segment to the nearest 1/16 of an inch. Put one end of the line segment at the 0 point on the ruler. Read the mark closest to the end of the line

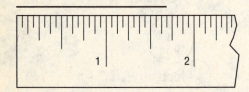

The line segment is $1^{11}\!/_{16}$ inches long.

Metric Rulers

Measure the length of the line segment to the nearest millimeter. Put one end of the line segment at the 0 point on the ruler. Read the mark closest to the end of the line.

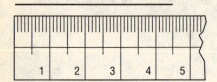

The line segment is 45 mm long.

Protractors

Most protractors are half circles and show degrees from 0° to 180°.

Put the center of the protractor on the vertex of the angle. Align one ray of the angle on the inner or outer 0° point on the scale. Read the measure of the angle on that scale.

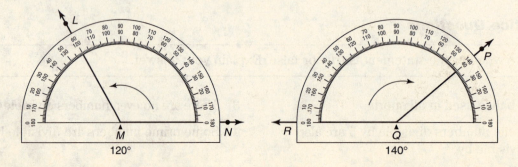

120°   140°

WEIGHT AND MASS

Mass is the amount of matter in a body. Weight is a measure of the force of gravity on a body. Mass is the same everywhere, but weight depends on its location in a gravitational field. That is, an object has the same mass whether on the moon or on earth. However, the object weighs less on the moon than on earth.

CUSTOMARY (ENGLISH) UNITS

Length

12 inches (in.) = 1 foot (ft)
3 feet = 1 yard (yd)
36 inches = 1 yard
1,760 yards = 1 mile (mi)
5,280 feet = 1 mile

Weight

16 ounces (oz) = 1 pound (lb)
2,000 pounds = 1 ton (T)

Capacity

2 cups = 1 pint (pt)
2 pints = 1 quart (qt)
4 quarts = 1 gallon (gal)

METRIC SYSTEM

The metric system uses common units of measure. The system uses prefixes that are powers of 10 or 0.1.

The common units used in the metric system follow:

Length—meter

Mass—gram

Capacity—liter

The prefixes used in the metric system follow:

1000	100	10	Unit	0.1	0.01	0.001
Kilo	Hecto	Deka		Deci	Centi	Milli

Notice that prefixes less than 1 end in *i*.

References for commonly used metric measurements

Unit	Description
Length	
Meter	A little more than a yard
Centimeter (0.01 meter)	The width of a paper clip (About 2.5 per inch)
Millimeter (0.001 meter)	The thickness of the wire on a paper clip
Kilometer (1000 meters)	About 0.6 of a mile
Mass	
Gram	The weight of a paper clip
Kilogram (1000 grams)	About 2.2 pounds
Capacity	
Liter	A little more than a quart
Milliliter	The amount of water in a cubic centimeter

Completed Example

Use your protractor and a ruler to construct an angle measuring 45°.

First construct a ray AB. Next place the center of the protractor at point A. Find the 45° measure and place a mark there. Call it point C. Now use the straight edge of the protractor and create ray AC.

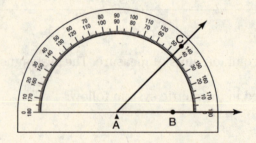

Practice Questions

1. 220 centimeters is equal to how many decameters?

2. How many feet equal 5.5 miles?

3. What is the length of the segment below to the nearest $\frac{1}{4}$ of an inch?

4. How many pounds equal 8 ounces?

5. How many ounces equal 2 tons?

6. What is the length of the segment below to the nearest centimeter?

7. How many inches in 3 miles?

8. 2.367 hectoliters is how many milliliters?

9. How many quarts are in $\frac{1}{2}$ gallon?

10. What is the measure of $\angle ABC$ below?

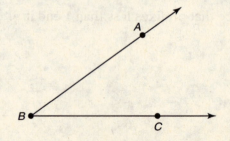

Answers on page 323

Completed Example

If it is 4:00 P.M. in North Carolina, what time is it in Nebraska?

Nebraska lies in two different time zones. If you are in the eastern Nebraska time zone, it is 3:00 P.M. If you are in the western Nebraska time zone, it is 2:00 P.M.

Practice Questions

1. What is colder, 0°C or 0°F?

2. If it is 10:00 A.M. in Washington State, what time is it in Maine?

3. Draw a picture of an analog 24-hour clock displaying 6:30 P.M.

4. If it is 9:00 A.M. in Minnesota, what time is it in Georgia?

5. 10°C is approximately how many degrees Fahrenheit?

6. 220°F is approximately how many degrees Celsius?

Answers on page 323

PROBLEM SOLVING

The problem-solving strategies of choosing a reasonable answer, estimating, choosing the operation, writing a number sentence, and identifying extra or needed information were discussed earlier in the review. This section shows you how to use more problem-solving strategies.

Estimate to Be Sure Your Answer Is Reasonable

You can use estimation and common sense to be sure that the answer is reasonable. You may make a multiplication error or misalign decimal points. You may be so engrossed in a problem that you miss the big picture because of the details. These difficulties can be headed off by making sure your answer is reasonable.

A few examples follow.

A question involves dividing or multiplying. Multiply: 28×72.

Estimate first: $30 \times 70 = 2,100$. Your answer should be close to 2,100. If not, then your answer is not reasonable. A mistake was probably made in multiplication.

A question involves subtracting or adding. Add: $12.9 + 0.63 + 10.29 + 4.3$.

Estimate first: $13 + 1 + 10 + 4 = 28$. Your answer should be close to 28. If not, then your answer is not reasonable. The decimal points may not have been aligned.

A question asks you to compare fractions to $\frac{11}{10}$.

Think: $\frac{11}{10}$ is more than 1. Any number 1 or less will be less than $\frac{11}{10}$. Any number $1\frac{1}{8}$ or larger will be more than $\frac{11}{10}$. You have to look closely only at numbers between 1 and $1\frac{1}{8}$.

A question asks you to multiply two fractions or decimals.

The fractions or decimals are less than 1. The product of two fractions or decimals less than one is less than either of the two fractions or decimals. If not, you know that your answer is not reasonable.

Stand back for a second after you answer each question and ask, "Is this reasonable? Is this at least approximately correct? Does this make sense?"

Check answers to computation, particularly division and subtraction. When you have completed a division or subtraction example, do a quick, approximate check. Your check should confirm your answer. If not, your answer is probably not reasonable.

Circle Important Information and Key Words
Eliminate Extra Information

This approach will draw your attention to the information needed to answer the question. A common mistake is to use from the question information that has nothing to do with the solution.

Example:

> In the morning, a train travels at a constant speed over an 800 kilometer distance. In the afternoon the train travels back over this same route. There is less traffic and the train travels four times as fast as it did that morning. However, there are more people on the train during the afternoon. Which of the following do you know about the train's afternoon trip?
>
> (A) The time is divided by four
> (B) The time is multiplied by four
> (C) The rate and time are divided by four
> (D) The rate is divided by four
> (E) The distance is the same, so the rate is the same

To solve the problem you just need to know that the speed is constant, four times as fast, and the same route was covered. Circle this information you need to solve the problem.

The distance traveled or that there were more people in the afternoon is extra information. Cross off this extra information, which may interfere with your ability to solve the problem.

> In the morning, a train travels at a constant speed over an 800 kilometer distance. In the afternoon the train travels back over this same route. There is less traffic and the train travels four times as fast as it did that morning. However, there are more people on the train during the afternoon. Which of the following do you know about the train's afternoon trip?

The correct answer is (A), the time is divided by four. The route is the same, but the train travels four times as fast. Therefore, the time to make the trip is divided by four. Rate means the same thing as speed, and we know that the speed has been multiplied by four.

Words to Symbols Problems

Before you solve a problem, you may have to decide which operation to use. You can use key words to help you decide which operation to use.

Key Words

Addition	sum, and, more, increased by
Subtraction	less, difference, decreased by
Multiplication	of, product, times
Division	per, quotient, shared, ratio
Equals	is, equals

You can't just use these key words without thinking. You must be sure that the operation makes sense when it replaces the key word. For example,

19 and 23 is 42	16 is 4 more than 12	30% of 19 is 5.7?
$19 + 23 = 42$	$16 = 4 + 12$	$0.3 \times 19 = 5.7$

three more than y	$y + 3$		The product of 3 and y	$3y$
y increased by 3	$y + 3$		3 times y	$3y$
y more than 3	$3 + y$		3% of y	$0.03y$
3 less than y	$y - 3$		3 divided by y	$\dfrac{3}{y}$
y decreased by 3	$y - 3$		y divided by 3	$\dfrac{y}{3}$
3 decreased y	$3 - y$		ratio of 3 to y	$\dfrac{3}{y}$
The opposite of y	$-y$		The reciprocal of y	$\dfrac{1}{y}$

Completed Examples

A. 18 divided by what number is 3?

$18 \div y = 3 \qquad 18 = 3y \qquad y = 6$

B. 25 less 6 is what number?

$25 - 6 = y \qquad y = 19$

C. A student correctly answered 80% of 120 mathematics problems. How many mathematics problems did he answer correctly?

$0.8 \times 120 = y \qquad y = 96$

The student correctly answered 96 problems.

D. The product of a number and its opposite is -25. What is the number?

$(y) \times (-y) = 25 \qquad y = 5$

The number is 5.

Practice Questions

Solve the problems.

1. What number decreased by 9 is 25?

2. What is 60% of 90?

3. Bob lives $\frac{2}{3}$ mile from Gina and $\frac{1}{2}$ mile from Sam. Bob's walk to the school is three times the sum of these distances. How far is Bob's walk to school?

4. The ratio of two gears is 20 to y. If the ratio equals 2.5, what is the value of y?

5. The sum of 5 and the reciprocal of another number is $5\frac{1}{8}$. What is the other number?

6. Car A travels at a constant speed of 60 mph for 2.5 hours. Car B travels at a constant speed of 70 mph for 2 hours. What is the total distance traveled by both cars?

Answers on page 323

FINDING AND INTERPRETING PATTERNS

Sequences

Arithmetic Sequence
A sequence of numbers formed by adding the same nonzero number.

3, 11, 19, 27, 35, 42, 50	Add 8 to get each successive term.
52, 48, 44, 40, 36, 32	Add (-4) to get each successive term.

Geometric Sequence
A sequence of numbers formed by multiplying the same nonzero number.

3, 15, 75, 375	Multiply by 5 to get each successive term.
$160, 40, 10, 2\frac{1}{2}$	Multiply by $\frac{1}{4}$ to get each successive term.

Harmonic Sequence
A sequence of fractions with a numerator of 1 in which the denominators form an arithmetic sequence.

$\frac{1}{2} \quad \frac{1}{9} \quad \frac{1}{16} \quad \frac{1}{23} \quad \frac{1}{30}$	Each numerator is 1. The denominators form an arithmetic sequence.

RELATIONSHIPS

Linear Relationships
Linear relationships are pairs of numbers formed by adding or multiplying the same number to the first term in a pair. Here are some examples.

(3, 12), (5, 14), (11, 20), (15, 24)	Add 9 to the first term to get the second.
(1, 6), (2, 12), (3, 18), (4, 24), (5, 30)	Multiply the first term by 6 to get the second.
(96, 12), (72, 9), (56, 7), (24, 3), (16, 2)	Multiply the first term by $\frac{1}{8}$ to get the second.

Completed Examples

A. What term is missing in this number pattern?

$$2 \quad 5 \quad 10 \quad 17 \quad \underline{\quad}$$
$$+3 \quad +5 \quad +7 \quad +9$$

26 is the missing term.

B. These points are all on the same line.
Find the missing term.

$$(-7, -15)\left(\frac{2}{3}, \frac{1}{3}\right)(2, 3)\,(4, 7)\,(8, \underline{\quad})$$

Multiply the first term by 2 and subtract 1.

The missing term is (8, 15).

Practice Questions

Find the missing term in each pattern below.

---

1. 4, 2, 0, −2, −4, _____ −8, −10

2. 4, 6.5, 9, 11.5, _____

3. 120, 60, 30, 15, _____

4. 1, 2, 6, 24, 120, _____

5. 5 9 13 17 _____

The points in each sequence below are on the same line. Find the missing term.

---

6. (4, 12), (2, 10), (10, 18), (18, 26),
(22, _____)

7. (100, 11), (70, 8), (90, 10), (40, 5),
(30, _____)

8. (3, 9), (7, 49), (2, 4), (100, 10,000),
(5, _____)

9. A meteorologist placed remote thermometers at sea level and up the side of the mountain at 1,000, 2,000, 5,000, and 6,000 feet. Readings were taken simultaneously and entered in the following table. What temperatures would you predict for the missing readings?

Temperature

0	1,000	2,000	3,000	4,000	5,000	6,000	7,000	8,000	9,000	10,000
52°	49°	46°			37°	34°				

10. Consider another example. A space capsule is moving in a straight line and is being tracked on a grid. The first four positions on the grid are recorded in the following table. Where will the capsule be on the grid when the x position is 13?

x-value	1	2	3	4	5
y-value	1	4	7	10	

Answers on page 323

ESTIMATION PROBLEMS

Follow these steps.

1. Round the numbers.

2. Use the rounded numbers to estimate the answer.

Completed Example

It takes a person about $7\frac{1}{2}$ minutes to run a mile. The person runs 174 miles in a month. What is a reasonable estimate of the time it takes for the person to run that distance?

Round $7\frac{1}{2}$ to 8.

Round 174 to 180.

$180 \times 8 = 1,440$ minutes or 24 hours.
24 hours is a reasonable estimate of the answer.

Practice Questions

1. A class took a spelling quiz and the grades were 93, 97, 87, 88, 98, 91. What is a reasonable estimate of the average of these grades?

2. To build a sandbox, you need lumber in the following lengths: 12 ft, 16 ft, 18 ft, and 23 ft. What is a reasonable estimate of the total length of the lumber?

3. Each batch of cookies yields 11 dozen. You need 165 dozen. What is a reasonable estimate for the number of batches you will need?

4. It takes 48 minutes for a commuter to travel back and forth from work each day. If the commuter drives back and forth 26 days a month, what is a reasonable estimate of the number of hours that are spent driving?

Answers on page 324

CHART PROBLEMS

Follow these steps:

1. Identify the data in the chart.

2. Add when necessary to find the total probability.

Completed Example

Table 1

	Air Express	Rail	Truck
5 pounds and over	0.07	0.34	0.18
Under 5 pounds	0.23	0.02	0.16

The table shows the percent of packages shipped by the method used and the weight classes.

What is the probability that a package picked at random was sent Air Express?

> Add the two proportions for Air Express.
> 0.07 + 0.23 = 0.30
> The probability that a randomly picked package was sent Air Express is 0.3.

What is the probability that a package picked at random weighed under five pounds?

> Add the three proportions for under five pounds.
> 0.23 + 0.02 + 0.16 = 0.42.
> The probability that a randomly chosen package weighed under five pounds is 0.42.

What is the probability that a package picked at random weighing under five pounds was sent by rail?

> Look at the cell in the table where *under five pounds* and *rail* intersect.
> That proportion is 0.02.
> The probability that a randomly chosen package under five pounds was sent by rail is 0.02.

Practice Questions

Use Table 1 above.

1. What is the probability that a package was sent by truck?

2. What is the probability of a package five pounds and over being randomly chosen?

3. What is the probability that a package five pounds and over picked at random was sent by Air Express?

4. What is the probability of randomly choosing a package under five pounds that was sent other than by rail?

Answers on page 324

FREQUENCY TABLE PROBLEMS

Percent

Percent tables show the percent or proportion of a particular score or characteristic. We can see from Table 1 that 13% of the students got a score from 90 through 100.

Completed Example

Table 1

Scores	Percent of Students
0–59	2
60–69	8
70–79	39
80–89	38
90–100	13

Which score interval contains the mode?

The largest percentage is 39% for 70−79. The interval 70−79 contains the mode.

Which score interval contains the median?

The cumulative percentage of 0−79 is 49%.
The median is in the interval in which the cumulative percentage of 50% occurs. The score interval 80−89 contains the median.

What percent of the students scored above 79?

Add the percentiles of the intervals above 79.   38 + 13 = 51
51% of the students scored above 79.

Percentile Rank

The percentile rank shows the percent of scores below a given value. We can see from Table 2 that 68% of the scores fell below 60.

Completed Example

Table 2

Standardized Score	Percentile Rank
80	99
70	93
60	68
50	39
40	22
30	13
20	2

What percent of the scores are below 50?

The percentile rank next to 50 is 39. That means 39% of the scores are below 50.

What percent of the scores are between 30 and 70?

Subtract the percentile rank for 30 from the percentile rank for 70.
93% − 13% = 80%. 80% of the scores are between 30 and 70.

What percent of the scores are at or above 60?

Subtract the percentile rank for 60 from 100%.
100% − 68% = 32%. 32% of the scores are at or above 60.

Practice Questions

Use Table 1 and Table 2 on pages 299 and 300.

Table 1

1. What percent of the scores are below 70?

2. In which score interval is the median?

3. What percent of the scores are from 80 to 100?

Table 2

4. The lowest passing score is 50. What percent of the scores are passing?

5. What percent of the scores are from 20 to 50?

Answers on page 324

FORMULA PROBLEMS

Concentrate on substituting values for variables. If you see a problem to be solved with a proportion, set up the proportion and solve.

Completed Examples

A. A mechanic uses this formula to estimate the displacement (*P*) of an engine. $P = 0.8\,(d^2)(s)(n)$ where **d** is the diameter, **s** is the stroke length of each cylinder, and **n** is the number of cylinders. Estimate the displacement of a 6-cylinder car whose cylinders have a diameter of 2 inches and a stroke length of 4 inches.

1. Write the formula. $P = 0.8(d^2)(s)(n)$

2. Write the values of the variables. $d = 2,\ s = 4,\ n = 6$

3. Substitute the values for the variables. $P = 0.8(2^2)(4)(6)$

4. Solve. $P = 0.8(4)(24) = (3.2)(24)$

    $P = 76.8$

The displacement of the engine is about 76.8 cubic inches.

B. The accountant calculates that it takes $3 in sales to generate $0.42 in profit. How much cost does it take to generate a profit of $5.46?

1. Write a proportion
Use *s* for sales. $\dfrac{3}{0.42} = \dfrac{s}{5.46}$

2. Cross multiply. $0.42s = 16.38$

3. Solve. $s = \dfrac{16.38}{0.42}$

    $s = 39$

It will take $39 in sales to generate $5.46 in profits.

Practice Questions

1. A retail store makes a profit of $3.75 for each $10 of goods sold. How much profit would the store make on a $45 purchase?

2. The formula for calculating average speed is $d/(T_2 - T_1)$. If T_1 (start time) is 5:00 P.M. and T_2 (end time) is midnight the same day, and 287 miles were traveled, what was the average speed?

3. A car purchased for $12,000 (**O**) depreciates 10% (**P**) a year (**Y**). If the car is sold in 3 years, what is its depreciated value if $V = O - POY$?

4. There is a square grid of dots. A figure is made of line segments that connect the dots. The formula for the area of a figure on the grid is $\frac{T-2}{2} + I$.

   T is the number of dots touching the figure, and *I* is the number of dots inside. What is the area of a figure with 14 dots touching and 5 dots inside?

Answers on page 324

PYTHAGOREAN THEOREM PROBLEMS

Follow these steps to solve this type of problem.

    1. Sketch and label the right triangle.

    2. Use the Pythagorean formula.

    3. Solve the problem.

Completed Example

A radio tower sticks 40 feet straight up into the air. Engineers attached a wire with no slack from the top of the tower to the ground 30 feet away from the tower. If it costs $95 a foot to attach the wire, how much did the wire cost?

    1. Sketch and label the right triangle.

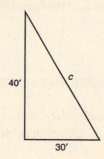

    2. Use the Pythagorean formula.

$$a^2 + b^2 = c^2$$
$$(40)^2 + (30)^2 = c^2$$
$$1{,}600 + 900 = c^2$$
$$2{,}500 = c^2$$
$$50 = c$$

The wire is 50 feet long.

    3. Solve the problem.

50 feet at $95 a foot.

$50 \times 95 = 4{,}750$. The wire costs $4,750 to install.

Practice Questions

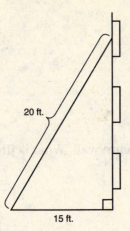

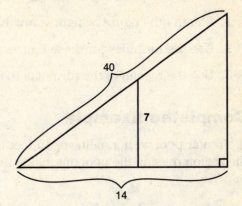

1. A 20-foot ladder is leaning against the side of a tall apartment building. The bottom of the ladder is 15 feet from the wall. At what height on the wall does the top of the ladder touch the building?

3. You are building a staircase. The wall is 14 feet wide and the stairs are 40 feet long. How high is the wall where it touches the top of the stairs?

4. A truck ramp is shaped like a right triangle. The base of the ramp is 300 feet long. The ramp itself is 340 feet long. How high is the third side of the ramp?

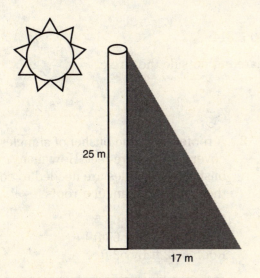

2. A 25-meter telephone pole casts a shadow. The shadow ends 17 meters from the base of the pole. How long is it straight from the top of the pole to the end of the shadow?

Answers on page 324

GEOMETRIC FIGURE PROBLEMS

Follow these steps to solve this type of problem.

1. Identify the figure or figures involved.

2. Use the formulas for these figures.

3. Use the results of the formulas to solve the problem.

Completed Example

A circular pool with a radius of 10 feet is inscribed inside a square wall. What is the area of the region outside the pool but inside the fence?

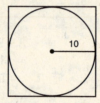

1. There is a square with $s = 20$ and a circle with $r = 10$. The side of the square is twice the radius of the circle.

2. Find the areas.
   Square: $(A = s^2)$ $(20) \times (20) = 400$
   Circle: $(A = \pi r^2)$ $3.14 \times 10^2 = 3.14 \times 100 = 314$

3. Subtract to find the area inside the square but outside the circle.
   $400 - 314 = 86$

Practice Questions

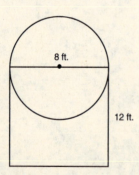

1. The dimensions of part of a basketball court are shown in the diagram above. One pint of paint covers 35 square feet. How much paint would it take to paint the inside region of this part of the court?

2. A roofer uses one bushel of shingles to cover 1200 square feet. How many bushels of shingles are needed to cover these three rectangular roofs?

Roof 1: 115 ft by 65 ft
Roof 2: 112 ft by 65 ft
Roof 3: 72 ft by 52 ft

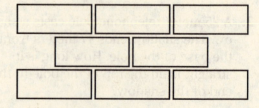

3. The bricks in the wall pictured here measure 2 inches by 4 inches by 8 inches. What is the volume of the bricks in this section of the wall?

4. A circular cone has a radius of 4 cm. If the volume is 134 cm³, what is the height?

5. The official basketball has a radius of 6.5 inches. What is the volume?

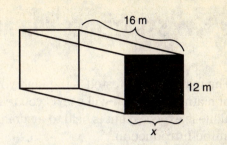

6. The rectangular solid shown here has a volume of 1,920 m³. What is the area of the shaded side?

Answers on page 325

INTERPRETING REMAINDER PROBLEMS

When you divide to solve a problem there may be both a quotient and a remainder. You may need to (1) use only the quotient, (2) round the quotient to the next greater whole number, or (3) use only the remainder.

Completed Example

Stereo speakers are packed 4 to a box. There are 315 stereo speakers to be packed.

Questions:

1. How many boxes can be filled?
2. How many boxes would be needed to hold all the stereo speakers?
3. How many stereo speakers will be in the box that is not completely full?

Divide 315 by 4.

$$
\begin{array}{r}
78\ \text{R}3 \\
4\overline{)315} \\
\underline{28} \\
35 \\
\underline{32} \\
3
\end{array}
$$

Answers:

1. Use only the quotient—78 of the boxes can be filled.
2. Round the quotient to the next higher number. It would take 79 boxes to hold all the stereo speakers.
3. Use only the remainder. Three stereo speakers would be in the partially filled box.

Practice Questions

At the quarry, workers are putting 830 pounds of sand into bags that hold 25 pounds.

1. How much sand is left over after the bags are filled?

2. How many bags are needed to hold all the sand?

3. How many bags can be filled with sand?

Answers on page 325

STRATEGIES FOR ANSWERING MATHEMATICS ITEMS

The mathematics tested is the kind you probably had in high school and in college. It is the kind of mathematics you will use as you teach and go about your everyday life. Computational ability alone is expected but is held to a minimum. Remember to use the general test strategies discussed in the Introduction.

WRITE IN THE TEST BOOKLET

It is particularly important to write in the test booklet while taking the mathematics portion of the test. Use these hints for writing in the test booklet.

Do Your Calculations in the Test Booklet

Do all your calculations in the test booklet to the right of the question. This makes it easy to refer to the calcuations as you choose the correct answer.

   This example should make you feel comfortable about writing in the test booklet.

   What number times 0.00708 is equal to 70.8?

   (A) 100,000 × 0.00708 = 708

   (B) 10,000 × 0.00708 = 70.8

   (C) 1,000

   (D) 0.01

   (E) 0.0001

   B

The correct answer is (B) 10,000

Draw Diagrams and Figures in the Test Booklet

When you come across a geometry problem or related problem, draw a diagram in the test booklet to help.

   All sides of a rectangle are shrunk in half. What happens to the area?

   (A) Divided by two

   (B) Divided by four

   (C) Multiplied by two

   (D) Multiplied by six

   Answer (B), divided by 4, is the correct answer. The original area is evenly divided into four parts.

Work from the Answers

If you don't know how to solve a formula or relation try out each answer choice until you get the correct answer. Look at this example.

What percent times $\frac{1}{4}$ is $\frac{1}{5}$?

(A) 25%

(B) 40%

(C) 80%

(D) 120%

Just take each answer in turn and try it out.

$$0.25 \times \frac{1}{4} = \frac{1}{4} \times \frac{1}{4} = \frac{1}{16} \quad \text{That's not it.}$$

$$0.40 \times \frac{1}{4} = \frac{4}{10} \times \frac{1}{4} = \frac{4}{40} = \frac{1}{10} \quad \text{That's not it either.}$$

$$0.8 \times \frac{1}{4} = \frac{4}{5} \times \frac{1}{4} = \frac{4}{20} = \frac{1}{5}$$

You know that 0.8 is the correct answer, so choice (C) is correct.

Try Out Numbers

Look at the preceding question.

Work with fractions at first. Ask: What number times $\frac{1}{4}$ equals $\frac{1}{5}$?

Through trial and error you find out that $\frac{4}{5} \times \frac{1}{4} = \frac{1}{5}$.

The answer in fractions is $\frac{4}{5}$.

$$\frac{4}{5} = 0.8 = 80\%$$

The correct choice is (C).

In this example, we found the answer without ever solving an equation. We just tried out numbers until we found the one that works.

Eliminate and Guess

Use this approach when all else has failed. Begin by eliminating the answers you know are wrong. Sometimes you know with certainty that an answer is incorrect. Other times, an answer looks so unreasonable that you can be fairly sure that it is not correct.

Once you have eliminated incorrect answers, a few will probably be left. Just guess among these choices. There is no method that will increase your chances of guessing correctly.

MATHEMATICS TARGETED TEST

These items will help you practice for the real CSET. These items have the same form and test the same material as the CSET items and test material. The items you encounter on the real CSET may have a different emphasis and may be more complete.

Instructions

Mark your answers on the sheet provided below. Complete the items in 40 minutes or less. Correct your answer sheet using the answers on page 326.

1	Ⓐ Ⓑ Ⓒ Ⓓ	9	Ⓐ Ⓑ Ⓒ Ⓓ	17	Ⓐ Ⓑ Ⓒ Ⓓ	25	Ⓐ Ⓑ Ⓒ Ⓓ	33	Ⓐ Ⓑ Ⓒ Ⓓ
2	Ⓐ Ⓑ Ⓒ Ⓓ	10	Ⓐ Ⓑ Ⓒ Ⓓ	18	Ⓐ Ⓑ Ⓒ Ⓓ	26	Ⓐ Ⓑ Ⓒ Ⓓ	34	Ⓐ Ⓑ Ⓒ Ⓓ
3	Ⓐ Ⓑ Ⓒ Ⓓ	11	Ⓐ Ⓑ Ⓒ Ⓓ	19	Ⓐ Ⓑ Ⓒ Ⓓ	27	Ⓐ Ⓑ Ⓒ Ⓓ	35	Ⓐ Ⓑ Ⓒ Ⓓ
4	Ⓐ Ⓑ Ⓒ Ⓓ	12	Ⓐ Ⓑ Ⓒ Ⓓ	20	Ⓐ Ⓑ Ⓒ Ⓓ	28	Ⓐ Ⓑ Ⓒ Ⓓ	36	Ⓐ Ⓑ Ⓒ Ⓓ
5	Ⓐ Ⓑ Ⓒ Ⓓ	13	Ⓐ Ⓑ Ⓒ Ⓓ	21	Ⓐ Ⓑ Ⓒ Ⓓ	29	Ⓐ Ⓑ Ⓒ Ⓓ	37	Ⓐ Ⓑ Ⓒ Ⓓ
6	Ⓐ Ⓑ Ⓒ Ⓓ	14	Ⓐ Ⓑ Ⓒ Ⓓ	22	Ⓐ Ⓑ Ⓒ Ⓓ	30	Ⓐ Ⓑ Ⓒ Ⓓ	38	Ⓐ Ⓑ Ⓒ Ⓓ
7	Ⓐ Ⓑ Ⓒ Ⓓ	15	Ⓐ Ⓑ Ⓒ Ⓓ	23	Ⓐ Ⓑ Ⓒ Ⓓ	31	Ⓐ Ⓑ Ⓒ Ⓓ	39	Ⓐ Ⓑ Ⓒ Ⓓ
8	Ⓐ Ⓑ Ⓒ Ⓓ	16	Ⓐ Ⓑ Ⓒ Ⓓ	24	Ⓐ Ⓑ Ⓒ Ⓓ	32	Ⓐ Ⓑ Ⓒ Ⓓ	40	Ⓐ Ⓑ Ⓒ Ⓓ

1. The sum of the measures of two angles is 90°. What do we know about these two angles?
   (A) They are right angles.
   (B) The are supplementary angles.
   (C) They are acute angles.
   (D) The are obtuse angles.

2. Three very bright light beams go out into space from the same spot on earth. None of the beams are parallel and none point in the same direction. What conclusion can we reach?
   (A) All three beams will cross at the same point.
   (B) Exactly two of the beams will cross.
   (C) At least two of the beams will cross.
   (D) At least two of the beams may be skewed.

3. Bob walked about 2,750 meters to school every day. About how many kilometers is that?
   (A) 2.750
   (B) 27.50
   (C) 275
   (D) 275,000

4. You buy 20 shares of stock on March 10 for $17\,^{7}/_{8}$ a share. You sell the 20 shares stock on May 5 for $19\,^{5}/_{8}$ a share. How much in dollars and cents did you make on the stock?
   (A) $75.00
   (B) $4.50
   (C) $37.50
   (D) $35.00

5. Alpha Centauri is about 4 light years from earth. Light travels about 186,000 miles in a second. About how far is it from Alpha Centauri to earth?
   (A) 23 quintillion miles
   (B) 23 quadrillion miles
   (C) 23 trillion miles
   (D) 23 billion miles

6. An unusual plant is 10 feet tall when planted and then, starting the next day, grows 20 percent of each of the previous day's final height. About how tall is the tree at the end of the fourth day after planting?
   (A) 19.4 feet
   (B) 20.7 feet
   (C) 18 feet
   (D) 16 feet

7. A block of stone is 9 feet wide by 12 feet long by 8 feet high. A stone mason cuts the stone to form the biggest cube possible. What is the volume of the cube?
   (A) 864 cubic feet
   (B) 144 cubic feet
   (C) 81 cubic feet
   (D) 512 cubic feet

Use this information for <u>questions 8 and 9</u>.

An archaeologist was investigating the books of an old civilization. She found the following table, which showed the number of hunters on top and the number of people they could feed on the bottom. For example, 3 hunters could feed 12 people. The archaeologist found a pattern in the table.

Hunters	1	2	3	4	5	6	7
Eaters	2	6	12	20	30		

8. Look for the pattern. How many eaters can 6 hunters feed?
   (A) 42
   (B) 40
   (C) 30
   (D) 36

9. What is the formula for the pattern:
   H stands for hunters and
   E stands for eaters?
   (A) $E = 3 \times H$
   (B) $E = 4 \times H$
   (C) $E = H^2 + H$
   (D) $E = 3 \times (H + 1)$

10. The school is planning a class trip. They will go by bus. There will be 328 people going on the trip, and each bus holds 31 people. How many buses will be needed for the trip?
    (A) 9
    (B) 10
    (C) 11
    (D) 18

1	2	3	4	5	6	7	8	9	10
11	12	13	14	15	16	17	18	19	20
21	22	23	24	25	26	27	28	29	30
31	32	33	34	35	36	37	38	39	40
41	42	43	44	45	46	47	48	49	50
51	52	53	54	55	56	57	58	59	60
61	62	63	64	65	66	67	68	69	70
71	72	73	74	75	76	77	78	79	80
81	82	83	84	85	86	87	88	89	90
91	92	93	94	95	96	97	98	99	100

Use this graph to answer <u>questions 13 and 14</u>.

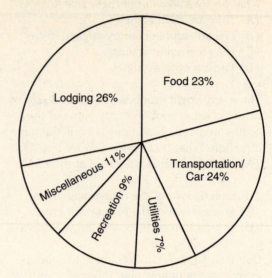

Jane's Monthly Budget

11. Cross off the multiples of 2, 3, 4, 5, 6, 7, and 8 in the above hundreds square. Which numbers in the 80s are not crossed off?
    (A) 83, 87
    (B) 81, 89
    (C) 83, 89
    (D) 81, 83, 89

12. Study the above shapes, and select A, B, C, or D, according to the rule:
    (small or striped) and large.
    Which pieces are selected?

(A)

(B)

(C)

(D)

13. Jane spends $2,600 in the month of March. How much did she spend on food?
    (A) $624
    (B) $598
    (C) $312
    (D) $400

14. Jane spends $2,600 in May. She needs $858 that month for transportation/car expenses, which is more than the budget allows. Any needed money will come from miscellaneous. When she recalculates her budget chart, what percent is left for miscellaneous?
    (A) 2 percent
    (B) 6 percent
    (C) 9 percent
    (D) 11 percent

15. The bakers make brownies and cookies in a ratio of 2 : 9. Today the bakers made 1,350 cookies. How many brownies did the bakers make?
    (A) 150
    (B) 300
    (C) 675
    (D) 2750

16. A candy manufacturer will make and ship 2,026,214,229,962,952 pounds of jelly beans this year. The manufacturer wants to ship the jelly beans in a single size package with no jelly beans left over. The package could hold either 1, 2, 3, 4, 5, 6, 7, 8, 9, or 10 pounds. Which answer below lists ALL the manufacturer's choices?
    (A) 1, 2, 3, 4
    (B) 1, 2, 3, 4, 6
    (C) 1, 2, 3, 4, 6, 8
    (D) 1, 2, 3, 4, 6, 8, 9

17. A tent standing on level ground is 40 feet high. A taut rope extends from the top of the tent to the ground 30 feet from the bottom of the tent. About how long is the rope?
    (A) 26.455 feet
    (B) 50 feet
    (C) 63.255 feet
    (D) 70 feet

18. $(123 + 186 + 177) \div (3) =$

    Which of the following statements could result in the number sentence given above?
    (A) The athlete wanted to find the median of the three jumps.
    (B) The athlete wanted to find the average of the three jumps.
    (C) The athlete wanted to find the quotient of the product of three jumps.
    (D) The athlete wanted to find the sum of the quotients of the three jumps.

19. Renee, Lisa, and Jan are all on the basketball team. Renee is the tallest player on the team. Lisa is not the shortest player on the team. Jan is not shorter than Lisa.

    Which of the following conclusions can be drawn from this statement?
    (A) Jan is taller than Lisa.
    (B) Jan is the second-tallest player on the team.
    (C) Jan is not the shortest player on the team.
    (D) Either Jan or Lisa is the second tallest player on the team.

20. If $x = 5/6$, which of the following inequalities is correct?
    (A) $\frac{5}{9} < x < \frac{7}{9}$
    (B) $\frac{5}{8} < x < \frac{3}{4}$
    (C) $\frac{3}{4} < x < \frac{7}{8}$
    (D) $\frac{7}{8} < x < \frac{15}{16}$

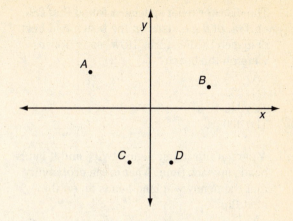

21. Which letter on the coordinate grid above could represent the point $(2, -5)$?
    (A) A
    (B) B
    (C) C
    (D) D

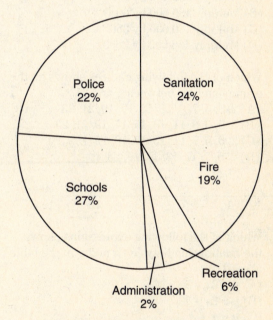

Tax money spent on town services.

22. A town collects $2,600,000 in taxes. The town needs $624,000 for police. Any needed money will come from sanitation. The percents in the circle graph are recalculated. What percent is left for sanitation?
    (A) 22%
    (B) 20%
    (C) 19%
    (D) 18%

23. The disaster relief specialist found that 289, or 85%, of the houses on the beach had been damaged by the storm. How many houses were on the beach?
    (A) 294
    (B) 332
    (C) 340
    (D) 400

24. A person flips a fair penny twice and it lands heads up each time. What is the probability that the penny will land heads up on the next flip?
    (A) 1
    (B) 1/2
    (C) 1/4
    (D) 1/8

25. Light travels about 186,000 miles in a second. How would you find out how far light travels in an hour?
    (A) Multiply 186,000 by 24.
    (B) Multiply 186,000 by 60.
    (C) Multiply 186,000 by 360.
    (D) Multiply 186,000 by 3600.

26. Which of the following choices shows all the prime numbers between 1 and 25?
    (A) 2, 3, 5, 7, 9, 11, 13, 17, 19, 21, 23
    (B) 3, 5, 7, 9, 11, 13, 15, 17, 19, 21, 23
    (C) 2, 3, 5, 7, 11, 13, 17, 19, 23
    (D) 3, 5, 7, 11, 13, 17, 19, 23

x	0	2	3	6	7	9
y	1	5	7	13	15	19

27. Which of the following expressions shows the relationship between x and y in the table above?
    (A) $y = 3x - 2$
    (B) $y = 2x + 1$
    (C) $y = x + 3$
    (D) $y = 2x - 2$

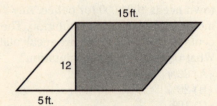

15 ft.

12

5 ft.

28. What is the area of the shaded portion?
    (A) 45 square feet
    (B) 270 square feet
    (C) 150 square feet
    (D) 180 square feet

29. $2n + 3n^2 - 5n \times 3 - 6n^2 =$
    (A) $-12n$
    (B) $-13n - 3n^2$
    (C) $13n + 3n^2$
    (D) $-6n^2$

30. Solve for x: $11x - 5 = -6 + 6x$
    (A) $x = 5$
    (B) $x = -5$
    (C) $x = \frac{1}{5}$
    (D) $x = -\frac{1}{5}$

31. The formula for converting a kilogram weight (K) to a pound weight (P) is $P = 2.2 K$. If a dog weighs 15.6 pounds, how many kilograms does the dog weigh?
    (A) 3.43 kg
    (B) 34.32 kg
    (C) 7.09 kg
    (D) 70.9 kg

32. Which is a linear factor of the following expression?
    $$6x^2 - x - 2$$
    (A) $(3x - 2)$
    (B) $(3x + 3)$
    (C) $(2x + 3)$
    (D) $(x + 2)$

33. What are the real roots of this equation?
    $$2x^2 - x = 3$$
    (A) (2, 3)
    (B) $(-1\frac{1}{2}, 1)$
    (C) (2, 1)
    (D) $(-1, 1\frac{1}{2})$

34. Choose the correct solution set for the system of linear equations.
    $$4x - 2y = -10$$
    $$2x - 4y = 10$$
    (A) $(\frac{1}{2}, -\frac{1}{2})$
    (B) $y = x + 3$
    (C) (5, -5)
    (D) the empty set

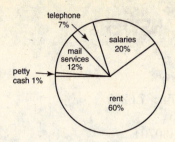

Federal Funding in 1994

35. The pie chart above represents the monthly expenses of a small business for August. In what area is the most money spent?
    (A) mail services, telephone, and salaries
    (B) salaries, telephone, and petty cash
    (C) petty cash and salaries
    (D) rent

38. The graph above represents the distribution of federal funding to Florida public schools in 1994. Which statement about the data is true?
    (A) West Palm represents the median amount.
    (B) Miami represents the mean.
    (C) Orlando represents the mean.
    (D) Jacksonville represents the mode.

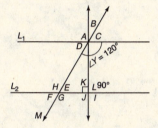

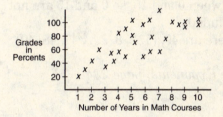

36. Which of the following statements is true about the diagram above?
    (A) Since $m\angle Y = 120$ degrees, $m\angle H = 120$ degrees
    (B) Since $m\angle L = 90$ degrees, $m\angle D = 45$ degrees
    (C) $m\angle C = m\angle B$
    (D) None of the above statements is true.

39. The graph shows the grade distribution on a standardized mathematics test. Which of the following best describes the relationships between test score and number of years in mathematics courses?
    (A) People who took fewer years of math scored highest.
    (B) People who took more math courses scored lower.
    (C) There is a negative relationship.
    (D) There is a positive relationship.

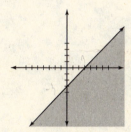

37. Identify the conditions that correspond to the shaded region of the plane shown above.
    (A) $x \geq 0$ and $y \geq 2$
    (B) $y = -x$
    (C) $x < 4, y > -2, y > x$
    (D) $x \geq y + 3$

40. Which graph correctly represents the conditions: $x \geq 5$ and $-5 < y < 5$.

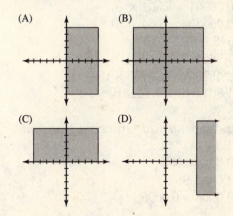

MATHEMATICS PRACTICE ANSWERS

Understanding and Ordering Whole Numbers, page 233

1. $2 < 3$
2. $4 > 1$
3. $8 < 9$
4. $1 = 1$
5. $7 > 6$
6. 9,037
7. 2,851
8. The hundreds place and the ones place each contain a 7.
9. 1, 2, 3, 4, 5, 6, 7, 8, 9, 10, 11, 12, 13, 14 The problem asks for the numbers between 0 and 15, so 0 and 15 are not included.
10. There are 49. (1, 2, 3, . . . , 47, 48, 49)

Positive Exponents, page 234

1. 241
2. 81
3. 8
4. 900
5. 35
6. 51
7. $4^6 = 4,096$
8. $2^5 = 32$
9. 44
10. 1,000
11. $4^4 = 256$
12. 72

Scientific Notation, page 235

1. $0.0564 = 5.64 \times 10^{-2}$
2. $0.00897 = 8.97 \times 10^{-3}$
3. $0.06501 = 6.501 \times 10^{-2}$
4. $0.000354 = 3.54 \times 10^{-4}$
5. $545 = 5.45 \times 10^2$
6. $7,790 = 7.79 \times 10^3$
7. $289,705 = 2.89705 \times 10^5$
8. $1,801,319 = 1.801319 \times 10^6$

Understanding and Ordering Decimals, page 236

1. $0.02 > 0.003$
2. $4.6 > 1.98$
3. $0.0008 > 0.00009$
4. $1.0 = 1$
5. $7.6274 > 7.6269$
6. 2.586
7. 90310.0704
8. The hundredths place and the hundred thousandths place each contain a 3.
9. 0, 0.1, 0.2, 0.3, 0.4, 0.5, 0.6, 0.7, 0.8, 0.9, 1.0
10. There are 99—0.01, 0.02, 0.03, . . . , 0.50, 0.51, 0.52, . . . , 0.97, 0.98, 0.99

Rounding Whole Numbers and Decimals, page 237

1. 23,500
2. 74.151
3. 980,000
4. 302.8
5. 495,240
6. 1500
7. 13.1
8. 200,000
9. 52
10. 23,500

Understanding and Ordering Fractions, page 239

1. $1\frac{2}{3}$
2. $2\frac{1}{7}$
3. $2\frac{2}{3}$
4. $\frac{41}{5}$
5. $\frac{55}{8}$
6. $\frac{68}{7}$
7. $\frac{3}{7} < \frac{4}{9}$
8. $\frac{5}{6} = \frac{25}{30}$
9. $\frac{4}{5} < \frac{7}{8}$

Order of Operations, page 241
1. $4 \times 5 + 4 \div 2 = 20 + 2 = 22$
2. $(5 + 7 - 9) \times 8^2 + 2 = 3 \times 8^2 + 2 = 194$
3. $((7 + 4) - (1 + 4)) \times 6 = (11 - 5) \times 6 = 36$
4. $6^2 + 3(9 - 5 + 7)^2 = 36 + 3 \times 11^2 = 399$
5. $51 - 36 = 15$
6. $40 + 4 - 4 = 40$
7. $^-50 + 7 = {}^-43$
8. $(49 + 16) \times 8 = 520$

Number Theory, page 244
1. 13: 1 and 13
2. 26: 1, 2, 13, and 26
3. 40: 1, 2, 4, 5, 8, 10, 20, 40
4. 23: 1 and 23
5. 24
6. 60
7. 35
8. 28
9. 6
10. 5
11. 32
12. 28

Whole Number Computation, page 246
1. 98,405
2. 27,079
3. 95,809
4. 66,184
5. 16,013
6. 34,099
7. 34,688
8. 42,209
9. 13,680
10. 27,482
11. 29,725
12. 5,256
13. 8
14. 4 R4
15. 29
16. 32 R2

Properties of Operations, page 247
1. Commutative Property $^6/_8 \times {}^7/_9 = {}^7/_9 \times {}^6/_8$
2. Associative Property
   $(2 + 3) + 4 = 2 + (3 + 4)$
3. The equation represents the distributive property.
4. Distributive property creates the expression $a(6 + 3)$.
5. The commutative property creates the expression.
6. (A) is not true for all real numbers. In fact the answer to $A \times (1/A)$ is always 1

Add, Subtract, Multiply, and Divide Decimals, page 248
1. 26.09
2. 72.617
3. 988.39
4. 5473.19
5. 8.2
6. 71.0096
7. 453.97
8. 1767.87
9. .6225
10. 163.45
11. 3680.538
12. 3761.514
13. 4.8
14. 9.6
15. 33.6
16. 125.63

Multiply, Divide, Add, and Subtract Fractions and Mixed Numbers, page 249
1. $\dfrac{5}{27}$
2. $\dfrac{1}{6}$
3. $13\dfrac{59}{64}$
4. $8\dfrac{8}{35}$
5. $\dfrac{6}{7}$
6. $\dfrac{18}{35}$
7. $2\dfrac{22}{91}$
8. $\dfrac{7}{19}$
9. $1\dfrac{2}{9}$
10. $1\dfrac{1}{5}$
11. $4\dfrac{1}{14}$

12. $12\frac{1}{2}$

13. $\frac{1}{21}$

14. $\frac{1}{40}$

15. $\frac{2}{3}$

16. $3\frac{58}{63}$

Square Roots, page 251
1. $\sqrt{256} = 16$
2. $\sqrt{400} = 20$
3. $\sqrt{576} = 24$
4. $\sqrt{900} = 30$
5. $\sqrt{1225} = 35$
6. $\sqrt{48} = \sqrt{16 \times 3} = 4\sqrt{3}$
7. $\sqrt{245} = \sqrt{49 \times 5} = 7\sqrt{5}$
8. $\sqrt{396} = \sqrt{36 \times 11} = 6\sqrt{11}$
9. $\sqrt{567} = \sqrt{81 \times 7} = 9\sqrt{7}$
10. $\sqrt{832} = \sqrt{64 \times 13} = 8\sqrt{13}$

Ratio and Proportion, page 252
1. 14 vacuum cleaners for 280 houses
2. 4 teachers for 32 children
3. 21 rest stops for 140 miles
4. Yes. $\frac{7}{9} = \frac{28}{36}$ because $7 \times 36 = 252 = 9 \times 28$

Percent, page 254
1. 35.9%
2. 78%
3. 21.5%
4. 4.1%
5. $11\frac{1}{9}\%$
6. 62.5%
7. 30%
8. $44\frac{4}{9}\%$
9. $\frac{29}{50}$
10. $\frac{79}{100}$
11. $\frac{213}{250}$
12. $\frac{487}{500}$

Three Types of Percent Problems, page 256
1. $\square \times 240 = 120$
   $\square = \frac{120}{240}$
   $\square = .5 = 50\%$

2. $.15 \times 70 = \square$
   $.15 \times 70 = 10.5$
   $\square = 10.5$

3. $.6 \times 300 = \square$
   $.6 \times 300 = 180$
   $\square = 180$

4. $\square \times 60 = 42$
   $\square = \frac{42}{60}$
   $\square = 70\%$

5. $\square\% \times 25 = 2.5$
   $\square\% = \frac{2.5}{25}$
   $\square = 10\%$

6. $40\% \times \square = 22$
   $\square = \frac{22}{.4}$
   $\square = 55$

7. $.7 \times \square = 85$
   $\square = \frac{85}{.7}$
   $\square = 121\frac{3}{7}$

8. $25\% \times 38 = \square$
   $.25 \times 38 = 9.5$
   $\square = 9.5$

9. $.35 \times \square = 24$
   $\square = \frac{24}{.35}$
   $\square = 68\frac{4}{7}$

10. $24 = \square \times 80$
    $\frac{24}{80} = \square$
    $\square = 30\%$

Percent of Increase and Decrease, page 257
1. Amount of increase $35 - $25 = $10
   $\frac{10}{25} = 0.4 = 40\%$

   Percent of increase = 40%

2. Discount: $100 × .25 = $25
$100 − $25 = $75
Sale price = $75

3. Discount $80 × 15% = $12
$80 − $12 = $68
New price = $68

4. Amount of increase $150 − $120 = $30
$\frac{30}{120} = \frac{1}{4} = 25\%$
Percent of increase = 25%

5. Discount $75 × 10% = $7.50
$75 − $7.50 = $67.50
Sale price = $67.50

6. Amount of decrease $18 − $6 = $12
$\frac{12}{18} = \frac{2}{3} = 66\frac{2}{3}\%$
Percent of decrease = $66\frac{2}{3}\%$

7. Amount of decrease $225 − $180 = $45
$\frac{45}{225} = 0.2 = 20\%$
Percent of decrease = 20%

8. Discount $150 = x − 0.25x$
$150 = 0.75x$
$x = 200
Original price: $200

Probability, page 258
1. There are 10 socks in the drawer. 7 of the 10 are not black.
$P \text{ (not black)} = \frac{7}{10}$

2. There are 6 goldfish; 2 of the 6 are male.
$P \text{ (male)} = \frac{2}{6} = \frac{1}{3}$

3. There are 52 cards in a deck. There are 4 kings and 4 queens.
$P \text{ (king or queen)} = P \text{ (king)} + P \text{ (queen)}$
$= \frac{4}{52} + \frac{4}{52} = \frac{8}{52} = \frac{2}{13}$

4. There are 6 different names.
$P \text{ (Carl and Phyllis)} =$
$P \text{ (Carl)} \times P \text{ (Phyllis)} =$
$\frac{1}{6} \times \frac{1}{6} = \frac{1}{36}$

5. $\frac{1}{2}$

6. This is an "and" problem. Multiply the probability.
$\left(\frac{1}{2}\right)\left(\frac{1}{2}\right)\left(\frac{1}{2}\right)\left(\frac{1}{2}\right)\left(\frac{1}{2}\right) = \frac{1}{32}$

Permutations and Combinations, page 260
1. There are 6 combinations of 2 people to sit in the chairs.
2. There are 5,040 possible arrangements of the 7 books on the shelf.
3. 67,600 $(26 \times 26 \times 10 \times 10)$
4. The positions on the bus are not specified. Order does not matter. This is a combination problem.

Four students   A B C D

ABC   ABD   ACD   BCD

There are four ways for three of four students to board the bus.

Statistics, page 261
1. mode 80
2. mean (average) 35.5
3. median 9 (Remember to arrange the numbers in order.)
4. 16 is the median, the mode, and very close to the mean.
5. mean 89
6. mode 30

Stem-and-Leaf and Box-and-Whisker Plots, page 262
1.
1	0, 3, 5, 7, 9
2	3, 6, 8, 9
3	3, 6, 8,
4	2, 2, 5, 7, 8, 9
5	3, 5, 6,
6	
7	5, 6, 7, 9
8	
9	2, 4, 6,
10	1, 5, 6

2. There is no score between 56 and 75.
3. 47
4. 42

Selecting Unbiased Samples, page 263

1. Good Sampling Techniques

   Randomly ask people at work about their child care needs.
   Randomly sample working parents of children ages 1–5.
   Randomly sample parents who have their children in day care.

   Poor Sampling Techniques

   Randomly sample women with children.
   Randomly sample people outside a supermarket.
   Randomly sample people who have no children.

Add, Subtract, Multiply, and Divide Integers, page 265

1. 15
2. 1
3. −69
4. −9
5. 1
6. 54
7. 22
8. −80
9. 99
10. −650
11. 1829
12. −1470
13. 15
14. −17
15. 44
16. −22

Polynomials, page 267

1. $3x^2 + 3x^2y + 10y$
2. $3x^2y + 24x + 3yx^2 + 7x^2y^2$

3. $(3x^5 + 3x^2 - 5x^2y + 6xy^2) +$
   $(3x^5 - 2x^2 + 4x^3y - x^2y + 3xy^3 - y^2) =$

   $3x^5 + 3x^5 + 3x^2 - 2x^2 - \underline{5x^2y - x^2y} +$
   $6xy^2 + 4x^3y + 3xy^3 - y^2 =$

   $6x^5 + x^2 - 6x^2y + 6xy^2 + 4x^3y + 3xy^3 - y^2$

4. $(x^4 - 4x^3 + 2x^2y^2 - 4xy^2) + (3x^5 -$
   $7x^4 + 3x^3 - 2x^2y^3 + 7xy^2) =$

   $x^4 \underline{- 4x^3 + 3x^3} + 2x^2y^2 \underline{- 4xy^2 + 7xy^2} +$
   $3x^5 - 7x^4 + 3x^3 - 2x^2y^3 =$

   $-6x^4 - x^3 + 2x^2y^2 + 3xy^2 + 3x^5 + 3x^3 -$
   $2x^2y^3$

5. $(6x^7 + 9x^4 - 3x^2y + 5xy^3) - (6x^8 - 15x^4 -$
   $3x^3y + x^2y) =$

   $(6x^7 + 9x^4 - 3x^2y + 5xy^3) + (-6x^8 + 15x^4$
   $+ 3x^3y - x^2y) =$

   $6x^7 + \underline{9x^4 + 15x^4} - \underline{3x^2y - x^2y} + 5xy^3 -$
   $6x^8 + 3x^3y =$

   $6x^7 + 24x^4 - 4x^2y + 5xy^3 - 6x^8 + 3x^3y$

6. $(7x^2 - 9x + 3xy^2 + 3y^3 - 12) - (x^3 - 9x^2$
   $+ 2xy^2 - 3y^5 - 18) =$

   $(7x^2 - 9x + 3xy^2 + 3y^3 - 12) + (-x^3 + 9x^2$
   $- 2xy^2 + 3y^5 + 18) =$

   $\underline{7x^2 + 9x^2} - 9x + \underline{3xy^2 - 2xy^2} + 3y^3 - 12 -$
   $x^3 + 3y^5 + 18 =$

   $16x^2 + 9x + xy^2 + 3y^3 - 12 - x^3 + 3y^5 + 18$

7. $(5x + 6)(x + 2)$

   Multiply the first terms. $(5x)(x) = 5x^2$
   Multiply the outer terms $(5x)(2) = 10x$
   Multiply the inner terms. $(6)(x) = 6x$
   Multiply the last terms. $(6)(2) = 12$

   Add $5x^2 + 10x + 6x + 12$

   Combine like terms $5x^2 + 16x + 12$

8. $(6x + 4)(3x - 8)$

   Multiply the first terms. $(6x)(3x) = 18x^2$
   Multiply the outer terms $(6x)(-8) = -48x$
   Multiply the inner terms. $(4)(3x) = 12x$
   Multiply the last terms. $(4)(8) = 32$

   Add $18x^2 - 48x + 12x + 32$

   Combine like terms $18x^2 - 36x + 32$

Formulas, page 270

1. πr^2
   $3.14 \times (9)^2 =$
   $3.14 \times 81 = 254.34$ m^2

2. $b = 3, h = 2.6$

$\left(\dfrac{1}{2}\right)(3)(2.6) = 3.9$

$4 \times 3.9 = 15.6$ in^2

3. Hexagon is 6-sided

6×5 ft = 30 ft perimeter

4.

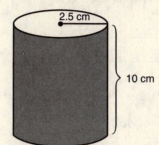

$\begin{array}{cccc} 2 & \pi & r & h \end{array}$

$2\,(3.14)(1.25)(10)$

$= 78.5$ cm^2

5. $(x + 5) + (x + 5) + x + x = 90$

$4x + 10 = 90$

$4x = 80 \quad x = 20$

length $= x + 5$

length $= 25$ ft

6. Area of each side $= 25$ cm^2

Cube is 6-sided

$6 \times 25 = 150$ cm^2

7. $x = 12$

8. $A = 32.5$ in.^{2}

9. $V = 4186.\overline{6}\left(4186\,\dfrac{2}{3}\right)$ cm^3

10. $V = 3375$ in^3

Solving Linear Equations and Inequalities, page 273

1. $y = -1$
2. $x = 2$
3. $y = -2$
4. $x = -2$
5. $n < 9$
6. $k < -3$
7. $x < 12$
8. $y > \frac{4}{7}$

Factoring Quadratic Expressions, page 274

1. B $3x - 2$
2. B $(6x + 2)$

Find Roots—Quadratic Equation, page 275

1. The roots of the quadratic equation are $(2, -\frac{1}{2})$.
2. The roots of the quadratic equation are $\dfrac{1 - \sqrt{21}}{4}$ and $\dfrac{1 + \sqrt{21}}{4}$.

Solve a System of Linear Equations, page 277

1. (A) is the correct answer.
   $x = -2, y = 1$ works in both equations.
2. (A) is the correct answer.
   $x = -4, y = 4$ works in both equations.
3. (B) is the correct answer. The ordered pair $(-1, 0)$ works in both equations.

Symmetry, page 279

1. The numerals 8 and 0 have line and rotational symmetry.

   The numeral 3 has only line symmetry.

   The other numerals have neither type of symmetry.

2. The most obvious pattern is shown below.

   $\begin{array}{cccccc} 2 & 3 & 4 & 2 & 3 & 4 \end{array}$

Parallel Lines, page 282

1. D $\angle$e and $\angle$i are vertical angles.
2. B $\angle$g measures 116. ($\angle$b and $\angle$g are congruent. $\angle$j and $\angle$g are supplementary angles.)

Geometry, page 284

1. trapezoid
2. $m\angle 2 = 135°$
3. $m\angle ABC = 50° = m\angle ACB$
4.

5. An octagon (8 sides) has two more sides than a hexagon (6 sides).
6. A right angle, which has a measure of 90°.

7. (Picture may vary)

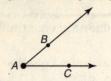

The new figure is ∠*BAC*.

8. (Picture may vary)

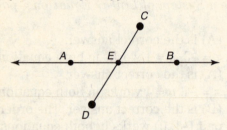

9. (Picture may vary)

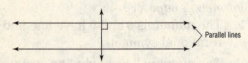

Parallel lines

10. The sum of the measures is 180° (m∠*A* + m∠*B* + m∠*C* = 180°).

Similar Triangles, page 286

1. Yes, the ratios of the lengths of corresponding sides are equal.

$$\frac{PR}{ST} = \frac{2}{4}; \frac{PQ}{SV} = \frac{5}{10}; \frac{2}{4} = \frac{5}{10}$$

2. The measures of corresponding angles are equal.
   Find the measure of the angle in *K*.
   Angle *b* in triangle *J* is the same size.
   180 − (50 + 55) = 75.
   The measure of angle *b* is 75°.

3. A. True. Both are right angles.
   B. False
   C. False
   D. False
   The triangles are not similar.

Coordinate Grid, page 287

1. *A* (3, −2)
   B (−2, −4)
   C (−5, 5)
   D (3, 3)
   E (0, 2)
   F (−5, 0)

2.

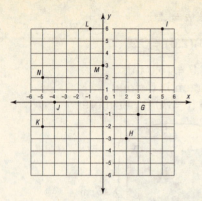

3.

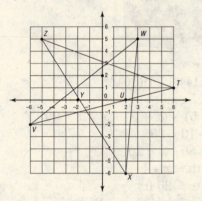

Graphing Equations on a Coordinate, page 289

1.

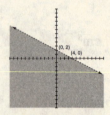

2.

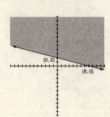

3.

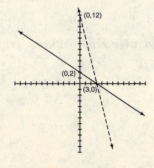

Logic, page 289
1. False—Some sports, such as hockey, do not use a ball.
2. True—For example, 35 is divisible by both 5 and 7.
3. False—For example, 12 is divisible by 3.
4. True—For example, 2 is both prime and divisible by 2.

Measurement, page 292
1. 0.22 decameters
2. 29,040 feet
3. $2\frac{3}{4}$ inches
4. $\frac{1}{2}$ pound
5. 64,000 ounces
6. 4 centimeters
7. 190,080 inches
8. 236,700 milliliters
9. 2 quarts
10. 35°

Time and Temperature, page 293
1. 0°F (0°C is 32°F)
2. 1:00 P.M.
3.

4. 10:00 A.M.
5. 50°F
6. 104°C

Words to Symbols Problems, page 295
1. 34; 34 − 9 = 25
2. 0.6 × 90 = 54
3. Add: $\frac{2}{3} + \frac{1}{2} = \frac{7}{6}$
   Multiply: $\frac{7}{6} \times 3 = \frac{21}{6}$
   Divide: $\frac{21}{6} \div 3 \frac{3}{6} = 3\frac{1}{2}$.
   Bob's walk to school is $3\frac{1}{2}$ miles.
4. $\frac{20}{y} = 2.5$ 20 = 2.5y   y = 8

5. $5\frac{1}{x} = 5\frac{1}{8}$ x = 8
   The number is 8.
6. Multiply: 60 × 2.5 = 150
             70 × 2 = 140
   Add: 150 + 140 = 290
   The cars traveled a total distance of 290 miles.

Finding and Interpreting Patterns, page 297
1. **−6** is the missing term. Subtract 2 from each term.
2. **14** is the missing term. Add 2.5 to each term.
3. **7.5** is the missing term. Divide each term by 2 to get the next term.
4. **720** is the missing term. The sequence follows the pattern $(1 \times 1)(1 \times 2)$ $(1 \times 2 \times 3)(1 \times 2 \times 3 \times 4)$...
5. **21** is the missing term. Add 4 to find the next term.
6. (22, **30**) is the missing term. Add 8 to the first term to find the second term.
7. (30, **4**) is the missing term. Divide the first term by 10 and add 1 to find the second term.
8. (5, **25**) is the missing term. Square the first term to get the second term.
9. The temperatures drops 3° from 52° to 49° and from 49° to 46°. If it drops at the same rate, the temperature drop at 3,000 feet would be 43° and at 4,000 feet would be 40° (followed by 37° and 34°). Continue to fill in the table accordingly, as follows.

Temperature

0	1,000	2,000	3,000	4,000	5,000
52°	49°	46°	*43°*	*40°*	37°

6,000	7,000	8,000	9,000	10,000
34°	*31°*	*28°*	*25°*	*22°*

10. Multiply three times the x value, subtract 2, and that gives the y value. The rule is y equals three times x − 2, so that the equation is y = 3x − 2. Substitute 13 for x:

$$y = 3(13) - 2 = 39 - 2 = 37$$

The capsule will be at position (13, 37).

Estimation Problems, page 298

1. Round all the scores and add the rounded scores.

   $90 + 100 + 90 + 90 + 100 + 90 = 560$

   Divide by the number of scores.
   $560 \div 6 = 93.3$
   93 is a reasonable estimate of the average.

2. Round the lengths and add the rounded lengths.

   $10 + 20 + 20 + 20 = 70$

   70 feet is a reasonable estimate of the amount of wood needed.

3. Round the number of dozens to the nearest 10.

   Divide the rounded numbers.

   $\dfrac{170}{10} = 17$

   17 is a reasonable estimate of the number of batches needed.

4. Round the number of minutes and number of days to the nearest 10.

   Multiply the rounded numbers.

   $50 \times 30 = 1,500$
   Divide to find hours.

   $1,500 \div 60 = 25$
   25 is a reasonable estimate of the number of hours.

Chart Problems, page 299

1. Add two proportions for truck.

   $0.18 + 0.16 = 0.34$

   The probability that a package picked at random was sent by truck is 34%.

2. Add the three proportions for 5 pounds and over.

   $0.07 + 0.34 + 0.18 = 0.59$

3. The proportion for Air Express over 5 pounds is 0.07.

4. Add proportions for under 5 pounds by Air Express and under 5 pounds by truck.

   $0.23 + 0.16 = 0.39$

Frequency Table Problems, page 300

1. Add the percentiles of the intervals below 70.

   $2 + 8 = 10$ 10% of the students scored below 70.

2. The median score is in the interval 80–89.

3. The percent of scores from 80 to 100 is
   $38 + 13 = 51$
   51% of the students scored from 80 to 100.

4. The question is asking for the number of scores that are above 50. The percentile rank next to 50 is 39. So 39% of the scores are below 50; 39% failed. $100 - 39 = 61$. 61% passed.

5. The percent of the scores from 20 to 50 is the percentile rank for 50, less the percentile rank for 20.

   $39 - 2 = 37$

   37% of the scores are from 20 to 50.

Formula Problems, page 301

1. $P =$ about $16.88
2. $s = 41$ mph
3. $V = \$8,400$
4. $A = 11$

Pythagorean Theorem Problems, page 303

1.
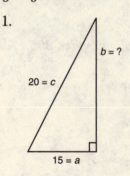

$a^2 + b^2 = c^2$
$(15)^2 + b^2 = (20)^2$
$225 + b^2 = 400$
$b^2 = 400 - 225 = 175$
$b =$ approximately 13.2 ft.

2.

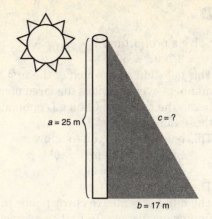

$a^2 + b^2 = c^2$
$(25)^2 + (17)^2 = c^2$
$625 + 289 = c^2$
$c^2 = 914$, c = approximately 30.2 m.

3.

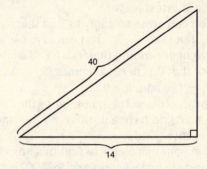

$a^2 + b^2 = c^2$
$(14)^2 + b^2 = (40)^2$
$196 + b^2 = 1,600$
$b^2 = 1,404$
b = approximately 37.5
The height is about 37.5 feet.

4.

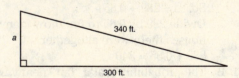

$a^2 + b^2 = c^2$
$a^2 + (300)^2 = (340)^2$
$a^2 = 115,600 - 90,000 = 25,600$
$a = 160$ ft
The ramp is 160 feet high.

Geometric Figure Problems,
page 304

1. Area of half the circle ($r = 4$)
    $\frac{1}{2}$ (3.14)(16) = (3.14)(8) is

    approximately 25.12 sq ft
    Area of the rectangle
    $12 \times 8 = 96$ sq ft
    Area of the entire figure
    $25.12 + 96 = 121.12$ sq ft
    $121.12 \div 35$ is approximately 3.5 pints
    Round up. You need 4 pints of paint.

2. Find the area of the roofs.
    Roof 1: 115×65 = 7,475 sq ft
    Roof 2: 112×65 = 7,280 sq ft
    Roof 3: 72×52 = 3,744 sq ft
    TOTAL 18,499 sq ft
    $18,499 \div 1,200 = 15.4$
    Round up. You need 16 bushels.

3. Volume of a brick = lwh
    $V = 2 \times 4 \times 8 = 64$ in^3
    8×64 in^3 = 512 in^3

4. Volume of a cone = $\frac{1}{3} \pi r^2 h$

    $134 \approx \frac{1}{3}$ (3.14)(4)^2 h

    $134 \approx 16.7\, h$
    $h \approx 8$ cm

5. Volume of a sphere = $\frac{4}{3} \pi r^3$
    $V = \frac{4}{3}$ (3.14)(274.6)

    $V = 1149.76$ in^3

6. Volume of a rectangular solid = lwh
    $1920 = (16)(12)\, w$
    $1920 = 192\, w$ $w = 10$
    Shaded area = $12 \times 10 = 120$ m^2

Interpreting Remainder Problems, page
305

1. 5 pounds
2. 34 bags
3. 33 bags

TARGETED TEST ANSWERS EXPLAINED

1. **C** Each angle must measure less than 90° to total 90°. Acute angles have measures less than 90°.

2. **D** We can't draw any conclusions about whether the light beams will cross or not. We just know that since they are not parallel and don't point in the same direction, at least two of them may be skewed (not touch).

3. **A** There are 1,000 meters in a kilometer. So, divide 2,750 by 1,000 to find the answer.

4. **D** The difference in the two stock prices $(19^5/_8 - 17^7/_8)$ is $1^3/_4$ dollars or $1.75. Multiply $1.75 by 20 to find the answer.

5. **C** There are about $(60) \times (60) \times (24)$ or 86,400 seconds in a day. There are about $(365) \times (86,400)$ or 31,536,000 seconds in a year. There are about $(4) \times (31,536,000)$ or 126,144,000 seconds in 4 years. Light travels about $(186,000) \times (126,144,000)$ or about 23,000,000,000,000 (23 trillion) miles in 4 years.

6. **B** 10 feet + 20% = 12 feet + 20% = 14.4 feet +

first   second

20% = 17.28 feet + 20% = 20.736 or

    third   fourth

about 20.7 feet.

7. **D** The maximum length of the side of the cube is the shortest of the three dimensions. The volume of the cube is 8^3 or 512.

8. **A** The correct answer is 42. The pattern increases by 4, 6, 8, 10, and then 12.

9. **C** This formula gives the correct answer. The formula $H \times (H + 1)$ is equivalent to this formula.

10. **C** Round the quotient (10) to 11 to have room for all the people to go on the class trip.

11. **C** This process crosses off all numbers but the prime numbers. The numbers in answer C are all the prime numbers in the 80s.

12. **D** The process yields the one piece that is both (small or striped) and large.

13. **B** Multiply 0.23 and $2,600 to find $598.

14. **A** Divide $858 by $2,600 to find the percent (33 percent) needed for transportation. Subtract the current transportation percentage from 33 percent to find the percent to be taken from miscellaneous (33% – 24% = 9%). Subtract 11% – 9% = 2% to find the percent left for miscellaneous.

15. **B** Solve a proportion. $^2/_9 = {}^x/_{1,350}$

$9x = 2,700$ $x = 300$

16. **D** This question asks which of the first ten numbers evenly divides the large number in the question. Choice D contains those numbers.

17. **B** This question asks you to apply the Pythagorean theorem $a^2 = b^2 = c^2$.

$$30^2 + 40^2 = 50^2$$
    The rope is 50 feet long.

18. **B** The number sentence corresponds to finding an average. To find an average, you add the terms and divide by the number of terms.

19. **C** Jan is either the same height as Lisa or she is taller than Lisa. Because Lisa is not the shortest player, Jan cannot be the shortest player.

20. **C** You can cross multiply to find that $^5/_6 > {}^3/_4$, but that $^5/_6 < {}^7/_8$. You can also use a calculator to find that $^5/_6 = 0.833$, and see that this decimal comes between $^3/_4 = 0.75$ and $^7/_8 = 0.875$.

21. **D** Only points in this quadrant of the coordinate grid have a positive x value and a negative y value.

22. **A** Use your calculator to find this answer. Divide to find what percent $624,000 is of $2,600,000. $624,000 \div 2,600,000 = 0.24 = 24\%$. The town needs 24% for police, 2% more than in the pie chart. Take the 2% from sanitation, leaving 22% for sanitation.

23. **C** This is another calculator problem. Think of the percent equation.

$85\% \times \square = 289$

So, $\square = 289 \div 0.85$

Divide 289 by 0.85 to find how many houses there were altogether.

$289 \div 0.85 = 340$

24. **B** The probability that a "fair" penny will land heads up is always 1/2 regardless of what has occurred on previous flips.

25. **D** There are 60 seconds in a minute and 60 minutes in an hour. So there are $60 \times 60 = 3600$ seconds in an hour. $186,000 \times 3600$ is about how far light travels in an hour.

26. **C** This is the correct list of numbers between 1 and 25 that are evenly divisible only by 1 and by themselves. The number 2 is the only even prime.

27. **B** Multiply x by 2 and then add 1. Some of the other choices work for individual values of x, but only this choice works for all the values of x.

28. **C** To find the area of a triangle, use the formula $A = \frac{1}{2} bh = 30$.

    To find the area of a parallelogram, use the formula $A = (bh) = 180$.
    Subtract: Area (parallelogram) – Area (triangle) = Area (shaded portion)
    $180 - 30 = 150$

29. **B** Use the order of operations to combine to simplest terms.
    $2n + 3n^2 - 5n \times 3 - 6n^2 =$
    $2n + 3n^2 - 15n - 6n^2 =$
    $-13n - 3n^2$

30. **D** Subtract $6x$ from both sides.
    $11x - 5 \, (-6x) = -6 + 6x \, (-6x)$
    $5x - 5 = -6$
    Add 5 to both sides.
    $5x - 5 \, (+ \, 5) = -6 \, (+ \, 5) 5x = -1$
    Divide both sides by 5.
    $5x/5 = -\frac{1}{5} \, x = -\frac{1}{5}$

31. **C** Use formula $P = 2.2K$
    $15.6/2.2 = 15.6/2.2 = K$
    $7.09 = K$

32. **A** Work back from the answers.
    $(3x - 2) \, (2x + 1) = 6x^2 - x - 2$

33. **D** Work back from the answers or set the equation equal to zero.
    $2x^2 - x - 3 = 0$
    Factor out and set each equal to zero.
    $2x^2 - x - 3 = 0$
    $(2x - 3) \, (x + 1) = 0$
    $2x - 3 = 0 \qquad x + 1 = 0$
    $2x = 3 \qquad\quad x = -1$
    $2x/2 = \frac{3}{2}$
    $x = 1\frac{1}{2} \qquad$ Real Roots = $\{-1, 1\frac{1}{2}\}$

34. **B** Follow the steps given on page 271.

35. **D** Rent represents 60% of the monthly expenses.

36. **A** $m\angle Y = m\angle H$ because they are alternate interior angles formed by transversal m.

37. **D** (A) Many points meet neither condition.
    (B) y never equals $-x$.
    (C) x is not always less than 4.
    (D) Correctly describes the graph.

38. **D** Figure out what the mean, median, and mode are for the data shown in the graph. The mode is 2 million (Tampa, Tallahassee, and Jacksonville). The mean (the average) of the funding is 2.4 million. The median of the data is 2 million. Given this information, only choice D can be true.

39. **D** There is a positive relationship between the test score and the number of years in math courses.

40. **D** The vertical axis includes 5 to –5. The horizontal axis includes 5 and greater.

PART V

Subtest III Review

7 VISUAL AND PERFORMING ARTS

TEST INFO BOX

13 Multiple Choice items   One-third of items
1 Constructed Response item   One-third of items

VISUAL AND PERFORMING ARTS ITEMS

Visual and Performing Arts multiple choice items look like this.

If you see a fresco, it is almost certainly

(A) on a canvas.
(B) in a church.
(C) on a board.
(D) on a wall.

Visual and Performing Arts constructed response items look like this.

Describe the different roles of the melody and bass notes in a song.

USING THIS CHAPTER

This chapter prepares you to take the Visual and Performing Arts part of the CSET. Choose one of these approaches.

I want a Visual and Performing Arts review.

❑ Read the Visual and Performing Arts review.
❑ Complete the Visual and Performing Arts CSET Practice Questions on page 351.

I want to practice Visual and Performing Arts questions.

❑ Complete the Visual and Performing Arts CSET Practice Questions on page 351.

I don't need any Visual and Performing Arts review.

❑ OK. If you're sure, skip this chapter.

VISUAL AND PERFORMING ARTS

Visual and Performing Arts topics on the CSET are partitioned into four domains, and this chapter is partitioned in the same way. However, the topics in this chapter overlap and you may find that a review in one domain helps with the other domains.

The visual and performing arts items are the most difficult to review for. Each of the four fields that comprise visual and performing arts is as extensive as history or science. This chapter gives a good overview of the types of material and the types of questions you will encounter on the CSET.

The visual and performing arts include dance, theater, music, and visual art. Five themes provide the focus for the visual and performing arts on the CSET: (1) artistic perception, (2) creative expression, (3) historical and cultural context, (4) aesthetic valuing, and (5) connections, relationships, and applications.

Artistic Perception

- Essential arts elements and vocabulary.
- Use language to discuss and respond to dance, theater, music, and visual arts.

Creative Expression

- Create a work of art or a performance; performing, and participating in the arts.
- Compose, direct, and perform a work of art.
- Communicate through original works of art.

Historical and Cultural Context

- The history and culture of the arts.
- The development of a visual and performing art.
- Human diversity as it relates to a performing art.
- The roles of actors, artists, composers, writers, choreographers, and dancers.

Aesthetic valuing

- Interpreting and drawing meaning from a work of art.
- Analyzing and critiquing works of dance, music, theatre, and visual art.
- Incorporate the elements of a performing art in an interpretation or analysis.

Connections, relationships, applications

- Integrate the performing arts with other disciplines.
- Career opportunities in the performing arts.
- Apply the lessons learned from the performing arts to life.

ON THE WEB

Visit http://www.cde.ca.gov/ci/vp/cf/ to view the complete California Visual and Performing Arts Framework.

Visit http://www.aep-arts.org/PDF%20Files/GAA%20Report.pdf to see the report "Gaining the Arts Advantage: Lessons from School Districts That Value Arts Education" for case histories of successful school arts programs.

DANCE

Dance is closely related to physical education. Many of the terms and concepts in physical education also apply to dance. Review the Physical Education section on page 357.

Dance means an intentional movement designed to express a thought, image, feeling, or reality. *A dance* is a sequential, rhythmic movement in two- or three-dimensional space. A dance has a beginning, a middle, and an end.

Dance medium refers to the types of movement used during dance, including space, shape, force, and time. *Space* refers to the outer space or sphere immediately around the body, and inner space, the real or imaginary space inside the body. *Shape* is the deliberate positioning of the body to create a particular appearance. *Force* is release of energy. Force is the energy that produces a dance. *Time* refers to tempo, beat, and accent during a dance.

Creative movement refers to children's dance movement, which is more exploratory and less purposeful than adult dance. Body movements during a dance may be locomotor or non-locomotor.

Kinesthetic perception describes the body's ability to sense movement. It refers to the muscles' retention of the movement and effort required to produce a dance.

Dancing means to move in a dance-like way. *Choreography* refers to the art of composing dances. A dance style describes the kind of dance associated with a particular style, location, or time period.

There are several types of dance, including ballet, tap, jazz, and modern. Improvisation refers to an unplanned dance.

Technique refers to the skills a dancer uses as she or he performs the steps and movements of a dance. The technique may depend on the particular style and form of specific dance training. The California Standards specifically mention the styles of dance associated with Alvin Ailey, Kathryn Dunham, Martha Graham, and Lester Horton.

Dance Forms

Ballet is a dance form that originated during the European Renaissance period. By 1650, the formal steps and body positions of ballet were established. Modern ballet originated in France, and ballet became fully developed in the 1800s. The California Standards specifically mention Jules Perrot (France), August Bournonville (Denmark), and Marius Petipa (Russia) as founders of modern ballet. The California Standards credit the continued development of ballet to Michel Fokine (Russia), to Kenneth MacMillan and Anthony Tudor (England), and to George Balanchine, Jerome Robbins, and Arthur Mitchell, all of the United States.

Ballroom dancing is social dancing that involves two dance partners. Social dancing likely began in Europe during the 1500s. There are four modern ballroom dances: Foxtrot, Quick-step, Tango, and Waltz (Viennese and modern). Latin dances include the Cha-Cha, Rumba, and Samba. Irene and Vernon Castle popularized ballroom dancing in the early 1900s.

Jazz dance developed in the United States from African-American jazz music as well as other ethnic music forms. Jazz dance features the improvisation and techniques of that music. The California Standards mention Lester Wilson, Jack Cole, and Bob Fosse as choreographers who developed jazz dance from its popular roots.

Modern dance is a theatrical dance form born in the 1900s. Modern Dance is a style of theatrical dance that moves away from the limitations of ballet and focuses on original movements derived from an expression of inner feelings. The California Standards identify Isadora Duncan (United States), Mary Wigman, and Rudolph Laban (Germany) as the founders of this dance form. The standards also identify Ruth St. Denis, Ted Shawn, Martha Graham, Doris Humphrey, and Charles Weidman as American pioneers of modern dance.

Tap dance involves a dancer who strikes the free foot against the floor to create a pleasing and intricate rhythm. Tap dance has many roots, including the flamenco, African-American dance, and Irish and English clogging.

Urban dance is a contemporary dance that includes break dancing and hip-hop.

DANCE OBJECTIVES

The following text summarizes dance objectives.

Artistic Perception

Motor Efficiency and Control
Explain the principles of kinesiology.

Space
Describe when actors are using personal or general stage space.

Time
Identify time concepts found in a dance.

Force
Explain internal force (tensions within physical structure of body) during a dance.
Explain external force (tensions created by gravitational pull on body) during a dance.
Explain range of movement qualities (sustained, percussive, vibratory, swing) during a dance.

Creative Expression

Create, perform, and participate in dance.
Compare and demonstrate the difference between imitating movement and original movement.
Describe and incorporate different dance forms (ABA, for example).
Coordinate movement music.
Develop partner and group skills.

Historical and Cultural Context

Identify dance styles from a variety of cultures.
Describe dance styles from historical and cultural perspectives.
Describe dance in various periods of history.
Identify major dance innovators and their innovations.
Explain the place of dance and movement in social contexts in selected cultures.
Discuss the dance that evolved into ballet, jazz, tap, and social forms.

Aesthetic Valuing

Aesthetic Perception
Explain the movements, motifs, and phrases of dance.

Creative Expression
Discuss dance form, noting relationship and manipulation of movement materials.
Interpret dance meaning.

Dance Heritage
Discuss dance history, its roles in society, its variety as related to cultural context, and its numerous contemporary styles and forms.

Viewing and Reviewing
Describe performances using the terminology of evaluation: intent, structure, effectiveness, and worth.

Discuss the character, theme, and meaning of a performance.

Connections, Relationships, Applications

Integrate dance with other art forms, other subjects, and with life's pursuits.
Describe how other arts disciplines are integrated into dance performances.
Identify potential careers in dance and in fields related to dance.

DANCE TERMS

AB   A dance with two distinct sections that share some common elements.

ABA   A dance in which the second section contrasts with the first section, and the third section is a shortened or lengthened version of the first section.

Accent   A strong movement or gesture.

Aesthetic criteria   Standards for judging a dance.

Alignment   A description of how the body aligns with the base of support and the line of gravity.

Axial movement   A nonlocomotor movement around a fixed body part, such as a foot.

Call and response   A second dancer(s) enters a performance in response to the first dancer(s), often associated with African dance.

Canon   A dance in which performers create the same movement, starting at different times, similar to a round in singing.

Choreography   The plan for a dance performance.

Contrast   Dances performed side by side to emphasize differences.

Folk   Dances associated with a specific culture and usually seen at social events or gatherings.

Genre   The particular dance form, such as ballet, jazz, or modern.

Improvisation   Dance created spontaneously.

Narrative   A dance embodies and follows a particular story.

Phrase   The organizational element of dance.

Pirouette   A complete turn while balanced on one foot.

Pulse   The underlying beat of a dance.

Retrograde   Dance sequence performed forward and then in reverse order.

Shape   How the body is positioned in space, such as straight, curved, or twisted.

Tempo   The speed of a dance.

ON THE WEB

Visit *http://www.cde.ca.gov/be/st/ss/damain.asp* for a grade-by-grade list of California Dance Standards.

Visit *http://www.pbs.org/wnet/freetodance/timeline/index.html* for a Public Broadcasting System time line and history of dance in America.

Visit the National Dance Association at *http://www.aahperd.org/nda/* for up-to-date information and links about dance education.

OTHER THINGS TO DO

Engage in some dance activities. Attend a dance performance and apply the overview and terminology here and at the web sites to analyze the play. Use some of your television viewing time to see additional dance performances.

MUSIC

Music can be thought of as organized sounds. Our culture has many different types of music, and there are various types of music from cultures all over the world. We usually classify our music in three categories.

1. Popular music is professionally composed, recorded, or performed live and represents the type of music of most current interest to the public.

2. Classical music was composed in the past and, while it is also recorded for sale, is usually performed by large orchestras in "symphony" halls.

3. Folk music usually has a rural origin, is usually not composed professionally, and is often transmitted by oral tradition.

Music consists of pitch, the actual frequency or sound of a note, and duration. A tone has a specific pitch and duration. Different tones occurring simultaneously are called chords.

Harmony is chords with a duration. A melody is the tones that produce the distinctive sound of the music.

Rhythm in our music refers primarily to the regularity of beats or meter. The most common meter in our music has four beats with an emphasis on the first beat.

Pitches separated by specific intervals are called a scale. Most music is based on the diatonic *scale* found on the piano white keys (C, D, E, F, G, A, B). The chromatic scale includes the seven notes of the diatonic scale with the five sharps and flats corresponding to the white and black keys on the piano.

Think of the piano. The piano represents the chromatic scale with groups of seven white keys and five black keys. Music is played using tones from this scale for varying durations.

Usually the melody consists of one note at a time and is played with the right hand. Harmony usually consists of chords and is played with the left hand. The rhythm of the music reflects the meter, and the arrangements and duration of notes.

Form refers to the overall structure of music. Patterns or sections of a musical may repeat or all parts of the pieces may be unique. Phrases or sections in a musical piece may complement one another or they may contrast.

Dynamics describes how loud or how soft the music is. The dynamic aspects of a musical work add to its expressive qualities. Terms such as *pianissimo* (play very softly) are used to refer to musical dynamics.

Tempo refers to the speed of a musical work. The tempo of a piece may vary in different sections of the piece to provide contrast and alert the listener to the various meanings that sections are meant to convey.

Texture refers to the "feel" the musical work imparts. Terms such as *staccato* (choppy) are used to describe the texture of a musical work.

Timbre describes the unique sound produced by different instruments, instrumental combinations and by the human voice. Families of instruments such as woodwinds (clarinet, saxophone) and horns (trumpet, trombone) have similar timbres.

MUSICAL NOTATION

Our musical notation uses a staff to represent notes. The clef placed at the beginning of the staff determines the pitches for each line and space on the staff.

Notes are written on the staff using the following notation. A flat (♭) lowers the note a half tone while a sharp (♯) raises the note a half tone. The natural (♮) cancels a flat or sharp. Rests indicate a time when no music is played. A note followed by a dot is increased in value by half.

𝅝	Whole-note	𝅘𝅥.	Dotted quarter-note
𝅗𝅥	Half-note	▬	Whole-rest
𝅘𝅥	Quarter-note	▬	Half-rest
𝅘𝅥𝅮	Eighth-note	𝄼	Quarter-rest
𝅘𝅥𝅯	Sixteenth-note	𝄿	Eighth-rest

The staff is partitioned into measures. A key signature of sharps and/or flats can be written at the beginning of a staff to change these notes throughout the piece. The key signature identifies the key the music is written in.

Some scales with flats in their key signatures are shown below:

F Major   Bb Major   Eb Major

Some scales with sharps in their key signatures are shown below:

G Major   D Major   A Major

A time signature is written at the beginning of each staff. The top number shows how many beats per measure and the bottom number shows which note gets a beat.

A clef is placed at the beginning of the staff on which notes appear. The most commonly used clefs are the G (treble) clef and the F (bass) clef.

G CLEF

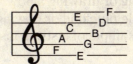

The notes on the lines from bottom are E, G, B, D, F ("Every Good Boy Deserves Fruit"). The notes on the spaces are F, A, C, E (spelling the word).

BASS CLEF

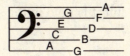

On a piano, the notes at and above middle C are on the G clef staff; while the notes at and below middle C are on the F clef staff. Look at the correlation between notes on the staff and the piano keys shown below.

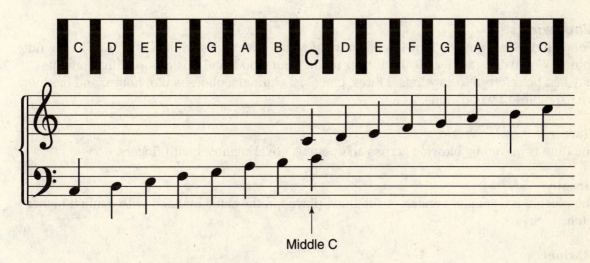

Middle C

Shown below is a typical staff with a G clef. The key is B flat major. There are three beats per measure and the quarter note gets one beat. The quarter note in the second measure has a natural, which means it is played as a B, and not the B flat indicated in the key signature. The half note in the third measure is played as F sharp.

ORCHESTRA INSTRUMENTS

Orchestra instruments are usually classified as strings, woodwinds, brass, and percussion. Following is a description of the most common orchestra instruments.

Strings

String instruments are played by plucking or drawing a bow across the strings. Notes are formed by holding the strings down while plucking or bowing. Violins, violas, cellos, and bass are examples of strings. A guitar is an example of a string instrument not usually found in an orchestra.

Violin

The violin is the smallest string instrument in the orchestra. It is held under the chin. You will find more violins in the orchestra than any other instrument. The musician playing the first violin is usually the concert master or concert mistress, the first assistant to the conductor.

Viola

The viola is a little larger than the violin, but it is held in the same way. It has a deeper pitch than the violin.

Cello

The cello rests on the floor in front of the musician and is still larger than the viola.

Double Bass

The double bass is the largest string instrument, about twice as large as the cello.

Woodwinds

Woodwinds are played by blowing. Most woodwinds have reeds while a few, such as the flute, do not. Woodwinds are usually no longer made from wood, and this group of instruments may just be referred to as winds. Flutes, piccolos, clarinets, oboes, saxophones, and bassoons are examples of woodwinds.

Flute

The flute is played by blowing across an opening, covering holes with fingers.

Piccolo

The piccolo is a smaller version of the flute, played in the same manner, with a much higher pitch.

Clarinet

The clarinet is a single-reed instrument with a wide range of notes.

Oboe

The oboe is a double-reed instrument that looks like the clarinet and is played in the same manner.

Bassoon

The bassoon is a large double-reed instrument that plays lower notes than the oboe.

Brass

Brass instruments have traditionally been made from "brass" or some other metal and are played by vibrating the lips against the mouthpiece. French horns, trumpets, trombones, and tubas are examples of brass instruments.

Trumpet

The trumpet player creates notes by blowing and pressing a combination of the three valves found on the instrument.

French Horn

The French Horn is played like the trumpet, but the opening (bell) of the French horn faces backwards. And the musician often puts his or her hand in the bell.

Tuba

The tuba has the lowest pitch of the brass instruments, and is played in a similar fashion to the trumpet, with the bell facing upward.

Trombone

The trombone is played by moving a slide, and so it has the widest range of notes in the brass section.

Percussion

Percussion instruments are played by striking. Cymbals, snare drums, timpani, and base drums are examples of percussion instruments. The piano and the xylophone are also examples of percussion instruments, and they are found in this section of the orchestra.

Cymbals

Cymbals are hit together and they produce a crashing sound.

Snare Drum

The snare drum is a small drum struck repeatedly to create accents in music.

Timpani

The timpanis (kettle drums) have a deeper sound than snare drums.

Bass Drum

The bass drum, the largest drum, is used to mark the beat in music.

In this century, music is produced electronically. In the past few decades, computers and other devices have been able to replicate exactly the sounds of almost every instrument. Today, a person can compose a musical piece on a computer and have the computer play that music using a full array of musical sounds without ever picking up an instrument. The full impact of this electronic music is yet to be realized.

MUSIC OBJECTIVES

The following text summarizes music objectives.

Artistic Perception

Sound Generation and Modification
Group sounds according to how they were produced.
Identify ways of changing the sound of a voice or an instrument.

Musical Elements

Identify *pitch* and pitch relationships.
Identify *rhythm* and discriminate among the rhythmic forms of musical works.
Describe and identify polyphonic, homophonic, and monophonic *harmonies*.
Describe the *form* of a musical work.
Describe and identify polyphonic, homophonic, and monophonic *texture*.
Identify the *tempo* of a musical work.
Describe how musical works combine elements to produce a particular timbre.

Notation Symbols

Identify a musical piece from its written form.

Creative Expression

Create, perform, and participate in music.
Compose and arrange music and devise melodies, and use electronic and digital technology.
Sing songs that represent various genres, styles, and cultures.
Play a musical instrument.
Compose short musical pieces.
Arrange simple musical pieces.

Aesthetic Valuing

Respond to, analyze, and evaluate music.
Derive meaning from music and musical performance.
Develop and apply a personal standard for evaluating music and musical performances.
Identify the aesthetic qualities of musical works.

Historical and Cultural Context

Cultural Musical Contributions

Describe how composers have drawn inspiration from regional and national cultures.
Explain the similarities and differences in styles, performance media, and tone colors in various cultures.
Describe how music is determined by the performance media.
Describe how the social and environmental influences of a cultural group determine the character of the music.
Explain how the function of music dictates the style and form.

Connections, Relationships, Applications

Integrate music with other art forms, with other subjects, and with life's pursuits.
Describe how other disciplines are integrated into musical performances.
Identify potential careers in theater and in fields related to music.

MUSIC TERMS

This glossary will help support and extend your music review.

A cappella   Sung without accompaniment.

Accompaniment   Voices or instruments that support a melody.

Adagio   Very slow tempo.

Allegro   Fast tempo

Aria   A song set off from the rest of an opera.

Articulation   How adjacent notes are connected.

Blues   A form of African-American folk music, characterized by simple, repetitive structures and a highly flexible vocal delivery; (2) the style of singing heard in the blues.

Canon   A musical form in which a melody is repeated in one or more parts.

CD-ROM (Compact disc-read only memory)   A compact disc technology that enables a personal computer to access digital text and images.

Chamber music   Music played by small ensembles, such as a string quartet, with one performer to a part.

Chord   Three or more tones sounded simultaneously.

Duet   Two singers or two musicians performing together.

Duple meter   The grouping of beats into sets of two.

Electronic music   Music in which some or all of the sounds are produced by computers or other digital devices.

Elements of music   Pitch, rhythm, harmony, dynamics, timbre, texture, and form.

Finale   Final movement of an instrumental work.

Folk music   Music indigenous to a particular ethnic group.

Forte   Loud

Genre   A particular type of music (examples include Dixieland, gospel, madrigal, march, and opera).

Harmony   Two tones sounded simultaneously.

Improvisation   Unrehearsed music.

Libretto   Contains the complete text of an opera, the literal meaning is "little book."

Melody   Sequence of single notes.

MIDI (Musical Instrument Digital Interface)   An interface that supports the synthesis of musical instruments on a computer.

Movement   One part of a piece of music consisting of several large parts.

Opera   A musical drama.

Overture   A musical, orchestral introduction.

Ragtime   Popular American piano music that led to jazz.

Rhythm   Combinations of long and short sounds that convey a sense of movement.

String quartet   Four musicians playing two violins, a viola, and a cello.

Symphony   A work for an orchestra in three to five movements.

Syncopation   Rhythm that emphasizes weak beats.

Tempo   The pace of a piece of music, usually reckoned by the rate of its beats.

Tone   A musical sound with the properties of pitch, duration, volume, and timbre.

ON THE WEB

Visit *http://www.cde.ca.gov/be/st/ss/mumain.asp* for the complete grade-by-grade Music Content Standards.

Visit the National Music Teaches Association web site at *http://www.menc.org/connect/links.html* for information about music in the schools and for some useful resource links.

OTHER THINGS TO DO

Immerse yourself in the music that is all around you. Go to live musical performances on a wide range of music types. Listen on the radio, use the music download resources on the Internet. Use the overview and the terms discussed here to analyze music as you listen.

THEATER

PARTICIPATION

Theater involves an audience. Theater is a formal presentation that may include a script, sets, acting, directing, and producing.

A *script* is a written description of a play or other performance. The script tells actors what to say, where to stand, and how to enter and leave a stage. *Actors* are the participants in a play or presentation. *Playmaking* means creating an original story and structuring, performing, and evaluating the presentation without a formal audience.

Acting includes the skills of speaking, movement, and sensory awareness. Acting requires preparation and rehearsal before presentation to the audience. Acting may also involve *improvisation* in which actors create their own spontaneous presentation in response to a problem or some other stimulus.

Production means to arrange for a theater performance. Producers coordinate all the technical aspects of the theater presentation. Producers may be concerned with the overall presentation or with technical aspects within a presentation. *Direction* means to coordinate the on-stage activities. Directors help actors practice and are concerned with the actual on-stage presentation.

EVALUATING DRAMATIC WORKS

Theater provides a natural basis for reflection and evaluation. The following criteria can be used to reflect on and evaluate a dramatic work.

Intent is the reason for a theater work. The intent reflects the objective or purpose for presenting the work.

Structure is the relationship among the different components of a dramatic work. These components include, but are not limited to, balance, coherence, conflict, contrast, emphasis, harmony, rhythm, stress, and transition.

Effectiveness refers to the impact of the dramatic work on the audience. An audience may be affected in many ways by a work, including being amused, elated, informed, interested, or moved.

Worth refers to the value of the work itself. That is, it refers to the amount of insight, knowledge, or wisdom found in a work.

THEATER OBJECTIVES

The following text summarizes theater objectives.

Artistic Perception

Process and analyze theater experiences.
Use the vocabulary of theater.

Use terms such as action/reaction, vocal projection, subtext, theme, mood, design, production values, and stage crew.

Be aware of the way theatrical productions can be used to mold thinking and for propaganda.

Creative Expression

Create, perform, and participate in theater, including acting, directing, designing, and playwriting for theater, film, videos, and electronic media productions.

Participate in improvisational activities.

Demonstrate an understanding of text, subtext, and context.

Create a character through appropriate facial and vocal expressions, gestures, and timing.

Historical and Cultural Context

Literature and History

Describe the theater including storytelling, improvisation, fairy tales, folklore, and myths.

Discuss theatrical history and the literature of the theater.

Culture

Discuss theater from many cultures and countries.

Discuss the social, psychological, and cultural impact of theater productions on contemporary culture.

Aesthetic Valuing

Function

Categorize music by function and purpose.

Underlying Structures

Observe the details of design principles (e.g., repetition, rhythm, balance, and variation on a theme).

Recognize and compare the three-dimensional composition details of forms from various viewpoints and angles.

Categorize and analyze the three-dimensional qualities of forms.

Discriminate visual characteristics.

Observe that things look different due to varying light, position, and motion.

Identify effects on visual impressions from changes in light, distance, atmosphere, position, recurring motion, lasers, and holograms.

Respond Aesthetically to Visual and Tactile Characteristics

Use various descriptors, analogies, similes, and metaphors to describe unique visual and tactile characteristics observed in works.

Connections, Relationships, Applications

Integrate theater with other art forms, other subjects, and with life's pursuits.

Describe how other art disciplines are integrated into theatrical performances.

Identify potential careers in theater and in fields related to theater.

THEATER TERMS

This glossary will help support and extend your knowledge of theater.

Actor   A person who plays a role.
Ad-lib   To speak lines not in the script.
Arena stage   A stage with the audience all around, such as a circus.
Audience   Those who watch a performance.
Auditorium   The audience section of a theater.

Black light   Ultra-violet light.
Blocking   The plan for actors' and scenery positions.

Cast   A list of characters along with the actors who play them.
Catwalk   A walkway above the entire width of the stage.
Character   The part an actor plays.
Characterization   The means used to develop a character.
Cold reading   Unrehearsed script reading.
Collaboration   A joint effort, usually in playwriting.
Context   The play's setting.
Costume   Stage clothing and attire.
Critique   Commentary about a performance.
Cue   A signal to an actor or others associated with a performance.
Curtain   The beginning or end of a performance.
Curtain call   Actor's additional bow at the end of a performance.

Dialogue   Spoken communication between actors.
Director   The person in charge of all aspects of creating a performance.
Downstage   The portion of the stage toward the audience.
Drama   Writing intended for a performance.
Drama elements   The plot, characters, theme, dialogue, music, and the spectacle.
Dress rehearsal   Rehearsal of the entire performance with full costumes and makeup.

Ensemble   A group of performers.

Flat   A canvas covered rectangular frame that is part of the set.
Flood   An unfocused beam of light.
Footlights   Lights in front of the stage floor.

Grip   Those who move scenery.

House manager   The person in charge of everything offstage.
House   The part of the theater where the audience sits.

Improvisation   Unscripted and unrehearsed performance.

Legs   Narrow vertical curtains.
Light board   The lighting control console.

Melodrama   A drama that includes exaggerated emotions and interpersonal conflicts.
Monologue   A dramatic presentation by one person.
Motivation   The reason behind an actor's performance.

Pantomime   A performance without words.
Pit   The area below the front of a stage often used by the orchestra.
Prompt   Helping an actor with his or her lines.

Reprise   Repeat of a musical piece previously played or sung.

Spike   A mark that shows the placement of set pieces.
Stage   Where actors perform.
Stage left, stage right   The actors' left or right when facing the audience.
Subtext   Unspoken meaning.

Thrust   A stage with the audience on three sides.

Upstage   The back of the stage away from the audience, or to "steal" a scene.

Wings   Sides of the stage not visible from the audience.

ON THE WEB

Visit *http://www.cde.ca.gov/be/st/ss/thmain.asp* for a grade-by-grade list of California theater standards.

Visit *http://www.aate.com/theatreinourschools.html* for information about theater education and for a wealth of additional links about theater in the schools.

Visit *http://www.tonyawards.com/en_US/index.html*, the official web site for the Tony awards. Tony awards are given each year for outstanding performance and participation in American theater.

OTHER THINGS TO DO

Immerse yourself in some theater experiences. Go to see a play and apply the overview and terminology here and at the web sites to analyze the play. Use some of your television viewing time to see additional plays and adaptations of plays.

VISUAL ARTS

Visual art includes paintings, photographs, prints, carvings, sculpture, and architecture. *Representational* art presents a recognizable representation of real people, places, or things. *Abstract* art presents nonrecognizable representations of real things or thoughts, perhaps using geometric shapes or designs. *Nonrepresentational* art is unrelated to real things or thoughts and represents only itself.

Visual arts are built around certain visual elements.

Points are represented by dots and are the simplest visual element. **Lines** are created when points move and may be horizontal, vertical, diagonal, straight, jagged, or wavy. Lines come in many thicknesses and lengths. Lines in a painting or drawing may suggest three-dimensional images or outline a shape.

Shapes are bounded forms in two-dimensional art. The boundary of a shape is usually a line, but it may also be created by color, shading, and texture. A shape may be geometric or fluid.

Space refers to the area occupied by the art. Paintings occupy two-dimensional space, while sculpture occupies three-dimensional space. Sculptors manipulate three-dimensional space and forms to create the desired effect, while painters often manipulate two-dimensional space to create the illusion of three-dimensional space.

Color: The colors of the spectrum are red, orange, yellow, green, blue, indigo, and violet. White is actually the combination of all the spectral colors, and black is an absence of color. Colors communicate mood (blue is cold, yellow is warm). Warm colors appear to expand a work's size while cold colors appear to contract its size. Color has three properties.

1. **Hue** is the color itself. It describes a color's placement in the color spectrum.
2. **Value** refers to the amount of lightness or darkness in a color. Low value shades are dark, while high value shades are light. You can raise the value of a color by adding white, and lower the value by adding black.
3. **Saturation** (also called chroma or intensity) describes the brightness or dullness of a color.

Perspective refers to methods of manipulating two-dimensional space to create the illusion of three-dimensional space. *Foreshortening* means exaggerating linear perspective by drawing the near parts of an object in close proximity to the far parts of the same object. *Linear perspective* means drawing objects smaller as they get further away. Still photographs naturally employ linear perspective.

PRINCIPLES OF DESIGN

These elements of design are frequently used to analyze and describe an artwork.

Balance refers to the equilibrium of elements that create a work. Balance can be achieved through both symmetrical and asymmetrical arrangements.

Symmetry is achieved when one half of an artwork more or less reflects the other half. Symmetrical works tend to create a sense of formality.

Asymmetry is achieved when color and the lightness of different parts of a work create a sense of balance. For example, a lighter area may balance a darker area. Asymmetrical works tend to create a sense of informality.

Rhythm refers to the repetition of elements in an artwork. Effective repetition of design elements tends to create a more dynamic work.

Dominance means to use color or positioning to draw the attention of the viewer to the most important element or elements in a work.

PAINTING

Painting techniques include oil, watercolor, gouache, and fresco. The paint for all of these techniques consists of a pigment (color), binder (e.g., egg, oil, wax), which holds the pigment together, and solvents (water, turpentine), which permit the paint to spread on a surface.

Oil is the primary painting form. The oil can be applied as thinly or thickly as desired and dries slowly so that the artist can rework it until the desired result is obtained.

Watercolor presents a thin wispy appearance and is widely used for landscape painting. Gouache is an opaque watercolor that is often applied to a board. Acrylic paints combine most of the advantages of oil paint with easy clean up. Acrylics are often applied with an airbrush.

ART OBJECTIVES

The following text summarizes art objectives.

Artistic Perception

Recognize Design Elements
Recognize and distinguish among the elements of line, color, value, shape, and texture. Recognize and discriminate between the impact of light and shadow on the other design elements.

Creative Expression

Create visual arts and participate in the visual arts.
Use a variety of media to communicate to create original works of art.
Show the illusion of depth on a two-dimensional surface.
Mix paints and show color relationships.

Historical and Cultural Context

Recognize Varying Cultural Themes
Name, compare, and contrast themes in selected works of art from various cultures.

Analyze the Creative Process
Identify that artists make art by conceiving an idea, developing and refining it, and giving form to the idea with art media.
Describe ways that historians, curators, critics, and anthropologists describe particular works.

Recognize the Artist's Role
Identify how artists who have achieved national and international recognition have influenced thinking.

Recognize Varying Cultural Styles
Identify the general style and period of major works of art and relate social, political, and economic factors that influenced the works.

Discriminate National Cultural Styles
Identify contemporary style trends in American art as reflections of diverse developments in our culture.

Recognize Visual Arts from World Cultures
Identify works of art from a variety of world cultures and recognize differences in media used by various cultures. Relate these differences to visual arts achievements.

Aesthetic Valuing

Analyze Design Elements
Use design elements (line, color, value, shape, and texture) to describe works of art.
Identify the interaction among design elements that give the work of art a particular emphasis.

Recognize Use of Design Elements
Describe art based on the way design principles are organized.
Explain how design principles contribute to the qualities of a work of art.
Recognize art media and processes.
Understand the use of specific media (oil, watercolor, clay, wood, stone, metal) that are used to create works of art and other art forms.
Explain a process related to a medium, such as watercolor, clay, or weaving, and how it is used in producing a work of art.

Recognize Artistic Mood
Explain the meaning of works of art in terms of mood, such as selected ideals
(e.g., courage and wisdom).
Describe aesthetic characteristics.
Employ descriptors, metaphors, and analogies to describe works of art.

Discriminate Artistic Style
Identify those qualities that indicate that two pieces of art have the same style.

Connections, Relationships, Applications

Integrate visual art with other art forms, other subjects, and with life's pursuits.
Describe how other arts disciplines are integrated into visual arts.
Identify potential careers in theater and in fields related to visual arts.

ANALYZING ART

Art appears in many incarnations, including paintings, photographs, prints, carvings, sculpture, and architecture. When asked to analyze any work of art, you can comment on the content, the form, the style, and the method used by the artist.

The *content* is what actually appears in a work of art. It is the subject matter of the art. Don't take the obvious subject matter for granted when considering your analysis. Choose descriptive words as you search for ways to capture the content of the image in front of you. For example, a landscape may contain peaceful blue skies, a raging river, cows and horses grazing, or seemingly endless grassy fields. A portrait may show a happy person or someone filled with concern or worry. A sculpture may show a smoothly muscled athlete. A building may have cascading stairs or a series of columns that thrust upward to the ceiling.

The *form* of a work of art is the order imposed by the artist. Form is the design of the work regardless of the content. A painting or photograph may show strong horizontal or vertical orientation. Perhaps the work is symmetrical, with one part a mirror image of the other. Some works may be tilted or asymmetrical.

The *style* refers to the artist's way of expressing ideas including formal styles such as gothic, high renaissance, baroque, or impressionist. In a painting or picture you can notice how the artist uses color. The colors may blend or clash. There may be an overall dark tone to the picture, or it may be light and airy. Perhaps the artist used dots of paint to produce the image.

The *method* is the medium used by the artist to create the work. It may be an oil painting or a watercolor. Perhaps the artist created prints or an etching. A three-dimensional work of art may have been sculpted, cast, carved, molded, or turned on a potter's wheel.

Keep these elements of content, form, style, and method in mind as you respond to the questions on the CSET.

GLOSSARY OF ART TERMS

allegory Art that represents or symbolizes some idea or quality.

amphora An egg-shaped Grecian urn.

ankh An Egyptian hieroglyph that represents life. See illustration.

Ankh

annealing Softening by heating glass or metal that has become hardened.

arch A curved span. See illustration.

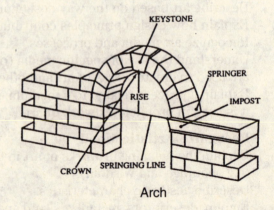

Arch

arebesque Very intricate designs based on plant forms.

atrium An open rectangular-shaped court, often in front of a church.

avant-garde Art considered ahead of its time.

baluster A small curved post or pillar.

balustrade A railing usually supported by balusters.

batten Strips of wood used as a base for plastering or for attaching tile.

belfry The top floor of a tower usually containing bells.

bevel To round off a sharp edge.

biscuit Unglazed porcelain.

bust A sculpture showing the head and shoulders.

calligraphy Decorative writing.

canopy A fabric covering.

casement A vertically hinged window frame.

ceramics All porcelain and pottery.

chalice An ornamental cup often used in religious services.

chancel The part of a church reserved for clergy.

collage Art created by pasting together many media including newspaper, fabric, and wood. A collage may also include paintings or drawings.

colors Many colors can be created by combining the primary colors. See illustration.

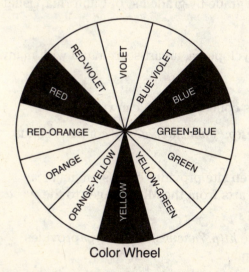

Color Wheel

column A free-standing, circular pillar. Several different styles exist. See illustration.

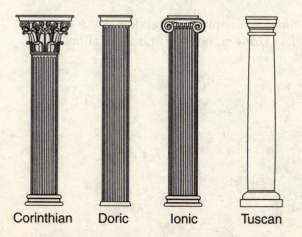

Corinthian   Doric   Ionic   Tuscan

course A row of bricks or stones.

cuneiform Wedge-shaped writing associated with Babylonians and Sumerians.

decoupage Cutting out designs to be used in a collage.

eclectic Drawing on many styles.

enamel Powdered glass bonded to a metal surface by firing.

engraving Inscribing a design on glass, metal, or some other hard surface.

etching Designs created on metal plates by applying acid to initial scratchings and the prints made from these plates.

filigree Gold or silver soldered to create elaborate, delicate patterns.

focal point The place on a work of art to which the eye is drawn.

foreshortened Objects painted or drawn as though they were seen from an angle projecting into space.

fresco A painting applied to wet plaster.

genre The type of painting—portrait, landscape, etc.

golden ratio The proportion of approximately 1.6 to 1, which is said to represent the most pleasing artistic proportion. For example, a window 3 feet wide would meet this proportion by being 4.8 feet high.

hieroglyphics Egyptian symbols representing letters or words.

illustration An idea or scene represented in art.

jamb The sides of a window or door.

kiosk A small booth with a roof and open sides.

linear A way of representing three-dimensional space in two dimensions.

louvers Shutter slats.

macrame Artwork made of knotted fabrics.

monolith A figure sculpted or carved from a single block of stone.

mural A painting made on or attached to a wall.

niche A wall recess.

obelisk A rectangular block of stone, often with a pyramidal top.

papier maché Paper (newspaper) soaked with water and flour and shaped into figures.

parquet A floor made of wooden tile.

perspective Representing three dimensions on a flat surface.

pigment The material used to color paint.

plaster Limestone and sand or gypsum mixed with water, which can be shaped and then hardened. Plaster can also be carved and is often used to finish walls and ceilings.

projection The techniques of representing buildings on a flat surface.

quarry tile Unglazed tile.

relief Carved or molded art in which the art projects from the background.

sarcophagus A stone coffin.

scale The relative size of an object, such as the scale was one inch to one foot.

sizing Gluelike material used to stiffen paper or to seal a wall or canvas.

stipple Dab on paint.

tapestry Fabric woven from silk by hand.

tempera A type of painting that binds the pigment with a mixture of egg and water or egg and oil.

uppercase Capital letters.

vihara A Buddhist monastery.

warp In weaving, the thick, fixed threads.

weft In weaving, the thin threads that are actually woven.

ON THE WEB

Visit *http://www.cde.ca.gov/be/st/ss/vamain.asp* for a grade-by-grade list of California Visual Arts Standards.

Visit *http://www.artcyclopedia.com/* for the Arts Encyclopedia, an art search tool with many useful links and other features.

Visit these museum sites. Each site has extensive arts collections you can view online.

The Los Angeles County Museum of Art web site *http://www.lacma.org/* contains about 50,000 artworks to view online.

The National Gallery of Art *http://www.nga.gov/* web site provides details on major achievements in painting, sculpture, and graphic arts from the Middle Ages to the present.

The San Francisco Museum of Modern Art web site *http://www.sfmoma.org/* provides information for modern art in many different formats.

OTHER THINGS TO DO

Involve yourself in art experiences. Go to an art show and apply the overview and terminology here and at the web sites to analyze the artworks. Draw something and think about the design elements discussed here.

VISUAL AND PERFORMING ARTS TARGETED TEST

These items will help you practice for the real CSET. These items have the same form and test the same material as the CSET items. The items you encounter on the real CSET may have a different emphasis and may be more complete.

Instructions

Mark your answers on the sheet provided below. Complete the items in 20 minutes or less. Correct your answer sheet using the answers on page 356.

1	Ⓐ Ⓑ Ⓒ Ⓓ	5	Ⓐ Ⓑ Ⓒ Ⓓ	9	Ⓐ Ⓑ Ⓒ Ⓓ	13	Ⓐ Ⓑ Ⓒ Ⓓ	17	Ⓐ Ⓑ Ⓒ Ⓓ
2	Ⓐ Ⓑ Ⓒ Ⓓ	6	Ⓐ Ⓑ Ⓒ Ⓓ	10	Ⓐ Ⓑ Ⓒ Ⓓ	14	Ⓐ Ⓑ Ⓒ Ⓓ	18	Ⓐ Ⓑ Ⓒ Ⓓ
3	Ⓐ Ⓑ Ⓒ Ⓓ	7	Ⓐ Ⓑ Ⓒ Ⓓ	11	Ⓐ Ⓑ Ⓒ Ⓓ	15	Ⓐ Ⓑ Ⓒ Ⓓ	19	Ⓐ Ⓑ Ⓒ Ⓓ
4	Ⓐ Ⓑ Ⓒ Ⓓ	8	Ⓐ Ⓑ Ⓒ Ⓓ	12	Ⓐ Ⓑ Ⓒ Ⓓ	16	Ⓐ Ⓑ Ⓒ Ⓓ	20	Ⓐ Ⓑ Ⓒ Ⓓ

A.

The Metropolitan Museum of Art, Gift of Mrs. Charles Stewart Smith, Charles Stewart Smith Jr. and Howard Casell Smith, in memory of Charles Stewart Smith, 1914. (14.76.37)

B.

The Metropolitan Museum of Art, Rogers & Fletcher Funds, Erving & Joyce Wolf Fund, Raymond J. Horowitz Gift, Bequest of Richard De Wolfe Brixey, by Exchange, & John Osgood & Elizabeth Amis Cameron Blanchard Memorial Fund, 1978. (1978.203)

C.

The Metropolitan Museum of Art, Gift of Mr. and Mrs. Joseph G. Blum, 1970. (1970.527.1)

1. Picture A expresses
   (A) anger.
   (B) pensiveness.
   (C) distraction.
   (D) assertiveness.

2. Picture A could be best described as
   (A) an abstract work whose primary meaning is the work itself.
   (B) a central figure surrounded by rectangular border.
   (C) an impressionistic work in which the figure represents an animal.
   (D) an 18th century American work.

3. Picture A is distinctive because
   (A) the border is decorated.
   (B) the figure is horned.
   (C) The sword has a carved, ornamental handle.
   (D) The figure is thrust forward.

4. Picture B depicts a
   (A) rocky shore.
   (B) seaport.
   (C) sloping shore.
   (D) turgid sea.

5. Picture B could be best described as
   (A) a bucolic scene.
   (B) an active scene.
   (C) a morning scene.
   (D) a languid scene.

6. Which of the following best describes Picture B?
   (A) A scene with people talking
   (B) A scene with children playing
   (C) A commercial scene
   (D) A scene dominated by the sky

7. Picture C primarily depicts
   (A) geometric contrasts.
   (B) a swirling sky.
   (C) a skyward needle.
   (D) a supported walkway.

8. Which of the following best describes Picture C?
   (A) A brick plaza sweeping by open latticed rectangles
   (B) A surreal world visited by real people
   (C) A visitors center at a spaceport
   (D) A central spire framed by sphere, semi-circle, and sky.

9. Picture C is most likely
   (A) an artist's rendering of buildings to be constructed.
   (B) a set for a futuristic movies.
   (C) a three-dimensional model of a NASA visitors center.
   (D) a picture of an actual structure.

10. Which picture best depicts determination?
    (A)
    (B)
    (C)

11. Which picture does not include a semicircular shape?
    (A)
    (B)
    (C)

12. Which picture shows multiple events?
    (A)
    (B)
    (C)

13. Which of the following is the name for the process of applying watercolors to a freshly plastered surface?
    (A) fresco
    (B) watercolor
    (C) mosaic
    (D) mural

14. When a mason refers to a course, he or she usually means
    (A) time spent as an apprentice.
    (B) a row of bricks.
    (C) a layer of plaster.
    (D) a stretch of lawn.

15. The songs "Frankie and Johnny," and "John Henry" are American examples of
    (A) blues.
    (B) jazz.
    (C) protest.
    (D) ballads.

16. The impressionist art movement, which included artists such as Monet and Renoir, was founded as a reaction against more classical styles and featured
    (A) abstract, linear works.
    (B) undetailed, but recognizable works.
    (C) blue and rose hues.
    (D) realistic, precise works.

17. Masks were worn regularly in Greek and Roman plays. A character wore the mask from the very beginning of the play
    (A) to conceal the actor's identity.
    (B) until the very last act, when it was removed.
    (C) enabling the actor to show a range of emotions.
    (D) removing any doubt about the characters eventual fate.

18. What form of dance do you associate with Alvin Ailey?
    (A) ballet
    (B) modern
    (C) rock
    (D) tap

19. In the key of C, which of these chords is a minor chord?
    (A) C E G
    (B) G B D
    (C) A C E
    (D) F A C

20. The Dutch artist Mondrian is best known for what art form?
    (A) abstract art
    (B) architecture
    (C) non-representational art
    (D) representational art

TARGETED TEST ANSWERS EXPLAINED

1. **D** The forward-leaning stance of the figure suggests assertiveness.

2. **B** The focus of the work is on the central figure, and the rectangular border is evident.

3. **D** The forward thrust of the figure is the distinctive aspect of this work.

4. **A** The rocks can be seen all around the shoreline.

5. **D** Languid means without animation, which this picture certainly is. (A) is incorrect because bucolic means an idealized country life, which this work does not portray.

6. **D** Most of the area of this picture is sky.

7. **A** The picture features part of a sphere, a pyramid, a semicircular bridge, and rectangles.

8. **D** The tall pyramid in the center is a spire, and the rest of the description is evident from the picture.

9. **D** Everything in the picture suggests reality.

10. **A** Determination is a human trait, and this picture, alone, represents a human.

11. **A** The cove in Picture B and the bridge and sphere in Picture C suggest semicircles.

12. **B** One boat is coming in near shore, while another boat sails offshore. There are other events.

13. **A** This is the correct name for that process.

14. **B** Each row of bricks is a course.

15. **D** Each of these songs tells a story, which makes them ballads.

16. **B** The clue in the question is the reaction against more classical works that featured more detail.

17. **D** The audience could tell what would happen to the actor from the type of mask.

18. **B** Alvin Ailey was an African-American modern dance choreographer and dancer.

19. **C** That chord is a minor chord in the key of C.

20. **C** This is a hard one. Mondrian was a non-representational painter known for his primary colors and vertical and horizontal bands.

⑧ PHYSICAL EDUCATION

TEST INFO BOX

13 Multiple Choice items   One-third of Subtest III items
1 Constructed Response item   One-third of Subtest III items

PHYSICAL EDUCATION ITEMS

Physical Education multiple choice items look like this.

Which of the following would be an appropriate way to practice a nonlocomotor skill?

(A) Hop in place.
(B) Leap over obstacles.
(C) Run around a circular path and stop in your original position.
(D) Hang from a bar or ring and then swing.

Physical Education short answer items look like this.

Choose one locomotor skill. Briefly describe three primary-grade learning activities for the skill.

USING THIS CHAPTER

This chapter prepares you to take the Physical Education part of the CSET. Choose one of these approaches.

I want all the Physical Education review I can get.

❑ Skip the Review Quiz and read the entire review section.
❑ Take the Physical Education Review Quiz on page 359.
❑ Correct the Review Quiz and reread the indicated parts of the review.
❑ Complete the Physical Education CSET Practice Questions on page 371.

I want a thorough Physical Education review.

❑ Take the Physical Education Review Quiz on page 359.
❑ Correct the Review Quiz and reread the indicated parts of the review.
❑ Complete the Physical Education CSET Practice Questions on page 371.

I want a quick Physical Education review.

❑ Take and correct the Physical Education Review Quiz on page 359.
❑ Complete the Physical Education CSET Practice Questions on page 371.

I want to practice Physical Education questions.

❑ Complete the Physical Education CSET Practice Questions on page 371.

PHYSICAL EDUCATION REVIEW QUIZ

This quiz uses a short answer format to help you find out what you know about the Physical Education topics reviewed in this chapter. The quiz results direct you to the portions of the chapter you should read.

This quiz will also help focus your thinking about Physical Education, and these questions and answers are a good review in themselves. It's not important to answer all these questions correctly, and don't be concerned if you miss many of them.

The answers are found immediately after the quiz. It's to your advantage not to look at them until you have completed the quiz. Once you have completed and corrected this review quiz, use the answer checklist to decide which sections of the review to study.

> Write the answers in the space provided or on a separate sheet of paper.

1. According to the NASPE, what reaction to new skills indicates that a person is a physically fit person?

   _____
   _____
   _____

2. Briefly describe the movement concept of flow.

   _____
   _____
   _____

3. What kinds of space does a child use while jumping rope?

   _____
   _____

4. Describe the slide in terms of some other locomotor skill.

   _____
   _____
   _____

5. What is the name for an a-rhythmic skip?

   _____

6. What is the difference between a turn and a twist?

   _____
   _____

7. Which manipulative skill does not use the arms?

   _____

8. What is the difference between aerobic and anaerobic exercises?

   _____
   _____
   _____

9. What four categories are used to categorize sport games?

   _____
   _____
   _____
   _____

10. Rolling is an example of what type of gymnastic activity?

    _____
    _____

11. What are the three gross motor areas of the body?

    _____
    _____

12. Describe how the field of motor development is concerned with the nature/nurture controversy.

    _____
    _____
    _____

13. What is the most abused drug?

    _____

14. What attaches muscles to bone?

    _____

15. What is the primary way to avoid tendinitis?

    _____

16. Briefly describe the ecological integration approach to teaching physical education.

    _____
    _____
    _____

ANSWER CHECKLIST

Answers are organized by review sections. Check your answers, and if you miss any questions in a section, review that section.

❑ *Overview, page 361*

    1. A physically fit person is able to learn new skills.

❑ *Movement Concepts, page 362*

    2. Flow describes the continuity of movement (e.g., free flow and bound flow).

    3. High space and personal space.

❑ *Locomotor Skills, page 363*

    4. The slide is a sideways gallop.

    5. An a-rhythmic skip is called hop and step.

❑ *Nonlocomotor Activities, page 363*

    6. A turn rotates the body or part of the body around the body's *vertical* axis. A twist rotates part of the body around *any* axis.

❑ *Manipulative Skills, page 364*

    7. Kicking is a manipulative skill that does not use the arms.

❑ *Self-image and Personal Development, page 364*

    8. Aerobic exercise uses oxygen in the blood. Anaerobic exercise does not use oxygen in the blood.

    9. The four categories are court, field, target, and territory.

    10. The roll is a weight transfer activity.

    11. The gross motor areas are the neck, the arms, and the legs.

    12. Motor development addresses how motor performance is related to heredity as opposed to learning and the environment.

❑ *Exercise Physiology, page 367*

    13. Heart rate is the most effective measure of the impact of exercise.

    14. Alcohol is the most abused drug.

❑ *Kinesiology, page 368*

    15. Muscles are attached to bones by tendons.

    16. A person avoids tendinitis by avoiding overuse of a tendon.

❑ *Social Science Foundations, page 369*

    17. The ecological responsibility approach emphasizes learning physical education skills to enable students to participate successfully with groups in the future.

Physical Education topics on the CSET are partitioned into three domains, and this chapter is partitioned in the same way. However, the topics in this chapter overlap, and you may find that review in one domain helps with the other domains.

OVERVIEW

The National Association for Sport and Physical Education (NASPE)

The NASPE Outcomes Project sets the stage for physical education. The following list of 20 outcomes from this project describes the characteristics of a physically fit person.

Possesses Skills
1. has movement skills including space awareness, body awareness, and relationships
2. is competent in a number of locomotor, nonlocomotor, and manipulative activities
3. is competent in combinations of these activities individually and cooperatively
4. is competent in many forms of physical activity
5. is proficient in a few forms of physical activity
6. can learn new skills

Stays Physically Fit
7. achieves, assesses, and maintains physical fitness
8. designs safe personal fitness programs using the principles of physical fitness

Regularly Participates
9. in health enhancing activity three times a week
10. in lifetime physical activities

Is Aware of the Implications and Benefits of Physical Education Involvement
11. identifies benefits, costs, and obligations of regular physical activity
12. recognizes risk and safety factors of regular participation in physical activity
13. applies concepts and principles to the development of motor skills
14. understands wellness is more than physical fitness
15. knows rules, strategies, and appropriate behavior for selected physical activities
16. recognizes that participation in physical activity can lead to multicultural, international understanding
17. knows that physical activity provides the opportunity for self-expression and communication

Values Physical Activity and Its Contributions
18. appreciates relationship with others that results from participation in physical activity
19. respects the role of physical activity in lifelong health
20. cherishes the feelings that result from regular participation in physical activity

The NASPE developed a set of content standards based on the seven objectives listed below.

- Demonstrates competency in many movement forms and proficiency in a few movement forms.

- Applies movement concepts and principles to the learning and development of motor skills.

- Exhibits a physically active lifestyle.

- Achieves and maintains a health-enhancing level of physical fitness.

- Demonstrates responsible social and personal behavior in physical activity settings.

- Demonstrates understanding and respect for differences among people in physical activity settings.

- Understands that physical activity provides opportunities for enjoyment, challenge, self-expression, and social interaction.

MOVEMENT SKILLS AND MOVEMENT KNOWLEDGE

Physical education has shifted from an emphasis on sports to an emphasis on movement and motor activities. Those who favor movement education place a greater emphasis on the aesthetic aspect of physical education than on the competitive aspect of physical education. Movement education is now the most important factor in most primary grade physical education programs and this influence is having an increased impact on physical education programs for the upper elementary grades.

The fundamental concepts and terms of a movement education program are quite different from those used to describe a traditional or sports based physical education program. These concepts and terms are presented below.

Movement Concepts

All movement can be described using these concepts or terms.

Space describes the place where the movement is performed. High space movements are performed in the air, or standing on tiptoe. Middle space movements are performed standing upright. Low space activities are performed when bending, crouching, kneeling, crawling, and so on.

Space can be partitioned into general space and personal space. Personal space is everything a child can touch without moving from his or her position. General space refers to all the other space. Personal space activities are necessarily confined to the area immediately around the child. General space activities that involve moving along a path will either be straight, curved, or zigzag.

A child crawling directly from one place to another is performing a low space, straight movement in general space.

Shape describes the relative position of different parts of the body. A body can assume a very large number of shapes. Children can try to make themselves square, tall, or round. Children trying to make their bodies look like a letter are exploring shape.

Time describes the speed at which a movement is performed. Time is often described in terms of other things or events. Children moving as slowly as a bird walking or as quickly as a bird flying are exploring time. Children clapping in a particular pattern are exploring the time concept of rhythm. In rhythmical movements each component has the same time value. In arhythmical movements each component has a different time value.

Force describes the body tension used with a movement. Children moving as softly as a gentle breeze or as strong as a thunderstorm are exploring force.

Flow describes the continuity of movement. *Free flow* movement is continuous, while *bound flow* is halting. Skipping from one place to another is an example of free flow, while the pattern skipping-halting from one point to another is an example of bound flow.

LOCOMOTOR, NONLOCOMOTOR, AND MANIPULATIVE SKILLS

Locomotor skills describe the movements that convey the body from one location to another. Nonlocomotor skills describe movements done in place in which the objective is body movement. Manipulative skills describe movements that have some effect on (manipulate) other things.

Locomotor Skills

Important locomotor skills are listed below. The skills are listed in the approximate order that they are acquired by children, although the age at which children develop these skills varies widely from child to child.

Crawl means a child is lying on his stomach but the upper part of his body is held aloft by his elbows, and he moves through space using his hips and elbows. The hands are not used when crawling.

Creep means using the hands along with either the knees or feet to move through space. *Cross-pattern* creeping or crawling means using opposite extremities (e.g., left knee, right hand). *Homolateral* creeping or crawling means using the extremities on the same side of the body (e.g., right elbow, right knee).

Walk means moving through space by transferring weight from one foot to the other foot. The feet move heel-ball-toes. At least one foot is always in contact with the surface while walking.

Run means moving through space by transferring weight (ball = toes) of one foot to (ball = toes) of the other foot. Both feet are frequently off the surface during a run. Arms swing in opposition (e.g., right leg forward, left arm forward) to the legs, and the arms are usually slightly bent.

Jump means to push the body upward (heel-ball-toes) from one or two feet until both feet are entirely off the surface. The knees are usually bent at landing, which usually occurs toe-ball-heel.

Leap is like an exaggerated run in which one foot pushes off then trails behind as the knee of the other leg leads forward. The foot of the leading leg lands and the action is repeated.

Gallop is an a-rhythmic combination of walking and running in which one leg remains in front and the other leg lags behind following the front leg.

Hop means to push the body upward (heel-ball-toe) from one foot and to land on the same foot (toe-ball-heel). The other foot does not touch the ground. Balance may be better maintained if the weight is shifted toward the leg that makes contact with the surface.

Slide is a sideward gallop. This movement skill does not refer to actions such as sliding across ice or down a slide.

Skip is an a-rhythmic combination of a hop and a step with the primary stress on the step. The leading foot alternates and both feet are briefly off the surface.

Nonlocomotor Activities

Important nonlocomotor skills are listed below. The skills are listed in the approximate order that they are acquired by children, although the age at which children develop these skills varies widely from child to child.

Stretch means to stretch muscles and extend a body part or parts away from the center of the body. A child standing in place and reaching upward with his or her arms is stretching.

Bend means that ball-and-socket or hinge joints are used to bring parts of the body together.

Turn means to rotate the entire body or a body part clockwise or counterclockwise around the body's vertical axis. A turn often, but not necessarily, involves turning the feet.

Twist rotates just a part of the body around some axis. For example, arms can be twisted but not turned. The neck can be twisted and turned.

Manipulative Skills

Important manipulative skills are listed below. The skills are listed in the approximate order that they are acquired by children, although the age at which children develop these skills varies widely from child to child.

Pull means to move something, usually with the arms and sometimes while walking, from one place to another toward the person doing the pulling.

Push means to move something, usually with the arms and sometimes while walking, from one place to another away from the person doing the pulling.

Lift means to move something, usually with the arms, from a lower to a higher position somewhat parallel to the person doing the lifting. *Carrying* is a locomotor activity that combines lifting and walking.

Strike is a strong movement from a bent arm position with the intent of hitting something or, when used with an implement such as a bat or a racquet, with the intent of hitting something with the bat or racquet.

Throw means to use a hand or hands to propel an object away from the body so that the object leaves the hands. A throw can be two-hand, one-hand, overhand, or underhand.

Kick means to use the instep of a foot to propel an object away from the body.

Bounce means to use one or both hands to strike a ball down toward the surface. Continuous bouncing is often referred to as *dribbling*. *Dribbling* can also refer to moving a ball with one or both feet.

SELF-IMAGE AND PERSONAL DEVELOPMENT

Physical fitness has always been a focus of physical education programs. The emphasis on fitness has increased in recent years and there has been a corresponding increased emphasis on fitness in physical education programs. Fitness is an important component of almost every physical education program.

Tests on elementary age children, secondary age children, and adults reveal low levels of cardiovascular performance, high levels of body fat, and an overly sedentary population. The main objective of the fitness approach to physical education is to improve cardiovascular performance through cardiovascular endurance. Cardiovascular endurance is the ability of the respiratory and circulatory systems to supply oxygen to the body through the bloodstream during prolonged exercise.

Cardiovascular endurance improves with *aerobic exercise* (exercise such as running, which uses oxygen in the blood). A person must usually reach and hold a threshold of training for about 20 minutes, a minimum of three times a week to maintain and improve fitness.

Fitness experts frequently emphasize the coronary problems, which occur later in life, that may be diminished by participation in a regular program of physical fitness. These coronary problems include *arteriosclerosis* in which plaque is deposited on artery walls, *congestive heart failure* in which the heart is too weak to supply sufficient blood to the body, and *coronary thrombosis* in which blood clots form that block a coronary artery.

These experts also point out that improved cardiovascular fitness has many positive benefits, including those listed below.

Benefits of Cardiovascular Fitness

- Lower heart rate and lower blood pressure
- Lower LDL (bad) cholesterol levels
- Higher HDL (good) cholesterol levels
- Reduced risk of heart attack
- Better chance of heart attack survival

Body composition, the ratio of body fat to overall body mass, is another important measure of fitness. A high percentage of body fat is also a risk factor for disease. Body composition can be determined by taking skin-fold measurements at various places on the body. More accurate measures of body composition are taken with hydrostatic weighing, which determines body weight normally and then underwater to get a very accurate measure of the percent of body fat.

But the fitness approach also seeks to improve the strength, endurance, and flexibility of participants. Fitness program proponents also point out that these programs create a leaner body with increased flexibility, strength, and endurance.

Flexibility means the range of motion at a joint. *Endurance* means a muscle's ability to contract repeatedly and efficiently. *Strength* is the amount of force that a muscle can exert. The compound ATP transfers and stores energy in the muscle cells. This compound is produced by aerobic exercise, anaerobic exercise (exercise such as pull-ups of maximum effort for short periods) and by the lactic acid produced during muscle contraction in anaerobic exercise.

These other attributes that are improved by fitness education also have many positive benefits, some of which are listed here.

Other Benefits of Fitness Education

- Reduced stress
- Reduced likelihood of heart attack
- Reduced likelihood of injury and disease
- Reduced likelihood of lower back problems
- Increased ability to work and perform motor skills.

Fitness programs also increase *agility* (the ability to quickly change bodily position), *balance* (the ability to maintain equilibrium), *coordination* (the ability to perform motor activities quickly when needed), and *power* (the ability to generate force quickly).

Play

Games begin as spontaneous, unstructured play. Games and sports develop from play. A child's participation in games and sports is frequently motivated by their early play experiences. But children frequently go off to "play" a game that is not particularly playful.

Children progress from watching others play to active and cooperative participation. Children's play is unbounded and frequently involves more creativity and imagination than actual physical activity. Children learn about their world as they play. Their experiences in early play both shape and reveal the types of social interactions they will evidence in life.

Games

Gradually as children play they develop their own rules and organization, and play develops into games. Most experts agree that the group of activities called games involve some form of competition using physical or mental prowess. The competition may be against a goal, and not between individuals or teams, but competition is always involved.

These experts say that noncompetitive games don't exist. They say there can be cooperation in a game, but there must be competition.

Competition is one of the most controversial aspects of games. To compete, to achieve competence, is a part of life. Accepting success and failure is a part of life. Competition fosters cooperation and respect. Those who learn how to compete effectively can have enjoyable, successful lives. Of course, competing successfully does not mean a person will win.

Children usually compete very constructively. But those not directly involved in the game may take competition too far. How many times have we all seen a parent or spectator press their child for performance even during informal games.

Games are not always the formalized games we are accustomed to. They are frequently unique to a group of children, or to a geographic area. However, every game has rules. The "appropriate" way to play the game is understood and adhered to by most participants. At the same time, rules for play are transmitted from older or more experienced children to their younger, less experienced friends.

Sports

Sports refers to organized, formalized games. Many of the rule-bound games that children play are not sport games. Children often participate in sport games such as basketball, field hockey, and soccer as a part of their social development.

The *primary rules* that define these games are well known and are usually written. Striking the ball with a bat is a primary rule of baseball. *Secondary rules* refer to the changes in the way these games are played to compensate for the age, varying skill, or varying number of participants and local playing conditions. Hitting a baseball off a stationary tee is a secondary rule of baseball to accommodate the developmental limitations of younger players.

Leagues in towns or in schools and professional leagues are examples of sports. A group of overseers regulates the league, umpires or referees officiate the games, and there are often special arrangements for spectators. There is usually some pre-game and/or post-game ritual.

Sport games require physical exertion and strategic thinking. Sport games are not games such as chess that involve only strategy or such as a state lotto that involve only chance. Experts use four categories to classify sport games: court, field, target, and territory.

Court games include the *divided court* games of tennis and badminton and the *shared court* games of handball or jai-lai. The basic idea in these games is to hit a ball or other objects so that the opponent(s) can't successfully return it.

Field games include baseball and softball. The basic idea in these games is to hit a ball so that defenders can't effectively retrieve it.

Target games include games such as golf and bowling in which the players are not direct opponents and games such as croquet and horseshoe in which the players are direct opponents.

Territory games include games such as football, soccer, basketball, and water polo.

An elementary school gymnastics program should be different from the competitive gymnastics we associate with older students and adults. Elementary school gymnastics fosters the development of the individual child. That is, the program is child oriented. Children do not compete with other children. Children do try to improve their skills, and their rewards are the progress they make.

In an elementary school gymnastics program, children make appropriate use of mats, low balance beams, slides, and low bars for hanging and swinging. Some elementary school gymnastics skills are described below.

Weight transfer means moving weight from one body part to another. Walking is a weight transfer activity, as is moving from a lying to a kneeling position.

Roll means to roll the body, first lying down around the body's vertical axis; then roll while in a compact egg shape; then a backward roll; and finally a forward roll. The roll is a weight transfer activity.

Balance means that a person's center of gravity is directly over the support base. The wider the base the easier it is to maintain balance. *Dynamic balance* refers to moving balance activities, while *static balance* refers to balance activities while stationary. The low balance beam is an excellent apparatus for balance activities.

Climb means pushing and pulling to a higher or lower position while maintaining balance. A jungle gym apparatus with sufficient underprotection is an excellent apparatus for climbing.

Hang and swing is usually performed on a bar no more than twice a child's height so that injury will not result from a fall.

Growth and Development

See pages 376–388 in the Human Development section for a complete review of the stages of growth and development and sensory-perceptual maturation.

Motor development in children follows some predictable patterns. Motor skills develop from the head down to the toes, from the waist out to the extremities and from the gross motor area (neck, arms, legs) to the fine motor areas (fingers, toes).

Motor Learning

Motor learning, and its subspecialties of motor control and motor development, are the basis for how children develop motor skills. Motor skills are the physical skills that children use for motor activities and other physical education and sports skills.

Motor learning describes *how* motor performance can be affected by attention and interest on the part of the child, and on the type of feedback and practice that the child receives. In particular, motor learning is about how the type, the frequency, and the timing of feedback influence the acquisition and maintenance of motor skills. Motor learning also addresses how factors such as aging and fatigue interfere with motor performance.

Motor development addresses *what* motor skills look like. That is, motor learning describes the essential qualities of motor skills. Motor development addresses how motor performance is related to heredity as opposed to learning and the environment. Motor development formulates the age or developmental stage at which a child is ready for particular motor activities.

Motor control addresses the *relationship* between the nervous system and muscular control, and how cognitive development and cognitive activities are related to motor skill development. Motor control formulates the schema that enables children to use motor skills once they have been learned. Motor control also establishes a relationship between the cognitive development, verbal instructions, and a child's ability to perform the motor skill.

Exercise Physiology

Exercise physiology is about how exercise affects the different body systems. The body must exercise to achieve physical fitness, and physical fitness must be maintained once it is achieved.

Exercise

Many body systems gain great benefit from exercise. In particular, exercise reduces the risk of cardiovascular disease. Physical activity also improves a child's muscular strength, muscular flexibility, bone strength, and self-image. Many experts believe that exercise can reduce the likelihood of lower back pain and fractures in adulthood.

The improvements noted above are best derived from high intensity exercise performed at regular intervals. However, experts believe that significant health benefits can be achieved from low intensity exercise. They note also that people are more likely to engage in low intensity exercise on their own.

Assessment

There are many sophisticated ways to effectively assess the impact of exercise. Heart rate, which can be assessed through pulse readings, is the most effective. Other involved observational systems also exist. Determining pulse should probably not be taught to elementary school students. Experts recommend that elementary school teachers use the amount of sweating or when students start hard breathing as general indicators of physical fitness.

Nutrition

Appropriate nutrition is required for a person to be physically fit. Inappropriate diets that increase HDL, cholesterol, sugar, or fat in blood have a devastating impact on body systems. Poor nutrition can devastate the circulatory system. Clogged hearts and blood vessels are the likely result, along with increased risk of diabetes and other diseases.

Drug and Alcohol Use

Inappropriate drug and alcohol use is devastating to body systems. Tobacco abuse and alcohol abuse represents the single largest health problem in this country. Tobacco devastates the respiratory system and results in cancer, emphysema, and other diseases.

Alcohol is the most abused drug and the most lethal drug. Alcohol disables the nervous system and is a factor in about 50 percent of traffic deaths and innumerable other accidental deaths in the country. Alcohol abuse creates many health problems that lead to premature death.

Abuse of other drugs is a factor in many other diseases. These drugs also disable the nervous system and are a factor in heart attacks, traffic deaths, and other accidental and premature deaths. Most nonprescription drugs are not monitored or controlled and there is no assurance of their contents. The devastating impact of drug abuse combined with uncertainty about the drug's contents makes nonprescription drug abuse particularly dangerous.

Kinesiology

Kinesiology is about how the body's muscles move the skeleton. The body moves itself through work performed by muscles.

Muscles are attached to bones by tough cords called tendons. A synovial membrane lines the area where bone and muscle meet and secretes synovial fluid to lubricate the area making it easier for tendons to move.

Injuries

Many injuries can be successfully prevented. Physical fitness, including muscle strength and flexibility, prevents injuries. A thorough warm-up and stretch and appropriate taping will help prevent most sprains (stretched or torn ligament) and strains (stretched or torn muscle). Bone strength developed through exercise and appropriate nutrition can help reduce the likelihood of a fracture (broken bone). Avoiding overuse can prevent tendinitis (inflammation of a tendon).

Safety Equipment

Appropriate safety equipment can help prevent many injuries. In particular, helmets and other headgear can help avoid skull fractures, concussions (swollen brain), and contusions (bruised brain). Mats and climbing equipment of the appropriate height can help avoid falls that can lead to fractures, loss of feeling, or paralysis (damage to the nervous system).

SOCIAL DEVELOPMENT

Physical education is a significant socializing agent and a powerful psychological force. Children learn to interact and develop psychologically through their play participation with other children. Play and games fill the days of most young children.

Social Status

A child's status in a school and community is frequently a function of his or her perceived athletic ability. Physical ability, and particularly the ability to participate in sports, is among the most valued attributes in our society. Children who show ability can receive favorable treatment combined with pressure to excel.

Children from lower socioeconomic levels are less fit than their higher socioeconomic counterparts. Children from more affluent families are more likely to participate in physical activity and sport.

Sex Related Differences

On average, boys are more physically fit and less sedentary that girls. Furthermore, girls tend to loose some of their fitness levels as they progress through the elementary school years, while boys tend to maintain their fitness level.

Social Approaches

There are several social approaches to teaching physical education. The *self-actualization* approach emphasizes matching the curriculum to the interests and motivation of students. The *ecological integration* approach emphasizes learning physical education to enable students to participate successfully with groups in the future. The *social responsibility* approach emphasizes establishing strong interpersonal relationships among students and learning to work together.

Responsibility Level

Sociologists have studied the responsibility level of physical education participants. They suggest five levels starting at irresponsibility (uncooperative) and progressing through self-control (cooperative nonparticipation), involvement (playing cooperatively), and self-responsibility (independent participation) to caring (helping others participate).

PHYSICAL EDUCATION TARGETED TEST

These items will help you practice for the real CSET. These items have the same form and test the same material as the CSET items and test material. The items you encounter on the real CSET may have a different emphasis and may be more complete.

Instructions

Mark your answers on the sheet provided below. Complete the items in 20 minutes or less. Correct your answer sheet using the answers on page 375.

1 Ⓐ Ⓑ Ⓒ Ⓓ   5 Ⓐ Ⓑ Ⓒ Ⓓ   9 Ⓐ Ⓑ Ⓒ Ⓓ   13 Ⓐ Ⓑ Ⓒ Ⓓ   17 Ⓐ Ⓑ Ⓒ Ⓓ
2 Ⓐ Ⓑ Ⓒ Ⓓ   6 Ⓐ Ⓑ Ⓒ Ⓓ   10 Ⓐ Ⓑ Ⓒ Ⓓ   14 Ⓐ Ⓑ Ⓒ Ⓓ   18 Ⓐ Ⓑ Ⓒ Ⓓ
3 Ⓐ Ⓑ Ⓒ Ⓓ   7 Ⓐ Ⓑ Ⓒ Ⓓ   11 Ⓐ Ⓑ Ⓒ Ⓓ   15 Ⓐ Ⓑ Ⓒ Ⓓ   19 Ⓐ Ⓑ Ⓒ Ⓓ
4 Ⓐ Ⓑ Ⓒ Ⓓ   8 Ⓐ Ⓑ Ⓒ Ⓓ   12 Ⓐ Ⓑ Ⓒ Ⓓ   16 Ⓐ Ⓑ Ⓒ Ⓓ   20 Ⓐ Ⓑ Ⓒ Ⓓ

1. Which of the following is the most accurate description of a fact about the movement concept of force?
   (A) Objects should be pushed away from the center of weight.
   (B) More muscle contraction leads to more force.
   (C) The sequence of body movements affects the amount of force.
   (D) The more contracted the arm, the more force it produces.

2. The NASPE physical fitness test of sit-ups is used to assess
   (A) the number of repetitions
   (B) lower back flexibility
   (C) abdominal strength
   (D) cardiovascular fitness

3. Which of the following is NOT an appropriate objective for a soccer lesson?
   (A) play soccer
   (B) chest trap a ball
   (C) kick a ball with the instep
   (D) foot trap a ball

4. Which of the following is most likely to result in maximum learning?
   (A) all time on task at a child's level of development
   (B) most time on task above the child's level of ability
   (C) all time on task above the child's level of ability
   (D) some time on task below the child's level of ability

5. The locomotor skill of jumping can involve which of the following?

   I. weight transfer from one foot to the other
   II. weight transfer from one foot to the same foot
   III. weight transfer from both feet to both feet

   (A) I only
   (B) I and III only
   (C) I, II, and III
   (D) Neither I, nor II, nor III

6. Which of the following nonlocomotor skills involves rotating the body parts around the body's vertical axis?
   (A) swinging
   (B) turning
   (C) twisting
   (D) bending

7. Which of the following is the most appropriate way to determine the fatness of a child?
   (A) overall weight
   (B) ration of weight to body type
   (C) sum of skinfold measurements
   (D) ratio of weight to height

8. Which muscle type is most prevalent?
   (A) tendons
   (B) skeletal muscles
   (C) smooth muscles
   (D) cardiac muscles

9. Which of the following does NOT affect body stability?
   (A) line of gravity
   (B) inertia
   (C) support base
   (D) center of gravity

10. Which of the following describes the body tension used with a movement?
    (A) strength
    (B) agility
    (C) force
    (D) contraction

11. Which of the following is a nonlocomotor skill?
    (A) bend
    (B) slide
    (C) push
    (D) kick

12. Which of the following is a benefit of cardio-vascular fitness?
    (A) lower HDL cholesterol levels
    (B) higher LDL cholesterol levels
    (C) lower blood pressure
    (D) higher alcohol tolerance

13. Which of the following coronary problems means depositing plaque on artery walls?
    (A) coronary thrombosis
    (B) arteriosclerosis
    (C) congestive heart failure
    (D) angina

14. Which of the following is NOT a category
    used to classify sport games?
    (A) court games
    (B) field games
    (C) target games
    (D) water games

15. Which of the following terms refers to moving
    balance activities in gymnastics?
    (A) flowing balance
    (B) dynamic balance
    (C) static balance
    (D) progressive balance

16. The roll is which of the following types of
    motion activities?
    (A) locomotor activity
    (B) nonlocomotor activity
    (C) weight transfer activity
    (D) dynamic balance activity

17. Motor development in children follows
    predictable patterns, including all of the
    following EXCEPT:
    (A) head to toes
    (B) waist out to extremities
    (C) gross motor area to fine motor area
    (D) fingers to shoulders

18. The patella refers to what skeletal part?
    (A) kneecap
    (B) thighbone
    (C) shinbone
    (D) hipbone

19. Joints are held together by
    (A) muscles
    (B) ligaments
    (C) tendons
    (D) membranes

20. Manipulative skills include all of the
    following EXCEPT:
    (A) bounce
    (B) kick
    (C) strike
    (D) twist

TARGET TEST ANSWERS EXPLAINED

1. **C** As an example, winding up to throw a pitch creates more force than not winding up.

2. **C** Sit-ups use the abdominal muscles.

3. **A** Playing soccer is not a soccer objective.

4. **A** Time on task is the key to maximum learning, and time on task at the child's ability level creates the maximum possible learning opportunities.

5. **D** A locomotor skill involves movement, which none of these choices include.

6. **B** A turn rotates the body around the body's vertical axis.

7. **C** Skin fold measurements determine how fat a child is; weight alone does not take body type or bone structure into account.

8. **B** There are more muscles that attach the body to the skeleton than any other type of muscle.

9. **B** Learning is greatest when instruction is at the child's ability level.

10. **C** Force is the tension that creates movement.

11. **A** Choices (B) and (C) are nonlocomotor skills while choice (D) is a manipulative skill.

12. **C** Lowered blood pressure is a prime benefit of cardiovascular fitness.

13. **B** Arteriosclerosis means depositing plaque on artery walls.

14. **D** Water is not a category used to classify games.

15. **B** Dynamic balance describes moving balance activities, such as activities on a balance beam.

16. **C** The roll transfers weight from one part of the body to another.

17. **D** Motor development in children does not begin with the fine motor activities associated with fingers.

18. **A** The patella is the kneecap.

19. **B** Ligaments hold joints together.

20. **D** A twist is a nonlocomotor skill.

⑨ HUMAN DEVELOPMENT

TEST INFO BOX

13 Multiple Choice items   One-third of Subtest III items
1 Constructed Response item   One-third of Subtest III items

HUMAN DEVELOPMENT ITEMS

Human Development multiple choice items look like this.

A child in the eighth grade is developing normally. According to Eriksen's theory of psychosocial development, what primary emotional crisis is the child going through?

(A) Intimacy vs. isolation
(B) Initiative vs. guilt
(C) Industry vs. inferiority
(D) Identity vs. identity confusion

Human Development constructed response items look like this.

The Swiss psychologist Jean Piaget believed that children learn through a process called equilibration. Briefly explain what Piaget meant and include an example.

USING THIS CHAPTER

This chapter prepares you to take the Human Development part of the CSET.

I want a quick Human Development review.

❑ Complete the Human Development CSET Practice Questions on page 389.

I don't need any Human Development review.

❑ OK. If you're sure, skip this chapter.

   Human Development topics on the CSET are partitioned into three domains, and this chapter is partitioned in the same way. However, the topics in this chapter are related to one another and you may find that review in one domain helps with the other domains. Additionally, the review in this chapter may help with the other chapters in this section.

COGNITIVE DEVELOPMENT

This section describes theories of learning and development.

Behavioral Development

Behaviorism was the first significant theory of development. Behaviorism is concerned with observable, measurable behavior and with those events that stimulate or reinforce the behavior.

Watson

John Watson originated the behaviorist movement during the early 1900s. His theoretical ideas centered around conditioned responses in children. Conditioned response means that a child was "taught" to respond in a particular way to a stimulus that would not naturally elicit that response. Watson's experiment to condition a child to fear a white rat that the child initially liked is most quoted in texts. Many claim that the success of the experiment was overstated.

Pavlov

Many trace the experimental basis for behaviorism to the Russian psychologist Pavlov who, in the 1920s, conducted classical conditioning experiments with dogs. Dogs naturally salivate in an unconditioned response to the unconditioned stimulus of food. Pavlov showed that dogs would salivate in response to any neutral stimulus. The neutral stimulus is called a conditioned stimulus, and the salivation that occurs is called a conditioned response.

Thorndike

Also in the early 1900s Edward Thorndike developed his own form of behaviorism called instrumental conditioning. Thorndike's work with animals led him to two significant conclusions.

- The law of exercise—a conditioned response can be strengthened by repeating the response (practice).

- The law of effect—rewarded responses are strengthened while punished responses are weakened.

Skinner

Skinner was the most influential behaviorist. Skinner referred to his approach as operant conditioning, which studied how voluntary behavior could be shaped. Operant conditioning relies on these basic mechanisms.

- Reward or positive reinforcement—Students are rewarded for repeating desired responses.

- Negative reinforcement—Students escape punishment by repeating desired responses.

- Extinction—Undesired responses are not reinforced.

- Punishment—Undesired responses are punished.

Skinner showed that he could condition very complex behaviors in animals. He believed that students learned when teachers gave immediate positive feedback for a desired behavior and used extinction or punishment for undesirable behaviors.

Jean Piaget

Jean Piaget is the most prominent of cognitive psychologists, who believe that students develop concepts through a series of stages. Stage theory is currently the most popular form of child development.

According to Piaget, children proceed through a fixed but uneven series of stages of cognitive development. His stages help us understand the general way in which students learn and develop concepts.

Action and logic versus perception are at the center of Piaget's theory. He believed that children learn through an active involvement with their environment. He also believed that students have developed a concept when their logical understanding overcomes their perceptual misunderstanding of the concept.

His conservation experiments explain this last point. In conservation of number, students are shown two matched rows of checkers. The child confirms that there are the same number of checkers in each row. Then one row of checkers is spread out and the child is asked if there are still the same number of checkers. Children who believe there are more checkers in one of the rows do not understand the concept of number because their perception holds sway over their logic.

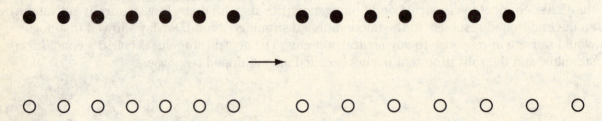

Piaget presents these four stages of cognitive development.

- Sensorimotor (birth to 18 months)—Children exhibit poor verbal and cognitive development. Children develop the idea of object permanence (out of sight not out of mind) during this stage.

- Preoperational (18 months to 7 years)—Children develop language and are able to solve some problems. Students' thinking is egocentric, and they have difficulty developing concepts. For example, students in this stage may not be able to complete the conservation of number task shown above.

- Concrete operational (7–12 years)—Students' thinking becomes operational. This means that concepts become organized and logical, as long as they are working with or around concrete materials or images. During this stage, students master the number conservation and other conservation tasks, but most students do not understand symbolic concepts.

- Formal operational (12+ years)—Children develop and demonstrate concepts without concrete materials or images. In this stage, students think fully in symbolic terms about concepts. Children become able to reason effectively, abstractly, and theoretically. Full development of this stage may depend on the extent to which children have had a full range of active manipulative experiences in the concrete operational stage.

Social Learning

Social learning theory is a fairly new field. Social learning theorists seek to combine behavioral and cognitive learning theories along with other types of learning.

Albert Bandura is the leading social learning theorist. He believes that a great deal of learning can take place through modeling. That is, students often act the way they see others act, or they learn vicariously by observing others. Bandura believes that verbal explanations and reinforcement are also important and that students become socialized through systematic modeling of appropriate behavior. Students can also develop cognitive skills by observing a problem-solving process and learn procedures by observing these procedures in action.

Psychosocial Development

Eriksen built on Freud's work and partitioned the life span into eight psychosocial stages. An emotional crisis at each stage can lead to a positive or negative result. The result achieved at each stage determines the development pattern for the next stage. Four of these stages fall within the school years.

Stage	Characteristic	Description
Kindergarten	Initiative vs. Guilt	Children accepted and treated warmly tend to feel more comfortable about trying out new ideas. Rejected children tend to become inhibited and guilty.
Elementary grades	Industry vs. Inferiority	Students who are accepted by their peer group and who do well in school and students who just feel that the above is true are more successful than those who do not feel good about themselves.

Stage	Characteristic	Description
Grade 6–9	Identity vs. Identity Confusion	Students who establish an identity and a sense of direction and who develop gender, social, and occupational roles experience an easier transition into adulthood than those students who do not establish these roles.
Grades 10–12	Intimacy vs. Isolation	Students who have passed successfully through the other stages will find it easier to establish a relationship with a member of the opposite sex. Those students who are unsuccessful at this stage may face an extremely difficult transition into adult life.

Moral Development

Kohlberg built on Piaget's original work to develop stages of moral development. Kohlberg proposed three levels of moral development with two stages at each level. His stages provide a reasonable approach to understanding moral development. Not everyone moves through all stages.

Preconventional Morality (preschool and primary grades)

Stage 1   Children do not demonstrate a conscience but do react to fear of punishment. Children are very egocentric.

Stage 2   Children still have no clear morality. Children concentrate on their own egocentric needs and let others do the same. Children may not be willing to help others meet their needs even though it would help them meet their own needs.

[Some children and antisocial adults may not pass this stage.]

Conventional Morality (middle grades through high school)

Stage 3   These children want to be good. They associate themselves with parents and other adult authority figures. They show concern for others and evidence a number of virtues and try to live up to expectations.

Stage 4   These children shift from wanting to please authority figures to a more generalized sense of respect for rules and expectations. These children see their responsibility to maintain society through a strict enforcement of society's laws.

[Many adults do not progress beyond this stage of development.]

Postconventional Morality (high school and beyond)

Stage 5   People at this stage differentiate between legality and morality. They have a more flexible view of right and wrong and realize that societal needs often take precedence over individual needs.

| Stage 6 | Very few people reach this stage. Those at stage six have pure, cosmic understanding of justice and dignity. These principles always take precedence when they conflict with what is considered legal or socially acceptable. |

Nature Versus Nurture

The relative effect of nature (heredity and genes) and nurture (environment and experience) on growth and development is still not resolved. Certain traits (sex, eye color, some forms of mental retardation, and susceptibility to some mental illnesses such as schizophrenia) are linked to genes and heredity. However, other developmental questions are not clear, and even studies of twins separated at birth have not yielded the kind of conclusive results needed to draw conclusions.

SOCIAL AND PHYSICAL DEVELOPMENT

The Family

The family remains the predominant influence in the early lives of children. However, the nature of the American family has changed, and for the worse.

Divorce rates are very high and some say that a majority of Americans under 40 will be divorced. American families are fragmented with about 30 percent of children living with a step-parent. About one-quarter of children are raised in one-parent families, and about two-thirds of these children live below the poverty level.

An increasing number of children, called latchkey children, return from school with no parents at home. School programs developed for these students cannot replace effective parenting.

In many respects, the school, social or religious institutions, peer groups, and gangs have replaced parents. This means that parents and families have less influence on children's values and beliefs.

The pressures of economic needs have drastically changed the American family. Less than 10 percent of American families have children, a mother at home, and a father at work. Over 30 percent of married couples have no children, and over 70 percent of mothers with children are working mothers.

Characteristics of Students

We can make some general statements about the students in a class. We know that 3–7 percent of girls and 12–18 percent of boys will have some substantial adjustment problems. Prepare yourself for these predictable sex differences.

Boys are more physically active and younger children have shorter attention spans. Respond to this situation by scheduling activities when students are more likely to be able to complete them.

A teacher's management role is different at different grade levels. Prepare for these predictable differences in student reaction to teacher authority.

In the primary grades, students see teachers as authority figures and respond well to instruction and directions about how they should act in school. In the middle grades, students have learned how to act in school and still react well to the teacher's instruction.

In seventh through tenth grade, students turn to their peer group for leadership and resist the teacher's authority. The teacher must spend more time fostering appropriate behavior among students. By the last two years of high school, students are somewhat less resistant and the teacher's role is more academic.

We know that many adolescents resent being touched and that teachers may anger adolescents by taking something from them. Avoid this problem by not confronting adolescent students.

We know that there will be cultural differences among students. Many minority students, and other students, may be accustomed to harsh, authoritarian treatment. Respond to these students with warmth and acceptance. Many minority students will feel completely out of place in school. These students also need to be treated warmly and also with the positive expectation that they will succeed in school.

Many other students may be too distracted to study effectively in school. These students may need quiet places to work and the opportunity to schedule some of their own work time.

Other factors, such as low self esteem, anxiety, and tension, can also cause students to have difficulty in school.

PHYSICAL DEVELOPMENT

Adequate nutrition in mothers is essential for proper fetal development. Adequate nutrition and exercise are essential for a child's physical growth. Inadequate nutrition can hamper growth and lead to inattentiveness and other problems that interfere with learning.

Alcohol and drug abuse by mothers can cause irreparable brain damage to unborn children. Children of drug-and-alcohol-abusing mothers tend to have lower birth weights. Low birth weight is associated with health, emotional, and learning problems. Alcohol and drug addiction, smoking, stress, and adverse environmental factors are among the other causes of abnormal physical and emotional development.

During the first 12 months after birth, the body weight of infants triples and brain size doubles. Infants crawl by about 7 months, eat with their hands at about 8 months, sit up by about 9 months, stand up by about 11 months, and walk by about 1 year.

From 12–15 months to 2.5 years, children are called toddlers. During this period, children become expert walkers, feed themselves, evidence self control, and spend a great deal of their time playing. This period is characterized by the word *no* and is also when children begin bowel training.

The preschool years span the time from the end of toddlerhood to entry into kindergarten. Children start to look more like adults with longer legs and a shorter torso. Play continues but becomes more sophisticated.

The elementary school years refer to ages 6–10 in girls but 6–12 in boys. During this period children enter a period of steady growth. Most children double their body weight and increase their height by one-half. Play continues but involves more sophisticated games and physical activities, often involving groups or teams of other children.

Adolescence begins at about age 10 for girls but at about age 12 for boys. The growth rate spurt begins during this time. Because this period begins earlier for girls than for boys, girls are more mature than boys for a number of years. Sexual and secondary sex characteristics appear during this time. Most adolescents rely heavily on peer group approval and respond to peer pressure.

HUMAN DIVERSITY

This section discusses human diversity and the implications of diversity for learning.

Age—Primary students should have more structure, shorter lessons, less explanation, more public praise, more small group and individual instruction, and more experiences with manipulatives and pictures. Older students should have less structure, increasingly longer lessons, more explanation, less public praise, more whole-class instruction, more independent work, and less work with manipulatives.

ACADEMIC DIVERSITY

Aptitude—Students exhibit different abilities to learn. You can provide differentiated assignments to enable students at different aptitude levels to maximize their potential.

Reading Level—Ensure that a student is capable of understanding the reading material. Do not ask students to learn from material that is too difficult. Identify materials at an appropriate reading level or with an alternative learning mode (tapes, material read to student). Remember that a low reading level does not mean that a student cannot learn a difficult concept.

Learning Disabled—Learning-disabled students evidence at least a 2-year discrepancy between measures of ability and performance. Learning-disabled students should be given structured, brief assignments, manipulative experiences, and many opportunities for auditory learning.

Visually Impaired—Place the visually-impaired student where he or she can most easily see the instruction. Use large learning aids and large print books. Use a multisensory approach.

Hearing Impaired—Ensure that the students are wearing an appropriate hearing aid. Students with less than 50 percent hearing loss will probably be able to hear you if you stand about 3 to 5 feet away.

Mildly Handicapped—Focus on a few, highly relevant skills, more learning time, and lots of practice. Provide students with concrete experiences. Do not do for students what they can do for themselves, even it takes these students an extended time.

Gifted—Gifted students have above average ability, creativity, and a high degree of task commitment. Provide these students with enriched or differentiated units. Permit them to "test out" of required units. Do not isolate these students from the rest of the class.

CULTURAL AND LINGUISTIC DIVERSITY

SES (Socioeconomic Status)—Socioeconomic status and school achievement are highly correlated. Overall, students with higher SES will have higher achievement scores. In America, SES differences are typically associated with differences in race and ethnicity. However, the achievement differences are not caused by and are not a function of these differences in race or ethnicity. Rather, achievement differences are typically caused by differences in home environment, opportunity for enriched experiences, and parental expectations.

Teachers frequently have a higher SES than their students. These students often behave differently than teachers expect. The crushing problems of poor and homeless children may produce an overlay of acting out and attention problems. All this frequently leads the teacher to erroneously conclude that these students are less capable of learning. In turn, the teacher may erroneously lower learning expectations. This leads to lower school performance and a compounding of student's difficulty.

A teacher must consciously and forcibly remind herself or himself that lower SES students are capable learners. These teachers must also actively guard against reducing learning expectations for lower SES students.

There are appropriate ways of adapting instruction for students with different SES levels. For high SES students, minimize competitiveness, provide less structure, and present more material. For low SES students, be more encouraging, guard against feelings of failure or low self esteem, and provide more structure. Do not lower learning expectations, but do present less material and emphasize mastery of the material.

Culturally Diverse—Almost every class will have students from diverse cultural backgrounds. Use the values embedded in these cultures to motivate individual learners.

Language Diverse—The first language for many students is not English. In addition, a number of American students speak local variants of the English language. Teachers frequently, and erroneously, lower their learning expectations for these students. There are a number of useful strategies for adapting instruction for these students.

A number of students are referred to as Limited English Proficiency (LEP) who need English as a Second Language (ESL) instruction. Teaching English as a second language can be accomplished in the classroom, but often requires a specialist who works with students in "pull-out programs." When teaching these students, use simpler words and expressions, use context clues to help students identify word meaning, clearly draw student's attention to your speech, and actively involve students in the learning process.

Successful Learning

Research indicates that the following factors are likely to lead to successful learning.

- Students who are engaged in the learning process tend to be more successful learners, particularly when they are engaged in activities at the appropriate level of difficulty.

- Students learn most successfully when they are being taught or supervised as opposed to working independently.

- Students who are exposed to more material at the appropriate level of difficulty are more successful learners.

- Students are successful learners when their teachers expect them to master the curriculum and use available instructional time for learning activities.

- Students who are in a positive, uncritical classroom environment are more successful learners than students who are in a negative, critical classroom environment. This does not mean that students cannot be corrected or criticized, but that students learn best when the corrections are done positively and when the criticisms are constructive.

- Students generally develop positive attitudes to teachers who appear warm, have a student orientation, praise students, listen to students, accept student ideas, and interact with them.

Motivation

Students learn best when they are motivated. The motivation interests the learner and focuses their attention on the lesson. It is also important to maintain students' motivation for the duration of a lesson.

The motivation for a lesson may be intrinsic or extrinsic. Intrinsic motivation refers to topics that students like or enjoy. Effective intrinsic motivations are based on a knowledge of what is popular or interesting to students of a particular age.

For example, you might introduce a lesson about the French and Indian War to older students by discussing the book and movie *Last of the Mohicans*. You might introduce a lesson on patterns to young children by picking out patterns in children's clothes. You might introduce a lesson on fractions to middle school students with a discussion about measuring.

Extrinsic motivation focuses on external rewards for good work or goal attainment. Extrinsic rewards are most successful when used in conjunction with more routine work. Extrinsic motivations may offer an appropriate reward for completing an assignment or for other acceptable performance. Establish rewards for activities that most students can achieve and take care to eliminate unnecessary competition.

For example, you might grant a period of free time to students who successfully complete a routine but necessary assignment. You might offer the whole class a trip or a "party" when a class project is successfully completed. Special education programs feature token reinforcement in which students receive or lose points or small plastic tokens or points for appropriate or inappropriate activity.

Motivation needs to be maintained during the lesson itself. Follow these guidelines for teaching lessons in which the students remain motivated. Lessons will be more motivating if you have clear and unambiguous objectives, give the students stimulating tasks at an appropriate level, get and hold the students' attention, and allow students some choices. Students will be most motivated if they like the topic or activities, believe that the lesson has to do with them, believe that they will succeed, and have a positive reaction to your efforts to motivate them.

Individual work gives a further opportunity to use intrinsic motivation. Use the interests and likes of individual students to spark and maintain their motivation.

The extrinsic motivation of praise can be used effectively during a lesson. For praise to be successful, it must be given for a specific accomplishment, including effort, and focus on the student's own behavior. Praise does not compare behavior with other students nor establish competitive situations.

INFLUENCES ON DEVELOPMENT

This decade finds our society beset with unprecedented problems of crime and violence, alcohol and drug abuse, sex, AIDS, high dropout rates, and child abuse. Many of these problems can be traced directly to poverty.

Crime and Violence

The number of serious crimes in the United States is at the highest level in memory. Students bring guns to school, and large urban areas report dozens of deaths each year from violent acts in school. Murder is the leading cause of death among African American teens. More than 70 percent of those who commit serious crimes are never caught. We live in a society where crime is rampant and crime pays.

Crime in school presents a particular problem for teachers. Some estimate that 3–7 percent of all students bring a gun with them to school. Students attack teachers every day in America. While this behavior is not defensible, attention to the principles of classroom management mentioned earlier can help in averting some of these incidents.

Substance Abuse

Alcohol is the most used and abused drug. Even though it is legal, there are serious short- and long-term consequences of alcohol use. Alcoholism is the most widespread drug addiction and untreated alcoholism can lead to death.

Tobacco is the next most widely used and abused substance. Some efforts are being made to declare tobacco a drug. Irrefutable evidence shows that tobacco use is a causative factor in hundreds of thousands of deaths each year.

Other drugs including marijuana, cocaine, heroin, and various drugs in pill form carry with them serious health, addiction, and emotional problems. The widespread illicit availability of these drugs creates additional problems. Many students engage in crimes to get money to pay for drugs. Others may commit crimes while under the influence of drugs. Still others may commit crimes by selling drugs to make money.

More than 90 percent of students have used alcohol by the time they leave high school. About 70 percent of high school graduates have used other illegal drugs. Awareness programs that focus on drug use can have some positive effects. However, most drug and alcohol abuse and addiction has other underlying causes. These causes must be addressed for any program to be effective.

Substance abuse has a devastating effect on the unborn child. Children born to substance-abusing mothers are addicted themselves. These babies frequently have low body weight and brain damage. These babies may be doomed to a life of physical and intellectual problems.

Sex

Many teens, and preteens, are sexually active. While many of these children profess to know about sex, they do not. It is in this environment that we find increases in pregnancies, abortions, dropouts, and ruined lives. Sex spreads disease. So we also note increases in syphilis, gonorrhea, and other sexually transmitted diseases.

About 10 percent of girls in school will become pregnant. Teenage pregnancy is the primary reason why girls drop out of high school. These girls seldom receive appropriate help from the child's father and are often destined for a life of poverty and dependence.

AIDS

AIDS stands for Acquired Immune Deficiency Syndrome. AIDS is a breakdown in the body's immune system caused by a virus called HIV. This virus can be detected with blood tests. People with HIV may take 10 years or longer to develop AIDS. Those who develop AIDS die.

The HIV virus is transmitted by infected blood and other bodily fluids. Sexual relations and contact with infected blood, including blood injected with shared hypodermic needles, are all examples of ways that AIDS can be transmitted. Some 2 to 5 percent of the teens in some urban areas may be HIV positive.

Students can try to avoid becoming HIV positive by reducing their risk factors. Abstinence from sex and never injecting drugs will virtually eliminate the likelihood that a teenager will become HIV positive. Less effective measures can be taken to help sexually active students reduce the likelihood of becoming HIV positive. Girls run a higher risk than boys of becoming HIV positive through sexual activity.

Acquiring the HIV virus is associated with drug and alcohol use. Even when students know the risks, and how to avoid them, alcohol and drug use can lower inhibitions and lead to unsafe practices.

Dropouts

About 10 percent of white students, 15 percent of African American students, and 30 percent of Hispanic students drop out of school. Dropout rates are worst in urban areas, with over half the students dropping out of some schools. High school dropouts are usually headed for a life of lower wages and poorer living conditions.

Many of these students feel alienated from society or school and need support or alternative learning environments. Intervention, counseling, and alternative programs such as therapeutic high school, vocational high schools, and other special learning arrangements can help prevent a student from dropping out.

Child Abuse

Child abuse is the secret destroyer of children's lives. Some estimate that between two and three million children are abused each year. Child abuse is a primary cause of violent youth, runaways, and drug abusers.

Physical and sexual abuse are the most destructive of the abuses heaped upon children. Contrary to popular belief, most child abuse is perpetrated by family members, relatives, and friends. Younger children are often incapable of talking about their abuse and may not reveal it even when asked.

In many states, teachers are required to report suspected child abuse. When child abuse is suspected, a teacher should follow the guidelines given by the school, the district, or the state.

ETHNICITY

The population of the United States is about 70 percent Caucasian, 10 percent African-American, 10 percent Hispanic, 6 percent Asian, and 2 percent Indian or Eskimo. Hispanics are the fastest growing ethnic group. By the year 2020 America's school population will be about evenly divided between Caucasian and non-Caucasian students.

About 15 percent of the families in the United States live below the poverty level. Some 30 percent of African American and Hispanic families do so, and an astonishing 65 percent of Native American families also live below the poverty level.

Minority Ethnic Groups

Hispanics

Hispanics come predominantly from Mexico and from other countries in Central and South America and the Caribbean. Many Mexican American families have been in this country for more than 100 years. Puerto Ricans form another large Hispanic group.

Language is the primary difficulty faced by this ethnic group. About half of the Hispanics in this country speak Spanish as their first language.

The nature of the Hispanic population varies by region. Most Hispanics in California or their forbearers are from Mexico. Many Hispanics living in and around New York City are from Puerto Rico or the Dominican Republic, while many Hispanics in Florida trace their ancestry to Cuba.

Hispanic students have more school problems than Caucasian students. Hispanics are disproportionately poor and low achieving.

African-Americans

African-Americans have been in this country for centuries, but they began their lives here as slaves. There is not a recent history of large-scale African immigration to the United States.

Their status as slaves and second-class citizens denied African-Americans the education, experience, and self-sufficiency needed for upward social mobility. Even when African-Americans developed these qualities, they were frequently discriminated against just because of their race. It took almost 200 years from the founding of this country for the Supreme Court to rule that overt school segregation was unconstitutional. Of course, de facto segregation continues to exist.

Many African-Americans have achieved middle class status. However, the overwhelming proportion of poor in urban areas are African Americans. The unemployment rate of young African-Americans can be near 50 percent in some areas.

Native Americans

Groups of Eskimos and other Native Americans have lived on the North American continent for over 25,000 years. Most Native Americans living today are ancestors of tribes conquered and put on reservations about 100 years ago.

During this time of conquest, treaties made with tribes were frequently broken. Native Americans lost their lands and their way of life. They were made dependent on the federal government for subsidies and were not able to develop the education, experience, or self-sufficiency needed for upward mobility.

Native Americans have the largest family size and fastest growth rate of any ethnic group. They also have among the highest suicide and alcoholism rates of any ethnic group.

Native Americans are disproportionally poor and disenfranchised. They live in poverty on reservations and are often alienated when they move off reservations to metropolitan areas.

Asian-Americans

Asian-Americans are predominately Chinese and Japanese together with recent immigrants from Korea and Southeast Asia. Asian-Americans represent a countertrend among American minorities. Their achievement and success tend to be above the national average.

Many recent immigrants do not have the educational background of other Asian-Americans. They tend to be more ghettoized and to attain a lower SES than other Asian-Americans.

However, overall, Asian students perform better on American standardized tests than non-Asian students. This finding holds also for those Asian-Americans who immigrated to this country unable to speak, read, or understand English.

Some researchers have said that a particular work ethic currently found in Asian countries together with a strong family structure are responsible for these trends.

HUMAN DEVELOPMENT TARGETED TEST

These items will help you practice for the real CSET. These items have the same form and test the same material as the CSET items and test material. The items you encounter on the real CSET may have a different emphasis and may be more complete.

Instructions

Mark your answers on the sheet provided below. Complete the items in 20 minutes or less. Correct your answer sheet using the answers on page 393.

1 Ⓐ Ⓑ Ⓒ Ⓓ	5 Ⓐ Ⓑ Ⓒ Ⓓ	9 Ⓐ Ⓑ Ⓒ Ⓓ	13 Ⓐ Ⓑ Ⓒ Ⓓ	17 Ⓐ Ⓑ Ⓒ Ⓓ
2 Ⓐ Ⓑ Ⓒ Ⓓ	6 Ⓐ Ⓑ Ⓒ Ⓓ	10 Ⓐ Ⓑ Ⓒ Ⓓ	14 Ⓐ Ⓑ Ⓒ Ⓓ	18 Ⓐ Ⓑ Ⓒ Ⓓ
3 Ⓐ Ⓑ Ⓒ Ⓓ	7 Ⓐ Ⓑ Ⓒ Ⓓ	11 Ⓐ Ⓑ Ⓒ Ⓓ	15 Ⓐ Ⓑ Ⓒ Ⓓ	19 Ⓐ Ⓑ Ⓒ Ⓓ
4 Ⓐ Ⓑ Ⓒ Ⓓ	8 Ⓐ Ⓑ Ⓒ Ⓓ	12 Ⓐ Ⓑ Ⓒ Ⓓ	16 Ⓐ Ⓑ Ⓒ Ⓓ	20 Ⓐ Ⓑ Ⓒ Ⓓ

1. Which of the following best describes the current state of the American family?
   (A) Most families don't have a working father, a mother at home, and children in school.
   (B) Most families today consist of two full-time working parents with children in day care.
   (C) Single parent families are headed by fathers.
   (D) Married people are choosing to start careers before they start families.

2. Research shows that modeling is an appropriate way of modifying behavior. Which of the following is an example of a good modeling technique?
   (A) Show students how to construct replicas of historic buildings.
   (B) Respond courteously to students' questions.
   (C) Demonstrate students' inappropriate behavior.
   (D) Stress the importance of appearance and show students how to dress.

3. Which of the following is an appropriate reinforcement of student behavior?
   (A) Grading on the basis of performance
   (B) Praising appropriate behavior
   (C) Explaining that students will lose privileges
   (D) Ignoring inappropriate behavior

4. Which of the following educational practices best reflects B.F. Skinner's model of learning?
   (A) Active involvement of students in learning
   (B) Token reinforcement of student's success
   (C) Problem solving as the central focus of instruction
   (D) Manipulative materials to help students learn

5. An adult honestly discusses her or his sexual abuse as a child. The adult does not say who the abuser was, but health professionals know that the abuser is most likely
   (A) a teacher or coach.
   (B) a relative or family member.
   (C) a convicted sexual abuser.
   (D) an intruder or thief.

6. Which of the following best depicts the way in which schools have reacted to America's multiethnic and multicultural society?
   (A) The academic atmosphere of our schools is not affected by the ethnic and cultural backgrounds of the students.
   (B) Recent immigrant groups are accustomed to the academic atmosphere of American schools.
   (C) There is no longer a need for schools to deal with the cultural differences of students.
   (D) The schools have noted a shift toward cultural pluralism.

7. Which of the following activities would engage the student at the highest level of *Taxonomy of Educational Objectives: Cognitive Domain*?
   (A) Evaluate a book
   (B) Understand a reading passage
   (C) Analyze a written paragraph
   (D) Apply a mathematics formula to a real situation

8. Repeated testing of a fourth grade student reveals an IQ in the range of 110–115 and two or more years of standardized achievement test scores are below grade level. Which of the following is the most appropriate interpretation of these test scores?
   (A) The student's achievement and potential match.
   (B) The student is mildly retarded.
   (C) The student is gifted.
   (D) The student has a learning disability.

9. When it comes to the general characteristics of elementary school students,
   (A) all ethnic groups adapt equally well to school.
   (B) boys have more adjustment problems than girls.
   (C) girls are more physically active than boys of the same age.
   (D) primary students rebel against the teacher's authority.

10. Maintaining discipline in seventh through tenth grade is particularly difficult because
    (A) students are reaching puberty.
    (B) students are peer oriented.
    (C) teachers are subject oriented.
    (D) teachers are authority figures.

11. According to researchers, which of the following is the most powerful overall motivation for students?
    (A) grades
    (B) privileges
    (C) learning
    (D) personal satisfaction

12. Behaviorism was the first significant theory of learning. Which of the following methods would be supported most strongly by behaviorists?
    (A) cooperative learning
    (B) inductive teaching
    (C) practice
    (D) inquiry learning

13. Piaget wrote that children learn through a process of equilibration. Which of the following classroom practices is most likely to promote this process in children?
    (A) Teachers teach skills while using manipulative techniques.
    (B) Students learn a concept through the repeat-practice method.
    (C) Students learn concepts vicariously.
    (D) Students actively learn concepts through their own experiences.

14. Which of the following summarizes Glasser's Reality Therapy approach to classroom management?
    (A) Students are left on their own to discover the harsh reality of their own mistakes.
    (B) The teacher establishes clear rules and the rewards or punishment that accompany acceptable and unacceptable behavior.
    (C) The teacher explains all positive and negative outcomes in terms of the real world.
    (D) Students help develop and then accept the consequences of any rule breaking.

15. Eriksen's stages of psychosocial development describe
    (A) the emotional crisis which, when resolved, leads to further development.
    (B) Freud's stages of development in more detail.
    (C) stages of cognitive development for males and for females.
    (D) the social skills needed to be successful at each level of schooling.

16. Which of the following does NOT describe the impact of physical and mental health on school learning?
    (A) Inadequate nutrition can lead to inattentiveness and other problems that interfere with learning.
    (B) Alcohol and drug addiction are causes of abnormal physical and emotional development.
    (C) Most adolescents rely heavily on peer group approval and respond to peer pressure.
    (D) Alcohol abuse by expectant mothers does little if any damage to the unborn child.

17. When a learning theorist says that children can learn vicariously this means that
    (A) children can learn by doing.
    (B) children can learn through a wide variety of activities.
    (C) children can learn if there is a clear structure.
    (D) children can learn from others' experiences.

18. All the following teacher actions are examples of cueing EXCEPT
    (A) flickering the lights quickly.
    (B) glancing directly at a student.
    (C) holding up an arm.
    (D) snapping fingers before asking a question.

19. Which of the following does NOT describe the American family?
    (A) A majority of families have mothers who work.
    (B) An increasing number of children are latchkey children.
    (C) Families are groups of people living together who are related to one another.
    (D) Less than 10 percent of American families have a mother (as a homemaker), a father (as the breadwinner), and the children.

20. Punishment can be an effective way to
    change students' behavior when
    (A) the whole class is involved.
    (B) it involves pertinent extra work.
    (C) it is used for limited and specific reasons.
    (D) it makes the teacher feel better.

TARGETED TEST ANSWERS EXPLAINED

1. **A** This choice accurately reflects the difficult state of American families.

2. **B** Modeling means a teacher acts as he or she wants students to act.

3. **B** Praise reinforces, while (D) ignoring inappropriate behavior is not reinforcement.

4. **B** Skinner was a behaviorist who believed in reinforcement.

5. **B** A relative or family member is most likely to be a child's sexual abuser.

6. **D** Schools have tended to embrace each student's culture.

7. **A** Evaluation is the highest level in Bloom's Cognitive Taxonomy.

8. **D** This description gives the classic definition of a learning-disabled child.

9. **B** As a group, boys have many more adjustment problems than girls.

10. **B** It is during these years that students turn most to peers for leadership.

11. **A** Grades are by far the most powerful student motivator.

12. **C** Behaviorists embrace practice and reinforcement, and would definitely not embrace any of the other choices.

13. **D** Piaget believed that students should learn actively through their own experiences.

14. **D** Glasser's theory is based on consequences for inappropriate behavior.

15. **A** Eriksen focused on emotional crises and their resolution.

16. **D** This question asks to identify the choice that is incorrect, as this choice is.

17. **D** Vicarious learning means learning from others' experiences.

18. **D** Cueing gives students time to prepare for a change in activity.

19. **C** This correct answer points out again the difficult state of American families.

20. **C** Punishment is most effective when it is used infrequently.

PART  VI

Two Complete CSETs
with Explained Answers

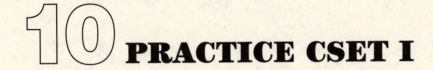 **PRACTICE CSET I**

TEST INFO BOX

On the real test, you may take one, two, or all three subtests in a five-hour period. You should take the practice subtests that you plan to take at the next CSET administration.

Take this test in a realistic timed setting. The setting will be most realistic if another person times the test and ensures that the test rules are followed. If another person is acting as test supervisor, he or she should review these instructions with you and tell you to "Stop" when time has expired.

SUBTEST 1 (page 387)   ~~| hr 40 min ea.~~

Reading Language and Literature	26 Multiple Choice and 2 Constructed Response
History and Social Science	26 Multiple Choice and 2 Constructed Response

SUBTEST 2 (page 411)

Science	26 Multiple Choice and 2 Constructed Response
Mathematics	26 Multiple Choice and 2 Constructed Response

SUBTEST 3 (page 427)

Visual and Performing Arts	13 Multiple Choice and 1 Constructed Response
Physical Education	13 Multiple Choice and 1 Constructed Response
Human Development	13 Multiple Choice and 1 Constructed Response

Once the test is complete, review the answers and explanations for each item as you correct the test.

Once instructed, turn the page and begin.

CSET I

Subtest 1

ANSWER SHEET

Record the answers to the multiple choice questions on this answer sheet.

1	Ⓐ Ⓑ Ⓒ Ⓓ	14	Ⓐ Ⓑ Ⓒ Ⓓ	27	Ⓐ Ⓑ Ⓒ Ⓓ	40	Ⓐ Ⓑ Ⓒ Ⓓ
2	Ⓐ Ⓑ Ⓒ Ⓓ	15	Ⓐ Ⓑ Ⓒ Ⓓ	28	Ⓐ Ⓑ Ⓒ Ⓓ	41	Ⓐ Ⓑ Ⓒ Ⓓ
3	Ⓐ Ⓑ Ⓒ Ⓓ	16	Ⓐ Ⓑ Ⓒ Ⓓ	29	Ⓐ Ⓑ Ⓒ Ⓓ	42	Ⓐ Ⓑ Ⓒ Ⓓ
4	Ⓐ Ⓑ Ⓒ Ⓓ	17	Ⓐ Ⓑ Ⓒ Ⓓ	30	Ⓐ Ⓑ Ⓒ Ⓓ	43	Ⓐ Ⓑ Ⓒ Ⓓ
5	Ⓐ Ⓑ Ⓒ Ⓓ	18	Ⓐ Ⓑ Ⓒ Ⓓ	31	Ⓐ Ⓑ Ⓒ Ⓓ	44	Ⓐ Ⓑ Ⓒ Ⓓ
6	Ⓐ Ⓑ Ⓒ Ⓓ	19	Ⓐ Ⓑ Ⓒ Ⓓ	32	Ⓐ Ⓑ Ⓒ Ⓓ	45	Ⓐ Ⓑ Ⓒ Ⓓ
7	Ⓐ Ⓑ Ⓒ Ⓓ	20	Ⓐ Ⓑ Ⓒ Ⓓ	33	Ⓐ Ⓑ Ⓒ Ⓓ	46	Ⓐ Ⓑ Ⓒ Ⓓ
8	Ⓐ Ⓑ Ⓒ Ⓓ	21	Ⓐ Ⓑ Ⓒ Ⓓ	34	Ⓐ Ⓑ Ⓒ Ⓓ	47	Ⓐ Ⓑ Ⓒ Ⓓ
9	Ⓐ Ⓑ Ⓒ Ⓓ	22	Ⓐ Ⓑ Ⓒ Ⓓ	35	Ⓐ Ⓑ Ⓒ Ⓓ	48	Ⓐ Ⓑ Ⓒ Ⓓ
10	Ⓐ Ⓑ Ⓒ Ⓓ	23	Ⓐ Ⓑ Ⓒ Ⓓ	36	Ⓐ Ⓑ Ⓒ Ⓓ	49	Ⓐ Ⓑ Ⓒ Ⓓ
11	Ⓐ Ⓑ Ⓒ Ⓓ	24	Ⓐ Ⓑ Ⓒ Ⓓ	37	Ⓐ Ⓑ Ⓒ Ⓓ	50	Ⓐ Ⓑ Ⓒ Ⓓ
12	Ⓐ Ⓑ Ⓒ Ⓓ	25	Ⓐ Ⓑ Ⓒ Ⓓ	38	Ⓐ Ⓑ Ⓒ Ⓓ	51	Ⓐ Ⓑ Ⓒ Ⓓ
13	Ⓐ Ⓑ Ⓒ Ⓓ	26	Ⓐ Ⓑ Ⓒ Ⓓ	39	Ⓐ Ⓑ Ⓒ Ⓓ	52	Ⓐ Ⓑ Ⓒ Ⓓ

Answers on page 440

1. Many English words follow common spelling patterns. Which of the following words has a pronunciation that does not follow the spelling pattern usually associated with that word?
   (A) Save
   (B) Axe
   (C) Sleigh
   (D) Neat

2. Phonemic awareness instruction is most effective with children when:
   (A) it focuses on many different types of phoneme manipulation
   (B) it is taught as phonological awareness
   (C) they learn the sounds along with the phonemes
   (D) the children understand that phoneme awareness is the same as phonics

3. Which of the following sentences is grammatically incorrect, but would be grammatically correct except for the irregular nature of English verb construction?
   (A) Blaire bringed the car to the mechanic.
   (B) Blaire hopped happily down the street.
   (C) Blaire were practicing a play.
   (D) Blaire speak to her friend yesterday.

4. Which of the following most accurately describes how the English language is linked to other world languages?
   (A) The English language was first developed about 2,500 years ago from the Spanish language.
   (B) Languages such as German and French contain many English words.
   (C) English uses the 26-letter Latin alphabet.
   (D) English developed first from languages in East Africa.

5. Based on recent findings, which of the following is the best approach to teach reading to young children?
   (A) Sight word programs
   (B) Literature-based programs
   (C) Phonics instruction integrated with literature-based approaches
   (D) Phonics programs

6. Based on recent findings, silent independent reading
   (A) has not been shown to improve reading achievement.
   (B) has been shown to improve reading achievement but not fluency.
   (C) has not been shown to improve reading achievement, but it has been proven to improve reading fluency.
   (D) has been shown to improve both reading achievement and fluency.

7. Which of the following is the best example of the phonemic awareness skill of phonemic identity?
   (A) A child recognizes the sound of "w" in the word "was."
   (B) A child recognizes the sound of the word "was."
   (C) A child recognizes the sound of "w" is the same as "was" and want.
   (D) A child substitutes the sound of "w" in "was" with the sound of "h" to form the new word "has."

8. Which of the following is NOT an effective text comprehension strategy?
   (A) Using graphic organizers
   (B) Careful detailed reading
   (C) Employing metacognition
   (D) Writing summaries

9. When we talk about teaching onsets and end rhymes to young children, we are talking about
   (A) written language that matches each syllable.
   (B) spoken language smaller than syllables but larger than phonemes.
   (C) written language found at the very beginning or the very end of a poem.
   (D) spoken language units smaller than a phoneme that combine to make up individual phonemes.

10. Which of the following sentences contains a possessive pronoun?
    (A) They were happy to have the day off.
    (B) John likes to ride his bike.
    (C) We don't know what to do with them.
    (D) They don't know whom to ask first.

11. In which of the following sentences is the underlined word used correctly.
    (A) The ropes helped the mountain climber with her <u>ascent</u>.
    (B) The runner <u>assented</u> the winner's platform.
    (C) The diver <u>ascented</u> to the lowest depths of the ocean.
    (D) The tree limb stood in the way of the cat's <u>assent</u> up the old oak tree.

Use the passage below to answer questions 12 and 13.

(1) Choosing educational practices sometimes seems like choosing fashions. (2) Fashion is driven by whims, tastes, and the zeitgeist of the current day. (3) The education system should not be driven by these same forces. (4) Three decades ago, teachers were told to use manipulative materials to teach about mathematics. (5) But consider the way mathematics is taught. (6) In the intervening years, the emphasis was on drill and practice. (7) Now teachers are told again to use manipulative materials. (8) Even so, every teacher has the ultimate capacity to determine his or her teaching practices.

12. Which of the following revisions to a sentence in this passage would be most likely to improve the style of the passage?
    (A) Sentence 1: The choice of educational practices sometimes seems like choosing fashions.
    (B) Sentence 3: The education system should not have to react to these forces.
    (C) Sentence 5: But consider mathematics and the way it is taught.
    (D) Sentence 8: Even so, every teacher can determine his or her teaching practices.

13. Which of the following describes the best way to rearrange sentences to improve the organization of the passage?
    (A) Move sentence 2 before sentence 1.
    (B) Move sentence 4 before sentence 3.
    (C) Move sentence 5 before sentence 4.
    (D) Move sentence 6 before sentence 5.

14. Base your answer to item 14 on this passage.

(1) Using percentages to report growth patterns can be deceptive. (2) If there are 100 new users for a product currently used by 100 people, then the growth rate is 100 percent. (3) It seems obvious that the growth rate of 100 percent would be better than the growth rate of 1 percent. (4) But a higher growth rate is not always better. (5) We must know the total number any growth percentage is based on to draw any conclusions.

Which is the topic sentence for this passage?
(A) Sentence 1
(B) Sentence 3
(C) Sentence 4
(D) Sentence 5

15. Which of the following is the best example of an invalid ad hominem argument?
    (A) "I must be right; most people agree with me."
    (B) "This is a matter of good and bad, right and wrong."
    (C) "You can't believe anyone like her."
    (D) "We don't need to hear from him; we all know the truth."

16. Most people feel at least some stage fright, particularly at the beginning of an oral presentation. The best strategy for handling this stage fright is to:
    (A) begin with a slow, well-thought-through introduction.
    (B) explain your nervousness to your audience.
    (C) make extra use of hand and arm movements.
    (D) use the whole stage; move actively to maintain your comfort.

17. The main reason reading directly from visuals such as slides makes a presentation ineffective is because:
    (A) the information on the visuals is not that important.
    (B) the audience can read the visual as well as you.
    (C) the audience can often not see the visuals.
    (D) you have to look at the visual to read and you lose eye contact with the audience.

Base your answers to items 18 and 19 on this excerpt from an oral presentation.

(1) Jean Piaget is world famous for his research on child development. (2) According to Piaget's research, children are at the concrete operational stage of development for most of their elementary school years. (3) However, in the early school years students are usually in the preoperational stage. (4) During the preoperational stage of development, students don't grasp many fundamental concepts. (5) Helping children make the transition from preoperational to concrete operational stages means striking a balance between not teaching a concept and teaching the concept with concrete materials.

18. Which of the following best characterizes this presentation?
    (A) It is primarily a narration
    (B) It is primarily opinion
    (C) It is primarily an exposition
    (D) It is primarily a reflection

19. Which of the following sentences when added to the presentation would make it primarily a persuasive presentation?
    (A) "Piaget conducted most of his developmental research on just a few children."
    (B) "Children may be hurt if instruction is not based on Piaget's stages."
    (C) "Primary teachers are most likely to encounter students who are at the preoperational stage."
    (D) "Piaget frequently collaborated with Barbel Inhelder."

20. Which of the following is usually the focus of an epic?
    (A) Profound feelings or ideas
    (B) Love and chivalry
    (C) Political ideas
    (D) A single mythological figure

Base your responses to items 21 and 22 on this story about the fox and the grapes.

A fox was strolling through a vineyard and after a while he came upon a bunch of grapes. The grapes had just ripened but they were hanging high up on the vine. It was a hot summer day and the fox wanted to get the grapes to drink a little grape juice.

The fox ran and jumped to reach the grapes, but could not reach them. Then the fox went a great distance from the grapes and ran as fast as possible and jumped as high as he could. He still did not reach the grapes. For over an hour, the fox ran and jumped but no luck. The fox was never able to reach the grapes and had to give up. The fox walked away sullenly proclaiming, "Those grapes were probably sour."

21. The structure of this story indicates that:
    (A) it is a legend
    (B) it is a fable
    (C) it is a lyric
    (D) it is a satire

22. The point made by this story is that:
    (A) height makes right.
    (B) the longer the run, the shorter the triumph.
    (C) it is easy to despise what you cannot get.
    (D) the fox would have done better by trying to solve the problem in another more clever way.

Use the poem "The Sullen Sky" to answer items 23 and 24.

The Sullen Sky

I see the sullen sky
Dark foreboding sky
Swept by dank and dripping clouds
Like ominous shrouds

A sky should be bright
Or clear and crisp at night
But it hasn't been that way
Oh dungenous day

That has been my life
And that has been my strife
I wish the clouds would leave
Ah, a sweet reprieve

23. Which of the following best describes the author's message?
    (A) The author's life is particularly impacted by rainy, cloudy days.
    (B) The author wants people to be free of worry.
    (C) The author is hoping life will get better.
    (D) The author lives on the coast where it is often rainy and cloudy.

24. What main literary technique does the author use to convey the poem's message?
    (A) Morphology
    (B) Alliteration
    (C) Allegory
    (D) Personification

Use this passage to answer items 25 and 26.

   I remember my childhood vacations at a bungalow colony near a lake. Always barefoot, my friend Eddie and I spent endless hours playing and enjoying our fantasies. We were pirates, rocket pilots,
(5) and detectives. Everyday objects were transformed into swords, ray guns, and two-way wrist radios. With a lake at hand, we swam, floated on our crude rafts made of old lumber, fished, and fell in. The adult world seemed so empty while our
(10) world seemed so full. Returning years later I saw the colony for what it was tattered and torn. The lake was shallow and muddy. But the tree that had been our lookout was still there. And there was the house where the feared mastery spy hid from
(15) the FBI. And there was the launching pad for our imaginary rocket trips. The posts of the dock we used to sail from were still visible. But my fantasy play did not depend on this place. My child-mind would have been a buccaneer wherever it was.

25. Which of the following best characterizes this passage?
    (A) An adult describes disappointment at growing up.
    (B) A child describes the adult world through the child's eyes.
    (C) An adult discusses childhood viewed as an adult and as a child.
    (D) An adult describes the meaning of fantasy play.

26. The sentence "The adult world seemed so meaningless while our world seemed so full" on lines (9) and (10) is used primarily to:
    (A) emphasize the emptiness of most adult lives when compared to the lives of children.
    (B) provide a transition from describing childhood to describing adulthood.
    (C) show how narcissistic children are.
    (D) describe the difficulty this child obviously had trying to relate to adults.

27. Use this map to answer the item that follows.

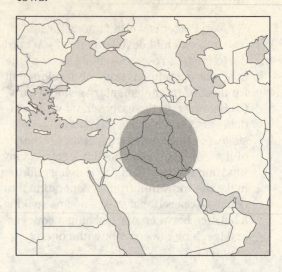

The shaded area on the map shown above best represents the location of which of the following ancient civilizations?
    (A) Egypt New Kingdom
    (B) Hellenistic Greece
    (C) Kush Kingdom
    (D) Mesopotamia

28. Which of the following best describes the area in which the Kush Kingdom developed?
    (A) Jungle
    (B) Desert
    (C) Plain
    (D) Mountains

29. Which of the following describes the primary impact of Confucius, who was born about 550 B.C.E. (B.C.), on Chinese life?
    (A) Regard for authority
    (B) An emphasis on religion
    (C) An emphasis on the way people thought, not the way they acted
    (D) A focus on rebelliousness

30. Use this list to answer the item below.

Civilization began on an Island
Home to the Myceneans and the Minoans
Invaded by the Dorians
Location of Sparta

The description given above best describes which of the following ancient civilizations?
(A) Assyria
(B) Egypt
(C) Greece
(D) Phoenicia

31. Which of the following best describes the impact of the Crusades, which took place from about 1100 to 1300 C.E. (A.D.)?
    (A) Richard the Lionheart conquered the "holy land."
    (B) Muslims and Jews were massacred.
    (C) The crusaders established the country of Turkey.
    (D) The pope moved from Rome to Constantinople.

32. Which of the following began shortly after the defeat of Antony and Cleopatra at the Battle of Acton, about 38 B.C.E. (B.C.)?
    (A) Roman Civil Wars
    (B) Pax Romana
    (C) Caesar was assassinated
    (D) decline of the Roman Empire

33. Feudalism in Japan was most like feudalism in Europe in that
    (A) shoguns were like lords.
    (B) Christians were persecuted.
    (C) leaders were overthrown by the people.
    (D) shoguns were like popes.

34. The Reformation in Europe led to which of the following developments?
    (A) The establishment of protestant religions in Spain.
    (B) The rediscovery of literature and art.
    (C) The painting of the Sistine Chapel.
    (D) The establishment of the Church of England.

35. Which of the following statements best summarizes aspects of the Mayan culture in Mexico?
    (A) The Mayans had human sacrificial ceremonies.
    (B) The Mayans had the most accurate calendar in the world at their time.
    (C) The Mayans extended their culture to the western coast of South America.
    (D) The Mayans were the predominant culture in South America before the arrival of Columbus.

36. When Christopher Columbus sailed he:
    (A) never returned to Europe from his explorations.
    (B) first established a settlement in what is now the state of North Carolina.
    (C) never reached the mainland of North America.
    (D) first established a settlement in what is now the state of Virginia.

37. Which line in the table given below correctly matches a description with the name of an event leading up to the Revolutionary War?

Line	Event	Description
1	Sugar Act	This act put a limit on the amount of sugar that the colonies could import.
2	Stamp Act	This act placed a tax on each legal document prepared in the colonies.
3	Boston Massacre	Several dozen colonial militia, including Crispus Attucks, were killed without provocation in the Boston Square.
4	Boston Tea Party	Hundreds of colonists dressed as Indians attacked the main tea warehouses around Boston Harbor and threw the cases of tea into the water.

(A) Line 1
(B) Line 2
(C) Line 3
(D) Line 4

38. Which of the following is the most accurate account of the battle leading up to the surrender of the British general Cornwallis at Yorktown in Virginia on October 17, 1781?
    (A) American troops trapped Cornwallis in and around Yorktown and forced him to surrender.
    (B) American troops and the American Navy surrounded Cornwallis at Yorktown and forced him to surrender.
    (C) French troops and American troops surrounded Cornwallis at Yorktown and forced him to surrender.
    (D) The French Navy and American troops surrounded Cornwallis at Yorktown and forced him to surrender.

39. During the state ratification process following the Constitutional Convention, the Federalist Papers were authored to support the ratification. In response, anti-federalists expressed their concerns, which were that:
    (A) there should be no federal or national government.
    (B) the Constitution replaced the Articles of Confederation, which formed a nation from only southern states.
    (C) the Constitution did not adequately protect individual rights.
    (D) the states could not properly ratify a document that established a federal government.

40. Use this excerpt from the Constitution of Article II, Section 1 to answer the item below.

    Article. II.

    [Section 1.] The executive Power shall be vested in a President of the United States of America. He shall hold his Office during the Term of four Years, and, together with the Vice President, chosen for the same Term, be elected, as follows:

    Each State shall appoint, in such Manner as the Legislature thereof may direct, a Number of Electors, equal to the whole Number of Senators and Representatives to which the State may be entitled in the Congress: but no Senator or Representative or Person holding an Office of Trust or Profit under the United States, shall be appointed an Elector.

    What is the impact of Article II, Section 1 on the election of the President of the United States of America?
    (A) The President of the United States is elected directly by the people of the United States foreign power.
    (B) The President of the United States is elected by a majority of the states.
    (C) The President of the United States can be elected by less than a majority of the voters.
    (D) The number of presidential electors is equal to the number of representatives.

41. The Declaration of Independence featured six self-evident truths including which of the following?
    (A) The right of the people to alter or abolish a destructive government
    (B) Equality of all who were not slaves
    (C) Freedom of religion, speech, press, assembly, and petition
    (D) Right to bear arms

42. In the table below, which line correctly lists a truth and a fiction about the event or person listed in the first column? For example, a correct listing of a truth about California is as follows. Truth: It has earthquakes. Fiction: It is on the east coast of the United States.

Line	Event or Person	Truth	Fiction
1	John Brown	Coordinated a raid in Harpers Ferry, Virginia	Captured by forces led by Robert E. Lee
2	Abraham Lincoln	Spoke against slavery	Spoke in favor of slavery
3	Dred Scott Case	Dred Scott has no standing in court	Dred Scott is property and not a citizen
4	Emancipation Proclamation	Issued by President Lincoln	Freed all slaves

(A) Line 1
(B) Line 2
(C) Line 3
(D) Line 4

Use this map to answer item 43.

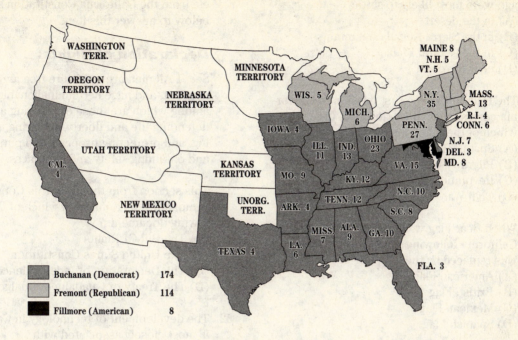

1856 Election map.

43. Which of the following conclusions can reasonably be drawn from the map above?
    (A) Were it not for Texas and California, Fremont would have won the election.
    (B) Buchanan was a strong supporter of the rebel cause.
    (C) Fremont was favored by those living in the northernmost states.
    (D) Fremont was favored by the states that fought for the Union in the Civil War.

44. In understanding the impact of the Civil War on all Americans it is worth noting that:
    (A) over six million prisoners were held in northern and southern camps.
    (B) the entire towns of Gettysburg and Atlanta were devastated and their entire populations were killed.
    (C) just as many men as women were killed during the war.
    (D) one in every thirty Americans was killed or wounded.

45. The Jim Crow South emerged following Reconstruction, in part because of
    (A) the Supreme Court's Decision in the Amistad Case that freed the slaves held on the ship.

(B) the Supreme Court's decision in *Plessy v. Ferguson* that ruled separate but equal accommodations were legal.
(C) the Supreme Court's decision in *Marbury v. Madison* that established the court's right to rule that federal actions were unconstitutional.
(D) the Supreme Court's decision in *Brown v. Board of Education* that essentially overturned the *Plessy v. Ferguson* ruling.

46. Which line in the table given below correctly matches a location in California with a description of that location?

Line	Location	Description
1	Sierra Nevada Mountains	Source of panned gold
2	Death Valley	Contains the Mojave Desert
3	Central Valley	Between the Coast Range and the Klamath Mountains
4	San Andreas Fault	At the Nevada border

(A) Line 1
(B) Line 2
(C) Line 3
(D) Line 4

47. Indian tribes in California about 5,000 years ago were most likely to settle
    (A) in the desert
    (B) in the Sierra Nevada mountains
    (C) in the Central Plain
    (D) near the coast

48. The founding of the first mission in California corresponds most closely in time with which of the following events?
    (A) Spanish Conquest in Peru
    (B) Pilgrims settle in America
    (C) Revolutionary War
    (D) Civil War

49. When Bear Flag was taken down in Sonoma, California following the Bear Flag Revolt, it was replaced by the
    (A) American Flag
    (B) British Flag
    (C) Mexican Flag
    (D) Spanish Flag

50. The internment of Japanese Americans during World War II was authorized by:
    (A) an Act of Congress
    (B) a Presidential Order
    (C) the Declaration of War against Japan
    (D) a Military Directive

51. Use Section 1 of Declaration of Rights article from the California Constitution shown below to answer this item.

Declaration of Rights.

Sec. 1 All men are by nature free and independent, and have certain inalienable rights, among which are those of enjoying and defending life and liberty, acquiring, possessing, and protecting property and pursuing and obtaining safety and happiness.

This section from the California Constitution is most like sections from which of the following documents?
    (A) The Bill Of Rights
    (B) The United States Constitution
    (C) The Declaration of Independence
    (D) The Treaty of Guadalupe Hidalgo

52. The development of technology in California is most closely associated with
    (A) Simi Valley
    (B) Silicon Valley
    (C) Central Valley
    (D) Transistor Valley

CONSTRUCTED RESPONSE ITEMS

Write your response on the response sheet that follows the item. Remember to write only in the lined area on the sheet.

Write a written response for each constructed response item. Remember that these constructed response items are rated using these three criteria.

Write your answer in the space provided on the numbered response form

> PURPOSE: Purpose means how well your response addresses the constructed response prompt.

> SUBJECT MATTER KNOWLEDGE: This means how accurate your response is.

> SUPPORT: This means how well you present supporting evidence.

Write your response for a group of multiple subject educators. The emphasis is on the subject matter in your response and not your writing ability. However, you must write well enough for evaluators to judge your response.

Assignment 1

Read the passage below. Then respond to the question that follows.

There was a time in the United States when a married woman was expected to take her husband's name. Most women still follow this practice, but things are changing. In fact, Hawaii has been the only state with a law requiring a woman to take her husband's surname. She may enjoy the bond it establishes with her husband, or want to be identified with their husband's professional status. Other women want to keep their own last name. They may prefer their original last name, or want to maintain their professional identity.

Some women resolve this problem by choosing a last name that hyphenates their surname and their husband's surname. This practice of adopting elements of both surnames is common in other cultures. As the modern woman increases her social standing, she will no longer need the pseudo support of her husband's surname. The future generations of women will offer their surnames to their new husbands at the nuptial table.

Discuss the bias in the passage above and the kind of language the author uses to express the bias. Be specific and give examples.

End of Assignment 1

Assignment 2

Use this brief summary of a child's phonemic awareness to answer the question below.

A child can recognize the /au/ in bow but cannot recognize that is the same sound as the /au/ sound in bough.

Briefly summarize the child's phonemic development and give specific examples of phonemic instruction that will help further that development.

_____

_____

_____

_____

_____

_____

_____

_____

_____

_____

_____

_____

Assignment 3

In 1861 the Civil War broke out in the United States. Use what you know about American history and respond to the following.

Name three important outcomes of the Civil War.

Choose one of these outcomes and describe how that outcome shaped the development of the United States.

End of Assignment 3

Assignment 4

The Native American population in California was reduced by over 70 percent during Spanish rule.

Name the primary cause of this decrease in population and describe in detail how it caused such a steep decline in the native population.

CSET I
Subtest 2

ANSWER SHEET

Record the answers to the multiple choice questions on this answer sheet.

1 Ⓐ Ⓑ Ⓒ Ⓓ	14 Ⓐ Ⓑ Ⓒ Ⓓ	27 Ⓐ Ⓑ Ⓒ Ⓓ	40 Ⓐ Ⓑ Ⓒ Ⓓ
2 Ⓐ Ⓑ Ⓒ Ⓓ	15 Ⓐ Ⓑ Ⓒ Ⓓ	28 Ⓐ Ⓑ Ⓒ Ⓓ	41 Ⓐ Ⓑ Ⓒ Ⓓ
3 Ⓐ Ⓑ Ⓒ Ⓓ	16 Ⓐ Ⓑ Ⓒ Ⓓ	29 Ⓐ Ⓑ Ⓒ Ⓓ	42 Ⓐ Ⓑ Ⓒ Ⓓ
4 Ⓐ Ⓑ Ⓒ Ⓓ	17 Ⓐ Ⓑ Ⓒ Ⓓ	30 Ⓐ Ⓑ Ⓒ Ⓓ	43 Ⓐ Ⓑ Ⓒ Ⓓ
5 Ⓐ Ⓑ Ⓒ Ⓓ	18 Ⓐ Ⓑ Ⓒ Ⓓ	31 Ⓐ Ⓑ Ⓒ Ⓓ	44 Ⓐ Ⓑ Ⓒ Ⓓ
6 Ⓐ Ⓑ Ⓒ Ⓓ	19 Ⓐ Ⓑ Ⓒ Ⓓ	32 Ⓐ Ⓑ Ⓒ Ⓓ	45 Ⓐ Ⓑ Ⓒ Ⓓ
7 Ⓐ Ⓑ Ⓒ Ⓓ	20 Ⓐ Ⓑ Ⓒ Ⓓ	33 Ⓐ Ⓑ Ⓒ Ⓓ	46 Ⓐ Ⓑ Ⓒ Ⓓ
8 Ⓐ Ⓑ Ⓒ Ⓓ	21 Ⓐ Ⓑ Ⓒ Ⓓ	34 Ⓐ Ⓑ Ⓒ Ⓓ	47 Ⓐ Ⓑ Ⓒ Ⓓ
9 Ⓐ Ⓑ Ⓒ Ⓓ	22 Ⓐ Ⓑ Ⓒ Ⓓ	35 Ⓐ Ⓑ Ⓒ Ⓓ	48 Ⓐ Ⓑ Ⓒ Ⓓ
10 Ⓐ Ⓑ Ⓒ Ⓓ	23 Ⓐ Ⓑ Ⓒ Ⓓ	36 Ⓐ Ⓑ Ⓒ Ⓓ	49 Ⓐ Ⓑ Ⓒ Ⓓ
11 Ⓐ Ⓑ Ⓒ Ⓓ	24 Ⓐ Ⓑ Ⓒ Ⓓ	37 Ⓐ Ⓑ Ⓒ Ⓓ	50 Ⓐ Ⓑ Ⓒ Ⓓ
12 Ⓐ Ⓑ Ⓒ Ⓓ	25 Ⓐ Ⓑ Ⓒ Ⓓ	38 Ⓐ Ⓑ Ⓒ Ⓓ	51 Ⓐ Ⓑ Ⓒ Ⓓ
13 Ⓐ Ⓑ Ⓒ Ⓓ	26 Ⓐ Ⓑ Ⓒ Ⓓ	39 Ⓐ Ⓑ Ⓒ Ⓓ	52 Ⓐ Ⓑ Ⓒ Ⓓ

Answers on page 452

1. Which of the following stages of skiing represents potential energy?
   (A) The skier is going to the top of the hill on a ski lift.
   (B) The skier is waiting at the top of the hill.
   (C) The skier pushes off from the top of the hill
   (D) The skier is skiing down the hill.

2. Use this portion of the periodic table to answer the question that follows?

6	7	8
C	**N**	**O**
12	14	16
14	15	16
Si	**P**	**S**
28	31	32
32	33	34
Ge	**As**	**Se**
73	75	79
50	51	52
Sn	**Sb**	**Te**
111	122	128

Which of these elements has 16 neutrons?
(A) C
(B) P
(C) Se
(D) Sn

3. Which of the following involves the most work?
   (A) Using all your might to try to lift a 50-story building.
   (B) Holding 100 pounds of weight perfectly still over your head.
   (C) Lifting 10 pounds over your head.
   (D) Dropping 100 pounds of weights to the floor.

Use this entry from the periodic table to answer item 4.

1
H
1

4. ^{3}H is an isotope of Hydrogen. What is the atomic mass of this isotope?
   (A) 1
   (B) 2
   (C) 3
   (D) 4

5. Use this table to answer the item below.

Line	Isotope	Neutrons	Mass in au
1	Carbon – 14	7	21
2	Carbon – 13	7	13
3	Carbon – 12	5	12
4	Carbon – 11	5	5

Which line in the table contains only accurate information about the Carbon isotope listed?
(A) 1
(B) 2
(C) 3
(D) 4

6. Which of the following best describes what happens to light when it strikes a flat mirror?
   (A) Light is reflected straight back from the flat mirror.
   (B) The light ray reflects back from the mirror at the same angle it strikes.
   (C) The light ray is refracted at many different angles back from the mirror.
   (D) The light is absorbed leaving only an image of the light waves to be viewed.

7. Written as a formula, Newton's second law of motion is (F)orce = (M)ass × (A)ccceleration.

   Which of the following is the best explanation of this law?
   (A) Something heavier will move slower than something lighter.
   (B) It is easier to move something if it has less mass.
   (C) The more acceleration you apply, the less mass there is.
   (D) The more mass there is means there is more force applied to it.

8. Which of the following best illustrates heat transfer through conduction?
   (A) A person feels heat when they stand near an electric stove.
   (B) A person feels heat when they stand in the sunlight.
   (C) A person feels heat when they stand in front of a hot air blower.
   (D) A person feels heat when they touch a steam radiator.

9. A ball is dropped and falls freely to earth. Which of the following graphs best represents the relationship between the velocity of the ball as compared to the time it has fallen?

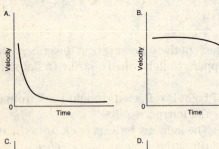

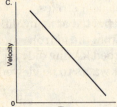
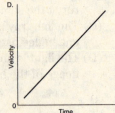

10. A green plant is placed in a terrarium and subjected to continuous light and to watering. Which of the following can we be sure will happen as a result of photosynthesis?
    (A) The plant will produce oxygen.
    (B) The plant will produce carbon dioxide.
    (C) The plant will produce water.
    (D) The plant will produce carbon monoxide.

11. Use the diagram below to answer the question that follows.

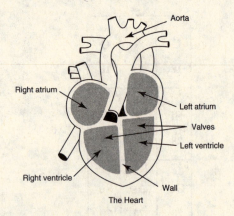

The Heart

From which chamber does oxygen-poor blood leave the organ shown to go to the lungs?
    (A) Left atrium
    (B) Left ventricle
    (C) Right atrium
    (D) Right ventricle

12. Which one of the body systems listed below includes a mechanical process?
    (A) Nervous System
    (B) Digestive System
    (C) Endocrine System
    (D) Immune System

13. An aphid is a slow-moving insect that sucks juices from plants. Some ants feed on "honeydew," excrement produced by the aphid. The ants protect the aphids and help the aphids get food. This relationship between these ants and aphids is best characterized by the term
    (A) mutualism
    (B) competition
    (C) parasitism
    (D) predation

Use the diagram below to answer items 14 and 15.

The diagram below shows a very simplified diagram of the kelp forest food web with the sea otter. The sea otter's favorite food is the sea urchin. The sea urchin's favorite food shown in the diagram is kelp.

```
┌─────────────────────────────────────────────┐
│         ┌───────────────────────┐           │
│         │      SEA OTTER         │           │
│    ┌────┴───────────────────────┴────┐      │
│    │  SEA URCHINS   SEA STARS         │      │
│ ┌──┴──────────────────────────────────┴──┐  │
│ │ SEAWEEDS   ALGAE   KELPS   PLANKTON     │  │
│ └─────────────────────────────────────────┘  │
└─────────────────────────────────────────────┘
```

14. It is most correct to say that energy in this food web:
    (A) flows in both directions.
    (B) flows upward in this food web.
    (C) does not flow in either direction.
    (D) flows downward in this food web.

15. Which of the following is the most likely short-term outcome if sea otters were hunted to extinction?
    (A) The number of sea urchins would be greatly reduced.
    (B) The number of algae would be greatly increased.
    (C) The number of kelps would be greatly reduced.
    (D) The number of plankton would be greatly increased.

16. Some cells respire aerobically while others respire anaerobically. Fermentation is an example of anaerobic respiration in that
    (A) the process occurs only during cell division.
    (B) the process does not require oxygen.
    (C) the process only occurs in aquatic animals.
    (D) the process produces oxygen.

17. Which of the following examples of cell reproduction results in a doubling of the number of chromosomes?
    (A) A human egg cell is formed.
    (B) A human sperm cell is formed.
    (C) A human cell enters the metaphase stage of mitosis.
    (D) Human sperm and egg cells combine.

18. In most cases, a plant must be pollinated before it can bear any fruit. Pollination is important because it provides:
    (A) sperm to fertilize the plant.
    (B) a rich culture in which seeds and fruits can develop.
    (C) the medium in which plant fertilization takes place.
    (D) a way to attract bees.

Use this diagram to answer item 19.

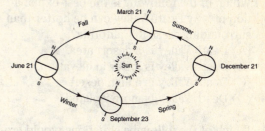

Seasons in the Southern Hemisphere

19. The diagram above demonstrates that seasons on Earth are due to:
    (A) the Earth's rotation.
    (B) the distance from the Earth to the sun.
    (C) the Earth's tilt.
    (D) the Earth's revolution.

20. The best way to characterize Earth's location in the Milky Way, our galaxy, is:
    (A) at the center.
    (B) near the outer edge.
    (C) near the top.
    (D) that we don't know.

21. The Fort Tejon earthquake in 1857 was probably the strongest earthquake in California during recorded history. The quake produced offsets along the San Andreas Fault showing that:
    (A) the earthquake is produced by a tilting of a major plate.
    (B) the plate west of the fault is moving toward the Pacific Ocean.
    (C) the earthquake is produced as one plate moves past another.
    (D) the earthquake is produced by a settling of a major plate.

22. A weather observer would use a hygrometer to measure which of the following?
    (A) Rainfall
    (B) Humidity
    (C) Wind speed
    (D) Air pressure

23. The hottest temperature of 134 degrees Fahrenheit in the Western Hemisphere was recorded in Death Valley.

    Which of the following is the best explanation of why Death Valley can be hotter than surrounding areas in California?
    (A) Death Valley is a desert area.
    (B) Death Valley is lower in elevation.
    (C) Death Valley is a high desert.
    (D) Death Valley is more isolated.

24. Which of the following situations would create the highest tides along the California coast?
    (A) A New Moon overhead
    (B) A strong westerly wind
    (C) A hurricane offshore
    (D) El Niño

25. A teacher wants to add salt to 100 milliliters of fresh water to match the salinity of sea water.

    About how much salt should be added?
    (A) 3.5 milliliters
    (B) 5 milliliters
    (C) 7.5 milliliters
    (D) 10 milliliters

26. A geologist is reviewing topographic maps for northern California, knowing that the maps will show:
    (A) the land features as viewed from the perspective of a hiker.
    (B) the rainfall and snowfall characteristics of a region.
    (C) the land features as viewed from above.
    (D) the location of cultural groups in the region.

27. An even number has two different prime factors. Which of the following could be the product of those factors?
    (A) 6
    (B) 12
    (C) 36
    (D) 48

28. Use this diagram to answer this item.

    What is the sum of the shaded regions?
    (A) $1\frac{1}{5}$

    (B) $1\frac{1}{10}$

    (C) $1\frac{12}{90}$

    (D) $1\frac{37}{180}$

29. Two types of elevators travel up and down inside a very tall building. One elevator starts at the first floor and stops every x floors. Another elevator starts at the first floor and stops every y floors.

    Which of the following is the best way to find at which floors both elevators stop?
    (A) Find the common multiples of x and the multiples of y.
    (B) Find the common factors of x and y.
    (C) Find the prime factors of x and y.
    (D) Find the divisors of x and y.

30. What is the value of the 7 in 1.37×10^{-2}?
    (A) $\frac{7}{10}$

    (B) $\frac{7}{100}$

    (C) $\frac{7}{1000}$

    (D) $\frac{7}{10,000}$

31. Use this number line to answer the item that follows.

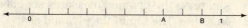

Which of the following could NOT be found on the number line between Point A and Point B?

(A) $\dfrac{27}{34}$

(B) $\dfrac{79}{86}$

(C) $\dfrac{81}{91}$

(D) $\dfrac{38}{54}$

32. The school received $5300 to use for eight different activities. A total of 91% of the money was allocated for seven of the activities, with the remainder used for the school trip. How much money was used for the school trip?
    (A) $477
    (B) $663
    (C) $757
    (D) $4,293

33. Use this list of numbers to answer the item that follows.

    524

    516

    528

    512

    502

    551

    The teacher demonstrates how to use front-end estimation to estimate the sum of these numbers. He ignores the numerals in the ones place and just adds the numerals in the hundreds and tens places.

    What is the difference between the teacher's estimate and the actual sum?
    (A) 6
    (B) 10
    (C) 18
    (D) 23

34. Which of the following best describes the arithmetic expression $1\dfrac{1}{4} \times \dfrac{1}{3}$?

    (A) There are 1¼ pounds of clay and we want to find an equal share for three people.
    (B) Each of three people has 1¼ pounds of clay and we want to find out how much clay there is altogether.
    (C) There are 1¼ pounds of clay and we want to find ⅓ more than that amount.
    (D) There are 1¼ pounds of clay and we want to find how much clay to take away to make ⅓ pound.

35. The landscaper recommended a mix of 3½ pounds of rye grass seed with ¼ pound of blue grass seed. If the lawn needs 5¼ pounds of rye grass seed, how many pounds of blue grass seed would that be?
    (A) ⅜ pound
    (B) 1⅛ pounds
    (C) 1½ pounds
    (D) 4⅛ pounds

36. Here is a multiplication problem with many missing digits.

    Each missing digit is represented by a □, although every □ does not represent the same number.

    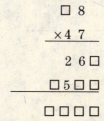

    What digit is in the tens place in the product of the two numbers?
    (A) 5
    (B) 6
    (C) 7
    (D) 8

37. Use this chart to answer the item below.

Diameter	Circumference
2	6.28
3	9.42
4	12.56
5	15.70

The table above shows the diameter and circumference of several circles. Which of the graphs below best represents this data?

A.

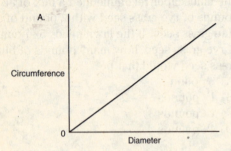

B.

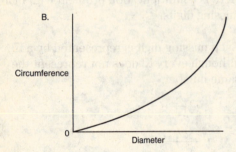

C.

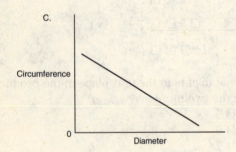

D.

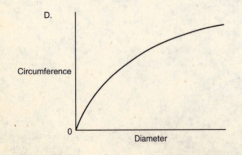

38. Cubes one centimeter on a side are used to form a square pyramidal shape. The bottom square on the pyramid measures six cubes on a side. The top of the pyramid shape has a single centimeter cube. How many centimeter cubes are used to make the pyramid?
(A) 81
(B) 91
(C) 100
(D) 216

39. Use this coordinate grid to answer the question that follows.

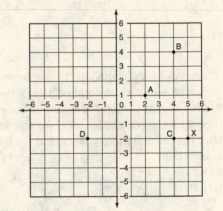

Point X is on a line with a slope of –1, meaning that which of the other points is also on that line?
(A) A
(B) B
(C) C
(D) D

40. A phone company has a rate plan of $0.29 a call and $0.04 a minute. Which of the following expressions could be used to find the cost of a call?
(A) (0.29 + 0.04)
(B) 0.04m + 0.29
(C) 0.29m + 0.04
(D) m(0.29 + 0.04)

41. Use this equation to answer the item below.

$$3x - 1/5\,(x + 5) = -x/5 + 33$$

Which of the equations below could have been a step on the way to solving the equation above?
(A) $3x = 33$
(B) $3x = 34$
(C) $13x = 156$
(D) $15x = 170$

42. Use this diagram to answer the item below.

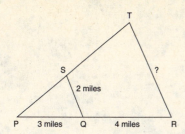

Engineers are building two bridges to span a deep canyon. They arranged the roads and bridges to form two similar triangles. △PQS is similar to △PRT. If the bridge from Q to S is two miles long, how long is the bridge from R to T?
(A) 3.0 miles
(B) 3.66 miles
(C) 4.66 miles
(D) 9.33 miles

43. Triangle ABC is an equilateral triangle. The length of side AB is 40 centimeters. What is the measure of angle B?
(A) 30 degrees
(B) 40 degrees
(C) 60 degrees
(D) 90 degrees

44. Use this diagram to answer the item below.

A 12-meter-tall pole is at right angles to the ground. Construction workers want to attach a wire at the top of the pole and then to a point on the ground five meters from the pole. How long will the wire be?
(A) $\sqrt{17}$ m
(B) $\sqrt{60}$ m
(C) 13 m
(D) 17 m

45.

A sphere with a volume of 36π is cut in half. One of the circles formed by the cut is shown above.

Which of the following is an accurate statement about this sphere if the formula for the volume of a sphere is $V = 4/3\pi r^3$?
(A) The surface area of the entire sphere is 18π.
(B) The area of each circle is 9π.
(C) The radius of each circle is 6.
(D) The surface area of half the sphere is 6π.

46. Use this diagram to answer the item that follows.

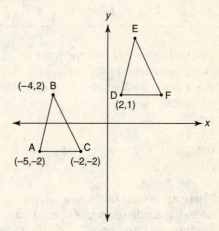

△ABC and △DEF are congruent. What are the coordinates at point E?
(A) (3, 4)
(B) (3, 5)
(C) (4, 4)
(D) (5, 5)

47. Cutting through a cylinder could produce all of the figures below, except

A.

B.

C.

D.

48. The car was set on cruise control to travel at a steady rate of 45 mph. The scale on the map for that area was 1 inch = 10 miles. What is the most likely length of the line on the map for the distance the car would travel in 90 minutes?
    (A) 3 inches
    (B) 4.5 inches
    (C) 6.75 inches
    (D) 27 inches

49. The area of a garden is 12 square yards. How many square feet is that?
    (A) 4
    (B) 36
    (C) 72
    (D) 108

50. Use this table to answer the item below.

January	February	March	April	May	June	July	August	September	October	November	December
3	7	6	4	8	7	8	6	4	3	2	2

   The table above shows the amount of precipitation each month, to the nearest inch. What is the median of these precipitation amounts?
    (A) 3
    (B) 4
    (C) 5
    (D) 6

51. There are 9 toll booths at a toll plaza. In one hour, the mode of the number of cars passing through a toll booth is 86; the median is 97, and the range is 108. From this information we can tell that:
    (A) at least 6 toll booths have fewer than 97 cars passing through.
    (B) the toll both with the most cars had at least 108 cars pass through.
    (C) most toll booths had more than 86 cars pass through.
    (D) most toll booths had 86 cars pass through.

52. A fair penny is flipped three times, and each time the penny lands heads up. What is the probability that this same penny will land heads up on the next flip?
    (A) 1/16
    (B) 1/8
    (C) 1/4
    (D) 1/2

CONSTRUCTED RESPONSE ITEMS

Write your answer on the response sheet that follows the item. Remember to write only on the lined area of the sheet.

Write a written response for each constructed response item. Remember that these constructed response items are rated using these three criteria.

Write your answer in the space provided on the numbered response form.

> PURPOSE: Purpose means how well your response addresses the constructed response prompt.

> SUBJECT MATTER KNOWLEDGE: This means how accurate your response is.

> SUPPORT: This means how well you present supporting evidence.

Write your response for a group of multiple subject educators. The emphasis is on the subject matter in your response and not your writing ability. However, you must write well enough for evaluators to judge your response.

Assignment 1

Read the passage below. Then respond to the question that follows.

An amateur grape grower intends to experiment with the impact of watering on grape production. At the beginning of the season the grower plants one group of Chardonnay grapes on one area of the hillside (Group 1) and a second group of grapes in another hill-side area several hundred yards from the first group (Group 2). Group 1 grapes are watered every day, while Group 2 grapes are watered just once a week. At harvest time the grapes from each group are weighed. The average weight of 100 grapes from Group 1 is more than the average weight of 100 grapes from Group 2. The grape grower concludes that more frequent watering is an effective way to grow grapes and plans to use this practice in future years.

Discuss the validity of the amateur grape grower's methods for determining the effectiveness of watering grapes and the validity of the grape grower's conclusion.

Use what you know about the factors that lead to plant growth and development to provide another explanation for the results the grape grower observed.

End of Assignment 1

Assignment 2

Use this diagram to complete this activity.

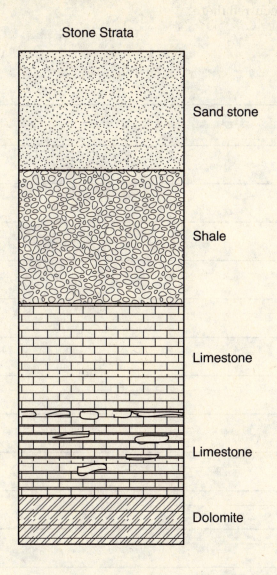

Stone Strata

Sand stone

Shale

Limestone

Limestone

Dolomite

In a recent search for aquatic fossils scientists found fossils for the animals shown below in the strata of the diagram.

Foraminifera (microscopic)   Shark Tooth   Gastropod (Snails)   Icthyosaur   Crinoid (Sea Lily)   Ammonite (Nautilus)   Pelecypod (Clam)

List five of the fossils in order from those that could have first appeared to those that could have appeared most recently.

What is there about the composition of the soil and rock layers that gives a clue about which fossils may have occurred there?

_____

_____

_____

_____

_____

_____

_____

_____

_____

_____

_____

_____

_____

_____

End of Assignment 2

Assignment 3

Use this diagram to complete the item.

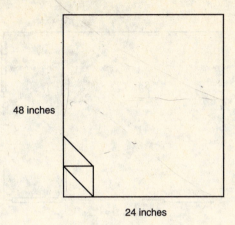

48 inches

24 inches

A printmaker wants to completely cover (tessellate) a poster shown above with triangles. You can see above one way that the work could be started. All the triangles must be congruent right triangles and the two legs must have whole number lengths.

Use what you know of geometry and the Pythagorean Theorem to do the following.
- List three different right triangles that could be used to completely cover the poster with no part of a triangle outside the poster boundary.
- List the fewest triangles with both legs the same length that could be used to cover the poster.

_____

_____

_____

_____

_____

_____

_____

_____

End of Assignment 3

Assignment 4

Use this room plan to answer this item.

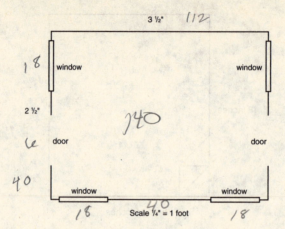

A contractor is going to paint the room shown above. The paint costs $28.03 a gallon. One gallon of paint covers about 400 square feet with one coat. One gallon can put a second coat on about 600 square feet. The ceiling is 10 feet high, doors are 8 feet high, and windows are 4 feet high. Doors and windows are 3 feet wide.

Find the number of gallons of paint to put two coats on the walls and the ceiling.
Find the cost of the paint to complete the work.

_____

_____

_____

_____

_____

_____

_____

_____

_____

End of Assignment 4

CSET I
Subtest 3

ANSWER SHEET

Record the answers to the multiple choice questions on this answer sheet.

1 Ⓐ Ⓑ Ⓒ Ⓓ	14 Ⓐ Ⓑ Ⓒ Ⓓ	27 Ⓐ Ⓑ Ⓒ Ⓓ
2 Ⓐ Ⓑ Ⓒ Ⓓ	15 Ⓐ Ⓑ Ⓒ Ⓓ	28 Ⓐ Ⓑ Ⓒ Ⓓ
3 Ⓐ Ⓑ Ⓒ Ⓓ	16 Ⓐ Ⓑ Ⓒ Ⓓ	29 Ⓐ Ⓑ Ⓒ Ⓓ
4 Ⓐ Ⓑ Ⓒ Ⓓ	17 Ⓐ Ⓑ Ⓒ Ⓓ	30 Ⓐ Ⓑ Ⓒ Ⓓ
5 Ⓐ Ⓑ Ⓒ Ⓓ	18 Ⓐ Ⓑ Ⓒ Ⓓ	31 Ⓐ Ⓑ Ⓒ Ⓓ
6 Ⓐ Ⓑ Ⓒ Ⓓ	19 Ⓐ Ⓑ Ⓒ Ⓓ	32 Ⓐ Ⓑ Ⓒ Ⓓ
7 Ⓐ Ⓑ Ⓒ Ⓓ	20 Ⓐ Ⓑ Ⓒ Ⓓ	33 Ⓐ Ⓑ Ⓒ Ⓓ
8 Ⓐ Ⓑ Ⓒ Ⓓ	21 Ⓐ Ⓑ Ⓒ Ⓓ	34 Ⓐ Ⓑ Ⓒ Ⓓ
9 Ⓐ Ⓑ Ⓒ Ⓓ	22 Ⓐ Ⓑ Ⓒ Ⓓ	35 Ⓐ Ⓑ Ⓒ Ⓓ
10 Ⓐ Ⓑ Ⓒ Ⓓ	23 Ⓐ Ⓑ Ⓒ Ⓓ	36 Ⓐ Ⓑ Ⓒ Ⓓ
11 Ⓐ Ⓑ Ⓒ Ⓓ	24 Ⓐ Ⓑ Ⓒ Ⓓ	37 Ⓐ Ⓑ Ⓒ Ⓓ
12 Ⓐ Ⓑ Ⓒ Ⓓ	25 Ⓐ Ⓑ Ⓒ Ⓓ	38 Ⓐ Ⓑ Ⓒ Ⓓ
13 Ⓐ Ⓑ Ⓒ Ⓓ	26 Ⓐ Ⓑ Ⓒ Ⓓ	39 Ⓐ Ⓑ Ⓒ Ⓓ

Answers on page 440

1. An elementary school teacher engages students in the following physical education activity.

> Students walk continuously around the gym floor.
>
> Then students walk around the floor stopping for five seconds every three steps.
>
> Students walk backward continuously around the gym floor.
>
> Then students walk backward around the floor stopping for five seconds every three steps.

This activity is most likely designed to help students:
(A) experience the difference between backward and forward locomotion.
(B) develop time-movement locomotor awareness.
(C) experience the difference between free flow and bound flow.
(D) warm up for subsequent physical activities.

2. Which of the following best describes the manipulative skill of striking?
(A) Strong movement from a best arm position
(B) Placing a bat or racquet against a ball
(C) An open-hand movement against a ball
(D) A purposeful semicircular leg or arm movement

3. In softball, which of the following will best help a batter strike the ball?
(A) Maintaining an upright stance in the batter's box
(B) Holding the bat above the shoulder
(C) Maintaining eye contact with the ball
(D) Holding the elbow of the upper grasping hand at right angles with the body

4. Which of the lines in the table shown below correctly pairs a physical activity with the type of skill?

LINE	ACTIVITY	SKILL TYPE
1	Jumping up toward a basketball backboard	Manipulative
2	Throwing a basketball	Locomotor
3	Stretching to receive a basketball pass	Non-Locomotor
4	Jumping to get a basketball rebound	Balance

(A) Line 1
(B) Line 2
(C) Line 3
(D) Line 4

5. Which of the following activities is an example of a manipulative skill?
(A) Pulling a rope
(B) Bending over
(C) Jumping up
(D) Turning around

6. A teacher is explaining the value of a cardiovascular fitness program. Which of the following would most properly be a part of the teacher's explanation?
(A) Lowers HDL cholesterol
(B) Raises LDL cholesterol
(C) Raises muscle strength
(D) Lowers heart rate

7. When designing an exercise program, experts say it is best to include:
(A) low-intensity exercise performed at regular intervals
(B) high-intensity exercise performed at regular intervals
(C) low-intensity exercise performed at unpredictable intervals
(D) high-intensity exercise performed at unpredictable intervals

8. Which of the following is the most appropriate way to monitor the impact of exercise on children?
(A) Monitor the child's pulse rate
(B) Observe how "hard" a child is breathing
(C) Take note of how much the child's eyes are dilated
(D) Feel the child's forehead to detect elevated body temperature

9. Which of the following choices is generally accepted as the best way to implement a self-actualization approach to physical education?
   (A) Emphasize the healthy competitive nature of team physical education activities.
   (B) Choose activities that will enable students to successfully participate with groups in the future.
   (C) Choose physical education activities that establish strong interpersonal relationships among students.
   (D) Match the physical education activities to the motivation and interest of the students.

10. When it comes to drug abuse, which of the following is most likely to be abused as children move through the school years into adulthood?
    (A) Alcohol
    (B) Cocaine
    (C) Heroin
    (D) Marijuana

11. Which of the following best describes a static activity for students?
    (A) Walking from one end to the other on a low balance beam.
    (B) A student balancing a book on his or her head as they walk from one end to the other of a high balance beam.
    (C) Holding a handstand on rings positioned about two feet above the child's height.
    (D) Standing on one leg with the other leg extended while on the gym floor.

12. Use these rules for Tee Baseball to answer the item below.

TEE BASEBALL

There are no pitches.

The person in the pitcher position throws a pretend pitch

The batter hits the ball from a batting tee.

Each player plays three innings in the field during a six-inning game.

There is a continuous batting order.

No scores are kept.

A coach may be on the field with the team.

Tee baseball is an example of a game that adapts the game of baseball by:
(A) not having a pitcher on the field during the game.
(B) using secondary rules to replace primary rules.
(C) limiting at-bats to when players are in the field.
(D) limiting the coaches to coaching while they are on the field.

13. Which of the lines in the table shown below correctly pairs a physical term and the definition of that term?

LINE	TERM	DEFINITION
1	Shape	Relative position of different parts of the body
2	Middle space activities	Activities performed when kneeling
3	Arhythmical movement	Movements performed to a steady beat
4	Force	Distance moved during a locomotor activity

(A) Line 1
(B) Line 2
(C) Line 3
(D) Line 4

14. Lisa sees Rita defending herself by fighting back after another student hits Rita with a book. Which of the following responses by Lisa would indicate the most advanced stage of moral development when compared to the other responses?
    (A) Lisa mentions to Rita that what she did was morally correct but against the school rules.
    (B) Lisa tells Rita that she should be careful because Rita might be punished for her actions.
    (C) Lisa finds a teacher and tells the teacher about what she observed.
    (D) Lisa tells Rita that Rita's parents would not approve of the fighting.

15. Which of the following is NOT a true statement about the nature versus nurture controversy about intelligence?
    (A) The nature part of nature versus nurture refers to heredity.
    (B) The nurture part refers to the environment and experiences.
    (C) Studying twins separated at birth has essentially cleared up this controversy.
    (D) It is difficult to isolate the interaction between these two factors.

16. A student has normal intelligence, but regularly scores more than two years below grade level in reading. Which of the following is the most likely explanation for these test scores?
    (A) The student has test anxiety.
    (B) The student has a learning disability.
    (C) The student has an emotional disability.
    (D) The student just performs better on intelligence tests than on achievement tests.

17. Which line on the following table shows a MISMATCH between a child's age and a child's actions?

Line	Age	Actions
Line 1	Grades 1 – 3	Students see the teacher as an authority figure.
Line 2	Grades 4 – 6	Students react well to teacher's instructions.
Line 3	Grades 7 – 9	Students resist teacher's authority.
Line 4	Grades 10 – 12	Students turn to peer group for approval.

    (A) Line 1
    (B) Line 2
    (C) Line 3
    (D) Line 4

18. Which of the following descriptions is *least* likely to require an intervention to help them with a transition to adult life?
    (A) A first grade student is very careful about trying out new ideas.
    (B) A sixth grade student exhibits a well-defined gender identity.
    (C) A third grade student feels he or she is accepted by their peer group when they actually are not.
    (D) A kindergarten student feels somewhat inhibited in school.

19. Children's tendency to ignore warnings about the dangers of drug abuse is most likely a result of:
    (A) a desire to be included in a group of friends.
    (B) an inability to conceptualize the real impact of drug abuse.
    (C) an insatiable desire for the euphoria caused by drugs.
    (D) a need to escape from an oppressed reality or a depressed life.

20. Sex-based differences in the physical growth of boys and girls is best characterized by which of the following choices?
    (A) Boys enter a period of steady growth around age 10
    (B) Girls enter a period of steady growth around age 8
    (C) Boys enter adolescence at about age 10
    (D) Girls enter adolescence at about age 10

21. Overall, children in school are most likely to achieve more as a result of
    (A) their intelligence
    (B) their sex
    (C) their SES
    (D) their study habits

22. Of the following choices, which is most indicative that a child is at the pre-operational stage of development?
    (A) The child demonstrates egocentric thinking.
    (B) The child is able to add and subtract numbers using manipulatives.
    (C) The child believes that a hidden object cannot be found.
    (D) The child can conserve numbers.

23. A child confides in the teacher and says that he has been abused, immediately leading the teacher to the conclusion that the abuser is most likely
    (A) a teacher, coach, or clergyman.
    (B) a relative or family member.
    (C) a convicted sexual abuser.
    (D) a stranger.

24. Students' lives are most influenced by their families, which are *least* accurately characterized by which of the following?
    (A) A majority of families have mothers who work
    (B) An increasing number of children are "latchkey" children
    (C) Less than 10% of American families have a mother (as a homemaker), a father (as the breadwinner), and children
    (D) Families are groups of people living together who are related to one another

25. Elementary school students frequently learn vicariously, meaning that the student
    (A) learns by doing.
    (B) learns through a wide variety of activities.
    (C) learns if there is a clear structure.
    (D) learns from others' experiences.

26. Which of the following best describes the role of ethnicity on a student's assimilation into society?
    (A) Asian-American students tend to perform worse on standardized tests than non-Asians.
    (B) Native Americans have the fastest growth rate of any American ethnic group.
    (C) A higher percentage of African-Americans live below the poverty level than any other American ethnic group.
    (D) Hispanics have the slowest growth rate of an American ethnic group.

27. The dance form ballet is based on
    (A) positions of the arms.
    (B) positions of the legs.
    (C) positions of the feet.
    (D) relative position of torso and legs.

28. Which of the activities listed below would be most likely to help elementary school students develop an aesthetic perception, an appreciation, of dance?
    (A) Ask students to view a dance performance and to identify the time and space elements in the performance.
    (B) Ask students to view a dance performance and to identify the cultural style of the performance.
    (C) Ask students to view a dance performance and to interpret the meaning found in the performance.
    (D) Ask students to view a dance performance and to interpret the history of the dance form.

29. An elementary school student knows about the pitch of a musical note. Which of the following will the child also need to know to fully understand the "note"?
    (A) chord
    (B) harmony
    (C) duration
    (D) timbre

30. Use the staff below to answer the item that follows.

    Which of the following songs begins with the five bars shown above?
    (A) "My Country 'Tis of Thee"
    (B) "Gray Squirrel"
    (C) "California!"
    (D) "The Star Spangled Banner"

Use the staff below to answer items 31 and 32.

31. In which key is this piece written?
    (A) B flat major
    (B) E flat major
    (C) F major
    (D) G major

32. Which of the following pairs of letters represents the piano chord played in the second measure? The right-hand note is represented by the letter on the right.

	Left Hand	Right Hand
(A)	D	F
(B)	F	F
(C)	F	D
(D)	G	F

33. As a part of a theater activity, an upper elementary teacher partitions the class into groups of three or four students. The teacher has a set of index cards that describe general situations. The teacher hands one of the cards to a group. Then the group has a few minutes to come up with a skit, which they then act out in front of the class. This activity most closely resembles what professional acting form?
    (A) stand-up
    (B) pantomime
    (C) comedy
    (D) improv

34. Each student in the class has an assignment to write dialog for a short story based on the other students in the class. Which of the following would be the most effective first step to take?
    (A) Write and rewrite until the dialog produced has the feel and texture of the students' everyday experiences.
    (B) Observe and listen to other students in the class.
    (C) Review other dialogs to find how to successfully structure their writing.
    (D) Review the rules for quotes and punctuation around quotes since the dialog will be almost entirely contained in quotation marks.

35. In a class, students will have the opportunity to produce and direct a brief dramatic work. Which of the following would best help distinguish the student's role as producer and the student's role as director?
    (A) The producer is responsible for planning and writing a performance, while the director is actually responsible for implementing the producer's overall scheme.
    (B) The producer follows the director's lead and makes arrangements for stage sets and props.
    (C) The producer is responsible once the performance begins, while the director is responsible for everything leading up to the actual performance.
    (D) The producer has overall administrative responsibility for the dramatic work, while the director has creative responsibility for the work.

36. A person viewing the visual art technique called a fresco is most likely viewing it
    (A) on a canvas.
    (B) in a church.
    (C) on a wall.
    (D) on a board or piece of wood.

37. Use the black and white image below of the painting by Winslow Homer to answer the item that follows.

["The Veteran in a New Field" by Winslow Homer. The Metropolitan Museum of Art. Bequest of Miss Adelaide Milton de Groot (1876–1967), 1967]

In this painting, the artist communicates the results of effort through:
    (A) the determination in the reaper's stance.
    (B) the fallen stalks of wheat.
    (C) the curved scythe handle.
    (D) the solitude of the reaper.

["Sunday Morning at the Mines." Crocker Art Museum, E.B. Crocker Collection. Dimensions 72 x 120 inches.]

38. The most famous painting of the California Gold Rush period is "Sunday Morning at the Mines," which shows
    (A) miners working deep in the gold mines on a day when most people were resting.
    (B) a contrast between carousing and Bible-studying miners.
    (C) a conflict between two groups of miners who have laid claim to the same mine.
    (D) a group of miners' wives waiting outside the mine entrance with lunch for their husbands, who are inside the mine.

39. In paintings, drawings, and architecture which naturally occurring proportion do artists frequently use to create the most pleasing appearance?
    (A) the harmonic balance
    (B) the chromatic sequence
    (C) the golden ratio
    (D) the symmetric proportion

CONSTRUCTED RESPONSE ITEMS

Write your answer on the response sheet that follows each item. Remember to write only in the lined area on the response sheet.

Write a written response for each constructed response item. Remember that these constructed response items are rated using these three criteria.

Write your answer in the space provided on the numbered response form.

> PURPOSE: Purpose means how well your response addresses the constructed response prompt.

> SUBJECT MATTER KNOWLEDGE: This means how accurate your response is.

> SUPPORT: This means how well you present supporting evidence.

Write your response for a group of multiple subject educators. The emphasis is on the subject matter in your response and not your writing ability. However, you must write well enough for evaluators to judge your response.

Assignment 1

A low balance beam used in primary grades is shown below.

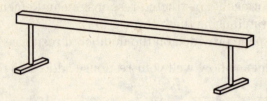

   Using what you know about physical education activities, describe two specific ways in which the low balance beam can be used to help primary grade children develop movement skills and concepts.

_____

_____

_____

_____

_____

_____

_____

_____

_____

_____

_____

_____

_____

Assignment 2

Use what you know about physical development to respond to the following.

Describe the physical developmental changes that occur in children between the ages of 6 and 12.

Review the changes in cognitive development that occur during these same stages.

_____

_____

_____

_____

_____

_____

_____

_____

_____

_____

_____

_____

_____

_____

End of Assignment 2

Assignment 3

Use the score below for the American song "Slavery is a Hard Foe to Battle," written in 1855 by Judson and sung originally by the Hutchinson family, to complete the activities below.

SLAVERY IS A HARD FOE TO BATTLE

Judson

Page from the sheet music "Slavery is a hard foe to battle." Music A-8636. Historic American Sheet Music. 1999. Rare Book, Manuscript, and Special Collections Library, Duke University. January 14, 2004. [http://scriptorium.lib.duke.edu/sheetmusic/]

Using your knowledge of music, write a response that:

- describes the genre, key, and tempo of this piece.

- explains how this piece could help upper elementary students explore a historic American period

_____

_____

_____

_____

_____

_____

_____

_____

_____

_____

_____

_____

_____

_____

_____

End of Assignment 3

PRACTICE CSET I

EXPLAINED ANSWERS

SUBTEST 1

1. **B** Words with <u>a</u> pronounced as in <u>a</u>xe usually do not end in "e." The word axe does not follow a regular spelling pattern. (A), (C), and (D) are all incorrect because each choice follows the regular spelling pattern for words pronunciation.

2. **C** Phonemic awareness is the ability to hear, identify, and manipulate phonemes in spoken words. (A) is incorrect because phonemic manipulation is just one part of phonemic awareness. (B) is incorrect because phonological awareness includes phonemic awareness, but also includes words and syllables. It is not effective to include words and syllables with phonemic awareness. (D) is incorrect because phonemic awareness is not the same as phonics.

3. **A** Substitute "brought" for "bringed." The word "bringed" would be appropriate, except for the irregular nature of English verb construction. (B), (C) are incorrect because the verbs "hopped," "practicing" are used correctly in the sentence. (D) is incorrect because, while a writer should substitute "spoke" for "speak," the problem is not caused by the irregular nature of English verb construction.

4. **C** English uses the 26-letter Latin alphabet and this is the clearest link among those presented to world languages. (A) is incorrect because English did not develop from Spanish. (B) is incorrect because most English words have foreign origins, including many German and French words. (D) is incorrect because English did not develop from languages in East Africa.

5. **D** According to experts, the research overwhelmingly supports the phonics program, alone, as the best approach to teach reading to young children. (A), (B), and (C) are all incorrect because research the programs listed, including the blended phonics approaches, are not as effective as phonics alone.

6. **A** Studies have consistently failed to confirm that silent reading helps students become better readers. (B), (C), and (D) are all incorrect because research does not show that silent reading improves either reading achievement or reading fluency.

7. **C** Phonemic identity means to recognize the same sound in different words. (A) is incorrect because it is an example of phoneme isolation. (B) is incorrect because it is an example of phoneme blending. (D) is incorrect because it is an example of phoneme substitution.

8. **B** Careful reading is not an effective text comprehension strategy. Good readers use strategies that are more flexible. (A), (C), and (D) are all incorrect because each of these choices presents an effective text comprehension strategy.

9. **B** This choice gives the definition of onsets and rhymes. For the word jump, "ju" is the onset and "ump" is the end rhyme. (A) is incorrect because onsets and end rhymes are smaller than syllables. (C) is incorrect because onsets and end rhymes are not directly related to poetry. (D) is incorrect because onsets and end rhymes are larger than phonemes.

10. **B** The pronoun "his" shows possession. The bike belongs to John. (A) is incorrect because the pronoun "They" does not show possession. (C) is incorrect because neither the pronoun "we" nor the pronoun "them" show possession. (D) is incorrect because neither the pronoun "they" nor the pronoun "whom" show possession.

11. **A** Ascent means the process of going upward, which is what the mountain climber is doing. (B) is incorrect because assented means agreed and it does not make sense for the runner to agree the winner's platform. (C) is incorrect because assented means to go up, but the diver is going down. (D) Assent

means to agree and it does not make sense for a cat to assent a tree.

12. **D** This sentence is too wordy. Replace the wordy "has the ultimate capacity to" with "can" to improve the style of the passage. (A) is incorrect because this change removes the parallel structure of the original sentence. (B) is incorrect because changing the words "driven by" to "react to" changes the meaning of the sentence and does not improve the style. (C) is incorrect because it alters the meaning from "consider the way mathematics is taught" to "consider mathematics" and it does not improve the style of the passage.

13. **C** The thought expressed in sentence 5 comes naturally before the thought expressed in sentence 4 and it makes sense to move it. (A), (B), and (D) are all incorrect because the sentences referred to in these choices are correct as placed in the paragraph.

14. **A** As frequently happens, the first sentence in the paragraph is the topic sentence. This topic sentence tells us the paragraph is about the deceptiveness of percent growth rates. (B), (C), and (D) are all incorrect because none of these choices communicates the main point of the passage.

15. **C** An ad hominem argument is an argument directed against a person and not against the person's position. (A) is incorrect because this choice contains an example of bandwagon. (B) is incorrect because it contains an either/or argument. (D) is incorrect because it contains an example of begging the question.

16. **A** There is nothing like being prepared for the introductory part of your presentation. This approach is most likely among those listed to get a speaker through initial stage fright. (B) is incorrect because you should never share your stage fright or uncertainty with an audience. (C) and (D) are incorrect because, while these can be effective techniques, these techniques are not likely to help alleviate stage fright.

17. **B** It can be an insult to read a visual aloud when audience members can read it for themselves. That does not mean you cannot summarize or call attention to visuals. (A), (C), and (D) are all incorrect because these choices are not the primary reason why you should not read directly from visuals.

18. **C** The main purpose of an expository presentation is to explain, and this presentation explains about Piaget and his operational stages. (A) is incorrect because a narration tells a factual or fictional story. (B) is incorrect because the presentation conveys only facts. (D) is incorrect because a reflection describes a scene, a person, or an emotion.

19. **B** The intent of a persuasive presentation is to convince the audience of a particular point of view. This sentence seeks to convince the audience to incorporate Piaget's ideas in their teaching. (A), (C), and (D) are all incorrect because they just continue the explanation, which is the hallmark of an expository presentation, not a persuasive presentation.

20. **D** An epic focuses on a single mythological figure. (A) is incorrect because a lyric is most closely associated with profound feelings or ideas. (B) is incorrect because this theme is most closely associated with a novel. (C) is incorrect because this theme is most closely associated with a romance.

21. **B** This is a version of a one of Aesop's better-known fables. (A) is incorrect because a legend is partially fiction but presented as fact. (C) is incorrect because lyrics are poems. (D) is incorrect because a satire uses irony and sarcasm to comment on the human condition.

22. **C** This choice paraphrases the moral of this story, often summarized as "sour grapes." (A), (B), and (C) are all incorrect because the sentiments expressed in these choices do not match the facts of the story.

23. **C** Things are not going well; however, the author hopes things will improve. (A) is incorrect because the reference to "this has been my life" in the last line indicates the poem is about larger issues. (B) is incorrect because nothing in the poem indicates any concern for others. (D) is incorrect because nothing in the poem indicates the author lives near the coast.

24. **C** (C) has a symbolic meaning. That is the case in this poem. (A) is incorrect because morphology is a branch of linguistics that studies morphemes. (B) is incorrect because alliteration is the repetition on an initial consonant. (D) is incorrect because personification attributes to an animal or object.

25. **C** This passage describes an adult's description of a setting, now as an adult and previously as a child. (A), (B), and (D) are all incorrect because none of these choices accurately describes the passage.

26. **B** This sentence provides a transition. It begins with a mention of the adult world and then ends with a description of the child's world. (A), (C), and (D) are all incorrect because these choices do not describe the primary purpose of the sentence.

27. **D** The shaded area east of the Mediterranean and east of the Red Sea corresponds to Mesopotamia. This region contains the Tigris and Euphrates rivers. Historians often identify Mesopotamia as the birthplace of civilization. (A) is incorrect because Egypt is located south of the Mediterranean and west of the Red Sea. (B) is incorrect because Greece is located on the northern shore of the Mediterranean. (C) is incorrect because the Kush Kingdom is located south of Egypt and west of the Red Sea.

28. **C** The Kush Kingdom developed in Africa on a plain along the Nile River. (A) is incorrect because the African jungles are found south of where the Kush Kingdom developed. (B) is incorrect because the Kush Kingdom developed in sub-Saharan Africa south of the Sahara desert. (D) is incorrect because there are no significant mountains in the area where the Kush Civilization developed.

29. **A** Confucius emphasized respect and regard for authority. (B) is incorrect because Confucius established a humanistic philosophy, but he did not set out to establish a religion, even though he came to be revered in China. (C) is incorrect because Confucius emphasized the way people act, not the way they think. (D) is incorrect because Confucius emphasized conformity and adherence to rules for behavior.

30. **C** Greek civilization began on the island of Crete and it was home to both the Minoans about 3000–1400 B.C.E. (B.C.) and the Myceans about 1600–1100 B.C.E. Greece was invaded by the Dorians 1100–800 B.C.E. Sparta is located in Greece. None of the other choices can claim these elements. (A) is incorrect because Assyria was located in Mesopotamia, an essentially landlocked region. (B) is incorrect because Egyptian civilization developed along the northern Nile River. (C) is incorrect because Phonecian civilization developed along the coast of what is now Israel and Lebanon.

31. **B** Both Muslims and Jews were massacred during the Crusades by the Christian invaders. (A) is incorrect because even though Richard the Lionheart spent most of his time in the Crusades while he was king, he never captured the Holy Land. (C) is incorrect because Turkish forces and the crusaders were combatants. (D) is incorrect because the "Great Separation" occurred in 1054, splitting the Catholic Church and establishing a second patriarch in Constantinople.

32. **B** The Pax Romana, 200 years of peace, began just after the Battle of Acton. (A) is incorrect because the Roman civil wars started after the Pax Romana. (C) is incorrect because Caesar was assassinated before the Battle of Acton. (D) is incorrect because the Roman Empire's growth began after the Battle of Acton.

33. **A** Feudalism refers to a European system in which lords protected vassals (knights) and then serfs in return for their service. The role of lords in this system very closely resembles the role of shoguns in Japan. (B) is incorrect because persecution is not an element of Feudalism. (C) is incorrect because the overthrow of leaders by "the people" may have occurred during Feudalism, but it is not a part of Feudalism. (D) is incorrect because a pope is a religious leader, and shoguns did have a religious role in Japan.

34. **D** The reform movement in Europe created Protestant religions, protesting Catholicism. Protestant religions spread to England and led to the creation of the protestant Church of England. (A) is

incorrect because the Reformation did not have a significant impact on religion in Spain, which remained a largely Catholic nation. (B) is incorrect because the rediscovery of literature and art occurred in the Renaissance, not the Reformation. (C) is incorrect because the Sistine Chapel was painted at about the same time the Reformation started, and it did not result from the Reformation.

35. **B** The very accurate calendar created by the Mayans, which features a circular design, is still in use today. (A) is incorrect because the Mayans did not have human sacrificial ceremonies. These sacrifices were found among the Aztecs. (C) and (D) are incorrect because the Mayans were located in Mexico, which is in North America.

36. **C** Columbus sailed the Caribbean and landed in what is now the Dominican Republic and the island of Hispaniola. He never reached the mainland. (A) is incorrect because Columbus did return to Europe during his explorations. (B) is incorrect because Sir Walter Raleigh established a settlement in North Carolina. (D) is incorrect because John Smith established the Jamestown colony in Virginia.

37. **B** This line includes an accurate description of the Stamp Act, which required a tax stamp for each legal document. (A) is incorrect because the Sugar Act taxed sugar in the colonies. (C) is incorrect because, while Crispus Attucks was killed in the Boston Massacre, five colonists, not dozens, were killed and there was provocation. (D) is incorrect because there were far fewer than a hundred colonists who boarded ships and dumped tea into the harbor.

38. **D** American troops trapped Cornwallis and his forces against the coast in Yorktown, Virginia, but the French fleet made it impossible for British forces to escape. (A), (B), and (C) are all incorrect because it was the combination of American troops and French naval forces that forced the British to surrender.

39. **C** The anti-federalists were not opposed to a federal government, but they were concerned that the Constitution did not protect individual rights. (A) is incorrect because the anti-federalists were not opposed to a federal government. (B) is incorrect because the Articles of Confederation were the first American constitution, and had nothing to do with the Confederacy of the Civil War. (D) is incorrect because many of those who preferred the Articles of Confederation did not feature a central government and were concerned whether individual states could act to form a central government. However, this was not a view held by the anti-federalists.

40. **C** This Article of the Constitution established the Electoral College. The popular vote chooses electors, not the president. The electors then vote for the president. In three recent presidential elections, a candidate received a majority of the electoral votes but did not receive a majority of the popular vote. (A) is incorrect because this article says that the people of the United States do not directly elect the president. (B) is incorrect because a plurality in a majority of the states is not enough to elect a president, even though most elected presidents do win in a majority of states. (D) is incorrect because as the article says, the number of electors is equal to the number of senators and representatives combined.

41. **A** This basic right was essential in order to formulate a document that abolished the British government. Look at the underlined portion of this excerpt from the Declaration of Independence.

> We hold these truths to be self-evident, that all men are created equal, that they are endowed by their Creator with certain inalienable rights, that among these are Life, Liberty and the Pursuit of Happiness. That, to secure these rights, Governments are instituted among Men, deriving their just powers from the consent of the governed. <u>That, when any form of government becomes destructive of these ends, it is the Right of the People to alter or abolish it.</u>

(B) is incorrect because the Declaration of Independence says that all men are created equal, with no exception for slaves, although delegates removed from a draft a section condemning the slave trade. (C) is incorrect because the First Amendment outlines these rights. (D) is incorrect because the Second Amendment mentions the right to bear arms.

42. **D** For a choice to be correct, the Truth must be true and the Fiction must be false. Only this choice shows a combination of a true statement and a false statement.

Line	Event or Person	Truth	Fiction
1	John Brown	This statement is true.	This statement is true. Robert E. Lee led the forces that captured John Brown at Harpers Ferry.
2	Abraham Lincoln	This statement is true.	This statement is true. Lincoln spoke in favor of slavery while he was in Illinois.
3	Dred Scott Case	This statement is true.	This statement is true.
4	Emancipation Proclamation	This statement is true.	This statement is false. The Emancipation Proclamation freed slaves in Confederate states.

43. **C** The map shading clearly shows that Freemont won in the northernmost states. (A) is incorrect because Texas and California did not have enough electoral votes to change the outcome of the election. (B) is incorrect because Buchanan did win in states that did not join the Confederacy and this is not the best choice from among the answers given and (D) is incorrect because not all of the states that favored Fremont fought for the Union in the Civil War.

44. **D** This very high rate of dead and wounded shows that the Civil War had an impact on all Americans. (A) is incorrect because this is about twice the number of soldiers who fought on both sides during the Civil War. (B) is incorrect because, while there was damage to these towns, it was nothing like total devastation. (C) is incorrect because the number of women killed in the war was a tiny fraction of the estimated 700,000 soldiers who died on both sides.

45. **B** Jim Crow Laws imposed racial segregation. The Supreme Court ruled shortly after the Civil War in *Plessy v. Ferguson* that it was legal to have "separate equal" accommodations, opening the door for segregationist legislation. (A) is incorrect because the Court's ruling in the Amistad Case was about 25 years before the Civil War began. (C) is incorrect because the Court's ruling in *Marbury v. Madison* was about 60 years before the Civil War. (D) is incorrect because the Court's ruling in *Brown v. Board of Education* was in 1954.

46. **A** The Sierra Nevada Mountains were the source of panned gold and the site of the discovery of gold at Sutter's Mill. (B) is incorrect; it is the vast Mojave Desert that contains Death Valley. (C) is incorrect because the Central Valley is between the Coast Range and the Sierra Nevada Mountains. The Klamath Mountains are north of the Coast Range at the Oregon Border. (D) is incorrect because the San Andreas Fault is near the California coast.

47. **D** Archaeological evidence indicates that most of these Native American settlements were near the coast. (A), (B), and (C) are all incorrect because, while there were eventually settlements in these areas, most of the early settlements were along the coast.

48. **C** The first Mission was established in 1769, just a few years earlier than the Revolutionary War. Just the approximate date of the first mission helps eliminate the other choices. (A) is incorrect because the Spanish Conquest in Peru was in the 1500s. (B) is incorrect because the Pilgrims settled in America during the 1600s. (D) is incorrect because the Civil War was in the late 1800s.

49. **A** The Bear Flag Revolt spanned a one-month period between Mexican and American control of California. (B) is incorrect because the British flag may have flown over California for brief periods, but not during this period. (C)

is incorrect because the Bear Flag replaced the Mexican flag. (D) is incorrect because the Spanish flag flew over California before the Mexican flag.

50. **B** The internment was authorized by Executive Order 9066 signed by President Franklin Roosevelt. (A) is incorrect because Congress did not act to authorize the internment. (C) is incorrect because the president issued the order after the United States declared war against Japan. (D) is incorrect because military directives did not authorize the internment.

51. **C** The heading "Declaration of Rights" and term "inalienable rights" followed by a list of these rights is most similar to the Declaration of Independence, which included the term "unalienable rights" followed by a list of rights. (A) and (B) are incorrect because the Bill of Rights and the United States Constitution establish rules for a government to follow, and are in that way unlike this section of the California Constitution. (D) is incorrect because the Treaty of Guadalupe Hidalgo was a "peace" treaty that ended the Mexican American War.

52. **B** Silicon Valley, south of San Francisco, and particularly Stanford University, is most closely associated with technological development in California. (A), (C), and (D) are all incorrect because the development of technology in California is not associated with any of these real and fictional locations.

CONSTRUCTED RESPONSE ANSWERS

Review the guidelines for writing constructed response answers on page 24.

1. The essential elements of this answer are that the bias is against women who prefer not to change their last name to their husband's last name. The author uses language such as "a law requiring women to take her husband's last name" and "identified with their husband's professional status" to express this bias.

2. The essential elements of this answer are that the child has difficulty because the word "bow" represents the standard spelling for the sound, but that "bough" is not a standard spelling. This child needs systematic phonics instruction to learn how to pronounce "bough."

3. The essential elements of this answer are that three important outcomes of the Civil War include: (1) the United States was a single country, (2) the XII, XIV, and XV amendments to the Constitution prohibited slavery, gave former slaves citizenship and voting rights, and that a period of reconstruction began in the South. There are other important outcomes.

4. The essential elements of this answer are that disease killed most Native Americans, while many others died of starvation. The main causes were the lack of immunity among Native Americans to European diseases and the unsuitability of Mission life for most Native Americans.

No book can effectively evaluate your answers, and you should show them to a college professor to receive a useful evaluation along with suggestions for improvement.

SUBTEST 2

1. **B** Energy is the ability to do work, and the sleigh skier at the top of the hill represents the most potential to create kinetic energy by skiing down the hill. (A) is incorrect because this choice does not represent any energy potential because there is no way to activate it. (C) is incorrect because a skier pushing off the top of the hill represents activation energy, not potential energy. (D) is incorrect because the skier skiing down the hill represents kinetic, motion, energy.

2. **B** To find the number of neutrons, subtract the atomic number (number of protons, shown at the top of each cell) from the atomic mass shown at the bottom of the cell. Among the elements listed as choices, element P has $31 - 15 = 16$ neutrons. Other elements have 16 neutrons, but none of these elements is an answer choice. (A) Element C has $12 - 6 = 6$ neutrons. (C) Element Se has $79 - 34 = 45$ neutrons. (D) Element Sn has $111 - 50 = 61$ neutrons.

3. **C** In science, work means movement of a body by force. This choice is the only one that involves movement. (A) and (B) are incorrect because these choices involve no movement, so there is no work. (D) is incorrect because no force is involved when an object is dropped, which means there is no work.

4. **C** The atomic mass of an isotope of an element can vary depending on the number of neutrons it has. The raised number (^{3}H) of the isotope gives the atomic mass. (A), (B), and (D) are incorrect because these numbers represent the mass of hydrogen isotopes ^{1}H, ^{2}H, ^{4}H, respectively.

5. **B** First, eliminate choices (A) Line 1 and (D) Line 4, because the mass does not match the isotope number. That leaves choices (B) and (C). The mass is equal to the number of protons plus the number of neutrons. You may remember, and you can see in the partial periodic table for question 2, that carbon always has 6 protons. That means choice (B) is correct, because 6 protons + 7 neutrons equals a mass of 13.

6. **B** The phrase most often used is "angle of incidence equals angle of reflection." Light rays reflect back at the same angle they strike the mirror. (A) In general, light is not reflected straight back. (C) Light refracts through a prism, but it reflects back from a mirror. (D) The majority of the light that strikes a mirror reflects back.

7. **B** This formula means, "the more mass there is, the more force you need to accelerate it." Less mass means you need less force. (A) A commonsense example of a heavy airplane moving faster than a lighter bicycle explains why this answer is incorrect. (C) is incorrect because making something go faster at this speed does not reduce its mass. (D) is incorrect because more mass does not mean more force will be applied to it.

8. **D** Conduction means heat transfer by direct contact, as described in this choice. (A) and (B) are incorrect because these choices give examples of heat transfer by radiation (no physical contact). (C) is incorrect because this choice gives an example of heat transfer by convection (moving air).

9. **D** Velocity is the rate at which an object moves. A free-falling object accelerates, increases velocity, at a constant rate. This graph best represents that the velocity of a falling body increases as time increases. (A) is incorrect because this graph shows that velocity decreases as time increases, with a time delay. (B) is incorrect because there is no time delay in the increase of velocity, as this graph shows. (C) is incorrect because this graph shows that velocity decreases as time increases.

10. **A** Photosynthesis in a green plant produces oxygen, along with carbohydrates (sugar and starch). (B) is incorrect because photosynthesis uses, but does not produce, carbon dioxide. (C) is incorrect because photosynthesis uses, but does not produce, water. (D) is incorrect because photosynthesis neither uses nor produces carbon monoxide.

11. **D** Oxygen-poor blood enters the lungs from the right ventricle. (A) is incorrect because oxygen-rich blood enters the left atrium from the lungs. (B) is incorrect because blood goes from the left ventricle to the body. (C) is incorrect because blood enters the right atrium from the body.

12. **B** The teeth help digestion through a mechanical process. Stomach muscle contractions during digestion are also a mechanical process. (A), (C), and (D) are all incorrect because none of these systems include a mechanical process.

13. **A** Both the aphids and the ants benefit from this relationship. That is the definition of mutualism. (B) is incorrect because ants and aphids do compete. (C) is incorrect because one organism does not benefit at the expense of the other. (D) is incorrect because one species does not eat the other.

14. **B** A fundamental truth of a food web is that energy flows upward as larger organisms eat smaller organisms. (A), (C), and (D) are all incorrect because these choices represent incorrect descriptions of energy flow in this food web.

15. **C** In the short term, the number of sea urchins will increase because sea urchins are the sea otter's favorite food. In turn, the number of kelps will decrease because they are the sea urchin's favorite food. (A) is incorrect because the number of sea urchins will increase with no sea otters to hunt them. (B) and (D) are incorrect because algae and plankton will decrease because increased numbers of sea urchins and sea stars eats them.

16. **B** Anaerobic respiration means respiration without oxygen. (A) is incorrect because anaerobic respiration is not related to cell division. (C) is incorrect because fermentation is the most commonly discussed example of anaerobic respiration. (D) is incorrect because anaerobic respiration does not produce oxygen.

17. **D** A human sperm cell and egg cell each has half the number of chromosomes normally found in an individual. When they combine, they form a zygote that has double the number of cells found in the sperm cell or the egg cell. (A), (B), (C) are all incorrect because cell reproduction through mitosis maintains the number of chromosomes found in the parent cell.

18. **A** Pollen contains the sperm that fertilizes the egg cells found in the plant. (B) and (C) are incorrect because pollen provides neither a rich culture nor a medium for plant development or fertilization. (D) is incorrect because pollination does not attract bees, although flowers on some plants attract bees to their pollen.

19. **C** Summer occurs in the southern hemisphere when that hemisphere tilts toward the sun, and summer occurs in the northern hemisphere when that hemisphere tilts toward the sun. (A) is incorrect because the Earth's rotation creates periods of daytime and nighttime. (B) and (D) are incorrect because the distance from the Earth to the sun, created by the Earth's revolution around the sun, does not create seasons.

20. **B** Earth is located at the outer edge of the Milky Way (A) is incorrect because the Earth is not located at the center of our galaxy. (C) is incorrect because the Earth is not located at the top of the Milky Way. (D) is incorrect because we do know where the Earth is located in the Milky Way.

21. **C** Plates move past one another to create offsets. (A) is incorrect because tilting of a major plate creates an uplift. (B) is incorrect because movement toward the coast creates a crack. (D) is incorrect because settling of a major plate creates a depression.

22. **B** A hygrometer measures humidity. (A) is incorrect because a rain gauge measures rainfall. (C) is incorrect because an anemometer measures wind speed. (D) is incorrect because a barometer measures air pressure.

23. **B** Death Valley's very low elevation explains why the temperature is higher there than in the nearby desert. (A) and (C) are incorrect because there are many desert and high desert regions that do not experience the extreme temperatures found in Death Valley. (D) is incorrect because there are many more

isolated areas that do not experience Death Valley's temperature extremes.

24. **A** Earth's tides result from the moon's position, and a new moon overhead creates the highest tides. (B), (C), (D) are all incorrect because the factors in these choices might create high waves, but the tides themselves would not be changed.

25. **A** Ocean water is about 3.5 percent salt. Adding 3.5 milliliters of salt to 100 milliliters of water would make the fresh water about 3.5 percent salt. Grams (G) are usually used to measure salt, but milliliters make the comparison easier. (B), (C), and (D) are all incorrect because adding these amounts of salt would not approximate the salinity of seawater.

26. **C** Topographic maps show an aerial view of land features. (A) is incorrect because a topographic map shows elevations, so although it would be useful to a hiker, it would not show things from a hiker's perspective. (B) and (D) are incorrect because topographic maps do not show rainfall or snowfall information, nor do they show information about cultural groups.

27. **A** The number 6 has two different prime factors, 2 and 3.
The product of 2 and 3 is 6 $2 \times 3 = 6$
(B), (C), and (D) are incorrect.
   (B) The number 12 has two prime factors, 2 and 3.
      The product of 2 and 3 is not 12.
   (C) The number 36 has two prime factors, 2 and 3.
      The product of 2 and 3 is not 36.
   (D) The number 48 has two prime factors, 2 and 3.
      The product of 2 and 3 is not 48.

28. **D** The first region has 2/5 shaded, the second region 5/8, the third region ¼.
   $2/5 + 5/9 + 1/4$
The denominators do not share common factors. Multiply them all to find the common denominator: $5 \times 9 \times 4 = 180$.
   $2/5 + 5/9 + 1/4 = 72/180 + 100/180 + 45/180 = 217/180 = 1\ 37/180$.
(A), (B), and (C) are all incorrect because these choices do not show the correct answer.

29. **A** The multiples of x and y will reveal at which floors each elevator stops. Find the common multiples to find at which floors both elevators stop.
For example, the multiples of 2 are 2, 4, 6, 8, 10, . . .
The multiples of 3 are 3, 6, 9, . . .
The common multiples we can see show that both elevators stop at the sixth floor. (B), (C), and (D) are all incorrect because the factors of a number are the same as the divisors of that number. Prime factors are factors that are also prime numbers. Divisors do not show at which floors elevators stop. The largest divisor of a number is the number itself.

30. **D** Begin by rewriting this expression: 10^{-2} means move the decimal point two places to the left.
   $1.37 \times 10^{-2} = 0.0137$
   The 7 is in the thousandths place. It has a value of 7/1000.
(A), (B), and (C) are all incorrect because these choices do not show this answer.

31. **B** The number line shows from 0 to 1 with a mark every 0.1 (1/10). The letter A is located at 7/10 (0.7) and B is located at 0.9.
Use your calculator to find the decimal value of each fraction.
(A) $27/34 = 0.79$ YES
(B) $79/86 = 0.92$ NO
(C) $81/91 = 0.89$ YES
(D) $38/54 = 0.703$ YES
Only choice B is not between Point A and Point B.

32. **A** 91 percent is spent on other things and 9 percent is left for the class trip.
   Use your calculator to find 9 percent of $5,300.
   9 percent of $5,300 =
   $0.09 \times \$5300 = \$477$
(B), (C), and (D) are all incorrect because these choices do not show the correct answer.

33. **D** Use your calculator.
   Find the estimate: $52 + 51 + 52 + 51 + 50 + 55 = 31\underline{10}$
   Now find the sum: $524 + 516 + 528 + 512 + 502 + 551 = 3133$
   Subtract: $3133 - 3110 = 23$
   The difference between the sum and the estimate is 23.
(A), (B), and (C) are all incorrect because these choices do not show the correct answer.

34. **A** Equal shares usually means division, but multiplying by 1/3 is the same as dividing by 3. This answer best matches the expression.

(B) The expression for this answer is

$1\frac{1}{4} \times 3$.

(C) The expression for this answer is

$1\frac{1}{4} \times 1\frac{1}{3}$.

(D) The expression for this answer is

$1\frac{1}{4} - \frac{1}{3}$.

35. **A** This is a proportion problem, and there are a few ways to approach it. Here's the more classic approach. It is a little easier to use decimals.
Write a fraction for what you know about the grass seed mix.

$\frac{3.5}{0.25}$ rye grass
blue grass

Now write a fraction with an unknown for the total amount of seed.

$\frac{5.25}{b}$ rye grass
blue grass

Write a proportion.

$\frac{3.5}{0.25} = \frac{5.25}{b}$

Cross-multiply.

$3.5\,b = 1.3125 \qquad b - \frac{1.3125}{3.5}$

$b = 0.375 \qquad$ That's 3/8.

(B), (C), and (D) are all incorrect because these choices do not show the correct answer.

36. **D** There is enough information to complete the entire problem.

$$\begin{array}{r} 3\,8 \\ \times\,4\,7 \\ \hline 2\,6\,5 \\ 1\,5\,2\,0 \\ \hline 1\,7\,8\,5 \end{array}$$

The digit 8 is in the ten's place.
(A), (B), and (C) are all incorrect because these choices do not show this answer.

37. **A** As the diameter increases, the circumference increases, and at a steady rate. That's because the formula for the circumference of a circle is πd. (B) is incorrect because this graph shows that the circumference increases at a faster rate than the diameter. (C) is incorrect because this graph shows that the circumference decreases as the diameter increases. (D) is incorrect because this graph shows that the circumference increases at a slower rate than the diameter.

38. **B** There are 36 cubes in the bottom square and the 25, 16, 9, 4 cubes on the fifth to second squares, with 1 cube on top.
Add 36 + 25 + 16 + 9 + 4 + 1 = 91
That is 91 cubes all together.
(A), (C), and (D) are all incorrect because these choices do not show this answer.

39. **A** The slope of –1 means the line goes generally from upper left to lower right on the grid.
That alone eliminates Points B, C, and D. A slope of –1 means move right one square for every square down. A line through Point A and Point X follows that pattern and shows the slope of that line is –1.

40. **B** This expression correctly shows multiplying $0.04 times the number of minutes plus the general charge of $0.29.
(A), (C), and (D) are all incorrect because these choices do not show this answer.

41. **B** Work out some steps for solving the equation.
$3x - 1/5\,(x + 5) = -x/5 + 33$
$3x - x/5 - 1 = x/5 + 33$
$3x = 34$
We can stop here. This step matches choice (B).
(A), (C), and (D) are all incorrect because these choices do not show this answer.

42. **C** Corresponding sides of similar triangles are proportional.
Write a proportion.

$\frac{3}{7} \qquad \frac{2}{x}$

Cross-multiply.
$3x = 14 \qquad x = 14/3 \qquad x = 4.66$
(A), (B), and (D) are all incorrect because these choices do not show this answer.

43. **C** Equilateral triangles, triangles with all sides the same length, have three 60-degree angles, regardless of how long a

side is. (A), (B), and (D) are all incorrect because these choices do not show this answer.

44. **C** Use the Pythagorean theorem to answer this question.

$a^2 + b^2 = c^2$, where c is the length of the wire.

$5^2 + 12^2 = c^2$

$25 + 144 = c^2$

$c^2 = 169$

$c = 13$

The wire will be 13 feet long.

(A), (B), and (D) are all incorrect because these choices do not show this answer.

45. **B** Eliminate choices (A) and (D). The question gives no information about the surface area.

Write the formula equal to the volume to find the length of the radius.

$4/3\pi r^3 = 36\pi$

$4/3r^3 = 36$

$r^3 = 27$

$r = 3$

That eliminates choice (C), so the answer is probably (B). Let's check.

The formula for the area of a circle is πr^2.

$\pi 3^2 = 9\pi$. That is Choice (B).

46. **B** Add (+1, +4) to get from Point A to Point B.

So add (+1, +4) to Point D (1, 1) and get (3, 5), which are the coordinates for Point E.

(A), (B), and (D) are all incorrect because these choices do not show this answer.

47. **C** There is no way to cut through a cylinder to produce rounded ends and straight sides.

(A) Cut through the diameter to create this shape.

(B) Cut through the diameter when the diameter and height are equal to create this shape.

(D) Cut diagonally through the cylinder to create this shape.

48. **C** To find the distance, write 90 minutes is 1.5 hours.

Then multiply 1.5 and 45 to find how far the car travels in 90 minutes.

$1.5 \times 45 = 67.5$ miles

Divide 67.5 by 10 to find the number of inches.

$67.5 \div 10 = 6.75$ inches

(A), (B), and (D) are all incorrect because these choices do not show this answer.

49. **D** One square yard measures 3 feet by 3 feet = 9 square feet.

12 square yards is $12 \times 9 = 108$ square feet.

(A), (B), and (C) are all incorrect because these choices do not show this answer.

50. **C** Arrange the rainfall amounts in order from least to greatest.

There are an even number of scores, so find the middle two scores.

2 2 3 3 4 <u>4</u> <u>6</u> 6 7 7 8 8

These scores are different;

find the average.

$4 + 6 = 10 \div 2 = 5$

The median is 5.

(A), (B), and (D) are all incorrect because these choices do not show this answer.

51. **B** The range is the highest number of cars minus the lowest number of cars. Even if no cars passed through one tollbooth, at least one tollbooth will have 108 cars pass through. (A) is incorrect because, if the median was unique, then five, not six, tollbooths would have less than 97 cars pass through. If the median repeated, you could not tell how many booths had fewer cars pass through without more information. In either event, this answer is incorrect. (C) is incorrect because the mode tells which number occurred most often and you cannot tell about how many numbers are above it or below it. (D) is incorrect because the mode could just be the numbers from two tollbooths.

52. **D** The probability that a fair coin will land heads up is 1/2, regardless of what has happened before the flip. (A), (B), and (C) are all incorrect because these choices do not show this answer.

CONSTRUCTED RESPONSE ANSWERS

Review the guidelines for writing constructed response answers on page 24.

1. The essential elements of this answer are that, while it seems intuitively correct, the grape grower's methods do not lead to the conclusion he or she presents. That's because factors such as superior soil, more sunlight, and other factors are not taken into account. The difference in the average weight of 100 grapes is small, and we can't tell if that difference is significant.

2. You may encounter items that appear very difficult, such as this one. Slow down and think the item through. The essential elements of this answer are that all of the fossils listed, except the shark's tooth and the Ichthyosaur, are very old and could date back 500 million years. The microscopic foraminifera could have appeared earliest. A shark's tooth could be as old as about 400 million years, and the Ichthyosaur fossil could date back about 250 million years. Sandstone rock layers are most likely to have been formed in conjunction with moving water, while the other rock layers are more likely to be formed in conjunction with standing water.

3. The essential element of this answer is that right triangles with these dimensions can cover the rectangle as follows.

leg	leg	hypotenuse
3	4	5
6	8	10
12	16	20

It will take a minimum of 12 of the largest triangles listed above to cover the rectangle.

4. The essential elements of this answer are that the dimensions of the room are 14 feet × 10 feet.

The ceiling is ten feet high.

The total area of the walls equals $14 \times 10 \times 10 = 1400$ square feet.

There are four windows with a total area $4 \times 3 \times 4 = 48$ square feet.

There are two doors with a total area $2 \times 3 \times 8 = 48$ square feet.

The total area of the walls to be painted equals $1400 - 96 = 1304$ square feet.

The total area of the ceiling is 140 square feet.

The total area to be painted is 1444 square feet.

First coat: $1444 \div 400 = 3.61$ gallons

Second coat: $1444 \div 600$ is approximately equal to 2.41 gallons

3.61 gallons + 2.41 gallons = 6.02

You can't buy two hundredths of a gallon. You'll buy 6 gallons or 7 gallons to be sure.

$6 \times \$28.03 = \$168.18$ or $7 \times \$28.03 = \$196.20$ to buy enough paint for the room.

No book can effectively evaluate your answers, and you should show them to a college professor to receive a useful evaluation along with suggestions for improvement.

SUBTEST 3

1. **C** The hesitation between movements introduces students to the idea of "bound flow," while the uninterrupted movement introduces students to free flow. (A) is incorrect because the five-second hesitation in the activity indicates that this choice is incorrect. (B) is incorrect because the movement time is the time required to complete a movement. (D) is incorrect because the activity has a specific objective; it is not just a warm up.

2. **A** The manipulative skill of striking does not require that something actually be hit. (B) and (C) are incorrect because striking is an action, not an outcome. Besides, if one of these were correct, they would both be correct. That does not happen on a multiple-choice test. (D) is incorrect because striking is not a semicircular movement.

3. **C** Maintaining eye contact with the ball will best help a batter strike the ball. (A) is incorrect because many effective stances are not upright. (B) is incorrect because good batters frequently hold a bat below the shoulder. (D) is incorrect because, while this can be an effective technique, it will not help unless the batter watches the ball.

4. **C** Stretching does not involve moving the legs, and so it is a non-locomotor task. (A) is incorrect because jumping is a locomotor task. (B) is incorrect because throwing is a manipulative task. (D) is incorrect because jumping is a locomotor activity.

5. **A** Manipulative skills typically involve the arms and legs. (B), (C), and (D) are incorrect because bending, jumping, and turning are non-locomotor activities.

6. **D** Generally, regular cardiovascular activity lowers heart rate. (A) is incorrect because HDL cholesterol is "good" cholesterol that may be raised by cardiovascular activity. (B) is incorrect because LDL cholesterol is "bad" cholesterol that may be lowered by cardiovascular activity. (C) is incorrect because cardiovascular activity itself does not increase muscle strength.

7. **B** The combination of high-intensity activities for an individual at regular intervals are the keys to an effective exercise program. (A), (C), and (D) are all incorrect because these choices do not include this answer.

8. **A** Pulse rate is the best way to determine if an exercise has become too demanding. (B) is incorrect because hard breathing is not as effective as pulse rate. (C) and (D) are incorrect because these choices do not include an effective way to determine if an exercise has become too demanding.

9. **D** Students will reach the highest level of self-actualization if they are motivated to participate and if the activities interest them. (A), (B), and (C) are all incorrect because these choices do not include the correct answer.

10. **A** Alcohol is a legal drug, and it is by far the most abused drug. (A), (C), and (D) are all incorrect because these illegal drugs are often abused but they are not the most frequently abused.

11. **D** This is the only activity listed that involves no movement. (A), (B), and (C) are all incorrect because all of these choices involve some movement.

12. **B** The list shows a number of secondary rules that make the game more appropriate for young children. (A), (C), and (D) are all incorrect because these choices do not characterize the adaptation in tee baseball.

13. **A** This is the correct match of term and definition. (B) is incorrect because middle space activities are performed while standing. (C) is incorrect because arhythmical activities occur at irregular intervals. (D) is incorrect because force refers to the body tension that accompanies an activity.

14. **A** People at the most advanced stage of morality distinguish between legality and morality. (B), (C), and (D) are all incorrect because these descriptions are associated with earlier stages of morality in which students associate with teachers, parents, and other authority figures.

15. **C** The study of twins has not cleared up the nature versus nurture controversy, which examines the roles of a person's genetic makeup and rearing environment in achievement. (A), (B), and (D) are all incorrect because these choices are true statements about the nature versus nurture controversy.

16. **B** This is what learning disability means, that a student's measured performance is two or more years below the level indicated by his measured ability. (A), (C), and (D) are all incorrect because these choices do not accurately characterize a learning disability.

17. **D** Students in this group have turned away, or started to turn away, from their peer group as a source of approval. This line alone represents a mismatch between age and actions. (A) and (B) are incorrect because children in the primary and middle grades do see the teacher as an authority figure and generally react well to a teacher's instructions. (C) is incorrect because, during these years, students resist a teacher's authority and turn to their peer group for approval.

18. **B** This choice alone represents an appropriate developmental trait and is least likely, among the choices given, to require an intervention. (A), (C), and (D) are all incorrect because these choices all represent deviations from appropriate development that are most likely, among the choices given, to require intervention.

19. **B** Children have little appreciation for their own mortality or their own vulnerability; they have great difficulty understanding the consequences of drug abuse. (A), (C), and (D) are all incorrect because these choices give reasons for using drugs but not the most likely reason that children ignore warnings about the dangers of drug abuse.

20. **D** Typically, girls enter adolescence about age 10, while boys enter adolescence a few years later. (A) and (B) are incorrect because the period of steady growth begins about age six for both boys and girls. (C) is incorrect because boys enter adolescence about age 12.

21. **C** Studies show that, overall, achievement is related more to SES (Socio Economic Status) than any other factor. This relationship may result from the enriched home environment that higher SES students enjoy. (A), (B), and (D) are all incorrect because, while these factors can be related to achievement, none correlates as highly as SES.

22. **A** Students' thinking is very egocentric during this stage, which extends from approximately 18 months to seven years of age. (B) is incorrect because this trait indicates that a student is at the concrete operational stage, which extends from approximately seven years to twelve years of age. (C) is incorrect because this trait indicates the student is at the sensorimotor stage, which extends from birth to approximately 18 months of age. (D) is incorrect because this trait indicates the student is at the concrete operational stage, which extends from seven years to twelve years of age.

23. **B** In the vast majority of cases, a child abuser is a member of the family. There are just so many more family members in a position to abuse children than there are of any other group. (A) is incorrect because the most widely publicized cases include those mentioned in this choice, but those mentioned here are not most likely to be abusers. (C) is incorrect because convicted sexual abusers may be more likely to repeat the abuse, but this is not the most common source of abuse. (D) is incorrect because children can be abused by strangers, but this is not the most common source of abuse.

24. **D** This choice least accurately characterizes the American family from among the choices given. This does not mean this choice is never accurate, just that it is not as accurate as the other choices. (A), (B), and (C) are all incorrect because these choices are the three most accurate characterizations of the American family among the choices given.

25. **D** Vicarious learning means to learn through others' experiences. (A), (B), and (C) are all incorrect because these choices do not accurately describe vicarious learning.

26. **B** The relatively small Native American population is growing faster than any other American ethnic group. (A) is incorrect because Asian-American students tend to be the top performers. (C) is incorrect because a higher percentage of Native Americans live below the poverty level than any other group. (D) is incorrect because the Hispanic population has one of the highest growth rates.

27. **C** Just observing ballet reveals that the dance form is based on the position of the feet. (A), (B), and (D) are all incorrect because these choices do not accurately describe the basis of ballet.

28. **A** Only this choice is related to an appreciation of dance and dance elements. (B) is incorrect because this choice is related to the cultural style of a dance. (C) is incorrect because this choice is related to the underlying meaning of dance and not the dance itself. (D) is incorrect because this choice is related to the history of dance.

29. **C** The real meaning of a note is found in the pitch, sound, and duration of that sound. (A), (B), and (D) are all incorrect because these choices are not related to the fundamental meaning of a note.

30. **A** These five bars show the distinctive beginning notes from "My Country 'Tis of Thee." (B), (C), and (D) are all incorrect because none of these songs mentioned in these choices begins with the notes shown in the question.

31. **C** A key signature for one flat on the staff with the G clef and one flat on the staff for the base clef is always F major.

    (A). The key signature B flat major is shown below.

(B). The key signature E flat major is shown below.

(D). The key signature G major is shown below.

32. **A** The second measure contains just one note on each staff. The left hand plays the "F" found on the staff with the Base clef and the right hand plays the "F" found on the staff with the G clef. (B), (C), and (D) are all incorrect because these choices do not correspond to the notes found on the staff.

33. **D** The students must improvise their acting using the general description on the card. (A) is incorrect because stand-up is a rehearsed comedic form. (B) is incorrect because pantomime uses only body movements. (C) is incorrect because the students do not have to create a comedic improvisation.

34. **B** The obvious answer is the correct answer. You should first know about what you plan to write about. (A), (C), and (D) are all incorrect because, while each show a useful step in creating the essay, none of them is the first step.

35. **D** The student's role as director is to create the performance, as opposed to the producer's overall responsibility. (A), (B), and (C) are all incorrect because these choices do not show the correct comparison between director and producer.

36. **B** A fresco is created in wet plaster on a wall. (A), (C), and (D) are all incorrect because these choices do not indicate where a fresco would appear.

37. **B** The fallen stalks of wheat communicate the results of effort. (A), (C), and (D) are all incorrect because the elements represented in these choices can be seen in the painting, but none of them communicates the results of effort.

38. **B** This image shows one group of miners carousing while another group is studying the Bible. (A), (C), and (D) are all incorrect because these choices do not accurately portray the artwork.

39. **C** The golden ratio is found throughout nature and architecture. That ratio is about 1 to 0.6. (A), (C), and (D) are not the pleasing and naturally occurring ratio referred to in the question.

CONSTRUCTED RESPONSE ANSWERS

Review the guidelines for writing constructed response answers on page 24.

1. The essential elements of this answer are that the balance beam can help a young child develop the skill of balance. A child standing still on the beam is developing static balance while a child moving on the beam is developing dynamic balance. The low balance beam is appropriate for young children because they cannot be injured by a "fall."

2. During these ages, children are in a period of steady growth. Most children double their body weight and increase their height by 50 percent. But development is not even, and adolescence begins at about age 10 for girls and 12 for boys. Most children experience a growth spurt during adolescence, when sexual and secondary sex characteristics appear.

According to Piaget's theory of cognitive development, children develop from the age of six when they are reliant on physical representations of concepts to twelve when many children can understand concepts abstractly.

3. Two sharps indicate that the key is G major. Inspection shows that there are four beats to a measure and the eighth note gets one beat. This piece is played in 4/8 time. The genre is the type of music, and this could be an anti-slavery song or an African-American song.

The piece gives insight into the reaction of African-Americans during a time of slavery.

No book can effectively evaluate your answers, and you should show them to a college professor to receive a useful evaluation along with suggestions for improvement.

11 PRACTICE CSET II

┌─────────────────────┐
│   **TEST INFO BOX**   │
└─────────────────────┘

On the real test, you may take one, two, or all three subtests in a five-hour period. You should take the practice subtests that you plan to take at the next CSET administration.

Take this test in a realistic timed setting. The setting will be most realistic if another person times the test and ensures that the test rules are followed. If another person is acting as test supervisor, he or she should review these instructions with you and tell you to "Stop" when time has expired.

SUBTEST 1 (page 457)

Reading Language and Literature	26 Multiple Choice and 2 Constructed Response
History and Social Science	26 Multiple Choice and 2 Constructed Response

SUBTEST 2 (page 473)

Science	26 Multiple Choice and 2 Constructed Response
Mathematics	26 Multiple Choice and 2 Constructed Response

SUBTEST 3 (page 487)

Visual and Performing Arts	13 Multiple Choice and 1 Constructed Response
Physical Education	13 Multiple Choice and 1 Constructed Response
Human Development	13 Multiple Choice and 1 Constructed Response

Once the test is complete, review the answers and explanations for each item on pages 498–513 as you correct the test.

Once instructed, turn the page and begin.

CSET II
Subtest 1

ANSWER SHEET

Record the answers to the multiple choice questions on this answer sheet.

1 Ⓐ Ⓑ Ⓒ Ⓓ	14 Ⓐ Ⓑ Ⓒ Ⓓ	27 Ⓐ Ⓑ Ⓒ Ⓓ	40 Ⓐ Ⓑ Ⓒ Ⓓ
2 Ⓐ Ⓑ Ⓒ Ⓓ	15 Ⓐ Ⓑ Ⓒ Ⓓ	28 Ⓐ Ⓑ Ⓒ Ⓓ	41 Ⓐ Ⓑ Ⓒ Ⓓ
3 Ⓐ Ⓑ Ⓒ Ⓓ	16 Ⓐ Ⓑ Ⓒ Ⓓ	29 Ⓐ Ⓑ Ⓒ Ⓓ	42 Ⓐ Ⓑ Ⓒ Ⓓ
4 Ⓐ Ⓑ Ⓒ Ⓓ	17 Ⓐ Ⓑ Ⓒ Ⓓ	30 Ⓐ Ⓑ Ⓒ Ⓓ	43 Ⓐ Ⓑ Ⓒ Ⓓ
5 Ⓐ Ⓑ Ⓒ Ⓓ	18 Ⓐ Ⓑ Ⓒ Ⓓ	31 Ⓐ Ⓑ Ⓒ Ⓓ	44 Ⓐ Ⓑ Ⓒ Ⓓ
6 Ⓐ Ⓑ Ⓒ Ⓓ	19 Ⓐ Ⓑ Ⓒ Ⓓ	32 Ⓐ Ⓑ Ⓒ Ⓓ	45 Ⓐ Ⓑ Ⓒ Ⓓ
7 Ⓐ Ⓑ Ⓒ Ⓓ	20 Ⓐ Ⓑ Ⓒ Ⓓ	33 Ⓐ Ⓑ Ⓒ Ⓓ	46 Ⓐ Ⓑ Ⓒ Ⓓ
8 Ⓐ Ⓑ Ⓒ Ⓓ	21 Ⓐ Ⓑ Ⓒ Ⓓ	34 Ⓐ Ⓑ Ⓒ Ⓓ	47 Ⓐ Ⓑ Ⓒ Ⓓ
9 Ⓐ Ⓑ Ⓒ Ⓓ	22 Ⓐ Ⓑ Ⓒ Ⓓ	35 Ⓐ Ⓑ Ⓒ Ⓓ	48 Ⓐ Ⓑ Ⓒ Ⓓ
10 Ⓐ Ⓑ Ⓒ Ⓓ	23 Ⓐ Ⓑ Ⓒ Ⓓ	36 Ⓐ Ⓑ Ⓒ Ⓓ	49 Ⓐ Ⓑ Ⓒ Ⓓ
11 Ⓐ Ⓑ Ⓒ Ⓓ	24 Ⓐ Ⓑ Ⓒ Ⓓ	37 Ⓐ Ⓑ Ⓒ Ⓓ	50 Ⓐ Ⓑ Ⓒ Ⓓ
12 Ⓐ Ⓑ Ⓒ Ⓓ	25 Ⓐ Ⓑ Ⓒ Ⓓ	38 Ⓐ Ⓑ Ⓒ Ⓓ	51 Ⓐ Ⓑ Ⓒ Ⓓ
13 Ⓐ Ⓑ Ⓒ Ⓓ	26 Ⓐ Ⓑ Ⓒ Ⓓ	39 Ⓐ Ⓑ Ⓒ Ⓓ	52 Ⓐ Ⓑ Ⓒ Ⓓ

Answers on page 498

1. Linguists' assertion that each phoneme is associated with a grapheme is not well represented by which of the following?
   (A) o
   (B) ay
   (C) ch
   (D) ho

2. When linguists talk about onset and rhyme, they mean:
   (A) the beginning stages of reading through rhyming words.
   (B) the initial consonant in a syllable and the part of the syllable that contains the vowel.
   (C) the beginning of a line of poetry and the end of the line of poetry that actually contains a rhyme.
   (D) the beginning of a word that does not show the rhyme and the end of the word which does rhyme.

3. Phoneme deletion activities promote phonemic awareness by:
   (A) breaking a word into separate sounds and saying each sound.
   (B) recognizing the sounds in a word that do not match the sounds in another words.
   (C) recognizing the word remaining when a phoneme is removed from a longer word.
   (D) substituting one phoneme for another to make a new word.

4. Phonics is the predictable relationship between graphemes and phonemes. In general, experts say:
   (A) systematic and explicit phonics instruction is the essential element of early grade reading programs.
   (B) literature based instruction that emphasizes reading and writing is the essential element of early grade reading programs.
   (C) sight word programs are the essential element in early grade reading programs.
   (D) basal programs that focus on whole word or meaning-based activities are the essential element of early grade reading programs.

5. According to recent research, which of the following approaches is most likely to improve a student's reading fluency?
   (A) round-robin reading in which students take turns reading a passage
   (B) monitored oral reading
   (C) silent independent reading
   (D) hearing models of fluent reading

6. Semantic organizers are most likely to help students:
   (A) understand the meaning of words, expressions, and sentences in relation to reference and truth.
   (B) identify the underlying structure of a story.
   (C) relate pictures and diagrams in the text to the text itself.
   (D) identify related ideas and concepts in a text.

7. Which of the following is the most effective way for children to develop phonemic awareness?
   (A) Become familiar with an appropriate number of symbolic phonemic spellings such as /b/ /eI/.
   (B) Focus on the unique sounds of each phoneme.
   (C) Learn how the building blocks of individual phonemes combine to form sounds that are more complex.
   (D) Learn phonemic awareness along with the letters of the alphabet.

8. Which of the following would indicate that a student is using a metacognitive approach to reading comprehension?
   (A) A student grasps the overall structure of a story.
   (B) A student summarizes the essence of a story.
   (C) A student adjusts his or her reading speed.
   (D) A student works cooperatively with others to comprehend a story.

9. It is most likely that a child has learned the meaning of a word
   (A) indirectly, through context clues
   (B) directly, through phonics learning experiences
   (C) indirectly, through everyday experiences
   (D) directly, through phonemic learning experiences

10. Which of the following sentences contains a subordinate clause?
    (A) When Dorothy takes a trip to the beach, she always feels happier.
    (B) Dorothy takes a trip to the beach, and she always feels happier.
    (C) A trip to the beach makes Dorothy feel happier.
    (D) I feel happier when I take a trip to the beach.

11. In which of these sentences is the underlined word used correctly?
    (A) The reduction from two lanes to one lane had no affect on traffic.
    (B) One positive effect of construction is decreased neighborhood traffic.
    (C) The bridge construction not really affect our lives.
    (D) The engineer is reviewing how car traffic effects the bridge's strength.

Use the passage below to answer items 12 and 13.

(1) All of my visits to the park came well before a series of fires that burned the park. (2) I have some very happy memories about the time I spent in Yellowstone National Park. (3) The United States National Park System is extensive and very large. (4) Although most of the land dedicated to the park system is in the western states.

12. Which of the following choices represents the most logical way to order the sentences from the paragraph above?
    (A) 4, 3, 2, 1
    (B) 4, 3, 1, 2
    (C) 3, 4, 1, 2
    (D) 3, 4, 2, 1

13. Which of the following revisions to a sentence in the paragraph would improve the overall style of the passage?

    (A) Sentence 1—All of my visits to Yellowstone Park came well before a series of fires that burned the park.
    (B) Sentence 2—I have some very happy memories about the time spent in Yellowstone National Park.
    (C) Sentence 3—The United States National Park System is extensive.
    (D) Sentence 4—Although most of the land dedicated to the park system is in the western United States.

14. Use this passage to answer question 14.

The computers in the college dormitories are actually more sophisticated than the computers in the college computer labs and they cost less. It seems that the person who bought the dormitory computers looked around until she found powerful computers at a low price. The person who runs the labs just got the computers offered by the regular supplier.

The best statement of the main idea of this paragraph is
    (A) it is better to use the computers in the dorms.
    (B) the computers in the dorms are always in use, so, for most purposes it is better to use the computers in the labs.
    (C) it is better to shop around before you buy.
    (D) wholesale prices are usually better than retail prices.

15. Use this passage to answer question 15.

In response to my opponent's question about my record on environmental issues, I want to say that the real problem with this election is not my record. Rather, the problem is the influence of my opponent's rich friends in the record industry. I hope you will turn your back on his rich supporters and vote for me.

What type of fallacious reasoning is found in this passage?
    (A) Nonsequitur
    (B) False analogy
    (C) Red herring
    (D) Begging the question

16. Some oral presentation experts suggest that a speaker should use rhetorical questions to capture the attention of an audience, meaning the speaker should ask questions
    (A) that engage audience members in a rhetorical response.
    (B) to determine audience members' knowledge of rhetorical techniques.
    (C) to which no response is expected.
    (D) that audience members already know the answer to.

17. As a rule, using a script instead of note cards to make an oral presentation can make the presentation:
    (A) more accurate.
    (B) more organized.
    (C) more detailed.
    (D) more monotonous.

Use this passage to answer questions 18 and 19.

(1) Using percentages to report growth patterns can be deceptive. (2) If there are 100 new users for a cereal currently used by 100 other people, the growth rate is 100 percent. (3) However, if there are 50,000 new users for a cereal currently used by 5,000,000 people, the growth rate is 1 percent. (4) The 1 percent growth is much larger than the 100 percent growth. (5) It seems clear that this growth rate of 1 percent is preferable to the growth rate of 100 percent. (6) While percentages provide a useful way to report growth patterns, we must know the initial number the growth percentage is based on.

18. Which of the sentences listed below includes a conclusion?
    (A) Sentence 1
    (B) Sentence 2
    (C) Sentence 4
    (D) Sentence 5

19. Which of the following people would most likely be concerned with a study such as the one described above?
    (A) A marketing specialist who conducts various types of market research
    (B) A sociologist who studies the actions and interactions of people
    (C) A nutritionist who helps people make decisions about which foods to eat
    (D) A supermarket manager who decides how much and what type of food to order each week

20. A class is studying an epic, meaning that the work under study might be:
    (A) King Arthur and the Knights of the Round Table
    (B) *Gulliver's Travels*
    (C) *The Odyssey*
    (D) Paul Bunyan

Use this passage to answer item 21.

Charles Dodgson, a non-American writing under the pen name Lewis Carroll, wrote *Alice's Adventures Under Ground* as a precursor to *Alice's Adventures in Wonderland*. In the book, Alice falls through a rabbit hole into a fantastic world filled with nightmares, illogic, and contradictions. The book is so filled with symbolism that a book titled *Understanding Alice* contains the original text with marginal notes explaining the symbolism.

21. The passage refers to the symbolism found in *Alice in Wonderland*, meaning that the story
    (A) was written in a foreign language.
    (B) contained many mathematical symbols.
    (C) contained no pictures.
    (D) has a figurative meaning.

22. *Alice in Wonderland*:
    (A) is based on a real character.
    (B) is categorized as an epic by English scholars.
    (C) includes primarily realistic characters.
    (D) was written to soothe children at a time when many children died at a young age.

Use the excerpt from the poem *The Walrus and the Carpenter* to answer questions 23 and 24.

Excerpt from *The Walrus and the Carpenter*
by Lewis Carroll

The Walrus and the Carpenter
Were walking close at hand:
They wept like anything to see
Such quantities of sand:
"If this were only cleared away."
They said, "It would be grand!"

"If seven maids with seven mops
swept it for half a year,
Do you suppose," the Walrus said,
"That they could get it clear?"
"I doubt it," said the Carpenter,
And shed a bitter tear.

"O Oysters, come and walk with us!"
The Walrus did beseech.
"A pleasant walk, a pleasant talk,
Along the briny beach.
We cannot do with more than four,
To give a hand to each."

The eldest Oyster looked at him,
But never a word he said:
The eldest Oyster winked his eye,
And shook his heavy head-
Meaning to say he did not choose
To leave the oyster-bed.

But four young Oysters hurried up,
All eager for the treat:
Their coats were brushed, their faces
washed,
Their shoes were clean and neat-
And this was odd, because, you know,
They hadn't any feet.
. . .
"The time has come," the Walrus said,
"To talk of many things:
Of-shoes-and ships-and sealing wax-
Of cabbages-and kings-
And why the sea is boiling hot-
And whether pigs have wings."

"But wait a bit," the Oysters cried,
"Before we have our chat;
For some of us are out of breath,
and all of us are fat."
"No hurry!" said the Carpenter.
They thanked him much for that.

"A loaf of bread," the Walrus said,
"Is what we chiefly need.
Pepper and vinegar besides
Are very good indeed-
Now if you're ready, Oysters dear,
we can begin to feed."

"But not on us!" the Oysters cried,
Turning a little blue.
"After such kindness, that would be
A dismal thing to do!"
"The night is fine," the Walrus said.
"Do you admire the view?"

"It was so kind of you to come!
And you are very nice!"
The Carpenter said nothing but
"Cut us another slice."
I wish you were not quite so deaf-
I've had to ask you twice!"

"It seems a shame," the Walrus said,
"To play them such a trick.
After we've brought them out so far,
And made them trot so quick!"
The Carpenter said nothing but
"The butter's spread too thick!"

"I weep for you," the Walrus said:
"I deeply sympathize."
With sobs and tears he sorted out
Those of the largest size,
Holding his pocket-handkerchief
Before his streaming eyes.

"O Oysters," said the Carpenter,
"You've had a pleasant run!
Shall we be trotting home again?"
But answer came there none-
And this was scarcely odd, because
They'd eaten every one"

23. When it comes to the characters in this poem, it is reasonable to say the
    (A) Walrus and the Carpenter followed the oysters to a deserted part of the beach.
    (B) Carpenter consumed more Oysters than the Walrus.
    (C) Oysters were like a pied piper for the Walrus and the Carpenter.
    (D) Walrus felt some guilt about eating the oysters.

24. Which of the following best characterizes the overall message of this poem?
    (A) Beware of the beach
    (B) Don't trust authority
    (C) Don't trust your elders
    (D) Don't trust walruses or carpenters

Use this poem to answer questions 25 and 26.

Solitude
by Ella Wheeler Wilcox

Laugh, and the world laughs with you;
　Weep, and you weep alone.
For the sad old earth must borrow it's mirth,
　But has trouble enough of it's own.
Sing, and the hills will answer;
　Sigh, it is lost on the air.
The echoes bound to a joyful sound,
　But shrink from voicing care.
Rejoice, and men will seek you;
　Grieve, and they turn and go.
They want full measure of all your pleasure,
　But they do not need your woe.
Be glad, and your friends are many;
　Be sad, and you lose them all.
There are none to decline your nectared wine,
　But alone you must drink life's gall.
Feast, and your halls are crowded;
　Fast, and the world goes by.
Succeed and give, and it helps you live,
　But no man can help you die.
There is room in the halls of pleasure
　For a long and lordly train,
But one by one we must all file on
　Through the narrow aisles of pain.

25. The style in this poem is best described as:
(A) analytical.
(B) sentimental.
(C) repetitive.
(D) free verse.

26. Ms. Wilcox likely chose the title "Solitude" because:
(A) she wrote her poetry in solitude.
(B) a person needs solitude to make appropriate life choices.
(C) it is what the poem shows you to avoid.
(D) as the poem indicates, reflection is the path to happiness and acceptance.

27. Which of the following is most closely associated with the development of civilization?
(A) The Upper Nile River and the Lower Nile River
(B) The Tigris River and the Euphrates River
(C) The Mediterranean Sea and the Red Sea
(D) The Caspian Sea and the Black Sea

28. Alexander the Great had the most lasting influence through
(A) the spread of Greek culture.
(B) the founding of Athens.
(C) tutoring of Aristotle.
(D) the founding of Rome.

29. Floods along the Nile River about 4,000 years ago were most responsible for which of the following?
(A) the destruction of agricultural land
(B) the establishment of cataracts
(C) the birth of geometry
(D) the construction of boats that could withstand the floods

30. Which of the countries listed below fits the following description?

This land juts out into one sea and has another sea next to it. It includes a large island off its tip and there are a great many other islands nearby.
(A) Egypt
(B) Greece
(C) Switzerland
(D) Austria

31. The key to the growth of Christianity as the religion of the Roman Empire:
(A) came following the slave rebellion led by Spartacus.
(B) is when Emperor Constantine embraced the religion.
(C) is found in its Judaic origins.
(D) came with the beginning of the C.E. (A.D.) era.

32. Which of the following describes a main impact of the end of Feudalism in Japan in the late 1800s?
(A) Lords lost their lands
(B) Samurai became more important
(C) Industrialism declined
(D) Shoguns gained power

33. Confucius influenced Chinese life by
(A) encouraging people to challenge authority.
(B) stressing conformity.
(C) focusing on the importance of the self.
(D) stressing free will.

34. In the caste system found in India:
    (A) a person must choose a caste at an early age.
    (B) all non-Hindus are untouchables.
    (C) a person must pay an expensive fee to move from one caste to another.
    (D) each caste has its own elected officials.

Use this map to answer questions 35 and 36

Some official languages of South American Countries

35. The native dialects spoken in western South America are most likely the result of:
    (A) the early Incan influence in that portion of South America.
    (B) the primitive nature of the countries in that part of South America.
    (C) immigration of Mayan Indians from further north in Mexico.
    (D) the proximity of Central America to this part of South America.

36. What accounts for the use of Italian as an official language in Southeastern South America?
    (A) the voyages of Christopher Columbus in the late 1400s
    (B) the exploration of the Americas by Amerigo Vespucci in the 1500s
    (C) Italian immigration in the 1700s
    (D) the voyages of Sir Francis Drake

37. Which line in the table given below correctly matches an early American colony with events surrounding that colony?

Line	Colony/ Colonizer	Description
1	Christopher Columbus	Columbus established a small settlement before returning to Europe.
2	The Lost Colony	John Smith established this colony near Roanoke, Virginia.
3	Jamestown Colony	Sir Walter Raleigh established this colony that came to rely on slaves for tobacco production.
4	The Pilgrims	The Pilgrims established a colony at Plymouth and drafted the Mayflower Compact.

(A) Line 1
(B) Line 2
(C) Line 3
(D) Line 4

Use this poster to answer question 38.

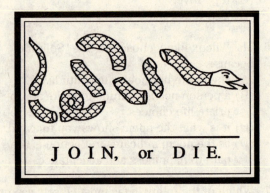

JOIN, or DIE.

38. This poster depicts
    (A) a threat to those who opposed British rule in the United States.
    (B) a call for more states to join the Confederacy during the Civil War.
    (C) the need for the American colonies to ratify the Constitution.
    (D) the need for the American colonies to unite against England.

39. Historians frequently refer to the Articles of Confederation as the:
    (A) document that started the Civil War.
    (B) first American Declaration of Independence.
    (C) list of grievances that stated Confederate state's concerns.
    (D) first Constitution of the United States.

40. Use this map to answer the following question.

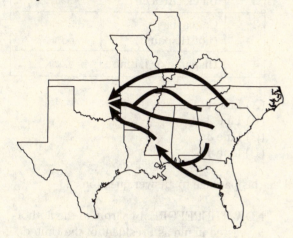

The map above best shows what events between the Revolutionary and Civil wars?
    (A) the migration of settlers from the east coast toward California
    (B) the forced removal of Native Americans to Oklahoma
    (C) the establishment of railroads from the east to the Midwest
    (D) the first wagon train trails to jumping off points in the Midwest

41. Which line in the table given below DOES NOT correctly match a person or people in the War of 1812 with a description of what they did?

Line	Person/People	Description
1	Francis Scott Key	Wrote the Star Spangled Banner
2	British Troops	Sacked and burned Washington, D.C.
3	Andrew Jackson	Fought the Battle of New Orleans
4	Commodore Perry	Fought the British in Baltimore Harbor

    (A) Line 1
    (B) Line 2
    (C) Line 3
    (D) Line 4

42. After the slave ship *Amistad* was seized by the American Coast Guard in 1839:
    (A) the Supreme Court ruled that the Africans aboard the ship were the property of their owners.
    (B) authorities learned that slaves aboard had revolted, killing several crew members.
    (C) the current president Van Buren and the past president Adams sided with the slave owners.
    (D) the Africans from the ship were given land to settle on in upstate New York.

43. Which of the following shows the correct order of listed events in United States History.
    I Reconstruction
    II Sherman's March to the Sea
    III Surrender at Appomattox Courthouse
    IV Approval of the XIII Amendment to the Constitution of the United States

    (A) I, II, III, IV
    (B) II, III, IV, I
    (C) II, I, III, IV
    (D) IV, II, III, I

44. What is the connection among the following items?

    • FDIC
    • Civilian Conservation Corps
    • Tennessee Valley Authority
    • Agricultural Adjustment Act

    (A) They are all programs enacted by President Herbert Hoover.
    (B) They are all programs enacted immediately after World War I.
    (C) They are all programs enacted by President Franklin Roosevelt.
    (D) They are all programs enacted immediately after World War II.

45. Which of the following factors is the main reason for many California earthquakes?
    (A) The North American Plate is moving west, pushing against the Pacific Plate.
    (B) The Pacific Plate is pushing against the North American Plate.
    (C) The Pacific Plate is scraping along the North American Plate.
    (D) The Pacific Plate is steadily rising.

46. In general, the various Native American groups in California
    (A) were advanced civilizations with several forms of written communication.
    (B) were isolated and not well organized.
    (C) were located mainly in the central valley where they could farm and hunt.
    (D) had just a few language groups.

47. The best description of the impact on California of the Spanish galleons that sailed from Manila is
    (A) they brought food and supplies to California.
    (B) they brought settlers and officials to several California ports.
    (C) the journey led to exploration of the California coast.
    (D) they provided a way of traveling up and down the coast of California.

48. Missions and presidios were built along to coast of California as far north as San Francisco. The first missions were built at approximately the same time as:
    (A) the Revolutionary War.
    (B) the Louisiana Purchase.
    (C) Mexican independence from Spain.
    (D) the Civil War.

49. During the construction of the transcontinental railroad, which of the following was the fastest way to travel from the east to California?
    (A) by stagecoach
    (B) by pony express
    (C) by ship and land travel across the Isthmus of Panama
    (D) by ship around Cape Horn and up the South American and Mexican coast to California

50. The progressive movement in California during the early 1900s:
    (A) was to improve schools for Latinos and Asians throughout the state.
    (B) was a reaction against railroad's control of government.
    (C) led to prohibition in the state.
    (D) proposed air pollution laws because of the very large number of cars already in the state.

51. Which line in the table below most correctly matches an ethnic group with the approximate percentage that group represents in the California population?

Line	Group	Percent of California Population
1	Asian	19%
2	Black (African)	7%
3	Caucasian (not Hispanic)	58%
4	Hispanic or Latino	42%

(A) Line 1
(B) Line 2
(C) Line 3
(D) Line 4

Use this passage to answer question 52.

NOW, THEREFORE, by virtue of the authority vested in me as President of the United States, and Commander in Chief of the Army and Navy, I hereby authorize and direct the Secretary of War, and the Military Commanders whom he may from time to time designate, whenever he or any designated Commander deems such actions necessary or desirable, to prescribe military areas in such places and of such extent as he or the appropriate Military Commanders may determine, from which any or all persons may be excluded, and with such respect to which, the right of any person to enter, remain in, or leave shall be subject to whatever restrictions the Sectary of War or the appropriate Military Commander may impose in his discretion.

52. This passage effectively
    (A) established secret flight test areas in California that eventually helped in the development of the stealth bomber.
    (B) established Japanese Internment Camps during World War II.
    (C) established a military defense zone at the United States–Mexican border.
    (D) created exclusion zones in San Francisco shortly after the San Francisco earthquake of 1906.

CONSTRUCTED RESPONSE ITEMS

Write your answers on the response sheets that follow each item. Remember to write only in the lined area on the sheet.

Write a written response for each constructed response item. Remember that these constructed response items are rated using these three criteria.

Write your answer in the space provided on the numbered response form.

PURPOSE: Purpose means how well your response addresses the constructed response prompt.

SUBJECT MATTER KNOWLEDGE: This means how accurate your response is.

SUPPORT: This means how well you present supporting evidence.

Write your response for a group of multiple subject educators. The emphasis is on the subject matter in your response and not your writing ability. However, you must write well enough for evaluators to judge your response.

Assignment 1

There are specific strategies for helping children develop phonemic awareness.

- List three of these strategies.
- Choose one strategy. Describe that strategy in detail and explain how the strategy will help students develop phonemic awareness.

_____

_____

_____

_____

_____

_____

_____

_____

_____

_____

_____

_____

_____

_____

_____

End of Assignment 1

Assignment 2

Native Californians came from tribes and groups with very diverse languages and no form of written language.

- List three specific reading and language problems that these children from these cultures might encounter in elementary school as a result of their background.

- Choose one of these problems and give two specific actions on the part of a teacher that could be successful in helping these students overcome the problems.

End of Assignment 2

Assignment 3

In the 1700s Revolutionary War broke out in the United States. Use what you know about American History and respond to the following.

- Name three causes of the Revolutionary War.

- Choose one of these causes and give a detailed description of how that cause led to armed conflict.

_____

_____

_____

_____

_____

_____

_____

_____

_____

_____

_____

_____

_____

End of Assignment 3

Assignment 4

The Bear Flag Revolt is a much-discussed aspect of California history.

- Use your knowledge of California history to describe briefly the revolt.
- Describe the importance of this revolt in California history.

End of Assignment 4

CSET II

Subtest 2

ANSWER SHEET

Record the answers to the multiple choice questions on this answer sheet.

1 Ⓐ Ⓑ Ⓒ Ⓓ	14 Ⓐ Ⓑ Ⓒ Ⓓ	27 Ⓐ Ⓑ Ⓒ Ⓓ	40 Ⓐ Ⓑ Ⓒ Ⓓ
2 Ⓐ Ⓑ Ⓒ Ⓓ	15 Ⓐ Ⓑ Ⓒ Ⓓ	28 Ⓐ Ⓑ Ⓒ Ⓓ	41 Ⓐ Ⓑ Ⓒ Ⓓ
3 Ⓐ Ⓑ Ⓒ Ⓓ	16 Ⓐ Ⓑ Ⓒ Ⓓ	29 Ⓐ Ⓑ Ⓒ Ⓓ	42 Ⓐ Ⓑ Ⓒ Ⓓ
4 Ⓐ Ⓑ Ⓒ Ⓓ	17 Ⓐ Ⓑ Ⓒ Ⓓ	30 Ⓐ Ⓑ Ⓒ Ⓓ	43 Ⓐ Ⓑ Ⓒ Ⓓ
5 Ⓐ Ⓑ Ⓒ Ⓓ	18 Ⓐ Ⓑ Ⓒ Ⓓ	31 Ⓐ Ⓑ Ⓒ Ⓓ	44 Ⓐ Ⓑ Ⓒ Ⓓ
6 Ⓐ Ⓑ Ⓒ Ⓓ	19 Ⓐ Ⓑ Ⓒ Ⓓ	32 Ⓐ Ⓑ Ⓒ Ⓓ	45 Ⓐ Ⓑ Ⓒ Ⓓ
7 Ⓐ Ⓑ Ⓒ Ⓓ	20 Ⓐ Ⓑ Ⓒ Ⓓ	33 Ⓐ Ⓑ Ⓒ Ⓓ	46 Ⓐ Ⓑ Ⓒ Ⓓ
8 Ⓐ Ⓑ Ⓒ Ⓓ	21 Ⓐ Ⓑ Ⓒ Ⓓ	34 Ⓐ Ⓑ Ⓒ Ⓓ	47 Ⓐ Ⓑ Ⓒ Ⓓ
9 Ⓐ Ⓑ Ⓒ Ⓓ	22 Ⓐ Ⓑ Ⓒ Ⓓ	35 Ⓐ Ⓑ Ⓒ Ⓓ	48 Ⓐ Ⓑ Ⓒ Ⓓ
10 Ⓐ Ⓑ Ⓒ Ⓓ	23 Ⓐ Ⓑ Ⓒ Ⓓ	36 Ⓐ Ⓑ Ⓒ Ⓓ	49 Ⓐ Ⓑ Ⓒ Ⓓ
11 Ⓐ Ⓑ Ⓒ Ⓓ	24 Ⓐ Ⓑ Ⓒ Ⓓ	37 Ⓐ Ⓑ Ⓒ Ⓓ	50 Ⓐ Ⓑ Ⓒ Ⓓ
12 Ⓐ Ⓑ Ⓒ Ⓓ	25 Ⓐ Ⓑ Ⓒ Ⓓ	38 Ⓐ Ⓑ Ⓒ Ⓓ	51 Ⓐ Ⓑ Ⓒ Ⓓ
13 Ⓐ Ⓑ Ⓒ Ⓓ	26 Ⓐ Ⓑ Ⓒ Ⓓ	39 Ⓐ Ⓑ Ⓒ Ⓓ	52 Ⓐ Ⓑ Ⓒ Ⓓ

Answers on page 504

1. Which of the following creates a chemical reaction?
   (A) mixing the hot water from two glasses in a single glass
   (B) mixing raisins and cashews
   (C) mixing water and cement
   (D) mixing sand and seashells

2. Which of the following is the most accurate statement about the atom of an element?
   (A) The atomic mass of an element is equal to the number of protons.
   (B) The atomic number of an element is the number of electrons.
   (C) Electrons move around an atom in a single orbit.
   (D) Two atoms of the same element may have different numbers of neutrons.

3. When describing the mass of an object it is most appropriate to say:
   (A) the mass of an object cannot change.
   (B) the weight of an object is proportional to its mass.
   (C) if two objects have the same specific gravity they have the same mass.
   (D) an object with a given mass always weighs the same.

4. Which of the following is the best example of heat transfer by convection?
   (A) A heating pad applied to an aching muscle
   (B) The sun warming a field of hay
   (C) A hot water radiator warming a room
   (D) A heat lamp warming horses in a cold barn

5. Which of the following involves changing the electrical charge of an object?
   (A) Rubbing a glass rod with a silk cloth
   (B) Using a twelve-volt battery in place of a six-volt battery
   (C) Using a twenty-amp fuse instead of a ten-amp fuse
   (D) Turning off the switch to an electric heater

6. When a white light is refracted through a prism, it can split into many colors, like the colors of a rainbow, showing that:
   (A) the colors only appear when light is refracted through a triangular object.
   (B) the prism has a colored filter that separates out these colors.
   (C) white light is formed by a combination of all these colors.
   (D) if all these colors were refracted through a prism a white light would come out.

7. When someone burns wood in a fire, the person is:
   (A) destroying matter
   (B) converting matter
   (C) breaking down elements
   (D) converting energy to mass

8.

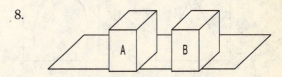

Two identical blocks with the same mass are on a flat frictionless surface. What happens when block A and B move toward one another and bump so that the blocks stay on that frictionless surface?
   (A) Block A touches block B and the blocks stop when they meet.
   (B) Block A touches block B and the blocks separate.
   (C) Block A touches block B and the blocks travel together in the direction block A was traveling.
   (D) Block A touches block B and only block B moves in the direction block A was traveling.

9.

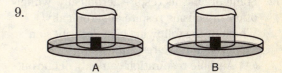

Identical beakers each have the same amount of water. The different solid objects placed in the beakers cause the overflow. The objects weigh exactly the same amount. What is the most likely explanation for the differing amounts of overflow?
   (A) The object in Beaker A has more mass.
   (B) The object in Beaker B is denser.
   (C) The object in Beaker A is denser.
   (D) The object in Beaker B has more mass.

10. The table below shows the temperature tracked for a 12-hour period. Which of the following graphs best illustrates this information?

Time	8 A.M.	9 A.M.	10 A.M.	11 A.M.	12 NOON
Temp	45°	55°	60°	60°	70°
Time	1 P.M.	2 P.M.	3 P.M.	4 P.M.	
Temp	75°	75°	70°	65°	
Time	5 P.M.	6 P.M.	7 P.M.	8 P.M.	
Temp	55°	50°	50°	45°	

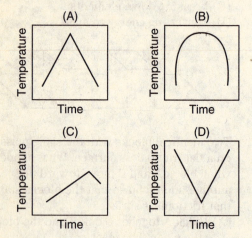

11. Which of the following best describes a function of the nose and the mouth in the respiratory system?
    (A) filter out oxygen
    (B) exhale carbon dioxide
    (C) heating air
    (D) expectoration

12. Some organisms respire aerobically, while other organisms respire anaerobically. Which of the following best describes an aspect of aerobic respiration?
    (A) Aerobic respiration can only occur outside earth's atmosphere.
    (B) Aerobic respiration produces the carbon bubbles in soft drinks.
    (C) Aerobic respiration takes place with oxygen.
    (D) Aerobic respiration produces oxygen.

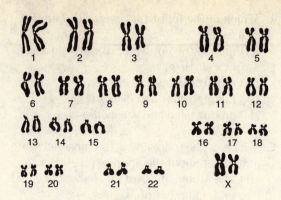

13. What conclusion could you reach about the person whose chromosomes are shown above?
    (A) The person is a man.
    (B) The person is a woman.
    (C) The person has an abnormal gene.
    (D) The person has more genes than usually found in humans.

14. Which of the following represents the correct sequence of events that happens during photosynthesis?

    I. CO_2 and water are broken down.
    II. Carbohydrates are formed.
    III. Sunlight is absorbed by Chlorophyll.
    IV. Plant emits O_2.

    (A) I, II, III, IV
    (B) I, III, II, IV
    (C) III, I, II, IV
    (D) II, IV, I, III

15. The destruction of the South American rain forests directly influences all of the following EXCEPT
    (A) animal habitats
    (B) rare plant species
    (C) climatic shifts
    (D) reproduction of natural resources

Use this table to answer questions 16 and 17.

AVERAGE OUNCES GAINED PER ANIMAL

Week	HF1	HF2
1	4	9
2	3	4
3	2	3
4	1	2
5	1	2
6	1	1

16. An experiment is set up to determine the effects of a new hamster food HF2 as compared to the effects of a current hamster food HF1. Each group receives the same quantity of food and the same attention. From the data above, choose the best conclusion for the experiment.
(A) HF2 group gained more weight
(B) HF1 group lived longer
(C) HF2 group gained more protein
(D) HF1 group got better nutrition

17. What appropriate criticism might a scientist have of this experiment?
(A) Averages should not be used in this type of experiment.
(B) The null hypothesis is not stated in the appropriate form.
(C) Hamsters are not found in enough homes for the experiment to be widely applicable.
(D) The experiment does not describe sufficient controls to be valid.

18. Which of the following contributes to the idea that DDT is not biodegradable?
(A) Insects and animals, other than pets, are poisoned by DDT.
(B) DDT is found in the carcasses of life forms.
(C) DDT is used as a pesticide in orchards.
(D) DDT has been found in riverbanks.

19.

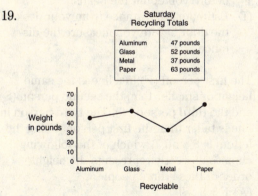

Saturday
Recycling Totals

Aluminum	47 pounds
Glass	52 pounds
Metal	37 pounds
Paper	63 pounds

Students visit the recycling center with their teacher and gather information about the recyclables collected during one day. The students organize the information and then sketch a graph shown above. Which of the following comments by the teacher would most help students continue with this project?

(A) "You should use a straight edge to draw the lines in your graph."
(B) "You should use a circle graph to show percents. This table and graph do not show percents of the whole."
(C) "You should use a bar graph when quantities are not related."
(D) "You should use kilograms instead of pounds for science results."

20. You are floating on a lake in a boat about 100 yards from the shore. You can hear someone talking at the shoreline. What is the best way to explain this phenomenon?
(A) Sound travels faster through air.
(B) Sound travels faster through water.
(C) Sound travels from the shore because of the materials the boat is made of.
(D) You hear the sound because of an echo.

21. Most earthquakes in California result from a process called plate tectonics. Which of the following best describes plate tectonic theory?
(A) Molten material from within the earth pushes up on portions of the earth called plates that put stress on the earth's surface.
(B) Certain roughly circular portions of the earth's surface called plates are subjected to pressure, causing them to move left or right.
(C) The earth's surface consists of a series of large land masses called plates that float slowly on the material beneath the surface.
(D) Over time, portions of the earth's surface crack or break away in a fashion similar to the way plates break when they are dropped.

22. What type of rock, millions of years from now, would most likely be formed from current animal remains?
(A) Gneiss
(B) Sedimentary
(C) Igneous
(D) Metamorphic

23. Meiosis is a very important cell reproduction process. This process always involves:
    (A) cells making carbon copies of themselves.
    (B) the formation of zygotes.
    (C) the creation of cells equal to all other in terms of DNA.
    (D) the formation of gametes.

24.

The two cats are the parents of these three kittens. How can this happen?
    (A) Both parents have recessive white genes.
    (B) One parent has a recessive white gene.
    (C) Both parents have dominant white genes.
    (D) One parent has a dominant black gene.

25. The half-life of uranium is 82 years. Approximately how much of the mass of uranium would remain after 330 years?

    (A) $\frac{1}{2}$

    (B) $\frac{1}{4}$

    (C) $\frac{1}{8}$

    (D) $\frac{1}{16}$

26. A scientist working in the Sierra Nevada mountains comes across some hail that had just fallen. The scientist cuts a piece of hail in half and finds a series of rings, much like tree rings. What information could the scientist find from the approximate number of rings?
    (A) How long the hailstone had been in the atmosphere
    (B) How long the hailstone was in space before falling to earth
    (C) How many miles above the surface of the earth the hailstone was before it began to fall
    (D) How many times the hailstone was blown from lower to higher altitudes

27. The salaries of four people in a company are listed below. Which choice is the best estimate of the sum of these salaries?

    Person 1: $45,250
    Person 2: $78,375
    Person 3: $52,540
    Person 4: $62,325

    (A) $237 thousand
    (B) $238 thousand
    (C) $239 thousand
    (D) $240 thousand

28. A primary objective of a school mathematics program is to estimate first to be sure a calculation is reasonable. Which of the following instructions to students by a fourth-grade teacher best meets that objective?
    (A) Estimate the answer to 6,294 + 7,892 before you find the answer with a calculator.
    (B) Estimate the answer to 900 + 9 before you find the answer with paper and pencil.
    (C) Estimate the number of beans in the jar before you count the beans.
    (D) Estimate the distance from your desk to the door before you measure the distance.

29. The first person (F) in a line is the same height or smaller than the second person (S) and the third person (T). The third person in line is taller than the first person. Using the letters F, S, and T, which of the following choices correctly represents the height order of these three people?
    (A) F > S > T
    (B) F ≥ S > T
    (C) T > S ≥ F
    (D) T > F ≤ S

30. What power of 10 would you multiply times 3.74 to get 374,000,000?
    (A) 10^6
    (B) 10^7
    (C) 10^8
    (D) 10^9

31. Which of the shaded regions below represents 2/3?

    A.

    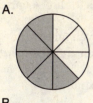

    B.

    C.

    D.

32. Store A has CDs in packs of three for $15.60. Store B sells the CDs for $6.00 each. How much will you save on each tape if you buy six tapes from Store A instead of six tapes from store B?
    (A) $3.40
    (B) $0.80
    (C) $1.80
    (D) $2.40

33. These are examples of a student's work.

    $$\begin{array}{r} 86.4 \\ 6\overline{)520} \end{array} \qquad \begin{array}{r} 81.7 \\ 9\overline{)736} \end{array} \qquad \begin{array}{r} 18.6 \\ 8\overline{)150} \end{array}$$

    The student continues to make the same type of error. Which of the following would be the student's answer to 124 divided by 5?
    (A) 2.2
    (B) 20.2
    (C) 22.5
    (D) 24.4

34. During a second grade mathematics lesson, the teacher presents this problem. There are 43 people on the camping trip. If five people can fit in a tent, what is the least number of tents needed.

Which of the following is the best strategy to solve this problem?
(A) guess and check
(B) interpret the remainder
(C) make an organized list
(D) choose the operation

35. Deena finished the school run in 52.8 seconds. Lisa's time was 1.3 seconds faster. What was Lisa's time?
    (A) 51.5 seconds
    (B) 54.1 seconds
    (C) 53.11 seconds
    (D) 65.8 seconds

36. A student has difficulty aligning partial products in multiplication, as shown below.

    $$\begin{array}{r} 119 \\ \times 258 \\ \hline 952 \\ 515 \\ 238 \\ \hline \end{array}$$

    Which of the following actions is the most appropriate for a teacher to take?
    (A) Reteach the concept of place value.
    (B) Give the student graph paper to write the multiplication computation.
    (C) Reteach two-digit multiplication and then return to three-digit multiplication.
    (D) Show students how to write placeholder zeros in blank spaces of the partial products.

37. A teacher wants to help students "discover" the approximate value for the constant pi (π). Which of the following activities is most likely to accomplish that goal?
    (A) Have students measure the radius and perimeter of a circle and then divide the perimeter by the radius.
    (B) Have students measure the diameter and perimeter of a circle and then divide the perimeter by the diameter.
    (C) Have students measure the radius and area of a circle and then divide the area by the radius.
    (D) Have students measure the diameter and area of a circle and then divide the area by the diameter.

38. A landscaper stacks firewood so that each row has one less piece than the row below it. If there are six rows and there are four pieces of firewood in the top row, how many pieces of firewood are in the entire stack?
    (A) 15
    (B) 21
    (C) 39
    (D) 49

39. Which of the following graphs shows a line with both x-intercept and y-intercept equal to 1?

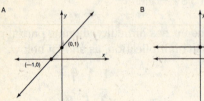
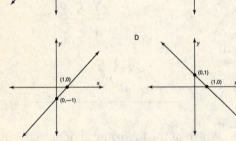

40. C is 5 more than half of B. Which of the following expressions states this relationship?
    (A) C + 5 = B/2
    (B) C = 1/2B + 5
    (C) C + 5 = 2/B
    (D) C + 5 > B/2

41.

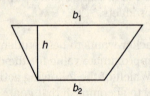

If the lengths of the bases in the trapezoid $A = \frac{h}{2}(b_1 + b_2)$ are doubled, what is the formula for the area of the new trapezoid, using the original height and base measurements?

    (A) $A = \frac{h}{2}(b_1 + b_2)$
    (B) $A = 2h(b_1 + b_2)$
    (C) $A = \frac{h}{4}(b_1 + b_2)$
    (D) $A = h(b_1 + b_2)$

42. Ryan ran 3 1/5 miles yesterday and 6 1/4 miles today. How many more miles has he left to run 16 miles?
    (A) a little less than six and three-quarter miles
    (B) a little more than seven miles
    (C) a little less than seven and one quarter miles
    (D) a little more than six miles

43. Some of the triangles are isosceles triangles.

    Some of the triangles are equilateral triangles.

    Which of the following conclusions is true?
    (A) Some of the triangles have three sides of equal length.
    (B) None of the triangles contains a right angle.
    (C) All of the triangles have three sides of equal length.
    (D) None of the triangles has two sides of equal length.

44.

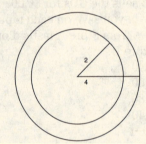

    What is the difference between the area of the inner circle and the area of the outer circle?
    (A) 2π
    (B) 4π
    (C) 6π
    (D) 12π

45. A teacher is helping young students learn about counting. The teacher uses shapes as counters and makes sure students point to a shape each time they say the next numeral. Why is the teacher using this approach?
    (A) The teacher wants to be sure students pay attention to what they are doing.
    (B) The teacher wants to be sure students develop eye-hand coordination.
    (C) The teacher is going to ask students questions about the shapes when the students finish counting.
    (D) The teacher wants to be sure students do not just say counting words.

46. The points (–4, +3) and (+4, –3) are plotted on the coordinate grid. At what point would a line connecting these two points cross the *y*-axis?
    (A) (+1, 0)
    (B) (0, 0)
    (C) (0, –1)
    (D) (–1, 0)

47. Light travels about 186,000 miles in a second. Which of the following choices shows how to find about how far light travels in an hour?
    (A) Multiply 186,000 by 24
    (B) Multiply 186,000 by 60
    (C) Multiply 186,000 by 360
    (D) Multiply 186,000 by 3600

48. It is Monday at 6:00 P.M. near the coast of California when you call your friend near the coast of New Jersey. It takes 5 1/2 hours before you finally get through to your friend. What time is it in New Jersey when you get through?
    (A) 8:30 P.M. Monday
    (B) 9:30 P.M. Monday
    (C) 2:30 A.M. Tuesday
    (D) 3:30 A.M. Tuesday

49. Beth's front walk is 58 feet long. If *y* stands for yards, which of the following number statements best represents the distance?
    (A) $19y + 0.1y$
    (B) $19y + 1/3y$
    (C) $19y$
    (D) $19.1y$

50. What is the average of 1/2, 2/3, and 5/12?
    (A) 19/12
    (B) 19/24
    (C) 19/36
    (D) 19/44

51. In a standard deck of 52 cards, what is the probability of being dealt a king, a queen, or a jack?
    (A) 1/3
    (B) 2/13
    (C) 3/13
    (D) 4/13

52.

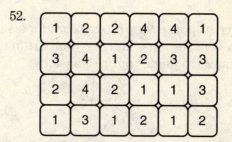

A ball is dropped randomly into the container shown above. What is the probability that the ball will land in a hole labeled with a composite number?
    (A) 8/12
    (B) 1/2
    (C) 1/3
    (D) 1/6

CONSTRUCTED RESPONSE ITEMS

Record your answers on the response sheets that follow the questions. Remember to write only in the lined area on the sheet.

Write a written response for each constructed response item. Remember that these constructed response items are rated using these three criteria.

Write your answer in the space provided on the numbered response form.

PURPOSE: Purpose means how well your response addresses the constructed response prompt.

SUBJECT MATTER KNOWLEDGE: This means how accurate your response is.

SUPPORT: This means how well you present supporting evidence.

Write your response for a group of multiple subject educators. The emphasis is on the subject matter in your response and not your writing ability. However, you must write well enough for evaluators to judge your response.

Assignment 1

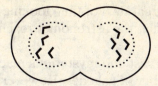

Every organism consists of cells. These cells must reproduce if living organisms are going to survive. Most often, cells reproduce through several stages. The diagram above illustrates one stage of a cell reproduction process.

Use what you know about cells and reproduction to name two reproduction methods.

Then use what you know about cell reproduction to name and briefly explain the cell reproduction process represented by the picture above.

_____

_____

_____

_____

_____

_____

_____

_____

_____

_____

_____

End of Assignment 1

Assignment 2

An amateur astronomer spends a great deal of time looking through a powerful telescope at stars and planets. After some thought, the astronomer reaches these conclusions.

> The universe we live in is a vast and mysterious place. We have developed telescopes that can detect a large number of galaxies. However, this is not very helpful. How can we decipher anything about our world by looking at stars so far away? Can we tell anything about the stars we can see in our own galaxy, the Milky Way? I would say that these distant galaxies and solar systems give us few clues to our own planet and solar system.

Discuss the validity of the amateur astronomer's conclusions.

Use what you know about astronomy, geology, and ecology to provide another conclusion about how useful distant galaxies and planets can be to give us clues about our planet and our solar system.

End of Assignment 2

Assignment 3

Pentominoes are shapes formed by five same-size squares. The entire set of pentominoes is shown below. The first pentomino, which looks like a rectangle, consists of five squares arranged in a row. The second pentomino, which looks like a T, has three squares across the top and two squares in the base.

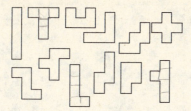

Create a drawing to show how to use three, four, or five different pentominoes to create a rectangle. Remember, a square is a rectangle. The drawing should accurately reflect the pentominoes but it does not have to be to scale.

Use what you know about area to describe the largest rectangle that might be created using all 12 pentominoes. You do not have to create the rectangle.

Assignment 4

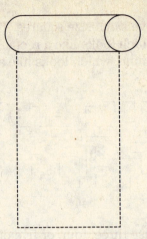

A cylinder is rolled three complete revolutions to create a rectangular shape 32 inches long and 12 inches wide.

Write an expression for the area of the rectangle in terms of the diameter of the cylinder. Show how you could use this expression to find a formula for the surface area of the cylinder?

CSET II
Subtest 3

ANSWER SHEET

Record the answers to the multiple choice questions on this answer sheet.

1 Ⓐ Ⓑ Ⓒ Ⓓ		14 Ⓐ Ⓑ Ⓒ Ⓓ	27 Ⓐ Ⓑ Ⓒ Ⓓ
2 Ⓐ Ⓑ Ⓒ Ⓓ		15 Ⓐ Ⓑ Ⓒ Ⓓ	28 Ⓐ Ⓑ Ⓒ Ⓓ
3 Ⓐ Ⓑ Ⓒ Ⓓ		16 Ⓐ Ⓑ Ⓒ Ⓓ	29 Ⓐ Ⓑ Ⓒ Ⓓ
4 Ⓐ Ⓑ Ⓒ Ⓓ		17 Ⓐ Ⓑ Ⓒ Ⓓ	30 Ⓐ Ⓑ Ⓒ Ⓓ
5 Ⓐ Ⓑ Ⓒ Ⓓ		18 Ⓐ Ⓑ Ⓒ Ⓓ	31 Ⓐ Ⓑ Ⓒ Ⓓ
6 Ⓐ Ⓑ Ⓒ Ⓓ		19 Ⓐ Ⓑ Ⓒ Ⓓ	32 Ⓐ Ⓑ Ⓒ Ⓓ
7 Ⓐ Ⓑ Ⓒ Ⓓ		20 Ⓐ Ⓑ Ⓒ Ⓓ	33 Ⓐ Ⓑ Ⓒ Ⓓ
8 Ⓐ Ⓑ Ⓒ Ⓓ		21 Ⓐ Ⓑ Ⓒ Ⓓ	34 Ⓐ Ⓑ Ⓒ Ⓓ
9 Ⓐ Ⓑ Ⓒ Ⓓ		22 Ⓐ Ⓑ Ⓒ Ⓓ	35 Ⓐ Ⓑ Ⓒ Ⓓ
10 Ⓐ Ⓑ Ⓒ Ⓓ		23 Ⓐ Ⓑ Ⓒ Ⓓ	36 Ⓐ Ⓑ Ⓒ Ⓓ
11 Ⓐ Ⓑ Ⓒ Ⓓ		24 Ⓐ Ⓑ Ⓒ Ⓓ	37 Ⓐ Ⓑ Ⓒ Ⓓ
12 Ⓐ Ⓑ Ⓒ Ⓓ		25 Ⓐ Ⓑ Ⓒ Ⓓ	38 Ⓐ Ⓑ Ⓒ Ⓓ
13 Ⓐ Ⓑ Ⓒ Ⓓ		26 Ⓐ Ⓑ Ⓒ Ⓓ	39 Ⓐ Ⓑ Ⓒ Ⓓ

Answers on page 510

1. An elementary school teacher asks students to perform the following tasks.

   > Take a little step
   >
   > Make a little hop
   >
   > Now, just a little bit faster
   >
   > Take a little step
   >
   > Make a little hop

   The teacher is most likely conducting this activity to help students
   (A) develop the concept of faster time movement.
   (B) learn about successive nonlocomotor activities.
   (C) learn how to skip.
   (D) develop an understanding of the word faster during locomotor activities.

2. Which of the following nonlocomotor skills involves rotating body parts around the body's axis?
   (A) swinging
   (B) turning
   (C) twisting
   (D) bending

3. When it comes to fatigue, five- to seven-year-olds:
   (A) fatigue quickly and recover rapidly.
   (B) fatigue quickly and recover slowly.
   (C) fatigue slowly and recover rapidly.
   (D) fatigue slowly and recover slowly.

4. Which of the following groups of locomotor skills should be taught first?
   (A) Walking, leaping, sliding, skipping, and hopping
   (B) Walking, running, leaping, jumping, and hopping
   (C) Walking, skipping, hopping, running and jumping
   (D) Walking, skipping, running, jumping, and sliding

5. All of the following are sound recommendations for operating a safe playground area, EXCEPT
   (A) Provide competent supervision within the playground at all times.
   (B) Inspect all equipment regularly.
   (C) Establish a list of safety rules and make sure each child follows them.
   (D) Choose equipment based on proven safety and practical value.

6. Which of the following would be an appropriate way to practice a nonlocomotor skill?
   (A) Hop in place.
   (B) Leap over obstacles.
   (C) Run around a circular path and stop in your original position.
   (D) Hang from a bar and then swing.

7. Which of the lines in the table shown below correctly matches a physical action with the sport in which it regularly occurs?

LINE	ACTIVITY	SPORT
1	Dodging	Swimming
2	Lateraling	Field Hockey
3	Putting	Tennis
4	Checking	Lacrosse

   (A) Line 1
   (B) Line 2
   (C) Line 3
   (D) Line 4

8. Which of the following would be the most appropriate way to improve the eye-hand coordination of a primary student?
   (A) Provide numerous highly organized team activities.
   (B) Provide for numerous pyramid-building activities.
   (C) Provide many different sized objects for the student to juggle.
   (D) Provide many different sized balls for the student to throw, catch, and kick.

9. Which of the following soccer skills should NOT be introduced to primary students?
   (A) foot trap
   (B) heading
   (C) instep kick
   (D) chest trap

10. Which of the following accurately describes a fact about the movement concept of force?
    (A) Objects should be pushed away from the center of weight.
    (B) More muscle contraction means more force.
    (C) The sequence of body movements affects the amount of force.
    (D) The more contracted the arm, the greater the force it produces.

11. All of the following are important in volley-ball EXCEPT a:
    (A) dink.
    (B) serve.
    (C) spike.
    (D) lay-up.

12. Scoliosis can create serious problems among elementary school children. In one school, children are screened for scoliosis as a regular part of the physical education program. This most likely means that the screener will use a:
    (A) treadmill.
    (B) plumb line.
    (C) chinning bar.
    (D) stethoscope.

Use the activity described below to answer the question that follows.

MOONBALL

Everyone stand in a circle.

Get a beach ball or a balloon with a cloth cover.

Toss the ball into the circle.

Keep hitting the ball into the air.

Keep the ball in the air as long as possible.

Count the number of hits aloud as you go.

Start again if the ball hits the ground.

13. The game is best described as a:
    (A) competitive game.
    (B) cooperative game.
    (C) locomotor game.
    (D) a non-locomotor game.

14. An elementary school child thinks that, when one of two matched rows of buttons is spread apart, the number of buttons has changed. According to Piaget, that child:
    (A) is in the sensorimotor stage.
    (B) has not experienced equilibration.
    (C) does not comprehend seriation.
    (D) does not conserve number.

15. When describing fifth and sixth grade students' moral development, a teacher is most likely to say they are children who:
    (A) are very egocentric and have no conscience.
    (B) have no clear morality.
    (C) associate with authority figures and show concern for others.
    (D) place personal motivation before moral concerns.

16. In order to understand children's psychosocial development, a teacher should know that Eriksen's stages of development describe:
    (A) the emotional crises that, when resolved, lead to further development.
    (B) Freud's stages of development in more detail.
    (C) stages of cognitive development for both males and females.
    (D) the psychological awareness and social skills needed for successful development.

17. A child's understanding that objects continue to exist after the object has been moved out of sight is called:
    (A) conservation of matter.
    (B) cause and effect.
    (C) object permanence.
    (D) stimulus and response.

18. During early development after birth, an infant's weight usually doubles by:
    (A) 3 months.
    (B) 6 months.
    (C) 9 months.
    (D) 12 months.

19. Which of the following is most consistent with constructivist theory of cognitive development?
    (A) Students should be actively involved with their own learning.
    (B) Student learning is based on reward and punishment.
    (C) Students should construct through the discovery technique all essential knowledge.
    (D) Teachers should construct learning for their students so that their students can emulate it.

20. What single factor correlates most significantly with achievement?
    (A) Socioeconomic status
    (B) Intelligence
    (C) Cooperativeness
    (D) Motivation

21. In general, a learning-disabled student is characterized by:
    (A) achievement scores significantly below intelligence scores.
    (B) intelligence scores significantly below achievement scores.
    (C) IQ scores below 90.
    (D) Achievement scores in the lower quartile.

22. The cognitive development of economically disadvantaged students tends to be lower than the cognitive development of other students, leading a psychologist to the valid conclusion that:
    (A) Economically disadvantaged students, as a whole, are usually less capable learners than other students are.
    (B) Minority teachers are more effective with minority students.
    (C) Learning expectations should usually be lowered for minority students.
    (D) Economically disadvantaged students usually have fewer enriched learning opportunities at home.

23. Vygotsky's view of child development can be generally characterized as a series of:
    (A) stages.
    (B) interactions.
    (C) challenges.
    (D) disputes.

24. A teacher using Gardner's multiple intelligences as the basis for instruction is most likely to engage in which of the following?
    (A) Implement interdisciplinary units.
    (B) Help students learn about each of the intelligences.
    (C) Eliminate assessments.
    (D) Allow students to determine the criteria for quality.

25. When it comes to the nature versus nurture controversy of human development, it is most accurate to say that:
    (A) the nature part refers to quality time spent out of doors.
    (B) the nurture part refers to the nutritional meals a child receives.
    (C) the nature part refers to a student's genetic composition.
    (D) the nurture part refers to a student's time spent helping others.

26. Piaget wrote that children learn through a process of equilibration. Which of the following classroom activities is most likely to promote this process in children?
    (A) Teachers actively teach skills while using manipulative techniques.
    (B) Children learn concepts through their own experiences.
    (C) Children learn by modeling others.
    (D) Children learn concepts vicariously.

27. What artistic principle is shown in this drawing?
    (A) golden ratio
    (B) foreshortening
    (C) etching
    (D) allegory

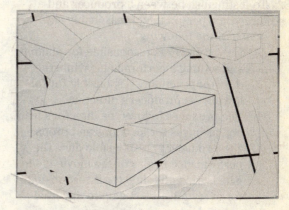

[Mercury Zone III. The Metropolitan Museum of Art, George A. Hearn Fund, 1976. (1976.21)]

28. This painting incorporates which of the following techniques?
    (A) Three-dimensional space
    (B) Regular geometric shapes
    (C) The curved lines of the three-dimensional figures contrast with the straight lines of the two-dimensional figures.
    (D) Two-dimensional space represents two- and three-dimensional space.

29. What color results from mixing two complementary colors?
    (A) a supplementary color
    (B) reddish brown
    (C) gray
    (D) a primary color

30.

What sequence of notes does the staff show?
    (A) A, B, G, B flat
    (B) A, B flat, G, B flat
    (C) A, B, G, B
    (D) A, B flat, G, B

31. The arena stage, completely surrounded by the audience, is most commonly used in:
    (A) small theaters.
    (B) college productions.
    (C) the circus.
    (D) the Asian theater.

32. To distinguish between a producer and a director, a person might reasonably say which of the following?
    (A) The producer is responsible for planning and writing a performance, while the director is actually responsible for following the producer's direction.
    (B) The producer follows the director's lead and arranges for locations and props.
    (C) The producer is responsible once the performance begins or the movie is finished, while the director is responsible for everything leading up to this final phase.
    (D) The producer has overall administrative responsibility, while the director has creative responsibility.

["Senil-Configurations" (Threshold Configuration) by Jean Arp. The Metropolitan Museum of Art, Gift of Arthur and Madelaine Lejwa to The Museum in honor of the citizens of New York, 1971. (1971.279)]

33. Which feature of the sculpture above enables the viewer to perceive several different images?
    (A) The light color of the sculpture against the dark background
    (B) Mounting the sculpture at eye level
    (C) The sculpture's dimensionality
    (D) The alternating curvature of the sculpture's boundary

34. Jazz music, developed by African-American musicians about 100 years ago, is characterized by:
    (A) chaotic sounds interspersed with individual solos.
    (B) a "battle" between two musicians to create the most pleasing sound.
    (C) popular songs interspersed with individual solos.
    (D) improvisation accompanied by repetition of chords from popular music.

35. Still photographs typically represent which of the following types of perspective?
    (A) aerial perspective
    (B) foreshortening
    (C) linear perspective
    (D) two-point perspective

36. Which of the following shows a correct association between a dance and its country of origin?
    (A) Italy: flamenco
    (B) Spain: tarantella
    (C) Japan: kabuki
    (D) France: waltz

37. Which scale corresponds to the white and black keys on a piano?
    (A) Chromatic
    (B) Diatonic
    (C) Harmonic
    (D) Piano

38. A middle grade teacher would like to integrate a lesson on art with haiku. Which of the following would least meet the teacher's needs?
    (A) Use the computer as an artistic tool to illustrate the haiku.
    (B) Provide a display of classical Japanese paintings for children to color.
    (C) Provide clay as a means to illustrate the haiku.
    (D) Provide paints and brushes so children can illustrate the haiku.

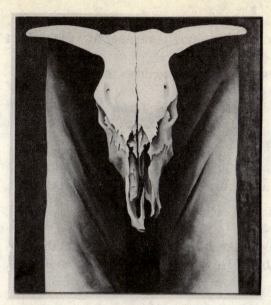

[The Metropolitan Museum of Art, The Alfred Stieglitz Collection, 1952. (52.203)]

39. This picture could be best described by saying:
    (A) it is an abstract figure on a rectangular background.
    (B) the nearly symmetric shape of the figure suggests that its completion is expected.
    (C) the Rorschach-like image suggests an underlying psychological theme.
    (D) the real-life object has an abstract quality.

CONSTRUCTED RESPONSE ITEMS

Write your response on the response sheet that follows each item. Remember to write only in the lined area on the sheet.

Write a written response for each constructed response item. Remember that these constructed response items are rated using these three criteria.

Write your answer in the space provided on the numbered response form.

PURPOSE: Purpose means how well your response addresses the constructed response prompt.

SUBJECT MATTER KNOWLEDGE: This means how accurate your response is.

SUPPORT: This means how well you present supporting evidence.

Write your response for a group of multiple subject educators. The emphasis is on the subject matter in your response and not your writing ability. However, you must write well enough for evaluators to judge your response.

Assignment 1

A fifth grade child with a learning disability participates in physical education activities.

- Use what you know to name three characteristics of the child that have an impact on their ability to participate in these activities.

- Use what you know about physical education to describe two teaching strategies for the child.

End of Assignment 1

Assignment 2

Children who are physically abused do poorly in school and may in turn become abusers themselves.

- Use your knowledge of human development to briefly describe this phenomenon.

- Further use your knowledge to briefly describe an intervention program that might help such a child.

_____

_____

_____

_____

_____

_____

_____

_____

_____

_____

_____

_____

_____

End of Assignment 2

Assignment 3

Perspective can introduce a feeling of depth in a painting.

- Use what you know about art to describe one way that an artist can create perspective in a painting.

- Make a sketch to demonstrate one of these forms of perspective.

_____

_____

_____

_____

_____

_____

_____

_____

_____

_____

_____

_____

_____

_____

_____

End of Assignment 3

PRACTICE CSET II

EXPLAINED ANSWERS

SUBTEST 1

1. **D** The letter combination "ho" is not a grapheme because it does not represent a phoneme. (A) is incorrect because the grapheme "o" can represent the phoneme in t<u>o</u>p. (B) is incorrect because the grapheme "ay" represents the phoneme in s<u>ay</u>. (C) is incorrect because the grapheme "ch" represents the phoneme in <u>ch</u>eck.

2. **B** The linguistic definition of onset and end rhyme is exactly as presented in this answer choice. Choices (A), (C), and (D) are all incorrect because they have nothing to do with the linguistic definition of onset and end rhyme.

3. **D** Phonemic deletion means to remove the phonemes from one word and to leave another word for students to identify. In an easy example, remove the /s/ from stack to form tack. (A) is incorrect because phoneme segmentation involves saying each phoneme in a word. (B) is incorrect because the technique of phoneme categorization involves recognizing a sound not found in another word. (D) Phonemic substitution is the term for the technique of substituting one phoneme for another to make a new word.

4. **A** Early grade students need systematic and explicit phonics instruction to become good readers. This approach is not the only approach that could be included; however, it is the only approach that must be included. Choices (B), (C), and (D) are all incorrect because they are examples of non-systematic phonics approaches. The evidence is clear that these non-systematic approaches are not as effective in early grades as systematic phonics approaches.

5. **B** Fluency is the ability to read accurately and quickly. Monitored oral reading that includes feedback from the teacher is the most effective way to help a student achieve fluency. (A) is incorrect because round-robin reading does not increase fluency, probably because each student

reads a relatively small part of the passage. (C) is incorrect because there is no current evidence that silent independent reading improves fluency or reading comprehension, although there is no final proof that it does not help. (D) is incorrect because, while students need to hear models of fluent reading, this approach is less likely to improve fluency than choice (B).

6. **D** Semantic organizers are a special type of graphic organizer that may look like a spider web and that helps students identify related events and concepts in a text. (A) is incorrect because semantic organizers are not related to the linguistic study of semantics described in this choice. (B) and (C) are incorrect because they describe some types of graphic organizers, but not semantic organizers.

7. **D** This approach is most effective because it helps children see how phonemes relate directly to their reading and writing. (A) is incorrect because there is never a reason to introduce children to phonemic symbols. (B) and (C) are incorrect because, while they can be effective phonemic awareness approaches, they are not the most effective approaches.

8. **C** Metacognition means thinking about thinking, and in this case thinking about reading. A student who adjusts his or her reading speed is thinking about the reading process and reacting appropriately. (A) is incorrect because understanding story structure is an effective comprehension technique, but it is not metacognition. (B) is incorrect because summarizing a story is another effective comprehension strategy that is not metacognition. (D) is incorrect because cooperative learning can be an effective way to learn comprehension strategies, but cooperative learning is neither an approach to reading comprehension nor a metacognitive strategy.

9. **C** Children are surrounded by a world of words and they learn most words by talking with others, overhearing conversations, and reading to themselves. (A) is incorrect because, although they are an important way for children to learn word meanings, context clues are just a part of the indirect experiences that lead to understanding a word's meaning. (B) and (D) are incorrect because explicit phonics instruction and phonemic awareness instruction are essential, but this is not the way children learn the <u>meaning</u> of most words.

10. **A** The subordinate or dependent clause is underlined below. This clause depends on the other clause in the sentence and it makes no sense on its own.

    <u>When Dorothy takes a trip to the beach,</u> she always feels happier.

    (B) is incorrect because each clause in this sentence makes sense on its own, so these are independent and not dependent clauses. (C) and (D) are incorrect because they have a single independent clause.

11. **B** "Effect" is usually a noun that typically means consequence. "Affect" is a verb that typically means act on. The word "effect" is used correctly as a noun in this choice to show that decreased traffic is a consequence of construction. (A) and (C) are incorrect because changing "affect" to "effect" would make these choices correct. (D) is incorrect because changing "effect" to "affect" would make this choice correct.

12. **D** Sentence 4 only makes sense after reading sentence 3. Sentence 1 only makes sense after reading sentence 2. Choice (D) alone shows this arrangement. (A), (B), and (C) are all incorrect because they do not show the correct sentence order.

13. **C** Replacing "extensive and very large" with "extensive" improves the style because the original phrase is too wordy. (A) is incorrect because there is no need to add Yellowstone to Sentence 1, since this proper noun appears a number of times earlier in the reordered paragraph. (B) is incorrect because removing the pronoun "I" from Sentence 2 does not improve the style. (D) is incorrect because replacing "states"

with "United States" changes the meaning slightly and does not improve the style.

14. **C** Most of this paragraph is devoted to a discussion of buying computers, not using computers. The person buying the dorm computers got a better deal because she shopped around. (A) is incorrect because the paragraph does not tell us the dorm computers are better to use, just that they are more sophisticated. (B) is incorrect because nothing in the paragraph indicates that the dorm computers are always in use. (D) is incorrect because there is no indication in the paragraph that either person bought the computers wholesale. Even though we might think this statement is generally true, it does not flow from the paragraph.

15. **D** Begging the question assumes that a statement is true without providing proof. In this passage the speaker states but does not prove that the problem is the influence of rich friends in the record industry. (A) is incorrect because an argument by nonsequitur reaches an unsupported conclusion. (B) is incorrect because a false analogy argument uses an analogy that does not match the situation. (C) is incorrect because a red herring argument uses an irrelevant point to divert attention from the position under discussion. The speaker does raise a point not directly related to the discussion, but the point is not irrelevant, just unproven.

16. **C** This is the definition of a rhetorical question, a question to which no response is expected. (A) and (B) are incorrect because a rhetorical question has nothing to do with rhetoric or rhetorical techniques. (D) is incorrect because audience members may or may not know the answer to a rhetorical question.

17. **D** Reading from a script can make the presentation more monotonous than when note cards are used. (A), (B), and (C) are all incorrect because using note cards can create just as accurate, organized, and detailed a presentation as using a script.

18. **D** Sentence 5 presents a conclusion about which growth rate is preferable. (A) is incorrect because Sentence 1 is the

topic sentence, but it is not a conclusion because it does not flow from other information. (B) is incorrect because Sentence 2 presents a hypothetical situation. (C) is incorrect because Sentence 4 is a summary statement about the information in Sentences (3) and (4), but it is not a conclusion because it does not go beyond the information given.

19. **A** A marketing specialist is most likely among those listed to be interested in the study described in the paragraph. The question is about the study, which describes growth rates for certain kinds of cereal. The question does not ask about the conclusion based on the study. (B) is incorrect because there is nothing in the study that addresses how people act or interact. (C) is incorrect because there is nothing in the study that would help a nutritionist decide which foods to recommend. (D) is incorrect because a supermarket manager could be interested in which type of cereal is most popular, but not in the study described in the paragraph.

20. **C** *The Odyssey* is an epic, which is a long narrative poem of grand sweep that focuses on a single heroic person who represents an entire nation. (A) is incorrect because the tales of King Arthur are a romance. This form of writing is closely related to an epic, but focuses on love and chivalry, and not heroic acts. (B) is incorrect because *Gulliver's Travels* is a satire in which the inhabitants of the various lands represented, and so mocked and ridiculed, leaders in England. (D) is incorrect because Paul Bunyan is a legend, a heroic story about an individual, but without the grand sweep and national identification associated with an epic.

21. **D** Any reference to symbolism in *Alice in Wonderland* refers to the story's figurative meaning. (A) is incorrect because Charles Dodgson was English and he wrote in English. (B) is incorrect because, while *Alice in Wonderland* includes mathematical ideas, it does not contain many mathematical symbols. The original work actually contained some pictures, but even if it did not contain pictures, the book's symbolism would not refer to the absence of this imagery, and so (C) is incorrect.

22. **A** This book is based on a real Alice, Alice Liddell. (B) is incorrect because *Alice* lacks the broad sweep and the heroic nature of an epic. (C) is incorrect because most of the characters in *Alice* are not realistic. (D) is incorrect because *Alice* was written well after the time referred to in this choice.

23. **D** The Walrus expresses his guilt in the next to last stanza, "I weep for you [the oysters], the Walrus said." (A) is incorrect because it was the oysters who followed the Walrus and the Carpenter down the beach. (B) is incorrect because the next to last stanza also reveals it was the Walrus who sorted out the largest oysters. (C) is incorrect because the Walrus and the Carpenter were like pied pipers as they led the oysters down the beach.

24. **B** The oyster's problem came from the undue faith in these representatives of authority. (A) is incorrect because the beach was the setting for this poem, but it was not the problem for these oysters. (C) is incorrect because an oyster elder did not fall for the Walrus's and Carpenter's deception, so trusting that elder would have been a good idea. (D) is incorrect because the traits of the Walrus and the Carpenter in the poem cannot be generalized to all walruses and all carpenters.

25. **B** The poem is sentimental and emotional as it urges readers to make choices that will bring them the full measure of life's opportunities. (A) is incorrect because the poem does not engage in analysis. (C) is incorrect because the poem does give many examples of appropriate choices, but it is not repetitive. (D) is incorrect because the poem uses a traditional rhyming pattern.

26. **C** The poem describes the actions that will bring you friends and colleagues and the actions that will bring you loneliness, with an emphasis on pursuing friendship. (A) is incorrect because we do not know if she wrote in solitude, but that is not the reason for the title. (B) and (D) are incorrect because the poem never recommends either solitude or reflection as a way of achieving happiness.

27. **B** Civilization is associated with a written language, which was most likely invented by the Sumerians about 5,000 years

ago near the confluence of the Tigris and Euphrates rivers. (A) is incorrect because the Nile River is certainly the center of important civilizations, but it is not where written language first appeared. (C) and (D) are incorrect because civilization did develop around the seas mentioned in the choices, but they are not the birthplace of civilization.

28. **A** Alexander the Great spread Greek culture as he conquered other lands after conquering Greece. (B) is incorrect because Athens was founded about 700 years before Alexander was born. (C) is incorrect because Aristotle tutored Alexander the Great. (D) is incorrect because Rome was founded hundreds of years before Alexander the Great was born.

29. **C** Flood along the Nile destroyed land boundaries, and mathematicians say that geometry and surveying were developed to reestablish these boundaries. (A) is incorrect because the floods actually added rich soil to agricultural lands. (B) is incorrect because the cataracts, waterfalls, along the Nile were long in existence and not established by the flowing. (D) is incorrect because, while this may have happened, the floods were much more responsible for the establishment of geometry.

30. **B** Greece alone meets this description. It juts out into the Mediterranean Sea, has a coastline along the Aegean Sea, has a large island off the southern tip of the mainland, and there are scores of Greek islands nearby. (A) is incorrect because the Nile Delta extends a little into the Mediterranean Sea, but it does not jut out. Egypt has a long coastline with the Red Sea, but there are not a great many other islands nearby. (C) and (D) are incorrect because Switzerland and Austria are landlocked.

31. **B** Shortly after Constantine's conversion, Christianity was decreed the official religion of the Roman Empire. (A) is incorrect because the slave rebellion came at the beginning of the C.E. (A.D.) period when Christianity was a fledgling religion. (C) is incorrect because, although many elements of Christianity are found in Judaism, these origins were not the key to Christianity's growth as the reli-

gion of the Roman Empire. (D) is incorrect because certainly there would be no Christianity without the birth of Christ, but his birth was not the key to Christianity's growth as the religion of the Roman Empire.

32. **A** In this case, the obvious answer is correct. As feudalism ended, the feudal lords lost their lands. (B) is incorrect because samurai were the lord's private soldiers, and as the lords lost their lands, the samurai became less important. (C) is incorrect because as the agrarian feudalism ended, industrialism increased. (D) is incorrect because the shoguns were the lords that lost power.

33. **B** Confucius stressed conformity. (A), (B), and (D) are all incorrect because these choices represent the opposites of Confucius's teachings.

34. **B** Technically, all non-Hindus in India are considered untouchables, even though there are exceptions. (A) is incorrect because a person is born into a caste, they do not choose it. (C) is incorrect because no fee can change your caste, although accomplishment might. (D) is incorrect because there are no elected officials for each caste.

35. **A** The Incas had an early culture in that region of South America. (B) is incorrect because the primitive culture does not explain the presence of a language. (C) is incorrect because Mayan Indians did not migrate to this area from Mexico. (A) is incorrect because areas further north and closer to Central America do not feature a native dialect as an official language.

36. **C** Italians who immigrated in the 1700s were there long enough to establish Italian as an accepted language. (A) is incorrect because, while Columbus is believed to be Italian, he never landed in southeastern South America. (B) is incorrect because Vespucci never landed in South America. (D) is incorrect because, while Drake landed in southeastern South America, he was English.

37. **D** This line in the table accurately describes the Pilgrims and the colony they established in New England. (A) is incorrect because, while Columbus never landed in America, he did establish a colony in what is now the Dominican Republic. (B) is incorrect because

Sir Walter Raleigh founded the Lost Colony. (C) is incorrect because John Smith founded the Jamestown colony.

38. **D** This famous poster reflects the sentiment "United we Stand, Divided we Fall." (A) and (B) are incorrect because the poster had the specific purpose described in Choice D. (C) is incorrect because the colonies were united before ratification of a Constitution became an issue.

39. **D** The Articles of Confederation was the first Constitution of the United States. This document was quickly replaced by the current Constitution. (B) is incorrect because the Articles of Confederation came after the Declaration of Independence. (C) and (D) are incorrect because the Articles of Confederation had nothing to do with the Civil War or with the Confederate States of America.

40. **B** The lines on this map represent the Trail of Tears, the forced removal of southern Native Americans to the Indian Territory, which is now Oklahoma. (A), (C), and (D) are all incorrect because the arrows begin only in southern states, and so they could not represent the westward movement of settlers, railroads, or wagon trains from the east coast.

41. **D** Perry was in charge of a small American fleet on Lake Erie. (A), (B), and (C) are all incorrect because they are accurate matches of a person or people with events during the War of 1812.

42. **B** Slaves aboard the *Amistad* revolted during a voyage to the United States and killed several crew members. (A) is incorrect because the Supreme Court eventually ruled in favor of the Africans. (C) is incorrect because Van Buren wanted the Africans deported, while John Quincy Adams represented them before the Supreme Court. (D) is incorrect because the Africans did not receive any land.

43. **B** This choice shows the correct time order. Think through the answer to this question. Reconstruction came after the Civil War. Sherman's March to the Sea was during the Civil War. That means the correct answer will show "I" after "II." Eliminate choice (A). The Surrender at Appomattox Courthouse came at the end of the war but before Recon-

struction. That means the correct answer will show "III" between "II" and "I." Eliminate choices (C) and (D). That leaves only choice (B), which is correct because the XIII amendment was ratified in 1865 and before Reconstruction began in 1866.

44. **C** These are just a few of the measures that FDR enacted during the depression. (A) is incorrect because Hoover did not enact these or any effective programs to combat the recession. (B) and (D) are incorrect because these programs were enacted in the 1930s.

45. **C** The Pacific Plate is moving slowly to the northwest, scraping against the North American plate along the San Andreas fault. (A), (B), and (D) are all incorrect because the North American Plate is not currently in motion and neither plate is currently rising.

46. **B** California Native Americans were widely dispersed and not well organized. (A) is incorrect because these civilizations were truly prehistoric, without any written language. (C) is incorrect because most California Native Americans were located near the coast. (D) is incorrect because there were many different language groups.

47. **C** The Spanish galleons sailed to Acapulco and did not land in California, but officials in Mexico explored the California coast to find a port where the galleons might land. (A), (B), and (D) are all incorrect because the galleons brought food and supplies to Mexico from Manila and did not land in California nor travel up and down the California coast.

48. **A** The first missions were built in the 1770s, about the time of the Revolutionary War. (B), (C), and (D) are all incorrect because all the other choices occurred after the first missions were built. The Louisiana purchase came about 30 years later, Mexican independence from Spain about 20 years after that, and the Civil War was about 40 years after Mexican independence from Spain.

49. **C** The fastest way was by ship to Panama, across the isthmus by land and by ship again to California. (A) is incorrect because the next fastest way was stagecoach, which took three or four weeks from Saint Louis. (B) is incorrect

because the Pony express covered the distance in about a week, but the Pony Express was not for travel. (D) is incorrect because travel by ship around the tip of South America could take six months.

50. **B** The progressive movement, a political movement, was a reaction against the stranglehold of railroads and other large companies on California government. (A) and (C) are incorrect because this movement was not related to the progressive education movement nor to the temperance movement. (D) is incorrect because the number of automobiles was growing much faster than the population; however, the progressive movement was not concerned with this issue.

51. **B** According to the most recent census results, about 7% of Californians are non-Hispanic Blacks. (A) is incorrect because about 11% of Californians are Asians. (C) is incorrect because about 47% are non-Hispanic Caucasians. (D) is incorrect because about 34% are Hispanic or Latino.

52. **B** This text is from Executive Order No. 9066, signed by Franklin Roosevelt, which established "Military Areas." The document does not mention Japanese, referring instead to "any or all persons," but the intent of this text and the rest of the document was clear to all. (A), (C), and (D) are all incorrect because the wording is innocuous enough that it might refer to any of these choices, but it does not. The secrecy of test flight areas are secured by other orders. There is no official military defense zone at the Mexican border. The federal government did not issue exclusion decrees after the San Francisco earthquake.

CONSTRUCTED RESPONSE ANSWERS

Review the guidelines for writing constructed response answers on page 24.

1. The essential elements of this answer are that there are many phonemic awareness activities, including the following.

   Phoneme isolation—recognize individual sounds in a word.

   Phoneme identity—recognize the same sounds in different words.

   Phoneme categorization—recognize a word with a sound that does not match the sounds in other words.

2. The essential elements of this answer are that these students must often learn English as a second language, that they do not possess the phonemic awareness found among English speakers, and that these students may have no experience with graphemes or with a system of phonics.

3. The essential elements of this answer are that the Revolutionary War was primarily caused by colonists' sense that they were literally second class citizens. The specific causes included the Sugar Act, the Quartering Act, the Stamp Act, the Townshend Acts, and the Boston Massacre.

4. The essential elements of this answer are that the Bear Flag Revolt consisted of a few settlers taking over a Mexican fort in Sonoma, California, with no resistance from those in the fort. The settlers flew the Bear Flag over the fort for about a month. The revolt is largely of symbolic significance, even though the Bear Flag remains an important symbol in California.

No book can effectively evaluate your answers, and you should show them to a college professor to receive a useful evaluation along with suggestions for improvement.

SUBTEST 2

1. **C** A chemical reaction forms a new substance. That is what happens when water and cement are combined to create concrete. (A) is incorrect because mixing two glasses of hot water does not create a chemical reaction, although chemical reactions can be formed when elements are heated, cooled, or burned. (B) and (D) are incorrect because when these kinds of things are "mixed," no chemical change takes place, and so no chemical reaction takes place.

2. **D** Atoms of the same element can have a different number of neutrons. The number of electrons and the number of protons is what defines an element. (A) is incorrect because the atomic mass of an element is the sum of the number of neutrons and the number of protons. (B) is incorrect because the atomic number of an element is the number of protons. (C) is incorrect because, in general, electrons move around in a number of orbits, although some atoms have a single orbit of electrons.

3. **B** The weight of an object varies depending on where it is in a gravitational field. However, weight is proportional to mass. For example, an object with more mass always weighs more than the object with less mass. (A) is incorrect because the mass of an object increases as it approaches the speed of light. (B) is incorrect because specific gravity describes the density of an object. However, two cubic centimeters of gold has more mass the one cubic centimeter of gold, even though both pieces have the same specific gravity. (D) is incorrect because the weight of an object varies depending on where it is in the gravitational field.

4. **C** Convection means heating through moving liquid or gas. The type of heat exchange does not depend on what is being heated. (A) is incorrect because a heating pad warms by conduction, direct contact. (B) is incorrect because the sun warms by radiation. (D) is incorrect because a heat lamp warms by radiation.

5. **A** Rubbing a glass rod with a silk cloth removes electrons and creates a negative electrical charge. (B), (C), and (D) are all incorrect because the electrical charge of an object refers to whether the charge is positive or negative. None of these actions has any impact on the charge of an object.

6. **C** The prism separates out all of the colors that white light consists of. (A) is incorrect because the colors of a rainbow appear when light is refracted through raindrops, so this statement must be false. (B) is incorrect because there is no colored filter in a prism, but the shape of the prism does help create the effect. (D) is incorrect because a prism separates colors, it does not combine them.

7. **B** Matter cannot be destroyed, but burning wood converts matter to energy, primarily in the form of heat and light. (A) is incorrect because matter cannot be destroyed, although it can be converted to energy. (C) is incorrect because elements cannot be broken down. (D) is incorrect because scientists have not been able to convert energy into mass.

8. **B** This experiment partially demonstrates Newton's Third Law of Motion (Conservation of Momentum). When the two blocks are pushed together, they move apart with equal force. (A), (C), and (D) are all incorrect because none of these reactions accurately depicts what is predicted by Newton's Third Law.

9. **B** If two objects weigh the same, the denser object takes up less space. That explains why there is less overflow. (A) and (D) are incorrect because objects that have the same weight also have the same mass. (C) is incorrect because the densest object creates the least overflow.

10. **A** This graph best represents the gradual increase and decrease in temperature, even though it does not reflect the repetition of 60 degrees at 10 AM and 11 AM and 50 degrees at 6 PM and 7 PM. (B) is incorrect because this graph shows the temperature went almost straight up at the beginning of the day, stayed high and then came almost straight down at the end of the day. (C) is incorrect

because this graph does not reflect the data in the table. (D) is incorrect because this graph reflects the opposite of the data shown in the table.

11. **B** The nose and the mouth serve two important respiratory functions. They inhale air, which contains oxygen, and exhale carbon dioxide. The second of these functions is the only one listed here. (A) is incorrect because the lungs, not the nose and mouth, filter out oxygen. (C) is incorrect because, although the mouth and nose do heat air, this is not a part of the respiratory cycle. (D) is incorrect because the mouth expectorates, but this is not a part of the respiratory system.

12. **C** Anaerobic respiration only occurs with oxygen. (A) is incorrect because aerobic respiration requires oxygen from the earth's atmosphere. (B) is incorrect because aerobic respiration is not responsible for these bubbles. (D) is incorrect because anaerobic respiration does not produce oxygen.

13. **B** The 23rd pair of a female's genes has XX chromosomes, as shown here. (A) is incorrect because the 23rd pair of a male's genes has XY chromosomes. (C) is incorrect because this choice cannot be confirmed from the information available in this diagram. (D) is incorrect because a person has 23 pairs of genes, as shown here.

14. **B** This choice represents the correct sequence for photosynthesis. First, carbon dioxide and water are broken down, then chlorophyll absorbs sunlight, then carbohydrates are formed, and finally the plants releases oxygen. (A), (C), and (D) are all incorrect because they each vary in some significant way from the correct sequence.

15. **C** Even the vastness of the rain forest cannot profoundly affect climatic shifts. (A), (B), and (D) are all incorrect because animal habitats, rare plant species, and natural resource reproduction can be directly affected by the deforestation of rain forests.

16. **A** In five of the six weeks, the HF 2 group of hamsters had the highest average weight gain. (B), (C), and (D) are all incorrect because there is no information in the chart about which hamsters

lived longer, got more protein, or got better nutrition. All we can tell is that the HF2 group gained more weight.

17. **D** This is the best choice among the answers given. The experiment does not describe any experimental controls. For example, the experimenter does not describe how experimenters ensured that the HF2 group received no special attention. (A) is incorrect because it is fine to use averages to compare groups. (B) is incorrect because any comment about a null hypothesis does not address the experiment itself. (C) is incorrect because this choice is just a false statement. There are enough hamsters to make this research useful.

18. **B** This answer demonstrates that DDT cannot be "broken down," even by living things. (A), (C), and (D) are all incorrect because they are all true statements about DDT, but they do not address the issue of whether or not DDT is biodegradable.

19. **C** Students should use a bar graph when quantities are not relayed by time. (A) is incorrect because the graph and table were made on site and an informal appearance is acceptable. (B) is incorrect because this choice describes when to use a circle graph, but a circle graph is not appropriate here. (D) is incorrect because it is fine to use pounds.

20. **D** Echoes frequently enhance sound production around bodies of water. (A) is incorrect because scientists report that sound travels faster through water than through air. (B) is incorrect because sound does travel faster through water, but this fact does not alter the volume and the person is not listening through the water. (C) is incorrect because the material the boat is constructed from, not described here, has no impact on how loud the voices are.

21. **C** Plate tectonic theory holds that the many plates that make up the earth's surface are constantly in motion. (A) is incorrect because molten material can cause volcanoes and even earthquakes, but this is not the description of plate tectonics. (B) is incorrect because this answer is partially correct, but the plates are not nearly circular and their movement is not just to the right or to

the left. (D) is incorrect because this answer is also partially correct when it says that portions of the earth's surface may crack. However, plate tectonics does not resemble the way dishes break when dropped.

22. **B** Sedimentary rocks form when the organic remains in sediment harden. (A) is incorrect because gneiss is a form of metamorphic rock. (C) is incorrect because igneous rocks form when molten lava crystallizes. (D) is incorrect because metamorphic rocks result when other rocks are put under extreme pressure.

23. **B** Zygote formation is a fundamental step in meiosis. (A), (C), and (D) are all incorrect because these steps are all common to mitosis, but not meiosis.

24. **A** The effects of a recessive gene may not appear in parents, but it may appear in their offspring if both parents carry the recessive gene. (B) is incorrect because both parents must carry the recessive gene for an offspring to inherit that trait. (C) is incorrect because if both parents have dominant white genes, the trait would appear in the parents. (D) is incorrect because this factor alone would not produce the results shown in the diagram.

25. **D** Divide 330 years by 82. That's about four. Uranium will lose half its mass about four times during those 330 years.

Multiply $\frac{1}{2}$ four times to find the answer.

$$\frac{1}{2} \times \frac{1}{2} \times \frac{1}{2} \times \frac{1}{2} = \frac{1}{16}$$

(A), (B), and (C) are all incorrect because these amounts do not result from the computation shown above.

26. **D** A new layer of water is added at lower levels and frozen as the hailstone is blown to an upper level. This process creates the rings. (A), (B), and (C) are all incorrect because none of these factors creates the rings in a hailstone.

27. **B** Use your calculator $45,250 + $78,375 + $62,325 = $238,490. $238,490 rounded to the nearest thousand is $238,000 or $238 thousand. (A), (C), and (D) are all incorrect because an accurate calculation does not produce any of these results.

28. **A** Students frequently make key entry errors when they use a calculator. If a student estimates first, he or she can tell if the answer is reasonable. (B) is incorrect because the answer is obvious, and an estimation is not nearly as important as Choice (A). (C) and (D) are incorrect because there is no calculation in these measurement examples.

29. **D** Use the letters F, S, and T for the first, second, and third person. The third person is taller than the first person is, so put T first. The first person's height is less than or equal to the second person's height, so use the symbol ≤. This all means T > F ≤ S. (A), (B), and (D) are all incorrect because none of these choices shows the correct order of people.

30. **C** Move the decimal point eight places to the right to get from 3.74 to 374,000,000. To accomplish this, multiply 3.74 by 10^8. (A) is incorrect because $3.74 \times 10^5 = 374,000$. (B) is incorrect because $3.74 \times 10^7 = 37,400,000$. (D) is incorrect because $3.74 \times 10^9 = 3,740,000,000$.

31. **B** This rectangle has nine regions the same size and six of these regions are shaded. That is the fraction 6/9. Write the fraction in simplest terms.

$$\frac{6}{9} = \frac{2}{3}$$

(A), (C), and (D) are all incorrect because these choices are not equivalent to the fraction 6/9.

32. **B** Three tapes cost $15.60 at Store A and $18.00 at Store B. The saving for all three tapes is $2.40. However, the saving for one tape is $0.90. (A), (C), and (D) are all incorrect because these choices do not show the correct answer.

33. **D** This student divides correctly but writes the remainder as a decimal. The correct answer to 124 divided by 5 is 24 R 4. (A), (B), and (C) are all incorrect because these choices do not show the error pattern.

34. **B** The answer to the division example is 8 R 3. In order to solve this problem, the student must interpret the remainder of 3 to mean that an extra tent is needed. That is, 9 tents are needed for the camping trip. (A), (C), and (D) are all incorrect because these choices do not show the correct strategy to solve the problem.

35. **A** Smaller numbers represent faster times. Subtract, 52.8 – 1.3 to find Lisa's time. (B), (C), and (D) are all incorrect because these choices do not show Lisa's time.

36. **B** This step is first because the student's difficulty is mechanical, not conceptual. The multiplication is correct, and the student tries to write the digits for the partial products in the correct places. Writing digits in the boxes on graph paper will usually solve this problem. (A) is incorrect because teaching place value will not help solve this mechanical problem. (C) is incorrect because the student does not have trouble multiplying. (D) is incorrect because the student is likely to write these digits in the wrong place as well.

37. **B** The formula for the circumference of a circle is C = πd. That means that dividing the circumference by the diameter will result in pi (π). The answer will be approximate because the student's measurement of the circumference and diameter will not be exact. (A) is incorrect because the student would have to divide the circumference by twice the diameter to approximate pi. (C) and (D) are incorrect because, as a practical matter, it is impossible to measure directly the area of a circle, and that makes this method impractical.

38. **C** There are four pieces in the top row. Add the number of pieces in all the rows, $4 + 5 + 6 + 7 + 8 + 9 = 39$. There are 39 pieces of firewood in the stack. (A) is incorrect because this is the sum of five rows of firewood. (B) is incorrect because if there had been one piece of wood in the top row, then there would have been 21 pieces in the entire stack. (D) is incorrect because this is the sum for seven rows.

39. **D** Read the graph to find an ordered pair where the first element is 1 (x intercept of 1) and another ordered pair where the second element is 1 (y intercept of 1). Graph D shows the ordered pairs (1, 0) and (0, 1). (A), (B), and (C) are all incorrect because these graphs do not show both an x intercept of 1 and a y intercept of 1.

40. **B** You can substitute the numerals and symbols for words

C is 5 more than half of B.
C = 5 + 1/2 B

This is the same as the equation C = ½ B + 5. (A), (C), and (D) are all incorrect because these choices do not show the correct equation.

41. **D** The formula for the area of a trapezoid is $A = \dfrac{h}{2}(b_1 + b_2)$.

The bases b_1 and b_2 are doubled in the new trapezoid. The formula for the area of the new trapezoid using the original values of b_1 and b_2 is

$A = \dfrac{h}{2}(2b_1 + 2b_2) =$

$\dfrac{h}{2} \cdot 2(b_1 + b_2) = h \cdot \dfrac{1}{2} \cdot 2(b_1 + b_2) = h(b_1 + b_2)$

(A), (B), and (C) are all incorrect because these choices do not show the correct formula for the area of the new trapezoid.

42. **A** 3 1/5 + 6 1/4 is a little less than 9 1/2. That leaves a little more than 6 1/2 miles left to go.

That is just like having a little less than 6 3/4 miles left to go.
You can also do the calculations
3 1/5 + 6 1/4 = 9 9/20
16 – 9 9/20 = 6 11/20   6 15/20 = 6 3/4
Ryan has less than 6 3/4 miles to run.

(B), (C), and (D) are all incorrect because these choices do not show the correct distance.

43. **A** This conclusion is supported by the first statement. (B) is incorrect because nothing in either statement leads to this conclusion. (C) is incorrect because of statement 2. (D) is incorrect because of statement 1.

44. **D** The formula for the area of a circle is πr^2.

Area of the inner circle = $\pi(2)^2 = 4\pi$
Area of the outer circle = $\pi(4)^2 = 16\pi$
$16\pi - 4\pi = 12\pi$

That is the area for the portion of the outer circle outside the inner circle. (A), (B), and (C) are all incorrect because these choices do not show the correct area.

45. **D** Just because a student can say counting words in order does not mean the student can count. The correspondence between the counting words and the objects is the important thing. (A), (B), and (C) are all incorrect because none of these choices is the reason the teacher is using the approach.

46. **B** The points are symmetrical and so the line passes through the origin, where the x axis and y axis cross. The coordinates for the origin are (0, 0). (A), (C), and (D) are all incorrect because these choices do show the correct coordinates.

47. **D** There are 60 seconds in a minute and 60 minutes in an hour, there are $60 \times 60 = 3,600$ seconds in an hour. The product $186,000 \times 3,600$ is a reasonable approximation of how far light travels in an hour. (A), (B), and (C) are all incorrect because these choices do not show the number of seconds in an hour.

48. **C** It is three hours later in New Jersey than it is in California. That means you start calling at 9:00 P.M. Monday, New Jersey time. It takes 5/12 hours to get through. Three hours is midnight in New Jersey and 2 1/2 hours more is 2:30 AM on Tuesday in New Jersey when you finally get through. (A), (B), and (D) are all incorrect because these choices do not show the time you got through.

49. **B** There are three feet in a yard. Beth's front walk is 58 divided by 3 = 19 yards and 1 foot. A foot is 1/3 of a yard. 19 yards 1 foot = $19y + 1/3y$. (A), (C), and (D) are all incorrect because these choices do not show the correct number of yards.

50. **C** $1/2 = 6/12$, $2/3 = 8/12$, $5/12 = 5/12$
$(6/12 + 8/12 + 5/12) \div 3 =$
$19/12 \div 3 = 19/12 \times 1/3 = 19/36$
(A), (B), and (D) are all incorrect because these choices do not show the correct fraction.

51. **C** In a standard deck of cards, there are 12 "face cards"—4 kings, 4 queens, and 4 jacks—out of 52 possible cards.
P (face card) = 12/52 = 3/13.
(A), (B), and (D) are all incorrect because these choices do not show the correct probability.

52. **D** A composite number has factors other than itself and 1. That means 4 is the only composite number in the container. Write a fraction to represent the number of fours—4/24.
Write the fraction in lowest terms—4/24 = 1/6.
(A), (B), and (C) are all incorrect because these choices do not show the correct probability.

CONSTRUCTED RESPONSE ANSWERS

Review the guidelines for writing constructed response answers on page 24.

1. The essential elements of this answer are that there are two primary methods of cell reproduction, meiosis and mitosis. These methods are explained in detail in the science section. The diagram shows the final stage of mitosis, when two new nuclei are formed.

2. The essential element of this answer is that observing stars give insight into how the universe was formed. It also offers a glimpse back in time and may help explain how our own sun will behave in the future. Observing stars may help us understand how our solar system was formed.

3. The essential elements of this answer are that there are a large number of ways to use 3, 4, or 5 pentominoes to form a rectangle. Three examples are given below.

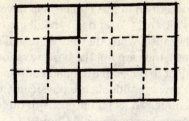

3 pentominoes make a 3 × 5 rectangle.

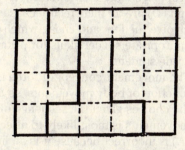

4 pentominoes make a 4 × 5 rectangle.

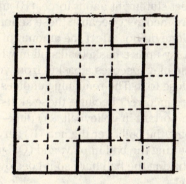

5 pentominoes make a 5 × 5 square.

The twelve pentominoes have a total of 60 square units, so the product of the sides of the rectangle will be 60 (2 × 30, 3 × 20, 4 × 15, 5 × 12, 6 × 10). The 6 × 10 rectangle cannot actually be formed, but you would not be expected to know that.

4. The essential elements of this answer are that if three rolls of the cylinder create a rectangle, then one side of the rectangle is $3d$. The area of the rectangle equals $3d \times 12 = 36d$. The expression is $A = 36d$.

One third of the rectangle is the long part of the cylinder's surface area ($12d$).

Each circle has an area equal to $2\pi\,(d/2)^2$. For two circles that's $4\pi\,(d^2/2)$.

Add: Surface area $= 12d + 4\pi\,(d^2/2)$.

No book can effectively evaluate your answers, and you should show them to a college professor to receive a useful evaluation along with suggestions for improvement.

SUBTEST 3

1. **C** Skipping involves a step and a hop in quick succession. (A), (B), and (D) are incorrect because none of these choices is the reason for teaching students to step and hop.

2. **B** A body turns around the body's axis, which goes from the top middle of the head straight down through the rest of the body. (A) and (D) are incorrect because neither choice represents a turn around the body's axis. Choice (C) is incorrect because twisting does not fully rotate the body around its axis.

3. **A** Young children tend to tire quickly, but also tend to recover quickly as well. (B), (C), and (D) are all incorrect because they do not accurately describe a child's reaction to exercise.

4. **B** The skills in this list are the five fundamental locomotor movements that form the basis for more complex locomotor skills. (A), (C), and (D) are all incorrect because galloping, sliding, and skipping combine several of the five skills listed in the correct choice.

5. **A** A playground is always accessible to children and it is impossible to provide constant supervision. (B), (C), and (D) are all incorrect because these choices all represent appropriate recommendations for running a safe playground.

6. **D** There is no movement along the ground, and that makes this choice a non-locomotor skill. (A), (B), and (C) are all incorrect because these choices are locomotor skills because they move the body from one place to another.

7. **D** In lacrosse, a check means trying to dislodge a ball from the opponent's stick. (A) is incorrect because dodging means moving quickly out of the way of someone or something, and this does not occur in swimming. (B) is incorrect because lateraling means a football payer throws the ball to another player who is even with them or behind them on the field. (C) is incorrect because putting means to tap a golf ball toward the hole.

8. **D** Eye-hand coordination is not fully developed in young children. The activities described in this choice help develop that skill. (A), (B), and (C) are all incorrect because, while they are all useful activities, they are not the best ways for a student to develop eye-hand coordination.

9. **B** Primary students are physically mature enough to use their heads to direct or propel a soccer ball. Choices (A), (C), and (D) are all incorrect because they involve the feet and chest, which are appropriate soccer skills for primary grade students.

10. **C** The movement concept of force is a function of body movements, so among the choices given the sequence of body movements is most likely to affect force. (A) is incorrect because it is an incorrect statement about force. (B) and (C) are incorrect because these actions alone do not affect the amount of force.

11. **D** A lay-up is a basketball skill in which the player scores a basket from very close to it. The remaining choices are incorrect because those skills are important in volleyball. (A) dink—tapping the ball over the net; (B) serve—putting the ball in play; and (C) spike—striking the ball hard so it goes over the net.

12. **B** Scoliosis is a misalignment of the spine. A plumb line will be exactly vertical, which will help reveal any spinal curvature. (A) is incorrect because a treadmill is used for athletic training. (C) is incorrect because a chinning bar is used to develop arm strength. (D) is incorrect because a stethoscope is used to listen to internal body sounds.

13. **B** In Moonball, all the students have the same goal, which is to keep the ball in the air. (A) is incorrect because Moonball is not a competitive game. All students have the same goal. (C) and (D) are incorrect because Moonball involves both locomotor and non-locomotor skills and it cannot be classified in either category.

14. **D** Conservation of number means that the child understands that the number of things is not changed just because the appearance of the arrangement changes.

(A) is incorrect because a child who cannot conserve number may be in either the sensorimotor or preoperational stage. (B) is incorrect because equilibration, the process of learning, is not related just to conservation of number. (C) is incorrect because a different Piagetian task assesses seriation.

15. **C** According to Kohlberg, most middle grade students associate with authority figures and do show concern for others. (A) is incorrect because this choice corresponds with the moral development of very young children. (B) and (D) are incorrect because these choices correspond with the moral development of primary grade children.

16. **A** Eriksen's four stages are described as the crises of (1) Initiative vs. Guilt, (2) Industry vs. Inferiority, (3) Identity vs. Identity Confusion, and (4) Intimacy vs. Isolation. (B) is incorrect because Eriksen built on Freud's work, but Freud did not describe stages in detail. (C) is incorrect because Eriksen does not describe stages of cognitive development. (D) is incorrect because Eriksen does not name specific skills needed for successful development.

17. **C** Object permanence is the name given to this trait, which signals a child's movement out of the sensorimotor stage. (A), (B), and (D) are all incorrect because none of these is the name for the trait described in the item.

18. **D** An infant's body weight usually doubles about when they reach the first year of life. (A), (B), and (C) are all incorrect because these ages do not accurately describe when a child's weight usually doubles, although it is common to believe that a doubling of body weight occurs before the first year of life.

19. **A** Constructivists believe that students should be actively involved in their own learning. (B) is incorrect because this choice describes the behaviorist view of learning. (C) is incorrect because active learning may involve the "discovery" of concepts, but this is not the essential element of constructivism. (D) is incorrect because constructivists believe that the active involvement of students, not the active involvement of teachers, is the key to learning.

20. **A** Research consistently shows that this single factor correlates most highly with achievement. (B), (C), and (D) are incorrect because, while they correlate with achievement in various degrees, the correlation is not marked as the correlation between achievement and SES. Recall that a correlation does not mean there is a cause and effect relationship.

21. **A** This is what learning disabled means; the measure of a student's learning is below the level predicted by the measure of a student's intelligence. (B), (C), and (D) are incorrect because the particular IQ or achievement score alone does not identify a learning-disabled student.

22. **D** Economically disadvantaged students are not less capable, but as a group economically disadvantaged students do have fewer home learning activities. (A), (B), and (C) are incorrect because these choices are false statements about economically disadvantaged students.

23. **B** Vygotsky viewed child development as a series of interactions. (A) is incorrect because Vygotsky, unlike Piaget, is not a stage theorist. (C) and (D) are incorrect because these choices are incorrect characterizations of Vygotsky's view of child development.

24. **A** Gardner's theory supports the use of interdisciplinary units. Gardner's theory posits that students have many intelligences, and interdisciplinary units promote utilization of these multiple intelligences. (B), (C), and (D) are incorrect because these choices do not reflect Gardner's theory.

25. **C** In this controversy, nature refers to the student's genetic makeup, their fundamental ability. Nurture refers to what happens to a child after they are born. (A), (B), and (D) are all incorrect because they are misstatements about nature and nurture.

26. **B** The process of equilibration is promoted most when children learn through their own experiences. (A) is incorrect because, while using manipulatives can support concrete learning, it does not necessarily support equilibration. (C) is incorrect because learning by modeling others does not support equilibration. (D) is incorrect because learning vicari-

ously, from others' experiences, does not support equilibration.

27. **A** The golden ratio is 1.6 to 1. This ratio is generally considered the most pleasing artistic proportion and it is found through nature and architecture. (B) is incorrect because foreshortening is an artistic technique. (C) is incorrect because etching is an artistic process. (D) is incorrect because allegory is a figurative literary device.

28. **D** The painting uses only two dimensions, but it represents both two and three dimensions. (A) is incorrect because the painting is two dimensional. (B) is incorrect because many of the shapes are irregular, have sides of different lengths. (C) is incorrect because there are no three-dimensional figures.

29. **C** Complementary colors are opposing colors on the color wheel. Mixing complementary colors produces gray. (A), (B), and (D) are all incorrect because mixing complementary colors does not produce the colors listed for these choices.

30. **D** The flat on the "B" line at the beginning of the staff shows that Bs on the staff are played as B flat. However, the natural before the second B note shows that note is played as a "B." (A) and (C) are all incorrect because neither of these represent the correct notes. (B) is incorrect because of the natural before the second "B" note on the staff.

31. **C** The arena stage is found most commonly in a circus, which has been a performing art since ancient times. (A), (B), and (D) are incorrect because none of the performance venues listed uses an arena stage.

32. **D** Generally, a producer has business and planning responsibilities, while a director has creative responsibilities. (A), (B), and (C) are incorrect because they contain incorrect explanations about the roles of a producer and a director.

33. **D** The curvature creates an illusion of several different images, including a "three-eared rabbit" and a "running ghost." (A) The light color helps perceive different images, but it does not create them. Neither (B), mounting at eye level, nor (C), the dimensionality, creates the illusion of different images.

34. **C** Jazz consists of popular songs interspersed with individual solos. (A), (B), and (D) are incorrect because they do not contain the most accurate description of jazz music.

35. **C** In linear perspective, the more distant objects appear smaller. A photograph represents perspective in exactly this way. (A), (B), and (D) are incorrect because they do not contain the perspective technique represented in a photograph.

36. **C** Kabuki is a popular folk dance in Japan. (A) is incorrect because flamenco is a Spanish folk dance. (B) is incorrect because the tarantella is an Italian dance. (D) is incorrect because the waltz is from Austria and Germany.

37. **A** The chromatic scale refers to the piano's black keys and the piano's white keys. (B) is incorrect because the diatonic scale refers to only the piano's white keys. (C) is incorrect because the harmonic scale refers to only a portion of the white and black keys on the piano. (D) is incorrect because there is no specific scale called the piano scale.

38. **B** Note the word LEAST in the item. This is the least effective method because this choice, alone, does not integrate haiku with the arts. (A), (C), and (D) are incorrect because these choices do describe effective ways of integrating haiku and the arts. Haiku is an Asian poetic form with three lines and a 5-7-5 syllabication pattern.

39. **D** The title of this painting by Georgia O'Keefe is "Cow's Skull." (A) and (B) might be reasonably correct answers were it not for the most correct answer, (D). (C) is incorrect because the figure does not resemble a Rorschach inkblot.

CONSTRUCTED RESPONSE ANSWERS

Review the guidelines for writing constructed response answers on page 24.

1. The essential elements of this answer are that learning-disabled children often have characteristics that include poor special orientation, clumsiness, and difficulty with motor proficiency. There are many effective teaching strategies, including using action games, tactile activities, balance, and body coordination.

2. Physical abuse accounts for about 20 percent of all child abuse and occurs when someone deliberately causes a child bodily harm. This type of abuse usually occurs when a parent hits a child or uses severe corporal punishment. Quick intervention to stop the abuse is essential because things grow progressively worse for the child and the abuser often intensifies the abuse and is less likely to respond to intervention. The best intervention is to involve the family in a way that improves parenting skills, coping skills, and offers positive models of discipline.

3. The essential elements of this answer are that the primary ways to create perspective are to make objects in the foreground larger than comparably sized objects in the background and to have normally parallel lines grow closer the further the lines recede into the background.

No book can effectively evaluate your answers, and you should show them to a college professor to receive a useful evaluation along with suggestions for improvement.

PART

Beginning a Career

in Teaching

12 GETTING A CALIFORNIA TEACHING CREDENTIAL

TEST INFO BOX

California Commission on Teacher Credentialing
1900 Capitol Avenue
Sacramento, CA 95814

Mailing address:
Information Services
P.O. Box 944270
Sacramento, CA 94244-2700

Phone: (12:00 pm to 4:45 pm Pacific Time)
(916) 445-7254
(916) 445-7256
(888) 921-2682 (Automated: Application status/Order materials)

Web Page Address: *www.ctc.ca.gov*
Email: credentials@ctc.ca.gov

The CCTC web page contains complete information about California teacher credentials, along with a wide range of other information of interest to teachers and prospective teachers. Credential applications are available at the web site.

It is best to send an email to the address above for teacher certification information. Access to Commission representatives is very limited. You may call to speak to a representative or to arrange an appointment.

MULTIPLE SUBJECT TEACHING CREDENTIAL

A Multiple Subject Teaching Credential enables you to teach any self-contained class from kindergarten through grade 12, primarily in elementary school, but also in adult classes and as a member of a core or teaching team.

California has two credentialing levels. You receive a Preliminary Credential when you meet basic credential requirements. You then have five years to receive a Professional Clear Credential. Emergency teaching permits are available at the request of an employer.

This section briefly summarizes the steps to receive a Preliminary Multiple Subject Credential. You must pass the CSET to meet the subject matter competency requirements for this credential and to meet the NCLB requirements to be a highly qualified teacher.

PRELIMINARY CREDENTIAL PROCEDURES

California Teaching Credential requirements may be subject to change. You should check with your college advisor or go to the California Teaching Credential web site (*www.ctc.ca.gov*) for the most recent information.

This section provides information about the Preliminary Teaching Credential. Information about the Professional Clear Credential is available from a college advisor or at *www.ctc.ca.gov*.

YOU COMPLETED A CALIFORNIA ACCREDITED UNDERGRADUATE OR GRADUATE PROGRAM

Your college or university must recommend you for certification and you must complete the required certification tests and the technology requirements. Check with your college advisor for complete information. The table below lists the colleges and universities in California with accredited teacher certification programs.

YOU COMPLETED A TEACHER CERTIFICATION PROGRAM OUTSIDE OF CALIFORNIA

Elementary school teachers who completed their professional preparation outside of California may apply directly to the Commission for their provisional credential. There are several different categories. Requirements for the Professional Clear Credential can be very complex and vary significantly for each of the categories listed below. Elementary teachers with five or more years of teaching experience have the fewest Professional Clear Credential requirements.

YOU HAVE THREE OR MORE YEARS TEACHING EXPERIENCE

Earn a baccalaureate or higher degree from a regionally accredited college or university. Complete an accredited elementary education teacher certification program, including successful student teaching, with a minimum grade of "C" on a five-point scale. Hold or be eligible for an elementary school teaching certificate from another state. Complete three or more years of full-time teaching experience in a self-contained classroom that includes rigorous performance evaluations of "satisfactory" or better.

YOU HAVE FEWER THAN THREE YEARS TEACHING EXPERIENCE BUT YOUR PROGRAM IS DEEMED TO HAVE EQUIVALENT STANDARDS

Most elementary school certification programs are deemed to have equivalent standards. Check with the CCTC. Earn a baccalaureate or higher degree from a regionally accredited college or university. Complete an accredited elementary education teacher certification program on or after January 1, 1997, from a state determined to have equivalent standards to the California Multiple Subject Teaching Credential. Hold or be eligible for an elementary school teaching certificate from another state.

YOU HAVE FEWER THAN THREE YEARS TEACHING EXPERIENCE AND YOUR CERTIFICATION PROGRAM DOES NOT HAVE EQUIVALENT STANDARDS

Earn a baccalaureate or higher degree from a regionally accredited college or university. Complete an accredited elementary education teacher certification program, including successful student teaching, with a minimum grade equivalent to "C" on a five-point scale. Hold or be eligible for an elementary school teaching certificate from another state.

YOU HAVE NATIONAL BOARD FOR PROFESSIONAL TEACHING STANDARDS CERTIFICATION

Qualify for an Early Childhood (ages 3–18)/Generalist, a Middle Childhood (ages 7–12)/Generalist, or an Early Adolescence (ages 11–15)/Generalist certification from the National Board for Professional Teaching Standards. You will actually receive Professional Clear Multiple Subject Teaching Credential and do not need to meet any additional certification requirements.

13 GETTING A TEACHING JOB

There are specific steps you can follow to increase your chances of getting the teaching job you want. There are no guarantees, but you can definitely improve the odds. Let's begin with a discussion of job opportunities.

WHERE ARE THE TEACHING JOBS?

There are teaching jobs everywhere! This writer served on the board of education in a small suburban town with about 80 teachers in a K-8 school district. It was the kind of place most people would like to teach. There were between two and five teaching openings each year, for six years. But you could hardly find an advertisement or announcement anywhere.

About the only people who knew about the jobs were administrators and teachers in the district and surrounding districts, the few people who read a three-line ad that ran once in a weekly paper, and those who called to inquire about teaching jobs. Keep this information in mind. It is your first clue about how to find a teaching job.

The *Occupational Outlook Handbook*, released by the federal government, predicts that teaching opportunities for elementary and secondary school teachers will increase faster than all occupations as a whole during the next 10 years. The book predicts a much faster increase in jobs for special education teachers.

Other sources predict an increased need for mathematics, science, and bilingual teachers during this same period. Experience indicates that the opportunities for teachers certified in more than one area will grow much faster than average as well.

Some publications predict that the population of elementary age school children will increase about 10 percent by 2010. There are about 315,000 public school teachers in California. A 10 percent increase would mean about 375,000 public school teaching positions in 2010.

The growth in the school age population and the increased retirement rate will produce a large number of teaching jobs during the next decade. You need only one.

JOB SEARCH CONTACTS

Schools and Districts

There are about 315,000 teachers, 27,000 administrators, 25,000 pupil services personnel, and about 6,250,000 students in just over 9,000 California public schools. The public school system is centered around district offices in each of California's 58 counties. There are about 700,000 students in about 4,500 private schools. About a third of these private schools have fewer than 50 students. Over one-quarter of California students need to learn English.

All of the information here is correct at press time. However, the California education system is a vast enterprise and changes occur regularly.

Begin your search with a California County map. Highlight the counties in which you would like to teach.

Education Data Partnership

The Education Data Partnership provides comprehensive online resources to help you locate school districts in which you might want to teach. It provides extensive information about each district and about every public school in that district.

Visit the Education Data Partnership at *www.ed-data.k12.ca.us*.

Click on Districts in the section titled reports.

The District Report page appears. Choose the county you are interested in from the drop-down list on the right. Choose a district in that county from that drop-down list on the right.

The Profile of District Report gives extensive information about that district and usually includes a link to the district's web site. Click on the Staffing tab to learn about the number of schools and the number of teachers in that district.

> The Teacher Salaries Report includes extensive information about salaries and benefits, along with other teacher demographic information.

> The List of Schools Report shows the name of every school in that district with contact information. Click on the address to locate the school on a map.

To learn more about individual schools, click on the Schools link at the top of the page. The Schools Report page appears.

> The Profile of School Report gives extensive general information as well as staffing and student information for each school.

As you become more experienced with the Education Data Partnership System, you will probably just use this report page along with the county and district lists from this book to do your research. There are many other reports available through this web site that will help you compare schools and help you learn more about California enrollment trends.

INDEX